BIG-BORE HANDGUNS

John Taffin

ECHO POINT BOOKS & MEDIA, LLC
Brattleboro, Vermont

Published by Echo Point Books & Media
Brattleboro, Vermont
www.EchoPointBooks.com

All rights reserved.
Neither this work nor any portions thereof may be reproduced, stored in a retrieval system, or transmitted in any capacity without written permission from the publisher.

Copyright © 2002, 2018 by John Taffin

Big-Bore Handguns
ISBN: 978-1-63561-846-4 (paperback)

Cover design by Didi Wahyudi

Cover image: *Foreground:* Colt Single Action Army .45 revolver, issued to the U.S. Cavalry early in 1874. Photo courtesy of Wikimedia Commons
Background: Western Accessories, by Antonio Gravante, courtesy of Adobe Stock

*For: Elyse, Laura, John Christopher, Jason Michael,
Katie, Whitney, Brian John, Hannah,
And always, Dot, she makes everything possible.*

CONTENTS

Acknowledgments 5
Introduction 6
CHAPTER 1   THE FIRST SIXGUNS 8
CHAPTER 2   COLT'S MODEL P: THREE LEGENDARY GENERATIONS 23
CHAPTER 3   COLT'S DOUBLE-ACTION SIXGUNS 45
CHAPTER 4   SMITH & WESSON: KING OF THE MAGNUM SIXGUNS 60
CHAPTER 5   50 YEARS OF RUGER: SINGLE-ACTION SATISFACTION 93
CHAPTER 6   RUGER'S BULL STRONG DOUBLE-ACTION REDHAWKS 116
CHAPTER 7   FREEDOM ARMS: SINGLE-ACTION PERFECTION 133
CHAPTER 8   TAURUS: RAGING BULLS FROM BRAZIL 173
CHAPTER 9   DAN WESSON: A BETTER IDEA 183
CHAPTER 10   MODEL 1911: COMPETITION FOR THE BIG BORE SIXGUN 200
CHAPTER 11   THE SINGLE SHOTS 223
CHAPTER 12   CUSTOM HANDGUNS 238
CHAPTER 13   CUSTOM STOCKS 274
CHAPTER 14   EL PASO SADDLERY 291
CHAPTER 15   HANDGUN RIGS 300
CHAPTER 16   HUNTING WITH HANDGUNS 315
CHAPTER 17   SIXGUN/LEVER GUN COMBINATIONS 330
Epilogue 344
Handgunner Directory 345
Index 347

ACKNOWLEDGMENTS

One does not put a book of this size and scope together alone. The following people have all contributed with such things as firearms, pictures, leather, stocks, ammunition, bullets, brass, action jobs, parts, custom work, and especially, encouragement. I am eternally grateful for their help.

Tedd Adamovich	Bob Baer	Bob Baker	Wayne Baker
Bart Ballew	Hamilton Bowen	Kelly Brost	Ed Brown
Bill Buckman	Dick Casull	Jim Clark Jr.	David Clements
Brian Combs	Brian Cosby	Larry Crow	Gordon Davis
Ed DeLorge	Ed Douglas	Ashley Emerson	Eddy Fernandez
Andy Fink	Ben Forkin	Mike Figueroa	Roy Fishpaw
Glen Fryxell	Derry Gallagher	Randy Garrett	Bill Grover
Mike Harvey	Rod Herrett	Jeff Hoffman	Pat Hogue
Andy Horvath	Teddy Jacobsen	Eddie Janis	J.D. Jones
Ken Jorgensen	Ken Kelly	Mike Kirkpatrick	Scott Kolar
Tony Kojis	Harvey Lane	Vicki Lawrence	Bob Leskovec
Larry Little	Dustin Linebaugh	Jim Lockwood	Rudy Lozano
Julie Magnuson	Bud McDonald	Don McMinn	Bobby McNellis
Ryan McNellis	Bob Mernickle	Dale Miller	Milt Morrison
Bob Munden	Terry Murbach	Bill Oglesby	Doc O'Meara
Walt Ostin	Joe Penner	Ron Power	Mike Rainey
Gary Reeder	Jim Riggs	Von Ringler	Paul Rosenberg
Dave Sample	Jay Sanders	Tom Sargis	Bob Serva
Rusty Sherrick	Raj Singh	Kelye Schlepp	Mark Shapel
Jim Stroh	Tim Sundles	Forrest Thompson	Lynn Thompson
Dwight Van Brunt	Rick vonDerHeide	Ray Walters	Syl Wiley

and Sam Sakamoto at Star Photo Service and Penn Baggett at the Baggett Ranch

INTRODUCTION

It has been six years since I sat down to write *Big Bore Handguns*. A lot of water goes down stream in six years and also much happens on the handgunning scene. The publishers and I were faced with the pleasant decision of whether to bring out a second edition of *Big Bore Handguns* or a totally new work. We have chosen the latter route and *Big Bore Handguns* will stay in print with this new work hopefully adding much new and useful information on handguns, ammunition, leather, and stocks. My goal is that readers will have two volumes rather than one to add to their reference library.

This new work also gives me a chance to correct a misconception. Two stories will illustrate this. We were in Mississippi shooting falling plates. It was colder than I ever expected in the South with the temperature at 30 degrees and the wind blowing 30 mph. The occasion was the Springfield Armory Seminar, and instead of the familiar single-action sixgun I am normally seen with, I was shooting one of Springfield's excellent 1911 platform .45 ACP's. "It's taking everything I've got to keep up with you. I thought you only shot single actions!" Those words came from one of my fellow gun writers who was surprised to find that I could also handle a 1911.

Now we switch to Texas in pursuit of the elusive Blackbuck. These antelope, which I consider the most beautiful in the world, are rarely ever standing either at close range or still. The joke in Texas is that a trophy Blackbuck needs only to be black and standing still. I was on the YO Ranch hunting with my guide, Don McMinn. It was the last possible hour of the hunt as I had to catch a plane out of San Antonio that afternoon. Suddenly, there was a real trophy. He was black and he

Author John Taffin.

was standing still, however, the range was at least 250 yards. I did not want to take that shot even though I had a solid rest. My guide encouraged me with "I've seen you shoot!" At the shot the Blackbuck went straight up in the air and came down dead. "You are the only hunter I've had that I would allow to take that shot."

I relate this story not because I am a great shot, far from it. However, Don had great confidence in the handgun I was using—a Thompson/Center Contender. This one happened to be a custom SSK Industries 6.5 JDJ with a Simmons 2-7X scope. It is almost impossible to miss with this combination and if anything goes wrong, it will be the fault of the shooter, not the handgun.

When it comes to handgunning, big bore sixguns remain my number one passion, but there is still room in my heart, soul, and spirit for others. I am a firm believer in matching both handgun and ammunition to the situation and conditions. This volume will reveal this and cover not only the best single- and double-action sixguns, but the best in semiautomatics and single shots as well.

A fellow once told me that there are at least a million people who would like to have my job. I have been truly blessed in being able to make a living doing something I enjoy so tremendously. It has been a dream come true. In addition to this, my third book, I also have well over 800 articles to my credit. This is not put forth to brag, but simply to acknowledge those who have made it possible. J.D. Jones, who believed in my ability as a writer when no one else would. He refused to allow me to give up. Cameron Hopkins, who hired me on the staff of American Handgunner when very few people had any idea who I was. Elgin Gates, who also believed in me and gave me the opportunity to do so much testing and writing for the long-range silhouette game. Jim Gardner, present editor of Guns magazine and Ron Huntington, editor of *American Handgunner*, both absolute pleasures to work with. Wayne Baker, who trusted me with one of their premium .454 revolvers way back when. Ned Schwing, editor of my first book who allowed me to do it my way. And, most importantly, Rev. Lewis Nauman, who showed a teenager the true way and what is really important in life. I made the choice he presented to me and I have never been sorry. Finally there is the love of my life, Dot. Without her nothing would be possible or worth doing. She has infinite patience and is perfectly happy living in what is more a combination hunting lodge and gun shop than the typical home. She is one in a million.

As exhaustive as this work is, it is nowhere near being complete. The problem with a book, even one of this size, is not the choice of what to place within its pages, but the difficulty of deciding what has to be left out. Not only is this necessary with the printed word, I also found myself having to cut 3,000 photographs down to the 300-400 that are contained herein. Hopefully, the right decisions were made all around. I hope you enjoy what you find and are able to learn from my experiences.

Good shootin' and God bless
John Taffin
Boise, Idaho

(**DISCLAIMER:** All loading data contained herein should be used with caution. The author is responsible only for that ammunition he personally assembles for use in his particular firearms. Because we have no control over your loading practices, nor the firearms you may choose for the use of such loads, neither the author, editor, publisher, nor manufacturers of components assume any responsibility for the use of any reloading data found in these pages.)

CHAPTER 1

THE FIRST SIXGUNS

June 8th, 1844. A massacre was about to begin. A force of 80 Comanches had surrounded 15 Texas Rangers under the command of John Coffee Hays. The Rangers with their single-shot rifles and pistols would be no match for the mounted Comanches. However, something had changed with the Ranger armament that the Comanches knew nothing of. Instead of single-shot pistols, the Rangers were armed with something that was completely new at that time—a five-shot revolver. Hays reported: "After ascertaining that they could not decoy or lead me astray, they came out boldly, formed themselves, and dared us to fight. I then ordered the charge; and, after discharging our rifles, closed in with them, hand to hand, with my five-shooting pistols, which did good execution. Had it not been for them, I doubt what the conse-

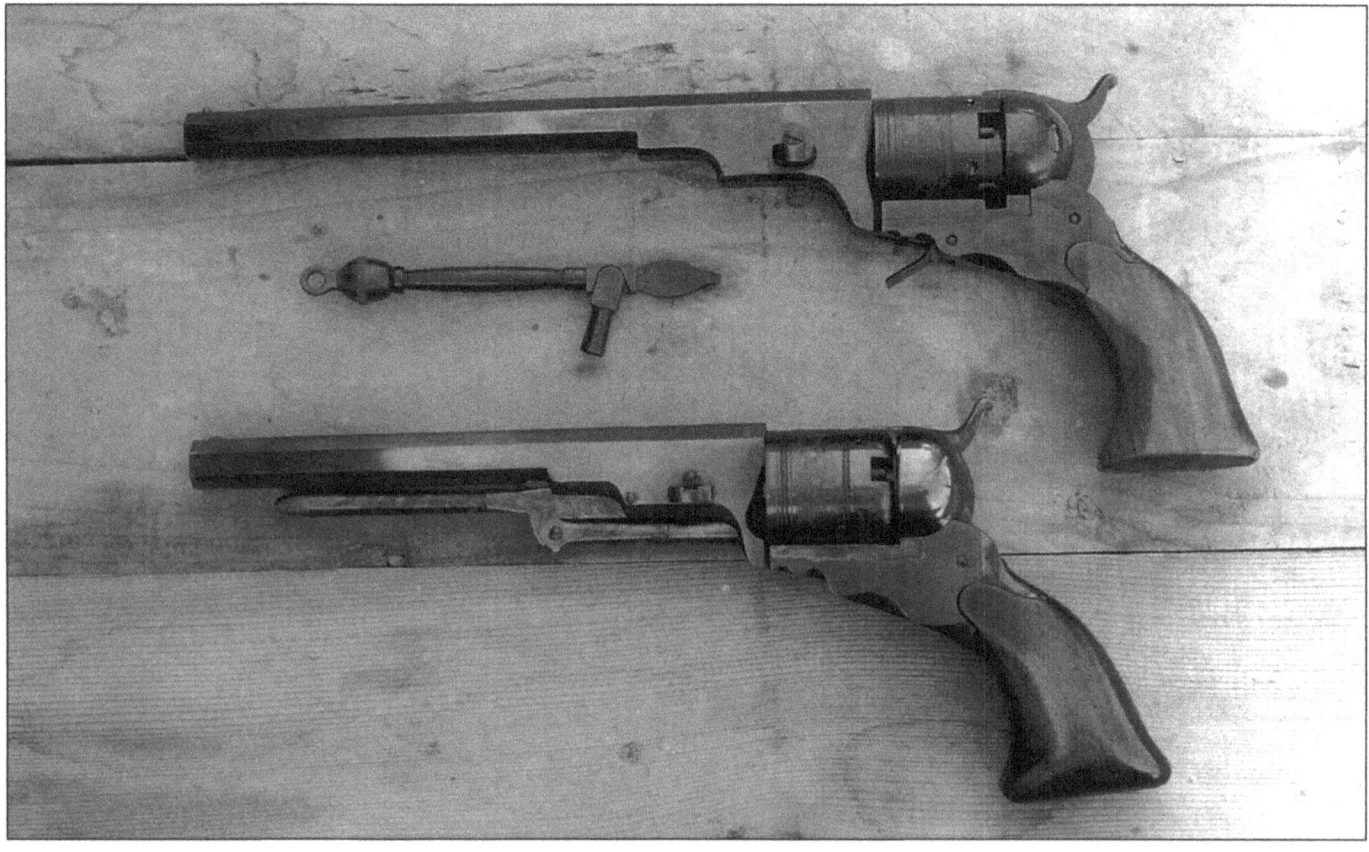

Sam Colt's Paterson was the first successful, and effective, revolver, literally changing the face of battle on the Texas frontier. Shown are replicas of .36 Paterson both with and without attached loading levers.

quences would have been. I cannot recommend these arms too highly."

When the battle was over, one Ranger was dead, one was wounded. The Comanches, however, had suffered 23 dead and 30 badly wounded. The upper hand was gained on the Indians that day, never to be relinquished. The difference was not tactics, nor courage. The difference was Samuel Colt's five-shot revolver. Each of the Rangers was armed with Colt's Model 1836 Paterson, the first successful repeating revolver.

Colt: The First Revolver

There are inventions and there are discoveries, and I choose to believe that some things are divinely or supernaturally inspired. The story may or may not be true, but it is a good one nevertheless. As a young boy, Samuel Colt served as a cabin boy on a paddle wheeler. As he watched the wheel turning he was inspired to carve a wooden model of what would turn out to be the first revolver. The five-shot Model 1836 was manufactured in a plant in Paterson, New Jersey, hence the name Paterson Model. It was a relatively small, five-shot revolver with a folding trigger. When the hammer was cocked the trigger came forward for firing. There was no trigger guard, and as such it is fairly awkward to handle for one used to current single actions. However in the 1840s it was a great advance over the single-shot pistols of the time.

Cartridges had not yet arrived on the scene so the Paterson, and all subsequent designs by Samuel Colt, were of the percussion, or cap and ball style. To load, powder was poured down the front of each cylinder chamber and a ball was then placed on the front of the cylinder chamber and seated solidly on the powder charge with a loading lever, or rammer, that was attached under the barrel. For the first Patersons, the loading lever was separate and the cylinder had to be removed to be charged. Once all chambers where loaded with both powder and ball in place, then and only then were percussion caps placed on the nipples at the rear of the cylinder.

It certainly did not take the Texas Rangers long to discover the importance of that repeating pistol. One of the men under Hays' command was another famous "Sam,"—Samuel Walker. When Texas became part of the United States in 1846 we soon went to war with Mexico. A new regiment of Rangers under Hays was formed with Walker also a member of this group. When the United States Army began its invasion of Mexico, Walker became a captain in the Army. Weapons were desperately needed, so Walker traveled to the East to raise both manpower and firepower for the First United States Mounted Rifles.

Sam Colt invited Sam Walker to visit his office in Paterson, New Jersey. He told Walker how valuable the Paterson revolver had been in the battle with the

The Paterson was short-lived, but it was replaced in 1847 by the 4 1/2-pound Walker Colt .44 that was "…effective on man or beast out to 200 yards."

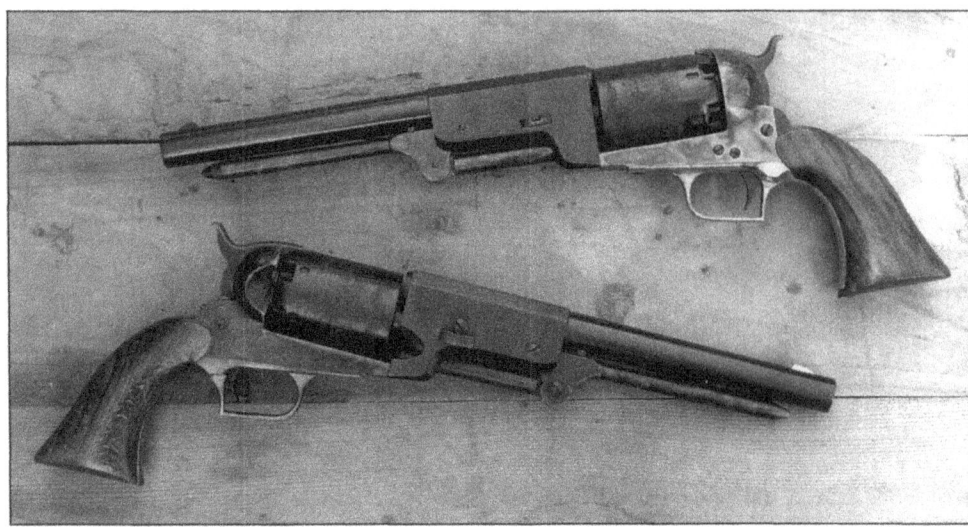

Armed with a pair of 1847 Walker's, such as represented by these replicas, "...a man on horseback could not be captured."

Comanches. Walker wanted more Patersons, but Colt had to inform him that none were available. Colt had gone bankrupt and was no longer producing revolvers. The two Sams but their heads together and designed a magnificent new fighting weapon—the first true sixgun—the 1847 Walker Colt. The small-calibered, five-shot, folding-trigger Paterson was replaced with a 4 1/2-lb., long-barreled, fixed-trigger with trigger guard, .44 caliber sixgun that would prove to be "good on man or beast out to 200 yards." The long legacy of big bore fighting handguns had begun.

The U.S. Army ordered 1,000 of the new "Walker Colts," even though Sam Colt had no manufacturing facilities. Colt contracted with Eli Whitney to produce

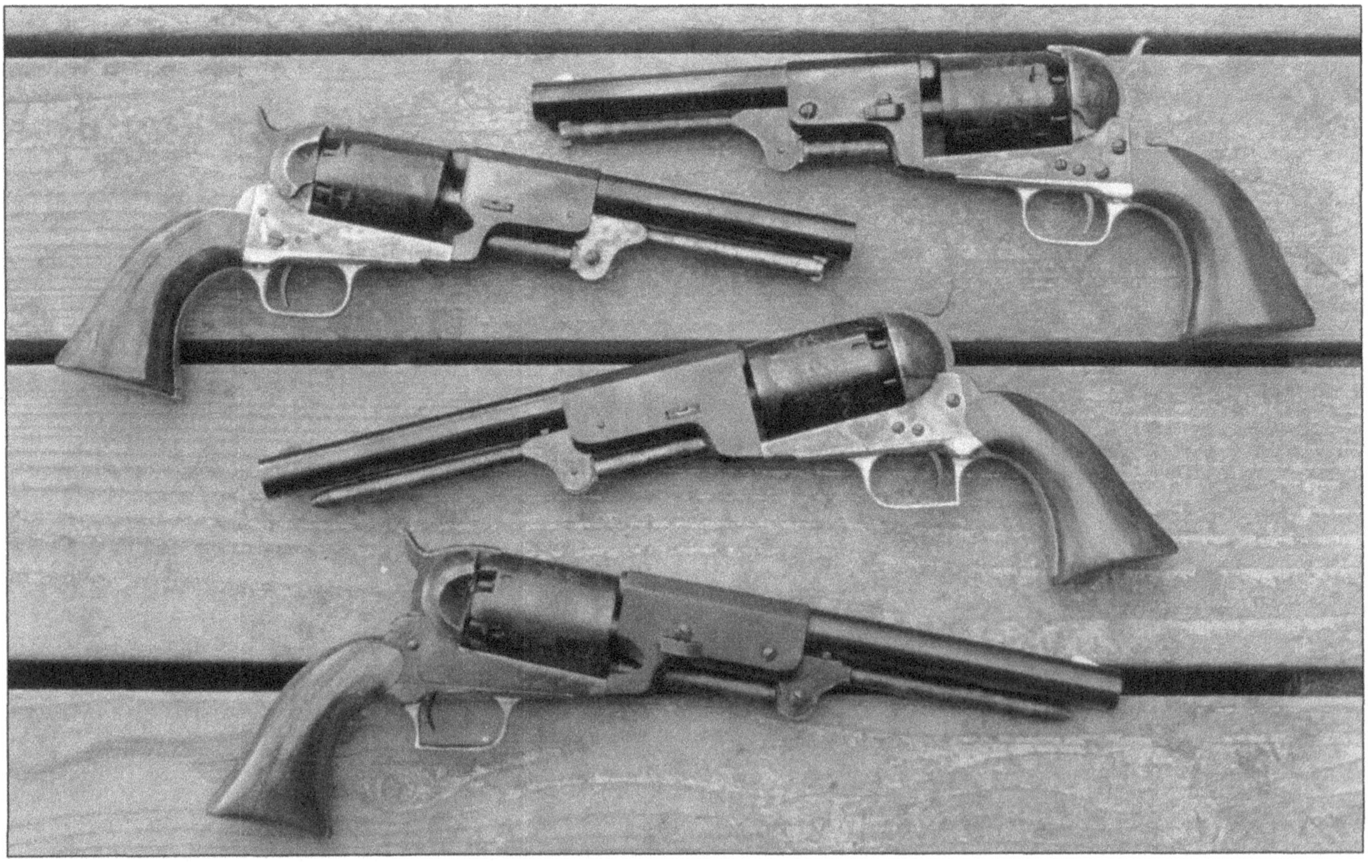

Original Dragoons and Walkers are too valuable to shoot, however, replicas such as these from EMF allow modern shooters to enjoy sixguns from the 1840s.

the Model 1847 Colts and he was back in business. Two of the first Walker Colts were shipped to Sam Walker. He never got much of a chance to use them as four days later he was killed, some reports say by being run though with a lance; others by rifle fire from ambush. Walker may have been killed, but his magnificent sixgun lived on. Even with black powder and a round ball, its load was so awesome that it would be nearly 100 years before a more powerful sixgun, the .357 Magnum of 1935, came along.

As good as the design advanced by Walker and Colt was, it was not by any means perfect. One problem was its weight and the other was the loading lever latch quite often unhinged when the big .44 was fired. Over the next three years the Walker Colt would be steadily improved with the 1st, 2nd, and 3rd Model Dragoons. The Walker was such a success that Colt was not only able to continue with the new improved models, but also to do it from a new factory in Hartford, Connecticut.

The Mexican War was over, but westward expansion was a reality and gold had been discovered in California, two events which created and sustained the demand for repeating belt pistols. The Dragoons were not only improved, they were also slightly better suited for belt carry than the Walker. The cylinder was shortened by 1/4 inch, the barrel length standardized at 7 1/2 inches, the weight was cut by 7 ounces, and the lock work improved.

The Dragoons would be produced from 1847 to 1861 in the Hartford facility in the three models mentioned. They are easily recognized one from the other as the 1st Model had a square back trigger guard and oval cylinder stop slots; the 2nd Model maintained the square back guard, however the cylinder stop slots were now rectangular; and the 3rd Model went to the now familiar round-backed trigger guard. The round-backed guard is found on all single actions except the Ruger Super Blackhawk, which debuted in 1959 with the square-backed trigger guard that Colt dropped from its .44 caliber sixguns way back in 1851.

With Colt firmly established in Hartford and both the Walker and Dragoons being firmly established as fighting handguns, Sam Colt looked at producing pistols that would be much easier to pack. The result was the .31 caliber Baby Dragoon and the Model 1849

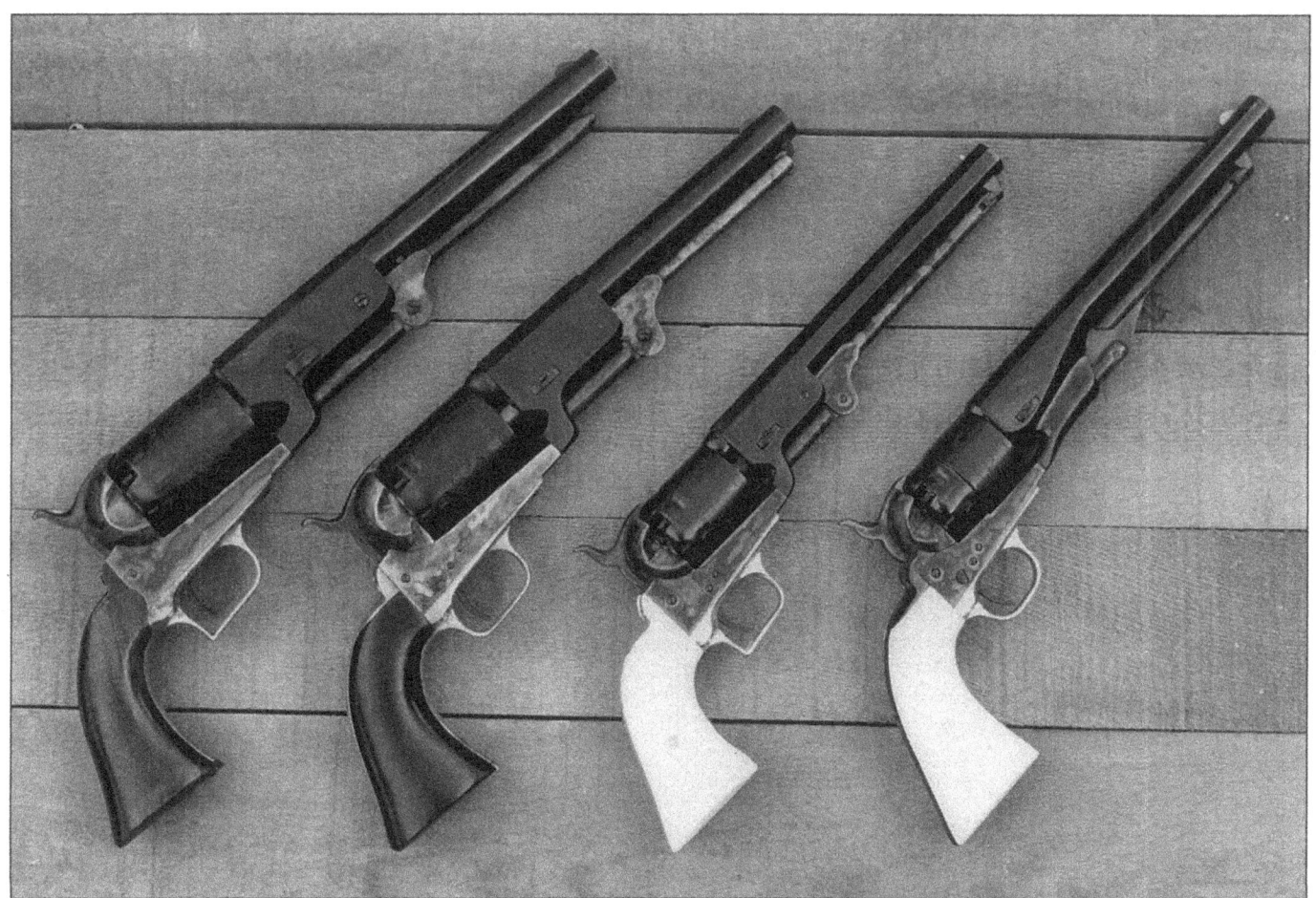

Modern replicas of the four great fighting cap and ball handguns from Colt: .44 Walker, .44 Dragoon (stocks by Scott Kolar); .36 1851 Navy, and .44 1860 Army. UltraIvory stocks by Eagle Grips.

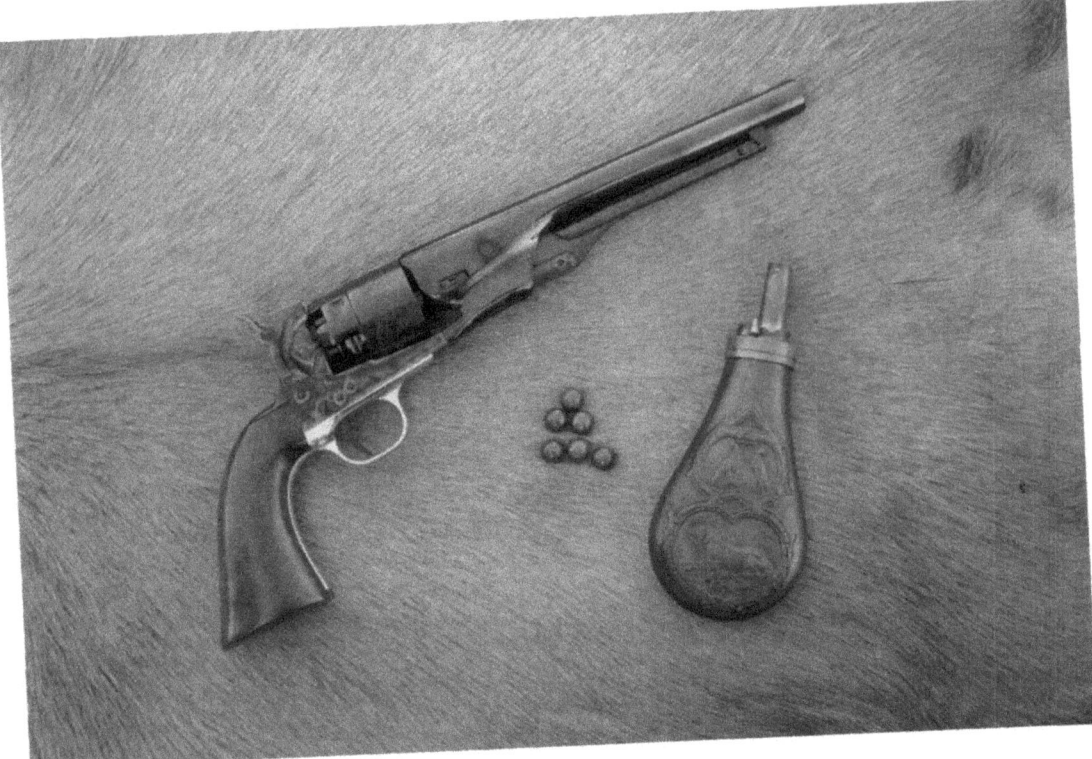

The pinnacle of Colt cap and ball sixguns is represented by this replica of the 1860 Army .44.

often referred to as the Wells Fargo Model. In 1851, Colt had 4-pound, .44 caliber belt pistols, and .31 caliber pocket pistols. Would it be possible to combine the two ideas into an easy to carry belt pistol? The answer of course, was yes and the result was one of the finest fighting handguns of all time—the .36 caliber Model 1851 Navy. The beginning of the age of the gunfighter had arrived!

The six-shot 1851 Navy shaved 1 1/2 pounds of packin' weight from the .44 caliber Dragoon while at the same time carrying a much more serious payload than the .31 caliber pocket pistols. With the advent of this single-action sixgun, the possibility now existed that a man could be just as dangerous with his sixgun holstered as with it in his hand, perhaps even more so. I've often heard it said that a quick draw was not possible with the leather that was available in the middle of the 19th century. I do not believe this at all! A close look at authentic leather from the time frame reveals such designs as the high riding Slim Jim, which made early percussion pistols not only comfortable to carry but provided easy access to the grip frame and hammer for a quick draw. Old pictures show leather that had been trimmed with a sharp knife to allow easy access to the sixgun. We must admit that leather of 150 years ago was certainly not capable of being as fast as the designs we have today. However, speed is relative, and a gunfighter that survived only had to be faster than his contemporaries.

Even with that I would hesitate to believe that such an accomplished sixgunner as Wild Bill Hickok, with his ivory-stocked single-action .36 Navies packed butts to the front in a sash around his waist, would have to give anything to a modern pistolero. History records that Hickok, along with such later gunfighters as Doc Holliday, was totally without fear, and in addition to skill, and probably even more important, had the necessary attitude and mindset. Hickok had everything he needed with his percussion .36 caliber Colts, and even when "better" sixguns came along he stayed with the tried-and-true. It is a tribute to his skill and reputation that he was killed not by a face-to-face confrontation, but shot in the back of the head by a coward. In his last fight, Wild Bill's Navy Colts were never drawn.

The crowning glory of Samuel Colt's genius, as well as the percussion era of the Colt factory, was the blending of the power of the .44 caliber Dragoon with the easy packin' quality of the .36 Navy. We are talking, of course, of the Model 1860 Army. The first models of the 1860 used the standard grip frame of the 1851 Navy Model as well as the 7 1/2-inch barrel length. The U.S. Army opted for an 8-inch barrel and the grip frame was changed by making it longer. Colt's first .44 sixgun, the Walker, weighed in at 4 pounds, 9 ounces; the original Dragoon .44s were reduced to 4 pounds, 2 ounces; and now the 1860 .44 Army came in at 2 pounds, 11 ounces. The streamlined look of the 1860 Army was carried over to the Navy Model with the Model of 1861 Navy .36.

With the outbreak of the War Between the States one year later and a large contract for 1860 Army sixguns, Colt's future was assured. However, Sam Colt would not live to see it as he died in 1862. This means that he had no hand in designing the most famous of

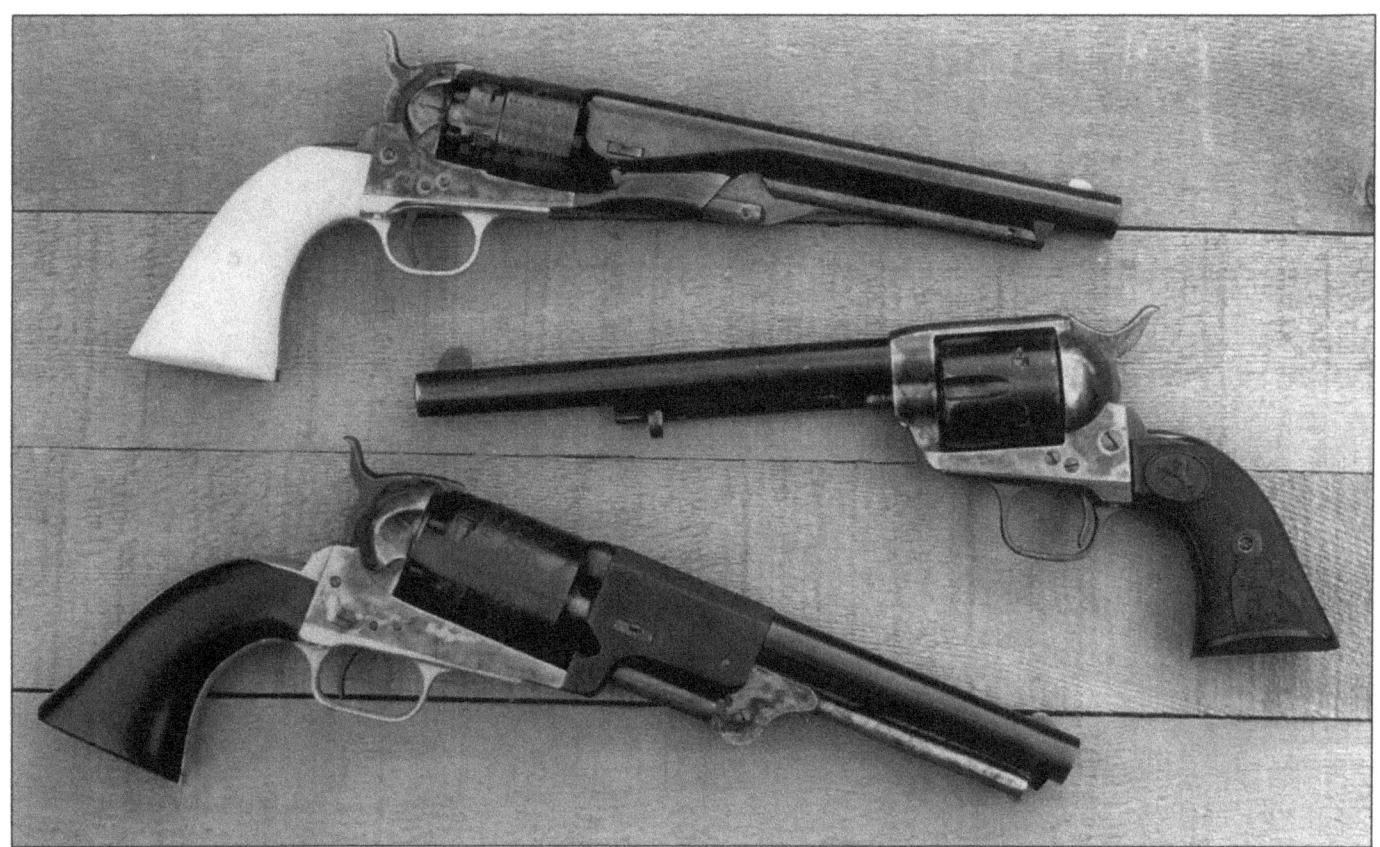

Today, thanks to modern replicas, we can enjoy shooting the first sixguns, such as the 1860 Army, the 1873 Peacemaker, and the 1848 Dragoon.

Colt's single-action sixguns, the Single Action Army of 1873. That distinction falls to another firearms genius, as we will see in Chapter 2.

Smith & Wesson

While Samuel Colt was establishing his dynasty in Hartford, Connecticut, another was beginning in Norwich, Connecticut. Horace Smith and Daniel Wesson were introducing two lever-action pistols that would become the first of many that would bear the "SMITH & WESSON" label. Those early guns are more commonly known as Volcanics. Smith and Wesson started the Volcanic Repeating Arms Company, which shortly thereafter became the New Haven Arms Company headed up by a shirt manufacturer named Oliver Winchester. His name, along with Colt and Smith & Wesson, was destined to become a household word.

The ammunition of the Volcanic pistol represented a transition between the percussion and cartridge-firing revolvers. Both .31 and .41 caliber Volcanic lever-action pistols used a hollow base lead bullet with the powder and primer contained in the bottom of the bullet. The lever-action Volcanic worked much the same as today's lever-action rifles with the ammunition contained in a tube under the barrel.

In 1857, Smith & Wesson introduced the first successful self-contained cartridge-firing revolver with the Model Number 1. This seven-shot, tip-up revolver was also the first .22 Rimfire. Europeans were already experimenting with self-contained cartridges when Daniel Baird Wesson invented the .22 Rimfire cartridge now known as the .22 Short. Strangely enough, Smith & Wesson used the Rollin White patent for a bored-through cylinder only after Colt had shown that it was not interested in the concept. As far as Samuel Colt was concerned, the future was percussion revolvers.

Smith & Wesson's first little revolvers were hinged at the top of the frame in front of the cylinder, and "tipped up" for loading and unloading. The Model Number 1 was followed by the Model Number 1 1/2 in .32 Rimfire, and the Model Number 2 chambered in .32 Rimfire Long. All of these featured a spur trigger and were quite popular as hideout guns during the Civil War.

While Smith & Wesson's business was brisk during the Civil War, it dropped off to almost nothing at the end of hostilities. However, Smith & Wesson was about to introduce one of the most significant models in sixgun history. Remember, the company still held that Rollin White patent for a bored-through cylinder, and had intended to use it earlier and produce a large-caliber cartridge-firing sixgun before the war broke out. It would be late 1869 before Smith & Wesson would introduce its .44 caliber, single-action sixgun. All of these would be of the same basic "top-break" design. They are hinged at the bottom of the frame in front of the cylinder with a locking latch at the top of the frame behind the cylinder and in front of the hammer.

One can only imagine the first meeting of the executives at Colt when Smith & Wesson brought out its first Model Number 3! Colt had turned down the Rollin White patent, thus ignoring the future and allowing Smith & Wesson to be the first to introduce a cartridge-firing, large-caliber sixgun. There were four basic Model 3 Smith & Wesson single actions manufactured from 1870 to 1912.

The Smith & Wesson American, 1870-1874, had a square butt with a rounded backstrap, 8-inch barrel, long ejector housing, locking latch mounted on the barrel, and chambered in .44 S&W American. One thousand of these were ordered by the United States Army. If you had been on frontier duty in the 1870s, would you have preferred a Smith & Wesson or Colt Single Action Army?

One of the finest single-action sixguns of the 19th century, this Smith & Wesson featured all the improvements asked for by the Russian government, including the .44 Russian cartridge, the first to feature an inside-lubricated bullet.

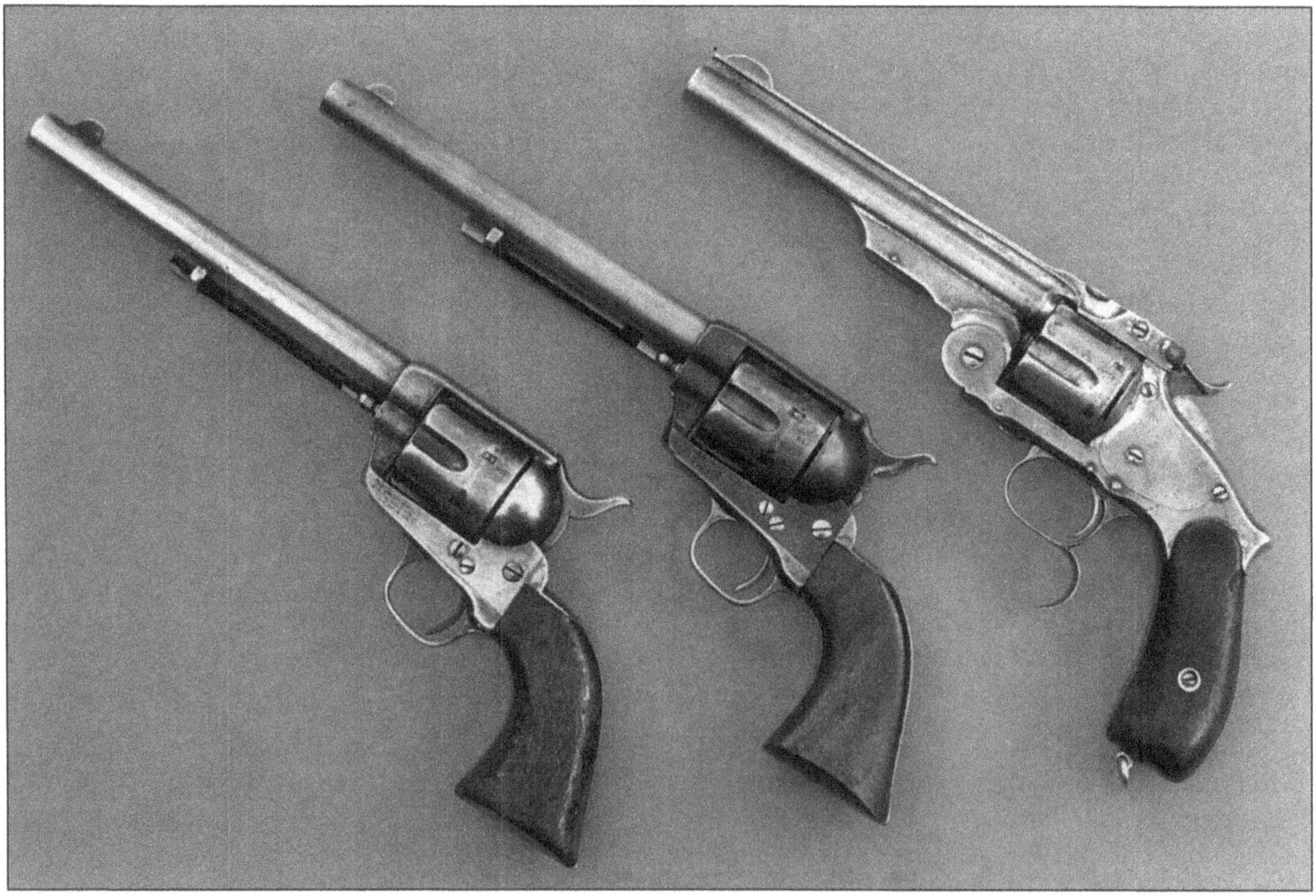

These original sixguns, a Colt .44-40 Frontier Six-Shooter, c. 1879; a Colt "U.S." .45 Colt, c. 1881; and a Smith & Wesson Model 3 .44 Russian, c. 1874, all saw service on the frontier.

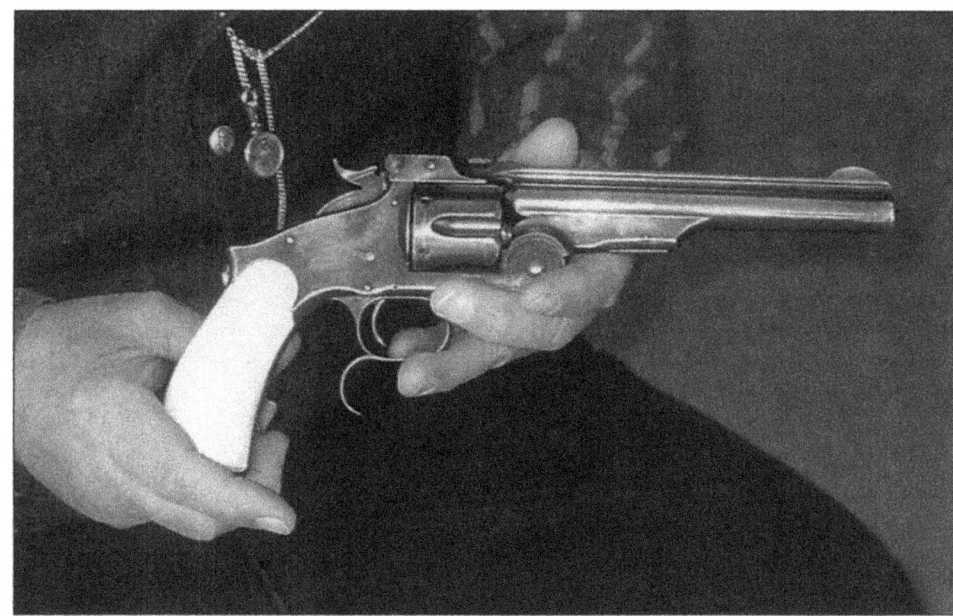

This original Smith & Wesson Model 3 Russian still performs well with black powder loads after 125 years of service.

The Russian Model, 1873-1878, had a round butt grip frame with a hump at the top to prevent the grip frame from sliding down in the hands when fired, 6 1/2- or 7-inch barrel, both long and medium length ejector housings, a spur on the bottom of the trigger guard, and a locking latch mounted on the barrel. The most important thing about the Russian Model was the ammunition it chambered.

The Russians were quite impressed with the Smith & Wesson Model 3. When the Grand Duke, Alexis, came to this country, he was presented with a special S&W American that accompanied him on a buffalo hunt hosted by William F. "Buffalo Bill" Cody and George Armstrong Custer. The Russians placed an order for 150,000 Model 3s to be chambered in a newly designed cartridge, which would become the .44 Russian. The .44 Smith & Wesson American utilized an outside-lubricated bullet with a smaller heel at the rear portion that fitted inside the brass case. The Russians changed this to an inside-lubricated bullet of uniform diameter. Instead of the cylinder being bored straight through, the portion that accepted the brass case was now larger than the throat, which accepted the bullet. With this significant change modern ammunition was born. In 1907 the .44 Russian was lengthened to become the .44 Special, which was then subsequently lengthened to the .44 Magnum in 1955.

The Schofield Model, 1875-1877, was an improved version of the American Model. Col. George Schofield was interested in a revolver that would be best suited

The great advantage of the Smith & Wesson break-top single actions was the loading and unloading speed.

These original Smith & Wessons, a .45 Schofield, two .44 Russian Models, and a New Model #3, are some of the finest single-action sixguns ever manufactured.

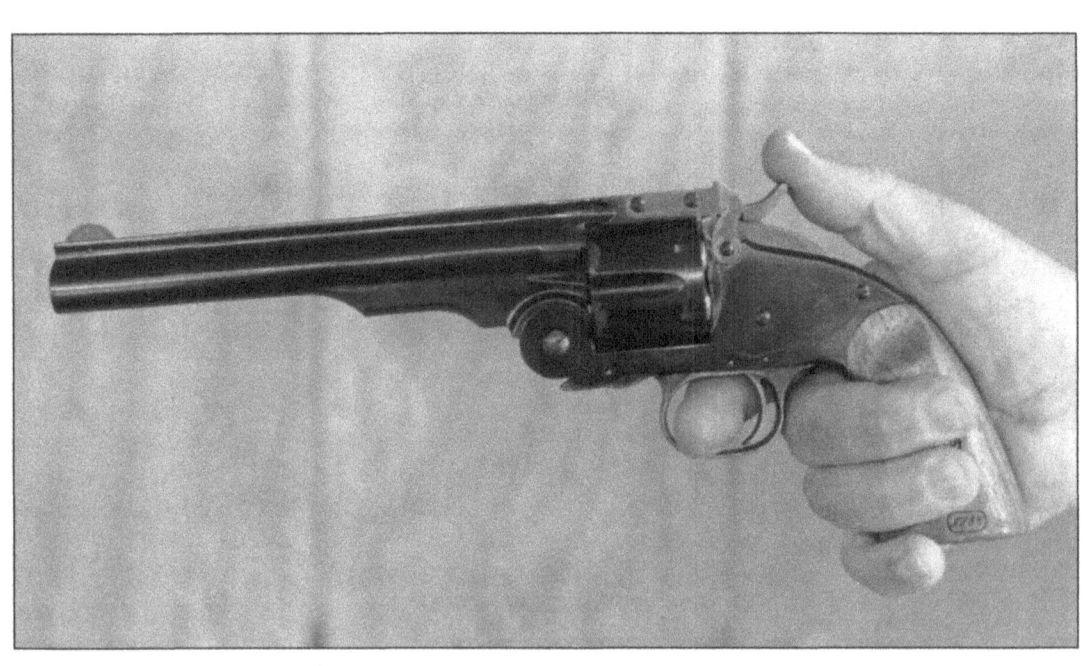

Smith & Wesson's Schofield Model, represented by S&W's current production Model 3, features a very comfortable grip and an easy to reach hammer.

THE FIRST SIXGUNS 17

These two original .45s from the 1870s, a Smith & Wesson Schofield (top) and a U.S. Cavalry Colt Single Action, both saw considerable service on the frontier.

The influence of the Colt Single Action Army can easily be seen in the Remington replicas, a 7 1/2-inch nickel-plated .45 Colt Model 1875 from Navy Arms (top), and a 5 1/2-inch .45 Model 1890 from Cimarron.

The finest Smith & Wesson single action, and perhaps the finest single action of the 19th century, is the New Model 3 chambered in .44 Russian.

for military use, and with his guidance two basic changes were made. The caliber was changed from .44 to .45, the latter being the standard caliber of the Colt Single Action Army that had been adopted by the U. S. Army in 1873; and the locking latch was moved from the barrel to the frame. By moving the latch it was now possible to open the Smith & Wesson with one hand as the thumb of the firing hand pressed down upon the top of the latch. Other models required the offhand to use the thumb and forefinger to lift up on the latch.

As the barrel of the Schofield Models swung down, all cartridges were automatically ejected, and the other hand could be used to remove fresh cartridges from the belt cartridge pouch and insert them in the waiting cylinder. All of this could now be accomplished in less time than it takes to tell about it and also be done relatively easily on horseback. There was a problem, however.

The Colt Single Action Army was chambered for the .45 Colt. Smith & Wesson cylinders were too short to accept this round and the extractor star of the Smith & Wesson Model 3 did not mate up well with the narrow rims of the .45 Colt cartridge. Smith & Wesson's answer was a new cartridge: the .45 S&W, or .45 Schofield. This round had a larger diameter rim for positive extraction and was shorter than the .45 Colt to work in the Smith & Wesson cylinders. The good news was that this same cartridge would also work in the Colt Single Action Army. The bad news, of course, was that the reverse was not true. By the end of 1877, the United States Army had purchased 8,000 Schofields and 15,000 Colt Single Action Armies.

The Schofield was short-lived as a military sixgun. Some authorities say the problem was that units outfitted with Schofields often received .45 Colt ammunition that would not chamber; others say Smith & Wesson was so busy with orders for the Russians that they no longer had any desire to manufacture Schofields. Many military models had the barrels cut to 5 inches and were sold to Wells Fargo and the civilian market.

The crowning glory of Smith & Wesson's single-action production was the New Model Number 3. Introduced in 1878, it would stay in production until 1912. The basic model had a round butt grip frame, short ejector housing, and a 6 1/2-inch barrel. Most of these were chambered in .44 Russian with a longer-cylindered version produced rarely in .44-40 and an extremely rare version (less than 100 made) in .38-40.

These are beautifully fitted and finished sixguns and are probably the finest single actions made during the frontier period. Much more sophisticated in their design than the Colt Single Action Army, this also worked against them as they were not nearly so rugged or so easily repaired. They were also more expensive to produce.

Remington

Before Smith & Wesson, even before Colt, there was Remington. Eliphalet Remington began producing both pistol and rifle barrels as early as 1816. For the next 40 years Remington supplied pistol barrels to gunsmiths and also made completed single-shot percussion pistols. By 1857, the same year that Smith & Wesson brought forth their first cartridge-firing revolver, "E. Remington" had been joined by "and Sons" and they were producing the first Remington percussion revolver. This revolver was designed and patented by Fordyce Beals and offered in both .36 and .44 caliber. Four years later, the 1861 Army and Navy sixguns were offered, based on W. H. Elliott's patents, and then two years later, the models arrived that we are most familiar with, the New Model .44 and .36 percussion revolvers.

The 1863 Model sixguns featured a base pin that could only be withdrawn far enough to allow the cylinder to be removed, and most importantly, safety notches were cut in the cylinder between the nipples.

While the Colt and Remington single actions are very similar in appearance, the author finds the balance, grip frame, and hammer reach on the Colt to be superior.

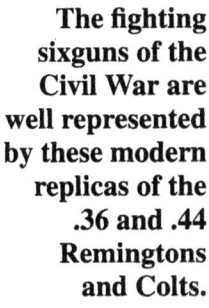
The fighting sixguns of the Civil War are well represented by these modern replicas of the .36 and .44 Remingtons and Colts.

Replicas of the .36 Remington Navy and .44 Remington Army have proven to be among the most accurate of the cap and ball revolvers.

This allowed the New Model Army .44 or Navy .36 to be carried safely fully loaded with six rounds if the hammer was rested in one of the notches.

All Remington .36 and .44 percussion revolvers feature a solid frame as found on currently manufactured cartridge-firing single actions, except replicas of the Colt Cartridge Conversions and 1871-72 Open Tops, rather than the open-top frame of all of Colt's percussion six-guns. This made the Remington a stronger revolver, however, for most shooters the grip of the Colt is more comfortable and the hammer is easier to reach.

In 1875, Remington joined Colt and Smith & Wesson in bringing out a cartridge-firing revolver. It is pretty obvious that either Colt or the U.S. Army, or both, looked at the Remington percussion revolvers before the Colt Single Action Army was produced in 1873, so the 1875 Remington looks much like a Colt Single Action Army. In looks, one of the main differences is the fact that the base pin of the Remington goes all the way to the end of the ejector housing and there is a web placed under the barrel. For my hands, the model 1875 still has the grip feel and hammer reach of the Remington percussion models, making it a little harder to handle than a comparable Colt.

The Remington model 1875 was chambered in .44 Remington, which is different than both the .44 Colt and .44-40. Four years later it would also be chambered in both .45 Colt and .44-40. Most 1875 Models came with a 7 1/2-inch barrel and a lanyard ring in the butt. An unknown number was purchased by the U.S. Army and 10,000 went to the Egyptian government. A variation of the Model 1875 is the Model 1890, which was manufactured without the web under the barrel. It came in 5 1/2- and 7 1/2-inch barrel lengths, and only in .44-40 caliber.

Merwin & Hulbert single actions were even more intricate in design than the Smith & Wesson. They were also more expensive to produce than the Colt Single Action Army. Still, many would argue that they are among the finest handguns ever produced.

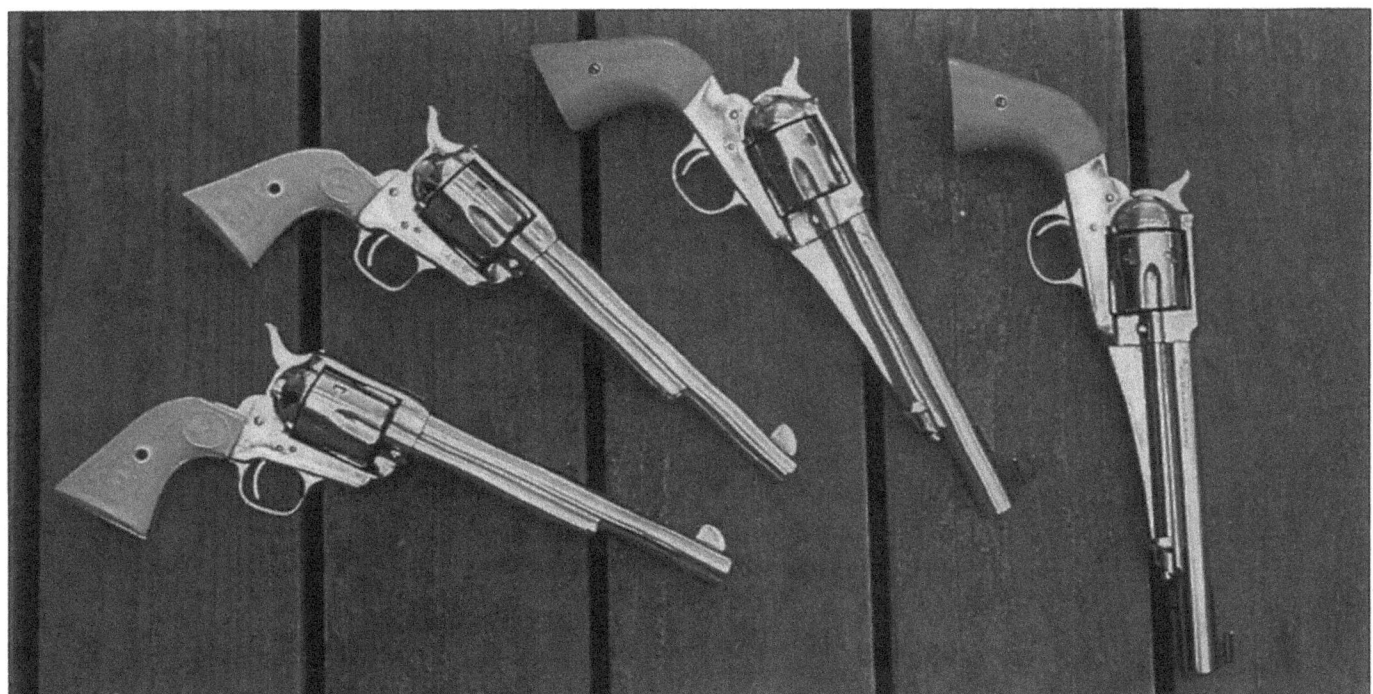

Both Colt and Remington were popular single actions in the latter quarter of the 19th century. Today's cowboy action shooter can enjoy them, thanks to such offerings from Navy Arms as these 7 1/2-inch nickel-plated replica Remington Model 1875s, and a pair of .44-40 nickel-plated "Colts" from EMF. The nickel plating helps with cleanup when black powder loads are used

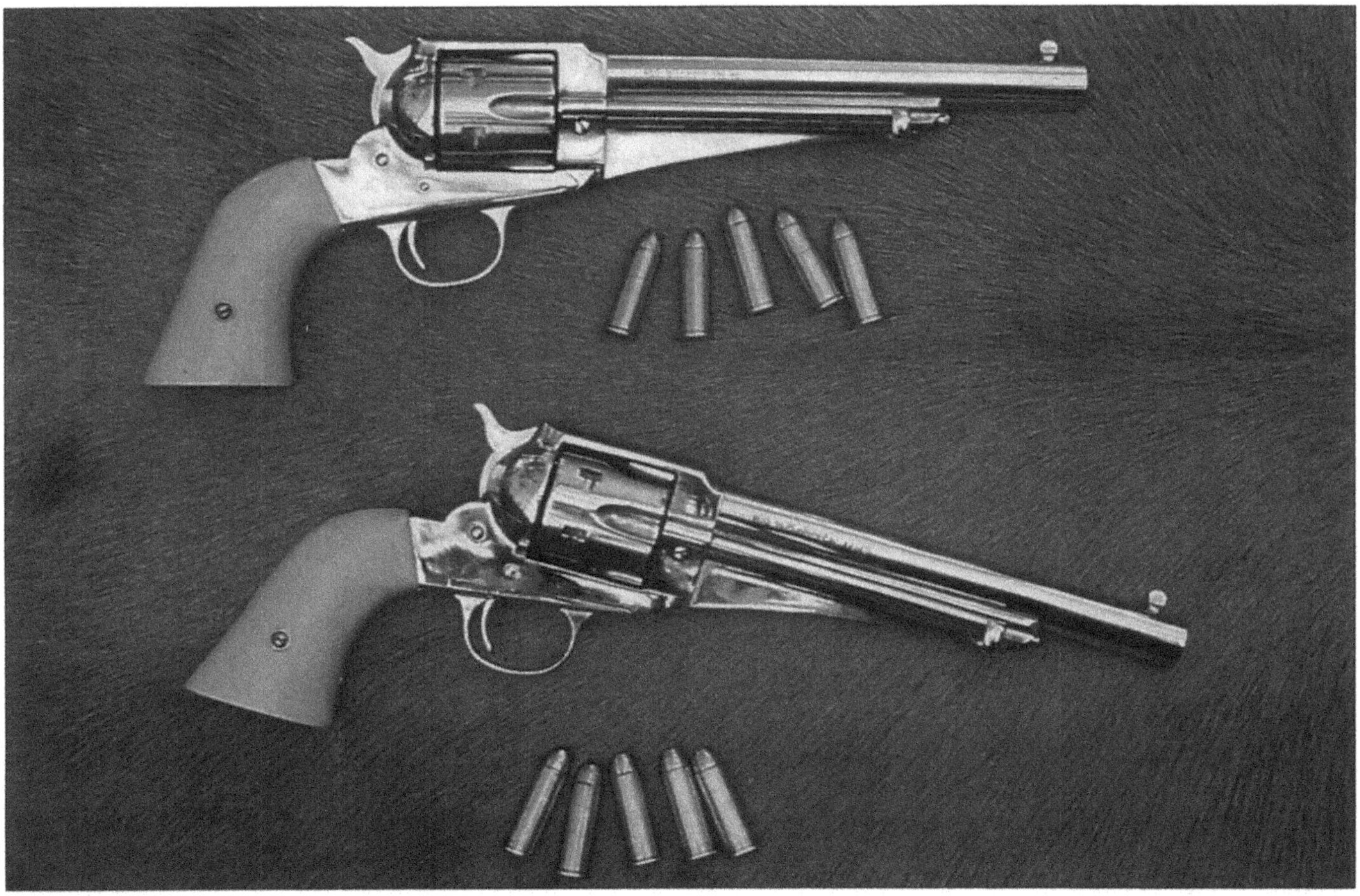

Remington's single action in its original form is too expensive to shoot, but Navy Arms offers nickel-plated authentically styled replicas in both .45 Colt and .44-40.

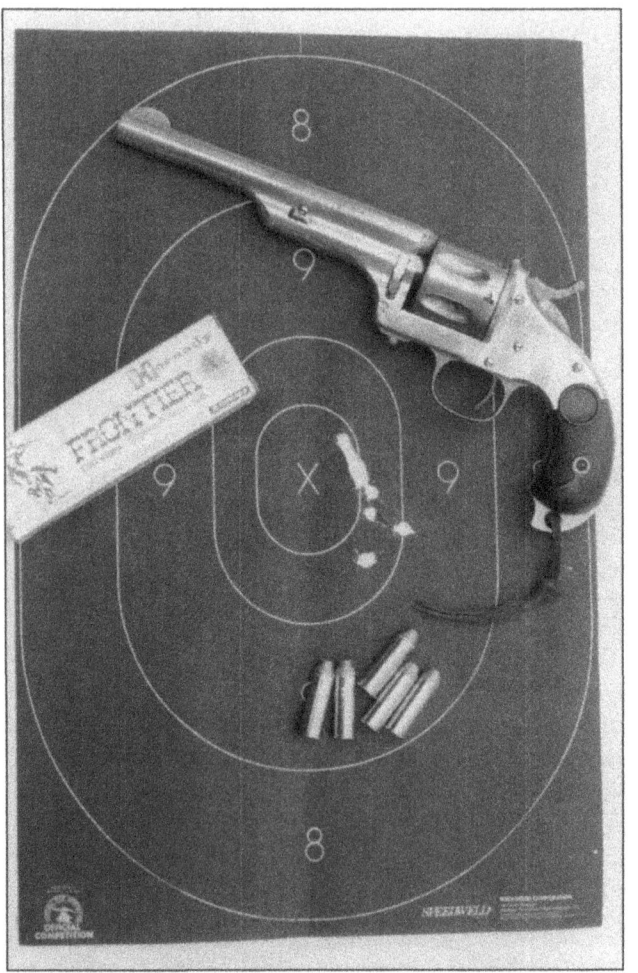

This 100-plus-year-old Merwin & Hulbert still shoots with black powder level loads.

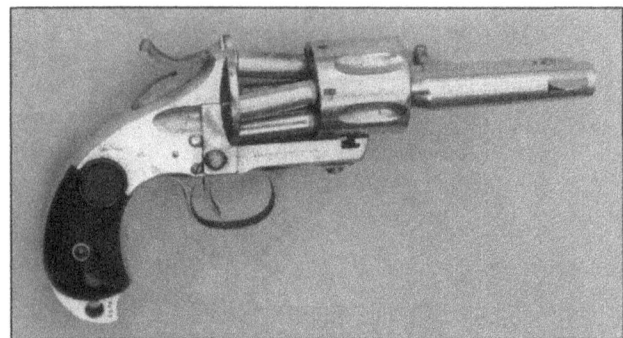

The automatic unloading of the Merwin & Hulbert is selective in that only empty cartridges will fall out.

Merwin and Hulbert

Perhaps the most fascinating of the early sixguns is the Merwin and Hulbert. Merwin and Hulbert were not the manufacturers but rather the sellers of these finely crafted sixguns turned out by Hopkins & Allen. The Merwin and Hulbert sixguns covered all the bases.

They were offered in both solid-frame and open top-frame versions, both single- and double-action models, and both full-size and pocket models. They were also way ahead of their time.

We have mentioned how quickly the Smith & Wesson Schofield could be unloaded and reloaded. The Merwin and Hulbert went one step further with selective extraction. When the barrel was unlatched at the top rear, and then rotated 90 degrees, the cylinder moved far enough forward so that only empty cases would fall out. It did not, however, reload as fast as the Smith & Wesson design as the barrel had to be re-latched and then fresh cartridges were inserted from the side when the loading gate was opened.

They were other models available, however, we have covered what I consider the most important. They all carry high price tags today and should be relegated to collector status only. Fortunately for shooters, most models are available in replica form. We will look at the double-action models of the 19th century from both Colt and Smith & Wesson in the chapters on these two sixgun manufacturing giants. There were also other manufacturers, however, Colt, Remington, and Smith & Wesson were the most important. If you had lived at that time, which one would you have chosen?

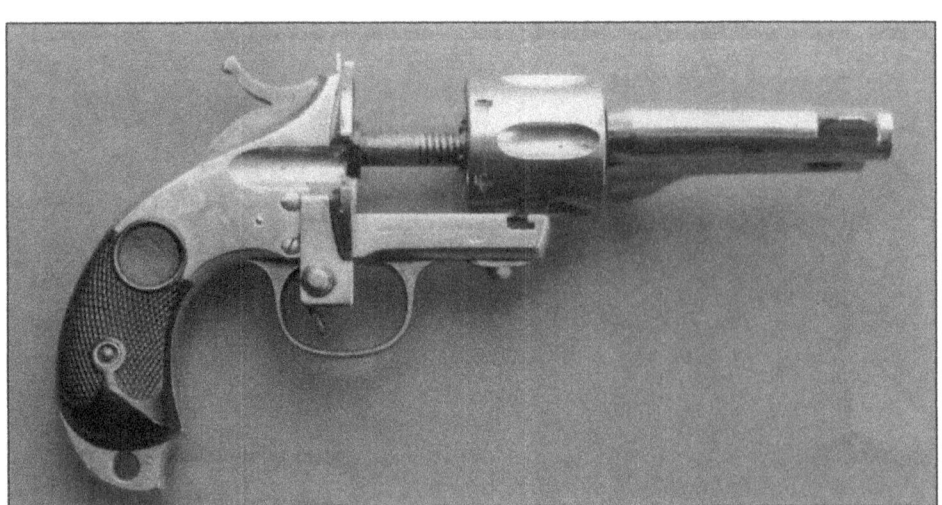

The cylinder of the Merwin & Hulbert rotates 90 degrees to the right for unloading.

CHAPTER 2

COLT'S MODEL P: THREE LEGENDARY GENERATIONS

In spite of the inadequacies, shortsightedness, and just plain foolishness of men, some things are simply just meant to happen. Such is the case of the Colt Single Action Army, the fabled Peacemaker. It was not born overnight, and in fact came into being only when the United States Army forced the issue. There were three major revolver manufacturers of the 19th century. Colt and Remington started with percussion or cap and ball sixguns and only switched to cartridge-firing revolvers when they realized they had no choice. The third manufacturer, Smith & Wesson, being much more progressive, started by producing a seven-shot, single-action, spur-triggered, tip-up revolver that was not only the first successful revolver to fire fixed ammunition, it was also the first firearm chambered in .22 Rimfire.

Smith & Wesson's Rollin White held the patent on bored-through cylinders that accepted fixed ammunition as opposed to the front-loading cylinders of Colt's sixguns. The Colt percussion revolvers were serious fighting weapons in .36 and .44 caliber, while Smith & Wesson built hideout guns in .22 and .32 Rimfire chamberings. The little Smith & Wessons were quite popular with officers during the Civil War and were often found under their military uniforms.

The immediate forerunners of the Colt Single Action Army, shown here in replica form, were the 1860 Army, the Richards Conversion, both with Eagle UltraIvory grips; and the 1871-72 Open-Top with Tiffany grips fitted by John Adams.

The natural evolution of the Colt Single Action 1860-1873: the .44 1860 Army, the .44 Richards Conversion, the .44 1871-72 Open-Top, and the .45 Single Action. UltraIvory grips by Eagle, Tiffany Grips by John Adams.

The first cartridge-firing revolver arrived in 1857, and Colt, which had by now produced the Walker, the 1st, 2nd, and 3rd Model Dragoons, and the 1851 Navy .36, virtually ignored the development of what would prove to be one of the most important firearms inventions in history, and instead continued to concentrate on percussion revolvers, resulting in a magnificent 1860 Army .44 three years later. This gun would certainly prove to be a financial success for the Colt Company as it was the official United States Army sidearm during the Civil War and for several years thereafter. As far as Colt was concerned, it was doing everything right and continued to believe cap and ball sixguns were still the future.

Actually, Smith & Wesson had planned to build top-break .44 caliber sixguns firing fixed ammunition during the early 1860s. However, this project had to be put on the back burner until after the war. The first big-bore cartridge-firing sixgun arrived as the .44 S&W American in late 1869. It was originally chambered in .44 Rimfire, the same ammunition that was then being used in two great lever guns, the Henry Model 1860 and the Winchester Model 1866, and .44 S&W, a centerfire cartridge. Although some units during the Civil War had purchased their own 1860 Henry rifles, it was never an official United States Army firearm. When the Army, which had been equipped with 1860 Colt Army revolvers since the advent of the Civil War, ordered 1,000 Smith & Wesson revolvers, it decreed that the cartridge be changed to a .44 caliber Centerfire. Hence, the .44 S&W emerged as the first centerfire cartridge chambered in Smith & Wesson revolvers.

It was probably this order from the military for the newfangled cartridge-firing sixguns that finally woke up the powers to be at Colt. In fact, their shortsightedness goes back even further as Colt had first crack at Rollin White and his patent. However, they were not interested, and White went to Smith & Wesson. Suddenly, Colt was left producing what would very soon prove to be an obsolete design. Colt could not get around the patent that allowed Smith & Wesson to build sixguns with bored-through cylinders, so it looked for other options until the 1860 Army Model parts would run out.

During the late 1860s, approximately 5,000 Colt cap and ball sixguns were altered to fire fixed ammunition by using the Thuer Conversion. Thuer's invention allowed a cartridge to be inserted from the front end of the cylinder, but it did not work very well and wasn't very successful. Colt had thousands of parts on hand for building 1860 Army Models. At the same time the United States Army had thousands of sixguns in use that fired round balls that were seated after the powder charge was placed in each cylinder and then each nipple had to be capped. Suddenly, this was a tremendously outdated and slow proposition.

Colt then turned to the Richards patent to convert cap and ball sixguns to the new fixed-ammunition style. The Richards Conversion can be recognized by an ejector rod that sticks out behind the ejector rod housing about 1 inch. The back end of the cylinders were cut off and a new section was fitted, or a completely new cylinder was built to accept rimfire cartridges. Colt was on its way to catch up with progress, but it would take the United States Army to push the company completely over the edge.

Serving the Army

In 1872, Colt introduced its first big-bore cartridge-firing sixgun. This was not a conversion, but a completely new revolver. However, Colt was still not quite ready to let go of the past. This Model 1871-72 Open-

It may be old but it still shoots! Five shots at 50 feet with a Colt .45 made in 1881. Grips are by Buffalo Brothers.

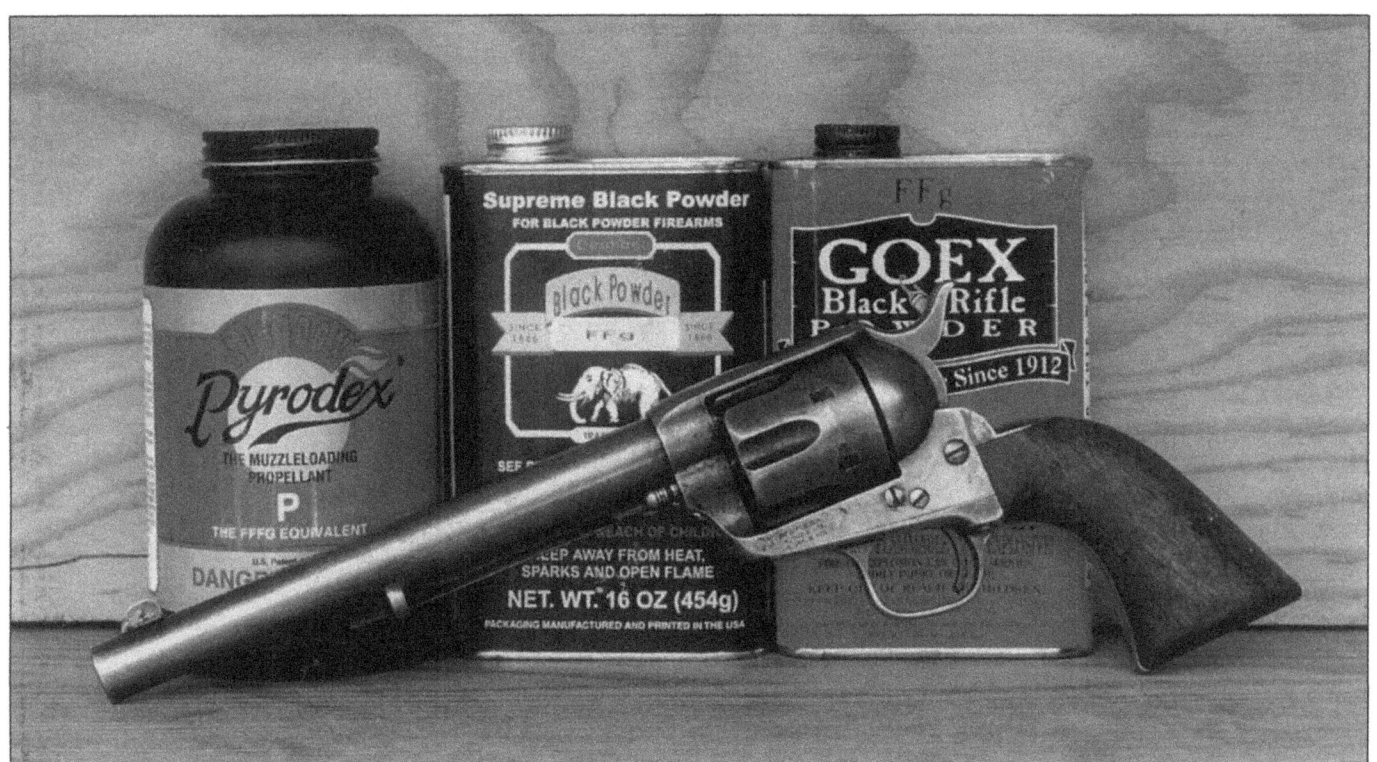

This .44-40 Frontier Six-Shooter left the Hartford plant in 1881 and is still used regularly today with black powder loads.

Oldies but goodies are the 7 1/2-inch .44-40 Frontier Six-Shooter from 1879 and a U.S. Cavalry Model dating back to 1881.

Top looks much like the basic 1860 Army cap and ball revolver with its open-top frame. Remington had been building solid-frame revolvers for nearly 15 years, and Smith & Wesson had gone with a break-top design with the frame extended over the top of the cylinder, but Colt tried to stick with the same design it had used since 1836. The Army wanted something more substantial.

The Army began tests in late 1872 to adopt a new sidearm. The design submitted by Colt was the Open-Top in .44 Rimfire. The Army wanted a solid-frame revolver and eventually decreed that it be in .45 caliber. Colt went back to the drawing board and the result was the Colt Single Action Army. We cannot credit Sam Colt with the design of the Model P, as it came to be known at the factory, since he had died 10 years earlier. His legacy is the lineup of cap and ball revolvers — the Paterson, the Walker, the Dragoons, the 1851 Navy, and the 1860 Army. The Colt Single Action would instead come from the inventive genius, and perhaps some supernatural inspiration on the part of William Mason.

The Colt Single Action Army was designed with one goal in mind: the Army contract. The original Single Actions submitted for testing were still chambered in .44 caliber. It is believed that the first one, possibly the first two, were chambered in .44 Russian, and the others in .44 S&W American, as that was the service cartridge of the time in the S&W Model 3 American. When the Army ordered 8,000 to 10,000 Single Actions, it specified that the caliber be changed to .45, and with such a lucrative contract Colt was certainly happy to oblige. It is evident that without the Army, we may never have had the Colt Single Action Army or the .45 Colt cartridge. Almost seems like it was a divine plan.

Since those first single actions were designed for military use, they were offered in a barrel length of 7 1/2-inch for cavalry use and to duplicate the balance and feel of the earlier 1851 Navy and 1860 Army. This Cavalry Model was joined by a 5 1/2-inch version that came to be known as the Artillery Model, but not until the 1890s. Colt had submitted .45 test guns to the Army in 1874 with barrel lengths of 5 1/2, 6 1/2, and 7 1/2 inches. The Army decided to stay with the longer barrel length. They were carried butt to the front in a full flap holster on the right side. A total of slightly over 37,000 7 1/2-inch Cavalry Model Colt's were ordered from 1873 to 1891. Barrels were replaced by Colt with new 5 1/2-inch barrels or cut to that length by armorers and officially adopted in 1895. This version received the "Artillery Model" designation informally when it was assigned to artillery batteries during the Spanish American War.

A century separates these two 7 1/2-inch Colt .44-40s. The top sixgun is a Third Generation from the 1970s, while the bottom Frontier Six-Shooter dates back to 1879. Beautifully carved leather is by Chaparral.

The U.S. Army had the Cavalry Model, 7 1/2-inch .45, known at the factory as the Model P, while the civilian market knew it as the Peacemaker. It would also become known as the Hogleg and the Equalizer. Civilians had a choice of either 5 1/2 or 7 1/2-inch .45s. Beginning in 1877, the Model P was offered in .44-40 as a companion piece to the 1873 Winchester. Single Actions so chambered were etched on the left side of the barrel with "Colt Frontier Sixshooter." The original 7 1/2-inch .45s had no caliber marking on the barrel, but rather a simple "45" on the left side of the trigger guard. Early .44-40s are found with a 45 trigger guard, which means they had been converted to the Winchester cartridge.

Someone decided to cut the barrel to a length even with the end of the ejector rod housing, and the 4 3/4-inch Civilian Model arrived. Many have tried to give Bat Masterson credit for the short-barreled Single Action Army as a letter exists in which he ordered a nickel-plated .45 Colt "... with a barrel even with the ejecting rod." However, both history and factory records show that the short-barreled Civilian Models were available at least three years before the Kansas lawman ordered his. In 1877, both 4 3/4- and 5 1/2-inch barreled Single Actions were sent to Colt's London office chambered in .450 and .455 Eley. The Model P would also eventually be chambered in two other English cartridges, the .450 Boxer and .476 Eley.

Personally, I prefer the 7 1/2-inch Cavalry Model for general use simply because it is easier for me to shoot accurately than with the shorter barrel versions. However, one has to admit that the 4 3/4-inch Colt Single Action Army is one of the finest-balanced sixguns, perhaps the finest, in existence. From a properly designed holster it may very well be the fastest sixgun for that all-important first shot. In the movies we may hear and see the hero besting the bad guy who went for his gun first. This is a myth perpetuated by Hollywood. All other things being equal, whoever went for his gun second usually finished second and one who practiced religiously could draw faster than anyone could react.

In addition to the standard barrel lengths of 4 3/4, 5 1/2, and 7 1/2 inches, customers could have just about any barrel length they wanted. When offered without an ejector rod housing, they became to be known as "Sheriff's Models" or "Storekeeper's Models," although at the factory they were simply recorded as "without ejector rod housing" versions. Long-barrel versions were also available, at an extra cost of course, but those known as "Buntline Specials," which had a folding leaf rear sight, are found only in the serial number range of 28,800-28,830. These are found mostly in .45 Colt, however, a few have surfaced chambered in .44-40.

If they could only talk! This Bisley Model .38-40 and Single Action .32-20 are both 100 years old and have seen lots of use, yet are still shooting superbly.

Growth of a legend

In these days of sophisticated target pistols it may be hard to believe that the Colt Single Action Army was once highly regarded as a target pistol. Beginning in 1888, shooters could have their Colt Single Action Army in a Flat-Top version complete with adjustable sights. Although crude by today's standards, they consisted of a rear sight in a dovetail slot that could be tapped for windage adjustment, and a blade front sight that could be raised or lowered and locked in place with a small screw. It was an improvement over the fixed sights of the original Single Action Army. It would only remain in production until 1895, as it was replaced by a better target pistol a year earlier. In 1894, the Flat-Top 7 1/2-inch Model P was fitted with a wide target hammer and trigger, and a special grip frame for target shooters.

The backstrap comes up higher along the back and deeper behind the trigger guard as well as the front strap being angled more to the front. The result was the Bisley Flat-Top Target Model named after the location of pistol matches in England.

The Colt Single Action was carried by gunfighters on both sides of the law. Jesse James, Cole Younger, John Wesley Hardin, Wyatt Earp, Doc Holliday, Bill Tilghman, Chris Madsen, Heck Thomas — the list goes on and on. My all-time hero, Theodore Roosevelt, carried a 7 1/2-inch Colt Single Action Army while ranching in the Dakotas. In 1916, before heading into Mexico after Pancho Villa, a young Army lieutenant picked up a fully engraved, ivory-stocked, nickel-plated 4 3/4-inch Colt Single Action Army in El Paso. That gun would become famous, carried in an S.D. Myres holster on the hip of General George S. Patton in World War II. It now resides in the West Point Museum and has two notches cut into the grip.

Frank Hamer, a former Texas Ranger, was called out of retirement to end the career of the infamous Bonnie and Clyde. As with most real-life heroes, Hamer has been treated unfairly by Hollywood, but the fact remains that he was a real one-riot, one-Ranger type of lawman. His favorite sidearm was "Old Lucky," a plain Jane Colt Single Action .45. And even as "modern" double-action sixguns and semi-automatics began to be more readily available, Hamer still very often packed his .45 loaded with five rounds and the hammer down on an empty chamber, with no extra ammunition or cartridge belt. When asked about this supposed lack of firepower, Hamer responded that if he couldn't get it done with five rounds, he was simply "guilty of sloppy peace-officering."

A most popular variation of the Colt Single Action Army was the Bisley Model shown in the three standard barrel lengths of 4 3/4, 5 1/2, and 7 1/2 inches.

There are those detractors who have said that Hamer went modern and carried a .45 Government Model the same as the rest of the posse on the quest for Bonnie and Clyde. Jim Wilson, my fellow gun writer and friend, and former sheriff of Crockett County, Texas, was able to contact Frank Hamer Jr., who substantiated that his famous father always carried two guns: his .45 Colt Single Action and a back-up. His normal back-up was a .44 Special Triple-Lock, but on his final assignment the .44 Special was replaced by a brand-new Colt .38 Super. His sixgun of choice, then and always, was his Colt Single Action Army.

The good guys' gun

Without the Colt Single Action, there would have been no heroes galloping across a silver screen during Saturday matinees all over the country in the 1930s and 1940s. Can we even begin to imagine Roy Rogers, Gene Autry, Hopalong Cassidy, Wild Bill Elliott or even John Wayne carrying anything but a Colt Single Action?

That most popular TV western, *Gunsmoke*, is still shown daily on cable TV nearly 50 years after its inception. The stories were great, the cast of characters was superb, and those in my generation really cared about the characters. Matt, Chester, Miss Kitty, Doc, Festus, and Newly were all very real to us. However, the real star of the show was often the 7 1/2-inch Colt Single Action (the early sixgun used was actually a Great Western) wielded by James Arness as Matt Dillon. When he drew that 7 1/2-inch .45 we all knew that wrong was about to be made right.

Speed mattered

We have mentioned the speed possible from a properly designed holster with a 4 3/4-inch Colt Single Action. In the hands of a trained expert there is no sixgun nor semi-automatic faster for the first shot than the Colt Single Action Army. The emphasis is definitely on "expert." This has been proven over and over again by countless trained shooters and personalities like Bill Jordan, Elmer Keith, and Skeeter Skelton, all men I have been privileged to know. However, they all carried double-action sixguns for the simple reason that after the first shot the double action quickly outpaces single-action sixgun.

Glenn Ford, in his starring role in *The Fastest Gun Alive* and most subsequent movies, carried his Colt Single Action in a rig quite different from other stars of the time. Ford's holster rode higher, and in front of it, sewed to the belt, was a thick piece of vertical leather. Ford would cock the hammer in the holster, fire the first shot as the gun came level, then swipe the hammer back on the piece of leather as the sixgun came forward and fired the second shot. Practical? No, but it certainly looked great in the movies!

Charles McDonald Heard, a teacher of fast draw for Hollywood heroes, went Ford one better. Heard cocked the gun in his specially designed holster for the first shot, caught the hammer by fanning with the thumb of his left hand for the second shot, then as his hand came around, swept the hammer back with the little finger for the third shot. This is done so fast that one cannot count the shots. Expert exhibition shooter Bob Munden not only does it with three shots, but can also do it with four, five, or six shots.

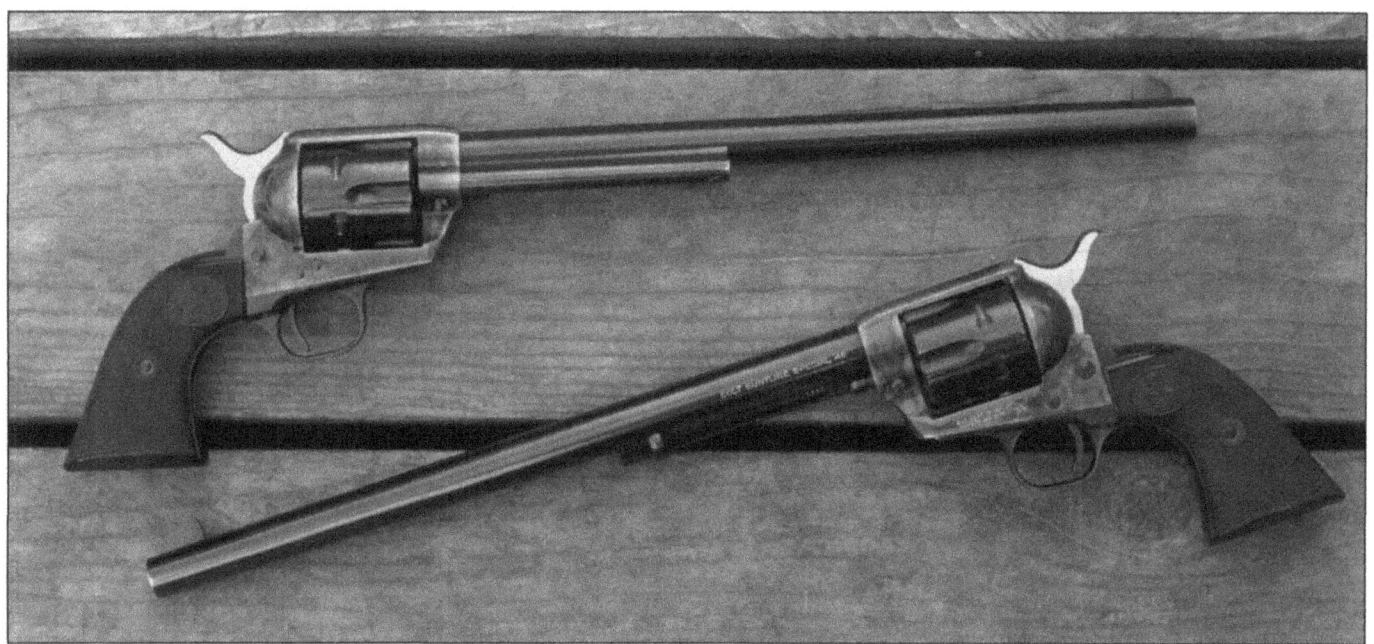

With the rising popularity of such TV westerns in the 1950s as Wyatt Earp, Colt reintroduced the Buntline Special with a 12-inch version chambered in .45 Colt.

Whether fitted with factory hard rubber grips or stags, the 4 3/4-inch Single Action Army is a natural pointer and probably the fastest gun from leather.

Hollywood often used fanning, or holding the gun with one hand with the trigger held back while the other hand slaps the hammer, for great effect. Of course, this was always done with blanks. Ed McGivern proved that the Colt Single Action Army actually could be fanned very accurately and he would put a cylinder full into a space that could be covered with one hand. However, he was definitely an expert and also used the relatively heavy .38 Special chambered Colt loaded with low-recoil .38 wadcutters to accomplish this.

End of an era

From 1873 until 1941 nearly 358,000 Colt Single Action Army sixguns were produced in more than 30 calibers. The five most popular, along with their approximate production figures, were: .45 Colt (158,885), .44-40 (71,391), .38-40 (50,621), .32-20 (43,264), and .41 Long Colt (19,676). Of the four basic models, the approximate numbers manufactured were Single Action Army (310,386), Single Action Army Flat-Top Target (917), Bisley Model (44,350), and Bisley Model Flat-Top Target (976). With the introduction of the Smith & Wesson .44 Special in 1907, the Colt 45 ACP in 1911, and the Smith & Wesson .357 Magnum in 1935, Colt eventually offered the Single Action Army chambered in these calibers with approximately 500 offered both in .44 Special and .357 Magnum, but only less than 50 chambered in .45 ACP.

The greatest production years for the Colt Single Action Army Model P were 1874 (14,800), 1883 (17,000), 1901 (17,000), 1902 (18,000), 1906 (15,000) and 1907 (16,000). The latter year would be the last time that the production amounts would run to five figures. Only once after this did the numbers exceed 4,000 Single Actions manufactured and that was in 1911. By the end of the World War I, shooters began to discover the newer Smith & Wesson and Colt double-action revolvers as well as the 1911 Model. By 1935 and 1936 production figures were down to approximately 100 per year. The combination of worn-out machinery, lack of demand, and the advent of World War II all worked to end the 68-year run of the Model P. At the time Col. Charles Askins summed it up best when he said, "Many an eye was dampened when the startling news was broadcast that Colt would discontinue manufacture of the grand old Peacemaker."

In the late 1940s, after the war, Colt did assemble approximately 500 Single Actions from parts it had on hand. Its official stance was that the Colt Single Action Army would be no more and it would be too expensive, costing approximately $100,000, to retool with the machinery. Even if it did spend the money, who would buy such an antiquated firearm when they could have a Colt Model 1911 in .45 ACP or .38 Super or a Smith & Wesson .357 Magnum, as well as several double-action Colt or Smith & Wesson .38 Specials? The market just wasn't there.

Welcome the westerns

Then something very strange happened and history took an unexpected turn and suddenly living rooms all around the country were filled with "B" westerns via the new medium of television. By the 1950s these old Hollywood productions were joined by new TV shows and the western was king of the entertainment industry. Shooters wanted revolvers like those used by Roy, Gene, and Hoppy, as well as the new heroes, Matt Dillon, U.S. Marshal, and that knight in black, Paladin.

Two new companies emerged to meet the demand. Ruger, which had started in 1949 with a very inexpensive .22 semi-automatic that performed like a target pistol, now read the public correctly and brought out a scaled-down version of the Colt Single Action Army with all coil springs and a virtually unbreakable lock work and chambered in .22 Rimfire. It was an immediate success. One year later, on the other side the country, Great Western in California began producing what were basically duplicates of the Colt Single Action Army except for a frame-mounted firing pin. It was not enough. Shooters still wanted real Colt Single Actions and in 1956 the Model P was resurrected as the Second Generation Single Action Army

Colt invested in all new machinery and began producing new model P's in both .45 Colt and .38 Special that were clearly the equal of the best of the first-generation Colts. I was fortunate enough to have grown up in the 1950s and was definitely a fan of western movies and single-action sixguns. My first handgun, like most kids in those days, was a Ruger Single-Six .22, which was quickly followed by my first centerfire revolver, a 4 3/4-inch .38-40 Colt Single Action made in 1899. So it was only natural that I would grab the first Second Generation Colt Single Action to arrive at my local gun shop. It was a 7 1/2-inch, blued and case-hardened example and cost me $125 at a time when I was making $1 per hour.

The Second Generation single actions came nowhere near lasting as long as the First Generation run, achieving less than 20 years by the time they were pulled from production in 1974. Only the .45 Colt would last for the full run, being offered in the

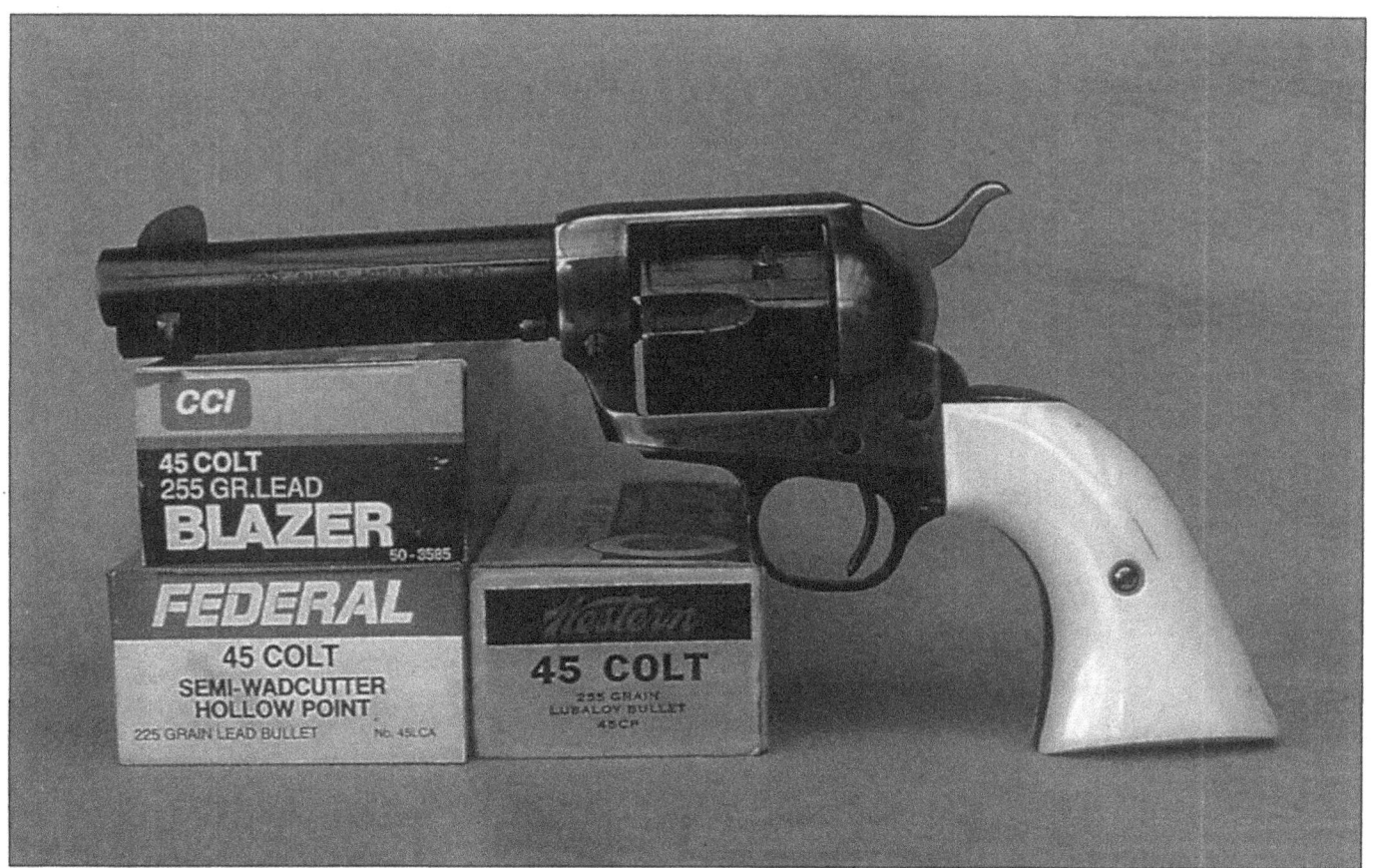

If ever a sixgun deserved to be called a classic it is the 4 3/4-inch Colt Single Action Army.

The single actions of the 1950s (from left): Ruger's .357 Magnum Blackhawk, a Great Western .357 Atomic, and a Colt Single Action.

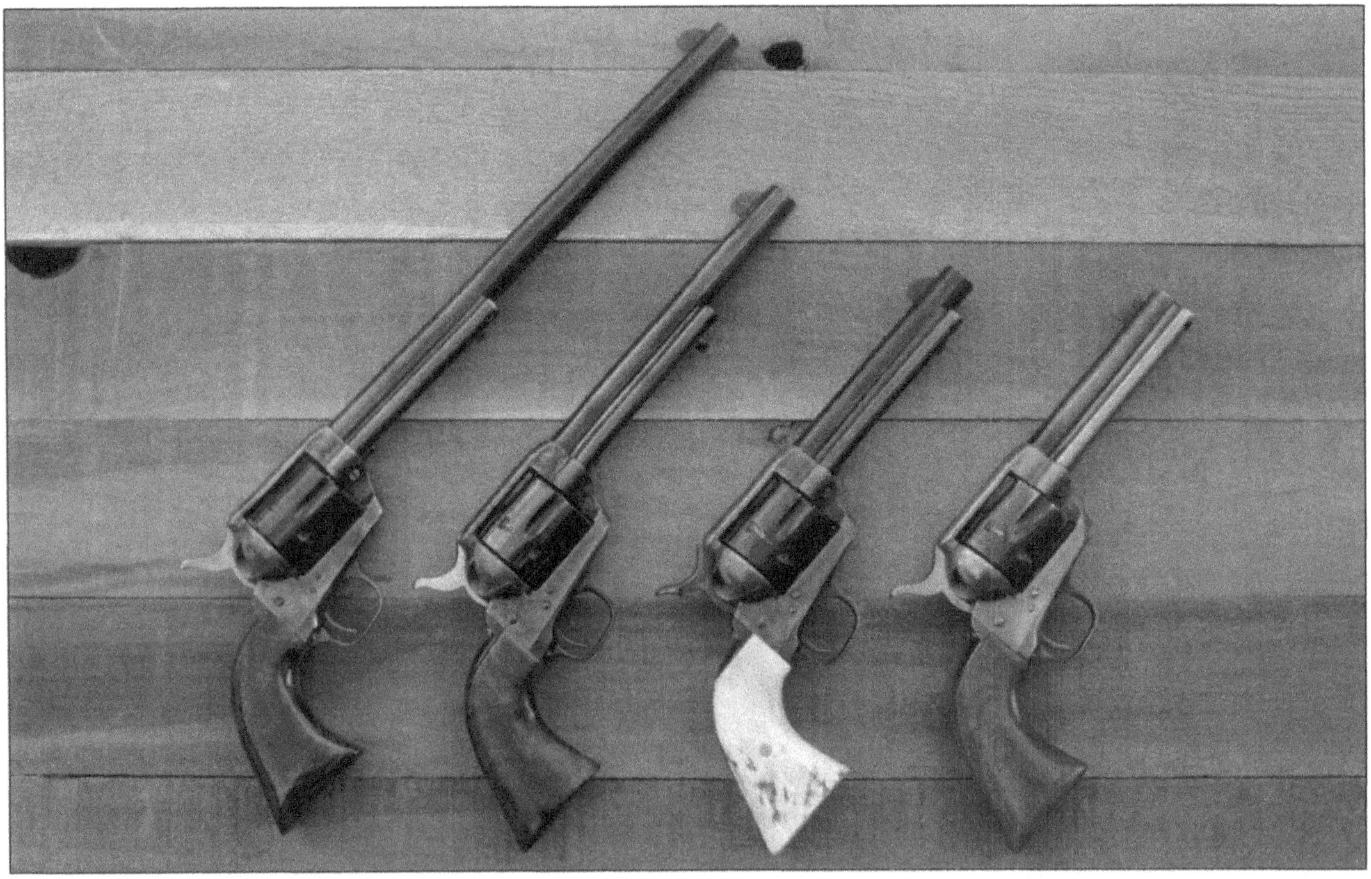

Second Generation Colt Single Action Armies were offered in barrel lengths of 4 3/4, 5 1/2, 7 1/2 and 12 inches.

One of the most beautiful sixguns to ever come from the Colt factory is the New Frontier. This 4 3/4-inch .45 Colt wears factory ivories.

A pair of favored sixguns for hunting are these Second Generation New Frontiers: a 7 1/2-inch .45 stocked by Bob Leskovec and a 7 1/2-inch .44 Special with ivory grips by Tony Kojis.

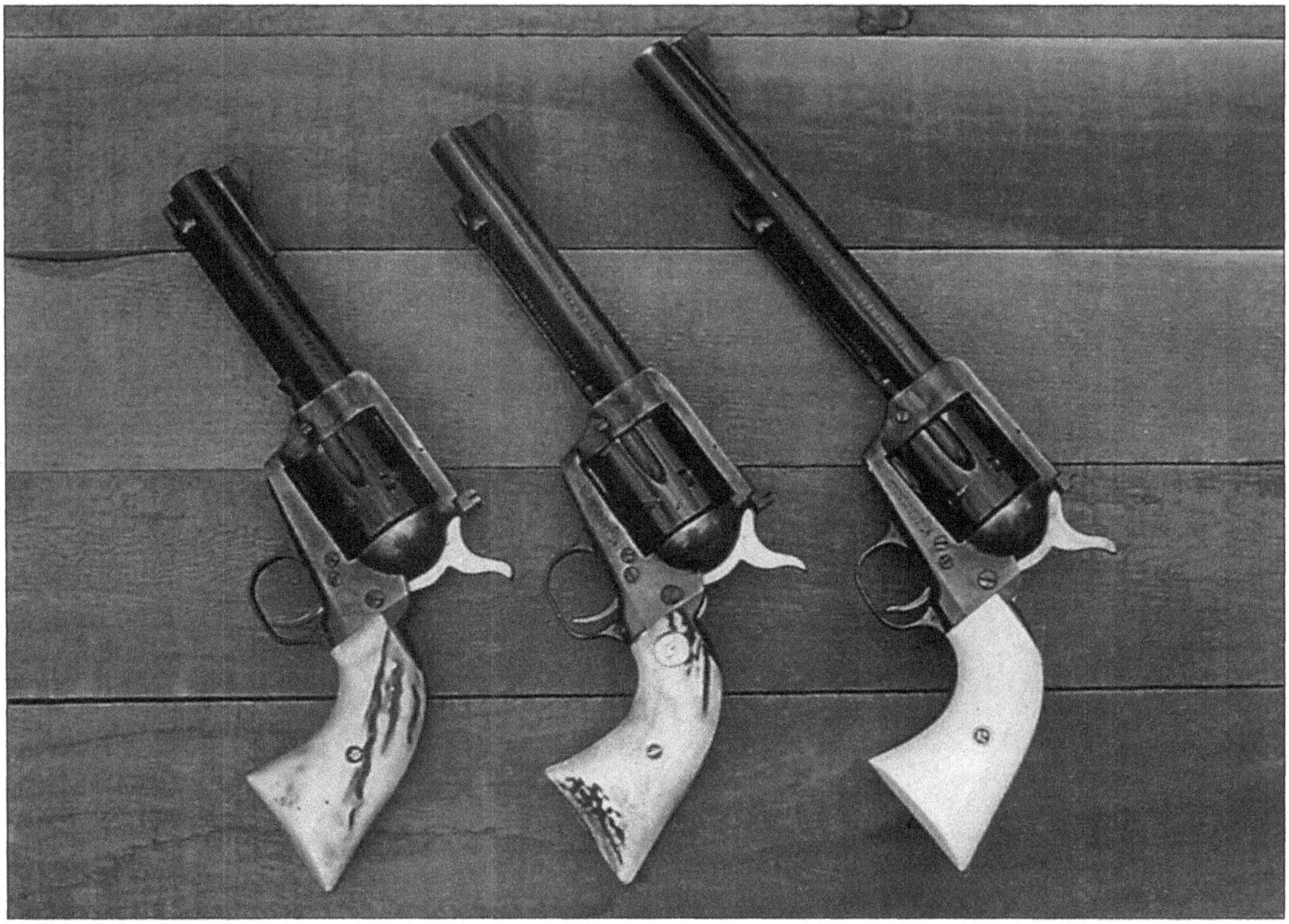

As with the Single Action Army, the barrel lengths of the New Frontiers were standardized at 4 3/4, 5 1/2, and 7 1/2 inches.

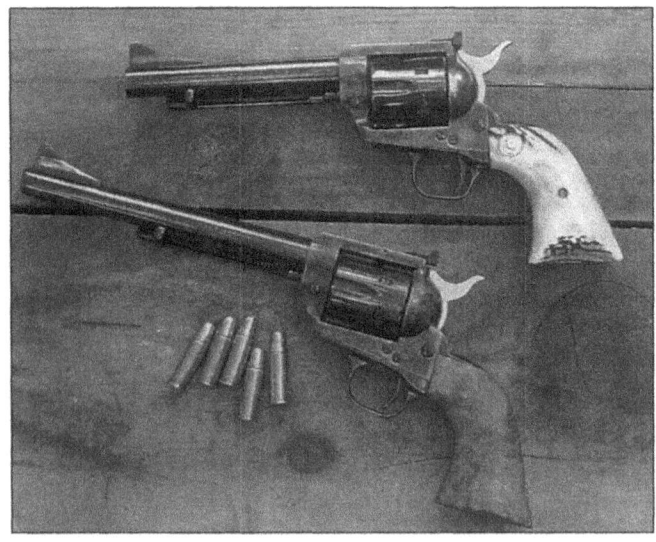

Excellent examples of the gun makers' art. These .44 Special New Frontiers, both Third Generations, are a 5 1/2 inch tuned by Tom Sargis, and a 7 1/2 inch tuned and stocked by Bob Munden.

three standard barrel lengths of 4 3/4, 5 1/2, and 7 1/2 inches and in either blue/case hardened or nickel finishes with approximately 37,000 being manufactured. They demand premium prices today with the 4 3/4-inch version at the top of the list. They were also offered in a 12-inch Buntline Special and a very rare 3-inch Sheriff's Model.

The .38 Special offered in the same standard barrel lengths and finishes as the .45 Colt would only last until 1964 with a total of approximately 11,700 being manufactured. There really was no need for the .38 Special after the .357 Magnum debuted in 1960. With a total production of approximately 17,375, the Magnum Model would last alongside the .45 Colt until 1974 in all the standard finishes and barrel lengths. The rarest of the Second Generation Colt's are those chambered in .44 Special. For some reason, although offered in both blue and nickel, the .44 Special was produced only in 5 1/2-inch and 7 1/2-inch versions with a total of approximately 2,230 Specials coming out of Hartford.

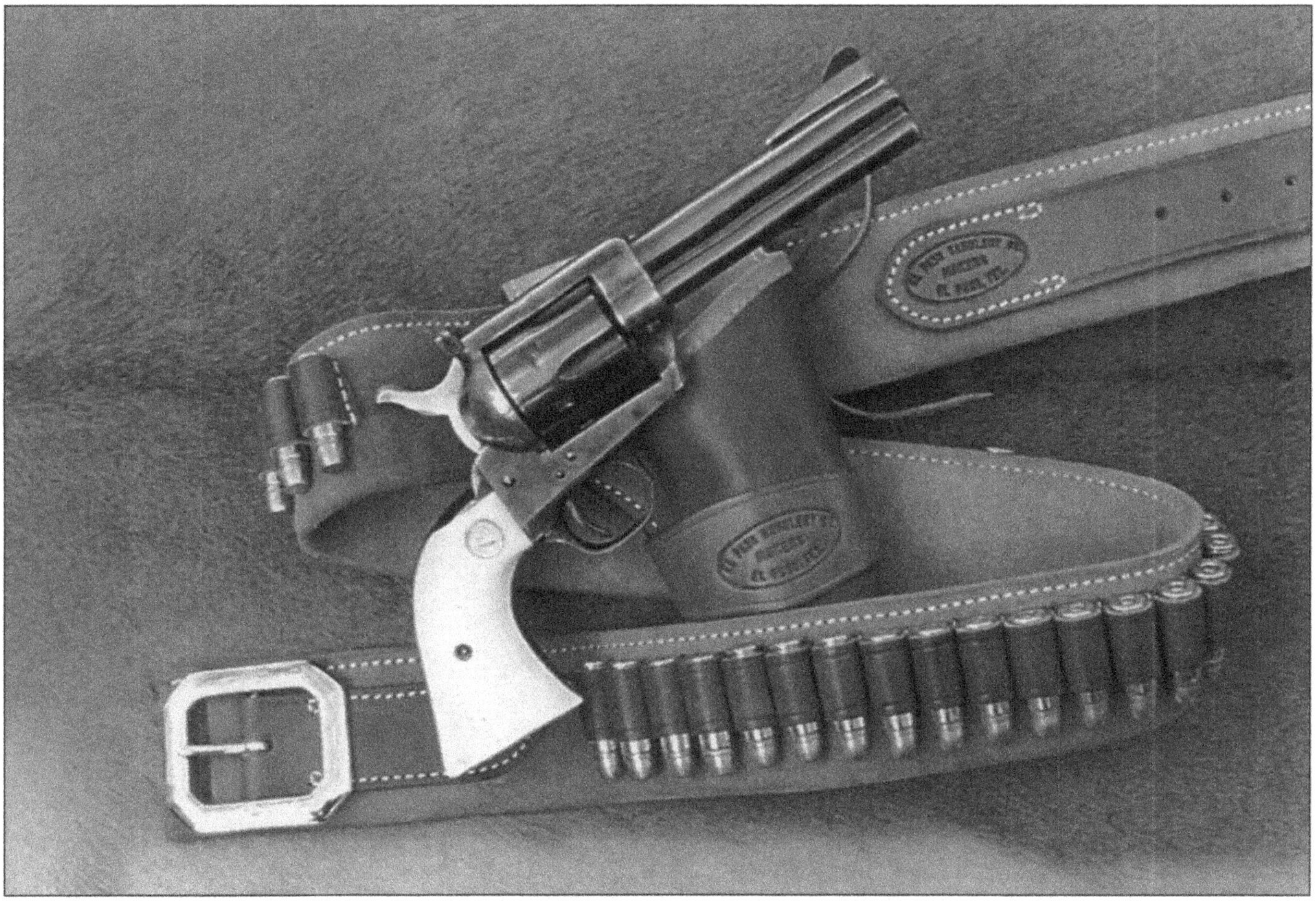

Classic sixgun, classic leather. El Paso's Duke rig and the 4 3/4-inch Colt New Frontier.

It not only looks good, it shoots good: the 4 3/4-inch .45 Colt New Frontier.

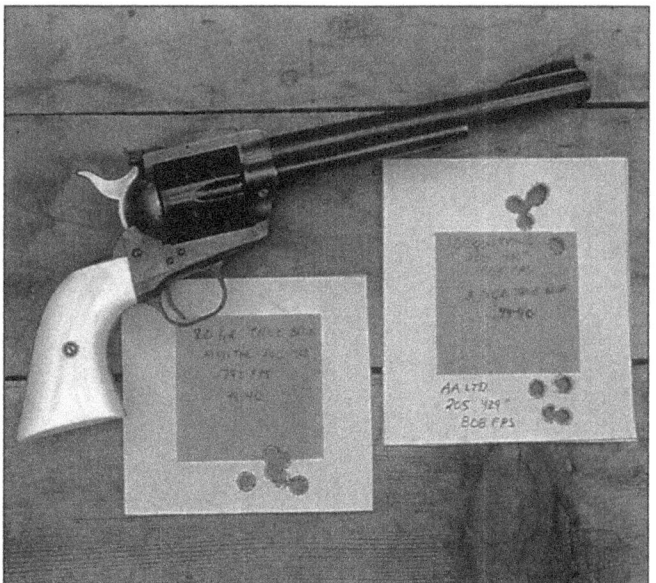

Who says the Colt Single Action is not a target pistol? This .44 Special New Frontier will shoot with the best of them.

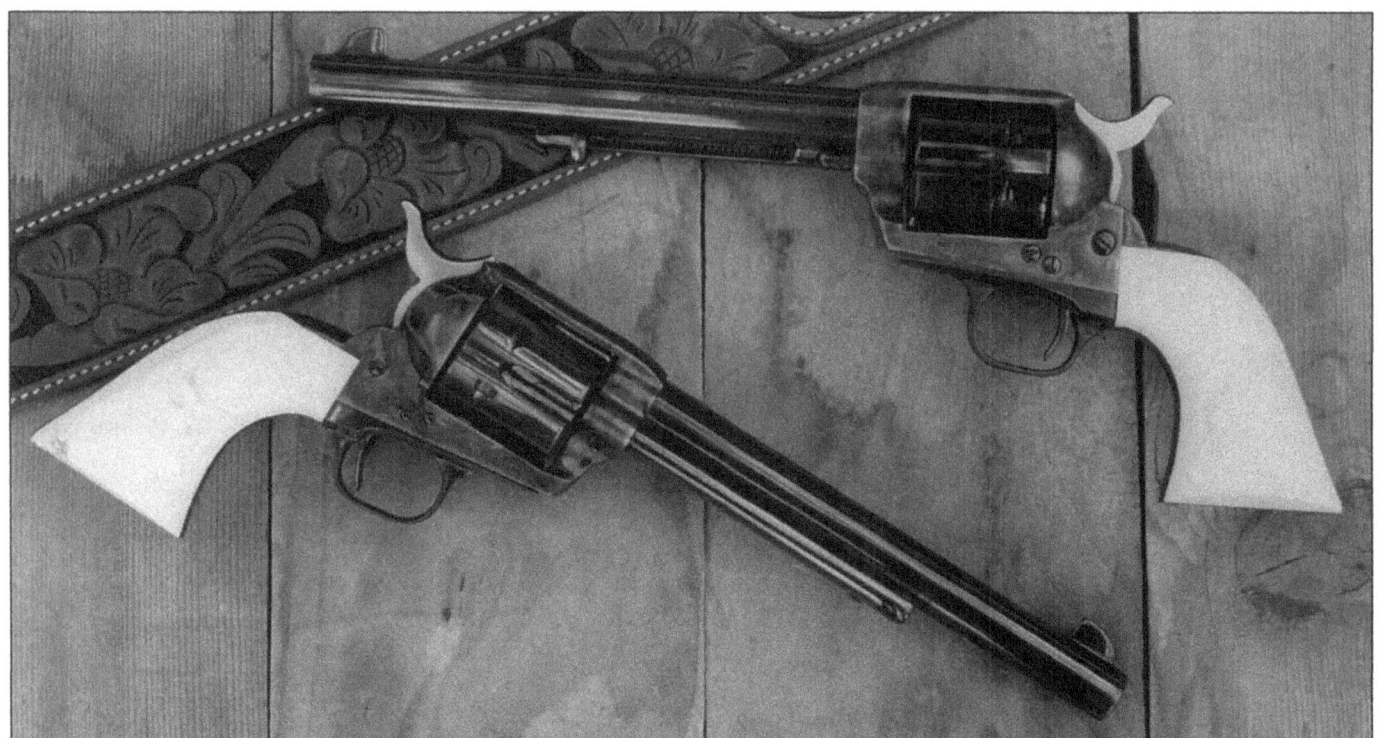

These beautiful Third Generation 7 1/2-inch Colt Single Action .45s have been tuned and smoothed by Bob Munden and stocked with ivory by Paul Persinger.

The author poses 1890s style with a 7 1/2-inch Colt Single Action Army.

Although they look like they came from the same era, the top sixgun is a Third Generation .44-40 totally rebuilt and antiqued by Peacemaker Specialists, while the lower gun is a circa 1917 .45 that Peacemaker Specialists also totally rebuilt on the inside and stocked with an older set of fleur-de-lis ivories.

These Civilian Model Peacemakers have all been totally rebuilt and stocked with stag horn and ivory by Peacemaker Specialists.

All three of these 7 1/2-inch Single Actions are chambered in .44 Special: a First Generation converted from .32-20, and a Second Generation that originally started life as a .38 Special, both conversions by Eddie Janis of Peacemaker Specialists; and a Third Generation stocked and tuned by Tom Sargis.

More than 100 years of Colt Single Action Armies are represented by, beginning at top right, a First Generation .45 Colt, a Second Generation .44 Special, a Third Generation .44-40, a Second Generation .45 Colt, and a Third Generation .38-40.

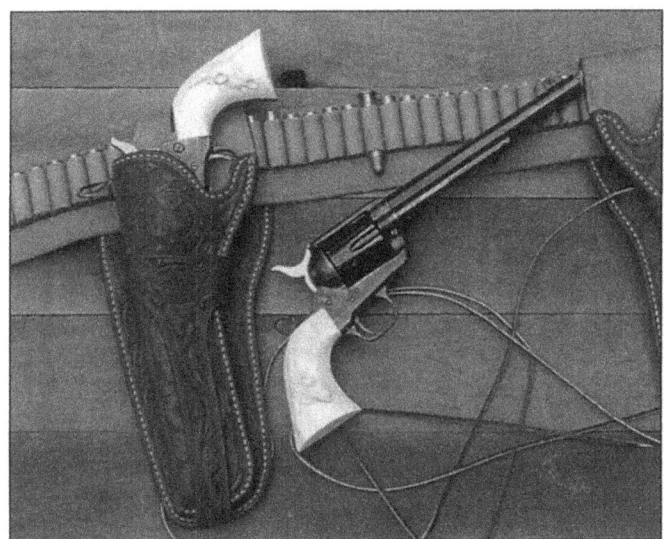

It doesn't get any better than this! A pair of 7 1/2-inch Colt Single Actions tuned by Bob Munden, ivory gripped by Paul Persinger, and with 1897 Sweetwater holsters by El Paso Saddlery.

The New Frontier

John Kennedy was elected in 1960 and with him came the beginning of his New Frontier. Colt sought to honor him by bringing forth its New Frontier Single Action Army. This was basically an upgrade of the old Flat-Top Target Model of the 1890s. The New Frontier of the 1960s had a fully adjustable rear sight, a ramp front sight, and flat-topped mainframe. They were exquisitely finished with a deep blue and vividly colored case hardening on the mainframe. The serial number range of the Second Generation New Frontiers is 3000NF to 7300NF.

The New Frontiers, which I consider the most beautiful Colt Single Actions ever produced, were also made in the same four calibers as the standard Colt Single Actions. Standard barrel lengths were also the same at 4 3/4, 5 1/2, and 7 1/2 inches, but neither the .38 Special nor the .44 Special were cataloged in the 4 3/4-inch version. The calibers, with their dates of manufacture and approximate production figures, are: .45 Colt, 1961-1974, 1,625; .38 Special, 1961-1963, 49; .44 Special, 1962-1966, 255; and .357 Magnum, 1962-1974, 2,178. Somewhere between five and 10 New Frontier Buntlines were manufactured in 1966-1967.

By 1974, the machinery was wearing out once again and the Colt Single Action Army and the New Frontier were both pulled from production. For the second time, the Colt Model P was no more. When production of the Second Generation Colts ended, the serial numbers had run from 00001SA to 73,000SA. The "SA" suffix had been added to the serial numbers to distinguish them from the pre-war Single Actions. That was the bad news. The good news was that Colt planned to resume production with new machinery.

The third generation

The Third Generation Colts arrived in 1976 with two minor changes to cut production costs. The design of the operating hand and the cylinder ratchet

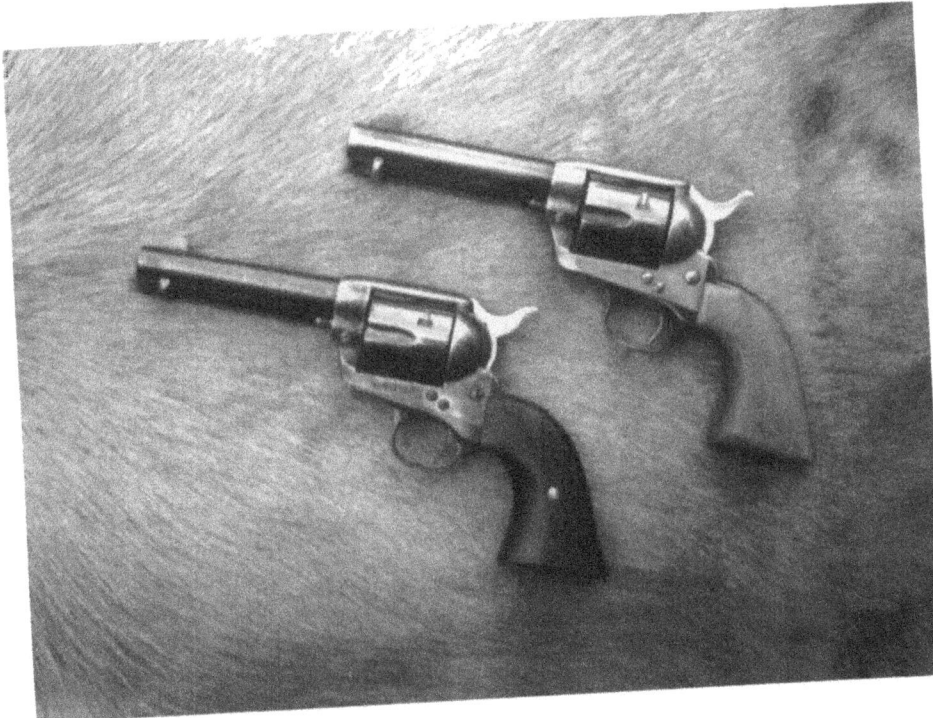

Although separated by more than a quarter of a century, this 1957 Second Generation .44 Special, cut to 4 3/4 inches and stocked by Tony Kojis, and the 1987 Third Generation .44 Special with black micarta grips by Charles Able, perform identically well.

Totally tuned and reblued by Bob Munden, stocked with stag by BluMagnum, this 5 1/2-inch .44 Special Single Action comes very close to perfection.

were both changed for easier assembly and less hand fitting, and the cylinder no longer had a full-length bushing. Instead, it had a press-in fit button bushing at the front end of the cylinder. The only other change from the original black-powder frame, which had a screw and entered the front of the frame to hold the cylinder pin in place, was the addition of a spring-loaded cylinder pin catch — a change that had occurred before World War I. That made three basic changes in more than 120 years. However, the third-generation Colts brought one non-operating change that seems to make little sense. The threads on the barrel shank and frame were changed from 20 TPI to 24 TPI, which means that Third Generation barrels could not be readily fitted to First or Second Generation models.

The Third Generation Colts would only last from 1976 until 1982, when production ended once again. The serial number range began with 80001SA, and switched to an SA prefix when 99,999SA was reached. During this brief run the Model P began with the .45 Colt and .357 Magnum, with the .44 Special added in 1978, and the .44-40, which had not been seen since 1941 (except for a special 100th anniversary commemorative run of 7 1/2-inch nickel-plated sixguns inscribed with "COLT FRONTIER SIXSHOOTER" in 1973), being added in 1980. The New Frontier also came back in 1978 with the beginning serial number

Two craftsmen worked their magic on this Third Generation .44-40. Engraving by Dale Miller, ram's horn stocks by Paul Persinger.

Four eras of the 7 1/2-inch Colt Single Action Army are represented (from left) by an original 1879 .44-40, a Second Generation .44 Special, UltraIvory grips by Eagle Grips; a Third Generation .44 Special, tuned and stocked by Tom Sargis; and a current production "Longhorn" .44-40 by American Western Arms.

being 01001NF. All Third Generation New Frontiers have five-digit serial numbers.

A total of approximately 8,543 Third Generation style .45 Colt New Frontiers were made in 4 3/4-, 5 1/2-, and 7 1/2-inch versions. Other calibers, barrel lengths and production figures were: .44 Special, 5 1/2 and 7 1/2 inches, 3,544; .44-40, 4 3/4 and 7 1/2 inches, 1,565; and .357 Magnum, 7 1/2 inches, 509.

As Colt began to phase out the Third Generation Single Actions in the early 1980s, numerous nonstandard models were offered, such as full blue or nickel New Frontiers, full blue Single Actions, unfluted cylinder models, and Buntline Specials in .44-40 and .44 Special. Three-inch Storekeeper's Models also surfaced in .44-40, .44-40/.44 Special, and .45 Colt. In 1984, the Colt Single Action Army became a Colt Custom Shop offering, and since that time, it has been offered in the three standard barrel lengths and both blue/case hardened and nickel, and in calibers .45 Colt, .44-40, and .38-40. Currently, the only offerings are 4 3/4- and 5 1/2-inch .45s and .44-40s in blue/case hardened or nickel. As this is written, Colt has just announced the re-introduction of the .357 Magnum Single Action Army.

A lifelong love affair

As a teenager, I purchased a First Generation 4 3/4-inch .38-40 in 1957 that dated back to 1899. That old Colt Single Action Army was in excellent shape, although with faded case colors. I added a pair of handmade one-piece walnut stocks and ordered a Lawrence Gunslinger outfit in black basket weave finish. Boy, I was proud of that sixgun. It cost me two weeks pay plus the leather, which added another weeks worth of work to the bill. I could barely afford to shoot more then a few rounds at a time in those pre-reloading days.

Marriage, three young babies, and college tuition all followed in rapid succession and it became a case of groceries or guns and all but a few of my sixguns got away. As I finished college and began to have a few more dollars coming in than going out, I looked for a replacement First Generation .38-40 for the one that had been sold. None ever surfaced at a reasonable price. When I heard that Colt would once again produce a .38-40 Single Action Army in the Third Generation series, my heart skipped a beat. After 35 years I finally had another 4 3/4-inch .38-40 Colt Single Action Army.

Purchasing a First Generation .38-40 was a real act of faith. Barrel grooves and chamber mouth diameters ran from tight to oversize and it was not uncommon to have a tight chamber and oversized bore, or vice versa. If everything fell just right and you were kind to your parents and lived right and were uncommonly

The Third Generation .38-40 will shoot! A little work with the file brings the groups right up to point of aim.

lucky, you just might get a .38-40 with the proper-sized barrel and cylinder. That problem disappeared with the Third Generation .38-40s as they are produced with tight barrels and cylinders and set up to use bullets sized at .400 inch. They do shoot extremely well. It has been worth the wait.

Just what is so special about the Single Action Army — a design that had its beginning nearly 175 years ago with the first Sam Colt designed single action? Why is it still around? Why is it still in demand? How can Colt continue to sell this "antiquated" sixgun that carries a retail price tag of more than $1,500? I could easily say for those that understand, no explanation is necessary; while for those that do not, no explanation is possible. But I will try.

Pick up a Colt Single Action and you'll discover true spiritual sixgun quality. The aesthetic value of the Colt Single Action Army cannot be approached by any other handgun. Slowly cock the hammer and listen. As the big hammer moves past the safety notch one hears a distinct "C"; the hammer travels past the half-cock and an audible "O" registers. As the hand pushes against the ratchet on the back of the cylinder, one who listens carefully can hear an "L"; and finally, as the hammer and trigger come together in the firing mode, a definite "T" resounds. Just the operation of the action of a Single Action Army spells C-O-L-T.

Pick up a Colt Single Action Army and let it speak to you. It will tell tales of frontier gunfights, buffalo hunts, Indian fights, trail drives, and stagecoaches. Hold onto it and you will hear the tinkling of a piano from the Longbranch Saloon; smell bacon and beans

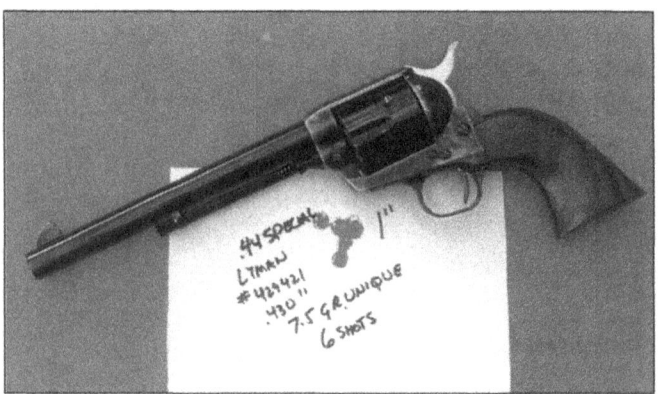

Tom Sargis tuned and stocked this .44 Special, which shoots like a target pistol with a Lyman Keith 250-grain bullet over 7.5 grains of Unique at 950 fps.

A charge of 6.0 grain of Unique with a 240-grain bullet duplicates the original .44 Special load and in this Colt Single Action Army shoots superbly and easily.

cooking over a campfire; see across endless miles of prairie grass; feel the wind on your face as the first snow falls in the high country; and taste steak and potatoes and a big slab of apple pie washed down by cups of steaming, hot, black coffee.

Greatness endures

Some may say that the Colt Single Action is outdated and fit for museum display only. They said the same thing about the Peacemaker with the coming of the first truly workable double-action revolver. They said it again in 1911 with the birth of the Colt Government Model semi-automatic. It was heard again in 1941 when the Colt was removed from production, and I heard it was ancient and not worthy of my time in the 1950s when I started shooting. I still hear it today and I still ignore it. There's no doubt the Colt Single Action is an ancient design. So is man. It has flat springs that will break, especially the hand and bolt springs. But even someone as fumble-fingered as I am and as devoid of gunsmithing skills can replace either.

There are those that still claim that the Colt Single Action Army is inaccurate and there is no way the long hammer fall can allow groups that will match modern double action and semi-automatic handguns. Don't believe it! With the right load, and in the right hands, a Colt Single Action .44 Special or .45 Colt of any generation will still group five shots within one inch at 25 yards even with old-fashioned fixed sights. And it will do it with 250-260 gr. bullets at 900-1000 feet per second with a gentle recoil that allows one to shoot all day in comfort.

No other big-bore sixgun is as easy to holster as a Single Action Army. It rides securely and simply in a minimum of leather. It balances in leather and it balances in the hand, so much so that I believe that the marvelous balance and design of the Colt is so perfect than it moved from the area of invention to that of discovery. In my mind it has never been equaled. The traditional Colt Single Action Army is one sixgun that comes from the factory with comfortable and usable stocks. The only reason to add custom stocks is for looks and for personalizing. The Colt Single Action Army is really easy to dress up by fitting it with custom stocks of fancy wood, stag horn, pearl, ivory, or ram's horn.

A defense weapon?

The question naturally arises as to whether a Colt Single Action is still a viable alternative for defensive use and/or concealed carry. It would be well to remind ourselves that for nearly 70 years the Colt Single Action, be it one of a cap and ball models or the Model P, was state-of-the-art when it came to self defense. Double-action revolvers arrived in 1877 with the Colt Lightning, were improved in the 1880s and 1890s and arrived at near perfection with the Smith & Wesson Triple-Lock .44 Special in 1907. Semiautomatics arrived in the 1890s and also reached near perfection before World War I with the Colt Government Model. In spite of these two great advances, many pistoleros, including Texas Rangers, held on to their Colt Single Actions well into the 20th century.

For those who seek a self-defense handgun, the double-action revolver must be rated as first choice. It is followed by the double-action semi-automatic, the 1911-style semi-automatic, and finally the single-action sixgun. No handgun is any faster for the first shot from leather than a Colt Single Action. There's no practical difference between action styles for that first shot. The order of preference is based on simplicity of operation. For the first two it is simply a matter of drawing the gun and firing. No matter which firearm is chosen, training is crucial and especially so with a Colt Single Action.

I would not encourage anyone to pick a Colt Single Action as their first choice for a defensive handgun or concealed weapon. However, if the choice is made, there are several things that are crucial. First, we must forget everything we have ever seen in the movies concerning the use of a Colt Single Action and start all over again. Gun handling in movies is about as far removed from reality as it is possible to be. Nearly everything movies teach about guns is both dangerous and virtually impossible. Secondly, one must be competent when it comes to both the operation of, and the reloading of, the single-action sixgun. Any handgun that is carried for self-defense purposes should be used for regular practice. Practice that not only includes shooting, but drawing from the carry position and also reloading. This is even more imperative with Single Actions than with other types.

Finally, we have the inherent danger that is built into a cocked Colt Single Action. If you carry a Colt Single Action for defensive use and have to draw this sixgun and cock it, then what? The gun is cocked and not fired. We must know what to do when it comes to lowering the hammer. In the case of the Colt, we are lowering the hammer on a live round. Now what? We must be trained to be able to return the single-action sixgun to a safe position with the hammer down on an empty chamber. Only in the movies does one lower the hammer on a live round and re-holster.

In the movies seemingly every one runs around with a cocked Colt Single Action. This is dangerous!! A double-action sixgun requires a pull of around 10 pounds to cock the hammer with the trigger and fire. A semi-automatic has a safety that can be left on until one is ready to fire and then the safety is pushed off. Not so with the Colt Single Action. Once that hammer is cocked, it is ready to fire and lowering the hammer places a loaded round under the firing pin. The most prudent use of a Colt Single Action for defensive purposes is to grasp it two-handed and cock the hammer with the off hand ONLY when it is deemed necessary to fire.

Colt Single Actions and New Frontiers carry hefty price tags. It makes no sense to heavy load them. Ruger Blackhawk and Freedom Arms sixguns are built for heavy-duty use, not Colts. Selected loads for both the Model P and the New Frontier are shown here, and while these are not heavy loads, they should still be used with the normal caution that accompanies a careful reloader. Cylinder walls of Colt Single Actions, especially the .45 Colt, are very thin. Don't push 'em!

For some reason, probably nostalgia, the standard Single Action Army sells for much more on the used market than the New Frontier, except in the more rare models, even though for an everyday working sixgun the adjustable sighted New Frontier is more practical and certainly the better choice for hunting.

SELECTED LOADS FOR THE COLT SINGLE ACTION ARMY

.45 COLT

BULLET	LOAD	MV 5 1/2"	MV 7 1/2"
Lyman #454424	7.5 gr. WW231	845	866
(260 grain)	8.0 gr. Unique	920	981
	9.0 gr. Unique	982	999
	20.0 gr. H4227	1040	1085

.44 SPECIAL:

Lyman #424421	6.0 gr. Unique	628	688
(250 grain)	7.5 gr. Unique	912	947
	16.5 gr. #2400	1107	1194
	17.5 gr. H4227	998	1056

.44-40 (.44 WINCHESTER CENTERFIRE)

Lyman #42798	8.0 gr. Unique		814
(205 grain)	9.0 gr. Unique		986
	10.0 gr. Unique		1107

.38-40 (.38 WINCHESTER CENTERFIRE)

BULLET	LOAD		MV 4 3/4"
Lyman #401043	8.0 gr. Unique		1022
(180 grain)	9.0 gr. Unique		1065
	10.0 gr. Unique		1235

CHAPTER 3

COLT'S DOUBLE-ACTION SIXGUNS

It was one of the worst cases of lust I had ever experienced. I first saw the picture of this beauty on the inside cover of a book at the downtown newsstand. I could not keep from looking at that picture. Over, and over, and over. I finally could not take it any longer. Something had to give. It was 1962 and I was married with two little kids and the third one on the way. There was very little time to get into any trouble of any kind as I was going to school full time and also working full time on the night shift at a local factory. Without my wife knowing it I found the time and rendezvoused with the new object of my affections.

On the way home from classes one day I stopped off at the company store and prepared to go over the edge. There it was, the same sixgun I had been dreaming about for several weeks. It was just about the most beautiful thing I had ever seen. No it was not a Colt Single Action, nor even a Smith & Wesson N-frame. There in the case was one of the new 4-inch Colt .357 Magnum Pythons. Not only could I not resist the Python, there next to it was a 6 1/2-inch Smith & Wesson .44 Magnum. My pay envelope would be a mite smaller every week for a long time. That purchase caused the first of only two "disagreements" Dot and I

Beginning in the 1890s, shooters had a choice of two new Colts: the Bisley Model (left) and the New Service.

It was very difficult to not heed the siren call of the first advertising for the 4-inch Python.

have had in 43 years. It wasn't the guns, but the fact that she felt we could not afford them at the time. She was right, of course.

The other clash came eight years ago when I bought another pair, not sixguns this time, but two malamute pups. They cost the same as that pair of sixguns 30 years earlier. This time it wasn't the money. She just didn't want to have the mess of puppies again, but I always wanted a pair of large dogs. Everything is fine with them now. They absolutely dote on her and as she is now home recovering from hip surgery, Red and Wolf spend their day surrounding and protecting her. (She loves 'em!) As you can guess, everything turned out O.K. I still have the picture, the Python and the Smith, the wife, who is as supportive as a wife can be when it comes to my avocation, the third baby was a boy, and we now have eight great grandkids.

The Colt Python

The Colt Python was the apex of Colt's double-action revolvers going back to 1877. Whoever wrote the advertisement for the Python that got me in trouble should win some kind of award for simplicity and strength. A simple picture of a 4-inch Python and three cartridges was powerful enough to send me buying: "THE COLT 4" PYTHON: NEW VERSION OF THE

At mid-20th century, anyone armed with any of these sixguns had chosen the best available: (left) Smith & Wesson's .357 Magnum and Combat Magnum; (right) Colt's New Service and Python.

Colt's Trooper, center, is basically a lighter and less finished Python (top and bottom).

FINEST HANDGUN EVER MADE. Hold .357 Magnum power in your hand, thumbstroke the wide spur hammer, look at the Royal Blue finish —this is Python, mister, the finest handgun around. But hold on — that 4-inch barrel says this is a new, all-purpose version of the world-famous handgun! It's the 4-inch Python, ideal for service, hunting or target work with either .357 or the ever-popular .38 Special ammo. You get the same fine accuracy and power in a versatile 4-inch barrel. And just as in every Python, you have handhoned contact parts, flawless action, and a heavier barrel with a ventilated rib to keep heat waves away from the sights. Your first few shots will tell you why the Python is accepted as the fastest, most accurate and best-looking handgun you can own. Where to see it? At your Colt registered dealer, of course. The magnificent 4-inch Python is sensibly priced at $125."

The Python has always been regarded as the Cadillac of Colt's double-action revolvers. As the advertising copy says, there are many shooters who value that it is the finest double-action revolver ever made. The roots of Colt's double actions go way back. Sam Colt himself had decided that both cartridge-firing and double-action sixguns were not to be. Even before Sam's death in 1862 there were double-action cap and ball revolvers such as the Starr and the British Deane and Adams. Colt felt that a double-action revolver simply could not have the accuracy of his beloved single action. William Mason was the guiding force behind Colt's Single Action Army, and he would also be the man responsible for Colt's first double-action revolver in 1877.

Today we have a situation where many arm themselves with semi automatics using high-capacity magazines and somehow think that the quantity of ammunition expended will take the place of training when it comes to being able to place that all-important first shot. Both Sam Colt in the 1850s and 1860s and the United States Army into the 1880s felt the same way and stayed with single-action revolvers. The prevailing idea was simply that a double-action revolver was not only more prone to breakage, but also encouraged the wasting of ammunition.

The "double-action" race commences

William Mason took another direction and in 1876, only three years after the Colt Single Action was adopted by the Army, this inventive genius introduced Colt's first double-action "self-cocking" revolver, the Model of 1877, the Lightning chambered in .38 Long Colt. This time, Colt jumped ahead of Smith & Wesson as the latter's first double-action revolver would not

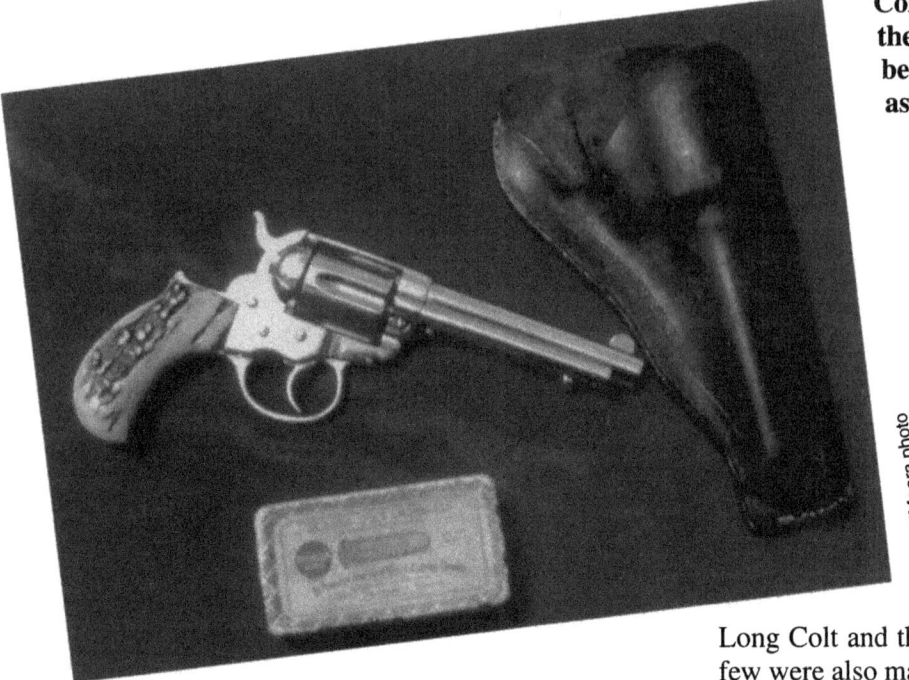

Colt's first double-action sixgun was the little .38 Long Colt Lightning. It became a favorite of such pistoleros as Billy the Kid and Doc Holliday.

surface until four years later. The Colt also proved to be a whole lot better looking, if not as sturdy, as the Smith & Wesson.

To come up with the Model of 1877, Mason basically scaled-down the Colt Single Action Army and in the process changed the mechanism to double action, meaning that it could be fired by simply pulling the trigger, or by cocking the hammer first. He also changed the grip frame to what is now known as the "birdshead" style with a small hump at the top of the backstrap to keep the grip from shifting in the hand when the gun was fired. This was just the opposite of all grip frames found on Colts from 1836 to 1873, which had a rounded backstrap to allow the grip to naturally roll in the hand under recoil.

The Model 1877 was available as the Lightning chambered in .38 Long Colt and the Thunderer in .41 Long Colt. A very few were also manufactured in .32 Long Colt. Although these were double-action revolvers, they still loaded through a loading gate on the right side, and unloaded with the use of an ejector rod exactly the same as the operations on the Colt Single Action Army. They were available both with and without ejector rod housings. The ejector-less "Sheriff Model" versions came in barrel lengths of 2, 2 1/2, 3 1/2, 4 1/2, and 6 inches while the standard models could be had with 4 1/2, 5, 6, 7, or

A popular chambering in the 1890s was the .41 Long Colt, as found in the double-action Thunderer and Army Special, as well as in the single-action Bisley Model.

7 1/2-inch barrels. Caliber markings are found on the left side of the barrel as "COLT. D.A.38," "COLT. D.A.41," or the very rarely encountered "COLT. D.A.32."

Mason maintained the same mechanical style of grip frame on the Lightning as found on the Model P. That is, the backstrap could be removed allowing the use of one-piece wooden stocks just as on the original Single Actions, and as with the originals, these were later changed to two-piece hard-rubber grips of black-checkered gutta percha.

Standard finish of the Model 1877 again copied the Single Action Army by being offered in both blue with a case-hardened frame and full nickel. They were, of course, also offered with custom stocks, such as ivory or pearl, and varying degrees of engraving. The major asset of the Lightning or Thunderer was not only the fact that it could be fired by simply pulling the trigger, its smaller grip frame also fit smaller hands much better than the full-sized Model P. This made it much more attractive to women and youngsters.

Its major drawback was the fact that the mechanism was very fragile. I can well remember when I first started looking seriously at sixguns in the 1950s that it was very easy to find a 19th-century Single Action Army in excellent mechanical shape, however, the search was much more difficult to find a like example among the 1877 Models. Its assets evidently outweighed its liabilities as the Lightning and Thunderer stayed in production until 1910.

Probably the most famous pistolero to carry and use an 1877 model was William Bonney. "The Kid" had small hands and found the grip frame and operation of the .41 Thunderer much more to his liking than the larger .45 Single Action Army. The dentist turned gunslinger, Dr. John Holliday, "Doc," was also known to carry a double-action Colt Model 1877 in a shoulder holster.

Elmer Keith was also quite fond of Colt's first double-action sixgun, at least in his early years. At the age of six he was impressed seeing an "old cowpuncher" who carried a .41 Thunderer in his left chaps pocket. Later he related, "We returned a Lightning model in .38 long caliber to J.H. Fitzgerald of Colt, and had him make it into a .41 with the barrel just to the end of the extractor. Colt did a beautiful job on it, but fitted to it what I will always believe to be an Army Special barrel. At any rate, the gun with barrel just to the end of the extractor made one of the fastest double actions of the old-timer type I have seen and I carried it for years out of sight in my left chaps pocket. It was also quite accurate with the 200-grain .41 Long Colt load either inside or outside lubricated. I preferred the inside lubricated 200-grain load. I later swapped it to an old gunfighter, Sam Russell, for a pair of .45, 4 3/4-inch-barreled, single actions with ox head carved pearl grips on each, together with belt and holsters. Sam simply would not let me keep that gun and was after it every time I rode in to Helena from the ranch. He finally got it."

There are two things here that speak very highly for the .41 Thunderer. First, of course, is the fact that Keith carried one for years. Secondly, a savvy old gunfighter like Sam Russell, whose pair of .45 Colts were confiscated by the judge when Russell was sentenced to prison for a shooting, had a friend steal those guns back so he could swap them to Keith for the Thunderer.

Full-size double action arrives

One year after the introduction of the Lightning and Thunderer 1877 Models, William Mason looked even closer at the Colt Single Action Army and came out with a full-sized double-action revolver. They are so close in size, in fact, that in later years Colt used leftover cylinders from the Model of 1878 in Colt Single Action Model Ps. These are easily recognized as the double-action cylinders had longer flutes than the production single-action cylinders.

Colt's first full-sized double-action revolvers still maintained a loading gate and an ejector rod, but the Colt was definitely starting to modernize as the mainframe and grip frame were now one solid piece. Early stocks were two-piece checkered wood, later ones checkered rubber, and of course fancy stocks of ivory

Colt's first big-bore double-action sixgun was the Model 1878. Carried in a skeletonized shoulder holster and chambered in .45 Colt, it was much favored by those who could not work a single action with any degree of speed.

and pearl were available on special order. Most models were fitted with a lanyard ring in the bottom of the butt. Barrel lengths on the 1878 Model were standardized at the same 4 3/4-, 5 1/2-, and 7 1/2-inch lengths of the Single Action Army, as well as being offered in the ejectorless versions with 3 1/2- or 4-inch barrels. Calibers offered were much the same as those found in the Model P, though not as numerous. They included: .45 Colt; the three Winchester Centerfires, .44-40, .38-40, and .32-20; the two Long Colts, .41 and .38; .44 Russian; .32 Long; and .22 Rimfire. As you might expect, some of these are extremely rare. For the English market, the Double Action Model 1878 was also chambered in .450, .455, and .476. Also very, very rare are Target Model 1878s.

After the Colt Single Action Army .45, the Army went to a kinder, gentler cartridge — the .38 Long Colt in the 1890s. It is believed that Theodore Roosevelt and his commanding officer, Leonard Wood, both carried .38 double-action Colts in the Spanish American War. However, the use of .38 caliber by the military was short-lived. The story, which may be true or not, was that the .38 proved to be less than effective on Moro warriors in the Philippines, so in 1902, the United States Army ordered 5,000 Colt Double Action revolvers on the 1878 platform. This model has been called both "Philippine" and "Alaskan" and is easily recognized from standard models by its oversized trigger guard. The latter designation makes more sense as the larger trigger guard would be compatible with gloves worn in the cold climate during winter duty in Army installations.

The Model of 1878 was advertised by Colt as the "New Double Action, Self-Cocking, Central Fire, Army, Six Shot, .45 inch caliber, Revolving Pistol. This pistol has the double hand or pawl, is made of the best quality steel and a superior workmanship, and is in all respects the best Double Action Pistol ever made. It takes the U.S. Regulation Cartridge, used by the U.S. Cavalry. It can be cocked by the thumb, if preferred, or can be cocked and fired by pulling the trigger."

The last 1878 Model would be shipped by Colt in the last month of 1907. The 1878 Model .45 was at least 50 percent more expensive than the Army-issued .45 Single Action, however, it was often personally purchased by Army officers. The highest serial number known is 51210. Among the owners of this first large-framed double-action Colt were Tom Horn and Buffalo Bill.

While Colt had gotten there first with a double-action sixgun, Smith & Wesson carried over the automatic and simultaneous ejection of fired cartridges and easy loading from its single-action models when it introduced a double-action revolver in 1881. At about this same time, William Mason of Colt was granted the first patents to provide for a swing-out cylinder. This cylinder operated on a crane that pivoted at the front of the frame and allowed the cylinder to be unlatched and to swing out from the frame. An ejector rod in the center of the cylinder was then pushed rearwards to eject all cartridges. Colt's first double action built on this principle arrived with the double-action 1889 Navy Model chambered in both .38 and .41 Long Colt with a 6-inch standard barrel

This Colt .45 1878 is the "Philippine" or "Alaskan" Model. The large trigger guard allows it to be used with gloves.

The Colt Official Police (above) would rival S&W's Military & Police for the position of most favored peace officer sidearm during much of the 20th century.

length. Civilian models were also additionally offered with 3- and 4 1/2-inch barrels.

This model would be followed by a line of double-action revolvers designed for Army and Navy use with the models of 1892, 1894, 1895, 1896, 1901, and 1903. Each succeeding model was slightly improved over the preceding version. These were also chambered in .38 and .41 Long Colt and eventually in .32-20 and .38 Special. The model most encountered seems to be the Army Special in .32-20. Stocks for these double-action models were normally plain walnut or checkered rubber. The final double-action Colt offered in this series was the Marine Corps Model of 1905 with a 6-inch barrel, rounded butt, and chambered in .38 Long Colt and .38 Special.

The New Service era

Meanwhile, Colt was also working on one of the greatest double-action revolvers ever produced. All mechanical ties with the Colt Single Action Army had now been severed and the New Service would be a large-framed double-action revolver with a swing out cylinder. Once again, Colt beat Smith & Wesson to the draw with a modern, large-frame, big-bore, double-action revolver as the New Service arrived in 1898, 10 years before the first Smith & Wesson .44

The Colt New Service was the largest sixgun made prior to World War II and was chambered in .45 Colt, .44-40, .44 Special, .38-40, .38 Special, and .357 Magnum.

Doc O'Meara photo

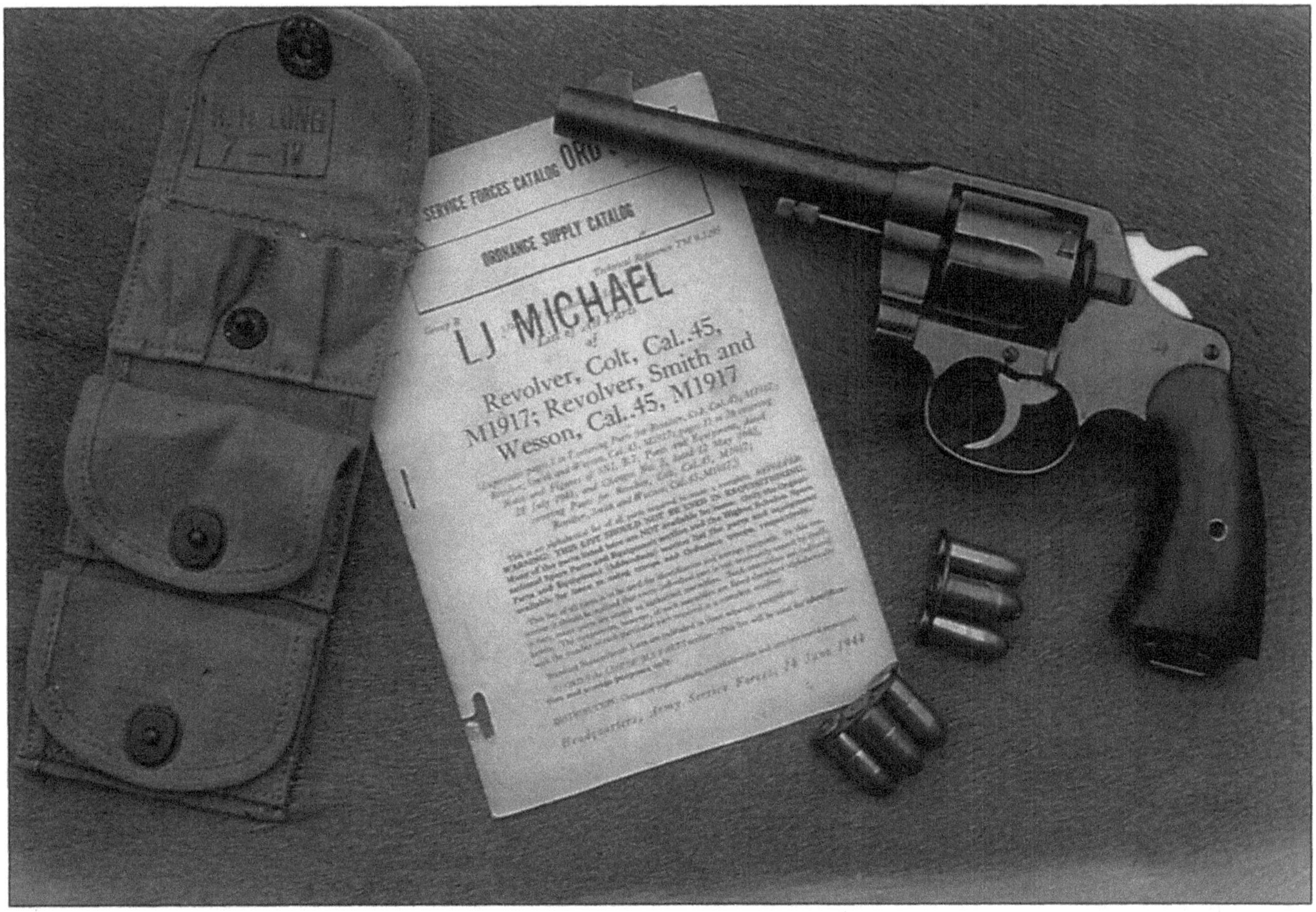

When the Colt 1911 could not be manufactured fast enough to supply the troops in World War I, the Colt New Service was chambered in .45 ACP and became the Model 1917.

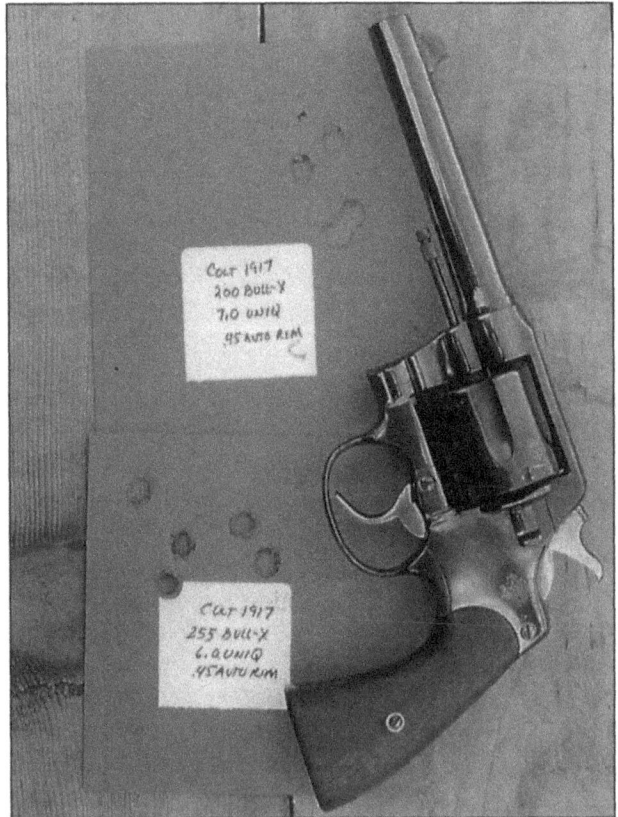

Even with its long cylinder, the New Service/Model 1917 provided more than adequate battle accuracy with the short .45 ACP.

This New Service "Russian and S&W Special .44" has been given a new lease on life by being completely rebuilt by Milt Morrison of Qualite Pistol & Revolver.

Special. Older model New Services had a strange look to them, with a narrow trigger guard that appeared to have been added on as an afterthought. This was changed after the turn of the century with a trigger guard that was the same width, and also looked to be part of the main frame. Early barrels were straight, which produced an awkward appearance where they mated with the main frame. The addition of a tapered barrel with a noticeable collar where it met the frame was a tremendous cosmetic improvement.

With the outbreak of World War I and our subsequent entrance into it, there was a great demand for sidearms and Model 1911 .45 ACP Government Models could not be made quickly enough. The answer to the solution, both at Colt and Smith & Wesson, was the 1917 Model. Colt supplied more than 150,000 New Service revolvers chambered in .45 ACP using half-moon clips. Since the .45 ACP cartridge is rimless, the use of two clips each holding three cartridges provided for head spacing and easy ejection. These sixguns found wide use in the civilian market after the war and thousands are still in use today. The .45 Auto Rim cartridge was designed with a thick rim to be used in these sixguns without the use of clips.

By the 1930s, Colt offered three versions of the New Service. A standard model with barrel lengths of 4 1/2, 5 1/2, and 7 1/2 inches and either blue or nickel finish was offered in all the big-bore calibers of the time, .45 Colt, .45 ACP, .455 Eley, .44-40, .44 Special, and .38-40. Shooters could also have a New Service chambered in the latest cartridge, the .357 Magnum or .38 Special, however, barrel lengths for these models were 4, 5, and 6 inches. Stocks were checkered walnut with a Colt medallion and sights were a standard fixed style with a square-notch rear.

Colt's advertising read, "The New Service is essentially a holster revolver for the man in the open — mounted, motorcycle and State Police; the hunter, explorer and pioneer. It is the arm adopted as standard by the Royal Canadian Mounted Police, and hundreds of city and state police organizations throughout the world. This arm has the well-known COLT GRIP, ample for the brawniest hand yet so formed that is easily grasped by a smaller hand." The emphasis here should be on a large-grip frame as I cannot operate a double-action New Service as easily as a Smith & Wesson N-frame, even though I have large hands. Colt was certainly right about this being a sixgun for both outdoor and duty use and it was adopted at the north and south ends of the country as the official sidearm of both the RCMP and the United States Border Patrol. The Mounties went with the .45 Colt, while for use along our southern border the choice was the .38 Special.

The Colt Single Action may have been the star of most western movies, but the New Service also shows up from time to time. A pair of 7 1/2-inch New Services were often found being worn by Wallace Beery in his movies. Jack Hoxie favored the New Service purchasing a consecutive numbered pair of engraved and pearl-stocked 7 1/2 inch .45s direct from Colt in 1934 and used them in all his movies after that date. Quite often one also sees New Services that have been fitted with phony ejector rod housings to make them look like Colt Single Actions in the hands of actors who cannot work a Single Action fast enough. Robert Mitchum carried a Colt Single Action all through *Five Card Stud*, and then switched to a New Service for the gunfighting scenes.

One of the finest double-action revolvers ever offered by any manufacturer at any time is the New Service Target Revolver. This beautiful version of the standard model was available in .44 Special, .45 Colt, and .45 ACP in a choice of either a 6- or 7 1/2-inch barrel. (The latter length chambered in .44 Special shoots like a rifle!) Stocks were checkered walnut, the trigger was checkered, as were the front and back straps, finish was a deep blue, and sights were adjustable with a choice of a Patridge or bead front sight.

The final version of the New Service was the deluxe target revolver, the Shooting Master. This 6-inch barreled revolver featured a "velvet-smooth" hand-finished action, sights and a top strap that were finished to eliminate glare, and a choice of calibers: .38 Special, .357 Magnum, .44 Special, .45 Colt, and .45 ACP. The Shooting Master represented the highest-quality revolver that Colt could build. Is also interesting to note, considering today's modern manufacturing techniques, that Colt emphasized that there were no castings found in any of their revolvers with everything being machined from solid bars of steel. Times have certainly changed!

With approximately 350,000 New Services, 150,000 of which where 1917 Models for military use, this largest of the Colt Double Actions rivals the pre-War Single Action Army for numbers produced, and did it in a time span that was 25 years shorter. The New Service met the same fate as the Single Action Army and both were removed from production with the beginning of World War II. The machinery for the New Service was

The three standard barrel lengths of the Colt Python are the original 6-inch, which was then followed by the 4- and 8-inch lengths. The bottom Python has interchangeable 4- and 8-inch barrels. Custom stocks are by BearHug.

stored in the Colt parking lot of all places and had rusted into worthless metal by the end of the war. We would never see the New Service again and it would be 50 years before Colt would build another large-framed, big-bore, double-action sixgun.

The big Magnums arrive

Smith & Wesson had introduced the .357 Magnum in 1935 when the country was deeply mired in an economic depression, however, Colt would chamber the .357 in both its New Service and Single Action before everything was shut down for wartime production. A whole lot more people wanted .357 Magnums than could acquire them. After the war, it would take a relatively long period of time before .357s, or any other revolver for that matter, would be available. It would be nine years from the end of the war in 1945 until Colt once again offered a .357 Magnum.

My first knowledge that there was even such a thing as a .357 Magnum came from the funny papers. Chester Gould, the creator of "Dick Tracy," had his hero armed with a Colt .357 Magnum. In 1953 Colt introduced the Trooper in .22 Long Rifle and .38 Special. The following year the Trooper was upgraded to a .357 Magnum that was simply called the "Colt .357." This first post-war Magnum from Colt featured either a 4- or 6-inch barrel, adjustable sights, a wide hammer, and most importantly, gave us a glimpse of what was to come.

In the 1950s, bullseye target shooting was the No. 1 handgun game and Colt's entry for punching tight little groups was the Officer's Model Match .38 Special. Colt was looking to make a heavier and better balanced Target Model .38 Special. When the heavy underlugged barrel with a full rib was attached to an Officers Model frame, the result was well over 3 1/2 pounds. Al Gunther was head of the project and reduced weight by drilling out the slot for the ejector rod, adding vents to the barrel rib, and reshaping the barrel profile to that found on the production Python. The first gun produced was in .38 Special with a 4 5/8-inch barrel. When the Python arrived, its concept had changed from a .38 Target Model to a .357 Magnum deluxe sixgun for outdoor and duty use.

Since this was the finest sixgun Colt ever produced, it was given a deluxe royal blue finish and a hand-honed action. Is one of the most accurate revolvers you're ever likely to encounter. It balances superbly with that heavy barrel that was a trendsetter in 1955 and is now practically a standard feature on all double-action revolvers. For me, the Colt grip frame has never been as comfortable as either the K- or N-frames from Smith & Wesson. However, this has now been somewhat corrected on a pair of Pythons with Skeeter Skelton Model stocks from Bearhug. Unfortunately, Deacon Deason of Bearhug has gone Home, and I know of no one currently producing this style of grip for the Python.

While the Python cocks oh so smoooothly for single-action shooting, the double-action operation has never felt quite as smooth to me as a tuned Smith & Wesson. This can be addressed, however. I know of only three men that could super tune a Python. Those men are Reeves Jungkind, Jerry Moran, and Fred Sadowski. I am most fortunate to have a 6-inch Python that was tuned by Sadowski and left to me by my dear friend and brother, Jack Pender. When Jack knew he would not come out of the hospital he offered me a choice of any one of three handguns: a Freedom Arms .454, a custom-built .41 Super Blackhawk by Jim Stroh, and the Python. I chose the Python due to the simple fact that Fred Sadowski is no longer around to tune Colts. Words cannot describe the buttery smoothness of a Sadowski-tuned Python!

The Python has always been chambered in .357 Magnum. However, there were others. For a short time, they were available in .38 Special and at least four other calibers were experimented with internally at the Colt factory. The .41 Magnum Python, the .256 Winchester Python, the .22 LR Python, and the wildcat .38/45 Python, were all experimental models that never left the factory. In addition to the royal blue finish, (which, like Smith & Wesson's Bright Blue, will never be seen again), Pythons were also offered in both a bright nickel, and an electroless nickel, and today, stainless steel. The original barrel length was 6 inches, followed by the 4 inches, 2 1/2 inches, and 8 inches. My original 4-inch Python now wears an 8-inch barrel, which makes it much easier for me to take advantage of its built-in accuracy. I also much prefer the longer barrels for hunting, and with the chambering of the Python this means small southern deer and varmints.

The Python has always been expensive to produce and the lockwork goes all the way back to the 19th century. Colt has made three efforts to modernize its .357 Magnum double-action lineup with the Trooper Mark III in the late 1960s, the Trooper Mark V in early 1980s and, probably one of their finest revolvers ever, the King Cobra in the late 1980s. All three are now gone. Only the Python remains.

One year after Colt introduced the Python, Smith & Wesson really exhibited one-upsmanship on a grand scale by bringing forth the .44 Magnum. The Python was built on the old .41 frame, which is too small for the .44 Magnum. Colt's proper size frame for the new .44 was, of course, the New Service. Alas, it was no more. The powers that be at Colt probably didn't think the .44 Magnum would last. It did! With both S&W and Ruger producing .44 Magnum sixguns through the 1960s and into the 1970s, Colt then decided to take a serious look at the big .44 chambering. One Colt Single Action, serial number GX 9234, was built chambered in .44 Magnum. It had a larger frame, longer cylinder, and a longer grip frame than the standard Colt Single Action Army. One gun was made, the project was shelved, and Colt continued to ignore the .44 Magnum, leaving the building of double-action .44 Magnums to Smith & Wesson and single-actions to Ruger.

The .44 Magnum takes off

It's about this time that a strange phenomenon took place. Hollywood gave us "Dirty Harry" movies with Clint Eastwood wielding a .44 Magnum and saying, "Make my day!" Suddenly, seemingly everyone wanted a double-action .44 Magnum. Never mind that most of those who wanted one had never shot a big-bore sixgun. The demand was there, and Smith & Wesson worked around the clock to try to satisfy it.

With prices soaring all out of reality with Smith & Wesson Model 29 .44 Magnums, it was time for other manufacturers to start producing double-action .44 Magnums. Both Ruger and Dan Wesson introduced thoroughly modern, bull-strong, heavyweight .44 Magnums in the early 1980s. Colt continued to produce .357 Magnum Pythons. Finally by 1990, Colt decided to give shooters a .44 Magnum. The new large frame sixgun, which arrived 50 years after the demise of the New Service and 35 years after the introduction of the .44 Magnum, was the Anaconda.

The .44 Magnum Anaconda had a standard barrel length of 6 inches, with a few being produced in 4-inch and 8-inch, and all of stainless steel. The Anaconda is not as heavy as either the Dan Wesson Model 44 nor the Ruger Super Redhawk. In fact, at 52 ounces, is only five ounces heavier than the original Smith & Wesson .44 Magnum. It is a good-looking double-action sixgun looking much like a larger King Cobra with a Python barrel. Anacondas are nicely polished with the top of the frame and the barrel being a non-reflecting dull gray.

Sights are King Cobra style; an adjustable rear sight with a white outline rear and a ramp style front sight with a red insert. A black post would be much better for my eyes. The Anaconda is perfectly suited for hunting, which makes the black post even more vital for my eyes as the red insert often washes out in bright sunlight. Factory grips are finger groove rubber and too small for my hands, which is of no great importance as any Anacondas I shoot are equipped with Bearhug's Skeeter Skeleton Stocks.

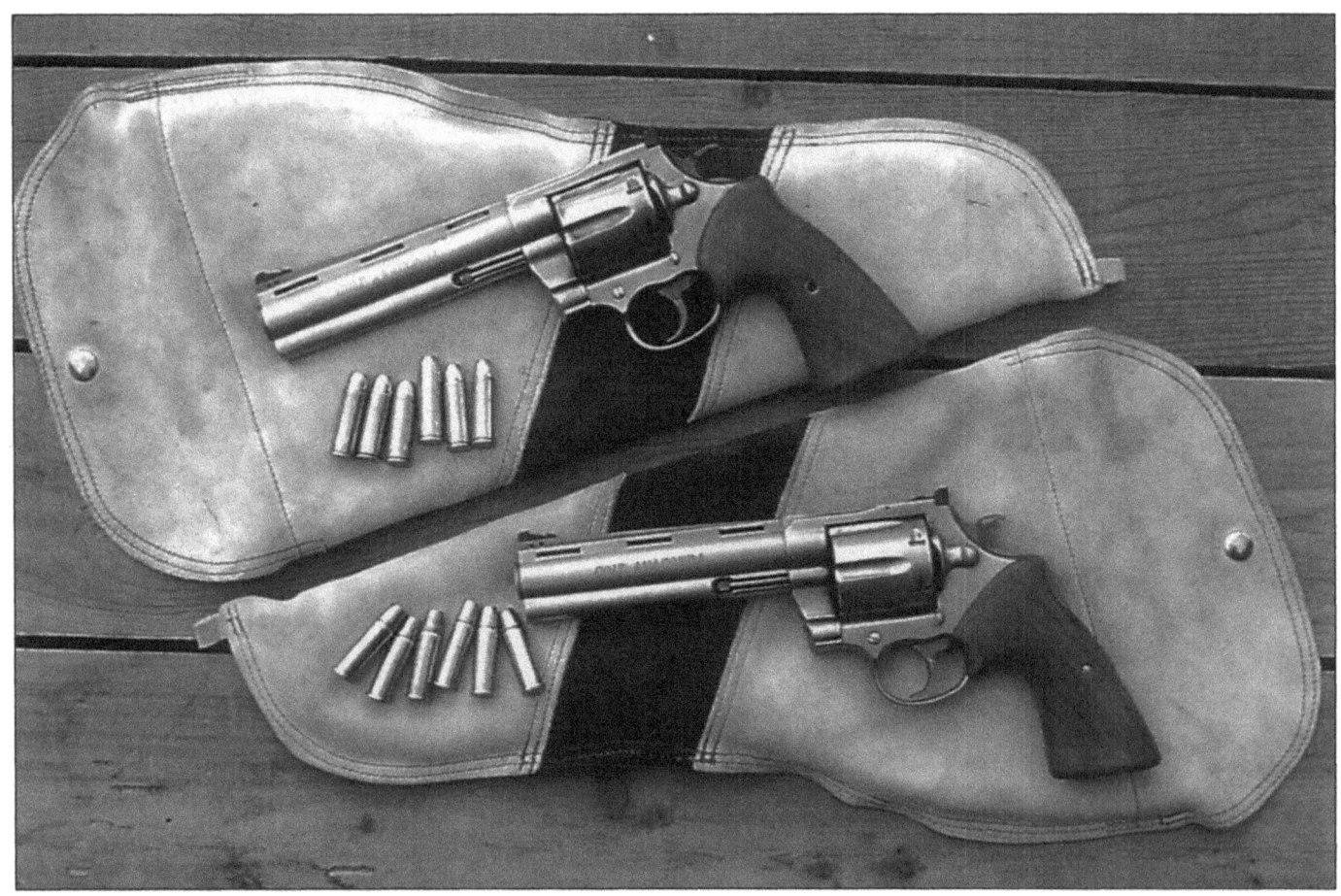

Colt's big-bore double-action sixgun of the 1990s is the Anaconda chambered in both .44 Magnum and .45 Colt. Skeeter Skelton stocks are by the late Deacon Deason.

COLT'S DOUBLE-ACTION SIXGUNS 57

The Anaconda (bottom) is a larger-framed revolver than a .41 framed Colt Python.

As fine as they come, this .45 Colt Anaconda has been tuned and polished by Teddy Jacobsen and stocked with bloodwood Skeeter Skelton stocks by Deacon Deason.

Once Colt solved the barrel problems from the very first production models, the Anaconda took its place with the very accurate sixguns.

El Paso's #1920 Tom Threepersons is an excellent carrying rig for the Colt Anaconda.

Think of a double-action .45 Colt and if you have been around for very long the first sixgun that should come to mind is the New Service. The Colt .45 was the No. 1 choice for New Services aimed for the civilian market. So it was only fitting and proper that the Anaconda be chambered in .45 Colt as well as the .44 Magnum. When I received my .45 Anaconda I found that the stainless-steel finish was not only better than that found on most stainless-steel sixguns, it was even nicer than that on the original .44 Magnum Anaconda.

The Anaconda is certainly no different than all modern double-action sixguns in that they come from the factory begging for the gentle touch of a premier gunsmith. I know no one better suited for this job than Teddy Jacobsen. Jacobsen works on both sixguns and semi-automatics and his work needs to be experienced to be believed. When the .45 Colt returned from Jacobsen, who by the way is an ex-peace officer who thoroughly understands the needs of those who carry a handgun for defensive purposes or as a duty weapon, I found that the double-action pull was now a smooth

Smith & Wesson introduced its .44 Magnum in 1956; the Colt Anaconda would arrive 35 years later. Skeeter Skelton stocks are by BearHug.

nine pounds, and the single-action, creep-free let-off was now set at 3 1/4 pounds.

To make this stainless Anaconda really personal and special, Jacobson polished the flutes in the cylinder, and then polished and jeweled both hammer and trigger. The final touch was to add a set of Bearhug Skeeter Skeleton Stocks of bloodwood. The entire package has become one of the best-looking Anacondas in existence.

The first .44 Magnum Anacondas had problems with accuracy, which turned out to be caused by bad barrels. That was taken care of quickly and all subsequent .44 Magnum and .45 Colt Anacondas have a reputation for excellent accuracy. I have found that both versions cover all the bases, shooting both cast and jacketed, as well as standard weight and heavyweight bullets well.

You'll notice that we have spoken of the Anaconda in the past tense. Unfortunately, before the dawn of the 21st century, the Anaconda was pulled from production. As this is written, we have heard that it is to be reinstated as a custom shop proposition. The New Service is dead, never to be seen again. Or so we thought. The new head of Colt, Gen. Bill Keys, dreams of bringing back the New Service also. May his dream come true.

SELECTED LOADS FOR THE PYTHON .357 MAGNUM 8" BARREL

BULLET	LOAD	MV
Hornady 140 JHP	17.5 gr. #2400	1608
	19.5 gr. WW296	1544
Speer 140 JHP	17.5 gr. #2400	1555
	19.5 gr. WW296	1489
Hornady 158 JHP	15.5 gr. #2400	1399
	17.5 gr. WW296	1339
Speer 158 JHP	15.5 gr. #2400	1305
	17.5 gr. WW296	1389
Sierra 170 JHC1	17.5 gr. H110	1277
	16.0 gr. H110	1297
Lyman #358156GC	15.0 gr. #2400	1543

SELECTED LOADS FOR THE .44 MAGNUM ANACONDA 6" BARREL /2X SCOPE

BULLET	LOAD	MV	4 SHOTS/25 YDS
Hornady 240XTP	25.0 gr. WW296	1515	1 1/4"
Hornady 265FP	23.0 gr. WW296	1283	1 1/2"
Hornady 300XTP	20.3 gr. H110	1208	1"
Sierra 240 JHP	25.0 gr. WW296	1465	1 1/4"
Sierra 300 JSP	21.5 gr. WW296	1069	7/8"
Speer 300 JFP	21.7 gr. H110	1198	1 1/4"
Lyman #431244GC	25.0 gr. WW296	1395	7/8"
Lyman #431244GC	22.0 gr. #2400	1484	3/4"
Lyman #431244GC	21.5 gr. AA#9	1365	3/4"
BRP #295GC	21.5 gr. WW296	1303	7/8"
RCBS #44-300SWC	21.5 gr. H110	1336	5/8"

SELECTED LOADS FOR THE .45 COLT ANACONDA 6" BARREL /2X SCOPE

BULLET	LOAD	MV	4 SHOTS/25 YDS
Lyman #454424	9.5 gr. Unique	1008	7/8"
Lyman #454424	22.0 gr. H4227	1127	1"
Lyman #454424	18.5 gr. #2400	1135	7/8"
BRP 300GC	21.5 gr. WW296	1087	1"
LBT 300LFN	18.5 gr. #2400	1120	1"
RCBS #45-300SWC	21.5 gr. H110	1123	1"
NEI 310.451KT	21.5 gr. WW296	1103	1"

CHAPTER 4

SMITH & WESSON: KING OF THE MAGNUM SIXGUNS

It is 1869. The Civil War has been over for four years and Colt, which became firmly established as the premier gun maker in the country thanks to a lucrative government contract for 1860 Armies during the conflict, is content to continue to produce the finest percussion revolvers possible. The .44 caliber 1860 had not only been used during the Civil War, it was also the standard sidearm for the United States Cavalry on the frontier. The cap and ball revolver had been the sidearm of choice for pistoleros since the Texas Rangers under John Coffee Hays surprised a large band of Comanches with what at that time was incredible firepower — the five-shot Colt Paterson sixgun.

Colt continued to improve the design and efficiency of its sixguns as it offered, in succession, the 1847 Walker, the First, Second, and Third Model Dragoons, the 1851 Navy, 1860 Army, and the 1861 Navy. While Colt was doing all this, a firearms revolution was about to occur. It started in 1857 with a young company by the name of Smith & Wesson offering the first successful cartridge-firing revolver with its .22 Rimfire Model #1. Rifle manufacturers were also looking at the new fixed ammunition and both the Spencer and the 1860 Henry were used by some northern units during the Civil War. Colt should have realized what was about to happen, but instead continued to ignore anything but

This beautiful example of Smith and Wesson's first top-break double-action .44 Russian from the 1880s, nickel-plated with ivory grips, gave no indication of the direction that the double-action Smith & Wessons would take beginning in 1899.

Doc O'Meara photo

the percussion system. It was about to receive a stunning surprise.

Twelve years after it offered the first revolver-firing fixed ammunition, Smith & Wesson introduced the first serious fighting sixgun to use brass cases rather than powder, round ball, and percussion cap. The original Smith & Wesson Model #1 had evolved into the Model #1 1/2 and #2 in .22 and .32 Rimfire, and now the Model #3 was a large-frame single-action .44 caliber revolver available in both .44 Rimfire, the same cartridge used in the 1860 Henry lever-action rifle, and .44-100, or .44 S&W American, a center-fire cartridge. The Smith & Wesson was a break-top design that unlatched in front of the hammer and pivoted at the bottom of the frame in front of the cylinder. The United States Army ordered 1,000 Model #3 Americans chambered in .44 S&W. For the first time, Colt saw the handwriting on the wall.

The U.S. government was not the only political entity to look at Smith & Wesson's new big bore sixgun. Grand Duke Alexis visited this country and was given a special engraved Model #3 with pearl grips with a value in 1871 of $400! It featured another chambering that would revolutionize ammunition, and the Duke used this sixgun (with very little effect) on a buffalo hunt hosted by Buffalo Bill and George Armstrong Custer. The Russian government had ordered Smith & Wesson Model #3s with what was a great improvement in ammunition. The .44 S&W used an outside-lubricated bullet that was the same diameter as the cartridge case with a heel at the base to fit inside the mouth of the case. The Russians reduced the diameter of the bullet to a uniform size to fit inside the cartridge case and cylinders were now chambered with two diameters; the back of the cylinder to accept the cartridge case and the smaller diameter in the front of the cylinder mated up with a now smaller bullet. The new round was the .44 Russian.

By 1872, Smith & Wesson had delivered 20,000 .44 Russian-chambered single-action sixguns to the Russian government. This was one year before Colt introduced the Single Action Army. One can only speculate on what would have been, had all of these guns gone to the U.S. Army instead of a foreign market. Colt got all the publicity while S&W filled a foreign contract. Had the Smith & Wesson stayed in this country, perhaps the Colt Single Action Army would have never been. Perhaps.

By 1878, the original American Model had steadily improved through the Russian Model #3, and the New

These three classic handguns were all manufactured within a 10-year period: (from left) Ivory-stocked .45 Colt Single Action Army, circa 1917; Smith & Wesson .44 Special Triple-Lock, first-year production, 1908; and Commercial Model .45 ACP 1911, circa 1914.

In 2001, Smith & Wesson celebrated the First Model Hand Ejector, or Triple-Lock .44 Special (bottom), by introducing the HEG (Hand Ejector Gold) .45 Colt, the first of the 21st-century Heritage Series.

Model #3 — the latter representing the highest point of single-action sixguns offered by Smith & Wesson and perhaps the finest single-action offered by any manufacturer during the 19th century. The vast majority of New Model #3s were chambered in .44 Russian with a standard barrel length of 6 1/2 inches. Both the .44 caliber chambering and the 6 1/2-inch barrel length would be used in no less than seven models of Smith & Wesson sixguns over the next 120 years.

The New Model #3 had a cylinder that was too short to accept the .44-40 that was a standard offering in Winchester's Model 1873. By this time, Winchester's .44 Centerfire was being offered in the Colt Single Action that was called the Frontier Sixshooter. To accommodate this cartridge, and also the .38-40, Smith & Wesson lengthened the cylinder by 1/8 inch. It did not, however, chamber the New Model #3 in .45 Colt. We have mentioned that this particular Smith & Wesson was probably the finest single action offered and one can only guess what would have happened had Smith & Wesson stayed with single actions instead of now following Colt's lead and offering a double-action revolver.

Colt introduced its smaller-framed Lightning Model in 1877, and four years later Smith & Wesson began its run as the most prolific of double-action sixgun producers. In 1881, a modified Model #3 was introduced, a double-action revolver chambered in .44 Russian as the .44 Double Action First Model. Smith & Wesson had built an experimental double action .44 10 years earlier, probably at the request of the Russian government. During the next decade numerous small-caliber double actions would be introduced by Smith & Wesson, but the .44 Double Action would be the beginning of the well-deserved title for Smith & Wesson as king of the double-action sixguns. By the turn of the century, Smith & Wesson would be the double-action sixgun by which all double-action sixguns would be judged during the 20th century.

While the Smith & Wesson single actions had been beautifully engineered with superb looks and balance, they lost something aesthetically in the transfer from a single-action operation to a double-action design. The addition of a larger trigger guard and the strange looking trigger that was necessary to turn the Model #3 into a double-action gave it a very strange look. This would be changed 25 years later when Smith & Wesson enlarged its .38 Military & Police Model of 1899 to become the .44 First Model Hand Ejector of 1907.

In addition to enlarging the frame of the Military & Police to produce the First Model Hand Ejector, also known as the New Century, two other improvements were made. A shroud was added to the bottom of the barrel to enclose and protect the ejector rod, which also served to improve the looks of the double-action revolver immensely. The second improvement, which would only last for less than 10 years, was the addition of a third lock. The M&P design locked at the rear of

This beautiful, ivory-stocked, gold- and nickel-plated Second Model Hand Ejector .44 Special belonged to Marshall Bill Tilghman.

The design that gave the First Model Hand Ejector its unofficial Triple-Lock name should have become a standard feature for all Smith & Wesson double-action revolvers for the next century. Instead, it fell way short with the Triple-Lock, lasting only through 15,375 revolvers from 1907-1915.

In 1915, the Triple-Lock sold for $21. Someone at Smith & Wesson decided that this was too expensive and looked for a way to cut costs. The third locking feature was dropped along with the enclosed ejector rod, and the Second Model Hand Ejector arrived just prior to World War I with a price tag of $19. So for a grand savings of $2 for each .44 Special Smith & Wesson sixgun we lost one of the grandest designs of all time. It was a true step backward in sixgun manufacturing.

the cylinder with a second lock at the front of the ejector rod added in 1902. Then a third lock at the front of the cylinder was machined at the front of the frame where the barrel and yoke came together to solidly lock the cylinder in place. This third lock gave the Triple-Lock Smith & Wesson its unofficial name.

The Triple-Lock Smith & Wesson

The Triple-Lock certainly has to be rated as one of the most important sixguns of all times not only for what it was but also for several directions it was destined to take in the future. Perhaps the most beautifully designed double-action revolver ever, it also is significant for the new cartridge it introduced: the .44 Smith & Wesson Special. S&W was on the threshold of something really sensational as far as big bore sixguns, however, this is another case of the manufacturer not knowing what it really had. The .44 Special was advanced as an improvement over the .44 Russian, a superb cartridge in its own right. To come up with the .44 Special, the .44 Russian case was lengthened from .97 inches to 1.16 inches and the powder charge was increased from 23.0 to 26.0 of black powder under a round-nosed 246-grain lead bullet. With the lengthening of the case the increase in the powder charge simply made the .44 Special a duplicate of the .44 Russian. When the switch was made to smokeless powder, the muzzle velocity basically stayed the same right at 700-750 feet per second. With the new cartridge case and the new strong, solid-frame .44 sixgun, the .45 Colt could easily have been matched or even surpassed. Alas, it was not to be.

The Triple-Lock was offered in both fixed- and adjustable-sighted models in barrel lengths of 4, 5, and 6 1/2 inches, in both blue and nickel finish. And while the vast majority are found in .44 Special, there were also a few manufactured in .38-40, .44-40 and .45 Colt.

The Second Model

Europe was at war in 1915 and the United States was about to join in. The .44 Second Model Hand Ejector would be used as a basis for Smith & Wesson's 1917 Army or .45 Hand Ejector of 1917. By this time the official sidearm of the U.S. Army was the 1911 Government Model .45, which could not be produced in the quantities needed to supply the United States Expeditionary Force. The machinery was certainly in existence to produce revolvers, and an engineer at Smith & Wesson solved the problem of using and ejecting rimless .45 ACP cases in a revolver cylinder with the use of half moon clips. Nearly 170,000 1917 models would be manufactured for the war effort. The same basic revolver would also be used to provide the British and Canadians with approximately 70,000 revolvers chambered in .455.

As with the First Model, the vast majority of Second Models would be .44 Special with a few made in .45 Colt, .44-40, and .38-40. However, they would last longer than the First Model, with the production running from 1915 until 1940. Many shooters tried to interest Smith & Wesson in bringing back the Triple-Lock, or at the very least once again providing a shrouded ejector rod. All requests fell on deaf ears until 1926, when a gun dealer in Texas, Wolf and Klar, placed an order for a run of Second Model Hand Ejec-

The Second Model Hand Ejector was modified in 1917 to accept the .45 ACP to arm the American Expeditionary Force as they marched off to Europe.

tors that would have an enclosed ejector rod. These sixguns would become the Third Model or the Model 1926. With less than 5,000 total being made from 1926-1941, the pre-War Third Models are much rarer than Triple-Locks.

The Model 1926 was manufactured predominately in .44 Special and was very popular with peace officers along the southwest border of the U.S. Texas Ranger Lone Wolf Gonzaullas carried a pair of .44 Model 1926 sixguns. After World War II, slightly less than 1,500 more Third Model Hand Ejectors were manufactured before it became the Fourth Model, the 1950 Target Model.

Sixguns chambered in .44 Special have been a special passion of mine ever since I discovered the writings of Elmer Keith in the 1950s. I have had both Colt Single Actions and New Frontiers, several 1950 Target Models, a first-year production Triple-Lock, and last year for my birthday, my wife presented me with a pair of unfired 4-inch Model 24 .44 Specials made in 1983. However, a suitable Model 1926 has always evaded me. By suitable I mean one in excellent shooting condition at a reasonable price. Most of those that have been encountered in excellent shape have always carried four-figure price tags. This has gone on since I acquired my first .44 Special in the 1950s.

It did not look like I would ever find "my" Model 1926 .44 Special. Then it happened. A reader who had been traveling through Oregon spotted a 4-inch, fixed-sighted Model 1926 .44 Special and immediately thought of me. He put me in touch with Gunners Central Oregon Traders in Redmond and I wound up with a beautiful Model 1926 .44 Special 99 percent-plus with Magna stocks. A faithful reader, an honest gun dealer, and everything came together perfectly like it was

The author enjoys shooting a Third Model Hand Ejector .44 Special that was made the same year he was.

The return of the enclosed ejector rod occurred in 1926 when Wolf & Klar ordered a special run of .44 Specials. These two particular sixguns date back to the late 1930s.

Two Classic sixguns from the Depression era that would evolve into the first two Smith & Wesson Magnums: the 1926 Model .44 Special (top) and the .38-44 Heavy Duty.

A favorite of true sixgun connoisseurs is the .44 Special such as these three 4-inch Smith & Wesson's: (clockwise from left) a re-chambered and re-barreled Highway Patrolman, a stainless-steel Model 624, and a 1950 Target.

meant to be. Now I know why those old Southwest lawmen liked the .44 Special "Wolf and Klar" Model so well. It is, as they say, silky smooth when operated in the double-action mode. With the older pre-War Smith & Wesson long action, once started, this double action sixgun almost seems to operate itself. With standard level .44 Specials recoil is very mild. And to top everything off, this great .44 Special was made the same year I was. Yes, we were definitely meant to be brought together.

In 1949, the Third Model was improved with a ribbed barrel, the new micrometer S&W rear sight, and the new post-War short action, which allowed for shorter hammer travel in both single- and double-action operation. The barrel rib and rear sight are definite improvements, but many shooters, myself included, prefer the old long action that was standard on Smith & Wesson revolvers for half a century.

The Fourth Model Hand Ejector, the Target Model of 1950, was chambered in .44 Special with a standard barrel length of 6 1/2 inches and is rarely found in 4 inches; very, very rarely with a 5-inch barrel. The fixed-sighted version was known as the 1950 Military Model. With the change to a numbering system instead of a name in 1957, the Target Model became the Model 24 while the fixed-sighted .44 was dubbed the Model 21. Both models were dropped from production in 1966 with approximately 1,200 Model 21s and 5,050 Model 24s having been produced. The Model 24 was resurrected for a short period of time, with 7,500 being produced in 1983-1984. The .44 Special Target Model was, and is, an excellent sixgun, however, in the mid-1950s it was used as the platform for a new sixgun and cartridge. More on this later. First we must back up and pick up the Smith & Wesson story at another point in history.

New guns for a new era

The 1920s. The Volstead Act, bootleg whiskey, speakeasies, flappers, the Jazz Age, talkies, then C-R-A-S-H!, the black day in October 1929 as the bottom dropped out of the stock market.

The 1930s. The Great Depression, the rise of the modern gangster, bank robberies, John Dillinger, Pretty Boy Floyd, Bonnie & Clyde, and suddenly peace officers were woefully outgunned, finding themselves

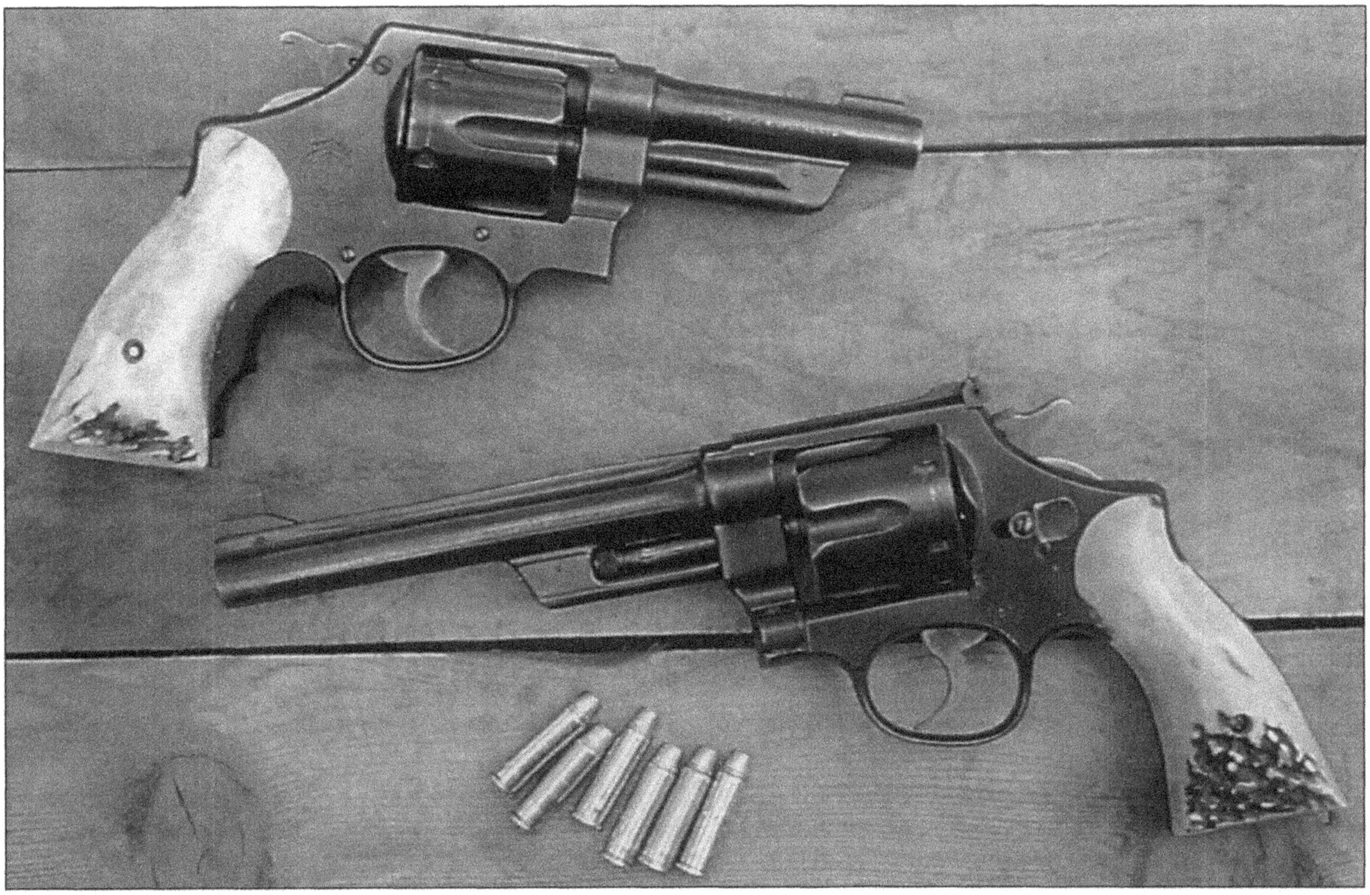

Before the .357 Magnum there were the Heavy Duty .38 Specials. The Standard Model .38-44 (top) was a favorite with peace officers, while the .38-44 Outdoorsman was most appropriately named.

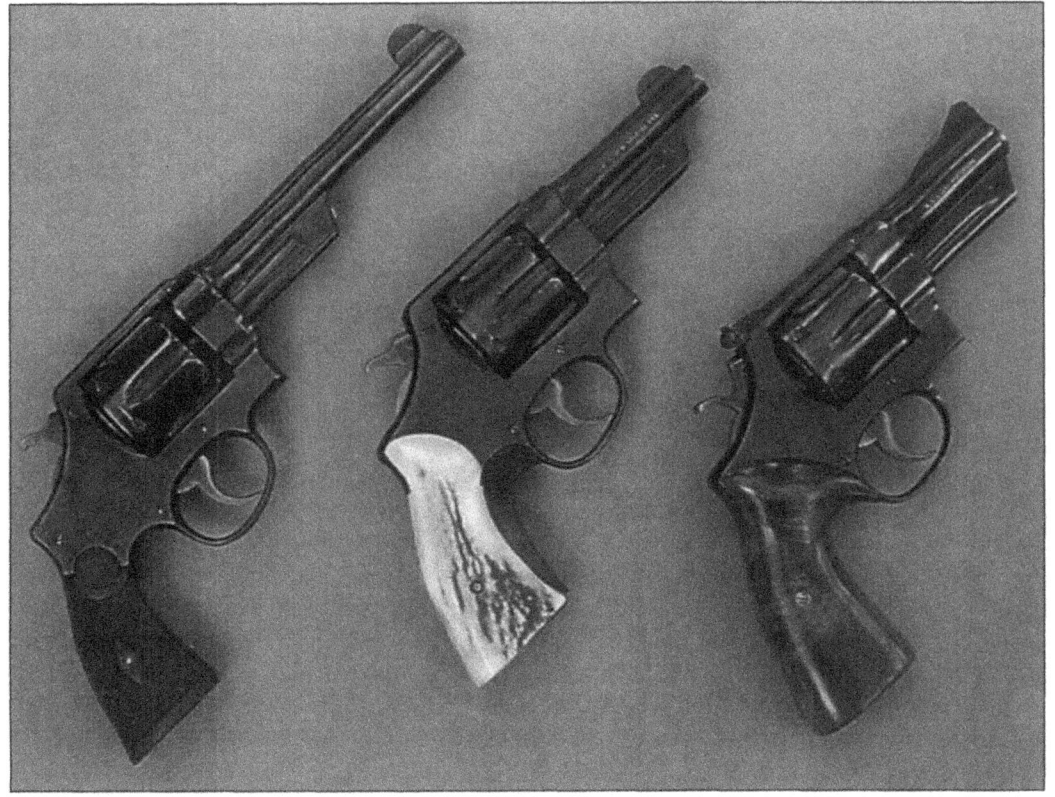

The natural evolution of Smith & Wesson's .357 Magnum consists of the Triple-Lock .44 Special (left) and the .38-44 Heavy Duty (center), which together resulted in the first Magnum, the .357, shown with grips by Roy Fishpaw.

Four aces from the Smith & Wesson deck are (from left) the .38-44 Heavy Duty, the .38-44 Outdoorsman, the 3 1/2-inch .357 Magnum, a favorite of General Patton, and the 5-inch .357 Magnum, Skeeter Skelton's favorite.

armed for the most part with .38 Specials, either Colt's Official Police or Smith & Wesson's Military & Police. The new breed of criminal had a fast automobile and was armed with .45s — both 1911 Government Models and Thompson's "Chicago Chopper," both of which had been discovered with military use in World War I.

Criminals escaping in cars presented a special problem and peace officers needed a handgun and ammunition that would pierce car bodies. A better weapon was definitely needed and Smith & Wesson heeded the call. The Military & Police had too small a frame to handle heavier .38 loads, while the Hand Ejector Model used larger but slower-moving bullets. The solution would be to put both ideas together and use the .44 frame, now known as the N-frame, and chamber it in a hotter .38 Special. Smith & Wesson had two choices: the Second Model or the 1926 Third Model. It wisely went with the Third Model with its heavy-duty fixed sights and fully enclosed ejector rod.

In 1930, a special Model 1926 came from Smith & Wesson chambered in .38 Super Police or .38/44. Available in both 4- and 5-inch models for peace officer use, the new sixgun, known as the .38/44 Heavy Duty, weighed right at 2 1/2 pounds. This sixgun was certainly appropriately named as it was the strongest revolver made by Smith & Wesson at the time and it handled the new .38/44 ammunition both with ease. It also maintained a relatively easy recoil, even though the muzzle velocity of the more efficient .38 Super Police round with its flat-nosed bullet was 300 fps faster than the old standard offering of a round-nosed bullet at 850 fps. With the First Model Hand Ejector in 1907, Smith & Wesson brought the revolver into the 20th-century. Sixgun ammunition soon began to follow it.

The .38/44 was a great sixgun in 1930. It still is. Most Heavy Duty models are found with 5-inch barrels. Four and 6 1/2-inch versions are also encountered, and a very few were made with 3 1/2- and 8 3/4-inch barrels. For an easy-shooting carry gun, I am very fond of the 4-inch I picked up at a bargain-basement price. It has a most businesslike look to it, and is everything a serious defensive double-action sixgun should be. That is, heavy-duty sights, standard trigger and hammer, a stout barrel with enclosed ejector rod, and for my personal tastes is fitted with staghorn stocks and a Tyler T-grip Adapter.

The fixed sights never get out of alignment and are no disadvantage for the sixgunner who uses one load exclusively. With its old long action and heavy cylinder, the .38/44 is even easier to shoot double action than the Model 1926 .44 Special, especially when using standard .38 loads.

One year after the arrival of the .38/44 Heavy Duty, the 6 1/2-inch version was fitted with adjustable sights and became the classic .38/44 Outdoorsman. Even though the country was deep in the Depression, 5,000 Outdoorsman Models were sold from 1931 to 1941. In all its versions, fixed-sights Heavy Duty and adjustable-sights Outdoorsman Models, pre-War and post-War, approximately 34,000 N-frame .38 Specials were manufactured.

By the mid-1930s, the .38 Special was about to make a great change. Two notable writers of the time, Elmer Keith and Phil Sharpe, both worked at developing loads even heavier than the factory .38/44 ammunition. Both men also designed their own bullet. For Keith, it was Lyman's #358429, a long-nose semi-wadcutter that dropped out of the mold when cast of a hard alloy at around 168 grains. Sharpe's design was Lyman's #358477, a 158-grain semi-wadcutter. (RCBS's #38-150KT is very close to Sharpe's design also.) Both men realized that this design was much more effective in transmitting energy to the intended target than the old round-nose design.

Keith used his bullet and 13.5 grains of #2400 in .38 Special brass. That load that even today is too hot for use in factory .38 Specials, except the heavy-framed .38 Specials of the time: the .38/44 Heavy Duty and Outdoorsman, and Colt's New Service and Single Action Army. In 1935, mainly because of Sharpe's work, the .38 Special case was lengthened by .135 inches and the cylinders of .38/44 Heavy Duty sixguns were specially heat treated to handle the 40,000-pound-plus pressure of the new round from Winchester, which was known as the .357 Magnum.

The sixgun was definitely coming into its own. Smith & Wesson brought the revolver into the 20th century with the Triple-Lock of 1907, and Winchester followed suit with the new ammunition. Remember, this was at the time when .44 Specials and .38 Specials clocked out at around 800 fps. Suddenly, there was a cartridge that drove a highly efficient, 158-grain, flat-nosed bullet at around 1500 fps from a long-barreled sixgun. No other round could even come close to the muzzle energy of the .357 Magnum.

Everything was not perfect, however. Both Keith and Sharpe had designed excellent bullets and both men also knew that they needed to be cast hard to prevent leading. Instead of a hard cast bullet, Winchester used a relatively soft swaged bullet that leaded barrels very quickly. Keith's bullet was too long to be used in the new .357 Magnum brass and crimped in the crimp-

Gone but not forgotten, the first and original .357 Magnum, 8 3/8-inch blue and nickel with stocks by BearHug; 5-inch stocked by Herrett's; and Roy Fishpaw gripped 3 1/2-inch version.

ing groove, so he was perfectly happy to continue to use .38 Special brass. With its shorter nose, Sharpe's design worked perfectly in .357 brass. The original .357 Magnum, as all previous large-frame Smith & Wesson double actions, used a relatively short cylinder that did not fill out to the end of the frame window. Keith's bullet was too long to use in the .357 cylinder; Sharpe's was not.

To promote the new gun and ammunition, Doug Wesson of Smith & Wesson used both to take several head of big game, including antelope, elk, moose, and grizzly bear. He was so enthused with the performance of the .357 Magnum that he went north to Alaska to hunt brown bear. He never did find one, and later in life he related that he was thankful he did not. It has been my good privilege to handle both of Doug Wesson's prototype .357 Magnums, one in 6 1/2-inch and the other an 8 3/4-inch-barreled version, when I visited Col. Rex Applegate in his private museum few years ago. I definitely felt that I was holding sixgun history in my hands.

Doug Wesson was not the only one to promote the new .357 Magnum. The first production model was presented to FBI director J. Edgar Hoover in 1935 and the 3 1/2-inch-barreled Magnum, the most businesslike looking sixgun of all time, very quickly became the favorite sidearm of FBI agents. That same year, a man who would become one of the most important figures in World War II, purchased a blue 3 1/2-inch Smith & Wesson with a bead front sight and fitted it with ivory grips. Lt. Col. George Patton was then stationed in Hawaii and in a few short years would be General Patton, commander of the Second Army. He carried both his fully engraved, nickel-plated, and ivory-stocked Colt Single Action .45 and his plain blue Smith & Wesson .357 Magnum in matching Border Patrol holsters from S.D. Myres of El Paso, Texas. For the most part, these guns were symbols of Patton's leadership status, but he did refer to his Magnum as his killing gun.

The original .357 Magnum had a barrel length of 8 3/4 inches, which was soon cut back to 8 3/8 inches to conform to the NRA rules for bullseye shooting which set the maximum allowable distance between sights. Barrel lengths were standardized at 3 1/2, 4, 5, 6, 6 1/2, and 8 3/8 inches with the three shorter lengths being especially popular with peace officers. The latter two were the top choices for hunters and outdoorsman. Two Border Patrolmen officers who were also gun writers favored the Smith & Wesson .357 Magnum. For Col. Charles Askins, it was the 4-inch version, while Skeeter Skelton preferred the 5-inch length.

Smith & Wesson's .357 Magnums were introduced in the midst of the Great Depression and even at the relatively high price of $60, the demand exceeded the supply. Those early guns were in fact custom made and carried both a serial number and a special registration number along with a registration certificate to attest to the fact. Instead of a heavy bull barrel as found on later models, the original .357 maintained the same slim, tapered barrel found on the early .44 Specials. A full-length barrel rib was added and the entire top of the rib, as well at the rear sight assembly, were both finely checkered to reduce glare — a nice touch that would only be found on the .357 Magnum. From 1935 to 1957, the original Magnum was known simply as the ".357 Magnum." With the coming of the computer age

The 5-inch Model 27 (bottom) is no longer produced, but the 5-inch 627 with an eight-shot cylinder remains.

and the depersonalizing of everything and everybody, even sixguns lost their names and became numbers, in this case the Model 27. That same year the Heavy Duty and the Outdoorsman, two soul-stirring titles, became the bland Model 20 and Model 23.

In 1960, the threads on the extractor rod were changed from right-hand to left-hand and the Model 27-1 had arrived. From 1961-1980, the .357 Magnum would be the 27-2 with several changes occurring in these two decades. With the elimination of the trigger guard screw, the four-screw model became the three-screw in 1961. The 6 1/2-inch barrel was dropped in 1967, and one year later the diamond stocks disappeared. Serial numbers gained an 'N' prefix in 1969; target stocks, target hammer, target trigger, and a patridge front sight became standard on 6- and 8 3/8-inch Magnums; and the 3 1/2- and 5-inch barrels were dropped in 1979, the same year that the 4-inch barrel was reintroduced. A further "improvement" occurred in 1982 as the 27-3 appeared without a pinned barrel and cylinders recessed for case heads. Four years later nickel-plated models were dropped. The year 1988 saw the model designation changed to 27-4 as the .357 Magnum began to receive the endurance package of all N-frame Smith & Wessons. One year later, 27-5 appeared with the longer stop notches in the cylinder, and in 1992 both the 4-inch and 8 3/8-inch barreled versions disappeared. One year later, all that remained was the 27-6 with a 6-inch barrel, Hogue grips, and the top strap drilled and tapped for scope mounts.

Slowly but surely the .357 Magnum was disappearing from the Smith & Wesson lineup. In 1994 the vanishing act was completed as one year short of its 60th anniversary, the original .357 Magnum was dropped off the pages of Smith and Wesson's catalog. I was way too young to be affected by the disappearance of the First Generation Colt Single Action Army in 1941. However, in 1994 I could definitely relate to Col. Charles Askins' statement regarding the old Colt that many an eye was dampened when the Peacemaker disappeared. All standard .357 Magnums are now gone with the exception of a few special runs, such as those with eight-shot cylinders, periodically coming from the Smith & Wesson Performance Center.

The Model 27

The Model 27 is certainly one of the greatest sixguns ever made and it would be difficult to argue with Smith & Wesson's Roy Jinks, who has called it the greatest handgun development of the 20th century. No shooting collection is complete without one Model 27, and collectors should at least have a 3 1/2-, 5-, and an 8 3/8-inch barreled .357 Magnum just to stay connected with sixgun history. The 5-inch is the most practical for everyday use and belt carry. The 8 3/8-

The barrel on this Model 627 .357 Magnum says it all: "357 Magnum-8 Times." Stocks are by Hogue.

inch is preferred for hunting and long-range shooting; I have used mine often in the past for silhouette shooting. And the 3 1/2-inch version, with its connection to the glory days of the FBI as well as General Patton, connects me to history and the Greatest Generation.

Most of my shooting with these sixguns has been done over the past 40-plus years with cast bullets and both .38 Special and .357 Magnum brass. Although I am confirmed big bore (.44 and up) fancier, I will admit that at least 95 percent of what I use a handgun for can easily be accomplished with a .357 Magnum in general, and the Smith & Wesson Model 27 in particular. With the excellent factory ammunition we have today, the .357 Magnum remains at the top of the list for one-shot stops as a defensive load, and also can be an effective hunting sixgun and cartridge in capable hands, although I would certainly restrict its use to animals the size of small Southern deer and down.

The Combat Magnum

By the mid-1950s peace officers began carrying other things on their belt besides a duty holster and sixgun. There arose complaints that the N-frame .357 Magnum was just too heavy to be carried comfortably all day. Before the advent of the .357 Magnum, many peace officers carried the much lighter .38 Special Military & Police model. This sixgun, Smith & Wesson's first modern double-action revolver introduced in 1899, was never adopted wholesale by the military, but certainly became a favorite of police officers all over the country. By 1940 more than 1 million Military & Police sixguns had been produced. Would it be possible to combine the smaller K-frame of the M&P with the .357 Magnum, that to that point in time had only been chambered in the larger N-frame?

SELECTED LOADS FOR THE S&W 8 3/8" MODEL 27 .357 MAGNUM

BULLET	LOAD	MV
Lyman #358156GC	15.0 gr. #2400	1,524
RCBS #38-150KT	7.5 gr. Unique	1,310
RCBS #38-150 KT	16.0 gr. #2400	1,493
Lyman #358429 (.38 Spl. brass)	13.5 gr. #2400	1,330
Hornady 158 JHP	15.5 gr. #2400	1,360
Speer 158 JSP	15.5 gr. #2400	1,372

One who thought so was Bill Jordan of the U.S. Border Patrol. He convinced Smith & Wesson that it could be done and the new sixgun should be the same size as the .38 M&P, but with a heavyweight barrel and a shrouded ejector rod. In 1955, Jordan's idea of the perfect peace officer's revolver came true with the introduction of the Combat Magnum. Until semi-automatics took over in the 1990s, the Combat Magnum would be the sidearm of choice by peace officers. The original Combat Magnum, which would become the Model 19 in 1957, had a 4-inch heavyweight barrel with a full-length rib, an adjustable rear sight, a Baughman front sight on a ramp base, a pinned barrel, the cylinder recessed for case heads, and very comfortable target stocks that fit most hands. Unlike the original .357 Magnum, the Combat Magnum utilized the cylinder window to good advantage, allowing the use of longer bullets, such as Keith's #358429. The whole package weighed 1/2 pound less that its N-frame counterpart. Eight ounces may not seem like much, but when carried all day, the difference is dramatic.

Just as with the original .357 Magnum, the Combat Magnum, which began with Bill Jordan's serial number K260001 in 1955, went through numerous "dash" model numbers and improvements. It became 19-1 in 1959 as the extractor rod thread was changed from right-hand to left-hand, as in all Smith & Wessons, to prevent the rod from unscrewing as the gun was fired. With the dawn of

A picture of changing times: (top right) the .38-44 Heavy Duty became the .357 Magnum in 1935. However, a call for a lighter .357 Magnum resulted in the .38 Special M&P (top left), becoming the .357 Combat Magnum in 1955.

Until the massive switch to semi-autos in the 1990s, this was the "peace officer's dream." The .357 Combat Magnum was inspired by Bill Jordan.

1961, Model 19-2 deleted the fourth screw, and one year later the 6-inch-barreled version arrived. The 19-3, a 2 1/2-inch Combat Magnum, arrived in 1966, and two years later diamond stocks were eliminated.

The Combat Magnum would sometimes freeze up as it got hot from sustained firing of heavy loads. This problem was addressed in 1977 as the gas ring was moved from the yoke to the front of the cylinder. Five years later, the 19-5 arrived with neither a pinned barrel nor a cylinder recessed for case heads. As with other Smith & Wessons, the endurance package began to arrive in 1988 with the 19-6, and in 1992 nickel-plated models were removed from production.

The last Combat Magnum, the 19-7, would be fitted with Hogue grips and drilled and tapped for scope mounts in 1994. It was changed to a round-butted grip frame in 1995, the 6-inch barrel was dropped in 1996, and a frame mounted firing was added in 1998. In 1999, the Combat Magnum received the same fate as the original .357 Magnum had suffered five years earlier when it was removed from production. I had some tears left over to use on this occasion.

My first Combat Magnum was the original 4-inch configuration simply because that was all that was available in 1960. It is still my favorite and is the lightest practical .357 Magnum for belt carry. A 2 1/2-inch nickel-plated Model 19, or its twin 66, gets the nod for concealed carry in a Derry Gallagher rig, while the 6-inch model is the easiest to shoot and also makes a practical lightweight sixgun for hunting small game, varmints, and small deer. One version of the 19/66 family, the 3-inch fixed-sighted Model 65, is also used for concealed carry and is my standard bedside sixgun.

Two Classic Smith & Wessons from 1955: the 4-inch .44 Magnum (left) and the 4-inch .357 Magnum.

The standard Combat Magnums (Model 19), 4- and 6-inch blued and nickeled. Stocks are by BearHug and BluMagnum.

In 1970, the Model 19 was joined by its stainless-steel counterpart, the Model 66. Fortunately, as this is written, the Model 66 still remains in production with a choice of 2 1/2-, 4-, and 6-inch barrels. It is now at 66-5 and with the necessity of modern manufacturing methods using CNC machinery, now has MIM (metal injected molded) trigger and hammer, and the firing pin mounted in the frame instead of the hammer nose.

Heavy loads and the .44 Special

The .357 Magnum came about to fill the need for a more powerful cartridge and a heavy-duty sixgun for law-enforcement use. The added benefit for sportsmen everywhere was a superb cartridge and sixgun for outdoor use. The .357 Magnum, advertised as "more powerful than any .44 or .45," would reign undisputed for 20 years. Let us correct this and say it was not challenged officially by any other factory chambering. However, there were voices that proclaimed there was something better.

We have mentioned the path of the .44 Special beginning as a ballistic twin to the .44 Russian using the same round-nosed bullet traveling about 750 fps, although chambered in the New Century Model of 1907. This was Smith's first large solid-framed double-action sixgun and was certainly capable of handling heavier loads than the breaktop designs of the home of the .44 Russian, that is the Model #3s and the Double

SELECTED LOADS FOR THE S&W 4" MODEL 19 COMBAT MAGNUM

BULLET	LOAD	MV
Lyman #358156GC	14.5 gr. #2400	1,312
	15.5 gr. H4227	1,236
Lyman #358429	14.0 gr. #2400	1,353
	14.5 gr. H4227	1,267
RCBS #38-150KT	14.5 gr. #2400	1,322
	15.5 gr. H4227	1,239
	7.5 gr. Unique	1,218
Speer 158 JSP	15.5 gr. #2400	1,227

Action New Model. Smith and Wesson did not recognize the capabilities of the new cartridge chambered in 20th-century sixguns but there were experimenters that certainly did.

When the production of the New Century, or Triple-Lock, ended in 1915, it was replaced by the less desirable Second Model without the third Lock and enclosed ejector rod. In 1926, the Second Model was modified to become the Third Model with a shrouded ejector rod housing once again. In 1950 this would evolve into the strongest .44 Special that Smith & Wesson ever offered, the Fourth Model Hand Ejector, or, as it is better known, the Model 1950 Target. The Target Model had a full-ribbed barrel such as that found on the .357 Magnum, adjustable sights, and the new post-War short action. This was the apex in .44 Special double-action sixguns. Although lacking the third locking feature of the original .44 Special, these were the finest sixguns Smith & Wesson could build and certainly stronger than the First Model from nearly a half-century earlier. This strength would be needed for the performance that would soon be demanded of the .44 Special Target Model of 1950.

Certainly the most vocal, though not the only voice, was that of Elmer Keith, who spent 30 years from the 1920s through the 1950s using his specially designed bullet, the Ideal, now Lyman, #429421 with heavy powder charges to obtain 1,100 to 1,200 fps muzzle velocity. Keith's bullet is a semi-wadcutter design casting out at about 250 grains from a hard alloy. Powders used in those days were #80, then the much better #2400, which even today remains as one of the best and one of the most popular powders for heavy loads in sixguns.

Keith led the way in trying to convince someone to bring out a heavily loaded .44 Special. His heavy loading of a .44 Special with his bullet, a basic design by the way that went back the turn of the century, would be THE heavy big-bore sixgun load of the first half of the 20th century, and still remains popular today in the proper sixguns. The bullet design may have gone back many years but Keith improved it by specifying three bands of equal diameter: a base band, a middle band that led into a deep crimping groove, and a full-calibered shoulder that rode outside of the cartridge case. In between the base band and the middle band was a

A Salute to Elmer Keith: a matched pair of Model 24 4-inch .44 Specials with Keith-style carved ivories by Bob Leskovec.

SELECTED LOADS FOR THE S&W .44 SPECIAL 1950 TARGET MODEL 6 1/2"

BULLET	LOAD	MV
Lyman #429421	15.5 gr. #2400	1,042
(250 gr.)	16.5 gr. #2400	1,190
	17.5 gr. #2400	1,219
	17.5 gr. H4227	1,029
	18.5 gr. H4227	1,115
	19.5 gr. H4227	1,148
	15.0 gr. AA #9	1,021
	16.0 gr. AA #9	1,090
	17.0 gr. AA#9	1,161
	12.5 gr. HS7	1,036
	13.0 gr. HS7	1131
	13.5 gr. HS7	1196
	7.5 gr. Unique	913
	8.5 gr. Unique	983

deep, square-cornered grease groove that would hold a generous amount of lubrication. The nose of the bullet was long with a flat point. Every semi-wadcutter today is generically referred to as a "Keith bullet," but very few actually follow his original design.

When Keith started heavy loading the .44 Special, the brass that was available was the old-style "balloon head" case that did not surround the primer pocket with brass. The "solid head" brass would not arrive until the 1950s. As one might expect, the balloon head style brass, which is also known as folded head brass, had more case capacity. This allowed Keith to use 18.5 grains of #2400 for his heavy loads. When the new brass arrived with less capacity he cut this load to 17.5 grains. He always recommended the use of standard pistol primers with his loads.

Keith's load is a 1,200 fps load to be used ONLY in heavy-framed .44 Specials. For me, this means to be used only in the Smith & Wesson 1950 Target, the special run of Model 24s and 624s from the 1980s, the Colt New Frontier, and Colt Single Action Army. THIS IS NOT A LOAD TO BE TAKEN LIGHTLY!! One should start at around 15.5 grains of #2400 and work up using a hard-cast bullet of the proper diameter. I have a Third Generation .44 Special Colt Single Action with one jugged chamber from this load. The other five chambers digest it perfectly and ask for more. The sixth chamber apparently had a bolt cut that was too deep and the fired brass was marked with an outline of this. That chamber has now been marked and since five rounds are all that should ever be carried in a Colt Single Action, it presents no real problem.

Had double-action sixgun development stopped in 1950 with the Target Model and Keith's heavy loads, we would still be in pretty good shape and able to handle most hunting chores. Keith was not a handgun hunter as defined today, that is, those that deliberately go after big game armed only with a handgun. However, he did kill a lot of game with his .44 Special for the simple reason that he spent most of his life outdoors and always carried a sixgun. For him it was a weapon of convenience and he had one buckled on for the vast majority of his life. For 30 years this meant his 5 1/2-inch #5SA Colt, a 7 1/2-inch King Custom SAA, a Triple-Lock, or a Model 1950 Target. All were .44 Specials and all were carried with his heavy load that he tried for 30 years with no avail to have produced by one of the major ammunition companies.

It is not always necessary, and certainly not desirable, to only shoot full power loads. For each of the big

PLEASURE LOADS: .44 SPECIAL S&W M24 6 1/2"/OREGON TRAIL 240 SWC

LOAD	MV	GROUP
6.5 gr. WW231	875	1 3/4"
5.0 gr. WW452AA	778	1 7/8"
5.5 gr. WW452AA	850	3/4"
7.5 gr. Herco	882	1 3/8"
8.0 gr. HS6	649	1 1/4"
5.0 gr. Bullseye	757	1 3/8"
5.5 gr. Bullseye	854	1 3/4"
11.0 gr. AA#7	808	1 1/2"
10.0 gr. HS7	850	1 1/2"

bores we will give proven "Pleasure Loads." These easy shootin' loads also give excellent accuracy. All groups are five shots at 25 yards with iron sights.

Keith was not the only well-known experimenter with a heavy-loaded .44. In the late 1940s, gunwriter John Lachuk went a step further with a .44 using cut-down .405 Winchester rifle brass to make his heavily loaded .44. Special cylinders were fitted to Colt Single Actions with the brass being made as long as possible to fill out the cylinder. Lachuk's wildcat used Lyman's Ray Thompson-designed gas-checked semi-wadcutter bullet, #431244 with a load of 22.5 grains of #2400 for what must have been an awesome load exhibiting tremendous recoil in Colt Single Actions.

The .44 Special Magnum

Keith's pleas for a heavily loaded .44 Special went unheeded for decades. Ammunition manufacturers were afraid, and rightly so, of what might happen if such loads were used in some older guns. Keith belief that lengthening the case, as had been done with the .38 Special to give us the .357 Magnum, would result in a .44 Special Magnum. This, of course, would require a new sixgun. To this end he spent a week at the Smith & Wesson factory in the early 1950s discussing the project, and then in December of 1955 he received word that his dream had come true. He was totally surprised to hear that Smith & Wesson would be sending him one of the first of the new .44 Magnums. The first new .44 sixgun had gone to Remington for testing, the second went to the American Rifleman, and Keith received the third 6 1/2-inch Smith & Wesson .44 Magnum.

Keith had spent 30 years asking for a 250-grain bullet at an even 1200 fps. Even he did not know what was possible as the engineers at Smith & Wesson and Remington were able to come up with a sixgun to handle the load, with a 240-grain bullet at 1450 fps. Keith was, of course, ecstatic about the new load and the new sixgun and retired his .44 Specials. He would carry a 4-inch .44 Magnum for the next 25 years. Using the same bullet he preferred in his .44 Specials, Keith worked up a load for the .44 Magnum using 22.0 grains of #2400. He preferred his hard cast bullets over the softer factory bullets.

The .44 Magnum was developed in partnership, with Remington working on the cartridge and Smith & Wesson providing the sixgun. The first four factory

Three great .44s from Smith & Wesson covering nearly one-half century: (from left) Triple-Lock .44 Special, 1908; Model 1950 Target .44 Special, and the .44 Magnum originating in 1956. Skeeter Skelton stocks on the latter two.

Loaded with .44 Specials, these two Smith & Wesson .44 Magnums, a pre-29 and a 29-2, will certainly do the job required of defensive sixguns.

prototype .44 Magnums were simply .44 Special 1950 Target Models with specially heat-treated cylinders and frames. Recoil with the 39-ounce Target Model was certainly excessive, and when the production model .44 Magnum surfaced a heavyweight bull barrel and a full-length cylinder was added to bring the weight of the 6 1/2-inch .44 Magnum up to an even three pounds. To complete the package, a target hammer and trigger were added along with a red ramp front sight and fully adjustable, white-outline rear sight.

The early Smith & Wesson .44 Magnums exhibited the precision fitting of the 1907 Triple-Lock without the third locking feature and were finished in S&W bright blue — a blue so bright and so deep you could see your ancestors in it. Unfortunately, it is no more, a victim of progress. The first guns were only available with the 6 1/2-inch barrel. The 4- and 8 3/8-inch barrels would follow shortly, so Keith had one cut to a barrel length of 4 1/2 inches and completely engraved and stocked by the old, and now long gone, Gun Re-Blu Company.

Evolution of the .44 Magnum

The first .44 Magnum I ever fired was one of the 4-inch models that a local gun store/outdoor shooting range rented out to all who wanted to try a really big-bore sixgun. We had been used to shooting .357

One of the great hunting sixguns of all time is the Smith & Wesson Model 29 equipped with custom stocks by Roy Fishpaw

The original 4-inch .44 Magnum from Smith & Wesson is second only to the Colt Single Action Army for esthetic value.

Magnums, .44 Specials, and both the .45s (Colt and Automatic Colt Pistol). We were teenagers and we were invincible, but we were not even close to being prepared for what we were about to experience. We all shot it, the recoil was absolutely awful, but we lied and said it was fun. It would take a lot of shooting and training before we would be able to handle the .44 Magnum.

Those original Smith & Wesson .44 Magnums were absolutely beautiful sixguns and were supplied by the factory in a fitted wooden case. They were purchased by outfitters, outdoorsman, guides, and handgun hunters. It was not long before very slightly used .44 Magnums were found for sale along with a box of cartridges with six empty cases and 44 loaded rounds. Some shooters learned very quickly that the .44 Magnum was a lot more than they wanted. When Maj. Hatcher of the NRA staff reviewed it, he said the recoil of the .44 Magnum Smith & Wesson was like getting hit in the palm of the hand with a baseball bat. Col. Askins chided him, saying Hatcher ought to have lace sewed on his shorts. Keith said the recoil was not as bad as shooting .38 Specials in a Chief's Special. I always wondered how Keith could handle the recoil in the S&W .44 Magnums, especially since he discarded the hand-filling target-style factory stocks for, as he called them, plainclothes stocks or the standard magna stocks that were found on the original .357

For more than 20 years, the standard barrel lengths for the .44 Magnum from Smith & Wesson were 4, 6 1/2, and 8 3/8 inches. For some reason, the 6-inch replaced the 6 1/2-inch length in 1979.

Both of these heavy underlug-barreled Model 629s wear Herrett's stocks. The top gun has Bo-Mar sights and both guns are superb long-range sixguns.

Magnums. I found out when I had the chance to handle his sixguns. He preferred carved ivory, and the carving fit perfectly into the crease in the shooting hand to help control recoil.

The .44 Magnum, as great a sixgun as it was, sold very slowly until three things happened. Two of these were real, and the other, "reel." The latter came from the movies with Clint Eastwood's "Dirty Harry" character creating a demand for .44 Magnums that the factory working round-the-clock could not satisfy. The other two were the rise of both long-range silhouetting and handgun hunting.

As with the other Smith & Wesson sixguns, the .44 Magnum also went through an evolutionary time period. In 1957, the .44 Magnum became a number with Model 29 stamped inside the crane beginning at serial number S179000. It was about the same time that the first of the long-barreled .44 Magnums arrived as the Model 29 joined the Model 27 .357 Magnum with an 8 3/8-inch barrel. These quickly became very popular with hunters and long-range shooters. It was about the same time in 1958 that a Chicago distributor, H.H. Harris, ordered 500 5-inch Model 29s. These are sixguns that are only rarely seen for sale on the used gun market.

One of the problems with those early .44 Magnums was the fact that the ejector rod screw would loosen under recoil, back out, and move forward, making it difficult or impossible to open the cylinder. In 1960, this rod was given a reverse left thread so it would tighten rather than loosen under recoil. With this change, the Model 29-1 arrived at serial number S270000. The 29-1 is quite rare, lasting only one year before being replaced by the 29-2 in 1961. With this arrival, the four-screw .44 Magnum became a three-screw model as a screw in the front of the trigger guard was dropped.

The Smith & Wesson .44 Magnum most likely to be encountered on the used gun market is the 29-2, as it lasted more than 20 years in production. During its time of production, the serial numbering was changed from an "S" prefix to an "N" prefix in 1969, while at the same time, the 6 1/2-inch barrel length was dropped and replaced by a half-inch shorter barrel. Why? The longer barrel not only looks better, it balances better in my hands.

In 1982, with Smith & Wesson being controlled by Bangor Punta, two major changes were made to cut costs. With the arrival of 29-3, the pinned barrel and recessed cylinder disappeared. Up to this point in time, all Smith & Wesson barrels were held tightly in place not just by thread pressure, but also by a pin that transversed the frame through a slot in the top of the barrel threads. With today's stronger brass, counterbored cylinders, or cylinders that completely enclose the rim of a cartridge case, are probably not needed. They also easily fill up with dirt and unburned powder granules and must be periodically cleaned or cases will not chamber. They may not be needed, but they are a sign of manufacturing quality and they are gone.

For years, Smith & Wesson refused to acknowledge a problem that definitely existed. The same problem also surfaced later with .44 Magnum sixguns from other manufacturers. The problem became especially prevalent when silhouette shooters started pounding hundreds of rounds of full-house loads down range in a single day. When a cartridge was fired, the cylinder would unlock, rotate backwards and when the hammer was cocked, the fired round would be back under the firing pin. At about the same time, handgun hunters discovered 300-grain bullets, whose use put a further strain on a basic mechanism design that went back to 1889.

To "correct" the problem, Smith & Wesson came out with a Silhouette Model in 1983. This model had a 10 5/8-inch barrel, a rear sight with a taller blade, and a four-position adjustable front sight to be set for the four distances encountered in long-range silhouetting. Nothing was done to correct the problem that occurred internally. Strangely enough, of all the Smith & Wesson .44 Magnums I have shot over the past 40-plus years, the Silhouette Model was the only one I ever encountered that unlocked and rotated backwards with regularity.

With a change of management, Smith & Wesson began to address some of the problems with the .44 Magnum Model 29. By now, both Ruger and Dan Wesson had heavy-duty .44 Magnum sixguns on the market that were designed around the cartridge. The Smith & Wesson had a distinctive disadvantage as it was built on a mechanical platform going back to 1899 and a frame size dating from 1907. S&W had to face the difficult choice: Scrap the 29 and start all over or try to fix what it had. It opted for the latter, and I am pleased that it did. To have scrapped it would have meant replacing a thoroughbred with a Clydesdale.

Smith & Wesson engineers changed the interior of the Model 29 by radiusing the studs to prevent cracking and cutting longer bolt slots in the cylinders that were matched up with larger bolts. The interior parts were changed so that they were prevented from moving under recoil and being battered loose. All of these changes came as part of the Endurance Package. The 29-4 from 1988 to 1990 began a change that was completed with the 29-5 in 1990.

In 1994, the 29-6 arrived drilled and tapped for scope mounts and fitted with Hogue grips. One year later, the square butt grip frame disappeared, replaced by the round-butt configuration. In 1997, the trigger was changed to MIM (metal injected molding). Finally, the 29-7 arrived in 1998. The serrations on the front and back strap were now gone, the hammer was now MIM and the firing pin was moved to the frame. In January of 1999, the last Model of the Magnificent 29 was laid to rest. The .357 Magnum, the Combat Magnum, the .44 Magnum — all gone. I don't have any tears left.

During the course of its production, the 29 also appeared with a full lug barrel with the Classic with 5-, 6 1/2-, and 8 3/8-inch barrel lengths, the Classic DX

The Model 29 .44 Magnum is gone, but the stainless-steel 629 remains. Smooth stocks on standard 629s by BearHug, checkered stocks on heavy-barrel models by Herrett's.

Forty years separate the introduction of these two .44 Magnums, which clearly illustrates the change in production of Smith's Magnum. The Standard Model 29 (top) with Skeeter Skelton stocks, represents the 1950s, while the stainless-steel, heavy-barreled, Hogue-stocked, Power Port version is a product of the 1990s.

with round butt grip frame and 6 1/2- or 8 3/8-inch barrel, and the MagnaClassic with a 7 1/2-inch barrel. There has also been a long list of commemoratives and special editions ordered by distributors over the years.

When Ruger, Dan Wesson, and Taurus introduced .44 Magnums, they all went with more weight than the original. The 8-inch Dan Wesson even had to have its weight shaved a couple ounces to make the four-pound limit under IHMSA rules. Ruger and Taurus have also added more weight with their two newer models, the Super Redhawk and the Raging Bull. Smith & Wesson added weight to the original Model 29 and its offspring, the 629, by going with a full underlugged barrel and also making recoil-soaking grips standard. All four manufacturers now use rubber grips. In spite of the fact that since the .44 Magnum arrived we have seen the advent of Heavy .45 Colt loads, the .454 Casull, and the .475 and .500 Linebaughs, all of which are heavier kickers than the .44 Magnum, the truth remains that the .44 Magnum still recoils, and recoils heavily. It is not a cartridge and sixgun to be taken lightly, even though there are so many larger calibers now that exhibit even heavier recoil.

All of the heavier .44 Magnums are certainly easier to shoot, however, my heart, soul, and spirit, still prefer the original configuration. The four-inch Smith & Wesson .44 Magnum comes very close to being as beautifully designed as a Colt Single Action. With its artistic lines, it is simply one great-looking sixgun. A pair of these matched up with a full floral carved rig is just about as good as it gets. With heavy loads the 4-inch .44 will certainly get your attention, and for my use I prefer to stay more with loads that are in the heavy .44 Special range. For hunting, the 8 3/8-inch gets the nod, and the 6 1/2-inch is really the most practical of the three. I like 'em all.

In the early days of the Smith & Wesson .44 Magnum, I mostly used the Keith load. Today, as I am wiser, and older, and my Smith & Wesson .44 Magnums are also older, I treat them and myself more gently. My most common loading is a 250- or 290-grain hard cast bullet over 10.0 grains of Unique for about 1,150 fps from a 6 1/2-inch barrel. Heavier loads listed are used very sparingly.

The forgotten .41 Magnum

We have looked at the .357 Magnum and the .44 Magnum, and now there's one Magnum left of the trio of Magnums produced by Smith & Wesson in the middle third of the 20th century. Both the .357 Magnum and the .44 Magnum followed natural paths; the third one did not and is often been looked upon as being "illegitimate." Nothing could be farther from the truth. The .357 Magnum came from a natural evolution of .38s starting with the .38s of the 1870s, the .38 S&W and the .38 Long Colt, followed by the .38 Special at the turn of the century, and the .38/44 Heavy Duty of 1930. The lineage of the .44 Magnum goes back even further from the .44 Henry of 1860 to the .44 American of 1869, then the .44 Russian of 1870 and the .44 Special that arrived in 1907.

SELECTED LOADS FOR THE SMITH & WESSON MODEL 29

BULLET	LOAD	MV/4"	MV/6 1/2"
Lyman #429421	9.0 gr. Unique	869	936
	10.0 g. Unique	1,057	1,134
(250 gr.)	24.0 gr. H4227	1,198	1,277
	20.0 gr. #2400	1,095	1,231
	21.0 gr. #2400	1,187	1,331
	22.0 gr. #2400	1,227	1,380
Lyman #431244GC	20.0 gr. #2400	1,154	1,295
(255 gr.)	21.0 gr. #2400	1,227	1,368
	22.0 gr. #2400	1,292	1,458
Hornady 240JHP	24.5 gr. WW296	1,168	1,318
Hornady 265JFP	23.5 gr. WW296	1,223	1,339
Speer 240JHP	24.5 gr. WW296	1,167	1,311
BRP 290 KT-GC	10.0 gr. Unique	1,076	1,148

PLEASURE LOADS: .44 MAGNUM S&W M29 6 1/2"/OREGON TRAIL 240 SWC

LOAD	MV	GROUP
7.5 gr. WW231	914	1 5/8"
6.0 gr. WW452AA	860	1 1/4"
7.0 gr. WW452AA	972	1 3/4"
8.5 gr. 800X	872	1 7/8"
8.0 gr. Unique	916	2"
8.5 gr. Unique	991	1 1/4"
8.5 gr. Herco	931	2"
7.0 gr. Bullseye	971	1 5/8"
13.0 gr. AA#7	917	1 1/2"
14.0 gr. AA7	1040	1 5/8"
8.0 gr. AA#5	640	1 5/8"
6.5 gr. HP38	851	1 5/8"
11.0 gr. Blue Dot	915	1 7/8"
12.0 gr. Blue Dot	992	1 5/8"

The .41 Magnum followed a different path. In the 1870s, Colt chambered the Model 1877 in .41 Long Colt; and both Winchester, in its Model 1873, and Colt, in the Single Action Army, offered the .38-40. Strangely enough, the .41 used a hollow-base bullet of .386-inch diameter, while the .38-40 had a larger .400-inch bullet. Three years before the .357 Magnum arrived, Colt had built at least one gun in .41 Special, but the project was shelved. Colt may have had the round to out-Magnum the .357 Magnum, but we will never know. Wildcatters such as Pop Eimer and Gordon Boser in the 1930s and 1940s both built custom sixguns in .40 caliber using cut-down .30-40 Krag and .401 Winchester rifle brass. In the early 1960s, the mail-order firm Herter's offered German-made revolvers chambered in the .401 PowerMag. None of these were a true .41 caliber.

Enter Elmer Keith. We have already seen his hand in the development of both the .357 Magnum and the .44 Magnum, and he also becomes the driving force for the .41 Magnum. He wrote in Guns & Ammo in 1963, "Since the early 20s, I have received many letters asking for a .41 Magnum cartridge for all police and peace officers. Until I had the .44 Magnum gun and load on the market and in general use, I never made a request to any of the loading companies or the arms industry for a .41 Magnum, because I felt the .44 was a better weapon and load. These requests have come from many of our most experienced old peace officers and gunfighters, men like Bill Jordan, M.A. Niles, the late Sam Russell (remember, he traded Keith two .45 Colt Single Actions for one 1877 .41!), Lt. Williamson, and many more I could easily name.... Many officers do not like the weight or the recoil of the heavily loaded 44 Special or the .44 Magnum, and the consensus is that a .41 Magnum is what is needed.... The cartridge case should be the same length as our present .357 and .44 Magnums. The bullet should be the Keith design of 200 to 210 grains in weight. The full load should carry a full jacket over the bearing-surface soft point at 1,400 to 1,500 fps velocity... The lighter load should be the Keith-design 200-210 grain cast or swaged lead alloy bullet, plain or copper-coated, at 1,100 fps.... This

The Middle Magnum, which certainly deserves more respect, the Model 57 .41 Magnum with stocks by BearHug.

load would be for general practice and for use where the big load was not needed. It would still be an excellent man-stopper, far better than the .357 load at its best.... Doug Hellstrom (of Smith & Wesson) feels as I do that the ideal police weapon would be a heavy-loaded .44 Special, not available commercially, or better the 4-inch S&W .44 Magnum, but he also realizes how hard it is to put over to most police organizations, whereas a .41 Magnum might well become the accepted police cartridge."

He talked to all the sixgun manufacturers who promised they would chamber the .41 Magnum if an ammunition company brought it out. From Smith & Wesson, the full-sized N-frame, and five-shot K-frame; from Ruger, a 4 5/8" Blackhawk and Super Blackhawk; and from Colt, the Python. Keith gathered help from two ex-Border Patrolmen turned gun writers, Bill Jordan and Skeeter Skelton, to help him lobby for the new cartridge and sixgun. The result for police use was the N-framed size, 4-inch Military & Police; and for hunters and outdoorsman, a 6-inch .41 Magnum built on the .44 Magnum frame. The new sixgun from Smith & Wesson became the Model 57.

The .41 Magnum was never really accepted as a police round. In its full-house loading in the Model 57 it is powerful and flat shooting, but for some reason has never been fully accepted by sixgunners. It remains the cartridge and sixgun of true connoisseurs. Had the .41 Magnum come between the .357 Magnum and .44 Magnum instead of after both of them it would probably have been accepted and received the recognition it deserves. Instead, it has been treated rather coldly, except by the same type of sixgunner that knows and appreciates the .44 Special. It is an excellent outdoorsman's and hunter's cartridge chambered in the Model 57. I have used the Smith & Wesson Model 57 on both deer and feral hogs and never in either case did they realize I was not using a .44 Magnum. The cartridge that Keith, Jordan, and Skelton really wanted for police use would arrive 25 years later in the .40 S&W, and not in a sixgun but in a semi automatic.

The Model 57 arrived in 1964 in either S&W bright blue or nickel with barrel lengths of 4, 6, and 8 3/8 inches. The original target style grips with a diamond around the screw hole, were dropped in 1968. It became 57-1 in 1982 with the dropping of both the pinned barrel and counter-bored cylinder. The nickel-plating option would be dropped in 1986. The beginnings of the Endurance Package came with the 57-2 in 1988 and were completed in 1990 with the 57-3. Two years later both the 4- and 8 3/8-inch barrel lengths were dropped. In 1993 the Model 57 was removed from production. Strangely enough, I have never owned or even fired a 6-inch Model 57, but I thoroughly enjoy both an 8 3/8-inch .41 Magnum for hunting, and the matched pair of 4-inch sixguns for general use.

Four great models, originally available in both bright blue and nickel plating, and now they're gone. The Model 28, the Highway Patrolman, available in both 4- and 6-inch models, was simply a workhorse version of the Model 27 without the checkering and with a matte blue finish. Nearly all of Smith & Wesson's production is now stainless-steel with several models now surfacing in the metals of the 21st century — titanium and scandium. It has become too costly to produce brightly finished blued sixguns and regulatory powers have driven away most nickel-plated sixguns. All is not lost, however, as the sixguns that Smith & Wesson now produces may not be as soul stirring as the older models, but they are stronger and in most cases where I have tested them head to head, even better shooters. All of the medium- and large-frame Smith & Wesson sixguns are produced on new CNC machinery and now feature MIM hammers and triggers and a frame-mounted firing pin. The Combat Magnum continues as the Model 66 with a choice of 2 1/2-, 4-, or 6-inch barrels; the .44 Magnum Model 29 has sired the stainless steel Model 629 with both standard and heavy underlugged barrels; and the Model 57 continues as the stainless steel Model 657.

In the late 1970s complaints arose about the durability of both the Model 19 and the Model 66 when used heavily with full-house .357 Magnums. Smith & Wesson addressed this problem by bringing out the L-frame Models 586/686 with a K-frame grip frame and durability comparable to the N-frame. The blued 586 has been dropped, but the stainless steel 686 has proven to be extremely popular, as durable as Smith & Wesson could have hoped, and in general could well be the most accurate double-action .357 Magnum ever built. While I hate to admit it, it is probably a better .357 sixgun than either the Combat Magnum or the original

SELECTED LOADS FOR THE S&W MODEL 57 8 3/8"

BULLET	LOAD	MV
Lyman #410459	17.0 gr. #2400	1,391
(220 gr. Keith SWC)	18.0 gr. #2400	1,421
	20.0 gr. #2400	1,521
	22.0 gr. H4427	1,410
	8.0 gr. Unique	1,041
	10.0 gr. Unique	1,292
Sierra 170JHP	20.0 gr. #2400	1,512
	24.0 gr. H110	1,503
Speer 200JHP	19.0 gr. #2400	1,404
	21.0 gr. H110	1,453
Hornady 210JHP	22.0 gr. H110	1,402
Speer 220 JFP	18.0 gr. #2400	1,346

PLEASURE LOADS: .41 MAGNUM S&W M57 6"/OREGON TRAIL 215 SWC

LOAD	MS	GROUP
6.0 gr. WW231	884	1 3/4"
6.5 gr. WW231	922	1 3/4"
7.0 gr. WW231	1,021	1 1/4"
5.5 gr. WW452AA	865	1 3/4"
6.0 gr. WW452AA	937	1 1/2"
6.5 gr. WW452AAA	969	1 3/4"
7.5 gr. 800X	868	1 3/4"
7.5 gr. Herco	915	1 1/2"
8.0 gr. HS6	756	1 3/8"
9.0 gr. HS6	882	1 3/4"
5.0 gr. Bullseye	810	1 3/4"
5.5 gr. Bullseye	849	1 5/8"
6.0 gr. Bullseye	879	1 3/4"
12.0 gr. AA#7	974	1 7/8"
8.0 gr. HS7	733	1 3/8"
9.0 gr. HS7	742	1 1/2"
10.0 gr. HS7	919	1 1/2"
6.5 gr. HP38	934	1 1/2"
5.5 gr. AA#2	829	1 1/4"
6.0 gr. AA#2	1,021	1 1/4"

They are all gone now! Classic 8 3/8-inch Smith & Wesson N-frames (from top left): .357 Magnum, .45 Colt, .41 Magnum, all with BearHug Skeeter Skelton stocks; .44 Magnum stocked by Roy Fishpaw.

.357 Magnum. With its heavy underlugged barrel, it not only balances well, it also dampens recoil well. It has been offered in 2 3/4-, 4-, 6-, and 8 3/8-inch barrel lengths as well as a seven-shot version. Excellence in a .357 Magnum sixgun.

In recent years, the .357 Magnum, which started out as a long-barreled, relatively heavyweight sixgun with warnings to the general shooter about its extraordinary performance and recoil, has now taken a turn to the opposite end of the spectrum. Sixguns like the very lightweight .357 Magnums such as the J-frame 340Sc Centennial and the 360Sc Chief's Special were composed of such alloys as titanium and scandium. For concealed carry use, these little 12-ounce J-frame revolvers loaded with 125-grain .357 Magnum-jacketed hollow points, can ride in a front pants pocket comfortably all day. For those who want a lightweight .357 as a belt gun, the same theme is carried out in the Model 386Sc Mountain Lite, with adjustable sights, a seven-shot titanium cylinder, 3 1/8-inch barrel, and Hi-Viz front sight. The same basic sixgun is also available in a five-shot .44 Special as the 396Ti Mountain Lite. For those that prefer a stainless steel .44 Special, Smith & Wesson also offers the Model 696, a five-shooter on the L-frame with a 3-inch underlugged barrel and adjustable sites. No one can rightfully accuse Smith and Wesson of not doing everything it can to produce some very interesting and excellent modern sixguns.

Possibly the best double-action .357 Magnum ever offered by Smith & Wesson, the Model 686 in both six- and seven-shot versions with Heritage Grips by Eagle and finger groove stocks by Hogue.

The .357 Magnums for the new century from Smith & Wesson are the Scandium Models 340Sc (bottom) and 360Sc.

With the great rising popularity of the .40 S&W as a duty weapon in the 1990s, and the advent of the popular 10MM, which was chambered in just about every manufacturer's semi-automatic, Smith & Wesson brought forth the Model 610 revolver that feeds on either cartridge by using half-moon clips. Available with both a 4-inch and a 6-inch heavy underlugged barrel, the round-butted, adjustable-sighted, stainless steel 610 is probably the most accurate of all the .40 S&Ws and 10MMs offered. Built on the large N-frame as a special run in the early 1990s, it has been in such demand that it returned in 1998. The Model 610 is an easy-to-handle, superbly accurate 10MM, and though it comes with half-moon clips to use with the rimless 10MM brass, I also achieve

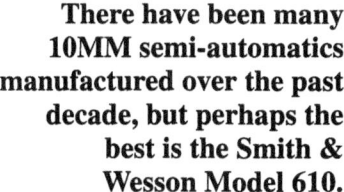

There have been many 10MM semi-automatics manufactured over the past decade, but perhaps the best is the Smith & Wesson Model 610.

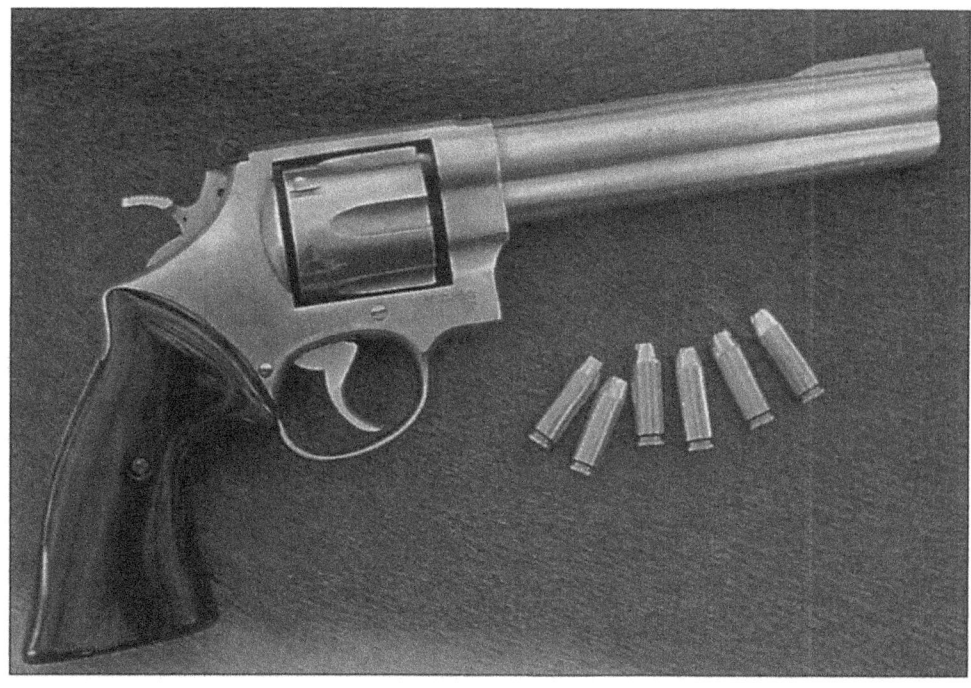

SELECTED LOADS FOR THE 10MM SMITH & WESSON MODEL 610 6 1/2"

BULLET	LOAD	MV	5 SHOTS/25 YDS
Hornady 155 JHP	Factory	1,325	1 3/8"
Hornady 170 JHP	Factory	1,218	1 3/4"
Hornady 200 JHP	Factory	1,061	1 7/8"
Hornady 170 XTP	12.5 gr. AA#7	1,307	1 3/4"
Hornady 200 XTP	10.5 gr. AA#7	1,086	1 5/8"
Hornady 200 FMJ	10.5 gr. AA#7	1,088	1 1/8"
Sierra 150 JHP	13.0 gr. AA#7	1,372	2"
Sierra 180 JHP	10.5 gr. AA#7	1,122	1 5/8"
Sierra 180 JHP	5.5 gr. WW231	957	1 5/8"
Speer 190 FMJ	10.5 gr. AA#7	1,110	1 3/4"
Speer 200 FMJ	5.0 gr. WW452AA	876	1 1/8"
RCBS #10MM-200	10.5 gr. AA#7	1,195	1 5/8"
RCBS #10MM-200	5.5 GR. WW231	1,052	1 1/4"

excellent results without resorting to their use. Of course, they would be mandatory in an action event, or more importantly, if the 610 sixgun is used defensively as punching out fired 10MM brass is almost as slow as emptying a single-action sixgun. Shooting the hottest 10MM loads in the round-butted, heavy-barreled Model 610 proves to be quite pleasant.

The best of the rest

There are other big-bore sixguns currently produced by Smith & Wesson worthy of being looked at even though they are not magnums, and those are the revolvers chambered in .45 ACP and .45 Colt. From the 1870s until the 1940s there almost seemed to be an unwritten code between the two major sixgun manufacturers, Colt and Smith & Wesson. Colts bailiwick was to be the .45 Colt while Smith would operate in .44 territory. Smith & Wesson had the first center-fire big-bore handgun in 1869 with the advent of the .44 S&W American. After the Colt Single Action Army was adopted as the official military sidearm, Smith & Wesson came out with the .45 Schofield in 1875. Adopted

Smith's other big bore six guns all with stocks by BearHug: (from left) Model 25-2 .45 ACP; Model 25-5, .45 Colt; and Model 57 .41 Magnum. Four-inch barrels are still highly regarded as defensive sixguns.

by the U.S. Army, it would be dropped two years later.

Until World War I forced both manufacturers to produce revolvers for wartime use chambered for the .45 ACP, each pretty much stayed in its own neighborhood. Up until World War II, Smith & Wesson produced a very few double-action sixguns in .45 Colt, while Colt produced a relatively few New Services and Single Action Armies in .44 Special. Smith was happy manufacturing First, Second, and Third Model Hand Ejectors in .44 Special while Colt was equally at ease with New Service and Single Action sixguns in its favored .45 Colt chambering. Find a Triple-Lock in .45 Colt or a first-generation Single Action Army in .44 Special and strike gold in the process! Colt still offers the .45 Colt in its Single Action Army, while Smith goes one better and also offers the other .45 Colt, the upstart .45 ACP, in its line of double-action sixguns.

As we recovered from the war-time production of the 1940s and entered a new era in the 1950s, Smith & Wesson introduced the Fourth Model Hand Ejector, the Model 1950 Target/Model 24 in .44 Special. This excellent sixgun was also chambered in .45 ACP as the Model 1950 Target/Model 26 with around 2,700 being manufactured before it disappeared from the Smith & Wesson catalog with a very few being manufactured in .45 Colt. The Model 1950 Target in .45 ACP was followed by the 1955 Target in the same chambering with the target hammer, target trigger, and bull barrel that would be standard on the new .44 Magnum coming forth in 1956. A special run of 10,000 Model 1955s would be offered as Smith & Wesson's 125th Anniversary Model in 1977 chambered in, of all things, .45 Colt.

One problem existed with these .45 Colt models in that Smith & Wesson used the short .45 ACP cylinder of the Model 1955 with precluded the use of .45 Colt bullets set in their proper crimping grooves. Bullets that worked fine in Colt Single Actions did not work in these double action sixguns. In order for the cylinder to function, bullets often had to be crimped over the shoulder rather than in the crimping groove. Smith & Wesson corrected all of this with the Model 25-5 .45 Colt. A dead ringer for the .44 Magnum (except for the caliber), Smith & Wesson's first catalogued standard production model in .45 Colt first saw the light of day in 1979.

The Model 25-2 ran side by side with the 25-5 for a one-two punch from Smith & Wesson in both .45 ACP/.45 Auto Rim chambering and also in .45 Colt. The former carries a short cylinder designed for the .45 ACP cartridge, while the latter has a cylinder, as in the .44 and .41 Magnums, that fills out the cylinder window.

It would be very difficult to find a big-bore double-action sixgun better suited for defensive use than a properly customized Model 1955 Target .45 ACP. All that is really needed is to cut the barrel to a length of four inches, and slim the target trigger and hammer to the contours of the less cumbersome and slicker-handling standard hammer and trigger. Throw in an action job by a skilled craftsman such as Teddy Jacobsen and

Especially popular as a packin' pistol is the Smith & Wesson Mountain Gun that has been offered in the .44 Magnum, .41 Magnum, and these two examples, both stocked by Herrett's, in the .45 ACP and .45 Colt.

With its slim tapered barreled and equipped with Eagle's Secret Service stocks, this Springfield Armory Commemorative .45 ACP (top) built on the Mountain Gun platform is actually more compact in some ways than the .357 Combat Magnum.

possibly replace the Baughman front ramp sight with a flat post Patridge sight and the perfect serious sixgun emerges. Just about every major manufacturer offers excellent defensive loads for the .45 ACP with highly rated stopping power statistics, all of which result in mild recoil and quick recovery between shots.

Chambered in .45 ACP, the Model 1955 allows the use of .45 ACP cartridges with or without the use of either half- or full-moon clips. The use of these clips, especially the full-moon style, results in the quickest reloading possible of a double-action sixgun. It rivals the speed of reloading with a semi-automatic. These sixguns will also accept .45 Auto Rim brass.

As .45 ACP cases are rimless, there is nothing for the ejector rod of the Smith & Wesson to grab onto for unloading. The use of .45 ACP cartridges without the clips requires the removal of the clips by using a fingernail or a rod of some kind to push them out. With clips or the use of the rimmed .45 Auto Rim brass, the ejector rod can be used as normal on a double-action sixgun.

The Model 25-5 in .45 Colt with a barrel length of four inches is also an easy packin', easy shootin' defensive sixgun. There are a number of excellent factory loads offered for use in the .45 Colt Smith & Wesson, namely Speer's 200-grain "Flying Ashtray" hollowpoint, Winchester's 225-grain SilverTip hollowpoint, and Federal's 225-grain lead semi-wadcutter. While not as fast as .45 ACP rounds in a full moon clip, the .45 Colt Smith & Wesson can be quickly reloaded with a speed loader.

A few years ago, Smith & Wesson made a special run of sixguns that are possibly even better suited for defensive use than the M25-2 .45 ACP or M25-5 .45 Colt. Call them Perfect Plus. These stainless steel sixguns were marked as Springfield Armory Commemoratives. Barrels on these 4-inch sixguns are of a pre-1955 slim style found on all Smith & Wessons prior to the bull barrels which came on the 1955 Target and .44 Magnum and 1956 .357 Combat Magnum. This makes them a little lighter for packin' and places the balance back in the hand rather than ahead of the cylinder.

Smith & Wesson may have dropped the Models 25-2 and 25-5, as they have with virtually all of the traditional square-butt, blue-finish, standard-barrel sixguns, but they have been replaced by the Models 625-2 and 625-5 in stainless with round butts and heavy underlug barrels.

The round-butted, full underlugged barrels have a couple of advantages over their ancestors. Most shooters will find them much easier to shoot with the heavier barrels that seem to hang on target, and though I prefer the old square-butt style of grip frame, I must admit that the round-butted grip frame allows the fitting of a greater range of custom grips.

The stainless finish also allows them to be carried close to the body in hot weather without fear of rust appearing on the finish. My close friend, the late Deacon Deason of BearHug Grips, was a long-time fan of the .45 Government Model. When the Model 625-2 arrived, his .45 Government Model was replaced by a three-inch M625-2. It was just as easy to conceal and he found, as many other shooters, that it was much easier to shoot, and it was not necessary to carry it cocked-and-locked. It was always at the ready with the hammer down and no safety to be concerned about.

Before the run of Model 25-5s ended, they were available in 4-, 6-, and 8 3/8-inch barrel lengths. The latter is one of my favorite sixguns for accurate sixgunning and just plain fun shooting. Loading with 260-grain Keith style semi-wadcutters at a muzzle velocity of 1,100 feet per second, it makes a practical close-range deer and black bear hunting handgun.

A few years back I ran an exhaustive test looking for what I call pleasure loads. That is, superbly accurate loads with 250 to 260-grain bullets, 210-220 grains in the .41 Magnum, and less than 1,000 feet per second muzzle velocity for the .44 Special, .41 Magnum, .44 Magnum, .45 AutoRim, and .45 Colt using Smith & Wesson sixguns. Surprise of surprises, the .45 Colt Model 25-5 proved to be the most accurate sixgun overall of all sixguns tested, which also included Models 29, 57, 24, and 25-2.

Smith & Wesson has offered the basic Springfield Armory Commemorative as a production sixgun with two of the finest .45s ever in the .45 Colt and .45 ACP Mountain Guns. These round-butted, slim, tapered 4-inch-barreled stainless steel sixguns make excellent packin' pistols.

The .45 Colt is superbly accurate in both Smith & Wessons chambered for the .45 Colt, namely the four-inch Model 25-5 and the 5-inch Model 625-5. A long-time favorite load of a 255-grain bullet over 9.0 grains of Unique clocked out right at 900 feet per second and grouped one inch or less. It would be hard to find a better load then this one for general use with the .45 Colt. For defensive use with the .45 Colt in these sixguns, my first choice has been Winchester's Silver-Tip hollowpoint at 800 feet per second with extra rounds carried in a speed loader.

Thirty-five years ago I adopted the full-house .45 ACP loading of a 200-grain bullet over 7.0 grains of Unique as my standard semi-auto load. Loaded in full-moon clips, this same load is an excellent performer in either a 4-inch Model 25-2 or a 5-inch Model 625-2. For defensive use in these sixguns, both Speer's 200-grain Lawman "Flying Ashtray" and Winchester's 185-grain Silver Tip-jacketed hollowpoints clocked out at 900 feet per second and gave excellent accuracy.

Both the .45 Colt and .45 Automatic Colt Pistol have a large and devoted following. The .45 Colt began as a 255-grain bullet at 850 to 900 feet per second over 40 grains of black powder. In the 1873 Peacemaker it replaced the 1860 Army with a 148-grain round ball at the same muzzle velocity. The Army soon found the full-house loading was too much for most soldiers to handle and went to a 230-grain bullet over 28 grains of black powder.

When the number one fightin' handgun of all time, the Colt 1911 Government Model arrived, its payload was a direct attempt to duplicate the old frontier military load in a semi-automatic. As a result, most Colt Single Action fanciers also espouse the Colt 1911 Government Model. Those that love the Single Action Army in .45 Colt or the .45 ACP Colt 1911 can find common ground in a Smith & Wesson chambered in either .45 Colt or .45 ACP.

For 2001 Smith & Wesson brought forth a 21st-century rendition of the 1907 Triple-Lock with a special Performance Center issue of blued Model HEG (Hand Ejector Gold) 6-inch sixguns with a slim tapered barrel in .45 Colt. These are now available in both .45 Colt and .44 Special as Heritage Models with case-colored

Smith & Wesson's heavy-barreled 625s, in .45 Colt (left) and .45 ACP, are both excellent shooters.

SMITH & WESSON .45 COLT

LOAD	4" MODEL 25-5 MV	GROUP	5" MODEL 625-5 MV	GROUP
Black Hills 255 LSWC	801	1 1/4"	789	1 3/4"
CCI Blazer 255 Lead	728	1 3/8"	736	1 1/2"
Federal 225 LSWC-HP	770	1 3/4"	769	1 5/8"
Winchester 255 Lead	737	1 7/8"	732	1 1/4"
Winchester 225 ST-HP	798	1 3/8"	783	1 5/8"
Bull-X 255/9.0 gr. Unique	887	1 1/8"	886	3/4"

All groups best five out of six shots at 25 yards.

PLEASURE LOADS: .45 COLT S&W M25-5 8 3/8"/OREGON TRAIL 255 SWC

LOAD	MS	GROUP
7.0 gr. WW231	790	1 3/4"
7.5 gr. WW231	875	1 3/4"
8.0 gr. WW231	926	1 3/8"
6.5 gr. WW452AA	831	1 3/4"
7.0 gr. WW452AA	893	1 3/4"
7.5 gr. WW452AA	947	1 3/8"
9.0 gr. 800X	861	1 3/4"

frames, along with a 1917 Model in .45 ACP/.45AR. These are beautiful sixguns reminiscent of revolvers produced before World War I.

Smith & Wesson is fast approaching its 150th anniversary of producing high-quality sixguns, from .22 Rimfire through .45 Colt. We have barely scratched the surface and only with the big-bore double-action sixguns. Detailed information on every handgun ever manufactured by Smith and Wesson, whether a production model, commemorative, limited edition, or a Performance Center issue, can be found in the greatest reference book on Smith & Wesson, The Standard Catalog of Smith & Wesson by Jim Supica and Richard Nahas, Krause Publications, 2001. It should be in every shooter's reference library.

SMITH & WESSON .45 ACP

LOAD	4" MODEL 25-2 MV	GROUP	5" MODEL 625-2 MV	GROUP
Black Hills 185 JHP	930	7/8"	969	1 7/8"
CCI Blazer 200 JHP	919	1 5/8"	898	1 3/4"
Federal 230 Classic FMJ	817	2 1/2"	798	2 1/4"
Federal 230 Hi-Shok	829	2 1/4"	816	2 1/2"
Speer Gold Dot 230 JHP	848	2 1/4"	840	2 1/4"
Speer Lawman 200 JHP	936	1 1/4"	936	3/4"
Winchester 185 ST-HP	900	7/8"	928	1 3/4"
Bull-X 200/6.0 gr. 452AA	970	1 1/2"	994	1 1/4"
Bull-X 200/7.0 gr. Unique	846	1 1/2"	844	1 1/8"

All groups best five out of six shots at 25 yards.

PLEASURE LOADS: .45 AR S&W M25-2 6"/OREGON TRAIL 255 SWC

LOAD	MV	GROUP
5.0 gr. WW231	741	1"
5.0 gr. WW452AA	818	1 1/2"
6.5 gr. 800X	787	1"
6.0 gr. Unique	855	2"
7.5 gr. Herco	919	1 1/4"
7.5 gr. HS6	723	1 3/4"
8.0 gr. AA#5	875	1 7/8"

CHAPTER 5

50 YEARS OF RUGER SINGLE-ACTION SATISFACTION

"God Bless Bill Ruger for putting Magnum rounds in single-action workin' guns!" I remember reading this quote in the middle 1950s in an article in *Guns* magazine. The piece was written by an old cowboy, trapper, ranger, etc., one Walter Rogers. Rogers, whom Elmer Keith mentions as a friend in his writings, had carried Colt Single Actions all of his life and in his later years Ruger had given him a nearly perfect single action — the .357 Blackhawk. After packin' Colts for so many years, Rogers found tremendous improvements in the then new big-bore single-action Ruger. The new Blackhawk from Ruger was "an upgraded Colt Single Action" with the flat-springs in the lockwork now replaced with virtually unbreakable coil springs, excellent adjustable sights made up of a Micro rear and a ramp front sight, and a heavy, wide, flat, top strap.

Experimenters like Elmer Keith, Gordon Boser, and John Lachuk tried to get Colt to modernize the Colt Single Action, but to no avail. Bill Ruger listened and reintroduced the Single Action at a time when American sixgunners were being primed for a single-action revival by TV westerns. Ruger had started in 1949 with an economically priced .22 semi-automatic that was eagerly accepted by shooters. Then in 1953, Bill Ruger, correctly reading the situation, brought out the .22 Single-Six, a scaled-down single-action .22 with a full-sized Colt-style grip frame. I doubt that even Bill Ruger could foresee the acceptance that his .22, and later centerfire Single Actions would find with the shooting public.

In a space of three years (1953-1956), Ruger introduced the .22 Single-Six, the .357 Magnum Blackhawk, and the .44 Magnum Blackhawk.

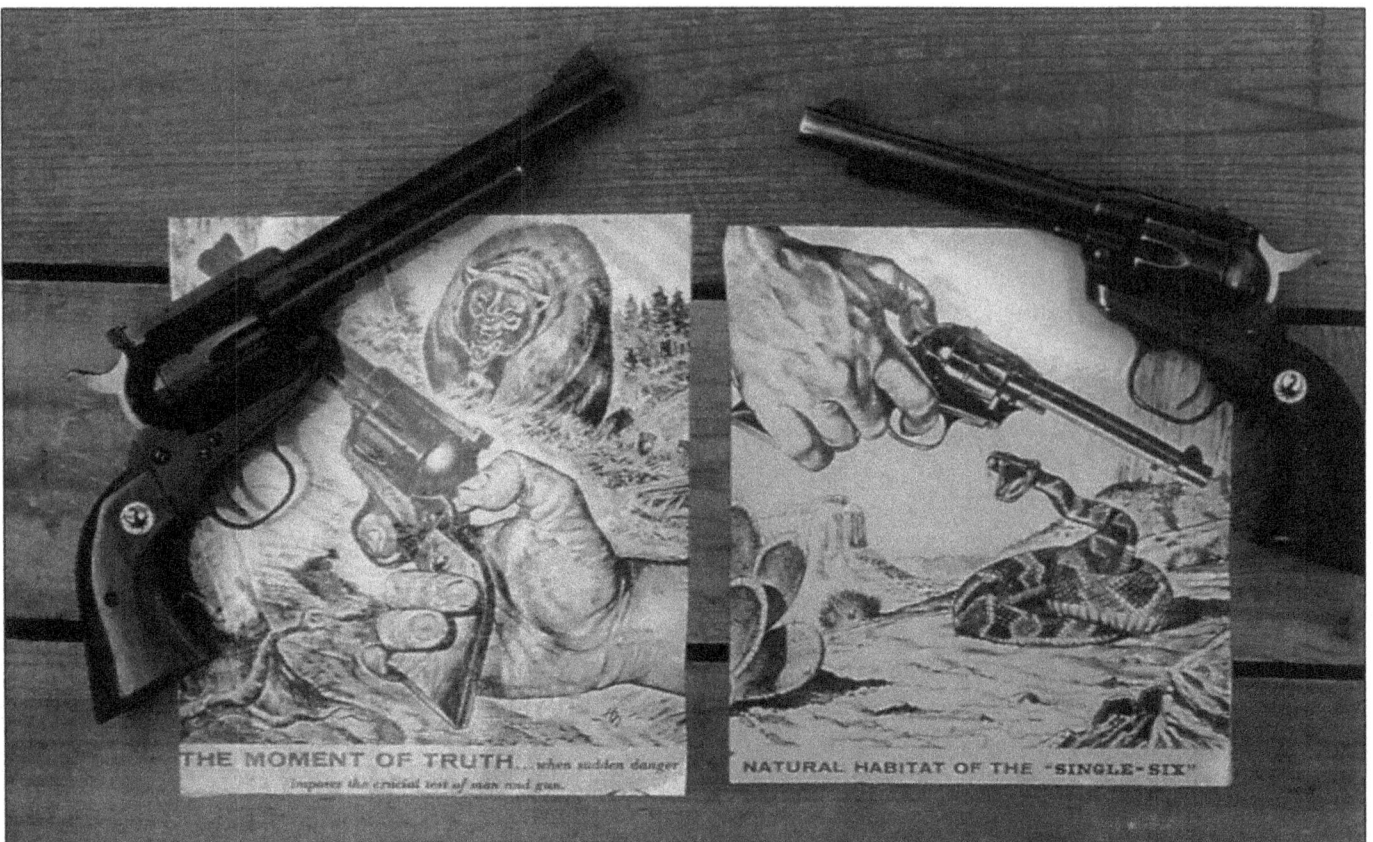

Advertising in the mid-1950s highlighted Ruger's single actions as the perfect sixgun for the outdoorsman.

Two years later, the first centerfire Ruger arrived as the .357 Magnum Blackhawk. Ruger had barely gotten a good start producing .357 Magnum Blackhawks when the .44 Magnum in the new Smith & Wesson arrived in 1956. Ruger went to work rechambering its .357 Blackhawk to the new ".44 Special Magnum." The .357 Blackhawk of the 1950s was built with a smaller frame and cylinder than the present .357 New Model. Keith told them that the gun was too small, but he would like to have one to use as a .44 Special. Before he was given the first .44 Ruger, factory testing proved him right when the .357/.44 blew.

The Flat-Top Blackhawk

Ruger went back to the drawing boards with the result being a larger sixgun, the first .44 Blackhawk, now also known to collectors as the Flat-Top .44 Magnum. That original .357 Blackhawk was basically the same size as the Colt Single Action Army. Just before the .357 Blackhawk came out in 1955, Great Western began producing the first Colt Single Action replicas in Los Angeles, and I have an old Great Western Frontier Model chambered in .44 Magnum that I found in a pawn shop with a price tag of $100. This sixgun had been around somewhere for over 30 years when I purchased it. The finish is practically gone, but the gun is sound and tight. It is the same frame size as the .44 Special and .45 Colt Great Western and Colt Single Actions. In fact, I can interchange cylinders between a .44 Special Colt and Great Western and this .44 Magnum. I have no idea what loads had been shot through this Great Western before I acquired it, but there is no way I would put full-house .44 Magnum loads through it. It will get mid-range .44 Magnums or .44 Specials for the rest of its shootin' life.

In some parts of the country, the Ruger .44 actually hit the shelves before the Smith & Wesson .44 Magnum. That was 1956 and the Smith & Wesson, beautifully finished and with a magnificently smooth action and trigger pull, sold for $140. As a teenager I was making $15 a week with a paper route at the time. The Ruger, not quite so nicely finished and fitted, sold for $96. One of the first Smith & Wesson .44 Magnum 4-inch models to hit my part of the country was rented out by a local gunstore/outdoor shooting range for all who wanted to try the big .44 Magnum. The recoil was absolutely awful, though few would admit it at the time. After graduating from high school, I bought the first Ruger Blackhawk in the area for the full $96 at a time when I was now up to making 90 cents an hour. To buy the Ruger I passed up a .45 Colt Single Action, with a full-ribbed barrel and a

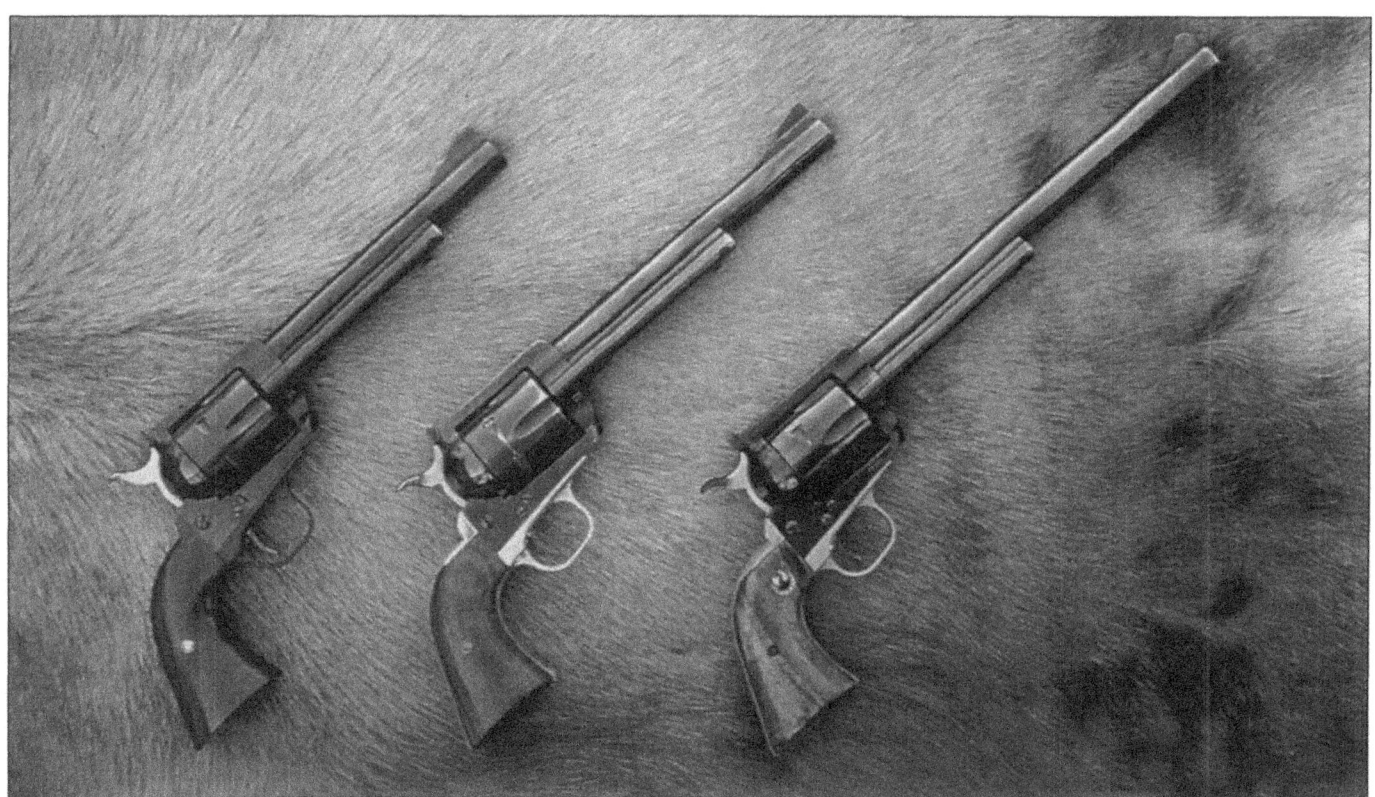

Ruger's .44 Magnum Blackhawk, the "Flat-Top," was in production from 1956-1963 in the three standard barrel lengths of 6 1/2, 7 1/2, and 10 inches.

Two very rare sixguns are Ruger's Flat-Top Blackhawks with 10-inch barrels and .357 (top) and .44 Magnum.

The author's first real packin' pistols from the 1950s: a 4 5/8-inch .357 Blackhawk (left) and a .44 Magnum Blackhawk custom cut to 4 3/4 inches.

King short-action job, for $125. I still have the Ruger, and I would not want to give it up at all, but just imagine what that Colt would be worth today!

I purchased a 6 1/2-inch Ruger Flat-Top .44 a few years back that came through a friend from a widow whose husband had been braver than most. He had fired 12 rounds, two cylinders full, of full-house factory loads before deciding it was too much for him. Two cylinders fired witnessed to the fact that he was twice as brave as many other shooters! I purchased my original .44 Flat-Top thinking the recoil would be less than the Smith & Wesson .44 Magnum. If anything it was worse. The Ruger Flat-Top Blackhawks were standardized at 4 5/8 inches for the .357 and 6 1/2 inches for both the .357 and .44 Magnum.

Those who frequent gun shows on a regular basis know that it is easy to find great guns. It is also easy to find great prices, BUT the rub is trying to find a great gun at a great price! I've walked a lot of aisles over many years at our local shows always looking for that certain sixgun. A few years back at one of the local gun shows I made it to the second aisle when I spotted the back end of a Ruger Flat-Top .357 Blackhawk amongst a whole bunch of guns of varying kinds and qualities. The price tag was extremely reasonable for a Flat-Top .357 and it looked as if I had found another sixgun to squirrel away for future conversion to .44 Special, .44-40, or .45 Colt.

As I looked at the Blackhawk, the barrel kept going. And going. And going. What I had in front of me was not just an ordinary Flat-Top .357 Magnum but a 10-inch barreled Ruger .357 Magnum. The deal was quickly struck (I did not even try to get the price down), the check was written, and I headed away with my treasure. Arriving home I went right to John Dougan's *Know Your Ruger Single Action Revolvers 1953-63*. I knew I had a rare sixgun, but I certainly did not know how rare. The .44 Magnum Flat-Top my wife bought for me to celebrate the successful completion of graduate school in 1971 was one of only 1,050 out of 30,000-plus .44 Magnum Flat-Tops manufactured from 1956 to 1963 that had 10-inch barrel. The .357 Magnum turned out to be even rarer. In fact, it is the rarest of all the Flat-Tops. Of the 42,600-plus .357 Magnums, much less than 1,000, probably only 500, were 10-inch models. Of these 500, Dougan estimates 50 10-inch Flat-Tops were made with eight-groove rifling. My find has eight-groove rifling, so call it one of about 50.

I did not buy it as a collector's item since the bluing was well worn, and when I shot it I also found that the front sight, as on many of the .357 Flat-Top Blackhawks, was too short, resulting in a sixgun shooting too high with my loads. I shipped it off to Milt Morrison at

Qualite Pistol & Revolver and had him re-blue it and fit a post front sight of the correct height. Now it not only looks good, it shoots to point of aim.

In 1953, Bill Ruger went against the idea that the single action was dead and brought out one of the great success stories in the firearms field: the .22 Single-Six. For nearly 50 years now this has been the outdoorsman's .22. The Colt Single Action Army had been dropped from production 12 years earlier in 1941. Ruger replaced the three flat springs of the Colt, two of which were prone to easy breakage, with virtually unbreakable coil springs. I've been shooting Ruger Single Actions since 1957 and have yet to experience a broken spring. The grip frame of the Ruger was a dead ringer for the classic Colt, while the rest of the gun was about 7/8 scale.

In 1955, as we have mentioned, Ruger really modernized the Colt Single Action with a full-sized centerfire single action in the only Magnum of the time — the .357 Magnum. The frame was flat-topped and held a fully adjustable Micro rear sight that mated up with a ramp-style front sight. The barrel length at 4 5/8 inches was nearly perfect for packin' for hunters, hikers, fisherman, guides, packers, outfitters, woods bums, you name 'em, the love affair with the .357 Blackhawk has not ceased for these four-plus decades. Walter Rogers was surely right.

Myself, I wanted a .357 Blackhawk so bad I could hardly stand it. Other teens had pictures of Jane Russell or Marilyn Monroe hanging over their beds. I hung a life-size picture of the Ruger .357 Blackhawk 4 5/8-inch from *Outdoor Life* on my bedroom wall in 1955 and drooled over it every day for two years. My father had died many years earlier, and my step-dad, a fine man, had gone through World War II and spent 18 months as a seriously wounded prisoner of war. When he was liberated and came home he never wanted to see a gun again. The two 9mm German handguns he brought home, a Luger and a Walther, were quickly sold. He changed in later years as he appreciated my guns, my hunting, and my writing career.

My family would not buy guns, but I soon got out of high school, found a job and then went Ruger sixgun crazy in 1956, purchasing a .22 Single-Six, followed almost immediately by a .357 Blackhawk and then the first .44 Magnum Blackhawk in our area. The Single-Six was $63.50, the .357 Blackhawk $87.50, and the .44 Magnum $96.

Some of the finest .44 Magnums made are these Flat-Top Rugers from the middle of the 20th century. Pictured are the three standard barrel lengths plus a custom packin' pistol with a 4 3/4-inch barrel.

In 1959 the Ruger .44 Magnum Blackhawk was improved to the Super Blackhawk, which more than four decades later still remains the greatest handgun bargain offered for the hunter and outdoorsman.

At the 90 cents an hour that I was making at the time in my first job, it took a long time to pay for those beautiful sixguns. Fifteen years later I would begin the same sequence again, this time providing my son with a .22 BearCat at age 10, followed by a .357 at age 13, and a .44 Magnum at age 18.

The .357 Blackhawk was the first really modern centerfire single action. Colt Single Action Armies were readily available at excellent prices, but the Ruger had three great advantages. It had adjustable sights and it also accepted easy shooting and easy-on-the billfold .38 Specials. When I did start reloading, a great deal of my heavy loads were assembled using the 170-grain Keith bullet, Lyman's #358429, over 13.5 grains of #2400 in .38 Special brass. This is still a great load, but only for .357 Magnum sixguns. The third advantage was that it was also literally unbreakable.

For those who have gotten into firearms within the last 10 years, or 20, or even 30, it may be difficult to understand the extreme importance of the Ruger Flat-Tops. Bill Ruger single-handedly brought back the single action and has continued to offer rugged, virtually unbreakable single-action sixguns for the past 50 years. I again certainly echo Walter Rogers' sentiments: "God bless Bill Ruger for giving us great single actions!"

The Old and New Models

The Ruger .357 Magnum Flat-Top (FT) was only offered for eight years before being replaced in 1963 by the Three Screw, or Old Model (OM) Blackhawk as it is now known to collectors. The main differences in the 1963 models are a change in the grip frame that gave more room behind the trigger guard, changing it from the standard Colt Single Action size, and distinctive protective ears on the rear sight that changed the Flat-Top profile. (This style of protected rear sight had begun in 1959 on the then-new Super Blackhawk, so there are no Flat-Top Super Blackhawks.) The ejector tubes were also changed from steel to an alloy. The original Colt Single Action-sized Flat-Tops were only produced in .357 Magnum, and plans were to offer both .44 Special and .45 Colt, but both of these were replaced by the other chambering in the original Blackhawks — the larger framed .44 Magnum. Old Models would be manufactured in .357 Magnum, in the same frame size as the original .357 Blackhawk. The .41 Magnum, .45 Colt, and .30 Carbine would utilize the .44 Magnum Blackhawk frame. All Old Model .44 Magnums are Super Blackhawks.

In 1973, the Old Model was replaced by the New Model with a transfer bar safety allowing six rounds to be safely carried in a centerfire single action for the first time. The New Model .357s are also on the .44 frame size so the .357 Blackhawk, while bull strong now, is no longer quite as slick and light as the Flat-Tops and Three Screws. The original .357 Blackhawks were offered in 4 5/8-inch and 6 1/2-inch barrels as standard with the very few 10-inch guns as mentioned. Since 1963, only the two shorter lengths have been offered. Strangely enough, no .357 Blackhawks have ever been cataloged in the 7 1/2-inch length.

Ruger has been one of the most prolific manufacturers of .44 Magnums and the Super Blackhawk has been a perennial best seller, but Ruger was completely surprised with the news of the new .44 Magnum. The story goes that a Ruger worker found several strange once-fired cases at a scrap yard and gave them to Bill

Ruger. Ruger traced them to Remington Arms and discovered the secret .44 Magnum project going on between Remington and Smith & Wesson. That was in late 1955. By early 1956, Ruger .44 Blackhawks were being manufactured and shipped, arriving on many gun shelves before Smith & Wesson's .44 Magnum. At about half a pound less than the Smith product, they kicked hard. In 1959, Ruger "improved" the .44 Flat-Top, adding protective ears to the rear sight, changing the grip frame from standard Colt Single Action size of a lightweight alloy to a steel Dragoon-sized grip frame, and standardizing at a barrel length of 7 1/2 inches. The Flat-Top would stay in production alongside the new Super Blackhawk until 1963, when it was dropped with the coming of what is now known as the Old Model Blackhawks.

During its seven-year run, the .44 Flat-Top was to go to serial number 29860 with most guns being 6 1/2-inch models. About 1,050 were 10-inch models and the 7 1/2-inch models number somewhere between the number of 10-inch .357s and 10-inch .44s, making them the second rarest Flat-Top Blackhawks. My first .44 Blackhawk, a standard 6 1/2-inch model, was soon cut to 4 5/8 inches and carried for many miles and many years in a Lawrence holster. I still have the .44 and the holster. The .44 now wears a 7 1/2-inch barrel and the 6 1/2-inch holster has been trimmed to fit a replacement old Flat-Top with the shorter barrel length. In the days, actually many years, when I could only afford one big-bore Magnum sixgun, it was the Ruger .44 Magnum 4 5/8-inch that did it all. Even after Smith & Wesson .44 Magnums were added in the early and mid-1960s, it was still the Ruger that was normally called upon until it was semi-retired by the addition to my working collection of a 10-inch .44 Flat-Top.

That 10-inch .44 Magnum Flat-Top was really my first real hunting handgun and it was carried for years in a Goerg shoulder holster, a great design that should still be in production. I very early learned that the long barrels were much easier to shoot. Less recoil, less noise, less muzzle blast all accompanied by a longer sight radius. In both the 10- and 4 5/8-inch Flat-Tops, I also learned early that the Keith load of 22.5 grains of #2400 with a 250-grain hard cast bullet kicked like crazy and I normally dropped back slightly to 21.0 grains. Today, my load of choice for these old sixguns is normally 10.0 grains of Unique.

One of the fondest memories of my shooting career is tied to the 10-inch .44 Flat-Top. It was February and too cold to shoot outside and I was getting very close to cabin fever. Something had to be done, so I headed for the local indoor range. This was in the days when bullseye shooting was king and everyone there was a serious paper puncher. This meant, at the very minimum, a High Standard .22 and a 1911 .45 ACP with target sights and the touch of master gunsmith. It was in this background that I pulled out the 10-inch Ruger .44 Flat-Top. Some snickered. Others were downright rude. I heard comments about that "cowboy gun." I loaded five rounds of .44 Specials with 250-grain bullets over 6.0 grains of Unique — a target load. Fortunately, I was a much better off-hand shot in those days and five shots later, using the .44 Special target loads as required, I had a one-hole group and all the snickering stopped.

When I acquired a 7 1/2-inch Flat-Top .44 Magnum, I knew this was it. I'm almost ashamed to say how much I paid for this one and how I got it! But here goes. A friend brought it over with the complaint that it would not shoot. I always love to hear this, as it is a rare sixgun that won't shoot. We went down to the same indoor range with the same .44 Special target loads and that "poor-shooting" .44 did its best and it also cut a one-hole group. He said that since I could make it shoot and he could not, he would still sell it. "But it is worth much more than you want for it!" I offered. "You're an honest man, so I will still sell it to you for the first price I asked." And with that I had a fine sixgun.

This surely was the finest Ruger sixgun ever made. It was not as easy to pack as the 4 5/8 inch .44, or as easy to hit with as the 10-inch Flat-Top. Nevertheless, it was a superb compromise, the nearly perfect sixgun. All it lacked was a steel grip frame to be perfect. It would not be until the advent of the Freedom Arms revolver that this fine sixgun would drop to second place.

For my somewhat biased choice, there are three superb 7 1/2-inch .44 sixguns out there and all will cost more than what I paid for my first car! (Of course it wasn't much of a car.) They are the Ruger Flat-Top .44 Magnum with less than 1,000 made; the Second Generation .44 Special New Frontier with less than 150 in existence (however, we are fortunate to have an ample supply of Third Generation New Frontiers in this chambering); and lastly, but certainly not least and still available, the Freedom Arms revolver in .44 Magnum. As an honorable mention, an Old Model Ruger Super Blackhawk, with its Dragoon-style grip frame replaced by a standard frame, is also a mighty fine sixgun.

Flat-Tops have not been made for more than 30 years now and I see no reason to try to make modern Magnums out of them. That is, I save my heavy magnum loads for the newer, larger-framed, and stronger .44 Magnums. No heavy loads with 300-grain bullets. No heavyweight jacketed bullets. Strictly traditional loads with traditional bullets.

Lyman, NEI, and RCBS all offer excellent Keith-style .44 bullets that weigh in right at 250 grains, lubed and sized and ready for loading. My heaviest .44 Mag-

SELECTED FAVORITE LOADS FOR RUGER FLAT-TOP SINGLE-ACTION BLACKHAWKS

BARREL LENGTH/CALIBER	BULLET/LOAD	MV/FPS
10" .357 Magnum	Lyman #358156GC/15.0 gr. #2400	1,555
10" .357 Magnum	Lyman #358429/13.5 gr. #2400*	1,449
10" .357 Magnum	RCBS #38-150KT/7.5 gr. Unique	1,375
4 5/8" .357 Magnum	Lyman #358156GC/15.0 gr. #2400	1,405
4 5/8" .357 Magnum	Lyman #358429/13.5 gr. #2400*	1,239
4 5/8" .357 Magnum	RCBS #38-150KT/7.5 gr. Unique	1,260
10" .44 Magnum	Lyman #429215GC/25.0 gr. #2400	1,514
10" .44 Magnum	Lyman #429421KT/21.0 gr. #2400	1,409
7 1/2" .44 Magnum	Lyman #429421KT/21.0 gr. #2400	1,398
7 1/2" .44 Magnum	NEI 260.429KT/21.0 gr. #2400	1,388
4 5/8" .44 Magnum	Lyman #429421KT/21.0 gr. #2400	1,347
4 5/8" .44 Magnum	Lyman #429421KT/10.0 gr. Unique	1,102

*Loaded in .38 Special brass

num Flat-Top load is normally 21.0 grains of #2400 for 1,350 feet per second in the short-barreled sixguns and 1,400 fps in the longer barrels. My favorite load these days is an easy-shooting 1,100-1,150 fps using 10.0 grains of Unique. Lyman's Thompson-designed gas check #429215 is a stellar performer at a cast weight of 220 grains and 25.0 grains of #2400. Ray Thompson was a professional outdoorsman and a design genius who came up with four superb gas check bullets for Lyman: #358156, a 155 grain .357 bullet; #429215; #429244, a 255-grain .44 semi-wadcutter; and #452490, an excellent 255-grain bullet for .45 Auto Rim and .45 Colt sixguns.

Today's Ruger single-action Blackhawks are bigger, stronger, and perhaps even built to closer tolerances. With the transfer bar safety they are certainly safer, especially for those who are not familiar with traditional single actions and the precautions that must be taken — number one of which is always let the hammer down on an empty chamber. But the old Flat-Tops are part of history and stir my soul almost as much as a fine Colt Single Action. That speaks highly for them.

The Ruger Bisley Model

We have mentioned Walter Rogers and his connection with Ruger Single Actions. In the early days of *Guns Magazine* in the 1950s, a couple of excellent articles were found authored by this grand old gentleman who must have been at least in his late 70s. Rogers was born about the time of the Gunfight at OK Corral and spent his lifetime as a cowboy, forest ranger, and out-

In the mid-1980s, the Ruger New Model Super Blackhawk became the Bisley Model with a new grip frame, hammer, and trigger.

Ruger's Bisley Model is cataloged only in 7 1/2-inch blue chambered in (from top) the .357 Magnum, .44 Magnum, .45 Colt.

doorsman. His firearms of choice, of course, were a Winchester lever-action rifle, he really liked the .25-35, and before Ruger came along, a Colt Single Action. Rogers' Colt was a trifle different than most encountered. It was strange looking sixgun known as the Bisley Model. For much of his life Rodgers carried that Bisley .45 in a homemade holster on a companion homemade combination cartridge and money belt. His sixgun was not 100 percent Bisley because the hammer spur had been modified to have the same shape as the Colt Single Action Army. Another fan of the Colt Bisley about the same time was Ed Bohlin, the saddle and holster maker to the Hollywood stars. Bohlin had short fingers and preferred the low-riding hammer of the Bisley to the standard Colt Single Action Army. If you watch carefully, it is often possible to notice a Bisley riding in the holster of many a 1930s "B" movie cowboy. Perhaps Bohlin had something to do with this.

Ruger got its inspiration for the Bisley Model from the original Bisley Colt, especially as modified by Elmer Keith back in the 1920s. Keith's modification was actually a combination of his own idea of what a perfect sixgun should be and that of Harold Croft, a gun enthusiast who visited Keith in the late 1920s. Croft had several sixguns made by altering Bisley grip frames. The two put their heads together and came up with a grip frame utilizing a Bisley backstrap and a

Two custom .45 Colt Ruger Vaqueros, a Bisley with Hogue's black micarta grips, and a standard model with grips by Bob Leskovec. These are excellent choices for general outdoor use.

Whether in .44 Magnum or .45 Colt, these 4 5/8-inch stainless-steel Blackhawks fit the author's definition of a packin' pistol. The leather is custom made by the author.

Colt Single Action trigger guard. The Bisley Model surfaced in 1894 when Colt brought forth a special six-gun for target shooters. The first guns went to England, where the target shooting matches were held at Bisley Commons in England. The new single action was advertised as the Colt's Target Revolver. It soon became known as the Bisley Model.

The big changes on the Bisley over the standard Colt Single Action Army were encountered in the grip frame shape and hammer and trigger. The original Colt Single Action Army rolled in the hand when fired, thus lessening the felt recoil. The Bisley was designed to set back in the hand and maintain the grip when used for target shooting. To accomplish this, the grip frame came up higher in the back and also much higher behind the trigger guard. To accomodate this new grip shape the frame of the standard Colt Single Action Army had to be altered slightly. About 1/8 inch in height was added along the back of the frame. To match with the new grip frame, the hammer was lowered and also fitted with a wide spur, and the trigger was also widened and given a radical curve in the oversized trigger guard of the Bisley. The wide hammer mated with a new main spring allowed easier cocking without disturbing the grip on the gun, and the wide trigger allowed for an easier let off when shooting bullseyes.

Ruger's Bisley Model is not a true copy of the Colt as to grip frame. The Ruger Bisley grip frame does not come up as high behind the trigger guard and the front strap is much straighter to avoid the ladle shape of the Colt. The result is a grip frame that actually handles recoil much better than a standard single-action grip. This is what Keith hoped to achieve with his grip shape back in the 1920s, and the idea has been carried out to near perfection by Ruger. The Bisley Blackhawk is nothing more than a standard Blackhawk with a redesigned grip frame. At first I, along with others, reported that the Bisley grip was a copy of Elmer Keith's old #5SA design, which was made by mating a Colt Bisley backstrap with a Colt SA trigger guard. Since then, I have had the opportunity to handle Elmer's #5SA and have found the grips are much smaller than the Bisley frame. I like the Bisley grip frame. It changes the recoil for me and avoids the knuckle dusting of the Super Blackhawk frame. I do get pinched on the trigger finger by the tip of the radically rounded trigger, but this can easily be taken care of by shortening and straightening the trigger

The Ruger Bisleys have proven themselves to be well built, strong, good-shooting sixguns. In fact, these revolvers seem to be put together with more care than normal. I purchased two Bisleys when they first came out, one in .45 Colt and the other in .41 Magnum. The barrel/cylinder gaps on these are .002 and .003 inches, respectively. I have since received two test Bisleys from Ruger, a .44 Magnum and a .357 Magnum, and they go .001 and .002 inches. This is exceptional for revolvers in the Bisley price range.

The Bisley has become the choice of custom gunsmiths such as John Linebaugh, Jim Stroh, David Clements, and Hamilton Bowen, for fitting with five-shot cylinders in .45 Colt, and .475 and .500 Linebaugh. The Bisley is chosen for its inherent strength and comfortable grip frame. Bisleys have only been catalogued in blue with 7 1/2-inch barrels, and this also marks the first and only time that Ruger has offered both the .41 and .357 Magnums in this barrel length. I would like to see them offered in the packin' pistol lengths of 4 5/8 and 5 1/2 inches, and 10 1/2 inches for the silhouetters and long-range shooters. Very recently there has been a special run of stainless-steel Bisley Models with 5 1/2-inch barrels in .44 Magnum and .45 Colt.

The .357 Ruger Bisley is about as comfortable a shooting .357 Magnum as one is likely to encounter. Many sixgunners are bothered by recoil even in .357s and this sixgun is a tremendous help for them. I see no point in anyone trying to shoot any sixgun that is more powerful than they can handle, and if the bottom line is a .357, this one can be loaded heavily and still not bother anyone with excessive recoil. For more than 30 years my favorite cast bullet for the .357 Magnum has been the Lyman #358156 gas check designed by Ray Thompson. This is an excellent performer in the .357 Bisley over 15.5 grains of #2400 for 1,587 fps. That nearly non-existant barrel/cylinder gap really helps. Another load that I like in the Ruger .357 Bisley is Lyman's #358627 210-grain Keith GC over 13.5 grains of #2400. This is normally a T/C Contender load and is hot even in the super-strong Bisley. Extraction is sticky with velocities at 1,519 fps. This is really pushing a .357 revolver, but is a good heavy-duty choice for a cast bullet hunting load.

The .41 Magnum Bisley has become a real favorite and I especially like the way this sixgun shoots at long range using Lyman's #410459 220 grain cast bullet over 19.5 grains of #2400. Velocity is around 1,500 fps. Switching to a heavyweight bullet in the .41, there is SSK's #275.411, which weighs out at 295 grains and coupled with 18.5-19.5 grains of H110 or WW296 does 1,300-plus fps. Either of these bullet/load combinations make excellent selections for hunting. While the .41 has never been as popular as its bigger brother, it is a fine cartridge in its own right and I do believe the problems that some have had with mediocre accuracy can be solved by using cast bullets sized to .411 inch. The Ruger .41 Magnum Bisley is probably the most pleasant of all .41 Magnums to shoot, with the exception of the mammoth Dan Wesson .41.

Ruger has been making .44s for a long time and they have made a lot of really good .44 sixguns. My favorite has always been the classic .44 Flat-top. The Bisley comes real close to challenging the Flat-Top as my choice of the best .44 Magnum. All it would take would be for Ruger to remove the warning stamping on the barrel and finishing everything off with a really top-quality blue.

It is no problem achieving a full 1,500 fps with 250-grain cast bullets in the Big Ruger, and brass taps out easily. Either the H&G 250-grain Keith or Lyman-Thompson #431244GC are excellent performers in the .44; 21.0 grains of #2400 being a little milder than the normal "standard" load of 22.0 grains but still giving 1,400-plus fps.

There are a number of excellent heavyweight bullets available that perform well in the Ruger Bisley .44:

SSK #310.429	22.5 gr. WW296	1,444 fps
NEI #295.429	24.0 gr. WW680	1,322 fps
Wilson 300BB	26.0 gr. WW680	1,373 fps
Wilson 295GC	21.5 gr. WW296	1,451 fps

For a really pleasant shooting heavyweight, try any of the above bullets at 9.0-10.0 grains of Unique. Velocities will be 900-1,100 fps, depending on the bullet.

Ruger gave new life to the .45 Colt when it first chambered the Blackhawk for the oldest of the big bores 30 years ago. For the first time it was possible to safely load the .45 Colt to 1,200 fps or more. When used with common sense, the Ruger Bisley makes a fine heavy-duty .45 Colt. I like 21.0 grains of #2400 with a 260-grain cast bullet for around 300 fps, but my favorite heavy-duty bullet/load combination in the Bisley .45 is NEI's #310.451 over 23.0 grains of WW296 for a little bit more than 1,200 fps. Definitely not a .44 Magnum heavyweight load, but a respectable load that does not give excessive recoil, and certainly more than adequate for any deer or black bear. For most of my shooting with the .45 Colt in the Ruger, especially with the Blackhawk and the standard grip frame, I use 300 to 325-grain bullets with 21.5 grains of H110 or WW296 for right at 1,200 fps from a 7 1/2-inch barrel.

Sierra, Hornady, and Speer all make jacketed hollow points for the .45 Colt at 240-, 250-, and 260-grain weights, respectively. While wasted in the Colt Single Action, they are perfect for the Bisley .45 Colt and will give around 1,250 fps when coupled with 25.0 grains of H110 or WW296. Bill Ruger has been responsible for a number of excellent sixguns. The Bisley is one of the best.

Ruger Blackhwks and Bisley Models are top choices for building custom sixguns. The frame size of the Bisley is the same as the Blackhawk or Super Blackhawk, but the grip frame handles the recoil of the heavy kickers, such as the Linebaugh cartridges, much better than the others. I had a 10-inch Super Blackhawk made up before Ruger brought out its 10 1/2-inch Model, and I have three packin' pistol Super Blackhawks, a 4 5/8-inch Mag-Na-Port Custom Predator, a 5 1/2-inch New Model, and a 5 1/2-inch New Model that has been converted to five-shot .45 Colt by Jim Stroh. The latter two sixguns both now wear Bisley grip frames, hammers, and triggers. I've also had several Flat-Top and Three Screw .357s converted to .44 Special. The .44 Special conversion on the smaller Old Model frame makes a particularly nice handling package.

It is only rarely that one encounters a .41 Magnum single-action sixgun. Only one model was available, the Ruger Blackhawk, until in very recent years Freedom Arms chambered both its Model 83 and Model 97 in .41 Magnum. Anyone who has ever owned more than two sixguns probably dreams of building that one perfect sixgun. I am particularly taken with a like for packin' pistols. A few years back I located a new Three Screw .41 Ruger with a 4 5/8-inch barrel at a local gun show with a bargain marked price. I offered even less and it was accepted. Now I have walked miles of aisles of enough gun shows without finding anything, that when a real bargain comes along I simply say "thank you Lord" and accept it gratefully.

The Ruger .41 shot well, so a stainless Old Army grip frame that had been in my parts box for more than a decade was fitted to it, along with my last blue steel ejector rod housing. Then it went off to Roy Fishpaw for a pair of his Circassian walnut grips that are guaranteed to make your mouth water. The extra weight of the steel parts really cut down the recoil, the grips make it handle better as well as look better, and the little .41 single action will handle just about any situation short of the big bears. So how much closer can one get to having the ideal sixgun? Of course, the pleasure is in the seeking, so the search never ends.

Currently, Ruger Single Actions are offered in .22, .32 Magnum, .30 Carbine, .357 Magnum, .41 Magnum,

One of the author's favorite, and certainly one of the most accurate Rugers, is this stainless-steel .44 Magnum New Model Super Blackhawk. Stocks are by BluMagnum.

Taffin's friend, hunting partner, and taxidermist, Rick vonDerHeide along with his son, Peter, took this wild boar with Ruger's New Model .44 Magnum Blackhawk.

.44 Magnum, .44-40, and .45 Colt. Special runs in the past include the .32-20/.32 Magnum Convertible, the 10mm/.38-40 Convertible, and the .44 Magnum/.44-40 Super Blackhawk Convertible.

Buckeye Sports, in conjunction with Ruger, offered a .38-40/10mm Convertible Blackhawk built on the large Super Blackhawk-sized frame. This .38-40 has a tight barrel, as evidenced by the fact that it shoots 10mm loads exceptionally well with its auxiliary 10mm cylinder installed. For the first time we had a properly chambered and barreled .38-40 sixgun that is also far superior in strength to any previously offered .38-40. Not as light or slick handling as an old Colt Single Action .38-40, the Blackhawk nonetheless was a welcome addition to the sixgunnin' world.

My first impression of the .38-40 Blackhawk was that it could use a little gunsmithing. Namely, shortening the barrel to 4 5/8 inches, replacing the overly thick factory stocks with a pair of slim walnut grips (both of which have now been accomplished), smoothing off the sides of the too-sharp trigger, and perhaps even flat-topping the frame. The result would be a beautiful-handling sixgun that is better than any .38-40 that ever left the Colt factory.

Lyman still offers an excellent bullet design for the .38-40, #401043. This is a flat-nosed design of 175 grains weight, which comes out at 180 grains with my alloy. Searches through gun shops and shows have produced two excellent, but out-of-production, Lyman bullet moulds in #40188: a 165-grain semi-wadcutter, and #401452, a Boser designed "Keith-style" 200-grain bullet for the .38-40 and .401 Special. Standard loads for the Ruger Blackhawk .38-40 have long been either 10.0 grains of Unique or 18.0 grains of #2400. These loads are in the 1,200-plus fps category with the 180-grain cast or the 180-grain jacketed bullet. They may be too heavy for any Colt Single Action, Bisley, or New Service .38-40.

The most accurate loads that I have found for the .38-40 Blackhawk are Lyman's #40188 with 10.0 grains of Herco (1250 fps), 10.5 grains of Blue Dot (1031 fps), and 6.5 grains of 452AA (990 fps). All of these are in the 1-inch category at 25 yards category. Not bad for a 125-year-old cartridge with a reputation for poor accuracy! Best loads with the slightly heavier bullet #401043 are 16.0 grains of #2400 (1119 fps), 18.0 grains of AA#9 (1207 fps), and 9.0 grains of Herco (1178 fps). Hornady's 170-grain XTP 10mm bullet, which has now been increased in weight to 180 grains, makes an excellent .38-40 bullet. I add a cannelure right behind the shoulder, load it over 18.0 grains of #2400, and the result is tight little groups at 1,286 fps.

Ruger SAs are not perfect. Most need the actions slicked up and the trigger pulls lightened. Economics and liability both preclude the offering of super-smooth actions and 3# trigger pulls. Ruger offers a conversion of all of their Old Model designs to the new transfer bar safety at no charge. All of the old parts are returned with the conversion on each customer's gun. This is a desired change for old sixguns with worn parts or those that may be handled by shooters who are not familiar with the safety problems of the old-style action. It is not generally known, but Ruger will also reblue older Rugers at the same time very economically. I've had two .357s done and the blue jobs are better than those on the new guns. They also refinish the aluminum grip frames at the same time.

The Super Blackhawk has been one of the real workhorses of the handgunning world. Ruger, early in the silhouetting game, brought back the long-barreled .44 by offering a 10 1/2-inch silhouette model .44. Around 1,000 Flat-Top .44 Blackhawks had been made with 10-inch barrels. The long-barreled Super Blackhawk became a favorite of silhouetters and hunters alike. Larry Kelly has long used the Super Blackhawk for his Stalker Conversions. Starting preferably with a stainless .44 10 1/2-inch, Kelly cuts the barrel to 8 3/8 inches, applies his Mag-na-Porting, tunes the action, adds sling swivels, and voila — a .44 Magnum that is identical to the one Kelly has used to take big game animals all over the world.

Without even being pressed, I will willingly admit that the Super Blackhawk and its companion, the Bisley Model, are the best bargains available today in .44 Magnum chambering. Retailing at right around $500, they are the hands-down favorite of those seeking reliability, accuracy, and economy. I am one who has never really cared for the Super Blackhawk grip frame as it feels all wrong to me and also thumps the knuckle of my middle finger with the square-backed trigger guard. I was very happy to see the introduction of the Bisley Ruger, as the grip frame is perfect for my hand. It feels much like the Freedom Arms single-action grip and, though larger, much like the original Keith #5SA grip found on Texas Longhorn Arms Improved Number Five. One thing about the Bisley grip, there is no middle of the road. A shooter either likes it or doesn't. I like it.

In addition to the Bisley, available only in blue finish with a 7 1/2-inch barrel, and the Super Blackhawk, which can be had in either 7 1/2 or 10 1/2-inch lengths, and in blue or stainless finishes, Ruger also offers a 5 1/2-inch blue or stainless-steel Super Blackhawk. It has a standard Blackhawk grip frame, albeit in steel rather than lightweight alloy as on the other Blackhawks. As expected, this rather lightweight .44 Magnum kicks like the proverbial mule. The Ruger 10 1/2-inch stainless-steel Super Blackhawk is one of my most accurate single actions this side of Freedom Arms. It has now gotten a satin finish from Gary Reeder, who also polished the trigger and hammer, tuned it, and engraved "JOHN TAFFIN THE SHOOTISTS" on the barrel. This sixgun will go to a grandson someday.

Evolution of the "best packin' pistols"

The legendary Colt Single Action Army arrived on the sixgun scene in 1873. It not only became the favorite of soldiers, frontiersmen, and shootists on both sides of the law, it was also the sixgun of choice for the outdoorsman. For most sixgunners, when equipped with

SELECTED LOADS FOR THE RUGER NEW MODEL SINGLE ACTIONS:

SIXGUN	BULLET/LOAD	MV
Bisley .45 Colt 7 1/2"	Lyman #454424/20.0 gr. #2400	1,291
	NEI #310.451 KT/22.0 gr. WW296	1,211
Bisley .41 Magnum 7 1/2"	Lyman #410459/19.5 gr. #2400	1,475
	NEI #275.410/18.5 gr. WW296	1,322
Bisley .357 Magnum 7 1/2"	Lyman #358156/15.5 gr. #2400	1,585
	Lyman #358429/14.5 gr. #2400	1,487
Super Blackhawk .44 4 5/8"	BRP 295 Keith/21.5 gr. WW296	1,335
	SSK 310TC/23.5 gr. WW680	1,304
Super Blackhawk .44 10 1/2"	BRP 295 Keith/21.5 gr. WW296	1,453

the shorter "Civilian" barrel length of 4 3/4 inches, it balanced perfectly — better, perhaps, than any handgun before or since. It was the first real cartridge-firing packin' pistol. It is a sixgun that was easy to pack, quick into action, and chambered for a cartridge that will get the job done. For the Colt Single Action, that caliber choice more often than not was the .45 Colt, .44-40, or .38-40.

The original .357 Blackhawk, with its barrel length of 4 5/8 inches, was the heir apparent to the title of "best packin' pistol" relinquished by Colt 15 years earlier with the ceasing of production of the Single Action Army. The .44 Blackhawk Flat-top was a grand sixgun, still is, but seemingly could not make up its mind as to what function it was to provide. At 6 1/2 inches, the barrel length was too long for a premier Packin' Pistol, and the 4 5/8-inch length was never a factory model in the original Blackhawk .44. When the Flat-Top was modernized to the Super Blackhawk in 1959, the standard barrel length offered this time was 7 1/2 inches, with no 4 5/8-inch length offered.

Like so many other sixgunners, I did what Ruger did not do and had both a Flat-top and Super Blackhawk .44 Magnum cut to the easy-to-pack shorter length. They have been special favorites for too many years.

When Ruger chambered its Blackhawk in .45 Colt around 1970, it corrected an earlier oversight and offered it with both a 7 1/2-inch barrel and the packin' pistol 4 5/8-inch length. A few years before, the Blackhawk was chambered in .41 Magnum and this, too, was offered in the 4 5/8-inch length. Still, this factory length in .44 Magnum was not offered, remaining a custom proposition. All that changed in the late 1990s. Ruger now offers almost a complete line of packin' pistols for the 21st century, with stainless-steel versions of 4 5/8 inches in .357 Magnum, .44 Magnum, and .45 Colt. A stainless-steel 4 5/8-inch .41 Magnum would complete the Packin' Pistol picture. Stainless-steel sixguns may not be as soul stirring as a deeply blued version, but two things are in this modern finish's favor. First, it is THE choice for the outdoorsman whose sixgun will be exposed to all kinds of weather. If it gets wet, minimum care is needed to keep it looking fine. If it is scratched, a little polishing will make it look new again. I always insist my wife take a stainless steel sixgun when she fishes as I know the inevitable will happen. Somewhere, sometime, whether crossing a log or wading in a pool, she will get dunked along with the sixgun. Stainless steel is the only answer for her. Secondly, when was the last time you saw a sixgun from the factory with an awe inspiring deep-blue finish? They rarely exist anymore. The Colt Royal Blue, Ruger's early Super Blackhawk blue finish, Smith & Wesson's Bright Blue are all faded into sixgun history.

Ruger's Blackhawk .357 Magnum has been around for more than four decades now. My first one was a 4 5/8-inch version with hard rubber grips purchased in 1957 for $87.50. It handled like a Colt Single Action with a grip frame that was identical. I was frustrated at the time at how easy the springs on a Colt SAA broke, not realizing that most of the Colt sixguns then available were built back around the turn of the century. They were fatigued in many cases and the metal just gave up. The Ruger .357 Magnum did not give up. The Blackhawk was virtually indestructible. Even though it was the same size as a Colt Single Action Army, it was bull strong. A real packin' pistol.

As we have mentioned, the Ruger .357 Blackhawk was "improved" with two changes in 1963. The grip frame was altered slightly to allow more room between the back of the trigger guard and the front of the grip frame. Old frames are marked XR-3. The new ones are XR3-RED. The second change was the addition of ears around the rear sight. The frame was no longer flat-topped, but rather had supports built into the frame on each side of the rear sight. The original Blackhawk/Flat-Top and the 1963 Three Screw/Old Model both operate the same as a Colt Single Action. Colt replicas still do with a half-cock notch on the hammer for loading. They are only safe to carry with five rounds and an empty chamber under the firing pin.

Two more significant changes would occur in 1973. The lockwork was changed completely to the New Model with a transfer bar safety and a cylinder that rotated when the loading gate was opened instead of by placing the hammer on half cock. This is a tremendous safety improvement over the old single-action style, but is decidedly less smooth than the originals. Any qualified gunsmith that understands Ruger Single Actions can smooth out a New Model to a state that will make your mouth water.

Finally, one year later in 1974, the .357 Blackhawk reached its highest development when it was introduced in stainless steel. There are, of course, several variations known to collectors in each of the major Blackhawk series (Flat-Top, Old Model, New Model, and Stainless Steel New Model), but they have very little importance to the average shooter. What is interesting is the fact that, from 1873 to 1941, Colt Single Action production, with both military contracts and civilian purchases, totaled approximately a third of a million units. Production of the Ruger Blackhawks, in less than 50 years, is already over 2 million!

In 1973, with the coming of the New Model Blackhawks, the Super Blackhawk also received the New Model lockwork with transfer bar safety and cylinder operation for loading and unloading by opening the loading gate. The 7 1/2-inch barrel remained standard, however, a longer 10 1/2-inch barrel was soon brought

SELECTED LOADS FOR THE RUGER NEW MODEL .357 MAGNUM
4 5/8" SS BLACKHAWK

BULLET/LOAD	MV	GROUP*
.38 SPECIAL:		
Lyman #358156/13.5 gr. #2400	1,345	2 1/8"
Lyman #358429/13.5 gr. #2400	1,376	2 3/8"
.357 MAGNUM:		
Lyman #358429/14.0 gr. AA#9	1,338	2 1/4"
H&G 173 Keith/14.0 gr. #2400	1,378	1 3/8"
Lyman #358156/15.0 gr. #2400	1,503	1 7/8"
Hrndy 125 XTP/20.0 gr. WW296	1,437	2"
Hrndy 158 XTP/14.0 gr. #2400	1,261	2 1/8"
Hrndy 180 XTP/13.0 gr. H110	1,061	1 5/8"
Speer 140 JHP/17.5 gr. WW296	1,304	1 1/2"
Speer 158 JHP/14.0 gr. #2400	1,257	1 3/8"

* Best five of six shots at 25 yards.

SELECTED LOADS FOR THE RUGER NEW MODEL .44 MAGNUM
4 5/8" SS BLACKHAWK

BULLET/LOAD	MV	GROUP*
.44 SPECIAL:		
RCBS 44-250 KT/17.3 gr. #2400	1,213	2"
Bull-X 240/8.0 gr. Universal	1,019	2 1/4"
.44 MAGNUM:		
NEI 260KT/10.0 gr. Unique	1,095	1 1/2"
Lyman #429421/20.0 gr. #2400	1,191	2 1/2"
Bull-X 240/20.0 gr. H4227	1,114	2 3/8"
Black Hills 240 JHP	1,216	2 1/2"
Black Hills 300 JHP	1,083	1 3/8"
Federal 240 Hi-Shok	1,256	2 3/8"
Federal 300 HC	1,193	2 1/8"
Garrett 280KT	1,275	2 3/4"
Garrett 310KT	1,203	2 3/4"
Winchester 250 Partition Gold	1,249	1 1/8"

*Best five of six shots at 25 yards

SELECTED LOADS FOR THE RUGER NEW MODEL .45 COLT
4 5/8" SS BLACKHAWK

BULLET/LOAD	MV	GROUP*
Federal 225 LSWC HP	754	1 1/2"
Winchester 225 SilverTip HP	750	2 1/4"
Bull-X 230 RN/5.0 gr. N100	710	2 1/2"
Bull-X 255/7.0 gr. WW231	725	2 3/4"
Bull-X 250 CSJ/6.0 gr. N100	757	2"
Oregon Trail 250/6.0 gr. N100	737	1 5/8"
Bull-X 255/9.0 gr. Unique	916	2"
Bull-X 255/10.0 gr. Unique	996	2 3/4"
Bull-X 255/18.5 gr. #2400	1,019	2"
Oregon Trail 250/10.0 gr. Uniq	1,010	1 7/8"
Oregon Trail 250/18.5 gr. #2400	1,010	2 1/2"
LBT 260 KT/10.0 gr. Unique	990	2 1/8"
Lyman #454424/18.5 gr. #2400	981	2 1/4"
Hornady 250 XTP/20.0 gr. #2400	1,175	2"
BRP 300 GC/21.2 gr. H110	1,008	1 1/2"
NEI 310 KT/21.2 gr. H110	1,100	1 1/4"
RCBS 300 SWC GC/21.2 gr. H110	1,075	1 1/2"
SSK 340 FN/212 gr. H110	1,150	2 3/4"

*Best five of six shots at 25 yards.

forth for hunters and silhouetters. Still, there were no packin' pistol lengths from the factory. The 5 1/2-inch barrel length came along in 1987 and, finally, in 1994 both blued and stainless 4 5/8-inch packin' pistols in .44 Magnum were introduced by Ruger. Strangely enough the short-barreled .44s were, and are, fitted with standard grip frames rather than the longer, square-backed Dragoon-style frames of the other Super Blackhawk barrel lengths.

Ruger Super Blackhawks are a super bargain in the handgun market. They deliver more in service and accuracy than their price tag would warrant. The 10 1/2-inch models in my experience have all been superbly accurate with two blued models and one stainless model being used for silhouetting and hunting. My long-barreled blue models are now a thing of the past. One has been rebarreled with a 5 1/2-inch Ruger barrel from 1976 marked "THE 2OOTH YEAR OF OUR LIBERTY." The other has now been built into a 5 1/2-inch .45 Colt by Jim Stroh. The 10 1/2-inch stainless version has been customized as mentioned earlier.

In 1971 Ruger brought forth the first Blackhawk in .45 Colt. We soon found we had a sixgun far stronger than the Colt Single Action Army as it was built on the .44 Magnum frame size capable of handling 260- and 300-grain bullets at 1,200 fps. The .45 Colt had been modernized. My original 7 1/2-inch .45 Blackhawk came with an extra bonus of an auxiliary cylinder that delivered excellent accuracy with .45 ACP hardball rounds. The Old Model .45 Colt Blackhawk only lasted for two years before it was replaced by the New Model in 1973. Unlike the .44 Magnum, the .45 Blackhawk has always been available in the 4 5/8-inch length and it came out in stainless steel in 1992. The cycle is now almost complete as we now have stainless-steel Blackhawks in .357 Magnum, .44 Magnum, and .45 Colt.

The .41 Magnum was made, at least cataloged, in stainless steel only in 1974. I've never seen one. All three stainless steel packin' pistols, .357 Magnum, .44 Magnum, and .45 Colt were ordered from Ruger for testing and subsequent purchasing. The number three was selected as that is how many they make and just also happens to be the number of grandsons I have to pass these onto someday.

All three sixguns look to be identical at first glance, but there are subtle differences. Both the .45 Colt and .357 Magnum have standard hammers while the .44 Magnum has the typical Super Blackhawk wide target hammer. All three have standard smooth triggers and the XR3-RED grip frame. Cylinders on the .44 and .357 Magnum are 1.702 inches in length while the .357 Magnum cylinder is .055 inch shorter. Both the .45 and the .357 have fluted cylinders. The cylinder of the .44 is unfluted.

Trigger pulls from the factory were fairly heavy at 5 1/4 pounds for the .357 and 4 3/8 pounds for the .44, while the .45 Colt came in at a more usable 3 3/8 pounds. After removing the grips, I then lifted one leg of the trigger return spring from its stud on the grip frame. This brought the trigger pulls down to 3 5/8 pounds for the .357 Magnum, 3 1/8 pounds for the .44 Magnum, and 2 1/2 pounds for the .45 Colt. One coil was then cut from the mainspring of the .357 Magnum, bringing it down to 3 1/4 pounds.

For my packin' purposes, these three sixguns are all carried in a holster I made myself that was patterned after the Tom Threepersons style with a safety strap that snaps over the hammer and a fully laced welt. It was made of heavy leather in the 1960s and gives every indication that it will last as long as the sixguns, and certainly longer than I will.

Favorite handloads for the three packin' pistols? For the .357 Magnum Blackhawk it is the Hensley & Gibbs 173-grain Keith bullet over 14.0 grains of #2400 for 1,375 fps. When I use .38 Special brass I prefer Lyman's #358156GC, the Thompson bullet, over 13.5 grains of #2400 for 1,350 fps.

For the bigger bores, the .44 gets 20.0 grains of #2400 or 10.0 grains of Unique under the Lyman #429421 Keith or NEI 429.260KT for 1,200 or 1,100 fps, respectively. Unique is my most commonly used powder for the .45 Colt in this Ruger, with 9.0 to 10.0 grains giving around 900 to 1,000 fps. For a more powerful loading for the .45 Colt I use the NEI #451.310, a 300-grain Keith bullet, or SSK's 340-grain flat nose, both over 21.2 grains of H110 for around 1150 fps. This is a most powerful load for a lightweight .45 Colt sixgun and is only for use in Ruger Blackhawks.

There are several factory loads for the .44 Magnum available that do well in the Ruger packin' pistol, including Garrett's 280 and 310, and Federal's 300-grain Hard Cast. The most accurate factory loads proved to be Black Hills 300-grain Jacketed Hollow Points at 1,100 fps, and Winchester's new Partition Gold 260s at 1,250. Both get close to one inch for five shots at 25 yards.

The "perfect packin' pistol" does not exist. The search for it is what keeps things very interesting. The Ruger Stainless Steel packin' pistols come close. Mighty close. I have now fitted both the .44 and .45 Rugers with stainless-steel Bisley Model grip frames, triggers, and hammers, while the .357 packin' pistol has been fancied up a mite by Gary Reeder and fitted with scrimshawed ivory micarta grips by Twyla Taylor for my wife's use.

The Vaquero

Dreams really do come true. Or as a wise sage once said: "Good things come to those who wait." Well, I waited and it took 35 years, but my dream finally came true, or close enough. My first Colt was a 4 3/4-inch

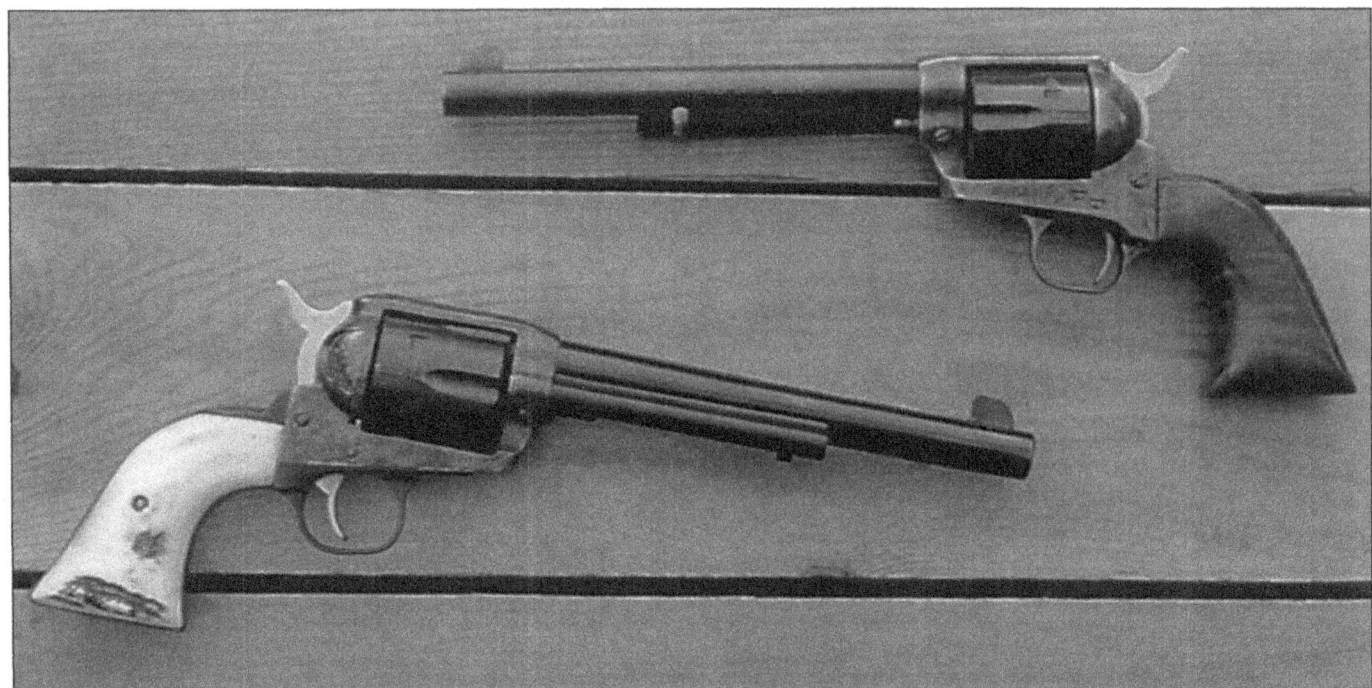

Ruger's great success story of the 1990s is the Vaquero (bottom), here compared to a Colt Single Action Army.

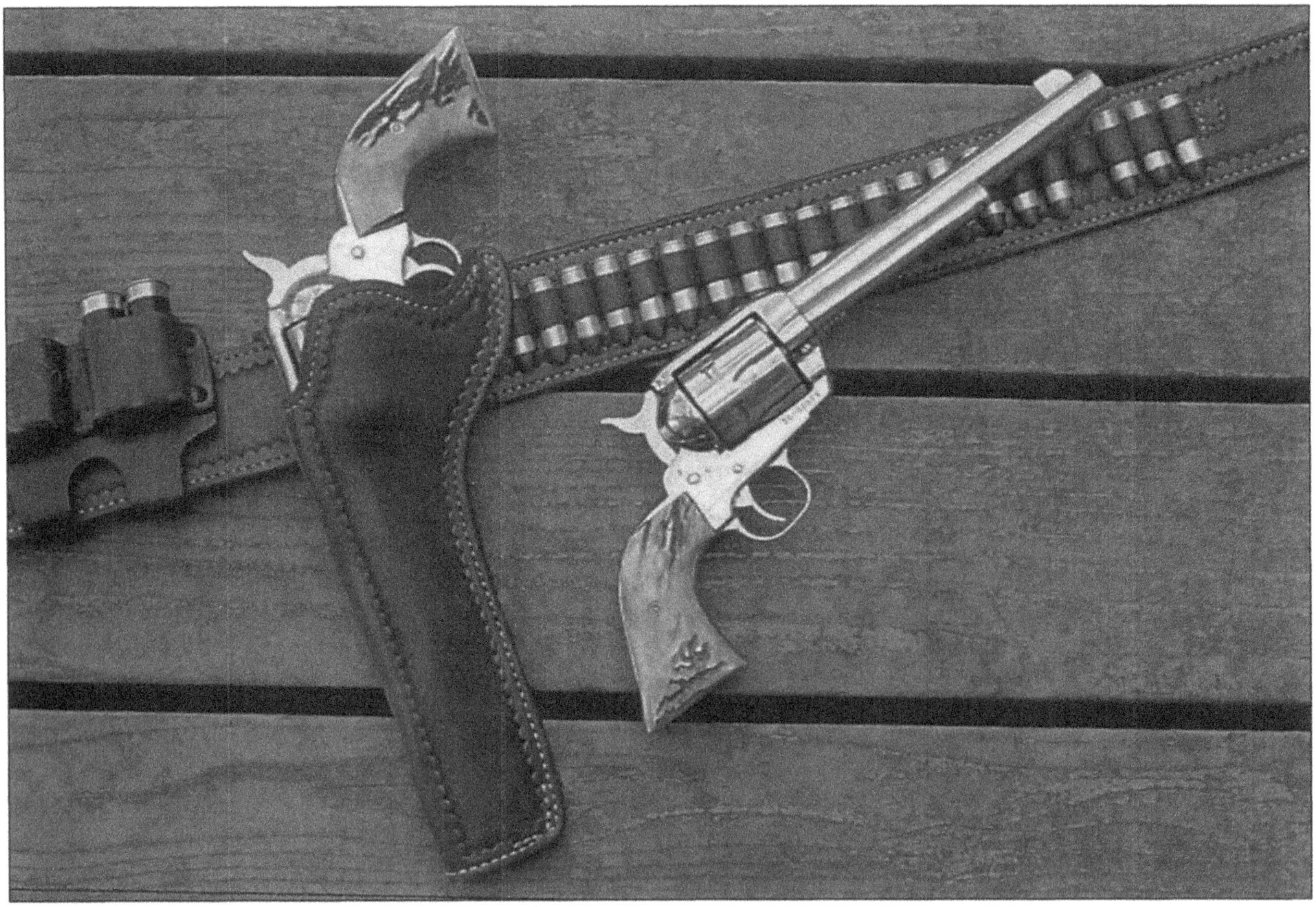

Two of Taffin's favorite sixguns for cowboy action shooting are these 7 1/2-inch stainless-steel, stag-gripped, .45 Colt Vaqueros. Leather is by the Leather Arsenal.

Rugged sixguns for cowboy action shooting or general outdoor use are these .45 Colt Rugers in the Bisley Vaquero and standard Vaquero models.

Single Action Army circa 1900, the so-called Civilian Model. What a beautiful old sixgun that was! I say was because in a weak moment I let it get away. The first centerfire Ruger, the .357 Magnum Blackhawk, became readily available in my area about this time and, while it did not have the beautiful esthetically flowing lines of the Colt, it was close and I was soon to find out, superior in one all important way. At the time, pre-war Colt Single Actions were plentiful and cost about the same as a new Ruger or Smith & Wesson Highway Patrolman. By the time I had .38 Special, .45 Colt and .41 Long Colt Single Action Armies added to the first .38-40, I discovered that Colt springs broke, especially hand and bolt springs, and Ruger coil springs did not.

It did not take me long to realize that the ideal situation would be a Colt Single Action Army with Ruger lockwork. That, of course, never happened. But we have come oh so close as Ruger has taken a giant backwards step forwards to offer a modern sixgun with a real 19th-century look. A few early Single-Sixes were finished with a case-colored frame, but never offered to the public. By "de-horning" the Blackhawk, it is made to look much like the original Single Action and becomes the Vaquero.

Ruger offers this classic-looking single action sixgun with fixed rather than adjustable sights for one great and over-riding reason: to provide a reasonably priced and rugged sixgun for cowboy action shooters. At the same time it has come up with an excellent packin' pistol for outdoorsman. All Blackhawks have come equipped with the familiar massive frame with an adjustable rear sight. The Vaquero, as the name implies, is a throwback to "those thrilling days of yesteryear." Ruger does not make very many, if any, marketing errors. Cowboy action shooting is big and the 19th-century fanciers can now have an authentic-looking single-action sixgun with virtually unbreakable lockwork and a transfer bar making it perfectly safe to carry loaded with six rounds. It is THE sixgun most encountered in the holsters of competitors at CAS matches.

The first Vaquero was the 7 1/2-inch Cavalry barrel length in .45 Colt. Even Ruger did not know how popular that Vaquero was going to be. It was stunned at the number of sales that first year. The company has rewarded shooters for their great acceptance of the Vaquero by now offering it in both blue with a case colored frame, and stainless, and in .357 Magnum, .44 Magnum, and .44-40, in addition to the original .45 Colt with most calibers available in barrel lengths of 4 5/8, 5 1/2, and 7 1/2 inches. There is also a Bisley Vaquero utilizing the grip frame, hammer, and trigger of the Bisley Model Blackhawk, and a Sheriff's Model with a round-butted grip frame.

Since all Vaqueros are fixed-sighted guns, it can be a real problem getting a gun that shoots to point of aim.

Not to worry. Plenty of front sight blade is afforded with the Vaquero to allow each individual sixgunner to "adjust" his/her sights by judicious filing for the particular load and hold he/she prefers. My original 7 1/2-inch .45 Vaquero shot three inches low with 300-grain bullets and 12 inches low with 225-grain bullets. I simply chose a load I intended to use the most often and filed the front sight blade to the proper height.

The stainless steel version of the Vaquero strikes me as the near-perfect outdoorsman's sixgun, especially for a packer or guide or woods bum who wants a strong dependable sixgun that will shoot one load to the preferred point of aim and distance with no worries about adjustable sights getting out of whack. My choice for this duty is a 4 5/8-inch .45 Colt or .44 Magnum, home gunsmith adjusted to hit point of aim with 300-grain bullets at 1,250 fps in the .44 or 1,100 fps in the .45 Colt.

A close look at the 7 1/2-inch-barreled Vaquero in .45 Colt reveals a sixgun that at 43 ounces is 10 percent heavier than its counterpart from Hartford, a similarly barreled Colt Single Action Army. The flat-top frame has been contoured and rounded off very nicely to provide a western-style single-action look and the traditional hog wallow style rear sight sets high enough that one can sight down the top of a Vaquero without cocking the hammer. The rear sight does not extend all the way to the back of the frame, but rather stops about 5/16 inch in front of the hammer face, resulting in a dished-out area that gives a flat-sight picture. I have found that blackening this area with spray-on sight black helps my groups immensely.

The front sight is shaped like a traditional Colt Single Action front sight and with a height of 3/8 inch affords plenty of latitude for filing in to one's load and hold as mentioned earlier. It is also shaped to provide a flat-black sight picture. The grip frame is Blackhawk-style and size, but is steel rather than the alloy found on most Blackhawks since 1955. Early ejector rod housings were an alloy; they are now steel. The firing pin is frame mounted as on all Ruger Blackhawks and the Vaquero is a transfer bar single action. That means it is loaded by opening the loading gate, which allows the cylinder to rotate with the hammer down.

The newest feature on the Vaquero is the case colored, not hardened, frame. The colors are somewhat

Ruger offers three stainless-steel 4 5/8-inch packin' pistols chambered in (from left) a .357 Magnum, .44 Magnum, and .45 Colt.

A favorite .44 Magnum of hunters, whether fitted with a scope or used with iron sights, is Ruger's Hunter Model.

subdued and show up best in certain lighting, but they are nowhere near as bright as those found on most Colt Single Action Armys, Cimarron Single Actions, or EMF Hartfords. Holding a Colt Single Action Army in one hand while clutching a Ruger Vaquero in the other really emphasizes the difference. A look at the price tag even emphasizes it even more. Therein lies the great popularity of the Ruger Blackhawks, whether they be standard Blackhawks, Super Blackhawks, or Vaqueros. They are priced within reach of any sixgunner! The legacy of Bill Ruger is not just great shootin' sixguns, but truly affordable great-shooting sixguns.

Shooting the Vaquero is pure single-action pleasure. It is a much stronger sixgun than the beloved Colt Single Action Army and safe to carry fully loaded with six rounds. That is not important to those of us who were raised with old-style single actions and know how to handle them, but it is tremendously important to new shooters.

I am a great fan of the Colt Single Action Army. It is a soul-stirrin', spirit kindlin', fast-heart-beatin' sixgun. I have been taken to task by more "modern" types for clinging to it as a viable defensive sixgun. I hold my ground on this. An extra added benefit is the fact that Colt Single Actions conjure up visions of bacon frying over a campfire during a drizzling rain in the mountains, and one cannot only smell powder smoke, but also cattle-raised trail dust each time one is picked up. Rugers have never had this capability. Until now. The bacon smell is a little lighter, the trail dust a little fainter, but it is there. Ruger has caught some of the spirit of the Old West with the Vaquero.

The Hunter Model

In 1992, Ruger offered the first Hunter Model Super Blackhawk. This version was fitted with a heavy bull barrel with an integral rib that featured scallops to accept Ruger scope rings, thus allowing this .44 Magnum to be very easily fitted with an LER scope. The finish was stainless steel only; the ejector rod and housing were longer than normal to assure easy removal of fired cases; and though the Super Blackhawk Grip frame was maintained, I would have preferred the Bisley Model grip frame, the square back trigger guard was rounded off.

This Ruger .44 Magnum made for an excellent hunting handgun. If one so desired, or bad weather condi-

SELECTED LOADS FOR THE RUGER VAQUERO .45 COLT 7 1/2"

BULLET/LOAD	MV	GROUP/25 YARDS
Oregon Trail 255/9.0 gr. Unique	975	1 5/8"
Oregon Trail 255/7.5 gr. WW231	865	2 1/8"
BRP 300GC/21.5 gr. WW296	1,192	2 3/8"
Lyman #454424/9.5 gr. Unique	1,080	2"
Lyman #454424/20.0 gr. H4227	1,089	2 1/4"
Lyman #454424/22.0 gr. H4227	1,252	1 1/2"
Lyman #454424/15.5 gr. HS-7	1,116	1 1/2"
Hornady 300 XTP/21.7 gr. WW296	1,194	1 1/4"

Two great bargains for the handgun hunter are Ruger's .44 Magnum Hunter Model (top) and the Bisley Model.

tions made it pertinent to do so, the scope could be removed easily with no other tool than a 50-cent piece to loosen the screws on the scope rings. The scope could also be replaced and would come back into zero. It was my good fortune to acquire one of the early Hunter Models and it has been used successfully in a number of hunting ventures. Stoked with 300-grain bullets at 1,200 fps or even faster, it is more than adequate for taking most big game cleanly.

Now that Ruger had the near-perfect hunting handgun, it did a most unexpected thing. It removed it from production!!! No explanation was ever offered as to why this was done, and in the meantime, scalpers were able to get anywhere from 50 to 100 percent over the original cost as the demand for these guns far outweighed their supply. Ruger has not made many mistakes in its half-century of existence, however this was a major one. Finally, it has corrected this error and the Hunter Model is available once again.

As far as I can tell the new models of this New Model Super Blackhawk are identical to the original versions, except the cylinder on the current version I have has much more play in it than my original Hunter Model. This was easily corrected with a call to Belt Mountain and a request for its #5 stainless-steel base pin to fit the Ruger Super Blackhawk. This base pin has a head reminiscent of that found on the base pin in

Keith's #5SA is made slightly larger in diameter than the Ruger base pin. It was an easy fix to remove the old base pin and replace it with the tighter-fitting Belt Mountain base pin. This is a custom feature, a do-it-yourself project that is recommended for any single actions that have too much play in the cylinder or are handicapped with a base pin that will not stay in under recoil. Belt Mountain pins also feature a locking Allen screw to help them stay in place. A good product.

As with many, perhaps most, factory new sixguns today, this Hunter Model had a too-heavy trigger pull. I say had as this condition is easily remedied on New Model Rugers by removing the grip panels, and then flipping one leg of the trigger return spring from its post on either side of the grip frame. This simple operation resulted in the reducing of the trigger pull from 5 1/4 pounds down to a near-perfect 3 1/4 pounds.

For test firing hundreds of rounds in a single sitting, I found it prudent to replace the standard factory grip pan-

These test groups show why Ruger's Hunter Model is such an excellent hunting handgun.

els with the more hand filling and secure Pachmayrs. These same grips are also a good choice for a non-slip surface when hunting in bad weather. This is also one instance where the addition of rubber grips does not detract from the appearance of the original factory sixgun as the laminated Ruger grips to my eyes are about as ugly as the proverbial mud fence. That is why my original Hunter Model wears staghorn grips.

The Ruger .357 Maximum

There remains one Ruger Single Action we have not mentioned: the Ruger .357 Maximum. Introduced in 1982 at the time that silhouettiing was really taking off, the Maximum featured a longer frame and cylinder to accept the 1.6-inch length case of the .357 Maximum cartridge. It was designed to shoot 180-grain .357 Magnum bullets as fast as 158s from the original Magnum to deliver more energy to 200-yard steel rams. It was killed by those who did not understand the cartridge and instead tried to drive lightweight bullets as fast as they could, resulting in top strap erosion. Ruger pulled the Maximum from production in 1984. It was an ignoble end to a fine long-range sixgun.

Single-Six, Flat-Top Blackhawk, Super Blackhawk, Old Model Blackhawk, New Model Blackhawk, Bisley Model Blackhawk, Vaquero, Bisley Vaquero, Hunter Model. All of these stand in great tribute to the genius of Bill Ruger. Not only has he given us 50 years of great single actions sixguns, one has to wonder if anyone could even afford a sixgun today had it not been for his introduction of modern manufacturing methods. Both are his legacy.

SELECTED LOADS FOR THE RUGER HUNTER MODEL .44 MAGNUM 7 1/2"

BULLET/LOAD	MV	5 SHOTS/25 YARDS
Boar Slammer 250/26.0 gr. H110	1,499	1 1/4"
Boar Slammer 320/18.0 gr. AA#9	1,247	1"
Boar Slammer 320/21.5 gr. H110	1,315	1 1/2"
BRP 290KT/10.0 gr. Unique	1,143	1 1/2"
BRP 290KT/21.5 gr. WW296	1,388	1 1/2"
CPBC 255PB/21.5 gr. WW296	1,401	1 1/4"
CPBC 320 LBT/21.5 gr. WW296	1,400	1 3/8"
CPBC 320 LBT/18.0 gr. AA#9	1,256	1"

CHAPTER 6

RUGER'S BULL STRONG DOUBLE-ACTION REDHAWKS

Ruger, after nearly 20 years of providing great single actions, first began offering double-action sixguns in 1971 with the Security-Six in both .38 Special and .357 Magnum. Four years later, the first stainless-steel Security-Six arrived. Up to this time, the double-action market had pretty well been dominated by both Colt and Smith & Wesson, both with basic designs that went back to the 19th century. The double-action Ruger featured a totally new design with the frame, crane, trigger guard, trigger, and hammer all machined from investment castings of chrome-

The Ruger Redhawk is offered in .44 Magnum and .45 Colt, both excellent hunting chamberings. The bottom sixgun is scope ready with Ruger rings, while the top gun utilizes a Buehler mount. Stocks are by BearHug.

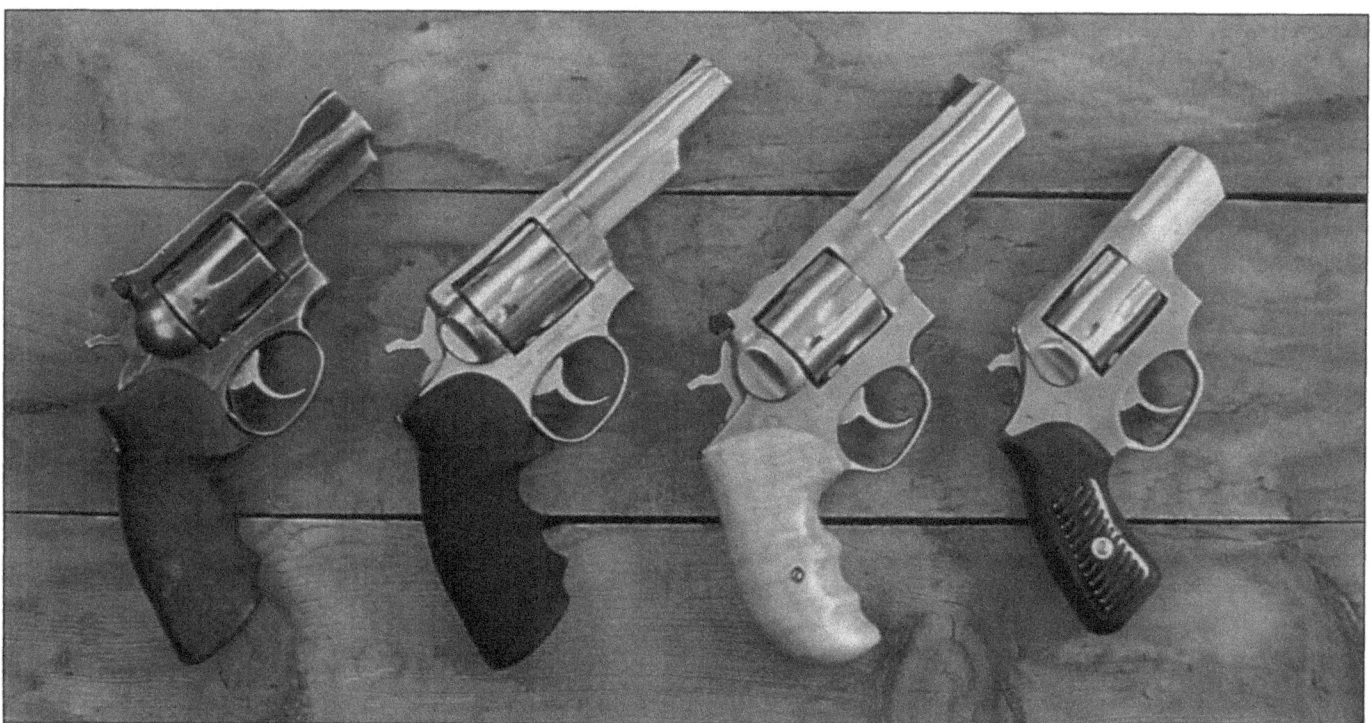

Ruger's medium bore sixguns include (from left) the Security-Six, Speed-Six, GP-100, and SP-101.

moly steel. All of the internal mechanism was contained in the trigger guard assembly instead of being exposed by removal of a side plate, and all that was necessary to take down a Ruger Security-Six was a coin as the only screws in the entire revolver were found in the rear sight and the grips.

The original grip angle was wrong for double-action shooting, so the top of the back of the grip strap was quickly changed to give a more prominent recoil shoulder and keep the Security-Six from climbing in the hand when fired. The Security-Six was a tremendous success with well over 1 million being produced before

Two custom Ruger Redhawks (left) cut to 4 inches pack as easy as the GP-100 shown in 4-inch stainless-steel and blued versions.

being phased out in 1988 in favor of the GP-100, which arrived two years earlier. Once the Security-Six was well established it was time for the Ruger to start looking at a truly big-bore double-action sixgun.

The Redhawk arrives

I first heard of a new Ruger double-action .44 Magnum at the NRA Show in 1978. The Redhawk was announced in 1979 and the first production sixguns were delivered in 1980. My first impression of the test sixgun received then was that it was a massive, business-like revolver and I liked its looks and feel in my hand. I was also surprised at how well it balanced with the weight of 52 ounces. Metal-to-metal fit was very good, the cylinder locked tightly, and the grips, a departure from the large, over-sized grips found on most double-action revolvers of the time, were smooth and comfortable.

The rear sight was a standard adjustable Ruger sight matched up with a front sight system with interchangeable blades held in place by a spring-loaded plunger that entered from the front of the full barrel rib. The trigger was smooth and the action had a very smooth double-action pull of 10 pounds, while the single-action pull was a too-heavy 5 1/2 pounds. I still have that original Ruger .44 Magnum, and while it has smoothed with use, it has always been difficult to get a light, crisp trigger on a Redhawk.

The ejector rod fits in a shroud under the barrel and does not lock at the end. Instead, the cylinder is locked at the front of the frame and at the rear. The cylinder on the Redhawk is massive, 31 percent larger

Taffin's Redhawk .44 Magnum (left), cut to 4 inches, it is round-butted compared to Smith & Wesson's Model 29 .44 Magnum.

than the Super Blackhawk with a barrel that is 19 percent larger in diameter. Over the past two decades the Redhawk has been proven to be an extremely strong sixgun. It was originally announced as being available in 5 1/2-, 7 1/2-, and 10 1/2-inch barrel lengths, but the latter never did appear. The two shorter lengths are available in both stainless steel and blue models. The 7 1/2-inch Redhawks are also available in a scope-ready version with scallops machined into the

The author visits the grand old man himself, Bill Ruger, in his office.

The cylinder on Ruger Redhawk .44 Magnum is long enough to handle the excellent 330-grain hunting loads from Garrett.

barrel rib to accept Ruger scope rings. The Redhawk was never popular with silhouetters, but it is the number one double-action sixgun choice for hunters who shoot heavy big-bore loads.

One of the most touted aspects of the then-new Redhawk was the grip shape. Frankly, I was skeptical that the grip shape was such that no fillers or adapters would be necessary to tame the recoil of full-house .44 Magnum loads. I have never been able to fire too many such rounds from a Smith & Wesson Model 29 with factory wooden stocks without being affected by recoil. I was pleasantly surprised to find that whoever designed the grip of the Redhawk knew what he was about. They certainly cannot be claimed to make firing full-power .44 Magnums fully comfortable — .44 Magnums kick and the Redhawk is no exception — but the Redhawk grip shape does help to reduce felt recoil.

The Redhawk was eventually chambered in both .357 Magnum and .41 Magnum, but both of these were dropped more than 10 years ago. In 1992, while on assignment touring gun makers in the East, I found myself in Bill Ruger's office to conduct an interview of the grand old gentleman of the firearms industry. I was ushered into his modest office, which was piled high with gun magazines of every description, and which also contained some notable firearms as well as a prototype semi-automatic pistol on his desk. He left word with his secretary that we were not to be disturbed. We were just talking about things in general, when we were inter-

Even when shooting a Ruger Redhawk, the author still packs a single action.

rupted by his secretary with a phone call that he was informed he had to take. Although I could only hear Bill's end of the conversation, I knew it was not good news. As I sat there, Bill Ruger received the tragic word of the seriousness of an illness to his son Tom.

After the phone call we discussed this and then went into the interview. Sharing something as difficult as this with a man makes one seem very close to him. I've had a very special feeling for Bill Ruger ever since, in addition to the appreciation I have always had for his firearms genius. In 1994, thanks mainly to Terry Murbach's contact with Sturm, Ruger, 52 Shootist Commemoratives, 4 5/8-inch stainless-steel Bisley Single-Sixes, were issued. All are marked "IN MEMORY OF TOM RUGER." This little gun is pictured on the bottom left hand corner of page 267 in Wilson's Ruger & His Guns.

Plenty of muscle

During our conversation I asked Bill Ruger about bringing out a .45 Colt Redhawk. I have no way of knowing if that had any bearing on the decision, but I at least like to think that the fact that we now have a Redhawk chambered in the grand old cartridge had something to do with our conversation that day. The Redhawk .44 Magnum has been recently joined by the .45 Colt in, at least as of this writing, stainless-steel models only. The Redhawk .44 Magnum is a very strong sixgun. It and its brother, the Super Redhawk, are probably the strongest double-action .44 Magnums ever offered to sixgunners. Since the .45 Colt is built on the same platform, it is also probably the sturdiest double-action .45 ever offered to shooters. The .45 Redhawk is available in both the easy packin' 5 1/2-inch version, as well as 7 1/2-inch models both with and without the factory scope option that consists of two scallops on the barrel that will accept Ruger scope rings.

When experimenters started heavy loading the .45 to take advantage of its larger case capacity with smokeless powders, the inevitable happened. Cylinders burst, top straps blew. Elmer Keith started his writing career in the 1920s describing a blow-up of a .45 Colt Single Action Army .45. That incident caused him to give up on the .45 Colt and take up the .44 Special for the heavy loads he wanted to use.

Some said then, still do, that .45 Colt brass was weak. Perhaps it was in its old original black powder loading. Perhaps it still was at Keith's time with folded, or balloon, head cases. However when Dick Casull started the experiments that lead to the .454 Casull, he used the standard .45 brass available at the time. The balloon head brass had given way to the modern solid head brass. This is exactly what we have today and exactly what Casull used.

Ruger's .45 Colt Redhawk shoots great!

When chambered in .44 Magnum, the Redhawk sometimes shoots even better.

The missing strength factor in Casull's work was not the brass case but the available sixguns. He blew several Colt Single Actions, then started fitting five-shot cylinders and finally built his own custom sixguns to house 230-grain bullets at 1,800 fps, or more, all in standard .45 Colt brass. It would be nearly 100 years after the advent of the Colt Single Action Army before we would see a single action strong enough to take advantage of some of the voluminous case capacity of the .45 Colt when using smokeless powder. That sixgun was Ruger's .45 Blackhawk.

These sixguns are certainly not as strong as Freedom Arms' five-shooters, so it behooves us to approach loading for the .45 Blackhawk with a great deal of common sense. Modern .45 Magnum-level loads began to appear in print with the advent of the Ruger Blackhawk. Some sensible, some not so sensible. I settled on a load consisting of a 300-grain bullet first loaded over 18.5 grains of #2400 for 1,100 fps and then 21.5 grains of either H110 or WW296. The latter does around 1,200 fps in a 7 1/2-inch Ruger Blackhawk. It is plenty for most of my needs and I rarely exceed it in the relatively lightweight .45 Colt Blackhawk. With the arrival of the Redhawk, we now have an even stronger .45 Colt wearing the Ruger name.

Ruger not only had an advantage in bringing its .44 Magnum double-action sixgun out at the right time, it also built its gun around the cartridge rather than chambering some existing model for the powerful .44 Magnum. This made it the strongest sixgun ever offered for the .44 Magnum up to that point. Ruger engineers were able to do this without giving us an extra heavy or clumsy sixgun. This strength factor also makes it a near-perfect .45 Colt. The only fault most of us can find with the Redhawk is the fact that it is, as we have said, difficult to get a really good trigger on Big Red. It is strange to read the account of the engineers and designers of the Redhawk as they talk about the smooth double-action trigger pull and good single-action pull. Not quite. My two latest Redhawks came with single-action trigger pulls that measure 6 3/4 and 6 1/4 pounds.

The Redhawk gains its strength in many ways. The threaded area of the frame is very thick, double what one finds in many other sixguns, and the massive cylinder is locked at the rear and front of the cylinder itself, rather than at the end of the ejector rod. The barrel carries a heavy rib and the top strap literally speaks of brute strength. Like the single-action Blackhawk, the double-action Redhawk just keeps going.

For shooting the .45 Colt in the Redhawk, I use a scope-ready 7 1/2-inch version, complete with Ruger rings for mounting a 2X Burris LER pistol scope, and 5 1/2-inch easy-packin' version. To help further soften recoil of some of the loads used in the 5 1/2-inch .45, a pair of Uncle Mike's finger groove grips replace the factory wood stocks when I intend to shoot a long string of heavy loads. I was fortunate to have a pair of grips from the late Deacon Deason of BearHug Grips laid back for the 7 1/2-inch .45 Colt Redhawk. Both sets of grips were appreciated with the loads that are used in both .45 Redhawks, including 265-grain bullets at 1,465 fps, 335-grain bullets at 1,275, and 360-grain bullets at 1,180.

The scoped .45 Redhawk has proven to be exceptionally accurate. Even more so in light of the heavy trigger pull. Of all the loads tested (five factory heavy-duty hunting loads, and 23 handloads using both cast and jacketed bullets and weights from 250 grains up to 335 grains), the average group size for five shots at 25 yards with all 28 loads proved to be just over one inch. I call that astounding accuracy.

Factory hunting loads tested included two from Buffalo Bore and two from Cor-Bon. Buffalo Bore's 300-grain Speer bulleted load clocks out at 1,367 fps over the sky screens of the Oehler Model 35P and places five shots in 3/4 of an inch at 25 yards. The Buffalo Bore 325-grain LBT load exhibits the same accuracy with a muzzle velocity of 1,392 fps. These are not faint-hearted loads! They are for use only in modern, heavy-framed .45 Colt sixguns. Cor-Bon's serious .45 Colt hunting loads include a 265-grain Bonded Core +P at 1,347 fps and a 300-grain Bonded Core +P at 1,271 fps. Both loads are right at one-inch for accuracy at 25 yards.

The above are for big-boned, heavy-muscled critters. For whitetails, my preferred .45 Colt load is Hornady's 250-grain XTP bullet over 20 grains of Alliant #2400. In the 7 1/2-inch Redhawk this load clocks out at 1,137 fps and has near pin-point accuracy with five shots in 7/8 of an inch. Cast Performance Bullet Company offers .45s from LBT bullet molds, and all loads with big game bustin' in mind are assembled with Winchester's 296 and CCI #350 Magnum primers. The 265 over 26.0 grains yielded 1,464 fps and a group of one inch; the 325, 21.0 grains, 1,234 fps, also one inch; the 335 with the same charge came in at 1,275 fps and 1 1/8 inch, while the super-heavy 360 over 19.5 grains grouped into 1 1/4 inches with a muzzle velocity of 1,180 fps. All of these loads will penetrate from here to Sunday.

The Redhawk has been a most popular hunting handgun in its original .44 Magnum chambering. So much so that it was joined rather than supplanted by the Super Redhawk as Ruger had planned. The Redhawk was simply in too much demand to drop. There is a large segment of the sixgun shooting population that holds to the idea that anything the .44 can do the .45 can do better. The .45 Redhawk is definitely for them.

The Redhawk .44 represents the .44 Magnum of the '80s; big and tough, able to withstand the recoil of not only standard .44 Magnums, but the new heavyweight bullet loads that were soon demanded by handgun hunters as well. Handloaders found that the durable Redhawk was capable of delivering 300-grain cast bullets at 1,500 fps from its 7 1/2-inch barrel, a load that gives maximum .44 Magnum penetration on large game.

In 1986, Ruger introduced the GP-100 that was, as Ruger said at the time, "Designed as the ultimate .357 Magnum police and personal defense use..." The GP-100 was the first double-action revolver from Ruger to use soft-cushioned rubber grips, and it also combined

The author shooting the .45 Colt Redhawk prior to a hunting trip.

SELECTED LOADS FOR THE .44 MAGNUM RUGER REDHAWK 7 1/2"

BULLET/LOAD	MV
Lyman #429421/22.0 gr. #2400	1,548
SSK 310 FP/21.5 gr. WW296	1,351
SSK 310 FP/23.5 gr. WW680	1,394
SSK 340 FP/19.5 gr. WW296	1,293
BRP 290KT/21.5 gr. WW296	1,297
BRP 290KT/22.5 gr. WW296	1,371

SELECTED LOADS FOR THE .45 COLT RUGER REDHAWK 7 1/2"

BULLET/LOAD	MV
Hornady 250 JHP/24.0 gr. H4227	1,087
Hornady 250 JHP/26.0 gr. WW296	1,292
Hornady 250 XTP/26.0 gr. H110	1,364
Speer 260 JHP/24.0 gr. H4227	1,124
Hornady 250XTP/20.0 gr. #2400	1,137
Hornady 300XTP/21.2 gr. H110	1,064
BRP 300 GC/21.5 gr. WW296	1,240
Swift 265 JHP/26.0 gr. WW296	1,415
LBT 260 KT/10.0 gr. Unique	1,059
LBT 260 KT/21.0 gr. #2400	1,294
CPBC 265 LBT/26.0 gr. WW296	1,464
CPBC 325 LBT/21.0 gr. WW296	1,234
CPBC 335 LBT/21.0 gr. WW296	1,275
CPBC 360 LBT/19.5 gr. WW296	1,180
Lyman 454424/18.5 gr. #2400	1,093
Lyman 452490GC/23.0 4227	1,165
Lyman #452490GC/20.0 gr.#2400	1,306
Lyman #457191/18.5 gr. #2400	1,108
NEI 310KT/21.2 gr. H110	1,217
NEI 325KT/21.2 gr. H110	1,208
Sierra 240 JHP/24.0 gr. H4227	1,058
Sierra 240 JHP/25.0 gr. WW296	1,250
Sierra 240 JHP/26.0 gr. WW296	1,301

the Redhawk locking system with the easy takedown that the modular system of Security-Six offered. According the Ruger, this sixgun offered "... a greater degree of accuracy, strength, reliability, and effectiveness than ever before realized in a double-action revolver." Time has proven that this was more than simply ad copy. The GP-100 is an excellent .357 Magnum revolver.

Making room for the Super Redhawk

Once the GP-100 was firmly established, Ruger saw fit to bring out an even larger Redhawk — the Super Redhawk. The Super Redhawk is not simply a Redhawk made bigger as one might have expected. Instead of just changing the Redhawk, Ruger used the GP-100 as the basis for its latest .44 Magnum. Actually, the Super Redhawk is a result of the blending of the best features of the GP-100 and the standard Redhawk.

Three major changes arrived with the Super Redhawk. First, for those who had complained about the poor trigger pulls of the standard Redhawk, the Super Redhawk used seperate springs for the trigger and hammer, going back to the hammer spring and strut used in its single-action revolvers. The result is a much smoother from-the-box trigger pull. In fact, while most Redhawks require either a gunsmith's tender care or much use to smooth out the trigger pulls, my first Super Redhawk came with an excellent trigger pull from the factory.

The second major change was found in the grip area. The Redhawk grip frame was replaced by the GP-100 stud that accepts the rubberized GP-100 grip panels. This could be either an improvement or a step backwards, depending upon one's point of view. The grip panels furnished on my first Super Redhawk were too small, leaving the sharp edges behind the trigger guard exposed. Even while wearing a shooting glove, one session of 600 rounds of full-house ammunition left me with a very sore and blistered middle finger on my shooting hand. I immediately surmised, sore finger and all, that grips panels that fitted the frame properly would solve this problem easily. So with my curiosity getting the best of me, I tracked down a GP-100 and confiscated the grip panels to try on the Super Redhawk. As hoped, the replacement panels were slightly larger and filled in the sharp edges behind Big Red II's trigger guard, thus alleviating the problem.

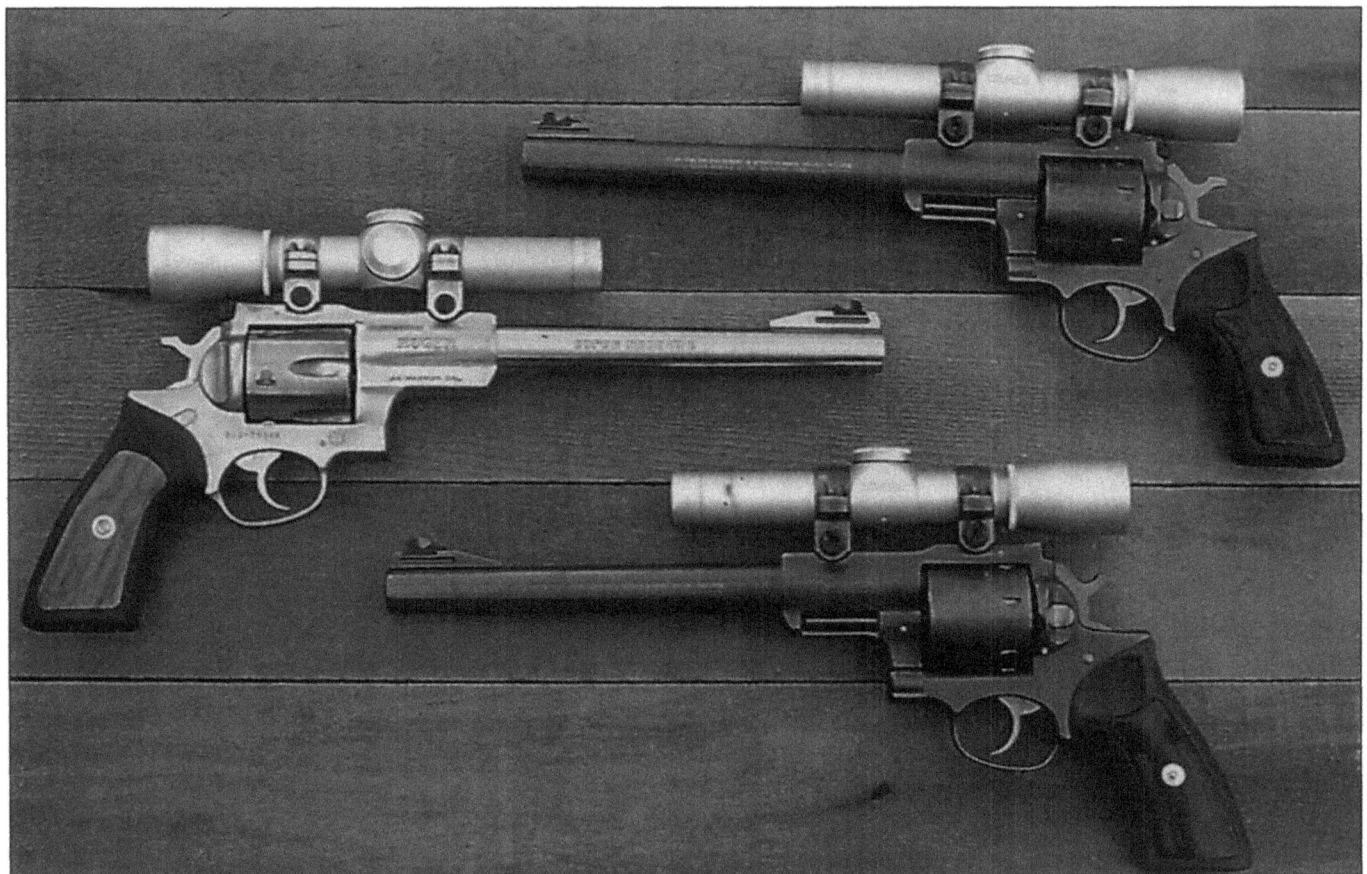

Ruger's trio of big-bore Super Redhawks chambered in .454 Casull, .44 Magnum, or .480 Ruger are all super heavy-duty double-action sixguns that will deliver the goods when it comes to hunting.

The third change was the most radical by far. The Ruger Super Redhawk has a distinctive profile not found on any other revolver. The frame itself has been extended forward of the cylinder so that the first 2 1/2 inches of the barrel are actually enclosed by the frame. This feature accomplishes two things: the frame is made heavier and stronger, and it allows the use of an integral scope mounting system on the frame rather than the barrel. The Super Redhawk comes with stainless scope rings that mount solidly on the frame using one large screw each and semi-circular recesses on each side of the frame. For added strength, a lug on the bottom of each ring mates with a recess on top of the frame. This allows each ring to be anchored from side to side as well as front to back. The rings install easily, and once the scope is zeroed in, will come back very close when the scope is removed and replaced again.

This easy on-again, off-again feature allows almost instant use of scope or iron sights, and makes the Super Redhawk very popular as a double-duty sixgun. A major selling point for the scope-ready Redhawk and Super Redhawk is the fact that they come already set up for easy scope mounting at no extra cost, thus saving scope users the $50 to $100, or more, that it normally costs to have a scope mounted properly.

The iron sights consist of a red insert front sight that is removable by depressing a plunger at the front of the sight base, thus allowing the use of replacement colored nylon front sights that are available as an option from Ruger. The rear sight has a standard Ruger white outline with adjustments that move the bullet impact approximately 3/4 inch at 25 yards. As barrel length is increased, the rear sight notch should be decreased in size to match the front sight. With the 9 1/2-inch Super Redhawk, the rear sight notch is much too wide for me and makes it difficult to align the sights precisely.

The 9 1/2-inch Super Redhawk is a massive .44 Magnum revolver with the following specifications: empty weight, 57 ounces; weight with rings and 2X Bausch & Lomb scope, 67 1/2 ounces; length, 15 1/8 inches; and height, 5 7/8 inches. Because of its weight, the Super Redhawk does an excellent job of dampening recoil of full-house .44 Magnum loads and with the proper-sized grips comes close to actually being almost pleasant to shoot. It is at least as pleasant as possible for a big bore revolver to be when shooting full-house loads. The 9 1/2-inch Super Redhawk has a decidedly muzzle-heavy feel, but the balance is good and I did not find myself having to struggle to keep the muzzle up. It just seems to balance naturally in my hands when shooting standing.

More than 40 different loads, with more than 1,000 rounds fired, were utilized in testing in my first Super Redhawk. Loads were classified into three categories: heavyweight cast bullet loads, standard weight cast bullet loads, and jacketed bullet loads. Initially, all firing was done at 25 yards with iron sights and loads were chronographed at the same time. Thirteen loads were then selected to be fired for group size at 50 yards after a 2X Bausch & Lomb scope was mounted on the Super Redhawk using the Ruger rings provided. Finally, the Super Redhawk was fired at long range using both iron sights and the 2X Bausch & Lomb scope.

At 25 yards, all loads stayed within 2 inches with a number of loads in the one-inch neighborhood. Since all loads were fired in one day using my aging eyes, I believe the new Redhawk is capable of even better groups than I accomplished. Also, firing for group size, and chronographing at the same time, is not conducive to best accuracy, at least for this shooter. It's somewhat like trying to walk and chew gum at the same time.

The Super Redhawk is a natural for 300-grain cast bullets and a number of loads show excellent accuracy. Using SSK's 310-grain flat-point bullet, cast hard, groups of 1 1/4 inches for five shots were accomplished using 21.5 grains of WW296, or 21.5 grains of H110, or 19.0 grains of #2400 plus all three averaged right at 1,450 fps. Any of these three loads combine accuracy with maximum muzzle energy for the .44 Magnum and still stay within recommended industry working pressures. The most accurate load with the SSK bullet proved to be 18.0 grains of Accurate Arms #9 giving one-inch 25-yard groups and still maintaining plenty of muzzle energy with a muzzle velocity of 1,300-plus fps.

Switching to another favorite heavyweight cast bullet, BRP's 290 grain Keith-style bullet, yielded much the same results as the SSK 310 grainer. Both 22.5 grains of WW296 and 18.5 grains of #2400 yielded groups of one inch at 25 yards and gave muzzle velocities in excess of 1,400 fps.

Both bullets were fired at 50 yards with the scope sighted Super Redhawk, and in spite of very heavy cross

Well-known handgun hunter J.D. Jones used one of his customized .44 Magnum Super Redhawks to take these two African warthogs.

winds, making it difficult to hold steady even on sandbags. Both bullets grouped under 2 inches. The load was 21.5 grains of WW296, which for me has become the standard .44 Magnum loading with 300-grain cast bullets. This load, like all loads tested, should be safe in any .44 Magnum revolver in good working order, but should be worked up to carefully with the shooter watching for any signs of excessive pressure.

Switching to standard weight cast bullets in Big Red II also gave excellent results and a few surprises. Using the standard Keith bullet, Lyman's #429421, cast at 250 grains, velocities exceeded 1,600 fps using either 22.0 grains of #2400 or 26.0 grains of H110. One-inch groups were accomplished with 20.0 grains of #2400 (1,366 fps), 24.0 grains of H110 (1,567 fps), or 26.0 grains of H110 (1,629 fps).

Both heavyweight and standard weight cast bullets were fired at long range using an unscientific, but often-used method — rocks on yonder hill. At a distance of 250 yards, again using the Bausch and Lomb scope sighted Super Redhawk, bullets showed a marked propensity for dropping into the same spot.

The .454 Casull

In 1999, Ruger chambered its biggest and baddest double-action sixgun for the .454 Casull. The Redhawk was surely Ruger's answer to the need for a big double action, so why the Super Redhawk? The Super Redhawk is not even a "bigger" Redhawk or an improved Redhawk; it is simply a stronger and different sixgun. The answer is found within the pages of R.L. Wilson's book, Ruger & His Guns. Trouble had arisen about the time that it had decided to change the Redhawk, so it had the grip and trigger mechanism of the GP-100. Before this could be done, a few Redhawks started blowing the barrel shanks at the threaded portion. To combat this the frame was extended to enclose about 2 1/2 inches of the barrel, which in turn made room for both of the scope rings on the frame rather than on the barrel. Now we know why the Super Redhawk is such a strange looking sixgun!

Then, about the time they decided to change the Redhawk to this configuration, it was discovered that the problem with the Redhawk was not a design flaw or even a weakness, but of all things it was being caused by the lubricant that was being applied to the threads of the Redhawk barrel before it was screwed into the frame. So what to do now? Do you drop a very popular sixgun, the Redhawk, because of a problem that did not exist? Do you forget the new design and stay with the Redhawk? Or do you bring out the new sixgun, the Super Redhawk, and still maintain the Redhawk in the line? Sixgunners everywhere are happy that Ruger chose the latter option.

Chambered in .44 Magnum, the stainless-steel Super Redhawk has indeed proven itself over the past decade to be everything it was claimed to be. It handles the heaviest .44 Magnum loads with ease and is also easy on the shooter with its weight of 4-plus pounds and cushioned grip panels, especially if a scope is added. I don't see any reason to go with the Super Redhawk unless one does plan to use a scope at least some of the time as it looks so strange without one!

SELECTED LOADS FOR THE RUGER SUPER REDHAWK .44 MAGNUM 9 1/2"

BULLET/LOAD	MV	5 SHOTS/25 YARDS
SSK 310 FP/21.5 gr. WW296	1,446	1 1/4"
SSK 310 FP/22.5 gr. WW296	1,498	1 1/2"
SSK 310 FP/21.5 gr. H110	1,442	1 1/4"
SSK 310 PF/22.5 gr. H110	1,515	1 3/4"
SSK 310 FP/18.0 gr. #2400	1,434	1 1/2"
SSK 310 Fp/19.0 gr. #2400	1,466	1 1/4"
SSK 310 FP/18.0 gr. AA#9	1,338	1"
SSK 310 FP/19.0 gr. AA#9	1,385	1 1/2"
BRP 290 KT/21.5 gr. WW296	1,394	1"
BRP 290 KT/19.5 gr. #2400	1,414	1"
BRP 290 KT/19.0 gr. AA#	1,375	2"
Lyman #429421/20.0 gr. #2400	1,366	1"
Lyman #429421/21.0 gr. #2400	1,582	1 1/2"
Lyman #429421/22.0 gr. #2400	1,625	1 1/2"
Lyman #429421/19.0 gr. AA#9	1,423	1 3/4"
Lyman #429421/20.0 gr. AA#9	1,477	1 1/2"
Lyman #429421/21.0 gr. AA#9	1,509	2"
Lyman #429421/24.0 gr. H110	1,567	1"
Lyman #429421/25.0 gr. H110	1,590	1 1/4"
Lyman #429421/26.0 gr. H110	1,629	1"
Speer 240 JHP/24.5 gr. WW296	1,438	1 3/4"
Speer 240 JSP/22.0 gr. #2400	1,461	1 3/4"
Sierra 240 JHC/17.5 gr. Blue Dot	1,501	1 3/8"

Comparing the .454 Casull to a .44 Magnum, which uses a 240-grain bullet at 1,400 fps, we see that the .454 Casull is .45 caliber and its 260-grain bullet has a muzzle velocity of 1,800 fps. To obtain this performance, one has to raise the 35,000-40,000 pressure range of the .44 Magnum up to 60,000 or more. That is very significant additional strain placed on a sixgun frame and cylinder.

The rumors of a .454 Ruger started circulating late in 1997. I was told all about it at the 1998 SHOT Show by someone who said they had the straight skinny on the project. It would be a single-action Bisley Model with a five-shot cylinder plus an auxiliary cylinder for .45 Colt. A single-action Bisley — a five-shooter with an extra cylinder? Sounded good to me. What did we get? A double-action Super Redhawk — a six-shooter with one cylinder. So much for those in the know!

The Super Redhawk, even though it is chambered in .454 Casull, and even though both Freedom Arms and Taurus use five-shot cylinders, is a true sixgun with six cartridge holes in the unfluted cylinder. I know the question will be asked so we will handle it right now. No, the .44 Super Redhawk should not be re-chambered to .454! When I called Ruger and asked what changes were made to accommodate the newer, higher-pressure cartridge, it informed me of two major changes. The steel used in the Super Redhawk .454 is of a higher grade than that used for the .44 Magnum model, and the heat treating is different. Neither of these can be duplicated by any gunsmith that would convert the .44 to .454 and Ruger, of course, will not convert any existing guns to .454.

In some ways, the .454 Super Redhawk looks like a .44 Super Redhawk, but in other ways doesn't. The same lines are there. The same strange profile of the main frame is maintained. But the overall effect is quite different. This is due to the color of the .454. I thought it had been coated with some high-tech finish, but a call revealed that, no, there was no coating, but it was simply the Target Grey finish that occurred when the components were tumbled. Also, the grips are different in that instead of wood-colored inserts, the rubber grips have black, laminated, grip panels. All of this gives a futuristic look.

There are a few other unseen differences. The barrel twist on the .44 Magnum Super Redhawk is 1:20, while the .454 version is slower at 1:24. The slower twist is designed to handle the faster and heavier bullets normally used in the .454. Due to the slightly larger holes found in the cylinder and barrel of the .454 Super Redhawk, the bigger version weighs in at 5 ounces less than the .44 Magnum Model's 57 ounces..

A difference that is easily noticed is the cylinder marking. This sixgun is marked for the use of .454 and .45 Colt ammunition in the same cylinder. Freedom Arms has always cautioned against this in its guns for one simple reason: If you fire a lot of .45 Colt ammunition, a ring will build up in the cylinder just ahead of the case mouth. If this is not cleaned out it makes the insertion of the .454 round difficult in the tight chambers of the Freedom Arms .454. It could also cause pressures to rise dramatically if it prevents the .454 crimp from opening as it should when the gun is fired. If one uses .45 Colt ammunition in the Super Redhawk .454, it would be prudent to scrub the cylinder out routinely.

The Super Redhawk has always been scope-ready and comes with stainless scope rings as standard equipment. These rings mount solidly on the frame using one large screw each and semi-circular recesses on each side of the frame. The rings install easily, and once the scope is zeroed in, it will come back very close when the scope is removed and replaced again. With nothing more than a quarter, 50-cent piece, or similar object, to loosen or tighten the base screws, you have almost instant access to either scope or iron sights. For those few that will use the Super Redhawk without a scope, I will mention again that the standard sights on the .454 Super Redhawk include a red insert front sight that is removable by depressing a plunger at the front of the sight base, thus allowing the use of replacement colored nylon front sights which are available as an option from Ruger. The rear sight is the standard adjustable white outline.

The .454 is a serious cartridge and one that must be approached seriously. I have fired thousands upon thousands of .454 rounds, and the same or more through various .44 Magnum sixguns. I am no stranger to the recoil afforded by the .475 and .500 Linebaugh, as well as the .475 and .500 Linebaugh Longs or Maximums. When I first tested the Super Redhawk in .454, I expected to be spending grueling moments at the shooting bench. I should not have spent any time worrying. The .454 Redhawk is a very easy, comparatively speaking, shooting big bore sixgun! Even so, I did not start at the top but worked my way up. First came heavy-loaded .45 Colt rounds with 300-grain bullets at 1,100 fps, then 340-grain bullets at 1,250, and then, and only then did I progress on to every factory loaded .454 at my disposal as well as a few of my favorite .454 handloads.

All shooting was done with the Burris 4X scope in place in Ruger's factory rings, which added weight and made the .454 Super Redhawk even easier to shoot. Any .454 kicks, but I kept felt recoil to a minimum with the use of Uncle Mike's shooting gloves paired with the rubber cushioned grips of the Super Redhawk. In all of my testing and chronographing over the Oehler Model 35P, absolutely no malfunctions of any kind occurred and all fired cases ejected easily from the Super Redhawk's cylinder.

SELECTED FACTORY LOADS FOR THE SUPER REDHAWK 9 1/2"

LOAD	MV
FACTORY .45 COLT LOADS	
Buffalo Bore HVY .45 Colt 325 LBT	1,403
Buffalo Bore HVY .45 Colt 300 JFN	1,416
Buffalo Bore HVY .45 Colt 260 JHP	1,592
Cor-Bon .45 Colt +P 300 BC	1,310
Cor-Bon .45 Colt +P 265 BC	1,395
FACTORY .454 LOADS	
Buffalo Bore 300 JFN	1,590
Buffalo Bore 325 LBT	1,593
Buffalo Bore 360 LBT	1,400
Cor-Bon 300 JSP	1,632
Cor-Bon 300 BC	1,511
Cor-Bon 320 PN	1,589
Cor-Bon 335 HC	1,569
Cor-Bon 360 PN	1,462
Winchester 260 Partition Gold	1,881
Winchester 300 JFP	1,646

As we have mentioned the Ruger .454 Super Redhawk is recommended for both .45 Colt and .454, so I started first with the .45 Colt handloads that I use mostly in Ruger Blackhawks. That is, 300-grain bullets that are heavier at around 1,200 fps. My normal powder charge for these is 21.5 grains of WW296 or H110. When I set the powder measure it weighed out at 21.2 grains which was fine with me.

My favorite bullets for this application are BRP's 300-grain gas check, LBTs 325-grain WFN (wide flat nose), two of NEIs standard Keith design, a 310- and a 325-grain semi-wadcutter, and finally SSK's really big .45 bullet, a 340-grain flat nose. Groups for five shots at 25 yards ran right at 1 inch for these loads with muzzle velocities from 1,100 to 1,250 fps. For most of us these are the only loads we really need as they will easily take care of critters in the deer, black bear, and wild boar class.

Next came the Heavy Duty .45 Colt factory loads from Buffalo Bore and Cor-Bon. Buffalo Bore's 300 Speer and 325 LBT loads both shot at around 1,330 fps and grouped at 1 1/8 and 5/8 inches, respectively. With Cor-Bon the choice is a 265 Bonded Core, a 300 Bonded Core and 300 Jacketed Soft Point. All of these are around 1,275 fps and grouped at 1 inch or less. Certainly nothing wrong with the way the .454 Super Redhawk shoots with .45 Colt loads, be they factory or home brewed.

Now we move up to the loads that are offered by both Winchester and Cor-Bon For the really big tough stuff, Winchester now offers ammunition with a 260 and 300 JFP that are dead ringers performance wise for the loads that were formerly offered by Freedom Arms. In the Super Redhawk these clock out at 1,745 and 1,544 fps, respectively, and group again at 1 inch or less. My favorite from Winchester for most hunting applications is the 260-grain Partition Gold that clocks out over the Oehler Model 35P at 1,803 (that's right, 1803!) fps.

To help further convince myself that the Super Redhawk really was an easy-shootin' sixgun, I handed it to my shooting friend Ray Walters and asked him to shoot it and tell me what he thought the load was. The Super Redhawk was loaded with six rounds of this Partition Gold 260-grain load. After firing a cylinder full, Walters guessed it was a 240 at 1,400 fps. He was quite surprised to find he was so far off the mark in his guess. It really does shoot easier!

The .480 Ruger

To celebrate the new century, Hornady and Sturm, Ruger have combined to place Bill Ruger's name on a cartridge for the first time. This new cartridge is the .480 Ruger chambered in a six-shot Super Redhawk. To be able to chamber the Super Redhawk in .454 two major changes had to be made. As we have mentioned, a higher grade of steel is used than in the .44 Magnum Super Redhawk, and it is also heat treated differently. This means that a .44 Magnum Super Redhawk cannot be re-chambered to .454, nor to the new .480 Ruger, which follows with these same changes. The .454 and .480 Ruger Super Redhawks are the same size and shape as the .44 Magnum Super Redhawk, however, while the latter is of a typical stainless-steel finish, the other two versions are Target Grey, a finish that occurs when the steel parts of the newer Super Redhawks are tumbled.

The .480 Ruger is offered in 7 1/2- and 9 1/2-inch versions, both stainless steel. Barrel twist is 1 in 18 inches with six grooves and a right-hand twist. They

Ruger's latest big-bore Super Redhawk is chambered in .480 Ruger.

weigh 53 and 58 ounces, respectively. The rear sight is the standard Ruger and is adjustable for both windage and elevation. The front sight features interchangeable inserts.

There is no such thing as a "comfortable-shooting" .44 Magnum or .454 Casull. However, an advertised weight of 58 ounces for the .44 Magnum and the .454 with 9 1/2-inch barrels, the added weight of the scope and rings, and the soft rubber grips place the Super Redhawk at the top of the list of the easiest-shooting big-bore sixguns. This attribute carries over to the new .480 Ruger. Most shooters will find all three chamberings in the easiest-to-shoot category, at least until recoil fatigue sets in during a long shooting session.

All three Ruger Super Redhawks, .44 Magnum, .454 Casull, and .480 Ruger were equipped with Leupold's excellent 2X LER Pistol Scope for testing. This rugged scope is one of the best to be found for handgun hunting with a revolver and offers all the magnification needed to suit the sensible range of a hunting sixgun. With the Leupold 2X in place, my groups with the .480 Ruger and factory ammunition averaged 1 1/2 inches at 25 yards and 2 inches at 50 yards.

Although I have placed these three Super Redhawks in .44 Magnum, .454 Casull, and .480 Ruger, at the top of the list of "easiest shooting" sixguns, it does not mean that they should be approached nonchalantly. They do kick. When I first tested the .44 Magnum Super Redhawk in 1987 I was almost invincible. Well, I was at least at the peak of my ability to both handle recoil and wring the best performance from a big bore sixgun. It was no problem to pound heavy loads down range hour after hour. By the time I got to the .454 Super Redhawk in 1999, the intervening years and thousands of heavy loads had taken their toll and even more so now two years later as I tested the .480 Ruger. What could be done before in matter of a few days now requires several weeks with a lot of recouping time in between. This was really driven home after three weeks of load development for the .480 Ruger when I spent the day with two new small bores, a .32 Magnum and a .32-20. I could literally drive tacks with the .32s. Are they more accurate than the .480? I think not, but rather it is a mental thing and I am not able to block out recoil as I was once able to do. Younger, stronger hands and wrists could probably cut the group sizes of the .480 in half.

What then is the .480 Ruger? Simply put, it is the .475 Linebaugh trimmed approximately 1/8 inch and chambered in the .454 version of the Super Redhawk. The .475 is a wildcat sixgun cartridge invented by John Linebaugh using .45-70 brass trimmed to 1.4 inches and loaded with 370-435 grain .475 bullets. Linebaugh uses the Ruger Bisley Model fitted with new, larger, five-shot cylinders. The .475 Linebaugh has now been legitimized with Buffalo Bore offering factory ammunition and Freedom Arms chambering its Model 83 in .475. As this is written the factory offerings in the .480

Ruger's first big-bore, double-action sixgun, the .44 Magnum Redhawk, top left, compared to Super Redhawk's in .454 (bottom left), .480 (bottom right), and .44 Magnum.

Ruger include Hornady's 325-grain XTP hollow point rated at 1,350 fps, and three hard cast loads from Buffalo Bore, a 370 hard-cast LBT at 1,000 and 1,300 fps, and a 410 LBT at 1,200 fps. By comparison, Buffalo Bore's 420-grain .475 Linebaugh is rated at 1,350 fps. This means the .480 compares to the .475 Linebaugh much as a heavy-loaded .44 Special compares to a .44 Magnum.

Make no mistake about it, a 325-grain bullet at 1,350 fps is a potent offering! This is not a cartridge to be taken lightly. However, some of the hype surrounding it should be taken very lightly. The .480 is a good cartridge and is certainly able to stand on its own merits without trying to make it look to be more than it is by using an apples-to-oranges comparison. I am referring to the myth that has already arisen that ascribes 40 percent-plus more energy to the .480 than the .44 Magnum. This simply is not true when comparing the .480 to serious hunting loads in the .44 Magnum or even the .45 Colt.

When we compare the .480 Ruger to all of the other serious sixgun cartridges used for hunting namely, .45 Colt. .44 Magnum, .454 Casull, and the .475 and .500 Linebaugh, we find that there are seven offerings in .45 Colt and/or .44 Magnum from Buffalo Bore, Cor-Bon and Garrett Cartridges that offer higher muzzle energies than the .480 Ruger when all loads are shot in 9 1/2-inch Super Redhawks.

It was my good pleasure to be part of the group that baptized the .480 Ruger on its maiden voyage into the hunting fields as Hornady hosted several gun writers on the prime pig hunting country of the Nail Ranch, north of Abilene, Texas. All of us used Hornady's .480 factory ammunition and Ruger Super Redhawks equipped with AimPoint red dot scopes. The first day found me teamed up with neighbor and fellow writer Brian Pearce. We spotted some shootable hogs in the afternoon of the first day and while the guide, Claud Clifton, and I went after a pair of hogs below us on the right, Brian pursued a big hog going over the hill on the left. Our pigs literally disappeared into thin air, but we heard a shot, and then another coming from Brian's direction. Claud headed cross country to get to Brian while I went back to get the pickup and meet them. By the time I got around and reached the truck, Claud was coming over the hill with the news that Brian had a pig down and we could drive around to it.

The first shot was around 75 yards and, although it was a good hit, the pig took off running and Pearce, who is an extremely good shot, hit him on the run again at around 100 yards. This time he went down to stay. The pig weighed 170 pounds and neither of the bullets had exited. I decided that if I got a chance at a smaller shootable boar I would take him to see what kind of penetration would result. About half an hour later I took a young boar of 125 pounds. At 50 yards I hit him behind the shoulder, he went about 10 feet and died. The 325-grain XTP-HP had penetrated completely.

The next day found me along for the ride with another friend and fellow writer, Jim Wilson, and his guide, Tim Mariner. It turned out to be one of my most memorable hunting days. While driving along a rim we spotted hogs way down below us. One old spotted boar had his head buried in a cactus plant and was totally oblivious to everything around him. Jim and Tim got out of the truck and as I watched they worked their way to the hog about 150 yards below us. While they were working their way down I had a perfect ringside seat to view what was about to happen. Due to the terrain, Wilson was able to work his way to within 50 feet of the old hog and take him with a head shot. He went down but not out and it took a second shot to finish him off. He weighed in at 190 pounds.

Pearce and I were traveling together and we discussed the trip and the results as we headed back home. Now such a small sample is not the best way to draw

Brian Pearce of *Handloader* magazine was the first to connect with the .480 Ruger on a hog hunt set up by Hornady and Ruger so writers could try out the new combination.

Jim Wilson of *Shooting Times* took this 190-pound hog with Hornady's original factory loading of a 325-grain jacketed hollowpoint at 1,350 fps.

conclusions, but we both agreed that the .480 Ruger had performed exactly as the 250-grain Winchester Medium Velocity .454 Casull on a hog hunt the previous year. I would like to see several other factory offerings from Hornady, including a 325-grain flat point at the same 1,350 fps muzzle velocity and a hard cast 400-grain bullet at 1,100-1,200 fps. The latter, already offered by Buffalo Bore, turns the .480 into a real big-game cartridge, as we shall see in subsequent chapters.

The Super Redhawk is a large sixgun and when scoped is probably easiest to carry in an Uncle Mike's shoulder holster. Even when used with iron sights it is still a lot of sixgun, weighing nearly 4 pounds with a very long barrel. I would not have believed it would be comfortable to carry in any hip holster. Enter C. Rusty Sherrick. Earlier Rusty had built a concealment rig to carry a Cimarron New Thunderer .45 with a 3 1/2-inch barrel. This rig is a modified pancake that rides high and straight and, being made of horsehide, keeps its shape and holds the sixgun securely without the need for retaining devices. For the Ruger Super Redhawk,

SELECTED LOADS FOR THE RUGER SUPER REDHAWK .480 RUGER 9 1/2"

BULLET/LOAD	MV	GROUP/5 SHOTS/25 YDS
Hornady Factory 325 XTP	1,349	1 1/2"
Hornady 325 XTP/25.0 gr. H110	1,337	1 1/2"
Hawk 350/23.0 gr. Lil' Gun	1,344	1 5/8"
Hawk 400/18.0 gr. Lil' Gun	1,195	1 5/8"
Hornady 400/18.0 gr. Lil' Gun	1,191	1 7/8"
Speer 400/18.0 gr. Lil' Gun	1,162	1 5/8"
CPBC 370/17.0 gr. H4227	805	1 5/8"
CPBC 370/18.0 gr. H4227	900	1"
CPBC 370/19.0 gr. H4227	985	1 1/8"
CPBC 390/21.0 gr. H110	1,210	1 5/8"
BRP 395/21.0 gr. H110	1,234	1 5/8"
BRP 395/20.0 gr. H4227	1,060	1 3/8"
CPBC 425/19.0 gr. H110	1,145	1 5/8"
CPBC 425/17.0 gr. H4227	912	1 3/8"
CPBC 425/18.0 gr. H4227	970	1 3/8"
CPBC 425/19.0 gr. H4227	1,005	1 1/4"
BRP 435/18.0 gr. H110	1,118	1 1/8"
BRP 435/19.0 gr. H110	1,178	1 1/2"
BRP 435/17.0 gr. H4227	938	1 1/4"
BRP 435/18.0 gr. H4227	995	1 3/4"
BRP 435/19.0 gr. H4227	1027	1"

Sherrick crafted a very lightweight crossdraw holster of horsehide with a half flap covered with sharkskin. It is a most attractive rig that rides high and comfortable on the waist belt on the off-side.

I welcome the .480 Ruger Super Redhawk (I purchased my test gun), and the .480 Ruger cartridge from Hornady is a reloader's dream. I have now worked up loads with bullets from 325 to 435 grains in weight in both cast and jacketed form and with six different powders. I expect the .480 to find wide acceptance among shooters and also serve to increase the popularity of the Super Redhawk even more. My unsolicited advice to Ruger, I have already mentioned the options I think Hornady should offer, is to chamber the .480 Ruger in the Bisley Model with a five-shot cylinder. Many shooters would like to have the option of packin' the .480 in a more compact sixgun and the Bisley would fit in right nicely.

Consider the double actions from Ruger — the Security-Six, the GP-100, the Redhawk, and the Super Redhawk — the second chapter in Bill Ruger's legacy of fine firearms.

CHAPTER 7

FREEDOM ARMS: SINGLE-ACTION PERFECTION

In the 1920s Elmer Keith discovered the .44 Special and began the experiments that would lead to the .44 Magnum 30 years later. In the early 1950s, Dick Casull began the experiments with the .45 Colt that would lead, also 30 years later, to the .45 Magnum. Early in his sixgunnin' life, Casull found he preferred the .45 Colt chambering in the Colt Single Action. He found, as many others since, that a big bore such as the old .45 was a much better killer on game than the then still relatively new .357 Magnum. In his experiments, Casull played with numerous calibers through the .44 Special and .45 Colt, but always came

The Freedom Arms Model 83 has been offered in four standard barrel lengths — 10, 7 1/2, 6, and 4 3/4 inches, plus a special 3-inch U.S. Marshals Commemorative in .454 only.

back to the .45. The other favorite sixgunner's big bore of the time, the .44 Special, was only available with folded head or balloon-type cases, while Winchester had just brought out solid head cases for the .45 Colt. This resulted in much stronger brass, which would be needed for the experimenting that was ahead.

The Colt Single Action was an excellent handgun then and even today still holds a very soft spot in the heart of many a sixgunner, the author included. But Colt SA cylinders are thin, almost paper thin in .45 Colt chambering. There is little or no margin of safety built in for heavier-than-standard loads as the design goes back to black powder days when pressures were relatively low. The early experiments in pursuit of a more powerful .45 saw Casull bulge many cylinders. The .45 Colt cartridge is a good one, but the walls between the cylinder chambers of the Colt Single Action were just too thin for what he wanted to achieve. Along the way, frame-mounted firing pins were used along with special barrels and heat-treated frames.

It was all to no avail, as cylinders burst and top straps blew. Ignition problems also developed, so primer pockets were reamed to accept rifle primers. This helped some, but not enough. The Casull experiments were far ahead of the powder capability of the time when nothing was yet available to deliver the velocities that Casull was looking for.

The problem was solved, for the time being at least, by going to duplex and triplex loading. The best powder available at the time was Hercules #2400, but it did not ignite satisfactorily. A triplex loading consisting of three Hercules powders Unique, #2400, and Bullseye was developed. The powders were loaded in sequence and were held in place by compression. Winchester's 296 and Hodgdon's H110 had not been developed yet, and its entrance onto the scene removed all need for duplex and triplex loads. All modern .454 loads are assembled without mixing powders.

The goal was to get a 230-grain bullet to a muzzle velocity of 1,800 fps. The brass could do it; the specially loaded ammunition could do it; the guns could not. A conventional six-shot cylinder was just not strong enough to contain the pressures that would be generated. The answer seemed to be a five-shot cylinder that would give greater strength and more metal between chambers. Casull soon saw the need for the extra strength and five-shot cylinders were made as large as possible while still fitting the frame window of the Colt Single Action. Using 4140 steel and five-shot cylinders, muzzle velocities of 1,300 fps were obtained.

By now, Casull still in his early 20s, became interested in heat treating and metallurgy and figured a way to heat treat frames to 40 Rockwell without warping them in the process. This was 1954, and with a Colt Single Action .45 with a special five-shot cylinder, results of 1,550 fps were obtained with 250-grain bullets. This was more than the soon-to-be-unveiled .44 Magnum would deliver. The power was there, but there was little margin of safety. In all of his experimenting, Casull was concerned with two things: ultimate power in a portable package, and the technology to make the guns completely safe. He wanted power plus a large margin of safety.

The .454 breakthrough

Casull started using special barrels from P.O. Ackley using a 1:24 twist rather than the conventional .45 Colt twist of 1:16. Accuracy increased significantly with the change of barrel twist. By 1957, Casull, in pursuit of his goal of power plus safety, decided to build his own single-action frame. Casull was at the point that he could engineer parts as needed, and using 4140 steel for the frame and 4150 steel for the cylinder, the first ".45 Magnum" was created. Casull had progressed from modified Colt Single Actions, to five-shot cylindered Colts, to a custom-built, five-shot single action. The .454 Casull had arrived.

By the early 1970s, the .454 was a catalog item as a production gun and a few magazine writers had the privilege of testing the .454 Casull. A few .454s were built by North American Arms, but it was 1983 before the first factory-produced Freedom Arms .454 Casull was sold to the public. Dick

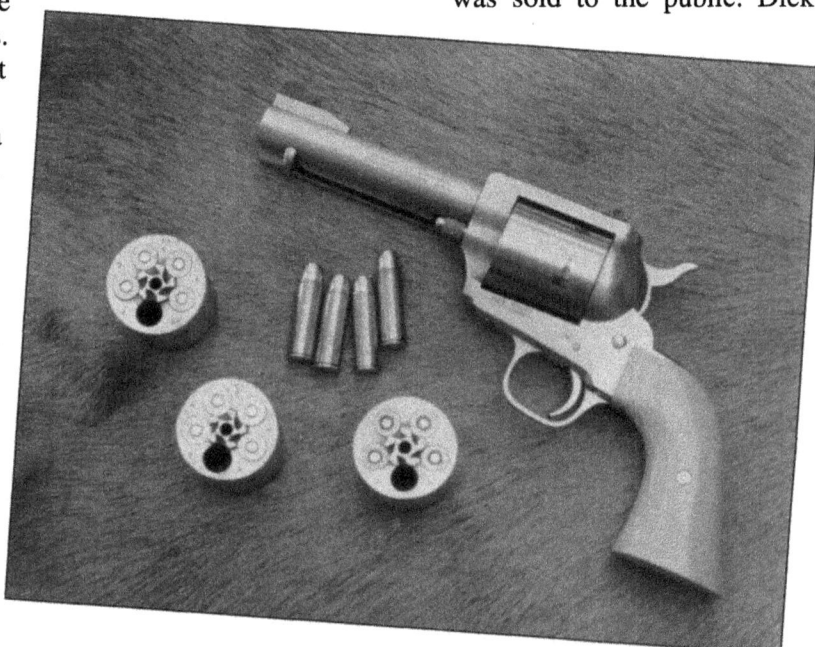

The great versatility of the Freedom Arms .454 packin' pistol with three extra cylinders chambered in .45 Colt, .45 ACP, and .45 WinMag.

Side-by-side size comparison of four great single-action packin' pistols (from top left): Colt New Frontier .45 Colt, Freedom Arms .454, Ruger Old Model .45 Colt Blackhawk, all with 4 3/4-inch barrels compared to the Freedom Arms Model 97 5 1/2-inch .45 Colt.

Casull teamed up with Wayne Baker at that time and the first Freedom Arms .454 was produced in a totally new plant in Freedom in the beautiful Star Valley area in the northwest corner of Wyoming. It is an area that is an outdoorsman's paradise, and also boasts of some of the most beautiful scenery in the world. It is the perfect setting for the building of the .454 Casull.

The Freedom Arms .454 Casull is a traditionally styled, but completely modern single-action revolver. Dick Casull's love and appreciation for the Colt Single Action can immediately be seen in the design of Freedom Arms .454 revolver. It is made of the most modern materials available, but looks and feels much like a traditional single action. One major difference is the five-shot cylinder that allows a lot of steel between the chambers.

The cylinder does not have the "play" that is common to most factory-produced revolvers. The reason is simple. Though they are made in a factory, .454s from Freedom Arms are really custom built. No long assembly lines here. All .454s are carefully, even meticulously, made by employees who care about turning out a quality revolver. Everything about it speaks of tremendous strength, and yet it is only slightly larger than other single-action revolvers.

Most modern single actions have a spring-loaded base pin catch to hold the cylinder pin in place. Ever chase a base pin from a regular single action across the landscape because it let loose under recoil? That cannot happen with the Freedom Arms Model 83 (named for the first year of production by Freedom Arms). A screw is threaded through the base pin and fits into a recess under the barrel. The base pin will not move under recoil. Being a single action, grip frame screws can loosen under recoil. A little Loc-Tite will take care of this. The Freedom Arms Model 83 is also such a precisely made piece of shooting machinery, that it absolutely must be cleaned regularly. There is simply no room for the dirt and crud that some of us allow to build up on the cylinder pin. The cylinder chambers are recessed to accept the case heads of .454 ammunition, so this area must also be kept clean.

The Model 83 grip is not the traditional SA grip that rolls up in the hand on recoil. If it were, it would probably roll right out of the hands with some of the heavy loads that are possible. The grip is much straighter than either the Colt Single Action or Ruger Super Blackhawk. For me it did take some getting used. My hand had been curled around a standard single-action grip almost daily for nearly 30 years before shooting my first Freedom Arms .454. The Freedom Arms .454 grip is an achievement in human engineering. It can actually make felt recoil in the .454 Casull feel less than that of .44 Magnums and heavily loaded .45 Colts in other single-action revolvers with the traditional Colt Single Action Army grip frame. At least for this sixgunner.

The Model 83 loads like the old-style single-action revolvers. Bring the hammer back to half cock, then open the loading gate and rotate the cylinder to either load or unload. Traditional, but also modern, the Model 83 is fitted with a safety bar that is put into operation by drawing the hammer back about 1/8 inch. The hammer is then held away from the frame-mounted firing pin. Since the safety is independent of the trigger, a smooth trigger pull can be had on the Freedom Arms revolver.

Whether being fed hard cast or Freedom Arms jacketed 260-grain bullets at 2,000 fps, or 300 grainers of the same persuasion at 1,700 fps, or even standard .45 Colt loads at 850 fps, the excellent accuracy of the .454 Casull is readily apparent. On one of my trips to the Freedom Arms factory, I was allowed the pleasure of test firing a picked-at-random .454 Model 83. All .454s are test fired before leaving the Freedom Arms plant. With the .454 Casull locked into the specially designed rest, I carefully placed the big revolver and its carrier forward, shot and returned it back into battery for each shot. The target came back from its abiding place 35 yards down range. The result? One ragged hole made with five shots. That speaks highly of the precision that is built into the Freedom Arms .454 Casull Premier Grade Revolver.

Premier Grade Casulls are available in the original .454 Casull chambering plus five others that we will discuss shortly. Standard barrel lengths for the Premier Grade Freedom Arms revolver are 4 3/4, 6, 7 1/2, and 10 inches. The shooter has the option of choosing either fixed or adjustable sights in all calibers and other barrel lengths are available on special order.

Just how powerful is the .454 Casull? I found out the first time I met with Dick Casull himself at the first Shootists Holiday in 1986. We met in Wyoming as I was spending time at the Freedom Arms plant going through the facilities, meeting the staff, and shooting various .454s. We were spending the afternoon running some of Dicks special-purpose loads through his 12-inch octagon-barreled personal .454 Freedom Arms Single Action. He had claimed 2,350 fps from this gun with his own 260-grain cast gas checked bullet over a stiff charge of WW296 ignited by Remington Bench Rest Rifle Primers. A 260-grain bullet at 2,350 fps would actually deliver a muzzle energy of 3,188 lbs.-ft. That would be 14 percent MORE muzzle energy than that generated by a .30/06 rifle using a 150-grain bullet. And this from a straight-walled pistol cartridge in a revolver with a 12-inch barrel!

I nervously nestled the .454 over sandbags, aiming through the skyscreens of my Oehler Model 33 Chronograph. The five shots averaged 2,346 fps! No wonder this load would shoot through 3/8-inch steel (as Dick had earlier demonstrated). After trying this load, Casull brought out his really big load, a 400-grain cast bullet at 1,600 fps. Compare this with the factory loaded .45/70 405-grain bullet that travels 1,300 fps from a 32-inch rifle barrel. Recoil from this load proved that I had some real power in my hand and the clock substantiated the claim: 1,606 fps.

Now both of these were, as mentioned, special loads for demonstration purposes. Factory ammunition is available from Buffalo Bore, Cor-Bon, and Winchester with both hard cast and jacketed designs in weights from 250 up to 360 grains for the Freedom Arms .454

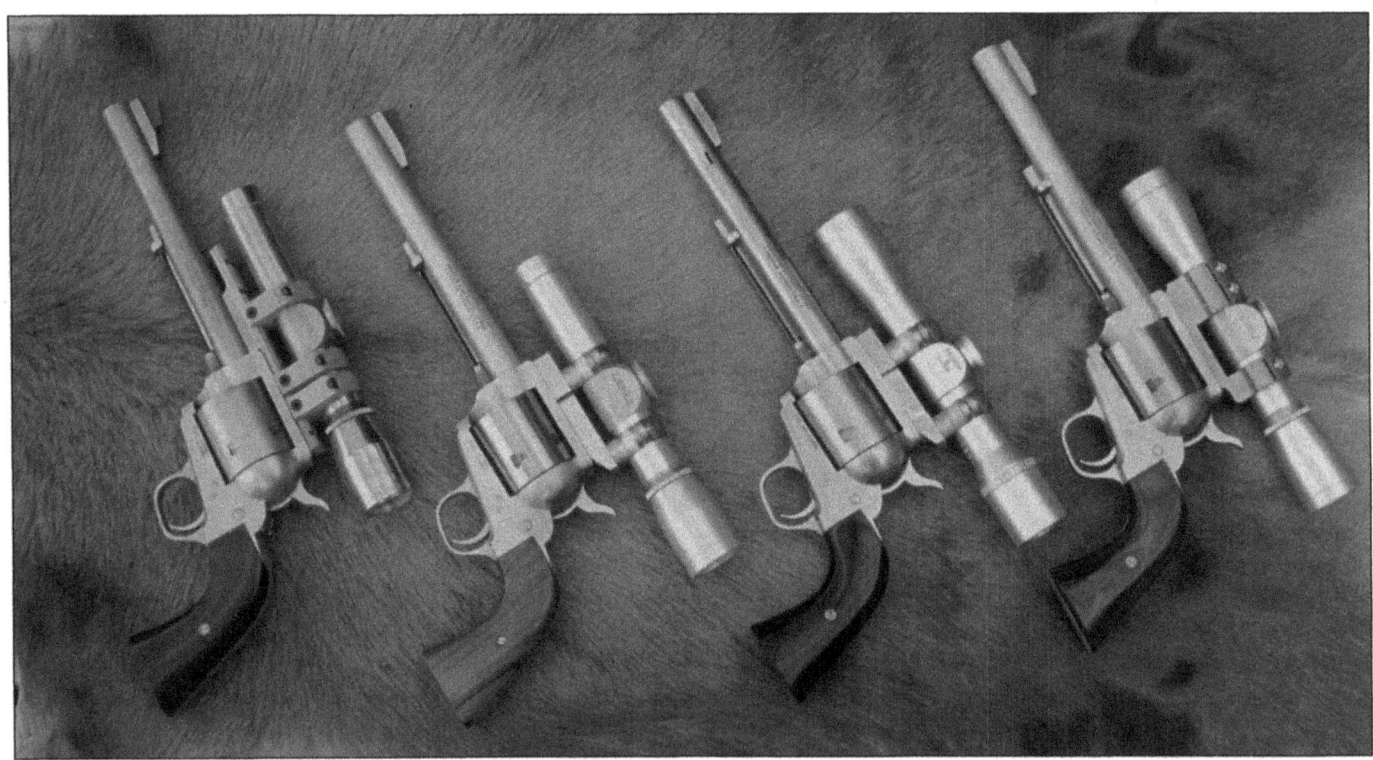

Chambered in .357 Magnum, .44 Magnum, .454 Casull, and .50AE, these 7 1/2-inch scoped Model 83s, when matched gun to game, can be used to take anything that walks.

Bob Baker, president of Freedom Arms, tests his products in the field. This Wyoming moose was taken with the .454 Casull.

Casull. Although all of Casull's early experiments were with standard .45 Colt brass, .454 brass is longer to preclude its use in .45 Colt sixguns. A cartridge developing up to 60,000 psi could be disastrous in a sixgun made to handle 15,000 psi. Jacketed bullets for the .454 are assembled with a heavy 1/32-inch jacket to both withstand the pressures generated by the .454 Casull and afford the deepest possible penetration on large game. Standard .45 Colt jacketed bullets have jackets that are too thin to handle the pressures of full-house loads in the .454.

The advent of the .454 gave sixgunners a revolver that not only rivals the single-shots in both muzzle energy and accuracy, it does it five times, not once. The Freedom Arms .454 Model 83 is the first revolver to offer both rifle-type energy and rifle-type accuracy to the handgun hunter. While the .44 Magnum has less energy than a .30-30 at 100 yards, the .454 Casull can be loaded above the muzzle energy of one of the most popular hunting rifle calibers, the .30-06. That makes the .454 a first-class hunting handgun by anyone's definition.

All this makes the Freedom Arms Model 83 .454, a true mouse-to-moose handgun with the accuracy to take the smallest game and the power to down the largest. It has been used successfully on Alaskan brown bear, African lion, Cape buffalo, and the largest of the game animals, the African elephant. Several .454 users have taken all the African "big five" with a Freedom Arms revolver. In addition, it has been used on all American game from pronghorn to mulies to whitetail to black bear to elk with complete success.

With the adjustable-sighted Freedom Arms Model 83 single-action revolver, there are a number of sight options. In addition to the standard sights consisting of adjustable rear and ramp front sight, various ramp front sight heights are available in both plain black and with orange inserts. The front sights fit into a slot on the ramp base and are easily interchangeable by loosening a socket-head screw at the front of the base itself. With four sight heights available, any adjustable sighted Freedom Arms .454 revolver can be sighted in with any load/bullet weight combination from 185-grain target loads to full-house 340-grain hunting handloads without having to raise the rear sight excessively.

Also available, and especially popular with hunters, are express sights. Consisting of a shallow V-notch rear and brass bead front, express sights are very fast for game shooting, and the front sights are also available in various heights for precision sighting in of each revolver and load combination. For competition use, especially for silhouetting, Freedom Arms revolvers can be equipped with Bo-Mar Silhouette Sights. These are the finest long-range iron sights ever made available for a revolver and consist of a Bo-Mar rear with very fine, positive clicks and a sharply undercut Patridge front sight designed to prevent glare and give the precise sight picture so necessary for long-range silhouetting.

Many would have us believe scopes do not belong on handguns. I disagree. The .454 is one revolver that will definitely outshoot its iron sights and thus is designed to be easily fitted with a scope. Many big-game hunters prefer scopes, not so much to stretch the range but rather to allow as little sighting error as possible. Due to the recoil that is involved with any large-bore, Magnum handgun, the Freedom Arms .454 requires a special scope mount base, and Freedom Arms can supply the extremely strong SSK T'SOB Scope Mount Base with three rings for extra holding power. For those who prefer a more compact scope mount base, stainless-steel bases are available that fit the rear sight channel. Freedom Arms is the only revolver that is designed so the scope mount base is in, as well as on, the revolver. This is accomplished by a projection on the bottom of the scope base that fits into the rear sight channel on the top strap. This provides for a very strong mounting system.

Standard barrel lengths of 4 3/4, 6, 7 1/2 or 10 inches are cataloged, with 7 1/2 inches being the most popular for hunting. Many hunters have gone to the 4 3/4-inch Freedom Arms revolver as a true back-up gun simply because it has the power that can be delivered immediately in a touchy situation. The range at which game can be taken and the type of game to be taken with the .454 will be limited only by the hunter's ability and desires. The .454 will deliver.

The original .454 from Freedom Arms is known as the Premier Grade. For those that want a less-expensive, no-frills sixgun, Freedom Arms offers the Field Grade. To bring the price down, Freedom Arms did three things, none of which sacrifices quality in any way. Instead of the highly polished finish found on the Premier Grade, The Field Grade carries a bead-blasted finish that eliminates many hours of careful polishing, which in turn cuts the cost significantly. All Premier Grade .454s are furnished with a special laminated grip that is meticulously fitted to the frame. This takes time and costs money. The Field Grade version is furnished with bolt-on Pachmayr grips, providing another cut in the total cost. The last change is the rear sight. A special base adapter is fitted to the frame to accept Ruger rear sights. Add them all up and the total savings is significant — several hundred dollars.

Barrel/cylinder gaps are held under .002 inch, and Field Grade Casulls have the same tightly chambered cylinders that are standard on Premier .454s. The same barrel stock is used, and all internal parts are the same. The only difference is the finish, the grip, the rear sight, and the price. All Field Grade .454s are fitted with Pachmayr grips but, black micarta grips are an option that can be fitted. They look extremely attractive when

Lynn Thompson of Cold Steel has hunted Africa extensively with the Freedom Arms .454, which took this Cape buffalo.

mated with the subdued bead-blasted finish of the stainless steel .454. Field Grade .454s can also be ordered with a custom action job and a trigger pull set at slightly over 3 pounds. Most shooters will want this desirable option. A third option available to customize the Field Grade to each individual shooter is a choice of sights. The Field Grade can be fitted with standard Premier sights, Bo-Mar Silhouette sights, Express sights with a V-notch rear and a gold bead front or, for those who want the ultimate in a hunting handgun, scope mounts.

One of my favorite hunting sixguns is a 7 1/2-inch Field Grade .454 Model 83. I went with the option of the black Micarta grips, regular sights, and an action job and it now wears a scope on a T'SOB mount. This is the sixgun I picked for my African hunt, as the Field Grade is about as close as one can get to perfection in an outdoorsman's revolver. It performs exactly the same as its more expensive counterpart, the Premier Grade. With the right load, groups will run 1 inch or less at 25 yards and long-range accuracy is excellent. This is one revolver that will definitely outshoot the iron sights it comes equipped with.

My first Freedom Arms .454 was a 10-inch model. It has had thousands upon thousands of heavy loads through it and is still as tight as the day it left Freedom, Wyoming, in 1986. At the other end of the spectrum is my do-everything Freedom Arms .454. Fitted with ivory Micarta grips, this 4 3/4-inch packin' pistol has three extra cylinders chambered in .45 Colt, .45 ACP, and .45 Winchester Magnum. It will go anywhere, do anything.

It is not always necessary, certainly not always pleasurable, to run the .454 at full throttle. The following loads are both comfortable enough to shoot all day and also give excellent accuracy. Groups are five shots at 25 yards.

SELECTED LOADS FOR THE FREEDOM ARMS .454 7 1/2" MODEL 83

BULLET: LYMAN #454628 260 GRAIN CAST GAS CHECK

LOAD	MV-4 3/4"	MV-7 1/2"	MV-10"
32.0 gr. H110	1,572	1,699	1,761
33.0 gr. H110	1,606	1,727	1,780
34.0 gr. H110	1,657	1,792	1,856
35.0 gr. H110	1,712	1841	1,888
36.0 gr. H110	1,801	1,926	1,986

BULLET: LYMAN #454629 300-GRAIN CAST GAS CHECK

LOAD	MV-4 3/4"	MV-7 1/2"	MV-10"
30.0 gr. H110	1,449	1,558	1,598
31.0 gr. H110	1,506	1,627	1,661
32.0 gr. H110	1,586	1,705	1,749
33.0 gr. H110	1,648	1,772	1,799

BULLET: SSK 340-GRAIN FLAT-NOSE

LOAD	MV-4 3/4"	MV-7 1/2"	MV-10"
28.0 gr. H110	1,435	1,585	1,610
29.0 gr. H110	1,468	1,631	1,656
30.0 gr. H110	1,513	1,672	1,706
31.0 gr. H110	1,591	1,758	1,776

BULLET: FREEDOM ARMS 260-GRAIN JACKETED SOFT POINT

LOAD	MV-4 3/4"	MV-7 1/2"	MV-10"
29.0 gr. H4227	1,322	1,430	1,510
30.0 gr. H4227	1,390	1,488	1,508
31.0 gr. H4227	1,442	1,548	1,556
32.0 gr. H4227	1,485	1,577	1,631
32.0 gr. H110	1,427	1,526	1,557
33.0 gr. H110	1,471	1,573	1,597
34.0 gr. H110	1,503	1,606	1,675

BULLET: FREEDOM ARMS 300-GRAIN JACKETED FLAT POINT

LOAD	MV-4 3/4"	MV-7 1/2"	MV-10"
27.0 gr. H4227	1,218	1,344	1,397
28.0 gr. H4227	1,305	1,406	1,475
29.0 gr. H4227	1,348	1,473	1,491
28.0 gr. H110	1,351	1,412	1,478
29.0 gr. H110	1,383	1469	1,494
30.0 gr. H110	1,450	1,529	1,570
31.0 gr. H110	1,559	1,631	1,674
32.0 gr. H110	1,628	1,717	1,743

PLEASURE LOADS FOR THE .454 FA M83 .454 7 1/2"/OREGON TRAIL 300FP

LOAD	MV	GROUP
8.0 gr. WW231	971	1 1/2"
9.0 gr. WW231	1,071	1 1/4"
10.0 gr. WW231	1,114	1 1/2"
7.0 gr. WW452AA	905	1 1/2"
8.0 gr. WW452AA	965	1 1/4"
9.0 gr. WW452AA	1,010	1 1/4"
7.0 gr. Bullseye	906	1 5/8"
8.0 gr. Bullseye	1,007	1 5/8"
9.0 gr. Unique	1,068	1"
10.0 gr. Unique	1,141	1 1/2"
10.0 gr. Herco	1,082	1 1/8"
10.0 gr. HS6	934	1 1/4"
13.0 gr. AA#7	1,043	1 5/8"
14.0 gr. AA#7	1,098	1 1/4"
10.0 gr. AA#5	957	1 1/2"

The .44 Magnum

For many hunters, the .44 Magnum is more than adequate for their needs. It is my number one choice for taking whitetails, as I do not need the power of the .454 for this duty. Many shooters are also already set up to reload and cast bullets for the .44 Magnum and hesitate to add more reloading dies, bullet moulds, etc. These same shooters, however, are willing to invest in a quality .44 Magnum such as the Freedom Arms Model 83 .44 Magnum.

The .44 Magnum from Freedom Arms is a five-shooter just as the Model 83 .454 and all subsequent Model 83s. No shortcuts are taken simply because the chambering is different and the pressure levels are lower. The .44 Magnum is made with the same exacting care that is used in its bigger brother, including line-boring the cylinder. This means reaming the cylinder chambers after the cylinder has been fitted to the frame and locked up under the same torque that is present when the revolver is fired. This results in a near-perfect barrel/cylinder/frame alignment.

The Freedom Arms .454 is the strongest handgun made and will handle loads far above conventional revolvers. The .44 Magnum is made of the same material, strength, and quality, and an extra added bonus to .44 Magnum shooters is the fact that .44 Magnum loads in the .44 Freedom Arms revolver seem much lighter in recoil than they do in most other sixguns. I should say they feel lighter to me, as felt recoil is highly subjective. However, for my hands the Freedom Arms handles felt recoil better than any other single-action grip except the Bisley Model Ruger.

With full-house .44 Magnum loads, the .44 Model 83 is much more pleasant to shoot than the full-house .454s and this is also a drawing card for many shooters who simply do not need the power that is possible with the .454 Casull. The Freedom Arms .44 Magnum, being as strong as the .454, is handicapped only by the capacity of the .44 Magnum brass itself. Handloaders will run out of case long before they even begin to approach the pressures that the Model 83 .44 Magnum is engineered to handle.

The Model 83 Freedom Arms Premier Grade .44 Magnum is available with either adjustable sights or fixed sights in barrel lengths of 4 3/4, 6, 7 1/2, and 10 inches. All custom options, such as custom grips, tuned action, scope mounts, etc., that are available on the .454 are also available on the .44 Magnum. It is also offered in the less-expensive Field Grade finish.

I have mentioned that the .44 Magnum is my number one choice for hunting whitetail deer. The revolver of choice is a 7 1/2-inch Model 83 .44 Magnum with a 2X Leupold scope and always loaded with Black Hills 240 jacketed hollow points. I have never varied from this ammunition choice as it has been such a stellar performer, taking more than two dozen whitetails in a row, many of them trophy bucks, with one-shot kills. The accuracy of the Model 83 .44 combined with the excellent performance of the Black Hills ammunition is all one could ask for.

When the .44 Magnum first became available from Freedom Arms, I had a 10-inch version set up with Bo-Mar sights for silhouetting. It performed remarkably well. Silhouetting has since disappeared in my area so it has simply become a favorite long-range revolver along with 10 1/2-inch Rugers in .357 Maximum and .44 Magnum. Strangely enough, and even though I have a definite affinity for packin' pistols I have never added a 4 3/4-inch Freedom Arms Model 83 .44 Magnum to my shooting battery. However, a 6-inch version with iron sights rides easily in a shoulder holster when the going is tough, such as pursuing mountain lions uphill in deep snow.

SELECTED LOADS FOR THE MODEL 83 FREEDOM ARMS .44 MAGNUM 10"

BULLET	LOAD	MV
Hornady 240 JHP	22.0 gr. #2400	1,578
	25.0 gr. WW296	1,557
Sierra 240 JHC	22.0 gr. #2400	1,601
	25.0 gr. WW296	1,594
Speer 240 JHP	22.0 gr. #2400	1,595
	25.0 gr. WW296	1,603
Lyman #431244GC	23.0 gr. #2400	1,750
	25.0 gr. W296	1,630
BRP 260 KT	23.0 gr. #2400	1,726
(260 gr. GC)	25.0 gr. WW296	1,595
BRP 290 KT	20.0 gr. #2400	1,504
(290 gr GC)	22.5 gr. WW296	1,483
SSK 340 FP	18.5 gr. WW296	1,285
(345 gr.)	19.5 gr. WW296	1,366

The .50 Action Express

The .50 Action Express was originally chambered in the Desert Eagle semi-automatic. It did not, however, take long for sixgunners to discover that the big .50 would make a pretty fair sixgun round. Hamilton Bowen regularly re-barrels Ruger Redhawks and Super Blackhawks to .50 caliber and fits them with five-shot cylinders of his own manufacture for the .50 Action Express. Factory .50 AE ammunition is available from Speer in a 300-grain jacketed hollowpoint and from IMI in both a 325-grain softpoint and hollowpoint. Velocities are around 1,300 fps from a 7 1/2-inch barrel.

Freedom Arms also chambers the Model 83 revolver in .50 Action Express and loads can be tailored specifically for the big Freedom Arms five-gun. With the 300-grain Speer jacketed hollowpoint, the .50 AE Freedom Arms will easily deliver muzzle velocities of 1,500 fps, and switching to the 385 grain LBT bullet, which is available from BRP, I have approached 1,600 fps. Recoil, as one might expect, is heavy to say the least. Needless to say, such loads are ONLY for the .50 AE Freedom Arms revolver.

Bullets designed for the .500 Linebaugh may not be used with the .50 Action Express as the Linebaugh takes bullets of .511-inch diameter, while the Action Express uses bullets that are a true .500-inch diameter. Keeping bullets in the rimless case with headspaces on the case mouth can be a real problem. Without a heavy crimp, I find that even with a scope mounted for extra weight, bullets start moving forward under recoil with the first shot and the fourth round will move significantly forward, though not enough to protrude through the front of the cylinder and tie up the gun. Since .50 AE brass is slightly tapered, one may be able to experiment with crimping the cases and not lose headspacing.

Speer offers a 325-grain Gold Dot jacketed hollowpoint and RCBS has a mold that drops a 340-grain flat-nosed bullet for use in the Freedom Arms Model 83 .50 Action Express. Either bullet is fine for hunting anything in North America short of the big bears. My most-used bullet for the .50 Action Express in the Freedom Arms sixgun is the BRP 385-grain flat-nosed LBT hard cast.

The .357 Magnum

The .454 is a heavy recoiling sixgun and everyone does not want that much recoil, nor do they need that much power. A natural part of the evolution of the Freedom Arms revolver then seemed to be the .44 Magnum with sales aimed at silhouetters and hunters who needed no more than the .44 could deliver.

SELECTED LOADS FOR THE FREEDOM ARMS MODEL 83 .50 AE 7 1/2"

BULLET	LOAD	MV
Speer 325 GDHP	26.0 gr. AA#9	1,330
	21.0 gr. Blue Dot	1,494
	34.0 gr. WW296	1,457
	26.0 gr. #2400	1,335
	31.0 gr. H4227	1,356
BRP 385 LBT	29.0 gr. H4227	1,327
	32.5 gr. H110	1,457
	26.0 gr. AA#9	1,372

The Freedom Arms Model 97 is available with fixed or adjustable sights and can be special ordered with an octagon barrel.

The Freedom Arms .357 Magnum is another great sixgun from Star Valley. The Silhouette Model has a 9-inch barrel instead of the 10-inch barrels available on the .454 and .44 Magnum as it will not make the 4-pound competition weight limit with a longer barrel. It handles all .38 Special and .357 Magnum brass loadings, as well as heavy-duty .357 loadings with heavyweight bullets.

The .357 Magnum is a standard Freedom Arms revolver that is built the same as the .454 and .44 Magnum, with the emphasis on precision and quality. With the .357 Magnum chambering in the Model 83, amazing things happen. We are talking 160-grain bullets at 1,750 fps, 180-grain bullets at 1,650 fps, and 200-grain bullets at 1,500 fps. To put that into perspective, look at some standard .357 Magnum loadings. These same jacketed bullets custom loaded for my pet 8 3/8-inch .357 Magnum, the original .357 from Smith & Wesson, will safely do 1,350, 1,250, and 1,050 fps, respectively. That is a dramatic difference to say the least.

It becomes even more dramatic when one compares the performance of the .357 Maximum/SuperMag with the possibilities in the Model 83 .357 Magnum. Remember, Maximum brass is .300-inch longer than standard .357 Magnum brass. The same bullets outlined for the Freedom Arms .357 Model 83 and .357 Magnum, max out at 1,500, 1,350, and 1,250 fps, respectively, in my 8-inch Dan Wesson .357 SuperMag. A look at the chart with muzzle velocities and muzzle energies puts all of this into proper perspective.

The 9-inch .357 Silhouette Model

I originally had a standard production Model 83 .357 Silhouette Model with a 9-inch barrel, standard impregnated hardwood grips, and Iron Sight Gun Works rear sight and sharply undercut black Patridge front sight for testing. The factory-produced .357 Model 83 has a groove diameter of .357 and 1:14 twist barrel, which is designed to stabilize the heavier 180-grain and 200-grain .357 bullets used for silhouetting and hunting. The argument continues over whether or not the .357 Magnum is a big game hunting handgun. For the first time we have a .357 Magnum that will utilize Hornady 158-grain XTPs at 1,750 fps and both 180-grain XTPs and Cor-Bons, will do 1,600-plus fps. Bob Baker, president of Freedom Arms, took the first game with the 357 Model 83, a black buck antelope on the YO Ranch with a 180 Cor-Bon at 1,600 fps. I followed with two Corsican rams, both of which dropped on the spot.

BULLET	.357 MAGNUM MV	ME	.357 SUPER MAG MV	ME	.357 FA M83 MV	ME
160 GR.	1,350	646	1,500	800	1,750	1,088
180 GR.	1,250	625	1,350	727	1,650	1,087
200 GR.	1,050	490	1,250	694	1,500	1,000

FIREARM: FREEDOM ARMS M83 .357 MAGNUM: 9"
CHRONOGRAPH: OEHLER MODEL 35P

FACTORY LOAD	MV	IRON SIGHTS 25 YARDS	4X LEUPOLD 50 YARDS
CCI LAWMAN 140 JHP	1,518	1 1/8"	1 1/8"
BLACK HILLS 158 JHP	1,374	1"	1 5/8"
FEDERAL 158 JSP	1,451	1 1/8"	1 1/4"
HORNADY 158 XTP-HP	1,386	1"	7/8"
HORNADY 158 XTP-FP	1,414	1 1/4"	1 1/8"
WINCHESTER 158 JSP	1,480	1"	3/4"

The 357 Model 83 can be loaded far above the performance of any other .357 Magnum or .357 Maximum/SuperMag revolver. But that is not its only claim to fame. It makes a superb .357 Magnum when used with standard loads and I suspect there are a lot of .357 Magnum shooters out there that want exactly that. Six factory jacketed bullet loads were tried in the standard Silhouette Model 83, and the results were an average, not the best mind you, but an average 25-yard five-shot group of 1.08 inch and an average 50-yard five-shot group of 1.25 inches. Those figures are miles above average for .357 Magnum revolvers and a direct result of the precision fit of the Freedom Arms revolvers.

Switching to handloads for that first 357 Model 83, I concentrated on super high-performance loads. All loads were assembled with Federal .357 Magnum brass and Remington #7 1/2 Benchrest Small Rifle primers. I cannot emphasize enough that these are heavy .357 loads and MUST NOT be used in any other firearm chambered for the .357 Magnum! It is impossible to damage the Model 83 .357 Magnum using these loads, but brass life will be very short, beginning with enlarged primer pockets. For best results these heavy loads should be assembled in brand-new brass only. This is one instance in which the brass is operating at maximum levels, not the revolver. In the following chart, 25-yard five-shot groups are with iron sights, 50-yard groups are with a 4X Leupold scope.

Cast bullet shooting in the 357 Model 83, as opposed to their use in the .357 Magnum or .357 Maximum/SuperMag, becomes a whole new field of experimentation. Cast bullets that perform well at 1,400 fps may or may not perform well when driven at the velocities possible with the Freedom Arms five-gun. I have run into the same situation when using some .45 Colt bullets in the .454. When the muzzle velocities exceed a certain level, accuracy disappears. My theory is that the bearing surface has to be just right or the bullets skid or strip on the rifling when driven at high speeds.

My old standard .357 Magnum loading consisting of the Lyman #358156GC over 15.0 grains of #2400 picks up considerable velocity over other long-barreled .357 Magnums. It exits the barrel of the .357 Model 83 at 1,641 fps and shoots very accurately with 1 1/4-inch groups at 25 yards and 1 1/2-inch groups at 50 yards. If I never used any other load, this load combination would make the Model 83 .357 Magnum a prized possession.

Switching over to 180-grain cast gas-checked bullets in the Model 83, I tried both the RCBS 38-180 FN and the BRP 180 grain gas check. Again, these loads are for use in the .357 Model 83 only!

SELECTED LOADS FOR THE FREEDOM ARMS MODEL 83 .357 MAGNUM 9"
JACKETED BULLET HANDLOADS

LOAD		MV	25 YARDS	50 YARDS
HORNADY 158 XTP-HP	21.0 gr. H110	1,753	1 1/4"	1 3/4"
	18.0 gr. AA#9	1,723	1 1/8"	2"
	18.0 gr. #2400	1,716	7/8"	1 5/8"
HORNADY 160 JTC-SIL	19.0 gr. AA#9	1,748	1 1/8"	1 3/4"
	20.0 gr. WW296	1,721	1 1/2"	1 3/4"
SPEER 180 FMJ	18.0 gr. AA#9	1,649	1"	1 1/4"
	20.0 gr. WW296	1,655	1 3/8"	1 5/8"
	17.0 gr. #2400	1,559	7/8"	1 3/8"
SPEER 200 FMJ	16.0 gr. AA#9	1,457	7/8"	1 3/4"
	18.0 gr. WW296	1,500	1 3/8"	1 1/2"
SPEER 180 SP	17.0 gr. AA#9	1,570	7/8"	7/8"
SIERRA 200 RN	17.0 gr. AA#9	1,522	1 1/4"	1 1/8"

SELECTED LOADS FOR THE FREEDOM ARMS MODEL 83 .357 MAGNUM 9"
JACKETED BULLET HANDLOADS

BULLET	LOAD	MV	5 SHOTS @ 25 YARDS
BRP 180 SWCGC	15.0 gr. AA#9	1,568	1 1/4"
	18.0 gr. AA#9	1,791	1"
	15.0 gr. H110	1,422	1 3/8"
	16.0 gr. H110	1,554	1 1/4"
	18.0 gr. H110	1,680	1 1/8"
	13.0 gr. #2400	1,436	1 1/4"
	14.0 gr. #2400	1,482	1"
	15.0 gr. #2400	1,607	1 1/8"
RCBS #38-180FNGC	15.0 gr. H110	1,402	5/8"
	16.0 gr. H110	1,550	1 1/8"
	13.0 gr. #2400	1,413	7/8"
	14.0 gr. #2400	1,458	1 1/8"
	15.0 gr. #2400	1,574	1 1/8"

The .41 Magnum

The .357 Magnum itself is rapidly approaching its 70th birthday and still remains the most popular of all of the Magnums; the .357 Magnum in the Model 83 opens a whole new chapter on the original Magnum.

The original chambering of the Freedom Arms Model 83 five-shot revolver was in .454 Casull, and it was later joined by the .44 Magnum, .357 Magnum, and .50 Action Express. It only seemed natural that the .41 Magnum be included in this lineup. Many have requested the .41 chambering, but it took a nudge from the Freedom Arms Collectors Association to accomplish it. If you are a fan of Freedom Arms revolvers, the Freedom Arms Collectors Association (FACA) may be of great interest. The *Five Shot Journal*, official publication of FACA, carries information on the history of Freedom Arms revolvers, interviews with key factory people, and field tests of various models. The first special offering through FACA for members was a specially marked and serial numbered Freedom Arms Model 83 .41 Magnum with the choice of a 7 1/2- or 10-inch barrel.

The first factory test gun in .41 Magnum from Freedom Arms was a 10-inch Model 83 fitted with black micarta grips and a Redfield variable LER Pistol Scope on an SSK T'SOB mount. As I discussed the .41 Magnum project with Bob Baker of Freedom Arms, I emphasized the fact that most factory .41 Magnums will not handle heavy bullets. That is, they simply will not shoot

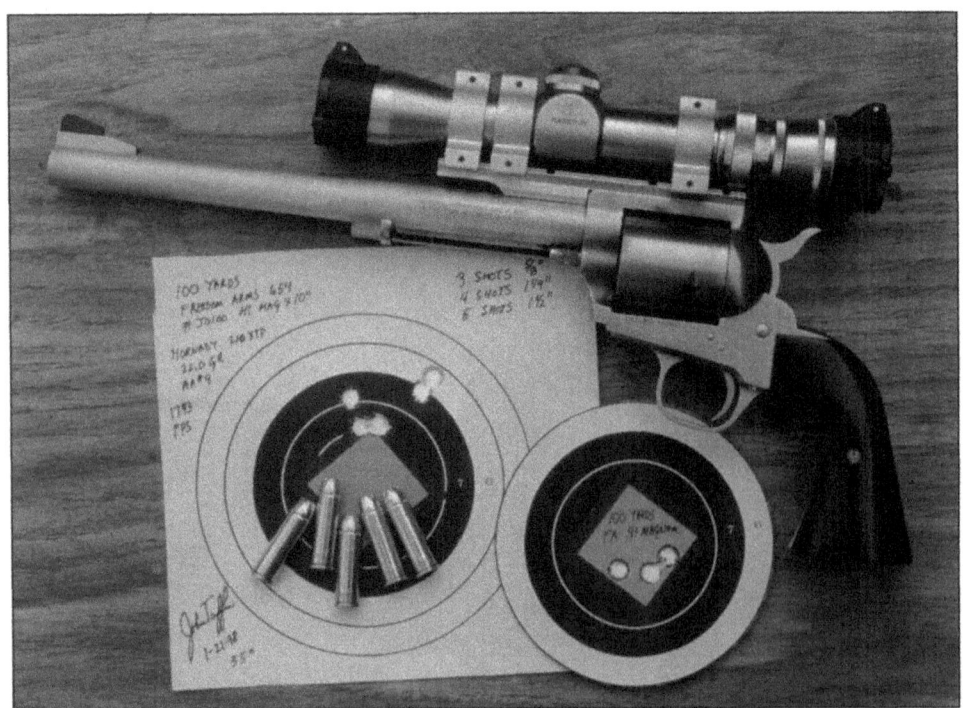

The Freedom Arms .41 Magnum could well be the most accurate .41 Magnum ever made. These groups were shot at 100 yards.

Big-Bore Handguns 145

Two of the greatest big-bore sixguns ever made, both .44 Magnums, arrived in the 1950s: Ruger's Super Blackhawk, 1959 (left), and Smith & Wesson's .44 Magnum. Both have been stocked by BearHug.

The latest big-bore cartridge chambering is the .480 Ruger. Here shown in Ruger's Super Redhawk, Taurus's Raging Bull, and the Model 83 .475 Linebaugh from Freedom Arms with an extra cylinder chambered in the .480.

For long-range shooting with a handgun it is difficult to beat the two single-shot offerings of Thompson/Center. The Encore (top) will handle rifle cartridges normally found in bolt-action rifles; while the Contender, bottom, handles most sixgun and lever gun cartridges.

Whoever said 1911s won't shoot have never handled a Kimber. This target was shot with Cor-Bon's 165 PowRBall through a lightweight Kimber .45 ACP.

The 1911 .45 ACP has been the most popular semi-automatic for more than 90 years. These examples (from top left) are an original Commercial Model Colt from 1914, a highly customized Combat Commander by Clark Custom Guns, a standard Colt Commander with Ed Brown grip safety, and a Series '70 engraved by Ed DeLorge with ivories by Bob Leskovec.

The epitome of the gunmaker's art is exhibited in the two Old Model Rugers. The top sixgun is a .41 Special by Hamilton Bowen, with stocks by BluMagnum. The bottom sixgun, a .45 Colt, has been re-worked to resemble the Colt New Frontier with grips of buffalo bone. The builder of this sixgun prefers to remain anonymous.

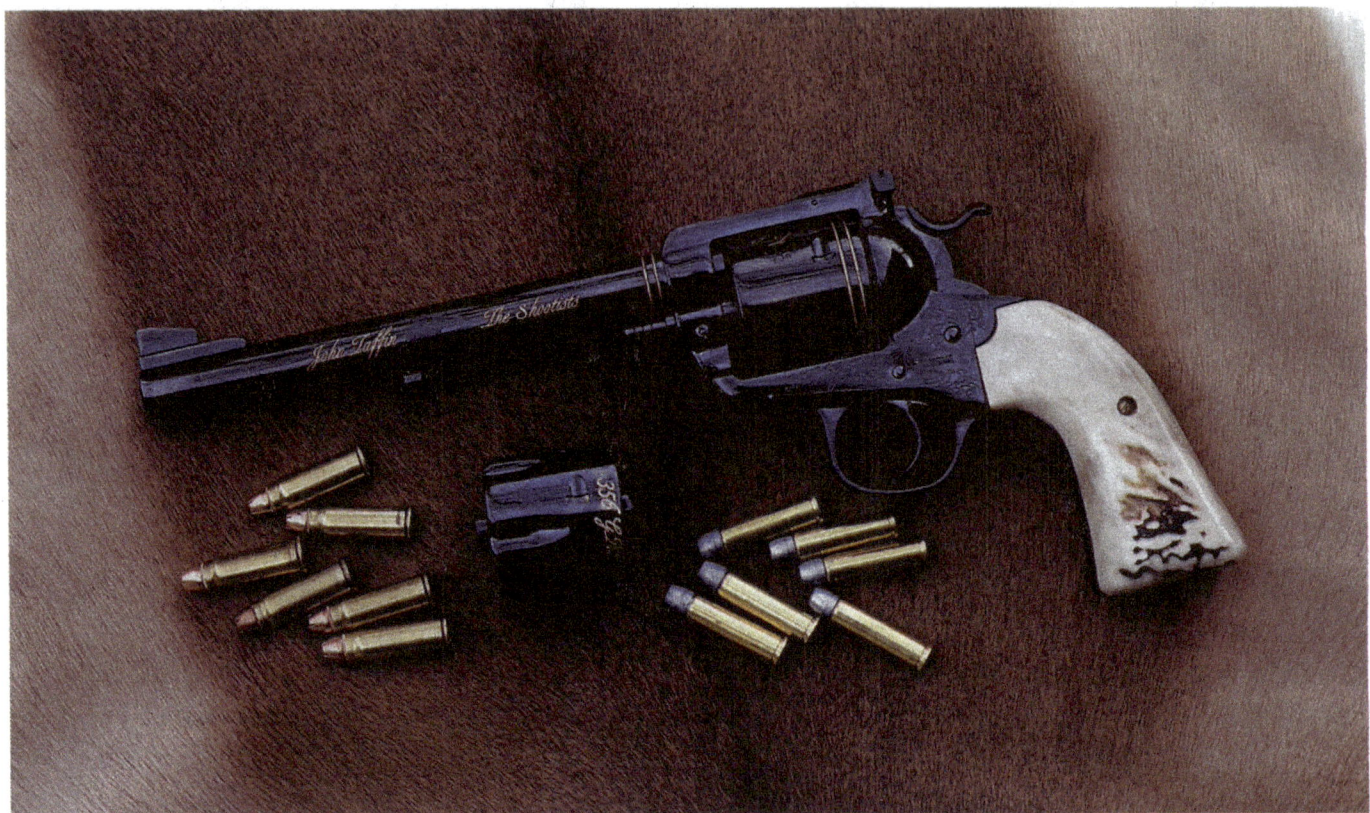

Gary Reeder fitted this .357 Magnum Ruger Bisley Model with an extra cylinder chambered in .356GNR, slightly rounded the grip frame, embellished the cylinder and barrel with gold trimming, and then re-blued the entire sixgun.

This Series '70 Colt .45ACP has been beautifully engraved by Ed DeLorge and stocked with ivory by Bob Leskovec.

Big-Bore Handguns 149

Life is too short to spend it with an ugly gun! A Series '70 engraved by Ed DeLorge and S&W .44 Magnum and Colt Single Action Army engraved by Jim Riggs.

The first choice among sixgunners for engraving is the Colt Single Action Army. Top is a Third Generation .44-40 engraved by Dale Miller and stocked with bighorn sheep by Paul Persinger; bottom sixgun is a Second Generation .45 Colt engraved by Jim Riggs and also stocked by Persinger with carved ivory.

It doesn't get much fancier than this! Carved ivory grips in the Keith-style by Bob Leskovec, left-hand sixgun of a matched pair of 4-inch S&W .44 Specials, and floral carved #1920 rig by El Paso Saddlery.

These five-shot single-action sixguns are built to handle the largest of big game. From top to bottom: a 5 1/2-inch .500 by John Linebaugh on a Ruger Bisley Model, followed by two 4 3/4-inch Freedom Arms Model 83s in .475 Linebaugh and .454 Casull. Ivory micarta stocks are by Charles Able.

Paul Persinger is a master when it comes to carving ivory. This longhorn skull resides on a 7 1/2-inch Colt Single Action .45.

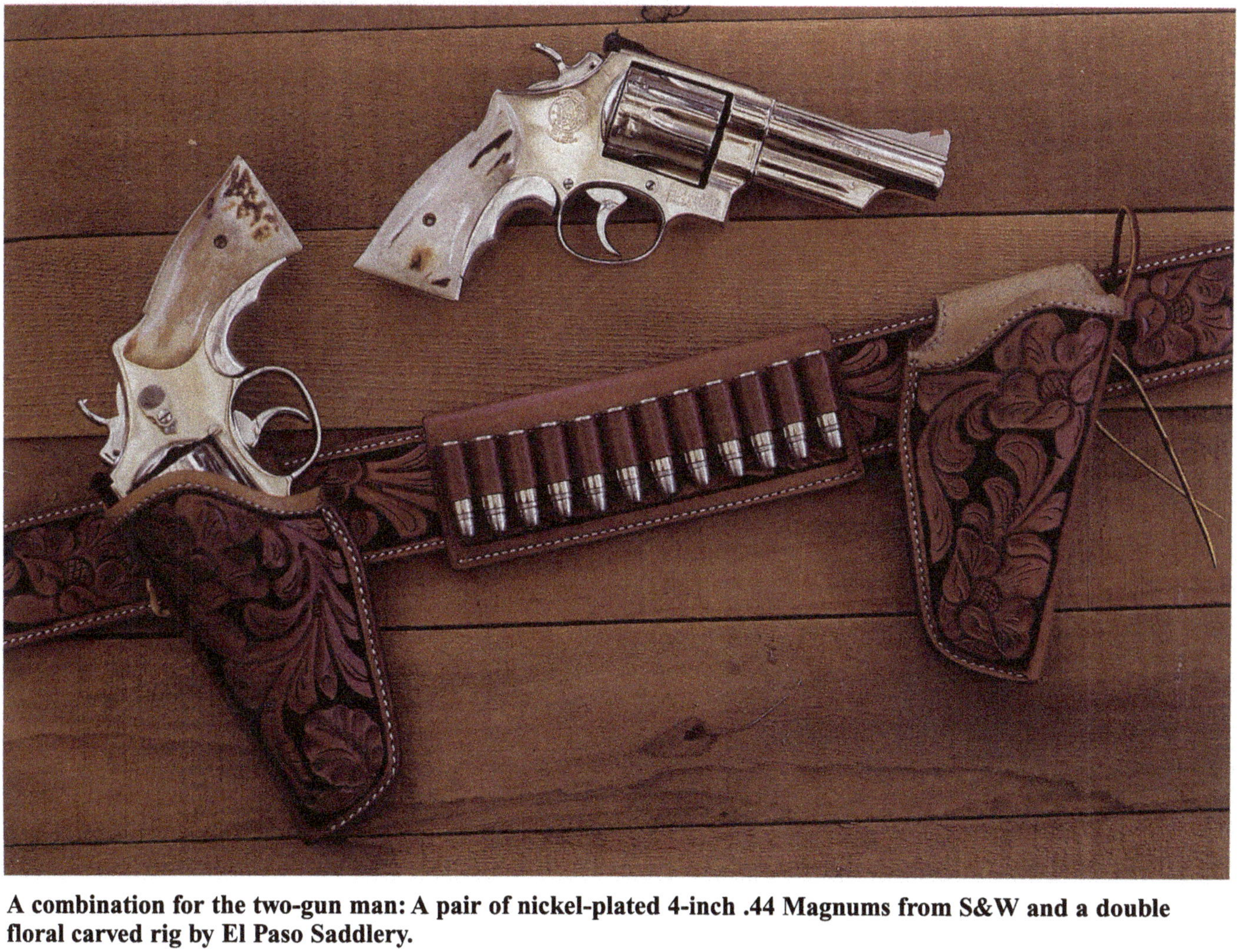

A combination for the two-gun man: A pair of nickel-plated 4-inch .44 Magnums from S&W and a double floral carved rig by El Paso Saddlery.

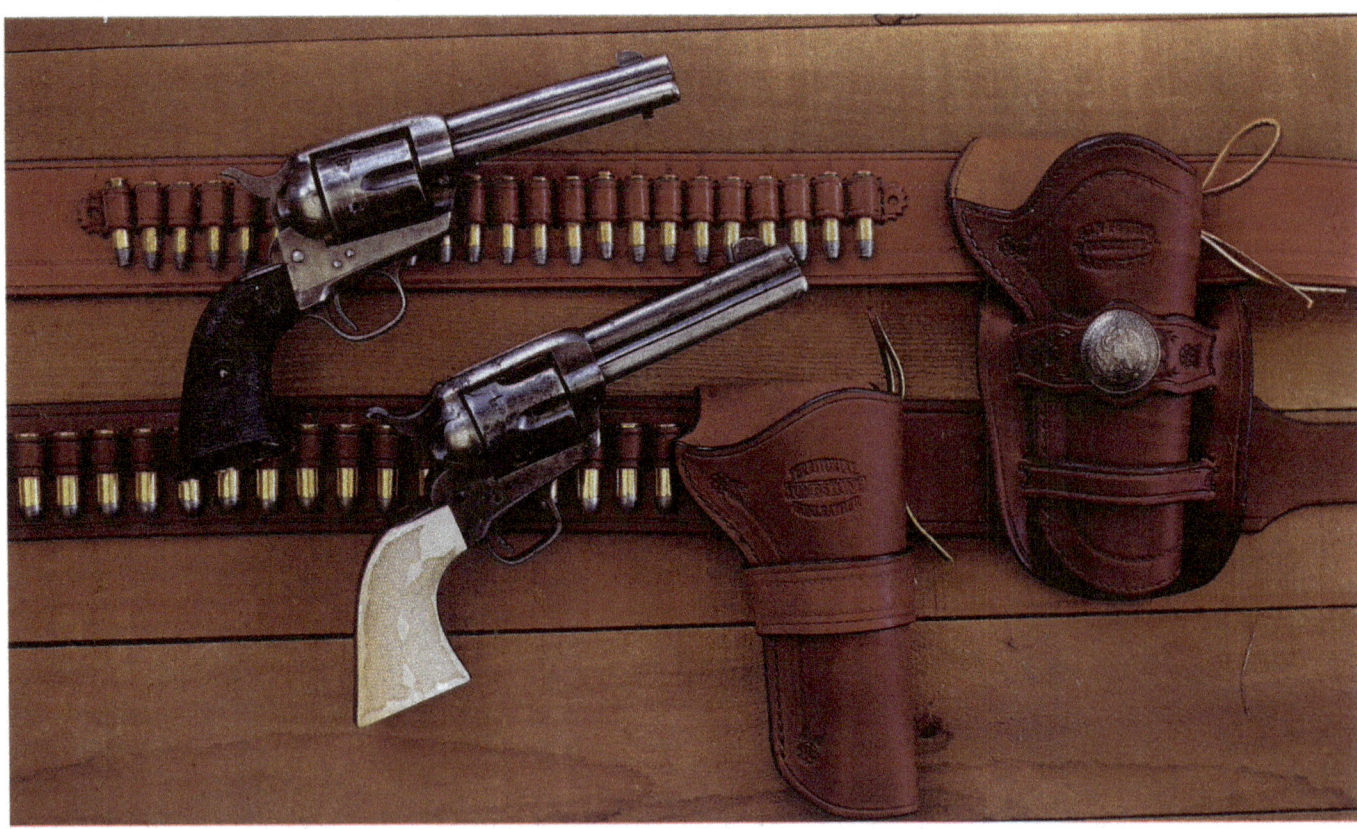

Period sixguns deserve traditional leather. This 4 3/4-inch .32-20 Colt, circa 1904, and the same model .45, circa 1917, ride in proper leather from San Pedro Saddlery.

A near-perfect set up for cowboy action shooting includes a pair of nickel-plated, stag-gripped, 4 3/4-inch Colt .45s and a double Prospector rig from Kirkpatrick Leather.

Big-Bore Handguns 153

Forty years ago, Andy Anderson offered his Gunfighter rig. It is available once again in superb form from Walt Ostin of Custom Gun Leather.

Nearly a century separates these 1911s. An original 1914 Colt is flanked by Springfield Armory's Mil-Specs in .38 Super and .45 ACP. Great guns all.

The past lives again with replicas. The Winchester Model 1873 .44-40 from Navy Arms, engraved Model P .44-40 from Cimarron, and El Paso Saddlery's Cheyenne rig.

Three great examples of three basic handgun styles: A double-action S&W .44 Special, a single-action Freedom Arms .475, and a semi-automatic Colt .45. Leather is by El Paso Saddlery.

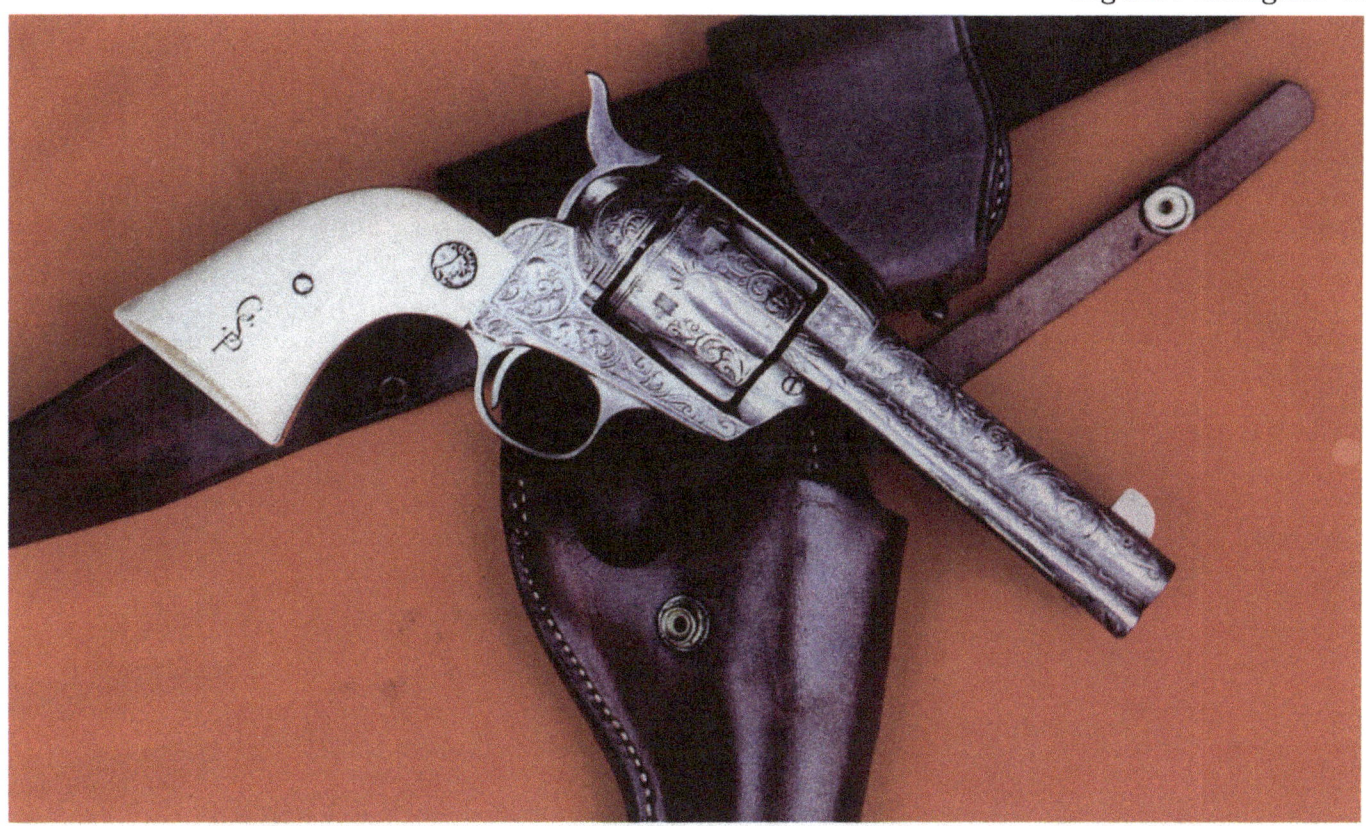

One of the most famous and certainly most recognizable Colt Single Action Armies is this .45 Colt that resided in its S.D. Myres rig on hip of Gen. George Patton in WWII.

Brian Cosby turned these Old Model Ruger Blackhawks into Colt-style single actions with traditional fixed sights, stag grips, nickel plating, and engraving by Michael Dubber.

Probably the most famous, as well as the most produced, holster is the Tom Threepersons. These are El Paso Saddlery's #1920 in floral carving and basket weave stamping for Colt Single Actions.

A favorite holster of the Texas Rangers for much of the 20th century was the Austin designed by Ranger Lee Trimble in the 1920s. These rigs in floral carving and basket weave stamping are El Paso Saddlery's #1930.

A .44-40 to be proud of, this Third Generation Colt was engraved by Dale Miller and stocked with ram's horn by Paul Persinger.

One of the most beautiful trophies Africa has to offer is the gemsbok. This magnificent animal was taken by the author on the Limpopo River with a Thompson/Center Contender chambered in 6.5 JDJ.

One corner of the author's family room exhibits trophies, eland, wildebeest, oryx, impala, and gemsbok, taken in South Africa with handguns.

Pistoleros gather in Colorado. Taffin, John Wootters, Bart Skelton, Jim Wilson, and Terry Murbach, all pack custom six-guns inspired by Skeeter Skelton.

Big-Bore Handguns 159

If they could only talk! Colt Single Actions from the Frontier Period are an 1879 .44-40 Frontier Six-Shooter and a U.S.-marked .45 Colt from 1881, with authentic leather by San Pedro Saddlery.

A pair of .44s from the 1870s are still in use with black-powder loads. The top sixgun is a Model #3 .44 Russian while the bottom sixgun is a .44 40 Colt.

This American bison was taken by Taffin using Buffalo Bore's .480 Ruger load with a 410-grain hard cast bullet in a 4 3/4-inch Freedom Arms.

Hamilton Bowen's salute to Elmer Keith is his rendition of the famous #5SAA complete with Mexican Eagle ivory stocks and full engraving. A most beautiful .44 Special sixgun.

The author and the Freedom Arms Model 83 .41 Magnum.

bullets much over 220 grains in weight very accurately. Some of the best hunting bullets for the .44- and .45-caliber revolvers are those in the 300-grain heavyweight range. They provide both excellent penetration and superb accuracy. When we tried to use comparable 250-grain and heavier bullets in those .41 Magnum sixguns available we often found the bullets would not stay on a 2-foot-square target at 50 yards! The problem had to be barrel twist and Freedom Arms has addressed this with a barrel twist of 1:14. Heavyweight bullets that used to provide shotgun-style patterns at 50 yards now stay right at 1 inch at that distance.

Five factory loads were tried in the first Freedom Arms Model 83 .41 Magnum, and the accuracy was superb. If a shooter never advances beyond standard factory loadings for the .41 Magnum, the Freedom Arms revolver will give the best possible accuracy for this cartridge that has too long been neglected. Both the Cor-Bon 265 grain Hard Cast and the new Federal 250 grain Hard Cast factory load designed for hunting will stay right at 1 inch at 50 yards. These loads are designed for the deepest possible penetration with the .41 Magnum and achieve muzzle velocities of 1,400 and 1,300 fps, respectively.

For assembling cast bullet reloads for the Freedom Arms .41 Magnums, I normally stay with heavyweights using BRP's 250-grain gas checked semi-wadcutter, a bullet for which we have had high hopes for. Those hopes were finally realized in the Model 83 and also with SSK's 275-grain flat point and LBT's 230-grain WFN. The latter is the same style bullet used in Cor-Bon's factory loading.

The Freedom Arms sixgun is the strongest single action ever offered and with that in mind I started experimental loads by beginning at the maximum recommended load for standard .41 Magnum revolvers. Again, I cannot emphasize enough that all loads are for use in the Freedom Arms .41 Magnum Model 83 ONLY!

As I started loading for the Model 83 .41 Magnum I knew the revolver would not be a problem strengthwise, but the brass and primers might. I used Starline brass throughout and never experienced a problem with sticking cases. All brass extracted easily. I recommend that all brass, including new unfired cases, be full-length-sized before loading. The first loadings were assembled with CCI's #350 Magnum Pistol Primers. At the top end these worked fine when fired outside in 30-degree weather.

For the first time we now have a local state-of-the-art indoor shooting range available. When I moved indoors to use the fine facilities at Shooting World, problems surfaced quickly. When shooting in a temperature closer to 70 degrees, primers on the heaviest loads cratered and flowed into the firing pin bushing, locking the Freedom Arms .41 up tight. Switching to CCI's harder #200 Large Rifle Primers solved this problem. Another caution is in order here. These loads were not fired in warm weather. When they are, a new set of problems could surface.

For seating rifle primers in the Starline's .41 Magnum brass, care must be used to see that they are seated flush or the cylinder of the Freedom Arms 83 will not rotate as the primer binds against the recoil shield. If this happens, do not force the cylinder to revolve. Instead, remove the cylinder, take out the rounds that caused the problem and replace them with cartridges that have the primers properly seated. Trying to fire "high primers" in a Freedom Arms, or any other revolver, can cause a cartridge that is not under the hammer to fire. Don't do it.

Powders used were two standards for heavy loads in Magnum sixguns, namely H110 and AA#9. With these powders I actually approached 1,700 fps with 250-grain bullets. All loads were assembled with Lyman's .41 Magnum dies using a heavy crimp. Heavyweight cast bullets such as BRP's 250 grain gas checked semi-wadcutter and SSK's 275-grain flat point must be crimped over the front shoulder to allow entrance into the tight chambers of the Model 83. This, of course, restricts powder capacity significantly, which in turn limits the muzzle velocities that can be achieved.

SELECTED LOADS FOR THE FREEDOM ARMS MODEL 83 MAGNUM 10-INCH

BULLET	LOAD	MV
Hornady 210 XTP	23.5 gr. H110	1,616
Hornady 210 XTP	24.5 gr. H110	1,685
Hornady 210 XTP	20.0 gr. AA#9	1,631
Hornady 210 XTP	21.0 gr. AA#9	1,657
Hornady 210 XTP	22.0 gr. AA#9	1,743
Hornady 210 XTP	23.0 gr. AA#9	1,774
BRP 250 GC	16.0 gr. H110	1,313
BRP 250 GC	17.0 gr. H110	1,373
LBT 411.230 WFN	22.0 gr. H110	1,533
LBT 411.230 WFN	23.0 gr. H110	1,624
LBT 411.230 WFN	24.0 gr. H110	1,684
LBT 411.230 WFN	20.0 gr. AA#9	1,619
LBT 411.230 WFN	21.0 gr. AA#9	1,701
LBT 411.230 WFN	22.0 gr. AA#9	1,720
SSK 275.411 FP	14.0 gr. H110	1,172
SSK 275.411 FP	15.0 gr. H110	1,236

After the loads were assembled I first fired them over the clock, recording muzzle velocities and checking for excessive pressure signs. I was somewhat limited in firing groups at 50 and 100 yards as the weather was wet and in the 35-degree range. My hands got cold very quickly.

I had been firing cast bullet loads at 100 yards and then switched over to jacketed bullets, namely Hornady's 210-grain XTP over 22.0 grains of Accurate Arms #9 for 1,750 fps. I fired the first round down the barrel to clean it out, fired round two on the target and saw it was about 6 inches above the aiming point, adjusted the scope accordingly, and fired the last three rounds. I could easily see those three rounds in the center of the orange diamond. The group looked really good!

I reloaded the cylinder of the Model 83 with five rounds and fired them on the next target. Looking through the scope I could clearly see all the holes clustered together right above the orange diamond. Upon measuring the groups my heart leapt with joy. What a sixgun! The first three rounds measured 7/8 inch! With the next five shots, three went into 5/8 inch, four into 1 1/4 inch, and all five were a most satisfying 1 1/2 inch! At 100 yards!! This is rifle accuracy!

This is not only the most accurate .41 Magnum I have ever had in my hands, it is one of the most accurate revolvers I have ever shot. Period. We now have in our hands, a sixgun that is not only chambered in the caliber that many consider the perfect deer cartridge, it is also capable of delivering rifle accuracy. The Freedom Arms Model 83 .41 Magnum is available in brushed stainless-steel Premier Grade finish or the Field Grade matte finish stainless steel with impregnated hardwood grips and adjustable sights in barrel lengths of 4 3/4, 6, 7 1/2, and 10. All models are scope ready. To install a scope, it is necessary to remove the rear sight and replace it with an SSK T'SOB or Freedom Arms base. Both are available from Freedom Arms.

The .475 Linebaugh

Now we had the Model 83 in .454, .44 Magnum, .357 Magnum, .50 AE, and .41 Magnum, with each subsequent chambering exhibiting less recoil than the original. What would be next? Seven years ago I was privileged to travel through the hills of eastern Idaho and drop down into the western part of Wyoming and Star Valley to the Freedom Arms factory to try out a new chambering. I knew right away we once again had a real tiger by the tail! And I was sworn to secrecy. The chambering was a special .475 Linebaugh. John Linebaugh's custom sixguns used .45-70 brass, which has a large rim diameter of .608 inch, or about 1/10 inch larger than the heads found on the .454. Freedom Arms revolvers feature

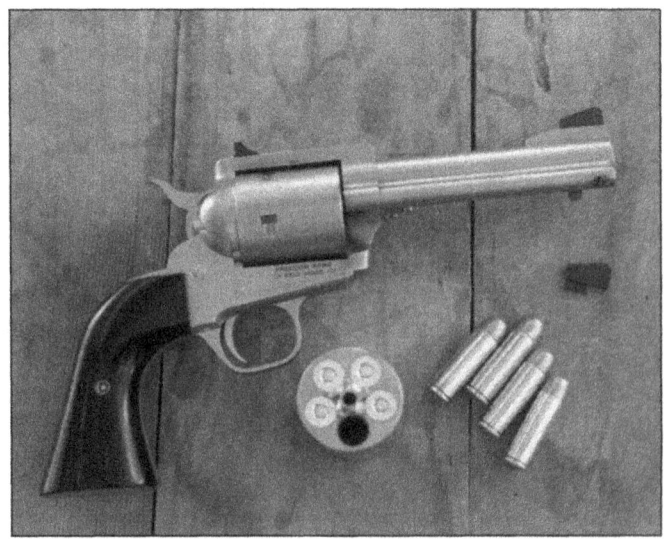

Another great packin' pistol from Freedom Arms: the Model 83 .475 Linebaugh with an extra cylinder chambered in .480 Ruger.

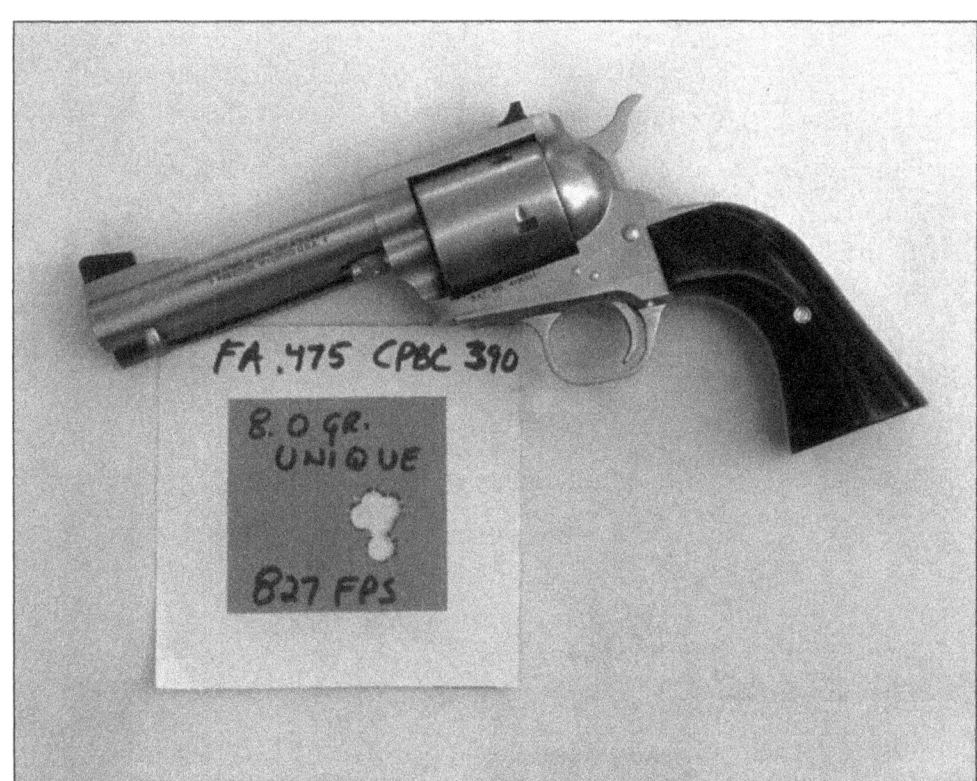

With a 370-grain cast bullet at 825 fps, this Freedom Arms Model 83 .475 not only shoots superbly, it is a very easy-handling sixgun for close-range deer hunting.

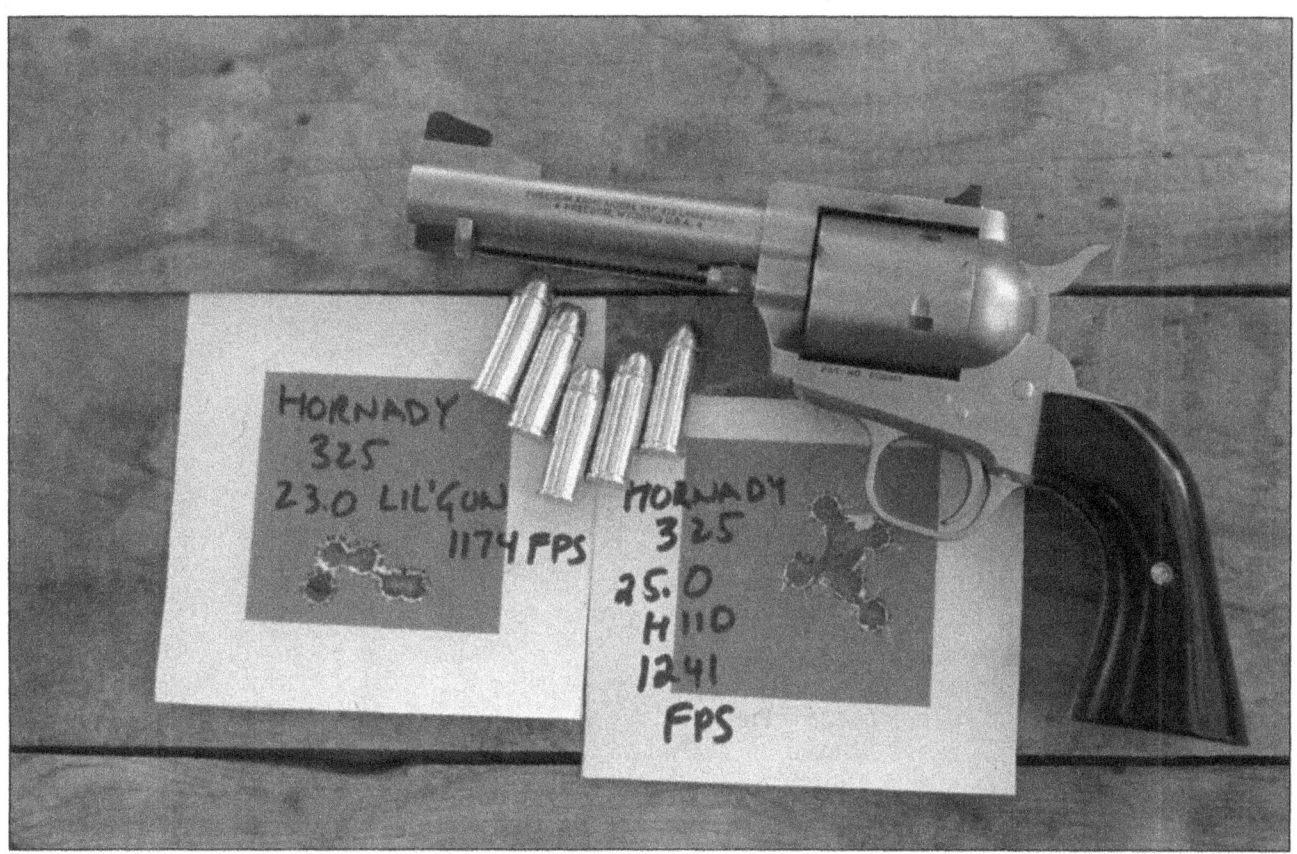

With Hornady's 325-grain jacketed hollowpoint and loads of around 1,200 fps, the .480 Ruger in the Freedom Arms Model 83 is another easy-handling whitetail deer combination.

The 4 3/4-inch Freedom Arms Model 83s chambered in .475 Linebaugh and .454 Casull are easy to pack and capable of taking any game animals.

recessed-case heads, meaning these cases were too large for use in the Freedom Arms cylinder. So case heads had to be turned down to fit. This also meant that brass would not be easily obtainable.

Unless someone came up with factory brass that would fit in the Freedom Arms .475 the project would probably never get off the ground. Enter Buffalo Bore.

Tim Sundles of Buffalo Bore is a hunter who likes big bullets from sixguns and leverguns. His line of ammunition includes heavy .45 Colt and Heavy .44 Magnum loads, both with 300-plus-grain bullets, .45-70 Magnum lever loads with 350- to 420-grain bullets, and for the first time, factory-produced rounds in both .500 Linebaugh and .475 Linebaugh. Starline is producing

The .475 from Freedom Arms is now sighted in and the author is ready to go hunting.

the brass for Buffalo Bore, which at this writing has both ammunition and brass available and both the Speer 400-grain PFP (plated flat point) and Hornady 400 XTP are available for the .475.

The Model 83 Freedom Arms revolver was introduced at the 1999 SHOT Show in Atlanta chambered in .475 Linebaugh. As with the other chamberings, the .475 is offered in both Premier Grade and Field Grade versions with both fixed and adjustable sights. It also has several options available, such as custom grips, action jobs, scope mounts, and special barrel lengths and configurations.

At my first shooting of the Freedom Arms .475 we were using handloads as nothing else was yet available. I was not caught unawares since in the past I had considerable experience with the really big-bore sixgun cartridges. We used heavy-loaded .44 Magnum and .45 Colt with 300-grain bullets. In the .454, up to 340-grain bullets at 1,800 feet per second. With the .475 and .500 Linebaughs, 400-grain bullets in custom sixguns; as well as the brutal Maximums, the .475 and .500 Linebaugh Longs. I had almost forgotten what the recoil of the .475 was like. My memory was jogged very quickly.

I've now had much more experience shooting the Model 83 .475 with factory loads from Buffalo Bore as well as handloads with both cast and jacketed bullets. The first question that comes up is how is the recoil of the .475 compared to the .454? Is it heavier or less? The answer is yes to both questions. The

The first really big critter to be taken with a .480 Ruger. The author took this 1,200-pound American buffalo with the 4 3/4-inch Freedom Arms .475 fitted with a .480 Ruger cylinder using Buffalo Bore's 410-grain cast bullet load.

recoil generated by the .475 is different than that created by the .454. The lesser caliber seems to have a quicker recoil, while the .475 gives a heavier push. With this in mind, it seems to me that the .475 is more punishing off the bench while the .454 is the winner of the baddest recoil when shooting off-hand. This is purely my interpretation of these big-bore chamberings with full-house loads.

The .454 uses bullets that are normally in the 260- to 300-grain weight range while the heaviest practical bullet for the .454 is around 340 to 350 grains. The weight range for the .475 is from 370 to 440 with Buffalo Bore's factory offerings at up to 420 grains. Those factory loads with the 420-grain LBT-LFN (long flat nose) clock out at 997 and 1,379 fps for the mid-range and full-house loadings. The former will handle most hunting chores even at what at first glance seems a rather sedate velocity. The key is bullet weight. Due to its mild recoil I expect this load to also be the best seller among Buffalo Bore's offerings. Buffalo Bore's other load is also a hard cast 420-grain bullet, LBT's WFN (wide flat nose), which as its name implies has a wider cross section at the nose. This is the one to use for maximum effectiveness on really big stuff. Both Hornday and Speer offer a 400-grain jacketed bullet loading at around 1,350 fps.

Bob Baker used the new .475 Linebaugh Model 83 to take this Alaskan brown bear.

SELECTED LOADS FOR FREEDOM ARMS MODEL 83 .475 LINEBAUGH 7 1/2"

BULLET	LOAD	MV
BRP 395 FP	25.0 gr. H4227	1,309
	27.0 gr. H110	1,419
BRP 435 SWC FP	23.0 gr. H4227	1,228
	25.0 gr. H110	1,374
	22.0 gr. Lil'Gun	1,276
CPBC LBT 370LFN	26.0 gr. Lil'Gun	1,459
	30.0 gr. H4227	1,445
	28.0 gr. H4227	1,367
	9.0 gr. WW231	935
CPBC LBT 420LFN	23.0 gr. Lil'Gun	1,359
	24.0 gr. H4227	1,254
CPBC LBT 440LFN	22.0 gr. Lil'Gun	1,313
	22.0 gr. H4227	1,143
	24.0 gr. H4227	1,260
	9.0 gr. WW231	919
	30.0 gr. H4227	1,383

I would expect the "light" loaded Buffalo Bore round to completely penetrate a deer, while the full-house loadings have already proven that they are real penetrators in really big stuff. This is the key in hunting really big game with a sixgun. The expansion is already built in due to the large caliber. I used Buffalo Bore's 410-grain .480 Ruger loading at about 1,100 fps from a 4 3/4-inch .475 Linebaugh Model 83 with a .480 cylinder fitted and shot completely through a 1,200-pound American Bison at 35 yards.

These are serious loads for a serious sixgun for serious applications. Recoil is very heavy and, with full-house loads, this is not a sixgun that most people will want to shoot for pure enjoyment. For what it is designed for, actually what both the cartridge and the revolver are designed for, it will virtually be unequalled. The Freedom Arms .475 Linebaugh is not a sixgun for silhouetting, concealed carry, or what we normally think of as self defense. It is not a sixgun that anyone will enjoy for plinking with the full-house loads. It is, however, a great assurance when carried on the hip or in a shoulder holster while in country where one could run into something big and mean and nasty, that bites.

Accuracy with the .475 Linebaugh has always been fine with the custom sixguns I have shot, and this factory-chambered specimen is no exception. Recoil, of course, is a major factor, but I found it no great problem to get groups right at 1 inch shooting at a range of 50 yards. This requires great concentration and all the strength I can muster. The addition of a Burris 4X scope on a SSK T'SOB mount not only aids me to shoot accurately, it also helps to tame recoil by adding a little weight to a 7 1/2-inch Premier Grade Model 83.

Reloading for the .475 raises several problems, all of which are easily solved, thanks mainly to RCBS. I have a set of .475 dies that were designed for the original .475 Linebaugh using cut-down .45-70 brass. The first thing I did was get on the phone to the RCBS customer service people and order a new shellholder for the smaller rim of the Starline brass. I thought this was all that would be needed. It was not! When I tried to seat the bullets using my seating and crimping die, the trouble really started. The die was so tight that bullets were ruined when seated. The thin jackets of some of the special bullets I had were squashed beyond use and a belt was raised up on hard cast bullets as they were seated. The original dies used in the past with Winchester .45-70 brass cut down to .475 length and they worked just fine. Starline brass is just thicker and heavier enough that the problem arose. The arrival of the new RCBS seating die solved the problem completely.

If you have access to my loading data for the .475 Linebaugh in custom sixguns built by John Linebaugh using cut down .45-70 brass, you are advised especially to proceed with caution. John's cylinders are longer and the brass was thinner. With the Freedom Arms sixgun the shorter cylinder means the bullets may have to be seated deeper, and the heavier brass combined with this cuts the case capacity enough that some powder charges will give greater velocity and also higher pressures with the Freedom Arms sixguns and Starline brass than they do with John's guns and brass. Again, simply proceed with caution and do not start at the maximum loads that I have listed in the past for the custom .475 revolvers. Both BRP and Cast Performance Bullet Co. offer great cast bullets for use in the .475 Linebaugh.

What then can the .475 Linebaugh Freedom Arms revolver be used for? Or what can one hunt with the .475? The answer, of course, is anything you want to. It will do the job!

The Freedom Arms Model 97 six-shot .357 Magnum (top) is available with an extra cylinder in .38 Special, while the five-shot .45 Colt (left) can be ordered with a second cylinder in .45 ACP.

To test the then new Model 97 .357 Magnum, Bob Baker took this Wyoming mule deer with a heavyweight hard cast bullet.

The Mid-Frame Model 97

The Freedom Arms single-action revolver, one of the finest, if not the finest, sixgun ever built, is now available in a version that is perfect for easy packin'. In the summer of 1996, at the Shootists Holiday, it was my privilege to test fire two new single-action revolvers. I was sworn to secrecy until such time as they could be finalized and officially announced. That time arrived in 1997 as Freedom Arms downsized its magnificent Model 83 to arrive at the Mid-Frame Model 97 sixgun. Test guns fired that summer were in a five-shot .45 Colt and a six-shot .357 Magnum. The first production guns arrived in 1997 in a six-shot .357 Magnum, with a 5 1/2- or 7 1/2-inch barrel, and with or without adjustable sights.

In the Mid-Framed Model 97 revolver, the first true six-shot sixgun from Freedom Arms, the original design and quality has been adhered to with the same painstaking attention to detail and precision. Barrels for the smaller gun are exactly the same stock as used on the full-sized Model 83 .357 Magnum. Each gun is made of stainless steel. Cylinders and barrels are line-bored. Each gun is precisely fitted to minimum tolerances. How then is the Model 97 different from the original?

First let us look at the size of the Model 97 compared to a Freedom Arms Model 83 in .357 Magnum and a Colt New Frontier chambered in .44 Special. Using the Hornady digital caliper, I came up with the following measurements: See chart page 153.

A check with the calculator shows that the Model 97 size is about 90 percent that of the Model 83. Comparing

The Freedom Arms Model 97 will fit holsters made for the Colt Single Action Army, such as these traditional rigs by San Pedro Saddlery.

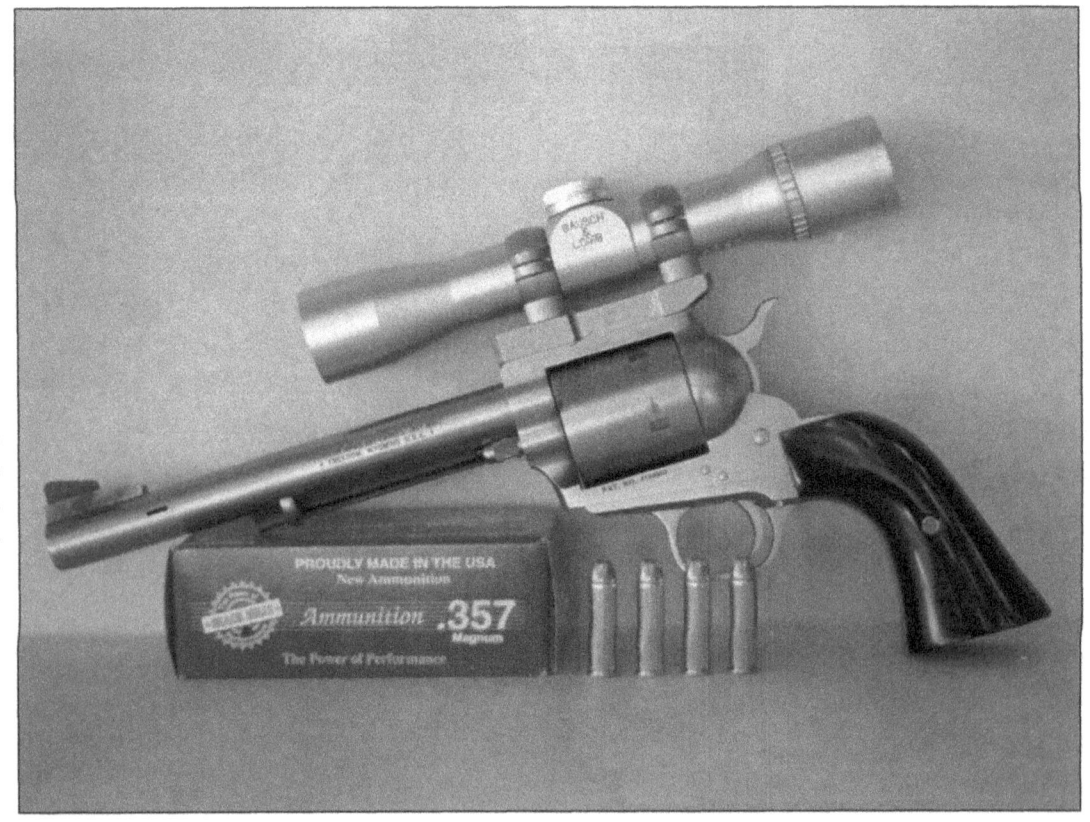

Taffin's turkey taker is the Freedom Arms .357 Magnum using Black Hills .357 Magnum jacketed hollowpoints.

O.D.	CYLINDER DIAMETER	CYLINDER LENGTH	BARREL
Model 97	1.5755"	1.6245"	.705" to .675"
Model 83	1.7505"	1.7905"	.790" to .750"
Colt New Frontier	1.650"	1.610"	.760" to .680"

top straps of these sixguns in their adjustable sighted model versions, we have the following dimensions:

	TOP STRAP WIDTH	TOP STRAP LENGTH
Model 97	.695"	2.168"
Model 83	.770"	2.897"
Colt New Frontier	.711"	2.527"

Again, the Model 97 comes in at 90 percent when comparing the thickness side to side of the top straps. When the Colt New Frontier is compared to the large-framed Freedom Arms revolver its size measures out at 92 to 94 percent. What does all this mean? Simply that the .357 Mid-Frame sixgun is slightly smaller than a Colt Single Action. It is therefore a standard-sized sixgun for standard loads. It will not handle the heavy-duty 180-grain .357 loads that are perfectly acceptable in the Model 353. This is a traditionally sized sixgun that will digest standard .357 Magnum loads all day and not complain. It is not a sixgun to be pushed to the limit and over as we are able to do with the large-framed Freedom Arms revolvers chambered in .454, .44 Magnum, .357 Magnum, and .50 Action Express.

Chambered in the .45 Colt and .41 Magnum, the Model 97 Freedom Arms revolver has a five-shot cylinder that allows more metal between chambers. The bolt slots are also between the chambers rather than underneath them, exactly as on the large-framed Freedom Arms revolvers. With this in mind, the .45 Colt Model 97 is about the same strength level as a six-shot Ruger Blackhawk .45, but nowhere near the strength level of the original Freedom Arms offering. This is exactly what makes this "little" sixgun so appealing. It is a sixgun for relaxing times, for hunting varmints and our smaller deer. It is for what I like to call desert roamin' and woods bummin', where a sixgun is needed but it does not need to be in the dinosaur-slayin' class.

Making the size of the Mid-Frame 90 percent of the large-framed Freedom Arms revolver results in a sixgun that is almost perfectly adapted to leather made for the Colt Single Action Army in the case of the fixed-sighted model, while the Colt New Frontier-sized holster accepts the adjustable-sized model. Holsters made for the Ruger Blackhawk will be slightly oversize but will do. Other than size and having six holes in the cylinder of the .357 Model 97 instead of five, there are some subtle differences in the Model 97 when compared to the Model 83 Freedom Arms revolver. The downsized parts in the action seem to impart a smoother feel, possibly due to having to move less weight and over a shorter distance. I like the feel to this sixgun's innards.

The trigger is smaller than the original and has more of a curve to its face. The only alteration I would make to this premier sixgun would be to straighten the trigger

A size comparison between the 5 1/2-inch Mid-Frame Model 97 in .45 Colt and the 4 3/4-inch Model 83 chambered in .454 Casull.

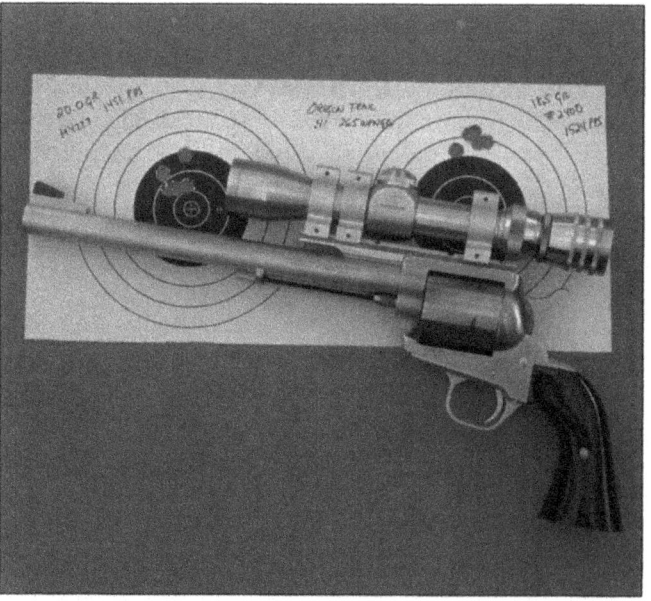

Notice the superb accuracy of the Freedom Arms .41 Magnum using Oregon Trails 265-grain cast gas checked bullet.

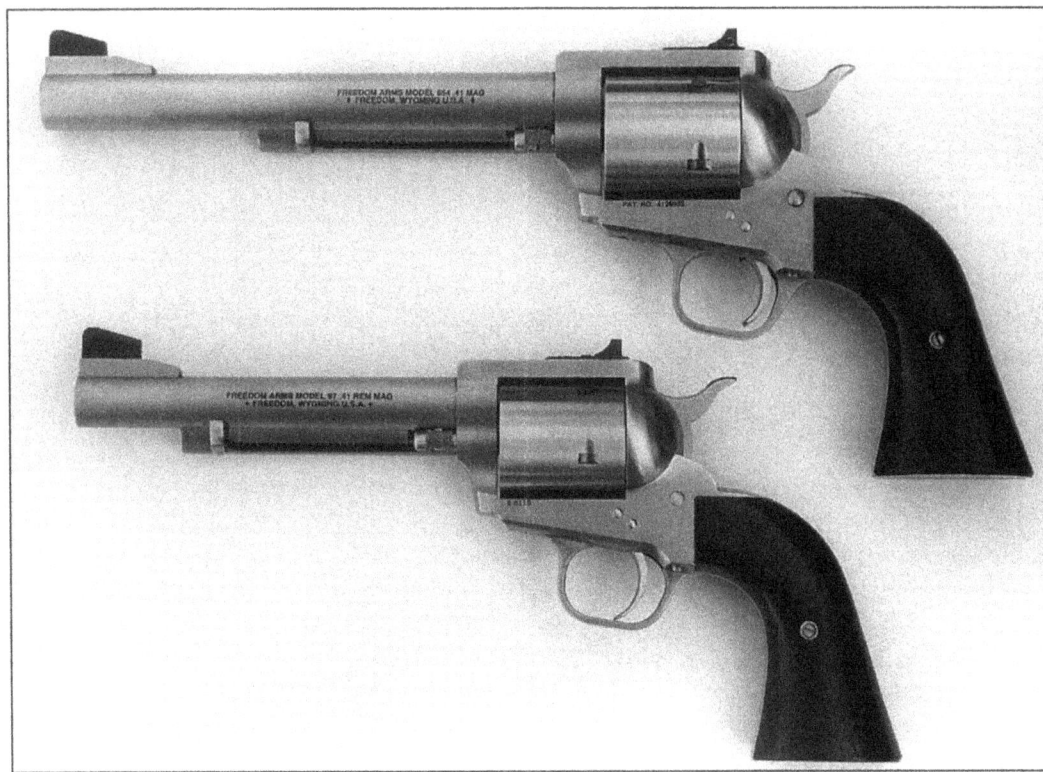

Freedom Arms has given new life to the .41 Magnum by chambering it in both the full-sized Model 83 and the mid-framed Model 97. Both versions are five-shooters.

at the bottom of it, just as the Ruger Bisley trigger, catches me at the bottom of my trigger finger. Straightening the trigger and rounding the bottom edge would result in a much more comfortable feel for me. The Model 97 carries a sliding safety in the face of the hammer. As the trigger is pulled the safety bar is in its upright position, it hits the firing pin, and the gun fires. However, if the hammer is let down slowly and carefully on a loaded round, the safety bar moves down and away as the trigger is released. Thus there is no contact with the firing pin on the primer of the loaded round under the hammer. It is a simple system that works, but normally I will do as the old time shootists did. That is, "load one, skip one, load four" as the chamber is rotated. This leaves the chamber under the hammer empty as the hammer is cocked and then lowered.

To my hand the smaller grip frame feels less like the original Freedom Arms grip shape and more like the old Colt Bisley from the turn of the century. The first test guns fired were mostly finished and finalized except for the grip shape. It required some real thought and planning to come up with a downsized grip shape that felt good and also handled felt recoil efficiently. Freedom Arms has succeeded.

The Freedom Arms grip frame is not as ladle-shaped behind the trigger guard, but when holding them, it is difficult for me to distinguish between the Colt Bisley and the Freedom Arms Model 97. The original Bisley grip frame was much better for handling recoil and also for deliberate shooting than the Single Action Army grip shape, while the latter had it all over the Bisley for quick shots from the leather.

The 7 1/2-inch .357 Magnum Model 97 feels mighty good in my hands. I specifically requested an adjustable-sighted 7 1/2-inch version for the initial testing of this new sixgun simply due to the fact that if pinned up against the wall, I would probably proclaim that 7 1/2-inch single actions are my favorite sixguns. I prefer adjustable sights also as fixed-sighted guns have a very narrow application as once they are sighted in for a particular load, any other loads require holding high or low on the intended target. Bullets of the same weight but differing velocities can have a wide range of impact points on target. For example, when this particular sixgun is sighted in to hit point of aim at 25 yards with 158-grain .357 Magnum loads at 1,300 fps or more, the 850-grain cowboy action shooting load strikes 5 1/2 inches high at 50 feet.

Sights on the adjustable sighted model are the same excellent sights found on the full-sized Freedom Arms revolver. They are designed to fit in the top strap, not on it, and they feature a locking system to keep the sights in total adjustment once a setting is dialed in. The rear sight is slightly miniaturized lengthwise to fit the shorter top strap, while the front sight blade is the same as found on the original revolver and also has the same interchangeable feature. The blade on the original 7 1/2-inch Model 97 .357 Magnum was slightly higher than I needed for my hold and eyes, and a shorter blade resulted in me not having to raise the rear sight as much. It's an easy adjustment that simply requires the Allen screw in the front of the ramp to be loosened, the old sight removed, a new sight inserted, and the screw retightened. Freedom Arms carries seven blade heights to cover any situation. For those who wish to scope the new sixgun, SSK has the necessary T'SOB mount to fit the adjustable-sighted sixguns only.

Being a traditional single-action sixgun, the Freedom Arms Model 97 loads by placing the hammer on half-cock, opening the loading gate on the right side, and inserting the cartridges one at a time as the cylinder is revolved by hand. To unload, the procedure is reversed, as the empty cases are removed with an ejector rod that rides on the right side of the barrel. The head on this ejector rod is large enough to allow easy removal without interfering with the holstering of the sixgun.

As soon as the .357 Magnum arrived, we all began trying to guess what the next chambering would be. A .32-20? Maybe .44 Special? Dare we even hope for a .45 Colt? Well, the second chambering was a five-shot .45 Colt—the most compact single-action .45 Colt ever factory produced. For 125 years the Colt Single Action Army in .45 Colt has been the best-balanced sixgun ever offered to the single-action sixgunners. The .45 Colt Model 97 from Freedom Arms is 1 ounce lighter than a 5 1/2-inch Colt SAA at 38 ounces, 2 ounces lighter than the same barrel length in the Colt New Frontier. It also has the same natural feel and pointability as the Colt. There all similarity ceases. The grip shape of the M97 is longer and straighter than the Colt SAA and could easily be argued to be an improvement over the finest grip shape ever devised.

The .45 Mid-Frame sixgun is slightly smaller than a Colt Single Action, and quite a bit smaller where it counts than the Ruger OM .45 Colt and Freedom Arms .454 Model 83. The .45 Colt Model 97 Freedom Arms revolver with its five-shot cylinder allows more metal between chambers, almost 90 percent more than a Colt Single Action and, unlike the Colt with its near paper-thin walls, the Freedom Arms Model 97 has the cylinder bolt slots between the chambers rather than underneath them, exactly as on the large-framed Freedom Arms revolvers. As previously noted, its five-shot cylinder makes the smaller Model 97 as strong as the Ruger .45 Blackhawk. However, I rarely will use the heavy .45 Colt loads tailored for the Ruger in the Freedom Arms Model 97. My heavy loads for the .45 Blackhawk are 300-grain hard cast bullets at 1,100-1,200 fps; for the Model 97 I am perfectly happy with 255-grain bullets at around 1,050 fps.

My favorite single action, my favorite sixgun in fact, is a .44 or .45 with a 7 1/2-inch barrel. I started with a pair of 7 1/2-inch Colt SAAs in fast draw as a teenager and the love of this style sixgun has stayed with me and simply grown stronger over the years. When I was informed by Freedom Arms that the .45 Colt version of the Model 97 was to be available, I could have easily opted for the 7 1/2-inch length. I did not. A small sixgun as big bores go, the cylinder diameter is smaller than a Colt Single Action Army by .075 inch. This is a sixgun that would carry easily in a shoulder holster on a weekend camping or fishing excursion. It is light enough to be welcome on a hiking trip. My wife is the fisherman in the family and she could very easily pack this sixgun for several days in comfort. This is a sixgun for enjoyable times. For plinking with the kids and grandkids, hiking in the Idaho mountains and forests, close-range varminting, and, if the chance presented itself, a deer at close range. Very close range. An awful lot of game, such as coyotes, deer, and black bear, have been taken with the standard .45 Colt load, including the old original blackpowder loading. The Freedom Arms Model 97 is right at home with this type of load, namely a 255-grain bullet at 800 to 1,000 fps. To maintain its easy packin' qualities, I went with a 5 1/2-inch

SELECTED LOADS FOR THE FREEDOM ARMS MODEL 1997 .45 COLT 5 1/2"

BULLET	LOAD	MV
Oregon Trail 255	20.0 gr. H4227	999
RCBS #45-250FN	8.0 gr. Unique	974
RCBS #45-250FN	20.0 gr. H4227	1,030
RCBS #45-250FN	7.0 gr. WW231	939
RCBS #45-255KT	18.5 gr. H4227	929
RCBS #45-255KT	6.0 gr. Red Dot	850
RCBS #45-255KT	6.0 gr. TiteGroup	889

SELECTED LOADS FOR THE FREEDOM ARMS MODEL 97 .357 MAGNUM 7 1/2"

BULLET	LOAD	MV
RCBS #38-150KT	15.0 gr. H4227	1,329
Speer 160 JHP	14.0 gr. #2400	1,360
Speer 158 JSP	14.0 gr. #2400	1,296
Speer 158 GD	14.0 gr. #2400	1,255

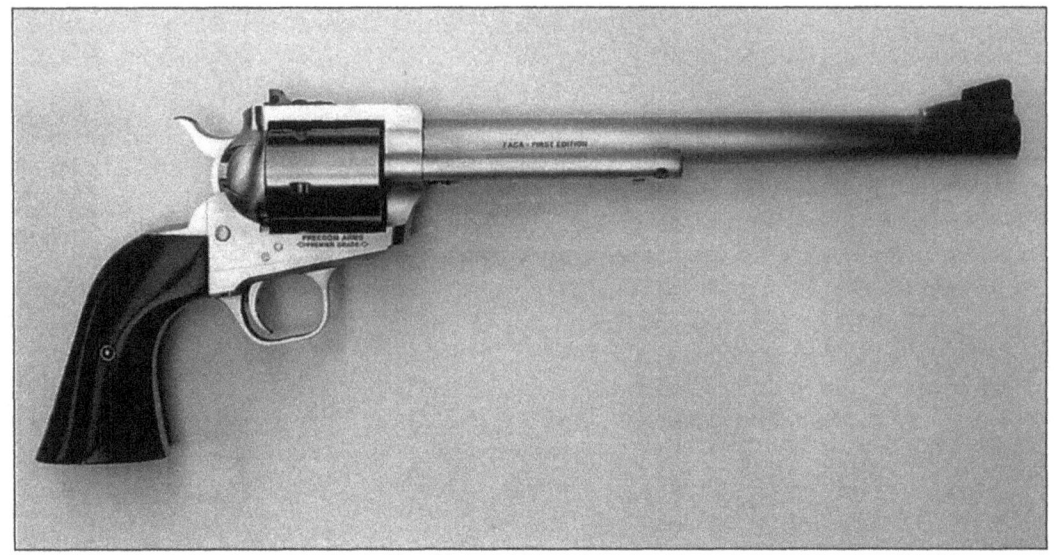

One of the perks of belonging to the Freedom Arms Collectors Association is being able to take advantage of special editions, such as this properly marked 10-inch Model 83.

barrel. To complete the package I ordered adjustable sights and black micarta grips.

For even more versatility, an added .45 ACP cylinder allows a whole range of target and defensive loads to be employed. With its interchangeable front sight system on the adjustable sighted models, the height of the front blade can be easily changed as one goes from 185-grain jacketed hollow point .45 ACP's to 260-grain hard cast .45 Colt loads.

Favorite loads for the Model 97 .45 Colt style definitely include Hodgdon's H4227 and 250-grain bullets. With RCBS's 45-250FN, a dead ringer for the original .45 Colt bullet of the 1870s, or Oregon Trail's 255 SWC and 20.0 grains of H4227, muzzle velocity is 1,000 fps and group size is right at 1 inch at a distance of 25 yards.

The Model 97 is now also chambered in .41 Magnum and, by the time you read this, will also be out in .22LR/.22 Magnum. I have not done extensive testing with the Model 97 .41 Magnum as of yet, but I did kill a Texas turkey with the prototype and friend Penn Baggett proclaims the .41 Magnum Model 97 as ideal for his work on the ranch.

In less than 20 years, Freedom Arms has been able to pretty much cover all the bases. The original Model 83 is chambered in .454, with extra cylinders available in .45 Colt, .45 ACP, and .45 WinMag; the three Magnums, .44, .41, and .357; two really big bores, .475 Linebaugh and .50 AE; and even .22/.22 Magnum. The Model 97 is already offered in .357 Magnum, with an extra cylinder offered in .38 Special; .45 Colt, with a .45 ACP cylinder as an option; .41 Magnum; and also in .22/.22 Magnum. All we need to complete the picture is a Model 97 Convertible in .32 Magnum/.32-20, and of course, a .44 Special.

We titled this chapter "Single-Action Perfection" knowing full well that little if anything manmade is perfect, including firearms. Perfection is an elusive goal that we strive to approach. Freedom Arms revolvers are about as close as we will ever come this side of The River.

CHAPTER 8

TAURUS: RAGING BULLS FROM BRAZIL

The .44 Magnum blasted onto the sixgunning scene in 1956 with Ruger's single-action .44 Blackhawk and Smith & Wesson's double-action that in those pre-model number days was simply known as the .44 Magnum. By 1963, a shooter had two choices in double-action .44s: a blued Smith & Wesson or a nickeled one. In single actions, the only choice was a 7 1/2-inch Ruger Super Blackhawk. As more and more sixgunners turned to handgun hunting and long-range silhouetting, a tremendous demand was placed upon manufacturers to supply more .44 Magnums. Smith & Wesson could not produce enough .44 Magnums to satisfy shooters and its pistols soon commanded black market prices. Only the arrival of other double-action .44s eased the price spiral.

Taurus, the far-sighted handgun supplier that gave us the "J-frame" nine-shot .22 and "K-frame" five-shot .44 Special, went Magnum by first unveiling its Model 44 at the 1993 SHOT Show, and then making it available to shooters the following year. The Taurus Model 44 is supplied in both blue and stainless finishes in 4-, 6-, and 8 3/8-inch models with all barrel lengths of the heavy underlug style with a built-in factory compensator. Stocks are a compact rubber. Sights are a micro click adjustable rear with a white outline and a red insert ramp front. It is easy to dial in the proper setting with the sights, but I have to blacken the red insert to be able to see it (a personal problem that does not apply to every shooter).

My first 8 3/8-inch test sixgun was high-polished stainless steel with a very smooth action in both double- and single-action modes. The hammer spur is a subdued target style with checkering that will not bite into the thumb while the face of the wide trigger is polished smooth. The single-action trigger pull, according to Brownell's Chatillon trigger pull scale, is 3 1/2

Taurus was the first manufacturer to offer a double-action .454 Casull. Unlike Ruger's six-shot cylinder, Taurus goes with five shots.

FIREARM	CYLINDER DIAMETER	CYLINDER LENGTH
Colt Anaconda	1.752"	1.752"
Ruger Redhawk	1.780"	1.754"
Smith & Wesson M29	1.715"	1.715"
Taurus Model 44	1.745"	1.696"
Wesson Model 44	1.758"	1.770"

pounds. The .44 Magnum Model 44, with the combination of small rubber grips, heavy underlug barrel, and compensator consisting of four small holes drilled on each side of the front sight, was found to be quite comfortable to fire compared to many other .44 Magnums. Having passed the invincible stage, I am now at the point in my shooting life when I have to be very careful about how much punishment I give the wrist of my shooting hand. But with the Model 44 I shot 200 rounds with iron sights and followed this up with 200 rounds the next day with a scope in place without any perceived lasting discomfort to said wrist.

Upon shooting the Taurus with iron sights at 25 yards, I soon realized that I had a very accurate sixgun in my hands! For example, varied loads such as the Lyman 250-grain hard cast Keith #429421 over 10.0 grains of Unique at 1,217 fps, RCBS's hard cast gas checked 300-grain #44-300 with 21.5 grains of H110 at 1,375 fps, and Northern Precision's 300-grain jacketed hollowpoint at 1,252 fps using 19.2 grains of VV #N110 all put four shots into less than 1 inch at 25 yards.

I used a Wiegand scope mount bolted to the top of the barrel rib of the Model 44 using the supplied steel bars that slip into the slots on the rib, and one of the new Burris 2X-7X Posi-Lock installed with Weaver rings. I shot the Model 44 at 100 yards resting on an Outers Pistol Perch, and shooting Black Hills 240-grain jacketed hollow points resulted in five shots going into 2 1/4 inches at 100 yards! Could it be duplicated? I waited two weeks and then shot the same Black Hills 240-grain XTP bulleted .44 Magnum loads again. Before the second shooting session the Model 44 was sent to Pat Hogue at Hogue's for a set of their exotic wood grips. Pat knows I normally do not like finger groove grips, but this time with a heavy sixgun and scope combination I opted for the finger groove grips that Hogues are famous for. The Model 44 arrived back with a beautiful pair of striped wood grips that had to be hand fitted by Pat Hogue as they did not yet offer grips for the Model 44. They do now, and the grips proved to be near perfect for the Taurus .44, giving quite a bit more security and comfort to my hand than the rubber factory grips.

The Weaver scope rings were slipped back on to the Weigand base, the Burris scope snugged up tight and I settled down at the Outer's Pistol Perch to try to duplicate the previously nearly unbelievable sixgun performance. I do believe I felt more stress shooting the .44 sixgun at 100 yards on paper this time than I normally do when getting ready to trigger a shot in a hunting situation! The original group was shot early in the morning when I was well rested and all was calm and still. The re-shot groups were fired late in the afternoon after a full day and my eyes were not so fresh and the wind was breezy. The results? Two groups were fired and I walked out to the target with ruler in hand. Group number one measured out with four shots in 2 inches and five shots in 3 inches, and the second group measured out to four shots in 2 1/8 inches and "opened up" to 2 5/8 inches with five shots. This is outstanding performance by anyone's standard.

I did a side-by-side comparison of the measurements of the length and diameter of the cylinders of five .44 Magnum double actions available to sixgunners. (see top of page)

These figures show the Taurus to be quite a bit larger in cylinder diameter than the Smith & Wesson, just slightly smaller than the Colt Anaconda and Wesson .44s, and a good .035 inch smaller in diameter than the Ruger Redhawk.

The Model 454

At the 1997 SHOT Show, Taurus became the first major company other than Freedom Arms to chamber one of its sixguns for the .454 Casull. The prototype model shown to gun writers did not cause any great stir of excitement, rather quite the opposite. It simply did not look like it was adequate to handle the high pressures involved in the .454 Casull. That gun did not even appear to have a forcing cone. As 1997 progressed, no articles concerning the testing of this gun came out in any of the gun magazines. Fast forward to SHOT Show 1998. A new Taurus sixgun was unveiled in .454 Casull along with a presentation by Taurus of the first .454 Casull Raging Bull to the designer of the .454 cartridge, Dick Casull. Taurus had done its homework after SHOT Show 1997, gone back to the drawing board, and came up with the best-looking double-action sixgun it had ever produced in the Raging Bull Model 454. This is one great-lookin' sixgun!

Available in a deep well-polished blue, high-polished stainless, or a frosted-matte stainless finish and in 5, 6 1/2- or 8 3/8-inch barrel lengths, the Raging Bull features a massive five-shot cylinder, a heavy top strap, a bull barrel

The author gives the .454 Raging Bull high marks.

with a full underlug and a ventilated rib, and excellently designed, user-friendly rubber grips. Sights, which are black on both the stainless and blued models, are fully adjustable with a post front sight that measures .120-inch in width and gives the best possible sight picture for this sixgunner. The front sight is pinned in place and conceivably could be easily replaced with one that is higher, lower, or of a different shape.

The cylinder is basically cut from a cube-shaped piece of steel with the diameter of the Model 454 Raging Bull measuring 1.770-inch mated with a length of 1.760-inch. The steel between the cylinder chambers measures out at .155-inch, while the outside walls of the chambers have a dimension of .110-inch in width. The top strap measures .630-inch in width and tapers in thickness from .305- to .289-inch back to front. The heavy barrel of the Raging Bull measures 1.650 inch top to bottom and from the muzzle end can be seen to taper from the center to the top and bottom. All models contain a built-in porting system consisting of a chamber that has four holes on each side of the front sight. This porting is approximately 1 1/4-inches in length, so a 6 1/2-inch barreled model is actually slightly over 5 inches as far as the rifling in the barrel goes, while the 8 3/8-inch model is effectively a 7-inch sixgun.

Operation of the Raging Bull is typical double action. Almost. It takes some getting used to the fact that the Model 454 has not just one but two cylinder latches that must be released at the same time to allow the cylinder to swing open. A typical double-action thumb latch behind the recoil shield must be pushed forward with one thumb while the other thumb releases a latch located on the crane in front of the cylinder. Thus, the Model 454's cylinder is effectively locked at both the front and back ends. Triggers are wide and smooth and the hammers are the semi-target type with user-friendly checkering. The finish on the hammers and triggers for the blued Model 454s is case colored while the stainless sixguns have what I assume to be plated parts. Firing pins are frame mounted with a trigger-activated transfer bar providing ignition.

Trigger pulls on test guns were found to be heavier than one would expect on a Taurus: 6 1/8 pounds for a 6 1/2-inch Model 454 in the single-action mode, and 5 3/4 pounds for the 8 3/8-inch Raging Bull, also in the single-action mode. There is a reason for this. The pressures inherent in full-house .454 loads require the use of rifle primers, which are tougher and harder to ignite than pistol primers. I had no problem with ignition using the Raging Bulls in the single-action mode. However, problems did surface when firing the Model 454's double action. Does this make a difference? Perhaps. I often hear those who may find them in a position of facing really dangerous game saying that they would prefer a double action to be able to fire quickly. One has to wonder if the key to such a situation is one well-placed shot or several quickly placed shots fired as fast as one can pull the trigger. A shooter might find it very difficult to hang onto a double-action .454 sixgun when fired one-handed, especially if the hand is wet.

The rubber grips of the Raging Bull could be very important here. These grips, combined with the porting system and the heavy weight of the Raging Bull, hold felt recoil to a manageable level. The grips accomplish their task in three ways. First, they taper properly from top to bottom, putting the major portion of grip material where it belongs on a double-action sixgun—at the top to prevent recoil from driving the grip down into the hand. Secondly, the grip material is soft rubber with finger grooves to provide a secure and comfortable gripping surface. Finally, the back of the grip contains a red-colored, cushioned insert to further lessen felt recoil in the palm of the hand. Due to the work of the porting system, the Raging Bull also comes straight back into the palm more than twisting upward or sideways. After several hundred rounds through both guns, I did not have any great pain in my recoil-ravaged wrists, but did feel as if my palm was slightly bruised. The porting, the weight of the Model 454, and the grips kept my discomfort to a minimum. I would not call the Raging Bull pleasant to shoot, but it rages a whole lot less than one would expect and that is no bull!

A word needs to be said here about porting. There are trade-offs when porting is used. Felt recoil is lessened, but noise is increased (you will NOT be the most popular shooter on the range!) and there is always the danger of material, especially when using cast bulleted loads, being thrown through the ports. Do not shoot any ported sixgun with anyone else in close proximity.

The Raging Bull .454s were test fired with seven factory loads from Cor-Bon ranging from the 265-grain Bonded Core all the way to the 360-grain Penetrator, Freedom Arms factory loads with both 260- and 300-grain jacketed flatpoints, and Winchester's 260- and 300-grain jacketed flatpoints as well as its new 260-grain Partition Gold Hollow Point loading. Accuracy was excellent in both guns when considering the recoil that is involved in firing several hundred rounds. The last five rounds fired resulted in the tightest group. Could it be that I was simply glad to be finished? That load, Freedom Arms' 260-grain jacketed flatpoint over 34 grains of H110, clocked out at 1,550 fps from the 8 3/8-inch Raging Bull and put four shots in 5/8 at 25 yards. My other handload of the BRP 300-grain bullet over 31 grains of WW296 clocked out at 1,530 fps from both guns and grouped four shots into 1 3/8 inch from the 6 1/2-inch Raging Bull and 1 1/8 inch from the 8 3/8-inch Model 454.

The Raging Bull is a double-action sixgun that will mostly be used in the single-action mode. It is a big, heavy, sixgun with the 6 1/2-inch model going 56-ounces empty and the 8 3/8-inch Model 454 almost off the postal scale at 62 1/2 ounces. Add in five rounds of 300-grain .454 ammunition and the weights go to 61 and 67 1/2 ounces, respectively. Neither of these test guns from Taurus would accept a .002-inch feeler gauge between the barrel and cylinder gap, and yet both cylinders have a greater amount of side-to-side play than I would like to see in a sixgun such as this. I would also like to see a larger cylinder bolt fitted in conjunction with a tighter cylinder.

The .44 Magnum

The Raging Bull has proven to be a raging success. Although it was first announced in a five-shot .454

Taurus's Raging Bull groups cast bullet loads exceptionally well, but for the author's use a higher front sight is required.

SELECTED FACTORY LOADS FOR THE TAURUS .454 CASULL RAGING BULLS

FACTORY LOAD	6 1/2" STAINLESS		8 3/8" BLUE	
	MV	GROUP/25 YDS	MV	GROUP/25 YDS
Cor-Bon 265 BondedCore	1,549	1 7/8"	1,632	1 3/8"
Cor-Bon 285 BondedCore	1,473	1 7/8"	1,540	1 1/8"
Cor-Bon 300 BondedCore	1,579	2 1/8"	1,632	1 3/8"
Cor-Bon 300 JSP	1,486	1 5/8"	1,564	1 7/8"
Cor-Bon 320 Penetrator	1,482	1 1/2"	1,548	2 1/8"
Cor-Bon 335 HardCast	1,463	1 7/8"	1,476	2"
Cor-Bon 360 Penetrator	1,405	2 1/2"	1,413	2 3/8"
Freedom Arms 260 JFP	1,657	1 1/4"	1,698	1 7/8"
Freedom Arms 300JFP	1,581	1"	1,586	1 1/8"
Winchester 260 P'tion Gold	1,744	7/8"	1,802	2 3/8"
Winchester 260 JFP	1,720	1 7/8"	1,790	1 1/2"
Winchester 300 JFP	1,622	1 7/8"	1,693	2 1/8"
Bull-X 255/9.0 gr. Uniq	887	1 1/8"	886	3/4"

Casull, as well as six-shot versions in .44 Magnum and .45 Colt, I personally have never seen one in .45 Colt and cannot say if any were ever actually produced. I have had considerable experience shooting both a blue and a stainless .44 Magnum Raging Bull as well as three of the .454 Casull's, an 8-inch blue model as well as two 6 1/2-inch stainless versions, one satin finished, and the other with the high-polish look of nickel. The only problem that has ever surfaced has been trying to ignite .454 Casulls with rifle primers when shooting double action. To the five Raging Bulls I have now added experience with the newest version chambered in the newest sixgun cartridge, the .480 Ruger.

We briefly mentioned the finishes available, three in all. Blued guns are a very attractive, deep, well-polished blue that is rarely found on factory sixguns today. The standard stainless steel versions are a glare-reducing frosted matte finish that most hunters will probably prefer, while the highly polished stainless-steel finish that looks a lot like nickel could be the choice of those wanting to be a little fancy. Raging Bulls are heavy sixguns with both the .44 Magnum and the .454 Casull weighing 56 ounces and the new .480 Ruger version 1 ounce lighter (all weights taken with 6 1/2-inch models). If I have any complaint at all about the Raging Bulls, it is the same complaint that can be issued for almost every sixgun, single-shot, and semi-automatic from nearly every manufacturer and that is the heaviness of the trigger pulls. Using the RCBS Premium Trigger Pull Scale, both the latest test guns in .44 Magnum and the .454 Casull measure 4 3/4 pounds, while the .480 Ruger is 8 ounces

Currently, Taurus offers the Raging Bull in (from left) .44 Magnum .454 Casull, and .480 Ruger. All chamberings are available in satin stainless, high-polish stainless, or bright blue.

Three relatively easy-shooting big-bore sixguns (from left): Taurus Raging Bull in .454 6-inch stainless and 8 3/8-inch blue, and .44 Magnum in 6-inch blue.

heavier at 5 1/4 pounds. A competent gunsmith is definitely called for here to bring these down to a more usable 3 pounds.

When we shoot big-bore sixguns with heavy loads we cannot escape recoil. Taurus has made its Raging Bulls as pleasant-shooting as possible with heavy-

SELECTED LOADS FOR THE TAURUS RAGING BULL .44 MAGNUM 6 1/2"

CAST BULLET LOADS	MV	GROUP
Black Hills 320 Hard Cast	1,183	2 1/8"
Cor-Bon 320 Hard Cast	1,205	1 5/8"
Federal 300 Hard Cast	1,260	1"
Garrett 280 KT-SWC	1,370	1 3/8"
Garrett 310 KT-SWC	1,258	1"
Garrett 310 Hammerhead	1,307	1 7/8"
RCBS 260 Keith/10. gr. Unique	1,174	1 3/4"
Boar Slammer 250/27.0 gr. H110	1,534	1 7/8"
BRP 290 KT-GC/10.0 gr. Unique	1,151	1 3/4"
CPBC 255PB/21.5 gr. WW296	1,397	1 3/4"
CPBC 320 LBT/21.5 gr. WW296	1,374	2 1/4"

JACKETED BULLET LOADS	MV	GROUP
Black Hills 240 JHP	1,247	1 3/4"
Black Hills 300 XTP	1,170	1 3/4"
Buffalo Bore 270 JFN	1,427	2 1/4"
Buffalo Bore 300 JFN	1,265	2 1/8"
Cor-Bon 240 JHP	1,455	1 5/8"
Cor-Bon 260 Bonded Core	1,413	1 7/8"
Cor-Bon 280 Bonded Core	1,299	1 7/8"
Cor-Bon 300 JSP	1,277	1 3/4"
Cor-Bon 305 Penetrator	1,244	1 1/2"
Federal 240 Hi-Shok	1,227	1 3/4"
Remington 240 JHP	1,365	2"
Speer 270 Gold Dot	1,285	2 1/2"
Winchester 250 Partition Gold	1,359	1 3/8"
Speer 300 JFP/21.7 gr. H110	1,226	2 1/8"

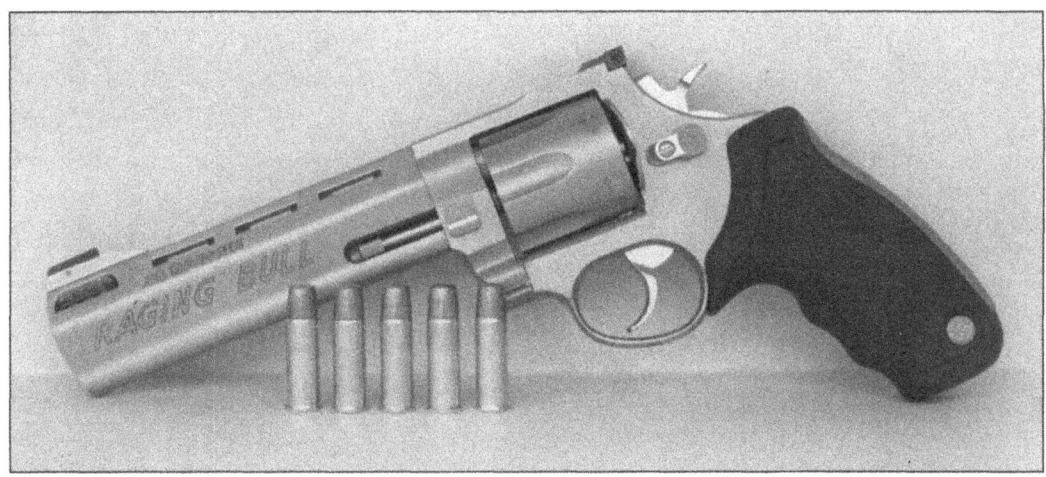

The Raging Bull from Taurus chambered in .44 Magnum and is one of the more pleasant-shooting .44 Magnums. The cushioned rubber grips go a long way to lessen felt recoil.

The author's first test Raging Bull .44 Magnum performed exceptionally well.

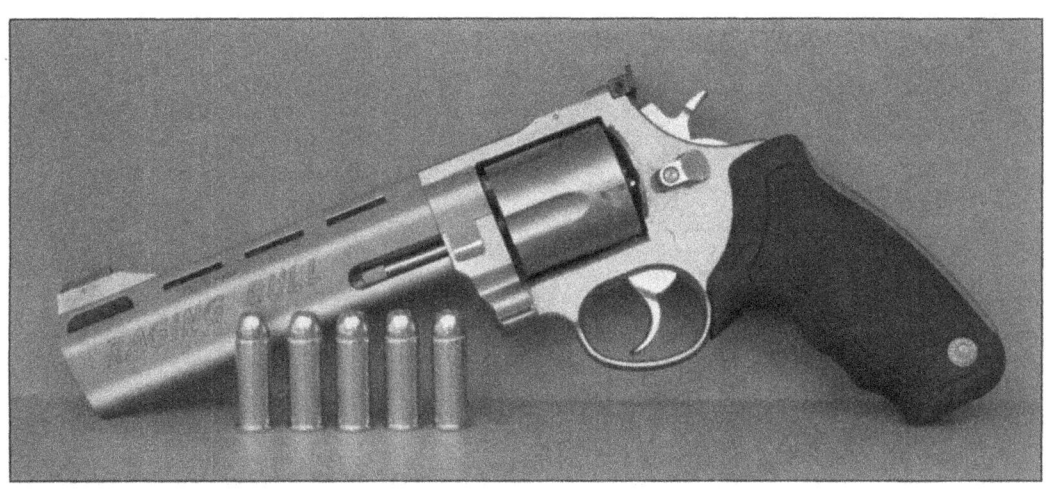

Taurus's latest Raging Bull is chambered in .480 Ruger and is a five-shooter.

All Raging Bulls lock at the front of the cylinder much like the old Smith & Wesson Triple-Lock.

Taurus's massive cylinder is chambered for five rounds in .480 Ruger and .454 Casull.

weight construction, ported barrels, and cushioned rubber stocks. Nearly all sixgun stocks that come on factory revolvers are small at the top and big at the bottom, which is obviously backwards to anyone who has ever shot heavy-recoiling revolvers. This poor design simply drives the gun down into the hand under recoil. The grips on the Raging Bull have been designed correctly — smaller at the bottom to provide a secure grip during recoil.

The .44 Magnum cartridge is fast approaching its golden anniversary as the "King of the Magnum Sixgun Cartridges." Even though "replaced" by several bigger and heavier cartridges, it is still the cartridge of choice for most big-bore sixgunners. The following loads were fired in the Taurus Raging Bull .44 Magnum with groups fired at 25 yards using iron sights (See chart on page 178).

The newest big-bore sixgun cartridge and the latest offering from Taurus in the Raging Bull is the .480 Ruger. The .480 has been personally tested in three different sixguns: the Ruger Super Redhawk, the Freedom Arms .475 fitted with an extra .480 cylinder, and the Taurus Raging Bull. It has proven to be an exceptionally accurate cartridge in all three sixguns and more than adequately powerful for most hunting purposes. Of the three cartridges offered by Taurus in their Raging Bull it would be my first choice. Groups are at 25 yards distance.

Taurus has been the leader of the pack in many ways often being the first to address shooters' wants and needs. The five-shot .44 Special mentioned earlier has now evolved into models in both .45 Colt and .41 Magnum. Very good move by Taurus.

The Raging Bulls have now been in the field for several years with good reports coming back from

All Raging Bulls feature a pinned front post sight and porting to reduce felt recoil.

The author found the Taurus Raging Bull in .480 Ruger relatively easy to shoot off hand using Hornady's 325-grain jacketed hollowpoint load.

Bigger and more powerful cartridges have come along, however, for most of us the .44 Magnum still does quite well.

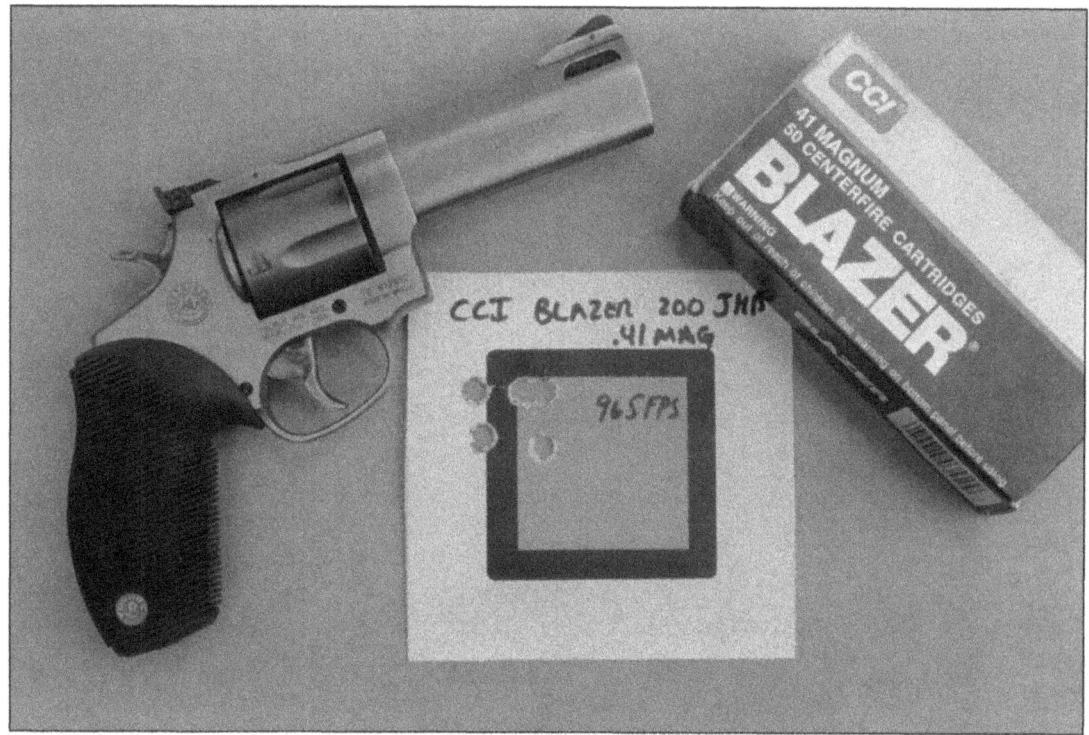

Taurus's lightweight big bore is the Tracker, here chambered in .41 Magnum.

SELECTED LOADS FOR THE TAURUS RAGING BULL .480 RUGER 6 1/2"

LOAD	MV	GROUPS
Buffalo Bore 370 LBT	987	2"
Buffalo Bore 370 LBT	1,226	1 3/4"
Buffalo Bore 410 LBT	1,154	7/8"
Hornady 325 JHP-XTP	1,286	1 1/2"
CPBC 370/11.0 gr. Unique	1,091	2"
CPBC 390/11.0 gr. Unique	1,065	1 3/8"
Hornady 400 JHP/18.0 gr. Lil' Gun	1,092	1 3/4"
Speer 400 JFP/18.0 gr. Lil' Gun	1,084	1 3/4"

those that own them. They are big, brawny, heavy, sixguns, and with others of their era, such as the Super Redhawk and Dan Wesson, are much more comfortable to shoot with full-house loads than sixguns that weigh a pound less, such as the Ruger Blackhawk, Freedom Arms Model 83, and Smith & Wesson Model 29. However, as the wise man said, "There is no such thing as a free lunch!" and with these heavier sixguns the price is paid more in the carrying all day than in the shooting. In general, the lighter a sixgun is the easier it packs, and of course, the heavier it is the easier it shoots. One simply has to decide which is of the greater importance.

The "Ribber" grips that are standard on the big bore Tracker help to reduce felt recoil whether the caliber is .41 Magnum, .45 Colt, or .45 ACP.

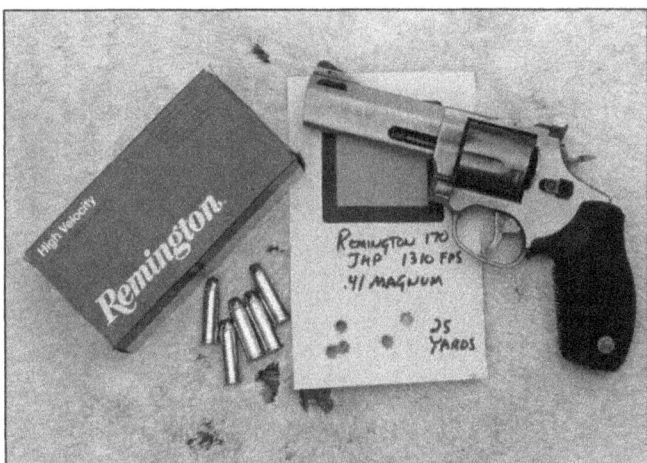

The .41 Magnum Tracker performs well with a varied assortment of factory ammunition.

CHAPTER 9

DAN WESSON: A BETTER IDEA

Many of us live in areas where quality handguns are easily obtainable with no restrictions as to how many we can own. However, others are burdened with restrictions that allow only one handgun, or one handgun per month, or too often, so much red tape that it takes seemingly forever to get the necessary permit to own a handgun. In the 1970s Dan Wesson was looking at a way to not only make a better sixgun but to also get around some of these stifling restrictions.

The answer was a revolver that could be made to accept barrels and cylinders in different calibers. Once the frame was acquired, that one frame would be all that was necessary, since it would accept barrel/cylinder combinations in .357 Magnum, .41 Magnum, .44 Magnum, .45 Colt, and .22 Long Rifle. Not such a bad idea even if one lives in a non-restrictive area. The guns would have the same trigger pull, grip, and feel for each caliber employed. The idea never achieved complete fruition, but thanks to Dan Wesson, the sixgun with interchangeable barrels became a reality.

Dan Wesson, great grandson of Daniel Baird Wesson, co-founder of Smith & Wesson, was born in Massachusetts in 1916. By 1938 he had joined the

For much of the 1980s and into the 1990s, the Dan Wesson revolver was "King of the Silhouette Range."

183

Two early long-range favored sixguns, especially for silhouettes: 10-inch barreled .357 SuperMag and .44 Magnum.

family company as a machine operator. The younger Wesson was named assistant superintendent in 1941 at a time when Smith & Wesson was in the dangerous predicament of being very close to bankruptcy. Wesson worked with president Carl Hellstrom through those hard times to save Smith & Wesson. In 1963, Dan Wesson was named plant superintendent, but trouble was immediately ahead. It came in 1966 with the acquisition of Smith & Wesson by Bangor Punta. This caused many problems for Smith & Wesson, including a decline in quality during the Bangor years. It also resulted in the last Wesson resigning from the company.

The early years

Dan Wesson was not without work, however, as he had formed his tool and die company 20 years earlier. In 1968, after leaving Bangor Punta's Smith & Wesson, Dan Wesson changed D.B. Wesson, Inc. to Dan Wesson Arms. By 1969, the new Dan Wesson .357 Magnum Model 12 arrived with its radical new design incorporating interchangeable barrels Those early six-

Although rarely seen with shorter barrels, the Dan Wesson 4-inch is an easy-to-pack double-action revolver, whether chambered in (from left) .357 Magnum, .41 Magnum, .44 Magnum, or .45 Colt.

guns from Dan Wesson had three problems: grips, barrel contour, and barrel locking nut. Add them altogether and they spelled ugly! The Dan Wesson .357 was the first revolver to offer interchangeable barrels, interchangeable grips and, praise the Lord, interchangeable front sights! But that first Dan Wesson model needed some cosmetic help.

Dan Wesson grips were quite different from the grips found on Colts and Smith & Wessons. Instead of two pieces of wood that bolted to two sides of the grip frame, the DW stocks were one-piece style that fit over a stud instead of a grip frame, and then bolted on from the bottom. If the first run of stocks were not too pleasing and did not fit real well, at least it was only a matter of time until fit was improved and different styles were offered. Until very recently, Dan Wesson revolvers were the only double-action sixguns that came from the factory with usable grips.

The really great offering from Dan Wesson was the interchangeable barrel system. The original idea may have been to be able to offer multiple guns for the price of one gun plus extra barrels, but the added bonus the shooter received was exceptional accuracy. The accuracy may have been designed into the gun, but I'm more inclined to believe that it was a fortunate by-product. To be able to offer interchangeable barrels, it was necessary to have a system that allowed the shooter to change barrels in the field. Anyone who has ever tried to change a revolver barrel knows how difficult this can be. If the barrel is loose enough to be easily changed, it can slowly rotate as it is shot. Dan Wesson abandoned the idea of a traditional barrel and instead provided a very skinny barrel (how can lightweight barrels shoot well?) that could be hand tightened and removed. No vise. No special tools. Great ingenuity!

The barrel is screwed into the frame until it bears against a feeler gauge of .002 to .006 inches, depending upon the caliber. Then a heavy shroud is placed over the barrel and a hole in the back of the shroud mates up with an aligning pin on the frame. A barrel nut is then screwed on the muzzle end of the barrel and, using a special wrench provided with each gun, is tightened against the shroud. The first barrel nuts were seemingly hanging on the end of the barrel, but by 1972 a concealed nut was being used and the Dan Wesson .357 had become a good-looking sixgun. In addition to a barrel that was locked at the front of the muzzle, the Dan Wesson cylinder latch was located not at the rear, but at the front of the cylinder. This also contributed to its exceptional accuracy.

Finding a niche: silhouetting

As long-range metallic silhouetting soared in the early 1980s, the Dan Wesson's fortunes rose with it. Conversely, when silhouetting started to decline, Dan Wesson rode the same downhill ride. Dan Wesson revolvers never really caught on with law enforcement personnel. Have you ever run into a constable on patrol carrying a Dan Wesson .357? And though they make fine, albeit heavy, hunting handguns, hunters never have really taken the big-bore DW to heart as much as lighter Rugers and Smith & Wessons. The saving grace was that everyone had to have Dan Wesson revolvers for serious silhouette competition in the 1980s. When silhouetting declined, Dan Wesson sales did likewise.

I was first introduced to the real capability of the Dan Wesson .357 sixgun when I watched a local shooter in the early 1980s clean everyone's clock using a DW .357 Magnum with a heavy 8-inch barrel. By this time, Dan Wesson was offering four styles of barrels: standard, heavy, standard ribbed, and heavy ribbed. When loaded with heavyweight bullets at moderate velocities, the heavyweight-barreled Dan Wesson .357 competed on an equal footing with the 10-inch Ruger Super Blackhawk .44 Magnum. Probably more than equal as less recoil gave the .357 DW a decided advantage.

After winning the state shoot in 1981 with a Ruger .44 Magnum, I switched to the Dan Wesson .357 Magnum with the 10-inch heavy barrel. Dan Wesson and Ruger were the only major revolver manufacturers to listen to silhouette shooters at the time. That Dan Wesson .357 would, (still does!) really shoot. I found out just how well the first few rounds through it. It is my practice to place any reloads with less than perfect cast bullets at the front of the ammo box and they are then used for warming up the gun. These are normally bullets that have obvious defects but somehow made it

A much younger author shooting an early Dan Wesson .44 Magnum. The experience was enjoyable and painless.

The author enjoying some long-range shooting with the 10-inch Dan Wesson .44 Magnum.

through the loading cycle and a visual inspection. I had loaded 210-grain cast bullets over a healthy charge of WW296 and put in five not-so-perfect rounds and proceeded to shoot at 25 yards off sandbags. I did not take any real particular care with the five shots, nor did I take a lot of time. As I looked at the target, I was more than pleasantly surprised to find one ragged hole! This was a sixgun!

The medium-framed Dan Wesson .357 Magnum, now known as the Model 15, or Model 715 in stainless, has undergone cosmetic changes over the years but remains the basic Model 12 first offered in 1970. It has been chambered in .38 Special, .357 Magnum, .22LR, .22 Magnum Rimfire, .32 Magnum, and .32-20. We are blessed in this country with some excellent .357 Magnum revolvers. I would rank the Dan Wesson Model 15, the Colt Python, and the Smith & Wesson Model 27 all in the same league, especially when all wear long barrels. They all handle quite differently, but are all superb examples of the gunmaker's art. For some reason, my 10-inch Dan Wesson .357 normally shoots slower than the 8-inch Python or 8 3/8-inch Model 27. It also shoots much better with cast bullets than with jacketed bullets. In fact, I did all of my silhouette shooting in the 1980s using this Dan Wesson with cast bullets.

The .44 Magnum

With the .357 Magnum solidly entrenched, Dan Wesson began experimenting with a large-frame revolver in .44 Magnum. In my file is a copy of a letter from Dan Wesson in April of 1977. I had written asking for a larger sixgun in .44 Magnum and .45 Colt and was told that "...the .44 Magnum is on the drawing board." Dan Wesson himself never saw the birth of the .44 Magnum as he died in the late 1970s. Unlike Smith & Wesson, which was able to use the N-frame that housed the .357 Magnum and .44 Special for its .44 Magnum, Dan Wesson had to go back to square one and build a new gun. The Model 15 .357 Magnum was too small to handle the .44 Magnum. When the .44 Magnum Dan Wesson came along it was a very large and beautiful sixgun, weighing in at

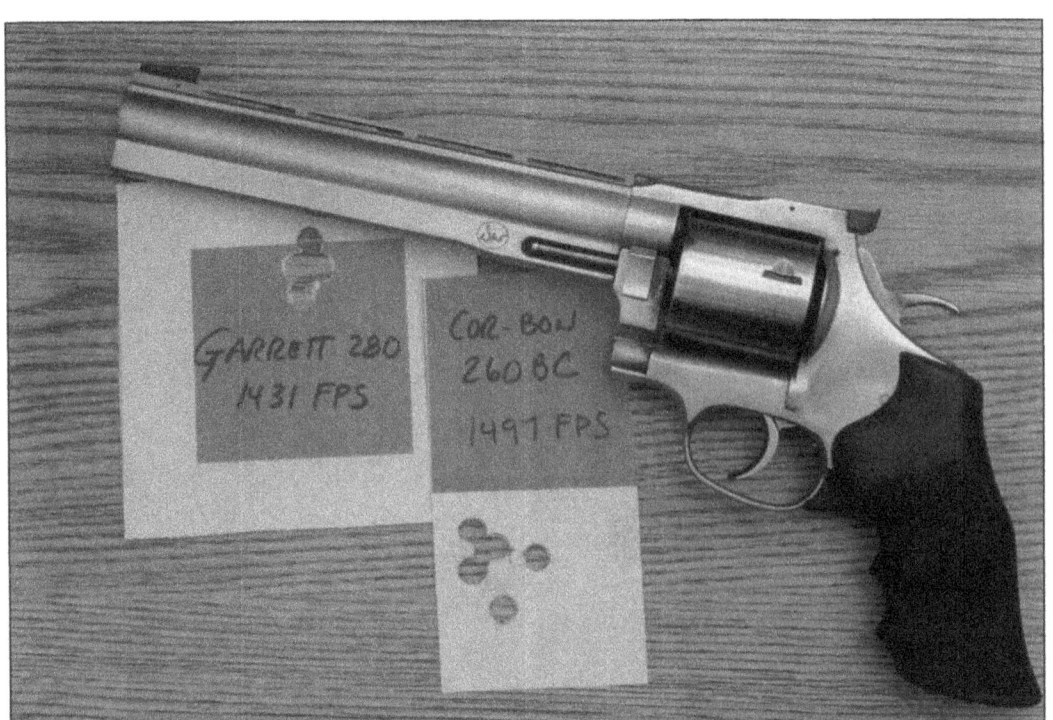

Dan Wesson's stainless-steel .44 Magnum handles heavy-duty factory loads from Garrett and Cor-Bon with ease.

The Dan Wesson .44 Magnum is exceptionally accurate with one of Taffin's favorite heavyweight bullet loads: BRP's 290-grain gas-check over 21.5 grains of H110 or 10.0 grains of Unique.

4 pounds with the 8-inch heavy barrel and a 10-inch standard barreled model.

The Dan Wesson .44 Magnum is an excellent .44 Magnum choice for anyone who is recoil conscious. The early Model 44 had ported barrels and shrouds, but these caused problems as crud from fired bullets worked its way between the barrel and shroud, making barrel changing quite difficult. The ports were not needed anyway. The 4-pound weight of the Dan Wesson Model 44 really tamed the .44 Magnum. The Model 44 has since been offered in the Model 744 stainless, the Model 41 and 741 .41 Magnum, and the Model 45 and 745 .45 Colt. All three of these calibers are relatively very pleasant to shoot in the big-bore Dan Wesson. This "pleasantness" is not without tradeoffs. A 3-pound sixgun packs easiest; a 4-pound sixgun shoots more comfortably. A pure case of personal choice.

The .45 Colt

Dan Wesson was the first company to bring us a large-framed, heavy-duty, double-action .45 Colt since the demise of the Colt New Service in 1941. The .45 Colt Dan Wesson is basically a .44 Magnum re-chambered and re-barreled, and looks identical to the .44 Magnum except for the stamping on the right side of the barrel shroud. In fact, I use my scope-mounted 8-inch .44 Magnum shroud on the .45 Colt DW when my shooting requires a scope.

Weighing in at just 3 ounces under 4 pounds, the .45 Colt Dan Wesson is an exceptionally pleasant big-bore to shoot, even when used with bullets of 300 grains or more. In fact, the Dan Wesson .45 Colt seems to prefer heavyweight bullets for best shooting. I have had excellent results with both the SSK 340-grain bullet and the LBT and NEI 350-grain bullets.

SELECTED LOADS DAN WESSON .44 MAGNUM 8"/BURRIS 1 1/2X-4X SCOPE

BULLET	LOAD	MV	50 YDS
Sierra 180JHC	26.0 gr. #2400	1,665	2 1/4"
Hornady 180JHP	29.0 gr. H110	1,524	2"
Speer 200JHP	28.0 gr. WW296	1,466	1 3/4"
Hornady 240JHP	24.0 gr. H110	1,412	1 1/2"
Speer 240JSP	22.0 gr. #2400	1,350	1 1/2"
Sierra 250JSP	24.0 gr. WW296	1,400	1 3/4"
Freedom Arms 260JSP	23.0 gr. WW296	1,447	1 3/4"
Hornady 265JFP	23.0 gr. H110	1,357	1 1/2"
Barnes 300JSP	20.5 gr. WW296	1,228	1 1/4"
Freedom Arms 300JSP	21.5 gr. WW296	1,300	1"
BRP 290KT	21.5 gr. WW296	1,303	1 1/2"
SSK #310\FP	21.5 gr. WW296	1,383	1 3/4"

With a weight of 4 pounds and the most usable factory stocks ever offered on a double-action sixgun, both the .44 Magnum and .45 Colt are relatively easy to shoot with minimum recoil.

The .45 Colt cartridge is a strange one in that even though it measures .480 inch at the base compared to the .44 Magnum's .455 inch, both have the same .505 diameter rim. This means that the extractor star of a .45 Colt DA revolver does not have much to push on to extract empty cases. If done carelessly, extraction will result in .45 Colt cases being bypassed and left below the extractor and in the chamber. I find that by holding the fired .45 Colt DW muzzle up and giving a sharp tap on the extractor rod, no problems are encountered in extracting empties. The loads listed here are for the .45 Colt Dan Wesson. They may be too heavy for smaller-framed .45 Colt revolvers.

The .41 Magnum

The Dan Wesson big-bore trio is rounded out with the fine, but in some ways still unappreciated Magnum, the .41. Only slightly less powerful than the .44 Magnum, the .41 Magnum can do just everything its big brother can short of the hunting of really large game. And it does it with less recoil. If .44 Magnum recoil is a problem with full-house Magnum loads, a heavy-barreled Dan Wesson .44 Magnum might be the choice. If that is still a little too much, the same sixgun chambered for the .41 Magnum could be the answer. The only problem I find with the .41 Dan Wesson is in trying to hold all of that 4 pounds-plus weight with one

SELECTED LOADS FOR THE DAN WESSON .45 COLT 8"

BULLET/LOAD	LOAD	MV
Lyman #454424	10.0 gr. Unique	1,082
(260 gr.)	20.0 gr. #2400	1,208
	21.0 gr. #2400	1,283
	22.0 gr. #2400	1,351
	23.0 gr. H4227	1,222
NEI #310.451	23.0 gr. WW296	1,193
BRP 305 gr. GC	21.0 gr. WW296	1,099
NEI #325.451	23.0 gr. WW296	1,236
LBT #350451FN	22.0 gr. WW296	1,174
SSK #345.451	22.0 gr. WW296	1,244

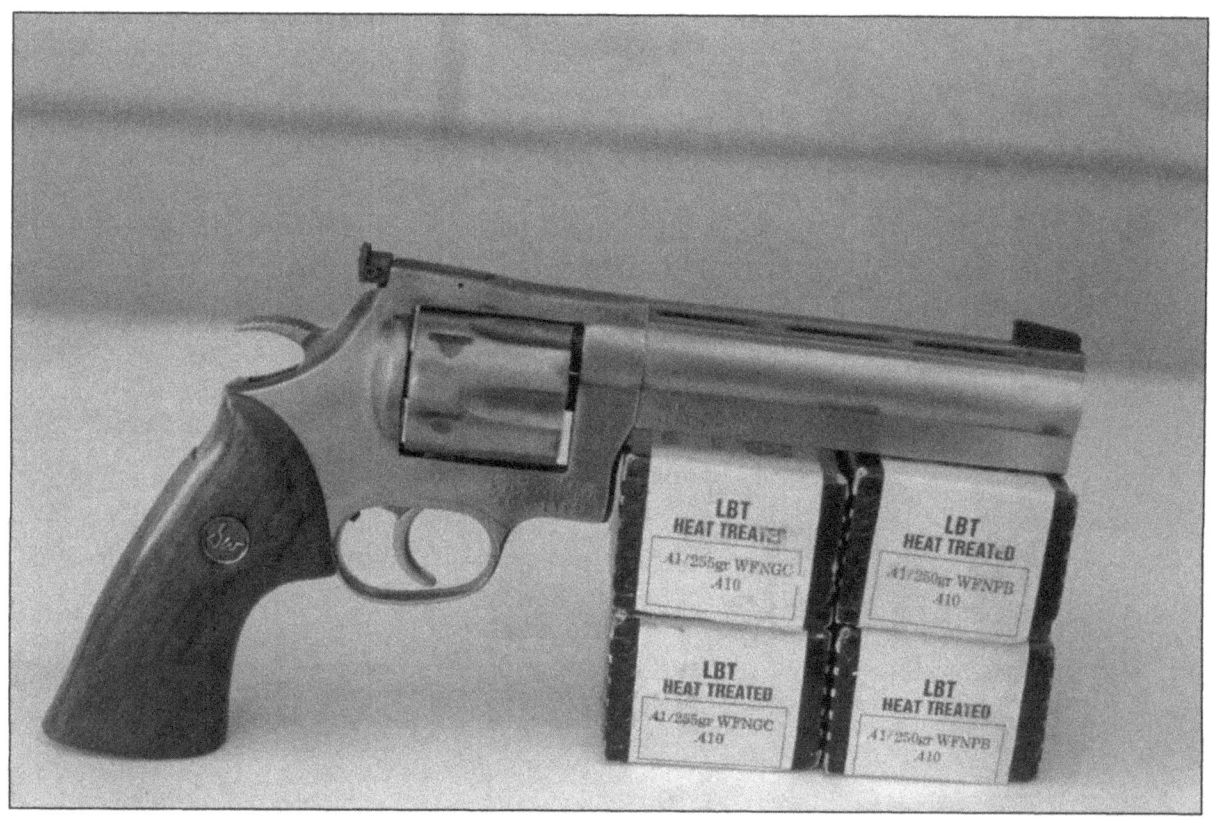

Dan Wesson's .41 Magnum is one of the few .41s that does well with heavyweight bullets, such as these from Cast Performance Bullet Company.

This target was shot with Cast Performance Bullet Company's 255-grain, .41 Magnum hard cast bullet. Exceptional performance.

The author and Hal Swiggett, friends and fellow Shootists, discuss the merits of the Dan Wesson .41 Magnum at the Shootists Holiday.

hand. Just like its two bigger brothers, the .44 Magnum and .45 Colt, the .41 Magnum is superbly accurate, and it is one factory .41 Magnum that will shoot heavier bullets with excellent accuracy. The following groups are for four shots at 25 yards.

The SuperMag

In the 1970s Elgin Gates came up with a number of exotic new 1.610-inch cartridges that he dubbed SuperMags. At this long length they were about .3 inch longer than standard Magnum cartridges, requiring the production of a totally new revolver with a longer frame and cylinder. At the time Gates had sample SuperMag cartridges in .357, .375, .44, .45, .50, and .60 caliber, but no revolver to shoot them in. After showing one of the company engineers a .357 SuperMag cartridge, he was told that "...the .44 Magnum was the most powerful cartridge that could ever be used in a revolver."

Gates related: "He stalked away, shaking his head at the thought of having to talk to nuts that came out of the woodwork at the trade shows. It's probably a good thing I did not show him the prints and prototypes of the .375, .445, .455, .505, and .610 I had in my pocket. It really would have blown his mind."

The SuperMag series of cartridges did become a reality thanks mostly to the combined efforts of Elgin Gates and Dan Wesson Arms. We now have Dan Wesson SuperMag revolvers available in .357, .375, .414, and .445 SuperMag chamberings. I was fortunate to be in on the beginning of each of the first three SuperMag cartridges — the .357, .375, and .445 — and to be able to assist with load development for all three.

The SuperMags came about with the rapid rise of silhouette shooting in the early 1980s. The three standard Magnum cartridges, .357, .41, and .44, are wonderfully accurate, but they lacked two things. They needed a flat trajectory and adequate case capacity to achieve the necessary velocity to both straighten out the rainbow trajectory arc and increase the knockdown power, especially on 200-meter, 60-pound steel rams that could often be stubborn going down. The SuperMag series of cartridges allows case capacity to be used to the ultimate and, in the .357 SuperMag, 200-grain bullets can be safely driven at speeds of 30-40 percent over the same weight bullet in a .357 Magnum. This flattens out the trajectory and cuts down on the sight adjustment that is needed going from 50-meter chickens to 100-meter pigs to 150-meter turkeys to 200-meter rams, plus gives the power necessary to send bent and wind-supported targets tumbling from their stubborn perches.

Most standard Magnum revolvers do not have enough sight adjustment to cover the 50- to 200-meter

SELECTED LOADS FOR THE DAN WESSON .41 MAGNUM 6"

BULLET	LOAD	MV	GROUP
BRP 260KT	18.0 gr. H4227	1,219	1 1/2"
	16.5 gr. #2400	1,290	1 1/4"
	17.5 gr. #2400	1,336	1 3/4"
	17.5 gr. H110	1,248	1/2"
CPBC 255 LBT	20.0 gr. H4227	1,179	1"
	18.5 gr. #2400	1,287	1"
	19.5 gr. H110	1,154	1"

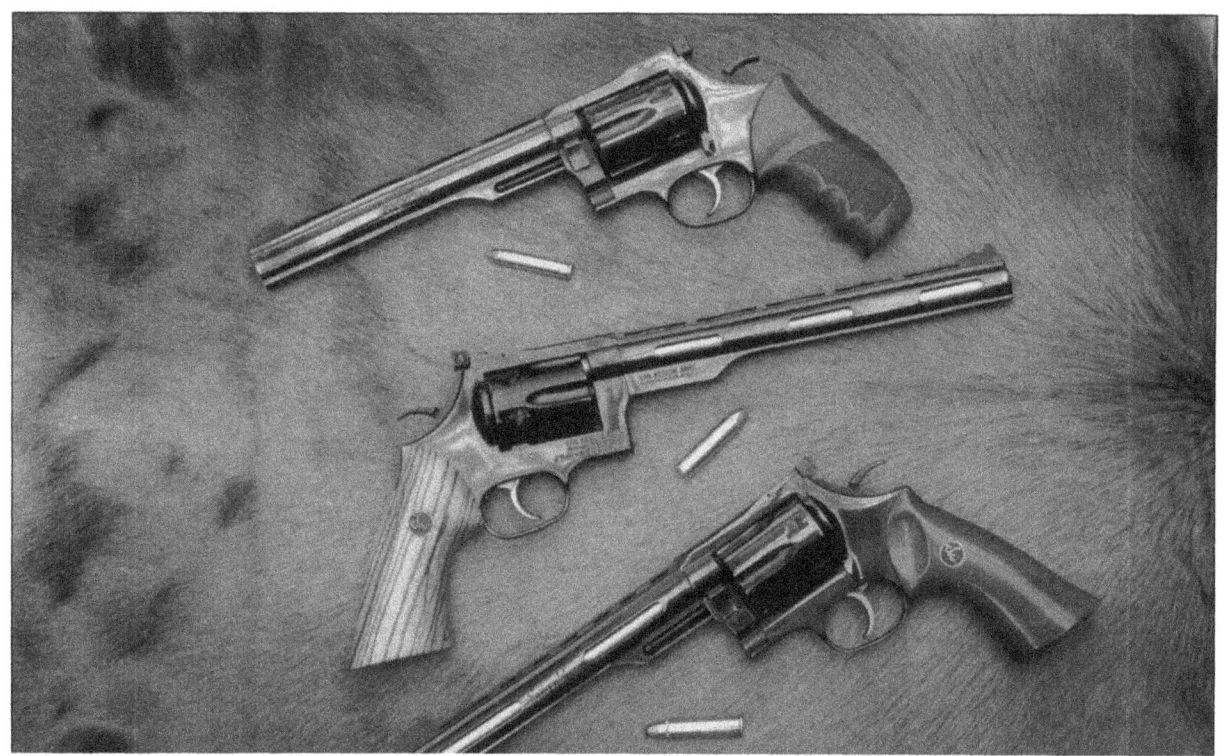

Dan Wesson introduced the sixgunning world to the SuperMags, .357, .375, and .445 all with 1.600-inch brass.

This compensated 4-inch .445 SuperMag is now known as the Alaskan Guide.

Dan Wesson offers its SuperMag revolver in .357 SuperMag, .375 SuperMag, .414 SuperMag, and .445 SuperMag.

ranges satisfactorily. In fact it is often necessary to either use different weight bullets at various ranges to compensate for this, or either hold under on the chickens or over on the rams. My early .357 Magnum load in a 10-inch Contender consisted of a 200-grain cast bullet at 1,400-plus fps. Beautifully accurate, flat-shooting, powerful, and a load that is duplicated in a revolver in the .357 SuperMag.

The .357 Maximum/SuperMag has the distinction of being the one new cartridge in my memory that many gun writers tried to kill off before it had a chance to prove itself with proper use. Early reloading attempts to make it into some type of ".357 Swift" in revolvers resulted in poor accuracy and the dangerous occurrence of bullets actually coming apart. Bullets designed for .357 Magnums, mainly 110-, 125-, 140-, and 158-grain versions, were not up to the pressure that was being applied to them in the new .357 SuperMag Dan Wesson or .357 Maximum Ruger Blackhawk.

Those writers who fall into this category simply did not understand the purpose of the .357 Maximum. Many shooters had found that standard .357 Magnums loads were not adequate for silhouetting, especially before the topple point rule was established. And even after the rule allowed targets to be set back for easier toppling, .357 shooters often found pigs and rams remained stubborn when supported by a strong wind coming from behind the targets. The .357 SuperMag/Maximum was designed to give .357 Magnum velocities to heavyweight bullets, not to see how fast a standard weight bullet could be driven. This was accomplished by stretching both cartridge case and cylinders by .3 inches.

The .414 SuperMag exhibits exceptional accuracy at 100 yards.

SELECTED LOADS FOR THE DAN WESSON .357 SUPERMAG 8"

BULLET	LOAD	MV-DW8"
RCBS #35-200FN	19.0 gr. H4227	1,468
RCBS #35-200FN	19.0 gr. WW296	1,489
Lyman #358627GC	19.0 gr. H4227	1,495
Lyman #358627GC	19.0 gr. WW296	1,526
Speer 180 FMJ	20.0 gr. H4227	1,371
Hornady 180 FMJ	20.0 gr. H4227	1,427
Speer 200 FMJ	19.0 gr. H4227	1,286

Those early "Swift" loads resulted in fast throat erosion, top strap cutting, and complaints from shooters and attempts to bury the cartridge by some gun writers. Dan Wesson packed an extra barrel with its .357 SuperMags. Mine is still packed in the box. The original barrel is fine and continues to be that way since it has always been used with proper loads.

While some were pronouncing the .357 SuperMag a failure, silhouetters were setting all kinds of long-range records with it. Serious shooters were not interested in lightweight/high-velocity loads. They were interested in accurate heavyweight bullet loads. That is, bullets in the 180-200-grain weight range that would shoot with silhouette accuracy at 1,300-1,500 fps. Many early long-range revolver silhouette records were set by the excellent-shooting Dan Wesson .357 SuperMag revolver.

Excellent bullets, both jacketed and cast, are available for the .357 Maximum. Early silhouetters went to RCBS's #35-200FN, a flat-nosed gas-checked bullet originally designed for the .35 Remington. This bullet had already seen much use by .357 Magnum silhouetters in both Dan Wesson revolvers and Thompson/Center Contenders, and it was a natural to carry over to the .357 Maximum. Two other excellent heavyweight cast bullets for the .357 Maximum are Lyman's #358627, a 210-grain, gas-checked Keith bullet, and RCBS's #35-180 SIL, a 180-grain gas-checked design. In the jacketed line, both Hornady and Speer offer 180-grain FMJs, and Speer also has a 200-grain FMJ bullet designed for maximum weight in the Maximum.

My favorite jacketed bullet loads for the .357 Maximum are assembled with 19.0-20.0 grains of H4227 with either the 180-grain Hornady or Speer Silhouette bullet, and 19.0 grains of H4227 with the 200-grain Speer FMJ. I have also had good results with the 19.0 grains of WW296 and the 180-grain full-metal jacketed bullets. These 180-grain bulleted loads are in the 1,300-1,400 fps range in the 8-inch Dan Wesson .357 SuperMag.

The first time I shot the .375 SuperMag in the then new Seville revolver, I experienced a sensation I had never achieved before from a sixgun. Elgin Gates had lent me his personal Seville .375 SuperMag and I was trying it out on rams. Normally when rams are shot with a revolver, there is an instant, that sometimes seems like an eternity, from the time the trigger is pulled until the bullet either strikes the dirt in a miss, or the target slowly changes color in the sun as it begins to slowly topple backwards. With all revolvers I had previously shot, .357 Magnum, .41 Magnum, .44 Magnum, and .357 SuperMag, there was time to recover from recoil and watch for the hit. With the new .375 SuperMag, it seemed that the target went down almost instantly. In fact, for the first time ever, I did not have time to see the ram topple. It was down. Right now.

The .375 SuperMag allowed the use of Hornady's .375, 220-grain rifle bullet at an incredible speed of 1,700 fps in the 10 1/2-inch Seville revolver. This completed changing the concept of the silhouette revolver that had begun with the .357 SuperMag. The flat trajectory and speed of the .375 SuperMag had heretofore only been found in single-shot handguns.

The .375 SuperMag, like its smaller counterpart, is 1.610 inches in length and originally brass had to be made from .375 Winchester or .30-30 Winchester brass, cut to length and filed in a trim die, and the .375 SuperMag remains a handgun cartridge that is factory chambered but for which no factory ammunition is available. It remains a reloader's proposition all the way. Since the .375 SuperMag is a tapered cartridge, carbide sizing dies are not available. I have had excel-

SELECTED LOADS FOR THE DAN WESSON .375 SUPERMAG 8"

BULLET	LOAD	MV
Hornady 220 JFP	23.0 gr. H110	1,267
	22.0 gr. H4227	1,258
	27.0 gr. WW680	1,364

SELECTED LOADS FOR THE DAN WESSON .445 SUPERMAG 10"
(All listed loads give groups of 1 inch or less at 25 yards.)

BULLET	LOAD	MV
Sierra 220 FPJ	34.0 gr. H4227	1,629
Speer 240 Silhouette	39.0 gr. WW680	1,626
Sierra 300-gr. JSP	35.0 gr. H110	1,472
SAECO 260 GC	32.0 gr. H4227	1,560
SAECO 260 GC	34.0 gr. H4227	1,648
SAECO 260 GC	37.0 gr. WW680	1,515
SAECO 260 GC	38.0 gr. WW680	1,540
SAECO 260 GC	39.0 gr. WW680	1,577
BRP 290 Keith GC	33.0 gr. WW680	1,468
BRP 290 Keith GC	36.0 gr. WW680	1,561
SSK 310 FP	29.0 gr. H110	1,469
SSK 310 FP	30.0 gr. H110	1,522

lent results with Redding .375 SuperMag dies and also have found .375 SM brass quite easy to make from .375 Winchester brass using a Redding trim die. No inside neck reaming is necessary unless the use of 250-grain or heavier bullets is desired.

Even before the .357 SuperMag became a viable revolver cartridge, experiments were being carried on using the SuperMag cartridge in re-chambered .357 Magnum Thompson/Center Contenders. It was about this time in 1981 that I met one such wildcatter, Lew Schafer. Schafer had been working on his .444 Schafer Magnum chambered in a Contender. The Schafer Magnum was nothing more than the .444 Marlin case swaged and turned on a lathe to have the same outside dimensions as the .44 Magnum. As soon as I heard that the Dan Wesson .357 SuperMag was coming, I contacted Schafer and he began to make plans to convert one to his other wildcat, the .44 Schafer UltraMag, made by trimming the .44 Schafer Magnum to 1.610 inches. We were shooting this new round in a 10-inch Contender at the time. With the Contender we were going to 2,200 fps with the Hornady 200-grain JHP, and 2,000 fps with the Sierra 220-and Hornady 240-grain bullets.

Schafer now had the cartridge, dies, chambering reamers, and test results, but no revolver. It would not take long to remedy this and the first .357 SuperMag Dan Wesson revolver to arrive in our area was never fired as a .357 but instead immediately re-chambered to .44 UltraMag and fitted with a shortened and re-threaded Dan Wesson .44 Magnum barrel and shroud. Using the 8-inch-barrelled .44 UltraMag, we shot 200-grain Hornady JHPs at 2,000 fps; 220 Sierras, 1,900 fps; 240 Hornady's, 1,800 fps; and the 265-grain Hornady jacketed flat point (an excellent hunting bullet) to 1,650 fps.

At the time, Schafer spent considerable effort trying to interest Dan Wesson in bringing out the .44 UltraMag, but to no avail. Schafer did first-class conversions but they were expensive because Dan Wesson 10-inch .44 Magnum barrels had to be cut shorter and re-threaded as the thread size of the SuperMag frame was different than that of the .44 Magnum frame. In 1988, the Dan Wesson .44 SuperMag became a reality as Elgin Gates worked with Dan Wesson to complete the SuperMag trio and also placed a healthy order with Dan Wesson for the new sixgun.

Problems arose early with the .445, as the .44 SuperMag was called, both guns and brass. The first guns had oversize cylinders and the brass was not properly annealed. All this has long since been corrected and present purchasers of guns and brass should not run into problems with either. I have received numerous inquiries about the availability of brass. It is now available through Starline.

As is the case with the other SuperMag cartridges, the .445 is a sub 1-inch, 25-yard revolver when used with the proper loads. Finding the proper loads may require some experimenting at both loading bench and shooting bench, but the potential is definitely there. The use of heavyweight bullets seems to further enhance accuracy and I particularly prefer bullets for the .445 in the 300-grain class.

Because of the large case capacity of the .445 SuperMag cartridge, powders can be quite position sensitive. That is, less than full cases of powder will allow the powder to shift around. Where it happens to be when it is ignited will determine the muzzle velocity. WW680 proves to be quite position sensitive to the tune of 200 or more fps and Accurate Arms 1,680 seems to be the least position sensitive. Reloaders have seen this phenomenon for years in trying to develop less than full-house loads for the .44 Magnum and .45 Colt. A session over the chronograph can be very enlightening.

A new era, a new direction

In the Golden Age of Silhouetting, the Dan Wesson sixgun was King! Most of us started with Rugers and

In addition to producing excellent sixguns, Wesson Firearms also offers an exceptionally well-designed shoulder holster. Custom stocks are by Herrett's.

Smith & Wessons, but as Dan Wesson listened to silhouette shooters and came out with better sights and longer and heavier barrels, the silhouette crowd flocked to the Dan Wesson products banner. As previously mentioned, my first true silhouette sixgun was the Dan Wesson .357 Magnum with a heavy 10-inch barrel. It was incredibly accurate and was followed by other Dan Wesson silhouette sixguns in .44 Magnum, .357 SuperMag, and the ill-fated .375 SuperMag. The .445 came along a mite too late for me to use in silhouetting much.

Dan Wesson's popularity with the silhouette shooters was a good news/bad news proposition. As long as there were plenty of silhouette shooters, Dan Wesson had a waiting market, but once that market started to drop, Dan Wesson was in trouble. Dan Wesson was caught in squeeze between two factors: the general decline in silhouette shooting clubs across the country, and the emergence of the Freedom Arms Model 83 Silhouette Model chambered in .357 Magnum. Many of the serious shooters that remained in the game took up the Freedom Arms revolver.

The handwriting was on the wall in the early 1990s and the doors of the Dan Wesson factory in Massachusetts closed. The company had gone through several hands beginning with Dan Wesson first. It went to the family when he passed on. They eventually lost control to an outside group, and then in the late 1980s the Wesson family regained control once again. Seth and Carol Wesson, as well as their sons Eric and Seth Jr, are all good people and it was gratifying to see them get control of the company back in family hands. Unfortunately, it was not to be. When I visited in the early 1990s, it was obvious the company was struggling. It was not too long after that the doors were closed and the Dan Wesson revolver was no more. A lot of us sixgunners were saddened by this, not only for the Wesson family personally, but also for the demise of a truly innovative sixgun.

All Dan Wesson revolvers from Wesson Firearms feature interchangeable front sights.

Wesson Firearms offers the Pistol Pack in a high-quality case.

Wessons were accurate, but they had several problems, often found in the same revolver. The front of the cylinder face and the back of the barrel were not always parallel to each other, making it difficult to set the cylinder gap. Cylinder chambers were often rough, and actions were almost always so. All of these problems, combined with the aforementioned decline in silhouetting, eventually killed the Wesson sixgun. But, as they say, that was then, and this is now. The Dan Wesson revolver is back and better than ever!

Dan Wessons are being produced once again, not in Massachusetts, but in New York. Using mostly new machinery, Bob Serva of Dan Wesson is turning out some beautiful sixguns if the examples I have fired over the past few years are any indication. The first sixgun I had from the "new" Dan Wesson was an 8-inch, heavy-barreled, stainless-steel Wesson .44 that had a smooth action, smooth cylinder chambers, and a barrel cylinder gap that featured parallel lines. All of these improvements are the result of Dan Wesson Firearms now producing guns on new machinery.

Gone are the rough chambers and they do not even have to polish the cylinder chambers to smooth them out. No more sticking case in the cylinder! The .44 Magnum was a real shooter. More loads than not were in the 1-inch category at 25 yards using iron sights. With scope in place, 1-inch 50-yard groups were also common using factory hunting loads, namely Black Hills 320-grain Hard Cast and Garrett's 280- and 310-grain Hard Cast Keith bulleted loads. Using the 8-inch Dan Wesson, Garrett's 310-grain Keith load would put five shots in 2 inches at 100 yards. Excellent performance for a .44 Magnum sixgun.

Dan Wesson is not only producing sixguns in the old standby .357 Magnum and .44 Magnum chamberings, but also the fourth SuperMag, the one that did not quite make it before. The .414 SuperMag is now a reality. Only a very few .414s were originally produced before the factory shut its Massachusetts doors.

Serva purchased Wesson Firearms in 1996. Included in the purchase was the tooling, patents, trademarks, and all remaining inventory. The old machinery was not purchased, but everything that was acquired by Serva was moved to upstate New York to an area that Serva describes thusly: "With its abundance of beautiful hills and mountains, woodlands and farmland, lakes, streams, and rivers, it is a mecca for wildlife as well as sportsman. It is also the perfect location to breath new life into the legendary Dan Wesson line."

The first problem that surfaced when Serva tried to move his new company in with his machining business was the fact that there was definitely a lack of space. Within a few months a new facility was located north of Norwich, New York, and the move was made. With the move and startup to produce new sixguns it became obvious that the old tooling would not do. It would be another year before all new tooling using high-tech machinery would result in the first revolver coming off the line in December of 1997.

For the next year, Serva continued to go forward with new CNC lathes and polishing equipment (Dan Wessons have always been well known for their fine finish) and the training of skilled workers. During this time the SRS-1 line of Super Ram Silhouette revolvers were introduced with plans to produce them in .22 Long Rifle, .360 (a shortened .357 SuperMag), .41

SELECTED LOADS FOR THE DAN WESSON .414 SUPERMAG 8"

BULLET	LOAD	MV	GROUP/25 YARDS
Factory 170 JHP		1,572	2"
Factory 220 FMJ		1,358	1 1/8"
Sierra 170 JHC	29.5 gr. H110	1,646	1 3/4"
Sierra 170 JHC	27.5 gr. H4227	1,535	2 1/4"
Sierra 170 JHC	27.7 gr. VV N-110	1,746	2 1/4"
Hornady 210 XTP	27.3 gr. H110	1,608	2"
Hornady 210 XTP	27.5 gr. H4227	1,524	1 7/8"
Sierra 210 JHC	26.0 gr. VV N-110	1,552	7/8"

Magnum, .44 Magnum, plus the SuperMag chamberings of .357, .375, .414, and .445.

With the training of workers and the acquisition of new equipment, production remained low throughout 1998. By 1999, the Model 360 and Model 460 both became reality, the .414 SuperMag arrived, and the Hunter Packs and Pistol Packs were reintroduced. My test Pistol Pack came in a fine-looking case trimmed in brass and leather with dual combination locks. Serva said it would remind me of a high-grade English-style gun case and it does.

Three SuperMags, .357, .375, and .445, came from Dan Wesson in the 1980s, three really big-bore Maximums, .458, .475, and .500, from custom 'smiths in the 1990s, and now Dan Wesson is back and producing the original three plus the .414 SuperMag once again. I do not know how many .414s were made before the doors were shut in the early 1990s, but I would guess less than two dozen.

The .414, as are the .357 SuperMag and the .445, is simply a stretched version of an existing Magnum chambering. The first two came from the .357 Magnum and .44 Magnum, while the .414 is the big brother of the .41 Magnum. My test .414 came with three barrels and shrouds in 4-, 6- and 8-inch lengths. It also came with two sets of grips from Hogue: one finger-groove rubber and the other, the one I prefer, is a laminated wooden stock, also with finger grooves. In the Pistol Pack is the mandatory barrel wrench and feeler gauge for changing barrels quickly and precisely. Dan Wesson still offers interchangeable front sights and several options are packed in with the frame, barrels, and shrouds in the Pistol Pack.

Factory loads provided with the .414 SuperMag from Dan Wesson consisted of a 170 jacketed hollow point for hunting and a 220 grain-full metal jacket for silhouetting. Both are loaded fairly mildly with the 170 clocking out at 1,572 fps and the 220 going 1,358 both from the 8-inch barrel. Handloads can improve performance dramatically, with the 170 at over 1,700 fps and the 220 over 1,450 fps.

My best handload turned out to be Sierra's 210-grain jacketed hollowpoint over 26.0 grains of VV N-110 for 1,550 fps and a five-shot group at 25 yards, using iron sights, of 7/8 inch. With cast bullets I went immediately to Cast Performance Bullet Company's 255-grain, gas-checked LBT bullet over 26.0 grains of H110 for over 1,600 fps. This combination should give excellent performance on big game.

Dan Wesson is also offering its big sixgun in a new chambering — the .460 Rowland. This new cartridge, originally designed for a semi-automatic, comes from Johnny Rowland, who hosts the "Shooting Show" radio program out of Louisiana. I met Rowland while hunting on the Y.O. one fall and then ran in to him again at the SHOT Show. Rowland was at the Clark Custom Guns booth and showing his new cartridge in both semi-automatics, the basic 1911 platform, and two revolvers that had been re-chambered to .460 Rowland, a Ruger Blackhawk and a Smith & Wesson Model 625. Clark offers a drop-in kit for putting a .460 Rowland together on a 1911 platform. I installed one of Clark's kits on a Springfield Armory platform and found I basically had a 1911 that was the equivalent of a 5-inch .44 Magnum sixgun.

This custom Model 460 Dan Wesson handles the .460 Rowland and the .45 Winchester Magnum using full-moon clips. It also accepts the .45 ACP and .45 Auto Rim. A most versatile revolver.

SELECTED LOADS FOR THE DAN WESSON .460 ROWLAND 8"

BULLET	LOAD	MV	5 SHOTS/25 YARDS
Factory 185 Nosler		1,509	1"
Factory 200 XTP		1,438	1 1/2"
Factory 230 XTP		1,351	1 1/4"
Speer 260 JHP	19.0 gr. AA#7	1,567	1 3/8"
Sierra 300 JFP	19.0 gr. AA#7	1,330	One hole!
Hornady 185 XTP	18.5 gr. AA#7	1,505	1 3/8"
Speer 200 JHP	17.5 gr. AA#7	1,499	1"
RCBS 255KT	14.3 gr. AA#7	1,254	1 5/8"
Nosler 185 JHP	17.0 gr. AA#7	1,398	1 1/8"

The .460 Rowland is a .45 ACP case that has been lengthened and also beefed up. The brass, from Starline, is head stamped ".460 ROWLAND," and is 1/16 inch longer than the .45 ACP. Factory loads for the .460 Rowland, all clocked in a 1911, are a 185-grain jacketed hollowpoint at 1,550 fps, a 200-grain jacketed hollowpoint at 1,450 fps, and a 230-grain jacketed hollowpoint at 1,340 fps. Rowland told me that the Dan Wesson chambered in .460 Rowland would use full moon clips and with bullets seated out would yield much higher muzzle velocities. He proved to be correct.

This sixgun handles four different cartridges. In addition to the .460 Rowland, the chambers will also accept the .45 ACP, the .45 Auto Rim, and the .45 Winchester Magnum. All except the Auto Rim require moon clips, be it 1/3, 2/3, or full-moon style. It certainly is handy to reach into a pocket for a reload consisting of a full-moon clip with six cartridges in place. One caution here, the full moon clips will not accept the .45 Winchester brass from Winchester, but will work fine with Starline brass. Accuracy with the .45 ACP and the .45 Auto Rim is nothing to get excited about. It is adequate, but I would reserve their use only for emergencies. The big cylinder of the Dan Wesson large-framed sixguns requires bullets from the relatively stubby little cases to jump quite a bit going from cylinder to barrel. Accuracy suffers in the trip.

Rowland supplied me with factory loads for the .460 Rowland, both semi-auto style and those with the bullets seated out for use in a sixgun. These loads, with their bullet weights and muzzle velocities from the revolver are: 185 Nosler, 1,509 fps; 200 XTP, 1,438 fps; and 230 XTP, 1,351 fps. When the 260 Speer is seated out to an overall length of 1.405 inches, and loaded over 19.0 grains of AA#7, muzzle velocity is 1,567 fps and five shots group in 1 3/8 inch at 25 yards. Switching to the Sierra 300-grain .45 JFP, with an overall length of 1.55 inches and loaded over 19.0 grains of AA#7, muzzle velocity is 1,330 fps and five shots group into one ragged hole at 25 yards.

The .360 DW

The latest cartridge from Dan Wesson is neither SuperMag nor standard Magnum case length, but rather a .357 Magnum case lengthened from 1.285 to 1.415 inches and chambered in its large frame, not Maximum frame, Wesson sixgun. The result is an accurate-shooting sixgun/cartridge combination that gets everything possible out of the .357 Magnum without going to an overly long cylinder and frame. The new cartridge and sixgun both bear the name "The .360 DW." Only the results are new as this cartridge uses the same bullets, primers, powder, and dies as the .357 Magnum (I use Redding's

The newest chambering from Wesson Firearms is the .360DW, an elongated .357 Magnum that takes full advantage of the cylinder on large-frame Dan Wesson sixguns. Stocks are by Hogues.

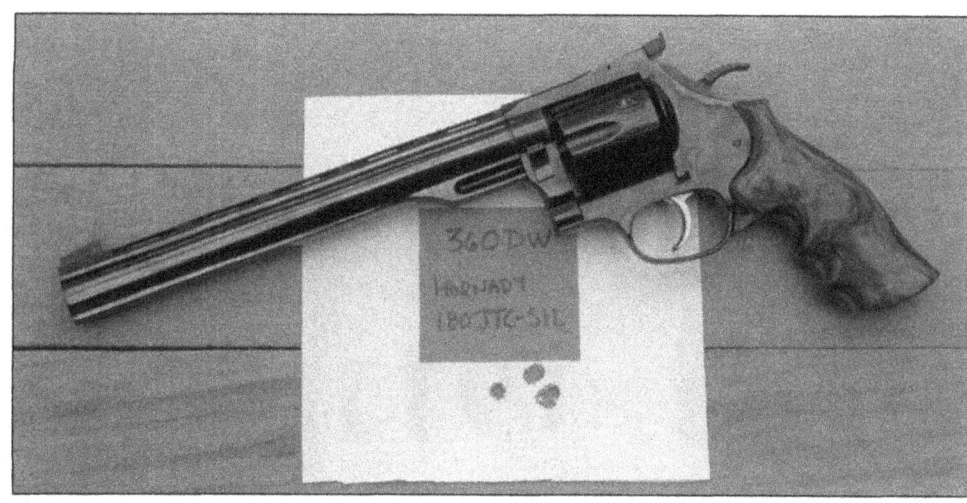

The new .360DW proves to be an accurate cartridge in the 10-inch Model 360.

excellent carbide dies). So if you already load for the .357 Magnum, everything necessary to use the .360 is already in place. Loaded ammunition as well as the new sixgun are available from Dan Wesson, while excellent brass comes from Starline.

My test sixgun is a 10-inch standard barreled Wesson Firearms .360 DW beautifully finished in the rarest of currently available factory finishes, deep blue! Dan Wesson has always been known for exceptional bluing and this Model 360 is no exception. As with all Dan Wessons of current manufacture from the company that has been totally revamped with new machinery, the .360 is of excellent quality. In the past few years I have tested new Dan Wessons in .44 Magnum, .460 Rowland, .414 SuperMag, .32 Magnum, .32-20, and now .360, and all have been well-fitted, well-timed and performed flawlessly.

The following data attests to the accuracy of the .360, even though the groups were shot without a scope and eyes that aren't as sharp as they once were. I was especially gratified by the results with the Cast Performance Bullet Company's 187-grain flat-point, gas-check design as this will be my bullet of choice with this sixgun.

Will the .360 fill a need? I feel it gives significant improvement over the .357 Magnum without excessive recoil or the use of an extra-long cylinder and frame. It certainly makes the .357 into an improved cartridge for hunting. One has to wonder what would have been had this sixgun/cartridge combination come about during the peak of long-range silhouetting.

I've been shooting Dan Wessons since the early days of silhouetting, going through the long-barreled .357 Magnum, .44 Magnum, .357 SuperMag, and .375 SuperMag. The .445 has proven to be an accurate powerhouse, and the .414 SuperMag, .460 Rowland, and .360 DW are all welcome additions to the Dan Wesson battery of big-bore sixguns. The sixguns coming from the new Dan Wesson are, in all ways, excellent sixguns.

SELECTED LOADS FOR THE DAN WESSON MODEL 360 10" .360 DW

BULLET	LOAD	MV	GROUP/5 SHOTS/25 YDS
360 DW/180 XTP-JHP		1,278	1 1/4"
360 DW/170 Sierra JHC		1,156	7/8"
360 DW/158 XTP-JHP		1,331	1 1/8"
360 DW/ 110 JHP		1,658	1 1/4"
Hornady 158 JHP	18.6 gr. WW296	1,213	1 1/4"
Hornady 180 JTC-SIL	17.0 gr. WW296	1,215	5/8"
Hornady 158 XTP-JHP	20.0 gr. H110	1,427	1 1/8"
Hornady 158 XTP-JHP	21.0 gr. H110	1,515	1 3/8"
Speer 158 Gold Dot HP	20.5 gr. H110	1,404	3/4"
Sierra 170 JHC	18.5 gr. H110	1,330	1 1/4"
Speer 170 GD-FP	18.5 gr. H110	1,300	1"
Speer 170 GD-FP	19.5 gr. H110	1,349	1 1/8"
Hornady 180 JTC-SIL	18.5 gr. H110	1,348	1"
CPBC 187 FP-GC	16.5 gr. H4227	1,236	1"
CPBC 187 Fp-GC	17.5 gr. H4227	1,338	1 1/2"
CPBC 187 FP-GC	17.5 gr. H110	1,361	1"
COBC 187 GC-FP	18.5 gr. H110	1,397	1 1/8"

CHAPTER 10

MODEL 1911: COMPETITION FOR THE BIG-BORE SIXGUN

For shooters, especially young shooters, the 1950s were a good news-bad news proposition. The good news was a great abundance of firearms with very little red tape or government regulatory hoops to jump through when buying them. The bad news was a lack of available money. On the plus side consider that from 1950-1956 Smith & Wesson introduced the 1950 Target in both .44 Special and .45 ACP, the 1955 Target .45, .357 Combat Magnum, and the .44 Magnum, all combined with the original .357 Magnum coming back into full production following World War II. The very young company of Sturm, Ruger gave us a .357 Blackhawk in 1955 followed by the .44 Magnum version one year later. Colt, the oldest handgun manufacturer, also introduced the Python .357 and the .45 Commander, and re-introduced the Colt Single Action Army. In retrospect, if I had known then how great the 1950s really were, I would have enjoyed them even more than I did.

By today's standards, these guns were all most reasonably priced with many costing less than $100. However, in the 1950s that was a lot of money. A lot of money! So for many of us a few new sixguns were backed by relatively inexpensive firearms that were either military surplus or available through the Director of Civilian Workmanship. The former included both Colt and Smith & Wesson 1917 revolvers from World War I, while the latter gave us 1903-A3 Springfields and Government Model .45s priced from $7.50 to $15.

For more than 90 years the Colt 1911 .45 ACP has been the .45 semi-automatic by which all others are judged. The 1911 at left is an original Commercial Model from 1914, and is shown with two of its offspring: a Clark Custom Commander, and a Kimber Compact.

Classic Colt 1911 .45s from top right: Clark Custom-built Commander, Commander, Ed DeLorge engraved Series '70, and 1914 Commercial Model.

Needless to say, a lot of us shot Springfields and Government Models. The old fellow that operated the elevator in the warehouse where I worked after high school kept us supplied with surplus .30-06 and .45 ACP military ball ammunition for $1 per box. We only had to work one hour to earn a box of ammunition.

This time period began my lifelong love of not only big-bore sixguns, but also the 1911 Government Model .45 ACP. I had several at the time marked Remington, as well as lesser manufacturers, and I terribly regret letting them get away. We definitely grow too soon old and too late smart. With the announcement of the coming of GCA '68, I very quickly purchased several 1911s, most notably three Commanders in .45 ACP, 9mm, and .38 Super, and I have never been without a 1911 since. The 9mm is long gone, but the other two remain and were soon backed up by a Series '70 Government Model .45. The Commander .45 ACP has now also been joined by a full-custom, all-steel Commander by Jimmy Clark that will shoot one-hole groups at 25 yards. The Series '70 Government Model has been engraved and satin-nickeled by Ed DeLorge and ivory stocked by Bob Leskovec.

One of my greatest buys of all is now a companion piece to this beautifully embellished .45. About 10 years ago, a fellow came to me at church and announced as a bank employee he was closing out an estate and said, "Would you like to buy a Colt .45 for $100?" at which point I interrupted him and uttered a resounding "Yes!" "But, don't you want me to tell you about it?" "Nope. I will take any Colt .45 for $100!" It turned out to not only be a Government Model, but a commercial model made in 1914. There was some pitting on the grip frame, so I had the entire frame bead blasted and satin nickeled, the slide was re-blued, and it shoots right to point of aim with military ball ammunition through what I assume is the original barrel.

When John Browning set his genius to work designing a semi-automatic pistol, the world already had the

When peace officers needed more powerful sidearms in the early 1930s, Smith & Wesson went with the .38-44 Heavy-Duty sixgun, while Colt developed the .38 Super in the 1911, which then evolved into the easier-to-pack 10-shot Commander.

It doesn't get much better than this; an Ed Delorge engraved 1911 carried in El Paso Saddlery custom leather.

As good as a 3 1/2-inch .357 Magnum? Or better? The 10-shot Colt Commander .38 Super.

The 1911 is one of the few semi-automatics worthy of engraving. This Series '70 .45 has been the engraved and satin nickeled by Ed DeLorge with ivory stocks by Bob Leskovec.

.30-caliber Broomhandle Mauser as well as the .30 and 9mm Lugers. The U.S. Army was more interested in a larger caliber and in the military trials to adopt a new pistol, the straight-gripped Colt .45 of 1905 was one of the participants. It was good, but not good enough, and no sidearm was adopted with all participants given the instructions to improve their designs. Browning went back to the drawing board and the result was the 1911 Government Model. As with William Mason and the Colt Single Action Army, one has to wonder if there could have been some supernatural intervention. Like that first Colt .45, the 1911 is such a masterpiece of design.

Except for wartime production, which required all available machinery, Colt had the 1911 design all to itself well into the 1970s. By this time shooters had really discovered the 1911 .45 thanks mainly to the writings of Jeff Cooper, who did for the .45 what Elmer Keith had done for the .44 Special and the .44 Magnum. There was also a great surge of interest in Combat Shooting. Colt could have led the way in providing high-quality 1911s. Instead it allowed quality to slip and was soon surrounded by many competitors as well as gunsmiths that could tune a Government Model to near perfection. One has to wonder how things would be different today if Colt had led the way instead of sleeping at the switch and then trying to play catch-up for the rest of the 20th century.

Literally dozens of manufacturers have offered 1911 designs over the past 20 years. Most of them are gone and to the credit of Colt, the original remains, though no longer at the top of the list. A look at the catalog section of the current edition of Gun Digest shows no less than 10 different manufacturers' names on Government Model-style pistols as well as a long list of double-action semi-automatic pistols that are a direct result of the popularity of the 1911 and the transition from revolvers to semi-autos for police use and self-defense.

In a book this size we cannot begin to look at all semi-automatic big-bore pistols, so it is necessary confine our examination only to some of those that I am both familiar with and have also test-fired extensively. Semi-auto's that are left out are not necessarily deemed to be less worthy, they are simply a victim of time and space. With that in mind we will look at some of the new heavy hitters on the 1911 platform, the 1911 pistols from the two top manufactures of 1911's, Kimber and Springfield Armory; and few other interesting developments that arrived before the 20th century bowed out.

We have seen a great deal of development of semi-automatics in the last two decades with new cartridges and an array of models too numerous to count. Most of them have been of the double-action variety. However, even with all the new technology the grand old 1911 is still king, is still the number one platform for custom 'smiths, and is certainly the "automatic" by which all others are judged. Has it ever really been improved upon, other than by taking the basic model and adding good sights, a good trigger, and possibly a beavertail grip safety? The Model 1911 in .45 ACP remains the epitome of what a fighting handgun should be.

The .38 Casull

It is easy, especially for a confirmed big-bore six-gunner such as myself, to consider revolvers as being much more versatile than the 1911. However, when I look with non-biased eyes I get a completely different picture. Two notable examples come to mind: the .38

The 1911 of the 21st century is this long-slide .38 Casull by Casull Arms capable of 1,800 fps with a 147-grain jacketed hollowpoint.

When fitted with a .460 Rowland Kit from Clark Custom Guns, the 1911 equals the muzzle energy of a 4-inch .44 Magnum.

Super and the relatively new .460 Rowland. With proper ammunition in a 1911, these two are the equivalent of a short-barreled .357 Magnum and .44 Magnum. The latest offering on the 1911 platform, the .38 Casull from Casull Arms, goes even further and leaves the .357 Magnum choking in the dust stirred up by a 147-grain jacketed hollowpoint at 1,800 fps!

I was able to test-fire the .38 Casull while taking a break for lunch during the 12th Annual Handgun Hunters Against Hunger Hunt on the YO Ranch in Texas. Well over 100,000 pounds of meat has been donated to the Salvation Army through this program. Since I was fortunate enough to take a 1,200-pound bison the first morning, I had time to enjoy shooting the .38 Casull at steel plates and 25, 50, at 100 yards using both a standard model and a compensated version. Recoil on the former is quite manageable, while the latter is not much worse than shooting a .22. The .38 Casull shoots so flat that I was able to use the same sight picture for all three distances.

The .38 Casull cartridge itself is a slightly shortened and necked-down .45 ACP. As such the magazine holds seven rounds and factory ammunition is offered in both 124- and 147-grain jacketed hollowpoint versions. This is a 6-inch long slide 1911 and has all the niceties as well as the quality of any handgun that bears Dick Casull's signature. The barrel of the Casull Arms Model CA3800 is Bar-Sto; sights are fully adjustable with the front sight on a locking dovetail; the ejection port is relieved; the grip safety is by Ed Brown; grips are checkered double-diamond exotic wood; and the recoil spring, as one might expect on such a powerful pistol, could hold up the rear end of 4X4 pickup, or at 30 pounds at least seems so. This is a beautifully made and flat-shooting pistol that will do the job on varmints and small deer. My buffalo was large enough to be a prize winner on this hunting trip, so I am now in possession of my very own .38 Casull.

The .460 Rowland

Wouldn't it be great if we could have a standard-sized 1911 that would deliver a .44 Magnum payload with no more recoil than a .45 ACP? This is now reality with the .460 Rowland that is handled by any standard 1911 using a drop-in kit from Clark Custom Guns. The concept comes from Johnny Rowland, who hosts the "Shooting Show," a radio program out of Louisiana. The .460 Rowland is simply a .45 ACP case that has

The author shooting a .460 Rowland. He found the weight and porting minimized felt recoil.

been stretched and strengthened. Starline is making the brass, head stamped ".460 ROWLAND," that is 1/16 inch longer than the standard .45 ACP brass and with a beefed-up interior. To come up with my .460 Rowland I used the Clark Drop-in Kit, a Springfield Armory 1911 main frame, and ordered the necessary parts to complete the gun from Brownells. A slide was needed along with several inner parts, such as a firing pin, firing pin stop, barrel link pin, and especially good sights. For the sights I chose a Bo-Mar adjustable rear sight and a Clark post front sight. A pair of cocobolo grips from Herretts completed the package. If one starts with a completed 1911, it is only necessary to change the barrel and replace the standard spring with the 24-pound spring found in the drop-in kit to come up with a .460 Rowland. Standard 1911 magazines work with the .460 Rowland.

Factory loads for the .460 Rowland are a 185-grain jacketed hollowpoint at 1,550 fps, a 200-grain jacketed hollowpoint at 1,450 fps, and a 230-grain jacketed hollowpoint at 1,340 fps. Fired in my completed .460 Rowland, the 185-grain factory load does 1,530 fps (and drops five shots into 5/8 inch at 15 yards), the 200-grainer does 1,436 fps and, and the 230 clocks out at 1,330 fps. For a comparison with .44 Magnum loads I fired the Federal 180 gr. JHP load from the 5-inch barrel of a Smith & Wesson Model 629 with the results being a muzzle velocity of 1,564 fps. Hornady's 200 XTP .44 Magnum loading clocked out at 1350, while Black Hills rendition of the 240-grain jacketed hollow point .44 load came in at 1247. For all practical purposes, the .460 Rowland with its 5-inch barrel equals, or surpasses, the .44 Magnum in a like barreled sixgun. Recoil? The Clark Drop-in Kit features a built-in comp that works. Really works. With it in place, the felt recoil of the .460 Rowland to me is less than that of standard .45 ACP. It is a different recoil, coming straight back rather than twisting, so it affects me less.

The .400 Cor-Bon

During the 1970s, wildcatters used the Browning Hi-Power chambered in a new .40 caliber, the .40 G&A using cut-down .224 brass and .38-40 jacketed bullets. It was the forerunner of what was to come forth in two decades. Seeking new ballistics and performance from the 1911 Government Model in the 1980s, SSK brought forth the .41 Avenger, a .45 ACP necked-down to .41 caliber. All that was needed to use this new caliber was a new barrel and a set of reloading dies. It was ahead of its time and never really got off the ground.

Peter Pi of Cor-Bon, designed the .400 Cor-Bon to make use of the vast array of .40-caliber bullets available, as well as the ease of converting nearly any semi-auto chambered for .45 ACP to .400 Cor-Bon by changing barrels. Nothing else, extractor, magazines, springs, guide rods, etc., needs to be changed and the semi-auto can easily be changed back to .45 ACP at any time. Dies for reloading the .400 Cor-Bon are available from RCBS. Simply run a .45 ACP case up through the sizing die and one has .400 Cor-Bon brass or already-formed .400 Cor-Bon brass is available from Starline.

With a standard 5-inch 1911 barrel, a 135-grain jacketed hollowpoint achieves 1,450 fps, the 150 JHP gives 1,330 fps, and the 165-grain jacketed hollowpoint comes in at 1,300 fps. AMT is offering the .400 Cor-Bon Accelerator, a stainless-steel, full-sized 1911 with a long slide and 7-inch barrel. Sights are fully adjustable Milletts with a white dot outlined rear sight and a

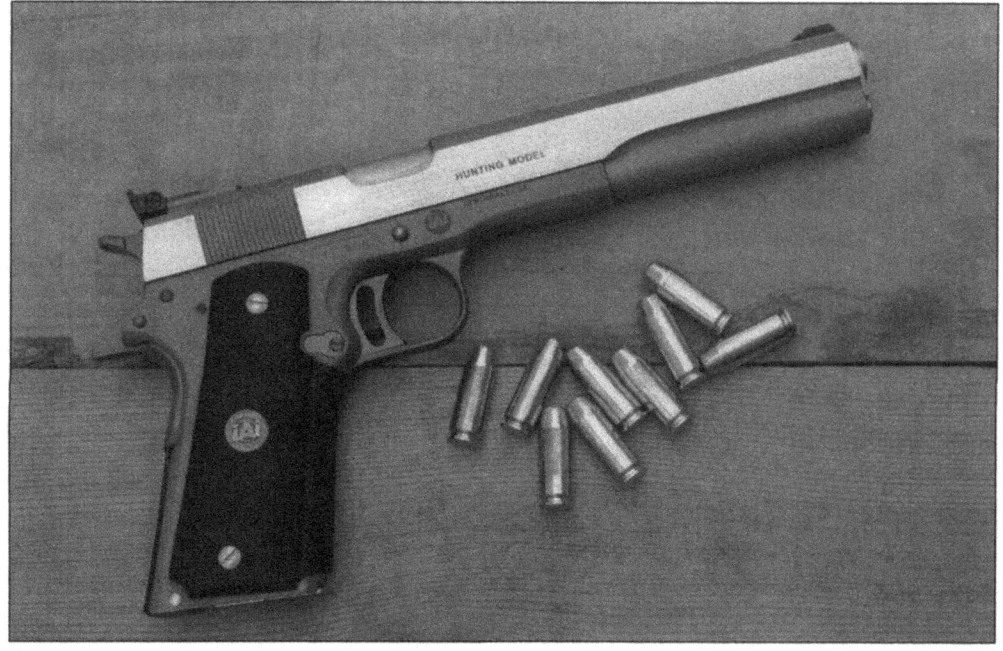

One can come very close to the ballistics of the .41 Magnum in a semi-automatic with the AMT Long Slide Javelina 10mm.

ramp front also with a white dot all for easy sight line up in a situation that demands quickness. Magazine capacity is the same seven rounds offered by any standard 1911 .45 ACP magazine. The safety is typical 1911 on the left side for right hander's use and the slide stop, also on the left, is large and easy to operate. Grips are pebble-grained rubber with a full piece wrapping around the front strap for a non-slip gripping surface.

Normally the torque of a semi-auto gets to my well-worn wrists more than a heavy recoiling sixgun, but the weight of the Accelerator at 46 ounces and the long slide kept torque to a minimum and I had no trouble with felt recoil with any of the loads tested. Those loads tested are all from Cor-Bon and put through the .400 Accelerator resulted in the 135 JHP doing 1,545 fps, and the 150 JHP and the 165 JHP both clocking out at 1,420 fps. This was in 35-degree weather, and muzzle velocity is higher in warmer weather. Five-shot groups with the above three loads for five shots at 25 yards averaged 2 1/8 inches with the 135-grain JHPs, 2 1/2 inches with the 150-grain JHPs, and 1 3/4 inches for the 165-grain JHPs.

More .40s from the '90s

As we have mentioned, the modern beginnings of the .40/10mm go back to the early 1970s with the creation of the .40 G&A. At the time, there were three semi-auto cartridges of any serious consequences available: the 9mm, the .38 Super, and the .45 ACP. The idea was to come up with a cartridge that combined the best qualities of the 9mm and .45 ACP. With the creation of the new .40 semi-auto cartridge, the statement was made that "...the .40 caliber was chosen because it can be shown mathematically that it takes about this size projectile to provide the cross-sectional area to achieve adequate stopping power at reasonable pistol velocities."

The .40 G&A was wildcatted using cut-down .224 Weatherby brass and 180-grain .38-40 bullets. Chambered in a Browning Hi-Power, maximum velocities were right at 1,250 fps. The .40 G&A went nowhere, but it opened the doors for the 10mm.

Being that it was built on the Browning Hi-Power, I have my doubts as to the fine Browning, which was designed around the 9mm, standing up to the pounding of the .40 G&A cartridge in its full-house loadings.

Enter the Bren Ten. In 1984, Jeff Cooper put his stamp of approval on a new semi-automatic from Dornaus & Dixon. The offspring combined some of the best features of the Czech-made CZ-75 9mm with the distinct advantage of a larger hole in the barrel. This was a semi-auto that was not chambered in .45 ACP and was a double-action semi-automatic. The new caliber was the 10mm and the new semi-auto, while a double action, could be carried cocked-and-locked. The name Bren Ten came from BR for the BRNO factory in Czechoslovakia and EN for the British Enfield factory. While "Bren Ten" made an easy-to-remember name for the new 10mm, the Bren Ten itself is no more as Dornaus & Dixon went into bankruptcy.

The gun died, but the cartridge did not, at least not then. Colt rescued it by chambering the Government Model, renamed the Delta Elite, and soon other 10mm handguns became available: Colt's Gold Cup Delta Elite, Springfield Armory's Omega, AMT's Javelina Hunting Model Long-Slide, LAR's Grizzly, and Thompson/Center's Contender. Smith & Wesson covered all the bases with the semi-automatic Model 1006 and the Model 610 sixgun, which operated with half- and full-moon clips just as the .45 ACP/AR-chambered Model 25-2/625-2. The Glock was soon offered in 10mm. Auto-Ordnance had the 1911A1 Government Model chambered for the Bren Ten. And the Parker from Wyoming Arms was available in stainless steel in

SELECTED LOADS FOR THE AMT JAVELINA 10MM 7"

BULLET	LOAD	MV	5 SHOTS/25 YARDS
Sierra 150 JHP	13.0 gr. AA#7	1,406	2 1/4"
Sierra 150 JHP	12.0 gr. Blue Dot	1,463	2 1/2"
Hornady 170 JHP	13.0 gr. AA#7	1,374	2"
Hornady 170 JHP	11.0 gr. Blue Dot	1,323	2 1/2"
Sierra 180 JHP	10.5 gr. AA#7	1,164	1 3/4"
Sierra 180 JHP	12.0 gr. AA#7	1,274	2 3/8"
Sierra 180 JHP	10.0 gr. Blue Dot	1,225	2 3/8"
Sierra 180 JHP	5.5 gr. WW231	959	1 7/8"
Speer 190 JFP	10.5 gr. AA#7	1,162	2 1/4"
Speer 190 JFP	5.5 gr. WW231	934	1 3/4"
Hornady 200 JFP	10.5 gr. AA#7	1,171	2 1/4"
Hornady 200 JFP	11.0 gr. AA#7	1,179	1 1/2"
Hornady 200 JFP	5.5 gr. WW231	948	1 3/4"
RCBS #10MM-200	11.0 gr. AA#7	1,281	1 1/4"
RCBS #10MM-200	5.5 gr. WW231	1,078	1 1/2"
Bull-X 175 GR. SWC	5.5 gr. WW231	1,096	1 3/4"

SELECTED LOADS SMITH & WESSON 10MM MODEL 1006 5"

BULLET	LOAD	MV	5 SHOTS/25 YARDS
Hornady 170 XTP	12.5 gr. AA#7	1,294	2 1/2"
Hornady 200 XTP	10.5 gr. AA#7	1,053	2 1/2"
Hornady 200 FMJ	10.5 gr. AA#7	1,066	3 3/4"
Sierra 150 JHP	13.0 gr. AA#7	1,335	2"
Sierra 180 JHP	10.5 gr. AA#7	1,111	3"
Sierra 180 JHP	5.5 gr. WW231	938	3"
Speer 190 FMJ	10.5 gr. AA#7	1,066	4"
Speer 200 FMJ	5.0 gr. WW452AA	850	3"
RCBS #10mm-200	10.5 gr. AA#7	1,156	1 5/8"
RCBS #10mm-200	5.5 gr. WW231	1,019	1 3/4"

3-, 5-, and 7-inch barrel lengths. I can think of no other instance in history where the original handgun died so quickly, and yet the cartridge lived on in so many persuasions, most of which also disappeared before the last calendar page on the century turned.

The AMT Javelina Hunting Model was a long-slide, 7-inch, stainless-steel, 10mm that had a great deal going for it. A typical Government Model-style semi-auto with an extended safety, slide release, and magazine release button, it gave an excellent sight picture with black sights fore and aft consisting of Millett rear sight and a ramp front sight. The trigger was adjustable.

Is/was the 10mm a hunting pistol? With the proper ammunition it is better than the .357 Magnum, but still a bit below the .41 Magnum. Using the 170 Hornady Jacketed Hollow Point, I developed a warm load of 13.0 grains of AA#7 for 1,374 fps from the 7-inch Javelina. This should do the job on small deer without any problem. This load should also be worked up to carefully starting at around 11.0 grains.

If the Javelina was/is an excellent 10MM candidate for a hunting pistol, then the Smith & Wesson 1006 is my choice as a defensive 10mm. I never cared for the original Smith & Wesson Model 39 and even less for the Model 59. The Second Generation semi-autos did nothing for me, but the Third Generation Smith semi-autos have pushed my button, especially in .45 ACP and 10mm. First came the 4506 in .45 and then the "improved" 1006 in 10mm. I say improved on the basis of two easily seen changes. The hooked trigger guard of the 4506 became slightly rounded and checkered on the 1006, and while the backstrap of the 4506 was curved, the 1006 backstrap was straight and felt much better in my hand.

The 1006 has excellent adjustable sights with the popular defensive three-dot sighting system and the protected rear sight is straight out of Wayne Novak. Comparing the slides of the two, the 4506 and the 1006 viewed from the top, shows that the 10mm version has been beefed up considerably. As with the Javelina, the only change I would make is the grip, again artistically speaking. This was somewhat more difficult to accomplish as it is a molded, wrap-around synthetic grip. However, Hogue managed to come up with a grip that was not overly bulky when made of wood. The 1006 proved 100 percent reliable, gobbling up everything that would fit in the magazine.

Pistoleros in the 1880s found they had an excellent defensive, hard hittin' but easy shootin', round when Colt and others began chambering sixguns for Winchester's .38-40 (.38 Winchester Centerfire). One hundred

The author enjoying shooting the Smith & Wesson 4006, representative of the new wave of semi-automatics and calibers of the 1990s.

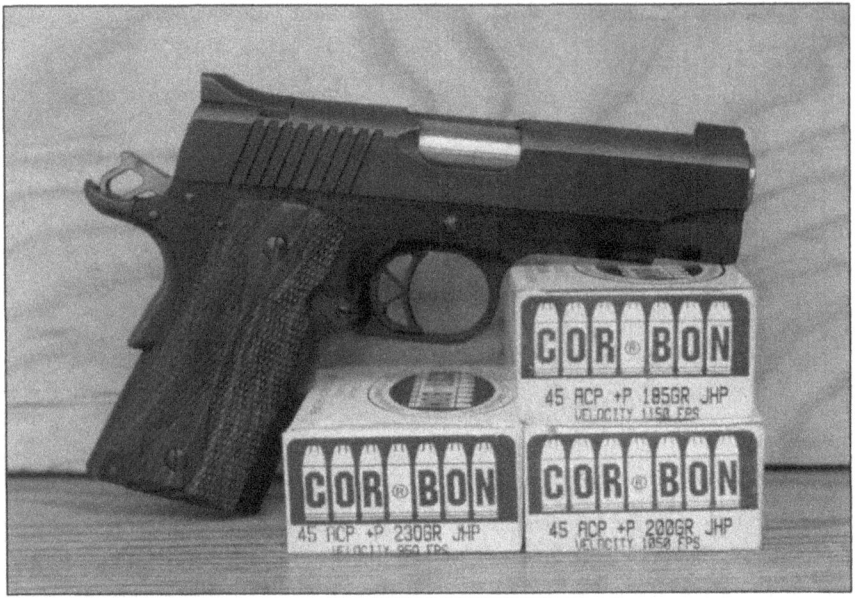

An excellent choice for the defensive use or CCW is Kimber's Compact .45. All handguns selected for such use should be loaded with factory ammunition such as that offered by Cor-Bon.

years later, history repeated itself. The .38-40 delivered a 180-grain bullet at 975 fps in 1880, and beginning in 1990 we saw the introduction of what many would declare is the perfect defensive handgun. This turns out to be the .38-40 in a more compact package — the .40 S&W. The .40's payload is the same 180-grain bullet at a factory-rated 950 fps. Ain't progress wonderful? With all our searching for the perfect defensive load over the last century, we wind up right back where we started. Could it be the sixgunners of old had the perfect cartridge and did not even know it?

What makes the .40 S&W modern is the fact that the .38-40, which was available in a five-shot, single-action, sixgun (leave an empty under the hammer, of course), is now available in 10-shot fairly compact semi-automatics that are easily concealable and use double-action design. The first shot is fired double action and subsequent shots are fired single action. Ten well-aimed shots can be fired faster in the S&W Model 4006 than five in the old Colt Single Action and then reloaded and fired 10 more times faster than the empties can be shucked one at a time from the Colt.

The .40 was touted as the cartridge, combined with excellent semi-autos such as the S&W 4006, that we expected would push the 9mm out as a defensive and law enforcement cartridge. It did just that! The Smith & Wesson .40 semi-automatic was the same size as the Third Generation 9mm's, but had a hole in the barrel that was an important 1 mm larger, .40 caliber instead of .36 caliber.

Kimber's lightweight CDP also carries well in the fancy carved Threepersons rig by El Paso Saddlery.

Cor-Bon's 165-grain PowRBall and Kimber's CDP .45 make a most efficient team.

The Kimber 1911

The Kimber .45s arrived in 1996 and in this short time this company, which started with the building of high-quality .22 rimfire rifles, has become one of the premier builders of 1911 semi-automatic pistols. In fact, it has surpassed all others in annual production numbers of such handguns. This says something about how quickly and how well it has been accepted by shooters. Kimber got where it is because it had a better idea: perfect the classic 1911 design using state-of-the-art computer technology and features that custom gunsmiths were adding after the original purchase.

When I first started shooting in the 1950s there was only Colt. I recently stopped at Shapel's, my local neighborhood gun shop, to see what it had to offer in the 1911 .45 ACP line. It had many Kimber .45s as well as several versions from their closest competitor, Springfield Armory. New Colts? None! They did have three nearly new 20-plus-year-old Series '70 Colts, two Government Models, and one Combat Commander, but nothing of recent vintage. I find this holds true throughout the valley in any gun shops I may visit.

The Kimber Custom Shop CDP (Custom Defense Pistol) is designed for serious defense use while at the same time being both user friendly and easy to pack with an aluminum frame and weight of 31 ounces.

Kimber starts with the machining of the frame from a block of 7075-T7 aluminum and mates it with a stainless-steel slide. As part of its standard custom gunsmithing, the frame and slide are given the "carry bevel" package that removes all sharp corners and edges, leaving nothing to snag on leather or clothing as well as being very friendly to fingers and hands. The front strap is checkered at 30 LPI, the mainspring housing is flat and also checkered, grips are double-diamond Rosewood, and are also checkered, all combining to provide a very secure grip.

Sights are Meprolight Tritium three-dot night sights, with both the front and rear being adjustable for windage by moving them in their dovetails. These dots really show up and, although I normally need glasses to see the sights, I do not need them to see these sights (something that could be very important in the middle of the night).

The grip safety is of the beavertail style and extends back between the thumb and trigger finger to prevent hammer bite. The hammer is Commander style, the safety is the extended ambidextrous style, the match grade barrel is 5 inches, the aluminum trigger is also match grade, the magazine well is beveled, slide serrations are angled and beveled, and magazine release, slide stop, grip safety, stock screws, and barrel bushing, are all of stainless steel. The stainless-steel parts and

SELECTED LOADS FOR THE KIMBER .45'S

BULLET	CUSTOM CDP MV	6 SHOTS/50 FEET	COMPACT MV
Black Hills 200 JHP	985	1 3/4"	903
Cor-Bon 165 +P Powerball	1,241	1 1/4"	1,188
Cor-Bon 185+P JHP	1,100	1 1/2"	995
Cor-Bon 200+P JHP	1,052	1 3/4"	933
Cor-Bon 230+P JHP	947	1 3/4"	865
CCI Blazer 200 JHP	960	1 3/4"	892
Federal 230 Hi Shok	875	1 1/4"	792
Hornady 185 XTP-HP	970	1 1/2"	889
Hornady 200 XTP-HP	909	1 1/2"	856
Remington 185 JHP	1,028	1 3/8"	953
Speer 230 GD-HP	859	1 1/4"	800
Bull-X 200 SWC/9.0 gr. AA#5	997	1 5/8"	947
Bull-X 200 SWC/6.0 gr. 452AA	978	1 3/8"	917
Bull-X 200 SWC/7.5 gr. Unique	1,016	1 3/4"	999

Rosewood stocks contrast very nicely with the flat-black aluminum frame.

A second, slightly older Kimber .45 that I have been using for a couple of years is the Compact model with a 4-inch bushing-less barrel and a shorter grip frame that is the same size as the Colt Officer's Model. This all-black gun has a steel slide matched up with an aluminum frame. I have replaced the black checkered grips with Rosewood double-diamond checkered grips from Herrett's Stocks. Sights on the Compact model are the same low-profile, dovetail-mounted, combat sights found on the Custom CDP, although these are plain black. As with the Custom CDP, the grip safety is of the beavertail style and the flat mainspring housing is checkered. The front strap is left smooth, and the thumb safety is found on the left side only. Weight is 28 ounces.

I find the CDP and the Compact model equally easy to shoot accurately with both guns basically shooting to point of aim with most loads tested. Most surprisingly, the CDP shot Core-Bon's 165-grain PowRballs at 1,240 fps, Black Hills 200-grain Jacketed Hollow Points at 985 fps, and Federal's 230 Hi-Shok's at 875 fps, all to the same point of aim. Many of the groups fired with the Custom CDP are in the 1-inch or slightly over category for six shots at a distance of 50 feet. That is outstanding accuracy for a defensive pistol. The best loads tested, giving groups of 1 1/4 inches at 50 feet, are Cor-Bon's 165-grain PowRball, Federal's 230 Hi-Shok, and Speer's 230 Gold Dot Hollow Point.

There are numerous excellent leather rigs to choose from for packing 1911s. For open carry with the Custom CDP, I go with a beautifully crafted El Paso Saddlery outfit consisting out of a 2 1/4-inch belt, a 1920 Tom Threepersons holster (both lined), and a double-magazine pouch. All three items are exquisitely floral carved with a dyed background. For concealment use the Custom CDP rides in Bianchi's Askins Avenger

"Over There, Over There ..." Springfield Armory Mil-Specs are a salute to the sidearms of the Doughboy and G.I. Joe. Appropriate leather is the Pike Rig from San Pedro Saddlery.

The author's search for an accurate full-sized 1911 in .38 Super ended with the Springfield Armory Mil-Spec.

designed by the late Colonel Charles Askins, while the Compact rides in an equally compact little horsehide holster by Derry Gallagher. Both .45s from Kimber also carry very well when placed behind the hipbone inside the pants belt alone.

Springfield Armory's 1911

Springfield Armory offers no-frills military-style 1911s, the Mil-Specs, in both .45 ACP and .38 Super. Both of these take me back to my teenage years when it was very easy to find government-issued .45s for $7.50 to $15 in the mid to late 1950s. My first 1911 in 1957 cost all of $7.50 complete with a flap holster. About this same time a young ex-Marine and handgun writer by the name of Jeff Cooper caught my attention with an article called "Trail Guns" in which he pictured a custom .38 Super with adjustable sights and special grips. I have wanted such a .38 Super ever since I saw that picture more than 40 years ago.

In the late 1960s I did purchase a Colt Commander .38 Super, which proved to be very disappointing. I could not keep all the shots on a 12-inch square target at 25 yards with that gun. It was put away until some time in the late 1980s when I finally sent it off to Bill Wilson. The addition of one of his barrels brought group size down from somewhere over 12 inches at 25 yards to less than 2 inches at the same distance. I now had a good-shooting .38 Super, but it was still not the full-sized 1911 that I dreamed about for so many years.

Springfield Armory's Mil-Spec 1911-A1 semi-automatics are made to stir memories of the original military 1911 .45 ACP's that have been part of the fighting hand-

As good as it gets with a full-sized 1911, the Springfield Armory Tactical TRP.

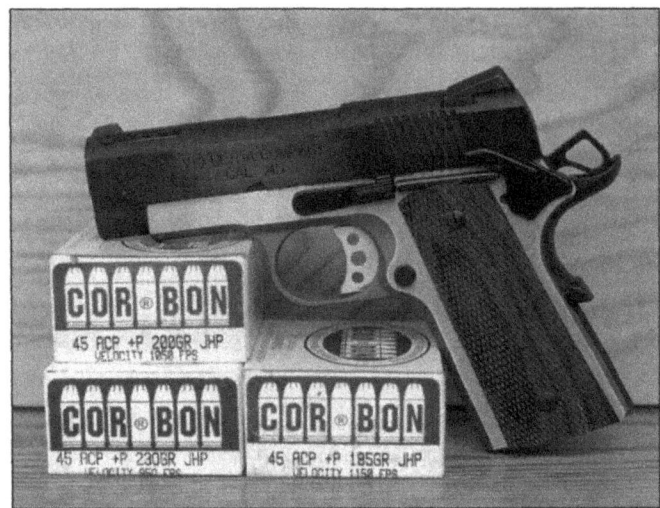

Another good choice for CCW use is Springfield Armory's V-10 Compact. Stocks are by Herrett's. The deep red color of the checkered stocks mates exceptionally well with the two-tone finish of the V-10.

gun scene for 90 years. These are military-style, Parkerized, 1911-A1s with a shortened trigger, arched mainspring housing, and the back of the top of the grip safety is slightly longer than that found on the original 1911. The short trigger is much easier to reach, the arched housing helps with pointability, and the change in the grip safety helps alleviate the hammer bite problem. The original Colt had a very small and narrow front sight mated up with a rear sight that, though drift adjustable for windage, had a very small notch. Springfield Armory has made one major change to the military version 1911s by equipping the Mil-Specs with three-dot sights that are big and bold and square and much easier to see. I have made only one change to both the .45 ACP and the .38 Super. Both guns now wear grip panels of exotic woods from Herrett's Stocks, fully checkered on the .38 Super and diamond checkered on the .45 ACP. They look great when contrasted with the flat black finish of the guns themselves, and they also help me to tell one from the other at a glance.

The 1911 .45 was designed to provide the same power as the military black powder load in .45 Colt Single Action Army in a modern semi-automatic, and as such was the only handgun that many peace officers of the old school felt was good enough to replace the Colt Single Action Army. The movie *The Wild Bunch* features a group of pistoleros that cannot quite make the changes necessary to survive during the first quarter of the 20th century and Bill Holden as Pike Bishop packed and used both a Single Action Army and the 1911. Being somewhat of a throwback myself I often carry these Springfield Armory Mil-Specs in a Pike Rig from San Pedro Saddlery of Tombstone, Arizona. This rig, consisting of a tapered belt, holster, and double cartridge case, all of oiled single weight leather except for the Mexican loop style holster, which is lined with pigskin, is an excellent and comfortable way to carry a 1911. Workmanship and material are excellent.

The Mil-Specs are no-frills 1911s while the satin stainless-steel Tactical TRP .45 ACP Model 1911-A1 from the Springfield Armory has all the following features: Hammer-forged, match-quality, throated

SELECTED LOADS FOR THE SPRINGFIELD ARMORY MIL-SPEC .38 SUPER 5"

LOAD	MV	8 SHOTS/50 FEET
Cor-Bon 115+P JHP	1,445	2"
Cor-Bon 125+P JHP	1,362	1 1/4"
Winchester 125 SilverTip HP	1,187	1 3/4"

SELECTED LOADS FOR THE SPRINGFIELD ARMORY MIL-SPEC .45 ACP 5"

LOAD	MV	6 SHOTS/50 FEET
Black Hills 185 JHP	915	2 1/2"
Black Hills 200 JHP	940	2 1/2"
Cor-Bon 185+P JHP	1,090	2"
Cor-Bon 200+P JHP	1,041	2 3/4"
Cor-Bon 230+P JHP	921	2 1/2"
CCI Blazer 200 JHP	947	1 3/4"
Federal 230 HiShok	918	1 1/4"
Hornady 185 XTP-HP	944	2 1/8"
Hornady 200 XTP-HP	893	1 7/8"
Remington 185 JHP	1,017	2 1/2"
Speer 230 GD-HP	839	1 3/4"
Bull-X 200 SWC/9.0 gr. AA#5	976	2 1/2"
Bull-X 200 SWC/6.0 gr. 452AA	997	1 1/2"
Bull-X 200 SWC/7.5 gr. Unique	1,016	2"
Bull-X 230 RN/5.0 gr. Bullseye	790	1 3/4"

SELECTED LOADS FOR THE SPRINGFIELD ARMORY .45 ACP'S

BULLET	TRP 45 MV	6 SHOTS/50 FEET	V-10 .45 MV
Black Hills 185 JHP	930	1 1/4"	818
Black Hills 200 JHP	945	1 1/8"	841
Cor-Bon 185+P JHP	1,090	1 3/4"	952
Cor-Bon 200+P JHP	1,037	1 3/8"	923
Cor-Bon 230+P JHP	944	1 1/2"	846
CCI Blazer 200 JHP	969	7/8"	860
Federal 230 Hi Shok	855	1 1/2"	768
Hornady 185 XTP-HP	949	1 1/2"	865
Hornady 200 XTP-HP	913	1 7/8"	816
Bull-X 200 SWC/9.0 gr. AA#5	1,021	1 3/8"	885
Bull-X 200 SWC/6.0 gr. 452AA	1,003	1"	883
Bull-X 200 SWC/7.5 gr. Unique	1,029	1 3/4"	944
Bull-X 230 RN/5.0 gr. Bullseye	805	1 7/8"	696

barrel; precision fitting of barrel, slide, and frame; lowered and flared ejection port; Delta lightweight hammer; ambidextrous and extended thumb safety; High Hand beavertail; Cocobolo grips, a dovetail front sight matched up with a Novak Low Mount rear sight, both with tritium dots; titanium firing pin and heavy-duty spring; beveled magazine well; flat mainspring housing of the 1911 style; carry bevel package; full-length guide rod, serrated front strap and mainspring housing, and a loaded chamber indicator consisting of a very tiny hole that allows one to see the rim of a cartridge if it is in the chamber. All this is in a factory 1911 that has not been worked over by a custom 'smith.

Weight of the TRP fully loaded with eight 230-grain hardball rounds is an ounce shy of 3 pounds, and I find this .45 ACP easy to shoot as well as exceptionally good shooting. Of all loads tried in the TRP, the best group was six shots in 7/8 inch for the CCI Blazer 200-grain jacketed hollowpoint at 969 fps. Right behind this at 1 inch was the CCI Blazer 200-grain TMJ at 926 fps. Both Hornady's 230-grain FMJ at 844 fps and Speer's 230 Lawman TMJ at 793 fps gave groups of 1 1/8 inches. My "combat" handload consisting of Bull-X's 200-grain SWC over 6.0 grains of WW452AA also grouped in 1 inch with a muzzle velocity of just over 1,000 fps. The Springfield Armory TRP also performed just as well with cast bullets as it did with jacketed bullets. It is an excellent choice for a duty gun or open-carry pistol.

At the other end of the spectrum we have one of Springfield Armory's concealed weapons offering — the all steel V-10 Ultra Compact. With its seven-round capacity even with its shortened grip frame, this little gun weighs in at 2 pounds 6 ounces. It came equipped with highly functional and comfortable Hogue wrap-around finger groove grips, however, I chose to equip it with Herrett's checkered Cocobolo grips. It is still easy to shoot with these grips in place and it also looks very attractive with the contrast of blue and stainless steel and reddish brown grips. It is easy to shoot with standard grip panels due to the porting consisting of five holes on each side of the front sight which works to keep felt recoil at a minimum even with +P factory .45 ACP loads in this 3 1/2-inch-barreled pistol. Another feature on the V-10 Ultra Compact is a Novak Low Mount rear sight that is drift adjustable for windage and locks in place with an Allen screw.

The new wave of .45/Glock

The Glock, which first saw the light of day in 1985, has now sold well over 1.5 million handguns. Someone is doing something right! No other handgun in history has spawned so many imitators in such a short time as Austria's Gaston Glock. I could not resist any longer. I

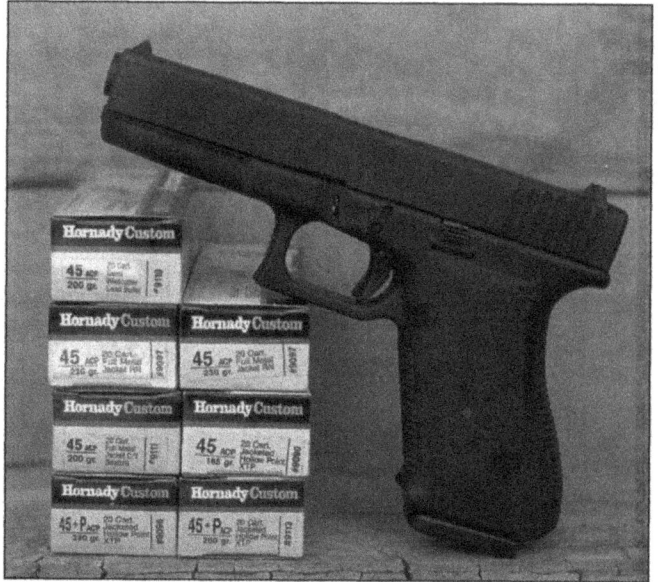

The Glock .45 ACP ain't pretty but it is highly efficient and provides maximum life insurance.

Fellow writer Chuck Karwan chooses the 10mm Glock as the number one choice for a defensive sidearm. It would be enjoyable, but difficult, to argue with him.

would have to get a Glock or two and shoot them in depth to see what the excitement is really all about.

Arrangements were made to acquire two Glocks, one chambered in 10mm and the other in the old standard, the .45 ACP. I also made arangements to attend a Glock Armorer's Class and Instructor's Workshop. To take part in the three-day Glock Workshop it was necessary to not only bring a Glock, proper holster, ear and eye safety equipment, but also 1,000 rounds of FACTORY ammunition. No reloads allowed for two obvious reasons: safety and the fact that this was to be a shooting workshop on how the Glock performed, not how some possibly unknown reloads worked. A request to Jeff Hoffman of Black Hills resulted in 1,000 rounds of Black Hills 230-grain .45 ACP ammo delivered to my doorstep. These were fired exclusively in the .45 Glock over the three-day period of the Glock Intructor's Workshop.

One of my concerns with the Glock has always been safety. We've all heard stories of police officers especially having "accidental discharges" including, at least one chief that put a round through the wall of his office. Is it really possible to fire a round when the Glock is holstered? Is the Glock more prone to "accidental discharges" than other handguns? These were questions running through my mind. I had fired the Glock in all calibers, but I did not understand its operation thoroughly.

The Glock is advertized as having a Safe Action trigger. After going through Armorer's Class I would say that there is absolutely no way to fire off a chambered round when the Glock is being holstered if IF YOUR FINGER IS OFF THE TRIGGER! As with any other semi-automatic, double-action, or single action sixgun, the Glock cannot fire until the trigger is pulled. It will not fire if the side of the trigger is hit or pressed. The trigger safety rides in the middle of the trigger and is a positive lock. There is no way to fire the Glock unless the trigger safety is pulled and there is also no way for inertia to fire the Glock if the gun is dropped as long as the trigger safety is intact.

As the trigger safety in the center of the trigger is pressed, the trigger is also pulled, the firing pin safety is released, the trigger bar moves forward, and the gun fires. This means there are three safeties in existence: the trigger safety, the firing pin safety, and the drop safety. Once the gun is fired, the trigger is reset and all other safeties re-engage. There are no external safeties to disengage as everything depends upon the operation of the trigger safety. After proper training, I now feel perfectly safe carrying a Glock properly holstered with a round in the chamber. But I do believe that any department that provides Glock semi-automatics without proper training in their use is doing its officers a real disservice.

The Glock Model 21 .45 weighs 25 ounces. Add a full magazine and the weight goes to 40 ounces for the .45, or about the same weight as an empty 1911 Government Model. My main hangup with the Glock has always been one of esthetics. They just look like a, well just like they sound, a Glock. After going through the Glock Armorer's School, I can also now attest to the fact that the interior of the Glock mirrors the exterior. There are no finely honed parts, nothing that would indicate that someone with great skill spent hours fitting beautifully machined parts. In fact, all parts are totally replaceable with new parts without any fitting of any kind. This is a handgun that is completely assembly-line friendly. Even I, as fumble fingered as I am, am now qualified as a Glock Armorer Entry Level and have been able to totally strip the Glock and replace everything in the right order and place without ever losing any of the parts and have done it numerous times. I can change the weight of the trigger pull with no tool other than the Glock punch to remove the pins that hold it all together. That alone speaks extremely well for the simplicity of the design of the Glock. If I can do it, anyone can do it.

During the three-day workshop, 14 of us (I was the only civilian) intimately learned the functioning of the Glock pistol. Two of us used .45 Model 21s and the rest

SELECTED LOADS FOR THE GLOCK MODEL 21 .45 ACP

LOAD	MV	4 SHOTS/25 YARDS
Black Hills 185 JHP	954	1 1/8"
Black Hills 230 JHP	851	2 1/2"
Black Hills 230 LRN	839	1 1/2"
CCI Blazer 230 RN	809	2 5/8"
CCI Blazer 200 JHP	946	2 1/2"
CCI Blazer 200 TMJ Match	904	2 1/8"
Hornady 185 XTP	902	1 1/4"
Hornady 200 XTP	872	1 3/8"
Hornady 200 Match	887	1 1/8"
Hornady 200 LSWC	945	3"
Hornady 230 RN	840	4"
Hornady 230 XTP +P	968	1 1/8"
Speer Lawman 200 JHP	963	2"
Winchester 230 JHP	807	2"
Winchester 230 FMC	807	2 1/8"
Winchester 185 SilverTip	901	2 1/4"
Bull-X 200 SWC/6.1 452AA	962	7/8"
Speer GDHP 185/8.9 gr. WAP	821	1"
Speer 400 JFP/18.0 gr. Lil' Gun	1,084	1 3/4"

went with 9mm's and .40 S & Ws. One skill encountered early was the idea of "resetting" the trigger. As the trigger is pulled, the gun fires, and the trigger is still in its rearward position. It is not necessary to allow the trigger to return completely to the original position. It only needs to be reset. That is, the shooter can feel the trigger come forward and click into place. This is trigger reset and allows the Glock to be fired much quicker and also more accurately. "Watch your trigger reset" was heard over and over again during our three-day shooting workshop.

For three days the Glock .45 and the Black Hills 230-grain ammunition performed perfectly. Never a malfunction at any time except those that were purposely induced by placing empty brass in the magazine for practice in clearing stoppages. For three days of extensive shooting at distances of 3 to 25 yards, most of which was at maximum speed (at least my maximum speed), I never once pulled a bullet off target, which to me is amazing and perfectly illustrates the pointability and ease of shooting the Glock in general and the .45 Model 21 in particular.

Before the training, I would not have considered carrying a Glock. That has all changed. I now feel totally confident in my ability with the Glock and also in the accuracy and reliability of the basic Glock pistol, again when used with proper ammunition and a proper holster. All my hardcore sixgunner friends need not worry. My personality hasn't changed totally. I won't salivate when I see a Glock as I do with a Colt Single Action Army. My heart won't do palpitations with a Glock as it does with a Smith & Wesson Triple-Lock. I won't try to fit the Glock with ivory grips or embellish it with engraving, nor will I carry it in a fancy floral carved holster. The Glock is built to be a weapon, not a piece of art. It receives a "100" for engineering and a "0" for intrinsic artistic value. It does not have one single sensuous line to its design. It is the same ugly duckling it has always been, but when loaded for battle and strapped on for serious business the ugliness disappears. I would not hesitate to use the Glock .45 to protect me and mine. In fact, it would probably be my first choice. I cannot give it any higher recommendation than that.

The new wave of .45/Ruger

Ruger's first entrance into the semi-automatic .45 ACP market was the P-90, a traditional single-column magazine style with a seven-shot capacity. Picking up the .45 Ruger for the first time gave me the feeling that it was lighter in weight and also slimmer in the grip area than Ruger's first centerfire semi-automatic, the 9mm P85. I was surprised to find that at 34 ounces the .45 is actually an ounce heavier than the P85. The grip frames are exactly the same.

Sights on Ruger semi-automatics are of the three dot variety. They have a single dot in the front post, which is pinned in place with two pins, something other manufacturers who sight pin should pick up on, and a dot on each side of the square notch rear sight. The white dots are designed for quick pickup in a combat situation and are not necessarily the best option for shooting tight little groups on paper. The rear sight is drift adjustable for windage and the rear sight is held in place with an Allen screw. Slide-to-frame fit of the P90 is very good with only the slightest amount of play, and barrel-to-slide fit is also tight with very little perceptible movement. Actually, both slide-to-frame fit and barrel-to-slide fit are as tight as many custom guns.

In 1990 Ruger introduced its first .45 semi-automatic, the P-90, left, which Col. Charles Askins promptly labeled the finest .45 of all time. The center pistol is Beretta's first .45, the Cougar, and on the right is the latest from Taurus, the PT145.

The trigger on the P90 is excellent with the double action pull being as good, no, make that better than that found on most double-action sixguns and the single-action pull, while somewhat creepy, is light and easy to handle. Grips are molded and grooved GE Xenoy 6123 resin and I was most happy to replace them with Hogue's custom wooden stocks. Functioning of the P90 can only be described as flawless. Because of the light weight of the Ruger P90 .45, a full 6 ounces less than a Government Model .45, I expected more felt recoil than I actually experienced. Firing the Ruger P90 can definitely be described as leaning heavily to the pleasant side.

The main purchasers of the Ruger P90 are the same shooters that have always felt that anything less than a .45 was a giant step down, and also the same shooters that have always been loyal Ruger supporters. A lot of P90s wind up in the hands of ordinary shooters who like big-bore semi-automatics. And when the prospective buyer of a double-action .45 semi-automatic sees

SELECTED LOADS FOR THE RUGER .45 ACP P90 5"

LOAD	MV	6 SHOTS/25 YARDS
H&G #68/7.2 gr. Unique	1,037	2 3/4"
Bull-X 200/6.1 gr. WW452AA	960	2"
Bull-X 200/5.0 gr. Bullseye	836	2"
Bull-X 200/7.5 gr. Unique	1,063	3 3/4"
Bull-X 225 RN/ 5.0 gr. Bullseye	798	1 3/4"
Lyman #454424/6.2 gr. Unique	907	2 3/8"
Speer 200 JHP/7.1 gr. Unique	946	2"
Blazer 200 TMJ	925	1 3/4"
Blazer 200 JHP	937	4"
Black Hills 200 JHP	942	3 1/2"
Black Hills 230 FMJ	778	3"
Black Hills 200 LSWC	838	2 1/4"
Cor-Bon 185 +P JHP	1,063	3"
Federal 185 JHP	881	1 3/4"
Federal 230 FMJ	781	2 1/2"
Hornady 230 FMJ-FP	829	2"
Winchester 230 FMJ	779	3"
Winchester 185 Silver-Tip HP	927	4 1/2"

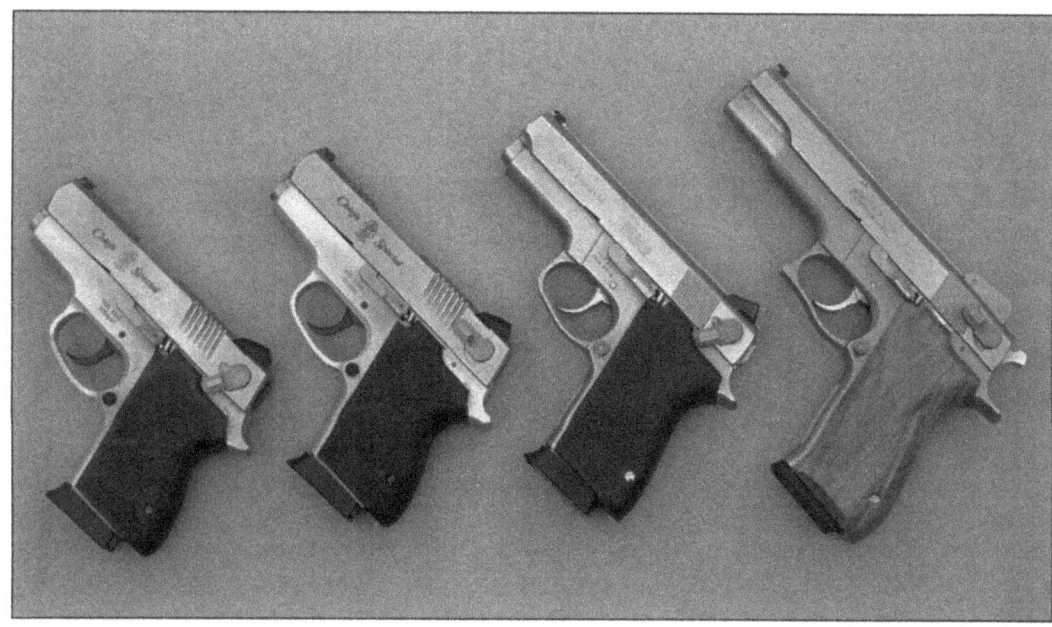

Smith & Wesson's new wave of semi-autos, a pair of very compact Chief's Specials, the 4516, and the full-sized 4506.

the price tag of the P90 compared to the price of a number of other .45 double-action semi-automatics, Ruger's first .45 ACP looks awfully good!

The new wave of .45/Smith & Wesson

Smith & Wesson began producing semi-automatics in the mid-1950s with the Model 39 9mm. In the 1990s, Smith's entry into the field of big-bore, double-action, semi-autos was the Model 4506. This big .45 features a fully adjustable rear sight with two white dots to match up with another white dot in the front sight, which is of the post type, slightly slanting forward.

The Smith & Wesson safety is ambidextrous and is pushed up with the thumb to release.

Smith & Wesson has offered full-sized 5-inch 10mm's and .45 ACPs as traditional double actions, Models 1006 and 4506; de-cocking lever Models 1026 and 4526; and double-action only Models 1046 and 4546. Full-sized Models with 4 1/4-inch barrels have also been available as 1066 and 4566 in traditional double action; 1076 and 4576 as de-cockers; and 1086 and 4586 were the double-action-only models.

Smith & Wesson's semi-automatics have easy-to-reach, smooth, double-action triggers. All are quite easy to operate one-handed. Double-action pulls are smooth with no discernable creep. A hooked trigger

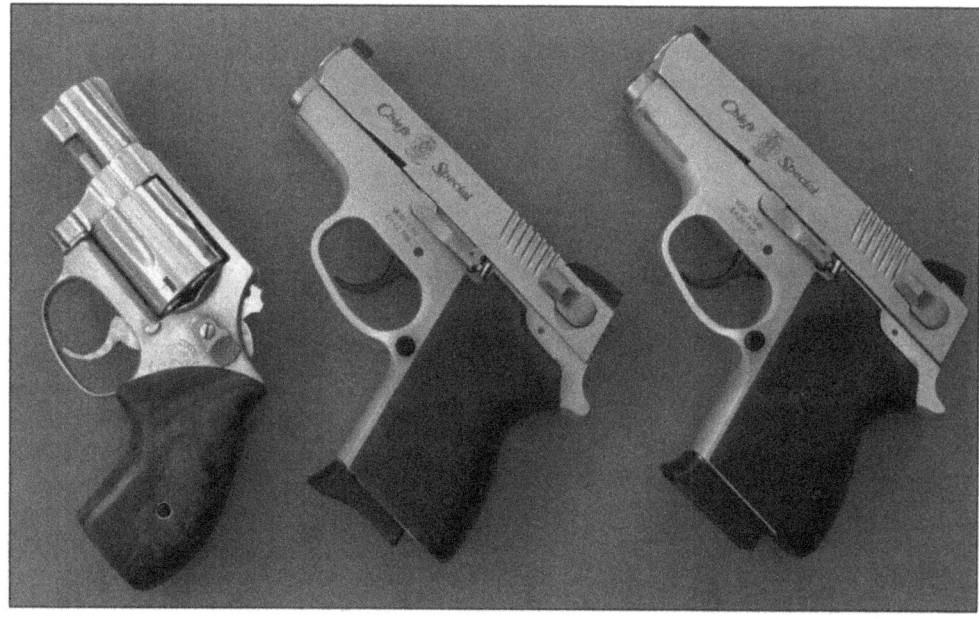

After 50 years the five-shot .38 Special Chief's Special has been replaced by the new Chief's Specials the CS9, and CS40.

SELECTED LOADS FOR THE .45 ACP S&W MODEL 4506 5"

LOAD	MV	6 SHOTS/25 YARDS
Bull-X 200/6.0 gr. 452AA	1,018	2 1/4"
Hornady 230JFN/6.5 GR. Unique	881	2 1/2"
Sierra 230JRN/6.5 GR. Unique	816	2 1/4"
Black Hills 200 LSWC	839	2 5/8"
Black Hills 200 JHP	964	2 3/4"
Blazer 185 TMJ Match	795	2 1/2"
Blazer 200 TMJ Combat	980	3"
Blazer 200 JHP	930	2"
Blazer 230 TMJ	863	2 1/4"
Cor-Bon 185 JHP +P	1,120	1 5/8"
Federal 185 JHP	804	1 3/4"
Federal 230 FMC	796	2 7/8"
Federal 230 Hi-Shok	866	2 1/2"
Winchester 185 Silver-Tip	918	1 3/4"
Winchester 230 FMC	795	2"
Winchester 185 Silver-Tip HP	927	4 1/2"

guard is found on the Smith & Wesson 4506 while that on the 1006 is rounded. Good move. Never did figure out what that hook was for!

I have used several Smith & Wessons both personally and for test articles over the years and found them all to 100 percent reliable; no jams, no stove-pipes, no failures to feed with any ammunition tested. Accuracy? All accuracy testing consisted of five shots fired at 25 yards using the spare tire of my Bronco as a rest. With all loads, Smith & Wesson's average group size was 2.5 inches.

The best loads proved to be Cor-Bon's Plus P 185 grain JHPs. Clocking right at 1,100 fps, the lightweight Cor-Bons grouped at 1 5/8 inches in the Smith & Wesson 4506. The Smith & Wesson also shot groups of 2 inches or less with Federal's 185-grain JHPs, Winchester's 185-grain SilverTip and 230-grain Full Metal Case loads. There is quite a difference in the loading of the 185-grain JHP's as Cor-Bon's clocks out at 1,120 fps over the Oehler Model 35P, while Winchester's registers 935 fps and Federal's is only 800 fps. This gives the peace officer or defensive-minded citizen a real selection to suit their particular needs and desired felt recoil level.

The 4516 followed the 4506 as Smith & Wesson's first answer to the need for a compact .45 semi-auto. Fully loaded, full magazine plus one up the spout, the 4516 with eight rounds of 200-grain JHP's weighs in at 2 pounds 7 1/2 ounces or, if one prefers, 39 1/2 ounces. The grip size of the Smith & Wesson fits the average hand and also allows easy access to the double-action trigger which, by the way, is better than that found on many double-action sixguns. I could live with the 4516 even if the trigger worked double-action for every shot.

The grip of the 4516 itself is a synthetic wrap-around style that fits my hand quite well, and this Smith & Wesson is fitted with an ambidextrous de-cocking lever and no grip safety. Sights are excellent even though of the fixed variety. The Smith & Wesson 4516 carries the Novak-style, low-mount, non-snag rear-sight with two white dots that matched up well with a post front with a white dot. As mentioned earlier, I prefer 'em on a defensive pistol as they aid my eyes quite a bit in seeing the sights quickly. Recoil is exceptionally mild even with full-house loads. In fact, felt recoil is again considerably less than a full-size Government Model .45. The top of the backstrap of the 4516 is quite broad and is no problem during firing. There is no hammer bite. The hammer of the Smith is guaranteed toothless as it is spurless and flush mounted with the frame when down.

Function is absolutely flawless. The 4516 feeds anything. Period. Well, I did not try empty cases. Accuracy from the short 3 3/4-inch barrel is quite astounding when one realizes that this is not a target pistol by any means but a quick-handling defensive pistol. Most groups, five shots at 25 yards, are in the 2- to 2 1/2-inch range. CCI's Blazer 200-grain jacketed hollowpoints go into 2 1/4 inches at 25 yards. The Smith & Wesson 4516 is no slouch in the cast bullet accuracy department, either, getting 1 3/4 inches with the RCBS #45-201 using 7.0 grains of Unique for a very satisfying 968 fps.

In 1950 the revolver was king. The number one peace officer's handgun of choice was a 4-inch Colt or Smith & Wesson double-action sixgun chambered in .38 Special or .357 Magnum. It was only natural that a companion pocket pistol also be a revolver. All this has changed over the past five decades with most departments long ago going to the semi-automatic as the number one sidearm. So it is only natural that a new batch of Chief's Specials be offered in semi-automatic form. They are the 9mm CS9, .40 S&W CS40, and .45 ACP CS45 from Smith & Wesson.

All three of the new series of Chief's Specials are built on a compact frame and in double-action persuasion with alloy frames and stainless-steel slides. The slide-mounted thumb safety is on the left side and grips are wrap-around style rubber from Hogue. All three also share a common bobbed hammer and .305-inch combat trigger, as well as an easy to see Novak LoMount rear two-dot sight mated up with a white dot front sight. Barrel length is 3 inches for the CS9 with both the CS40 and CS45 being 1/4 inch longer.

Both the CS9 and CS40 are eight-shooters with a magazine capacity of seven rounds, while the CS45 carries six rounds in its magazine, making it a seven-shot big bore. All three come equipped with an extra magazine. The original Model 36 Chief's Special weighs in at 20 ounces; the new Chiefs are rated at 20.8 ounces, 24.2 ounces, and 23.9 ounces for the CS9, CS40, and CS45, respectively.

The CS45, with 13 different loads tested, averaged 1 3/4 inches for six rounds at 50 feet. For the biggest Chief's Special the most accurate loads proved to be Cor-Bon's 165- and 185-grain +P JHP's at a little over 990 fps and CCI's Blazer 200-grain JHP load at 860 fps. The .45 ACP remains the king of defensive loadings. Both of Cor-Bon's 165 and 185 +P JHP loadings are right at 1,000 fps from the biggest of the little Chief's Specials. For the CS45, which in all likelihood will be the most-carried of the new Chiefs, the Gould & Goodrich leather of choice is the #801 Yaqui Slide. Simplicity in itself, this design features a holster that is about as compact as leather can be with a belt slot, and a folded-over strip of leather to hold the barrel and trigger guard of the CS45. Two adjustable tension screws are provided at the trigger guard and a loop cutout of the back of the holster allows for placement perfectly over a pants belt loop for added security.

It is easy to conceal a sixgun or semi-automatic in cold weather, but it becomes much more of a logistics problem as the weather warms up. The tendency is to go to smaller and smaller weapons as less clothing is worn. A so-called travel vest or a mesh vest is a dead giveaway for concealed carry anymore, but a western-style vest such as worn by many of the cowboy shooters is not. The combination of the CS45 and the Gould & Goodrich version of the Yaqui Slide can easily be concealed under a vest as the barrel on the CS45 protrudes less than 1 inch below the belt line. Concealability is one thing semi-autos have all over sixguns. Even as I type this, the CS45 is riding in its Yaqui Slide under my Wahmaker vest.

The new wave of .45/Beretta

Beretta, whose 9mm replaced the 1911 .45 ACP as the standard military sidearm, is now offering its first .45. The Cougar, with a capacity of eight rounds in the magazine plus one in the chamber, is a double-action semi-auto that is carried, as most double actions semi-autos, with the hammer down and the safety on. To fire this .45, the ambidextrous safety is pushed forward, the trigger is pulled in the double-action mode, then it switches to the single-action mode for the rest of the rounds. If it is cocked with a round in the chamber, it is made safe by once again engaging the safety, at which time the hammer drops forward. It should go without saying that on any semi-auto with a hammer drop safety, the muzzle should still be pointed in a safe direction when it is engaged. The old rule of "don't point at anything you do not intend to shoot" still holds.

The Cougar weighs 36 ounces fully loaded with nine rounds of CCI Blazer 200-grain JHPs. The sights on the Cougars, both of which are adjustable for windage by drifting them in their dovetail slot, are of the white-dot variety for quick pickup. The Cougar is carried in an inside-the-pants holster or a belt holster, both of which carry a reinforced tab around the top of the holster body to keep it open for easier re-holstering and a tension screw at the welt to adjust the snugness of the fit.

With 14 different factory loads from Black Hills, CCI, Cor-Bon, Omega Star, Remington, and Winchester fired at 50 feet, groups run from 1 3/4 to 2 3/4 inches in the Cougar with no malfunctions of any kind. Perfect performance all the way through.

When I first started shooting and also reading about sixguns, I knew that semi-autos were unreliable. Many of the gun writers of the time told me so. I can't vouch for then, but I can state unequivocally that today's semi-autos will perform perfectly if they are fed quality ammunition. This is one thing they all have in common, whether the parts are blued steel, stainless steel, polymer, or alloy. They flat out work. Always.

The most powerful semi-automatic offered to handgunners is the massive Desert Eagle .50 Action Express with power and accuracy to satisfy any hunter.

These semi-automatics are built with the handgun hunter in mind, the Desert Eagle and the LAR Grizzly.

The Desert Eagle

The IMI Desert Eagle .50 Action Express represents the new batch of very large semi-automatics that are chambered for the longer and larger-than-normal cartridges normally found in self-cockers. It is imported exclusively by Magnum Research. Ammunition is also available in a 300-grain hollowpoint version from Magnum Research bearing the Samson label, and 325-grain hollowpoint ammunition is also available from Speer along with both brass and 325-grain bullets for reloading. The first of the really large-caliber production semi-automatics was a long time coming for a couple of reasons. The Persian Gulf War put everything scheduled to come out of Israeli Military Industries on hold for nearly a year. The .50 had been promised to shooters at the 1991 SHOT Show and was not delivered until after the 1992 SHOT Show. This delay was unforeseen and could not have been anticipated by Magnum Research.

A second roadblock came from a little-known law on the books that says handguns may not be over 1/2 inch in bore diameter. If interpreted as written, the original .50 Action Express would have been legal as the bore diameter was .500 inch, but the groove diameter was .511 inch. Whoever was making the decisions ruled that the original .50 AE was illegal and it was back to the drawing board. As now manu-

Browning's best: the H-Power in 9mm and .40 S&W with stocks by David Wayland and leather by Milt Sparks.

factured, the Desert Eagle .50 Action Express takes bullets of .500 inch in diameter rather than .511, so bore diameter is now around .49 caliber and groove diameter is .50 caliber and neither is over 1/2-inch size limit.

Desert Eagles first arrived in .357 Magnum, followed by the .44. They became the first successful .44 Magnum semi-automatic, which in turn was followed up by chambering to the .41 Magnum. Standard barrel length of all models is 6 inches, with 10 and 14 inches available. All of the above are available in blue — really a dull black — and stainless-steel finishes. The owner of a Desert Eagle in .357, .41, or .44 Magnum can purchase a conversion kit for all models to change calibers. Millett adjustable sights are also available, although the standard model comes with fixed sights.

The .50 Desert Eagle is a L-A-R-G-E handgun with every part of it speaking of hugeness and strength. The slide, measuring approximately 1 3/4 inches in height and 1 1/4 inch in width, is a lot of steel and weight and is a major factor in packing so much power in a semi-automatic pistol. The barrel is over an inch in diameter at the rear with a heavy square rib on top, slotted to accept scope rings. The front of the barrel is trapezoidal in shape with the base being 1 1/4 inches in width. Even the .50 caliber hole does not look large in the massive barrel of the Desert Eagle. The rifling of the barrel is polygonal with a 1 in 19 twist. Overall length is 10.60 inches, height is 5.90 inches and unloaded weight is 66.5 ounces. An ambidextrous safety is provided that is difficult for me to operate while maintaining a shooting grip due to my relatively short fingers. Someone with a longer thumb should have no trouble flicking the safety off without changing the grip position of the hand. The large area on the back of the grip, combined with a large, wide tang, does much to spread recoil over the largest possible area.

Having considerable experience with both .357 Magnum and .44 Magnum Desert Eagles, I have found both to be very accurate semi-automatic pistols. The .50 AE falls into the same category. Unlike the recoil-operated 1911s, all Desert Eagles, including the .50 Action Express, are gas operated and should only be used with jacketed bullets as lead bullets can gum up the works considerably. Factory recommendations are for the use of standard weight jacketed factory ammunition only, with 158-grain .357 Magnum ammunition. This follows through with 210-, 240-, and 300-grain in the .41 Magnum, .44 Magnum, and .50 Action Express, respectively. Lightweight bullets and lighter-than-standard loads may or may not operate the action of the Desert Eagle in all calibers.

As to the mechanical operation of the Desert Eagle, I quote from the factory manual: "Prior to firing the pistol, the bolt is locked by three lugs in the barrel assembly. Upon firing the pistol, propellant gases pass through a hole underneath the bore of the barrel into the gas cylinder and push the piston, which in turn moves the slide backwards. During this movement the bolt is unlocked and carried to the rear by the slide, but not before the pressure in the chamber is reduced. When the bullet has left the barrel the empty cartridge is extracted and ejected with the continuing movement of the slide and bolt to the rear. At the same time, the slide pushed the hammer downward into the cocked poistion, where it is retained by the sear. The recoil springs are compressed. When the recoil springs expand, they drive the slide and bolt forward. During this movement the bolt cannot rotate due to the stabilizer pin which retains it. When the bolt scoops another round from the magazine and inserts it into the chamber, the locking lugs on the bolt come into contact with the recesses in the barrel and the bolt is rotated thus locking the cartridge in the chamber."

The Desert Eagle is a big brute of a gun to say the least, and as with the LAR Grizzly, I feel a little inadequate trying to wrap my stubby fat fingers around the grip frame. My thumb and middle finger just barely touch each other as I take a shooting grip on the wide grip of the Desert Eagle. Recoil is healthy and this is not a gun for the timid by any means, but the combination of gas operation and a pistol that weighs over 65 ounces empty and more than 4 1/2 pounds fully loaded makes this big handgun one of the more pleasurable of the big-bore pistols to shoot.

A comparison of the Desert Eagle with some of the other big-bore handguns yields the following results. Instead of muzzle energy figures which are slanted

CALIBER	BULLET WEIGHT	MV	TKO
.44 Magnum	240 gr.	1,400	21.0
.44 Magnum	300 gr.	1,400	26.6
.454 Casull	260 gr.	1,800	30.2
.454 Casull	300 gr.	1,600	31.0
.475 Linebaugh	385 gr.	1,400	36.0
.500 Linebaugh	400 gr.	1,300	38.0
.50 Action Express	300 gr.	1,350	28.9
.50 Action Express	325 gr.	1,330	30.9
Nosler 185 JHP	17.0 gr. AA#7	1,398	1 1/8"

SELECTED LOADS FOR THE DESERT EAGLE .50 ACTION EXPRESS 6"

LOAD/SPEER 325JSP	MV	5 SHOTS/25 YARDS	5 SHOTS/50 YARDS
30.0 gr. H110	1,316	1"	1 7/8"
30.0 gr. WW296	1,320	1 1/8"	1 3/4"
31.0 gr. H4227	1,362	1"	1 3/4"
26.0 gr. #2400	1,304	1"	2"
21.0 gr. BLUE DOT	1,323	1"	1 1/8"
26.0 gr. AA#9	1,345	7/8"	2 3/8"
22.0 gr. AA#7	1,286	7/8"	2 3/8"

towards the lightweight high velocity rounds, many shooters of the really big guns use the Taylor Knockout Formula, or KO, to realize a comparison of the power of the big bores. John "Pondoro" Taylor was an African hunter of no little renown who devised the formula as a true picture of the capabilities of big-bore rifles. When applied to handguns, the numbers mean nothing. They are simply an attempt to rank the effectiveness of large-bore handguns. (Caliber x bullet weight x muzzle velocity by 7,000 = TKO).

With the Taylor formula the .50 Action Express is above the full-house .44 Magnums, just slightly below the .454 Casulls, and overshadowed by the .475 and .500 Linebaughs. If there is a hitch in this formula it is that it does not consider penetration. If deep penetration is needed, the .44 Magnum, .454 Casull, .475 and .500 Linebaugh will all out-penetrate the .50 Action Express. Accuracy of the .50 Action Express is excellent with the capability of one-hole groups at 25 yards.

The Desert Eagle .50 Action Express is big and bad and mean and brute ugly. When it is fired the ugliness turns beautiful very quickly as one watches tight little groups form on paper or rocks disappear on yonder hill. It will never win an esthetics contest when pitted against the likes of the Colt Single Action Army or Smith & Wesson .44 Magnum. It is not a gun with great flowing lines or soul-stirring feel. No one is going to look at a Desert Eagle and think full coverage engraving. What it is is a gun that is a real kick to shoot, no pun intended, and a gun that many shooters will gather a whole lot of pleasure just from shooting and having such instant power at hand. It will certainly do the job when called upon for hunting big game at reasonable ranges.

I cannot close out this chapter without mentioning one of my favorite semi-automatics, John Brownings improvement on the 1911, the Browning Hi-Power. With this design, the grip safety was dropped and capacity went from a seven-round to a 13-round magazine. For years, the 9mm of the original Browning has been looked down upon as too small and too light. However, with modern ammunition, it snaps at the heels of the .357 Magnum in a short barrel. In addition, the Browning is now also chambered in the .40 S&W. A pair of Brownings remain favorites, not only because they are so enjoyable to shoot, but also because they each wear custom stocks by Dave Wayland, a good friend and brother Shootist who has now gone home.

Today's crop of big-bore semi-automatics gives shooters an almost unlimited number of variations for self defense, concealment use, hunting, or just plain shooting. Once in a great while progress really is positive.

CHAPTER 11

THE SINGLE SHOTS

During the middle of the 20th century, writers like Elmer Keith did their best to convince shooters that handguns were viable firearms for hunting. Of course for Keith, handgun meant sixgun. And for him it was a weapon of convenience, not one that was necessarily chosen as the primary hunting tool. He spent most of his life with a sixgun belted around his middle as well as being outdoors during that time, so sixguns and the taking of big game just naturally went together.

When Al Goerg came along and began the hunting trips that would lead to his book, *Pioneering Handgun Hunting*, he branched out to the use of single-shot pistols, even building some of his own. One that he came up with was a single-shot .257 Roberts on a Remington Rolling Block. He didn't know that is was illegal to build a pistol from a rifle. It got a little sticky for him with that one.

Goerg was simply ahead of his time and, although he didn't know it, was setting the stage for what was about to come. One of the major factors in the rise of the popularity of both handgun hunting and long-range silhouetting over the past 3 1/2 decades has been the excellent single-shot handguns offered by Thompson/Center. Beginning with the Contender, then the black powder Patriot, on to the magnum-power, muzzle-loading Scout, and now the Encore, handgun hunters have been able to choose a Thompson/Center single-shot pistol for any quarry from mouse to moose to mammoth. At the same time long-range silhouetters found they had a pistol in the Contender that was worthy of the game.

More than 165 years ago, way back in 1836, the sixgun arrived and buried the single-shot pistol for all time. The repeating handgun was such a great step forward that certainly no one would ever go back to a sin-

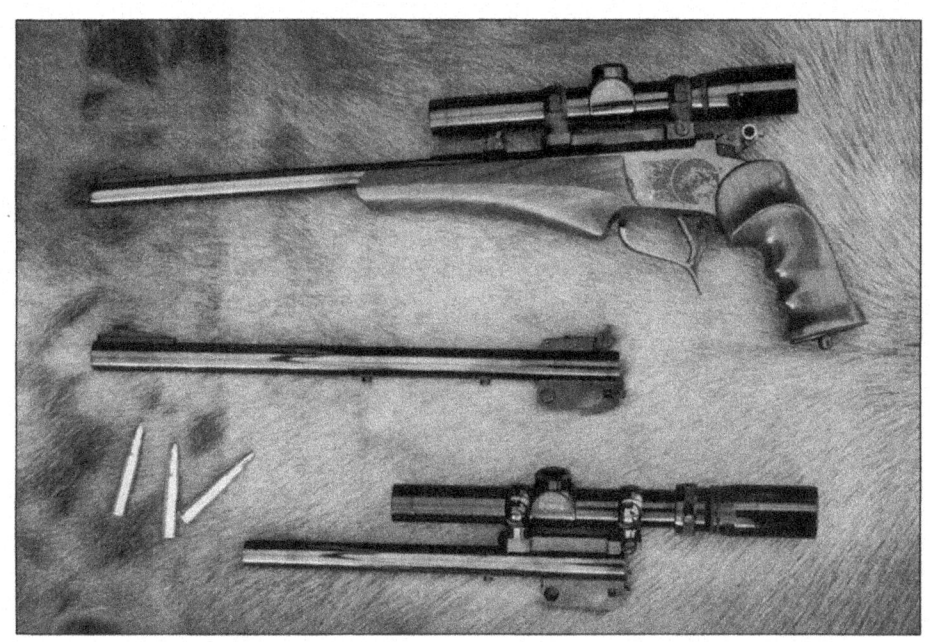

Three standard barrel lengths in the Contender have been 10-inch, Super 14-inch, and Super 16-inch. Steve Herrett designed the excellent stocks.

gle-shot pistol for any use. The revolver continued to progress through the .44 Walker, the .44 Dragoon, the .36 Navy and .44 Army Colts, into the cartridge-firing .44 Smith & Wesson and .45 Colt Single Actions, then on to the double-action sixguns and semi-automatic pistols personified by the Model of 1911, perhaps the finest fighting handgun ever devised. By the first quarter of the 20th century we had such grand sixguns and semi-automatics that there simply could never again be a use for single-shot pistols. It was dead and buried, never to rise again.

The Contender

Everyone knew this, but somehow Warren Center missed this fact, and in the 1960s, in the midst of all the development of better and better .357, .44, and .41 Magnum sixguns, Warren Center brought out a break-open, single-shot pistol that accepted interchangeable barrels. Some of the first barrels were offered in the easy-shooting, and soft-recoiling .22 Long Rifle and .38 Special. To change barrels one simply had to remove the forearm, open the action, remove the hinge pin, lift off the barrel, replace it with the next barrel, and reverse the process. Center certainly did not know what he had, as witnessed by those first chamberings, and why would anyone want a single-shot pistol to shoot .22s and .38s when we had such grand semi-auto .22s and superb target revolvers in .38 Special?

I was hooked on sixguns in the 1960s and hardly gave the Contender, as it was called, a second glance. You couldn't put ivory stocks on it, carved leather holsters for such a handgun did not make much sense and, unlike the Colt, Ruger, and Smith & Wesson sixguns of the time, it did nothing to stir my heart, soul, or sixgunnin' spirit. For hunting I used a .44 Magnum sixgun, a Smith & Wesson or Ruger. When silhouetting arrived

The .35 Remington in the Super 14 Contender will outshoot most lever guns and is an excellent choice as an all-around hunting pistol.

After 35 years of excellent service the Contender has now been upgraded to the easier-opening G2. It also operates like the Encore as it does not have to be reopened to be recocked. Barrels and forearms interchange with original Contenders. Grips do not.

One of the most potent offerings from Thompson/Center in the Contender is the .375 Winchester. The muzzle brake is a welcome addition.

on the scene, I used a .44 Magnum sixgun, again starting the game with sixguns marked Ruger and Smith & Wesson. I saw some shooters using those funny-looking, break-in-the-middle, single-shot pistols, but it looked to me like a passing fad and I intended to just keep using my sixguns for everything. Besides, I had five or six quick shots to their one. I was yet to learn about "One Good Shot!"

Some things simply are meant to be and when one is stubborn, then fate intervenes. In my case, Dot, my wife, intervened and bought me a Christmas present. Now over the years she has given me some grand gifts, beginning with a Smith & Wesson .44 Special on our first Christmas together and such great sixguns as a Second Generation Colt New Frontier .44 Special on the occasion of our anniversary, and a matched pair of Smith & Wesson .44s for my birthday. She certainly knew what I liked. It almost always said "44 Special" on the barrel, and had a cylinder that turned.

However, the above mentioned Christmas present was not a .44 Special. It was not even a sixgun. Oh, it was a handgun. At least some said it was, but I had my doubts. That unexpected gift was a .30-30 Thompson/Center Contender Super 14. My first thought was "What in the world am I gonna do with this thing?" I certainly could not tell my wife I was disappointed. I couldn't sell it. I would have to at least try to use it.

The shelves in my reloading room were filled with loaded rounds for sixguns, .357, .44 Magnums and Specials, .45 Colt, and I had to go out and buy factory .30-30s to shoot the new whatever it was. I took a few shots to get it sighted in and then I set up a long-range silhouette ram target at 200 meters, and bolted it down. Back at the firing line I then assumed the Creedmore position, lying on my back with knees drawn up, right elbow on the ground, and the Contender held in my right hand and resting along my right leg. Slowly and deliberately I would shoot, pull back on the lever at the bottom of the trigger guard, remove the fired round, insert the next round, and close the action until five shots were carefully squeezed off as I sighted on the ram. Those first five shots on metal from the .30-30 Contender at the 200-meter ram made a group that could be covered with my hand. I looked down at the Contender Super 14 in my hand, and it had suddenly turned into a beautiful handgun!

It was not only beautiful, it was unbelievable — a handgun that would outshoot many rifles. I had my first unlimited silhouette gun that doubled as a hunting handgun. A second Contender was added in the shape of a 10-inch .357 Magnum and I had the perfect production gun. In all the years I shot silhouettes, I tried a lot of different sixguns, almost a new test revolver each month, but these two Contenders were never replaced.

About this same time I became acquainted with J.D. Jones and soon had SSK barrels chambered specifically for hunting in the big-bore .430 JDJ and .45-70. I was

How about a lever gun/single-shot combination such as the Marlin 336 and Thompson/Center Super 14 in .35 Remington? ...

hooked on Contenders. I don't shoot silhouettes anymore, but I do shoot Contenders a great deal in the game fields. I've used them on everything from Idaho ground squirrels to a 1,500-pound African eland. They don't replace my sixguns, but they are a welcome addition to my shooting collection.

The Contender has been a constantly changing handgun as far as chamberings are concerned with just about every safe factory caliber being offered at one time or the other. Standard barrel lengths have been mostly 10 and 14 inches, with a few calibers being offered in the Super 16 length of 16 1/4-inches.

A look at the calibers offered 30 years ago shows that the Contender had not quite found its niche. One could actually purchase Contenders chambered for .38 Super and 9mm! The hunting chamberings offered were .30-30 and .44 Magnum plus the wildcats from Steve Herrett and Bob Milek, the .30 Herrett and .357 Herrett, both based on the .30-30 case. The longest barrel length offered was 10 inches. In 1978, the Super 14 emerged and the Contender began to be taken very seriously as a hunting handgun. The original chamberings in the Super 14 were .30-30, .30 Herrett, .357 Herrett, .41 Magnum, .44 Magnum, and .35 Remington — all serious hunting cartridges.

My now scoped-sighted Super 14s in factory chamberings of .30-30, .35 Remington and .375 Winchester are sighted in for 150 yards. Reloader 7 seems to be an excellent choice for loading these three cartridges in the 14-inch barreled Contender. For the .35 Remington

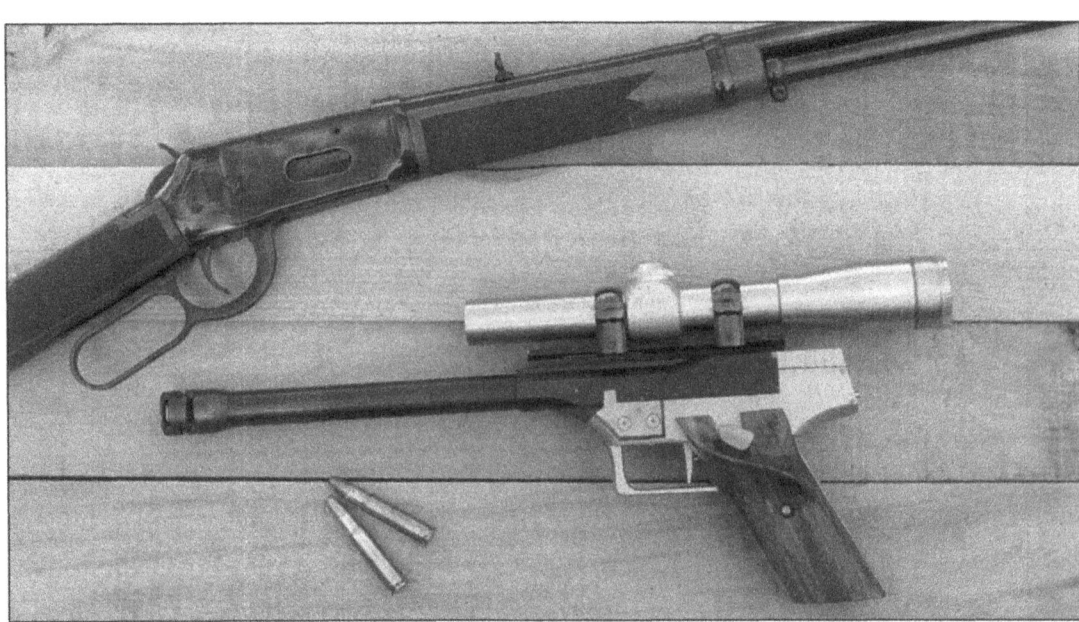

Or Winchester 94BB and RPM in .356 Winchester? ...

Or even the Winchester 94BB and Contender for the .375 Winchester?

I prefer 32.0 grains of RE-7 and Hornady's 180-grain Single-Shot Spire Point for 1,983 fps and three-shot groups at 50 yards of less than 1/2 inch. In the .375 Winchester, the powder charge with RE-7 is upped to 36.0 grains under Hornady's 220-grain JFP for 1,947 fps and groups under 1 inch at 50 yards.

When I used the Super 14 .30-30 for silhouetting, I used Hornady's 150-grain jacketed spire point at 1,950-2,000 fps. Now that it is strictly a hunting handgun, the bullet weight remains the same, but I have switched to Speer's 150-grain jacketed flatpoint for 2,062 fps over 28.0 grains of RE-7.

As we have seen from the original chamberings, when the Contender first emerged, T/C did not really know what a great handgun the Contender could become. The first chamberings were very light-recoiling handgun cartridges. Equipped with a lightweight octagonal barrel and a grip shaped like a saw handle, the Contender really got the shooter's attention by the time it was chambered in .44 Magnum. The felt recoil was awful and it was not long before a heavy bull barrel was made standard and the grip was expertly redesigned by Steve Herrett to make the heavy-kickin' version of the Contender manageable.

SSK Industries has been a leader in offering custom chamberings in the Contender beginning 30 years ago with the .430 JDJ, a .444 Marlin trimmed by .010 inch., and the .45-70. Presently SSK offers dozens of chamberings in the Contender, including the .257 JDJ, 6.5 JDJ, .309 JDJ, 338 JDJ #2, and .375 JDJ. A man equipped with a 6.5 JDJ and a .375 JDJ is ready for anything. More about J.D.'s custom T/C's shortly.

My longest hunting shot with a Contender occurred with the 6.5 JDJ. My hunting load for my 14-inch custom-barreled Contender in this chambering is 34.0 grains of AA2520 under Speer's 120-grain JSP for right at 2,400 fps. This is a warm load and is to be approached with the usual caution. It is superbly accurate and has recorded more than two dozen straight one-shot kills over the past 10 years. Eight years ago I was on the last day of a hunt for blackbuck antelope on the Y.O. Ranch in Texas. I just could not get a shot and time was running out. Suddenly, I had a chance. There was a decent blackbuck at 250 yards. Too far, I felt. My guide encouraged me to take the shot, so I took a solid rest, put the crosshairs on the beautiful little antelope, and squeezed the trigger ever so carefully. The antelope went straight up in the air and came down, dead. My guide said after the shot that I was the only hunter he ever had that he would allow to take such a long shot with handgun. It wasn't me; it was the Contender. If I ever have a failure with this gun I know it will be me and neither the gun or load. This buck is pictured on page 457 of Speer's *12th Edition Reloading Manual*.

My most gratifying shot with the Contender came in Africa. I was in an area that had never been hunted with a handgun. The trackers had never seen such a thing as my 12-inch T/C chambered in .375 JDJ. In fact, the head tracker made some very disparaging remarks about my handgun in his language. I asked what was said and it was translated as "Gun no good. Barrel too short." Then we got a chance on wildebeest, which, along with zebra, are very hard to kill, especially with one shot. We spotted a big bull at about 100 yards. At the shot, the Wildebeest dropped in his tracks. The tracker was all smiles and after that he thought that if he could see it, I should be able to kill it.

The Patriot

This T/C pistol is certainly well named as it is reminiscent of the single-shot handguns that were the defensive and offensive weapons around the time of the Revolutionary War. Reminiscent it may be, but this is a thoroughly modern pistol with double-set triggers and fully adjustable sights. The sights consisting of T/C rear with a square notch and a post front sight surrounded by protective ears preclude this from being an easily holstered handgun. The front sight sits in a dovetail, so it can be easily tapped from side to side if the rear sight does not have enough windage adjustment.

The Patriot is extremely attractive with its blued octagon barrel, figured walnut stock and brass-trimmed trigger guard, butt plate, and forearm cap. The brass and walnut are nicely set off by the case coloring on the hammer and lock. It shoots just as good, or better, than it looks. It is designed for a .440 round ball. I use Speer's swaged round ball and T/C patches over 30.0 grains of Goex FFFg or Pyrodex P for 993 fps and 935 fps, respectively. This does not represent a whole lot of power, so the Patriot is best reserved for small game and varmints. Unfortunately, the Patriot is not currently in production and is in high demand by those who shoot muzzleloaders in competition so they are very hard to find. The last one I found had been shot with black powder and never cleaned. Of course the barrel was ruined. If you happen to stumble across one, my advice is buy it!

The Scout/209X50 Magnum

Thompson/Center's Scout is the blackpowder equivalent of the Contender. It is a single-shot, 4-pound pistol with a barrel length of 10 inches. The front sight is a black post on a removable ramp, the rear sight is fully adjustable for windage and elevation, and the rear sight can be removed and a scope mounted in its place. When loaded with a percussion cap in place, the hammer does not rest on the nipple, but is blocked completely unless it is fully cocked.

The Scout is the most powerful percussion pistol ever offered to the handgun hunter. Recoil is more than that experienced in firing, say, a Super Blackhawk with full-house .44 Magnum loads. This is a serious hunting handgun! In .54 persuasion, 90 grains of Pyrodex RS (Do not use Pyrodex "P" in the Scout) and a 230-grain round ball with T/C patches yields 1,585 fps. Switching to the 435-grain Maxi-ball and the same charge gives 1,253 fps.

A 435-grain Maxi-ball at 1,250 fps churns up 1,510 lbs.-ft. of muzzle energy, while a 230-grain round ball at 1,585 will result in a muzzle energy of 1,281 lbs.-ft. By comparison, a 300-grain hard cast bullet at 1,300 fps from a .44 Magnum yields a muzzle energy of 1,125 lbs.-ft. Again, I say this is a serious hunting handgun. And now it has been replaced by one that is even more efficient, the upgraded 209X50 Magnum with a closed-breech design that uses shotgun primers instead of percussion caps. It is based on the platform of the newest Thompson/Center pistol, the Encore.

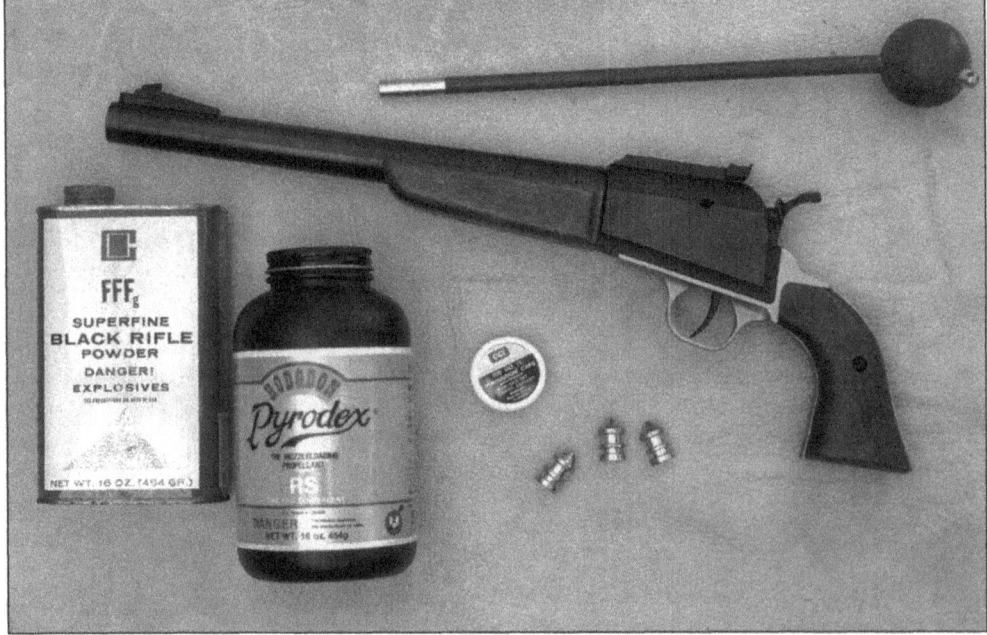

An excellent choice for black powder handgun hunting is the Thompson/Center Scout in .50 or .54.

The Contender (left), in this case with Pachmayr grips and custom SSK barrel, compared to the Encore chambered in .308.

The Encore

T/C's latest offering for the handgun hunter is the Encore, a totally new single-shot design. As with the Contender, the Encore features interchangeable barrels, however, Contender barrels and Encore barrels are not compatible. The Encore is larger than the Contender but seems to balance every bit as well as its older and smaller brother. There is a reason for the Encore's larger size. The Contender is limited to cartridges in the magnum sixgun pressure range (35,000 to 40,000). The Encore will handle the high-pressure rifle cartridges such as the .30-06. It is in fact chambered in .30-06 as well as .223, .22-250, 7BR, and my two favorites .308 and 7-08. In the .308 chambering, factory loads in the 150 to 165-grain weight range clock out right at 2,500

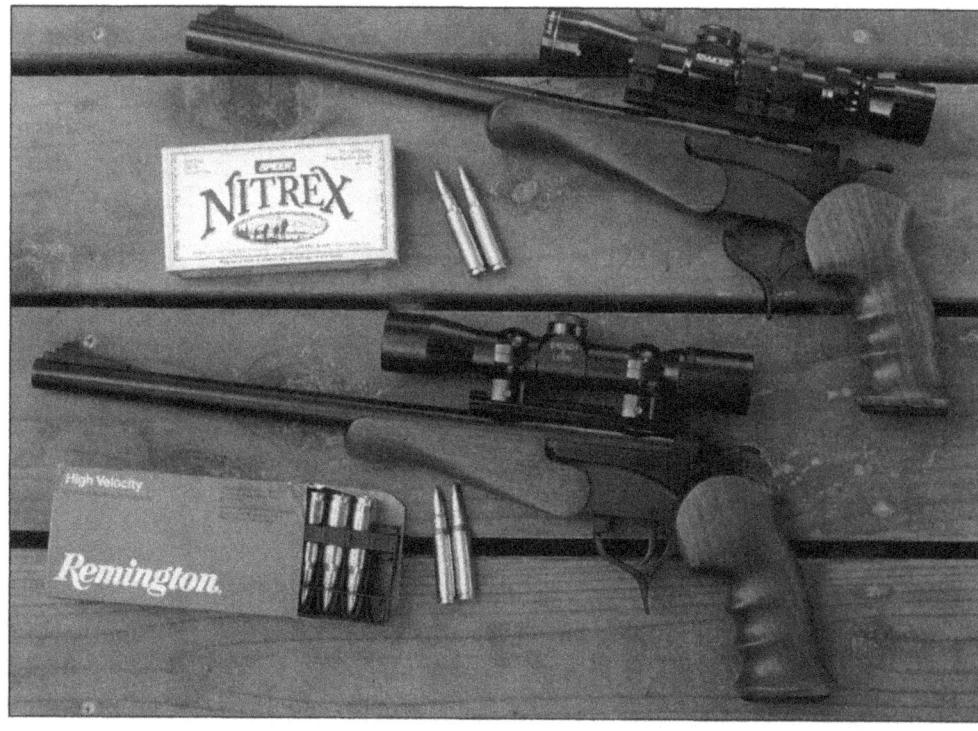

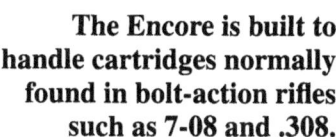

The Encore is built to handle cartridges normally found in bolt-action rifles such as 7-08 and .308.

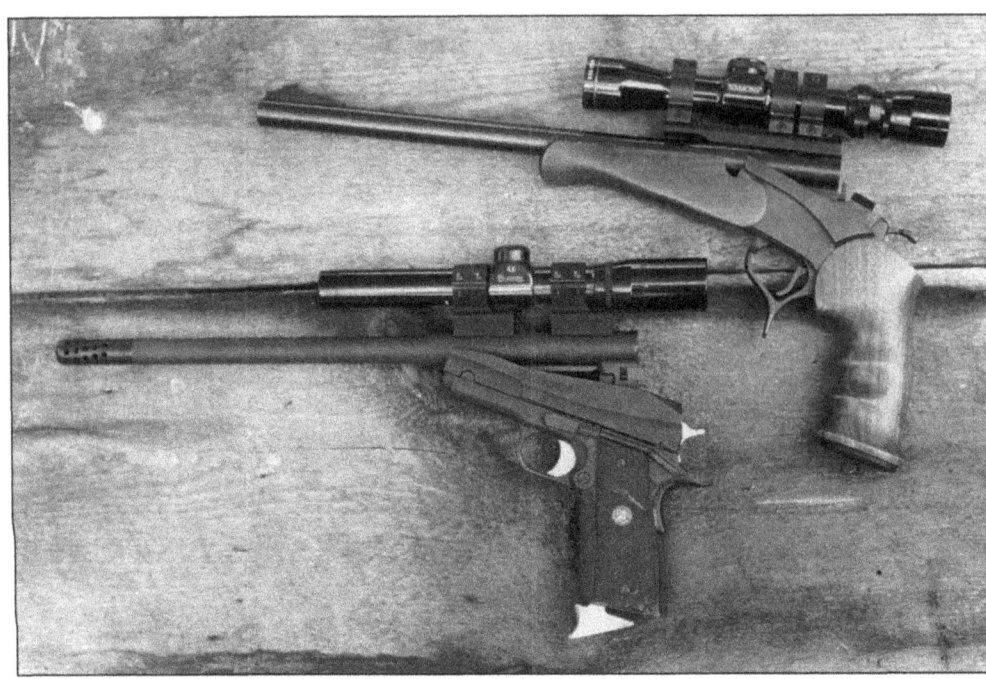

Two superbly accurate single-shot 7-08 hunting handguns: the Thompson/Center Contender (top) and the Springfield Armory Single Shot (S.A.S.S.).

fps muzzle velocity, while the 7-08 accomplishes the same with Remington's 140-grain jacketed soft points. The latter is absolutely deadly on deer-sized game.

Both of these Encores are set up for long-range handgun hunting with the excellent Simmons 2.5-7X LER scope on the .308 in a T'SOB mount, while the 7-08 wears a Bausch & Lomb 4X LER scope in the T/C factory mount. The 7-08 has been one of my favorite "handgun" rounds in the Remington XP-100. The Encore fires the same round in a much trimmer and easier to handle package.

Not only does the Encore use different barrels and handle higher pressures than the Contender, it also has a different safety system. The Contender is set up with a moveable lever on the top of the hammer to select rimfire, centerfire, or a safety hammer block. To use the Contender, the hammer is cocked and the safety lever must be moved to the proper position. If the gun is not fired, the safety must be engaged, the hammer left down, and then the Contender must be opened to re-cock the action. The Encore has been totally simplified with a rebounding hammer, no external safety, and it does not have to be re-cocked if the hammer is let down without firing the gun.

The Contender is chambered in such cartridges as .30-30, .35 Remington and .375 Winchester. These cartridges, all originally chambered in traditional lever action rifles, are in the below-40,000 CUP pressure level. Using higher-pressure cartridges will stretch the frame or worse. Such cartridges as the .444 Marlin and .45-70, while big-bore cartridges capable of downing the largest game at close range, actually operate at mild pressures for most loads with pressures well under 40,000 CUPs.

While the Contender is a "lever action level" single-shot pistol, the Encore moves into the strong bolt-action category. Now we are in the 50,000-plus CUP range. A few simple measurements reveal the obvious strengthening of the single-shot Thompson Center as we go from the Contender to the Encore. Measuring the barrel diameters at the breech with the Hornady Electronic Digital Caliper I come up with a diameter of .805 inch for a .30-30 Contender barrel compared to 1.000 inch for a .308 Encore barrel. That is an increase of 25 percent The frame is thicker on the Encore also, measuring 1.255 inches to the Contender's .910 inch, for an increase of more than 35 percent.

Wildcats for the Contender are built mainly on brass, such as the .225 Winchester or .444 Marlin, both of

This is the kind of accuracy that one can expect from a scoped Contender at 50 yards, or longer.

which are rimmed cartridges. The Encore is already being wildcatted with several necked-down, necked-up, and blown-out offerings on the rimless .30-06 case. Two other significant differences are found when comparing the Contender to the Encore. The latter is much easier to open, at least the two examples I have tried, compared with several Contender frames. It requires very little pressure on the tang to open the action, while Contenders, especially the older models, require a goodly amount of Wheaties for breakfast before operating. This has been enough of a problem in the past that the Contender has now been redesigned to the Contender G2 with an easier-to-open action and the safety features of the Encore, including not having to break open the action before the hammer can be recocked. In a hunting situation, I have often found myself cocking, then letting the hammer down, and having to open the action to reset the mechanism before recocking the original Contender. This occurs for various reasons, such as deciding to pass on the particular animal, or not having a clear shot as the animal moves. The Encore and the new Contender G2 makes this phase of hunting so much easier.

As with the Contender, The Encore comes with removable iron sights and is furnished drilled and tapped for scope mounting. The Encore, as with the Contender, is available in both blue and stainless. Wood for the Encore is a walnut forearm mated up with an excellently designed finger groove stock. With the cartridges that the Encore is capable of handling, the smooth wood grip may prove to be too slippery for security when shooting heavy-kickin' loads, so T/C has come up with a rubber grip and matching forearm.

The Encore is also available factory ready for hunting, and this single-shot is made for hunting, make no mistake about that. The Hunter Package consists of a 15-inch .22-250, .270, or .308 barrel without iron sights, but with a 2.5-7X T/C Recoil Proof Pistol Scope mounted on a Weaver-style base. Both grips and forearm on the Hunter Model are black rubber rather than the walnut supplied on the standard Encore.

With the Contender, I find that up to the .35 Remington, felt recoil is not excessive. However, both the .375 Winchester and .45-70 can really get to this shooter and I prefer a muzzle brake with these cartridges. With the Encore, the 7-08 is the top level of "pleasant shooting" loads, while the .308 begins to talk to me. When attending the Handgun Hunters International Hunt and World's Champion Pistol Shoot on the YO Ranch one September, I had the opportunity to shoot a .308 Winchester with an SSK Arrestor muzzle brake installed. This brake is user friendly in that it does not vent to the sides and is extremely effective, bringing the recoil down to a pleasant shooting, even a mild level.

As with the Contender, the Encore also features the interchangeable barrel system allowing more than one barrel to be used with a frame. Both provide an easy changing of barrels by simply removing the forearm, tapping out the hinge pin, removing the barrel, replacing it with a different barrel and then reversing the operation. All of this can be accomplished in just a few minutes. With a look at the previously mentioned dimensions, it should be obvious that although both the Contender and Encore feature interchangeable barrels, Contender barrels will not fit Encore frames, nor will Encore barrels fit Contender frames.

Some other notable single shots

Two single shots arrived in the early 1960s offered as long-range varmint handguns. Ruger's single-shot Hawkeye was made by replacing the cylinder of the Blackhawk with a swing-out breech block and chambered in the then new .256 Winchester. Instead of experimenting with other calibers, Ruger eventually dropped the Hawkeye, which now demands big collector prices. It would certainly have handled anything in the length and pressure of the .30-30.

Remington's single-shot pistol was the bolt-action XP-100 in .221 Fireball. Unlimited class silhouetters soon had converted the XP-100 to several factory rifle cartridges, such as the .308, as well as many wildcat long-range chamberings. I used an XP-100 7-08 for hunting for quite

SELECTED LOADS FOR THE THOMPSON/CENTER ENCORE 15"

LOAD	MV	3 SHOTS/100 YDS
.308/Cor-Bon 150 Single-Shot	2,543	1 1/2"
.308/Hornady 150 SP	2,580	1 3/8"
.308/Hornady 165 SP	2,490	1 3/4"
.308/Speer 165 Grand Slam	2,538	1 1/2"
.308/Winchester 150 Ballistic ST	2,574	One hole
.308/Winchester 168 Ballistic ST	2,417	3/4"
.308/Winchester 180 Fail Safe	2,434	1"
.308/Winchester 180 Power Point	2,327	1 3/4"
7-08/Cor-Bon 130 Single Shot	2,614	1 3/4"
7-08/Remington 120 HP	2,825	1 7/8"
7-08/Remington 140 SP	2,560	7/8"

The Remington XP-100 has been a very popular long-range handgun for unlimited class silhouettes as well as handgun hunting.

some time and found it deadly accurate, but the T/C Contender in 6.5 JDJ was easier to pack and won out as my favorite for game in the deer/elk size range.

In 1981, world renowned gunsmith George Hoenig designed an ingenious single-shot pistol that used the main grip frame of the 1911 Government Model. This bolt-action single-shot action replaced the barrel and slide of the 1911 and bolted on by going through the magazine well. Hoenig's prototype was a beautifully crafted .22 Hornet with a light, slim barrel designed for hunting varmints. With the burgeoning popularity of both long-range silhouetting and handgun hunting at the time, Pachmayr took over the manufacturing and distribution of what became known as the Dominator in 1985.

I used the Dominator in the early days of silhouetting in .357 SuperMag with excellent accuracy, and also in 7-08, which was a deadly combination for hunting. Hoenig had an excellent idea and it is regrettable that his design lost so much of its elegance through mass production There was no way that the Pachmayr Dominator could compete with the Thompson/Center Contender and after a few years Pachmayr removed it from production. I still have my Dominator conversion units, but both 1911 frames have become 1911 Government Models once again. Springfield Armory tried to resurrect the idea with S.A.S.S, the Springfield Armory Single Shot, offering several rifle and sixgun cartridges in a solid unit that also met the same fate as the Dominator.

In the early days of silhouetting a most popular single-shot pistol was the Merrill. Merrill shooters were always easily recognized by the cleaning rod hanging out of their back pocket. The rod was for removing stuck cases that resisted the Merrill's weak extractor. In a move that I'm sure had more to do with personalities than performance, the Merrill, by now the RPM XL, was effectively banned when cleaning rods were disallowed for removing fired cases.

That rule finally went the way of the price ceiling, which worked to keep the Freedom Arms revolver out of competition and now both Freedom Arms and RPM handguns are not only regularly seen, they are usually in the winner's circle. Jim Rock, owner of RPM and the

George Hoenig's original single-shot .22 Hornet on a 1911 grip frame (bottom) is compared to a production run Pachmayr Dominator.

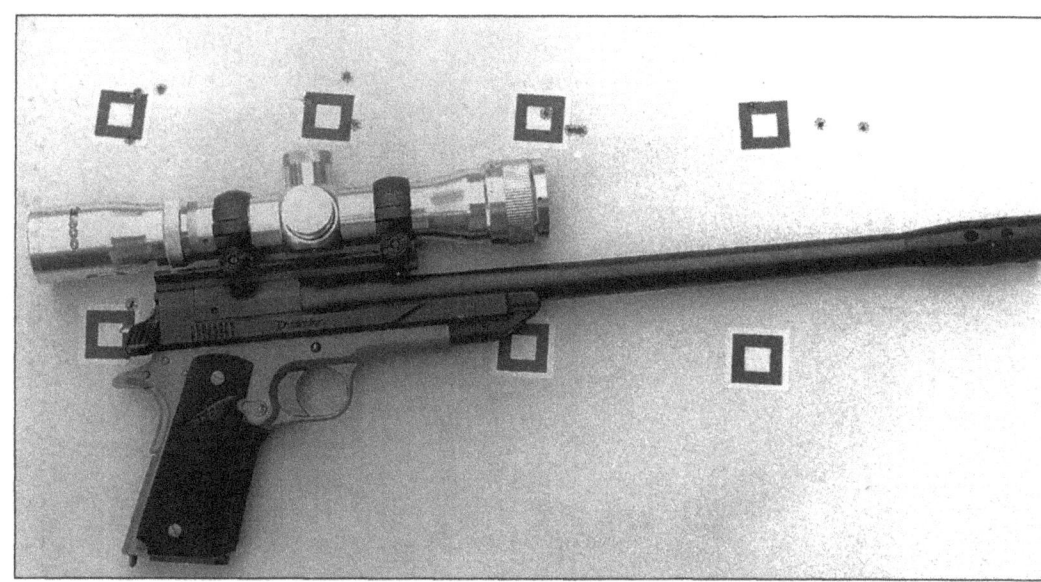

These 100-yard groups were shot with the Pachmayr Dominator chambered in 7-08.

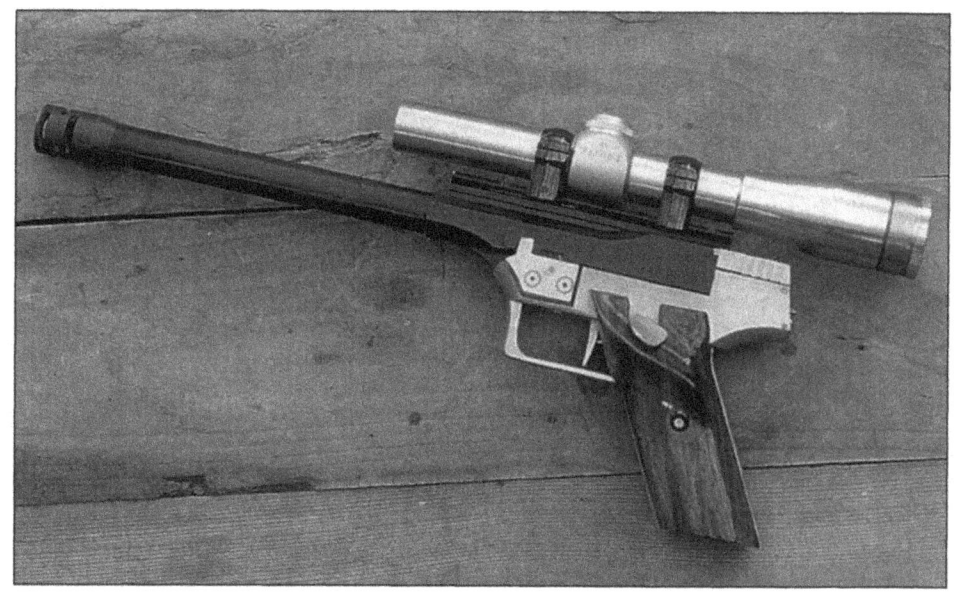

This RPM single-shot pistol by Jim Rock is chambered in the very potent .356 Winchester.

SSK offers hundreds of wildcat chamberings in the Contender. These are in .257 JDJ and .338 WoodsWalker.

number one senior shooter in the country, shoots a Freedom Arms revolver in the revolver class.

RPM pistols are now fitted, and can be retrofitted, with a positive extractor that removes the most stubborn fired case. My RPM XL is fitted with a 12-inch barrel and a compensator that is entirely welcome when firing the .356 Winchester. Fitted with a good quality pistol scope, the RPM XL will outshoot many (most?) out of the box rifles.

As a single-shot pistol, the RPM is of the break-open style with a lever on the right side that allows the barrel to pivot at the front of the frame for loading and unloading. On this particular RPM, the frame is satin nickel while the barrel is blue with both nicely set off by walnut grip panels. The grip angle is reminiscent of the old Colt Woodsman except it is much larger. The right grip has a palm swell and heel rest, while the left grip panel carries a thumb rest. All in all, it is a most comfortable feeling grip. The front of the frame is squared off and provides a perfect spot for the index finger on my off hand. In .356 Winchester, this is definitely a two-handed handgun.

The safety of the RPM is a lever that rides above the thumb rest on the left grip. It must be pressed to allow the RPM to fire. On the back of the frame is a cocking indicator that tells at a glance or feel if the RPM is ready to fire. The trigger carries an adjustable built in stop and is set at the factory for a smooth pull of 28 ounces. The RPM frame can be fitted at the factory with other barrels with any sensible caliber, including a number of RPM original wildcats. The .356 Winchester, being only slightly less potent than the excellent .358 Winchester, can certainly handle anything that walks on American soil.

While most single shots are of the break-open style or built on a rifle-type bolt action, M.O.A. goes a different route with their excellent line-up of lever activated single-shot handguns. This falling-block action allows a single-piece receiver of tremendous strength. Barrels are all Douglas and free floated to help insure accuracy. The M.O.A. also has a unique safety button that allows the loading and unloading only when it is in the safe position. The gun cannot be fired until it is cocked and the safety then moved downwards.

The M.O.A. comes equipped with precision sights for silhouetters, but is also drilled and tapped to accept

The author took this beautiful African trophy, a gemsbok, at 180 yards with one shot from the SSK Custom Contender chambered in 6.5 JDJ.

the M.O.A. scope mounts. Barrel lengths offered are 8 1/2, 10 1/2, and 14 inches with a list of calibers offered that is almost endless including the .308 and 7-08, the .358 Winchester, the .350 Remington, and the .375 H&H, with muzzle brakes of course. For those that prefer sixgun cartridges, nearly everything is offered, including the .454 Casull. For those that prefer a handgun for varmints, the M.O.A. is also offered in such easy-shootin' small bores as .22 Hornet, .223, .22-250, and .243. Other calibers are available on request. If it is safe, M.O.A can build it.

SELECTED LOADS FOR THE .356 WINCHESTER RPM XL 12"

LOAD	MV
Winchester 250 FP	1,881
Speer 180 FP/48.0 gr. AA2520	2,167
Hornady 180 SSP/44.0 gr. AA2015	2,256
Hornady 200 SP/46.5 gr. AA2520	2,135
Speer 220 FP/44.5 gr. AA2520	2,015

One of the few animals to ever take two shots from one of Taffin's super accurate Contenders, this eland from South Africa was taken with the .375 JDJ.

The single shots of SSK

I don't believe there is anyone, anywhere, at anytime, that can equal the knowledge of J.D. Jones of SSK when it comes to big handguns and big handgun cartridges. For more than 30 years, he has been experimenting with Contenders, and now Encores from Thompson/Center and was the first to realize just what these single-shots were really capable of achieving. His experiments are not simply in the shop, but in game fields literally all over the world. The first Contenders may have been chambered in .22 LR and .38 Special, however, SSK has offered more than 200 calibers in the Contender, making it without a doubt the most versatile and effective hunting handgun ever offered. SSK has custom barrel profiles, finishes, and serial numbers as well as chamberings from mild to wild. The most popular calibers offered are the .226, 6mm, .257, 6.5mm, .270, and 7mm JDJs all on the .225 Winchester case; and the .309, 8mm, .338 #2, .358, .375, and .416 JDJs all on the .444 Marlin brass. I have used the .257, 6.5, and .375 very successfully in hunting fields around the country as well as Africa. They flat out work!

Now that the Contender has been joined by the stronger Encore, J.D. already provides truly awesome chamberings of the latter. A look at Wildcats on the Contender and Encore as offered by SSK will give a revealing picture as to what can be expected from the Encore. My favorite SSK chambering in the Contender for medium-sized game is the 6.5 JDJ, which is on the .225 Winchester case. My standard load achieves 2,400 fps with Speer's 120-grain spire point. Using the same bullet in the new 6.5 Mini-Dreadnought on the .220 Swift case in the Encore increases the muzzle velocity by 400 fps. I don't believe it can dispatch game any faster, but it will surely flatten out the trajectory even more.

Three potent Wildcats on the .444 Marlin case in the Contender are the .309 JDJ, .338 JDJ #2, and the .375 JDJ. These, respectively, have muzzle velocities of 2,300 fps with a 150-grain bullet, 2,300 with a 200-grain bullet, and 1,900 fps with a 270-grain bullet. The latter has been the standard by which all handgun cartridges for hunting large dangerous critters has been judged. Switching to the Encore and using the .30/06 as the parent case, we have the .30/06 JDJ with a 150-grain bullet at 2,900 fps, the .338/06 JDJ with a 200-grain bullet at 2,700 fps, and the .375/06 JDJ using a 270-grain bullet at 2,400 fps. These are serious velocities! Note the .30/06 JDJ does more than most .30/06 rifles!

Any cartridge with the case head size and pressure level of the .300 Winchester Magnum can be safely chambered in the Encore. This means such previously big rifle chamberings as the .300 and .338 WinMags, the .375 H&H, .416 Taylor, .416/348 JDJ, .500 Alas-

J.D. Jones, founder of SSK Industries and Handgun Hunters International, took this 54-inch kudu just before dark with the .375 JDJ-chambered Contender.

kan, even the .458 WinMag can be handled by the Encore. We should emphasize that, although the Encore is up to it, the shooter may not be! Many of the old Nitro Express chamberings can be used in the Encore. As with the Contender, SSK offers everything from plain to fancy, barrel configurations of plain, bull, fluted, even antique cannon style, custom finishes, muzzle brakes that work, and T'SOB scope mounts, the best in the business for heavy-kickin' handguns.

The single shots of Gary Reeder Custom Guns

For several years I had heard of Gary Reeder and saw his work advertised, but never met him personally. Two years ago we met on a handgun hunt where I found that Reeder not only specializes in building hunting handguns, he also tests them in the field himself (tough work!). While many custom shops are a one-man operation turning guns out one at a time, Reeder Custom Guns is the Henry Ford of the custom gun line with a large staff turning out a large quantity of custom sixguns and single shots. For those that prefer single shots, Reeder uses both the Thompson/Center Contender and the Encore as the platform to build everything from .22 Hornet to .458 Winchester as well as

Another rare and unique trophy taken by J.D. Jones with the Contender in .375 JDJ. This is, in fact, the only known Gobi argali ever taken with a handgun.

WILDCATTING THE THOMPSON CENTER SINGLE-SHOT PISTOLS

15" ENCORE	14" CONTENDER
6.5 Mini-Dreadnought (.220 Swift)	6.5 JDJ (.225 Winchester)
120 gr. @ 2,800 fps	120 gr. @ 2,400 fps
140 gr. @ 2,700 fps	140 gr. @ 2,100 fps
.30/06 JDJ (.30-06)	.309 JDJ (.444 Marlin)
150 gr. @ 2,900 fps	150 gr. @ 2,300 fps
165 gr. @ 2,750 fps	165 gr. @ 2,200 fps
180 gr. @ 2,650 fps	180 gr. @ 2,200 fps
.338/06 JDJ (.30-06)	.338 JDJ #2 (.444 Marlin)
200 gr. @ 2,700 fps	200 gr. @ 2,300 fps
250 gr. @ 2,480 fps	250 gr. @ 2,100 fps
.375/06 JDJ (.30-06)	.375 JDJ (.444 Marlin)
220 gr. @ 2,650 fps	220 gr. @ 2,100 fps
270 gr. @ 2,400 fps	270 gr. @ 1,900 fps
300 gr. @ 2,650 fps	300 gr. @ 1,930 fps

several exotic chamberings such as the .356GNR on the .41 Magnum case, and the .338GNR, .350GNR, and .378GNR, all on the .405 Winchester case.

In the Contender, Reeder's Custom Calibers and their parent cases include 7mm (7x30), .30 (.30-30), .338, .350, and .378, all on the .405 Winchester and the .450, and .475 GNRs, on the .45-70 brass. Want to take something really big? Reeder goes with the .470 Nitro Express necked down to form the .450KNR, or the .348 Winchester case formed to the .416GNR or .450GNR. Reeder's Ultimate Encore has 30 different chamberings, including the .475 GNR, while the beautiful, short-barreled Kodiak Hunter is offered in .454 Casull and .50 Action Express.

There are still handgunnners, and especially handgun hunters, who do not consider the single-shots to be "handguns." It took me quite awhile to discover the potential of the single shots, the precision; the long-range accuracy; the rifle-style muzzle energy. Granted, no single-shot pistol will ever stir my soul as does a classic sixgun, but they are all part of the great world of handgunning. If I can understand this, there is hope for all.

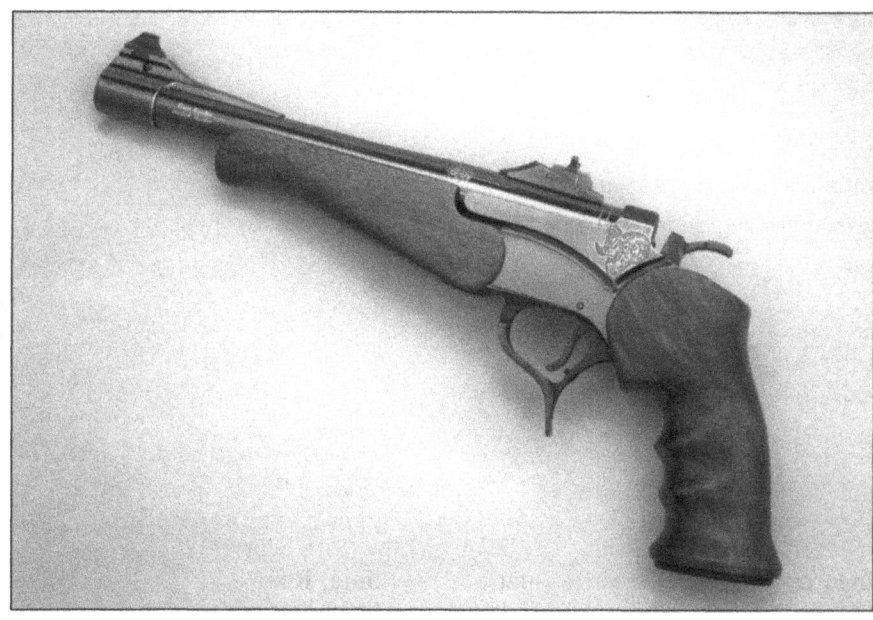

Gary Reeder Custom Guns offers a full line of custom Contenders and Encores. This Alaskan Hunter is chambered for the .50 Action Express.

CHAPTER 12

CUSTOM HANDGUNS

As a kid I spent many an hour looking through the pages of *Outdoor Life* and *American Rifleman* dreaming of hunting trips and guns. With *Outdoor Life* it was a real chore to wait every month (even tougher to come up with a quarter to buy it!) to see what exotic place Jack O'Connor would be found in and also with what great trophy he would be pictured. *American Rifleman* carried the works of Elmer Keith and especially intriguing to me were the sixgun articles. Single-action sixgun articles with customized big-bore revolvers. Keith was always the experimenter in those days and brought us the works and ideas of Croft, Houchins, Sedgely, and their peers. Those articles in the early '50s were so good that I eventually traced back and acquired copies of all of Keith's sixgun stories going back to the 1920s. They are still a valuable resource.

By 1957, graduation had passed and I was out in the world and discovering daily the wonders of sixguns. As I looked in the gun case, my eyes and spirit were caught by two single actions. One was the then brand-new Ruger Blackhawk, now known to collectors as the Flat-Top, in the equally new .44 Magnum chambering — the first of its kind in the area. The price tag was $96, or just about 2 1/2 weeks' pay for this teenager. The other single action was a little more expensive, representing about a month's pay at $150. Oh, but it was beautiful! Although it was at least 50 years old, it had been extensively customized and this Colt Single Action Army .45 now had a full-length rib, target hammer, tasteful engraving and a high-polish blue finish.

Today I can easily tell anyone in the same situation to simply "Buy 'em both!" but the reality was that whichever I chose would take quite a while to pay off.

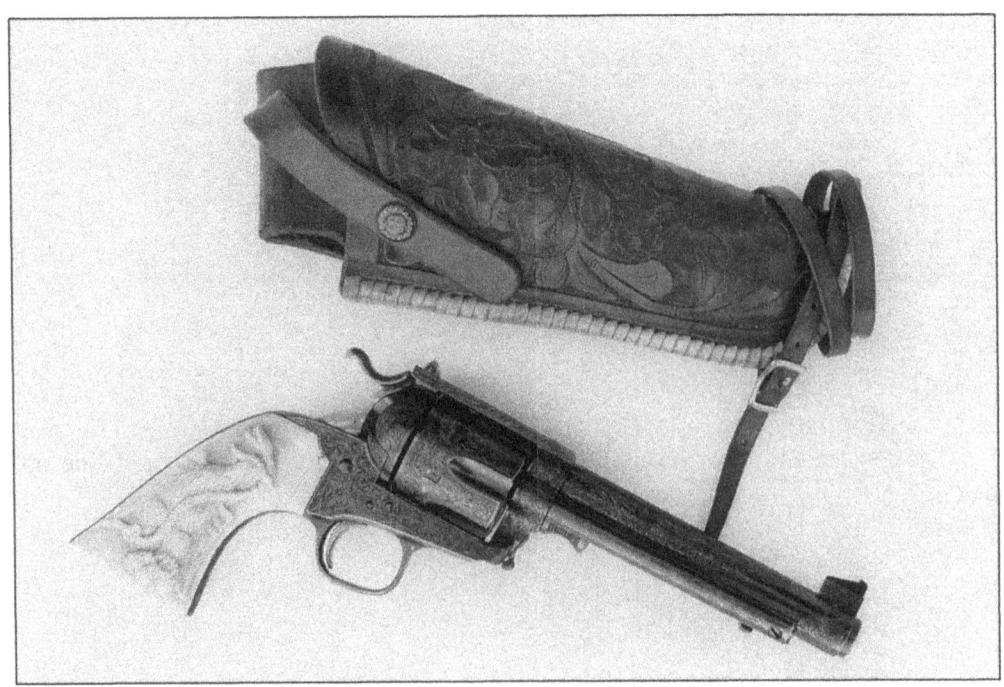

A true Heritage Handgun. This pistol is easy to recognize as Elmer Keith's #5SAA .44 Special that he had built in the 1920s. The holster is a Lawrence #120 Keith. Both have been in the Keith family for more than three-quarters of a century.

Prior to World War II custom gunsmiths often fitted S&W rear sights to Colt Single Actions. Jim Stroh now does the same thing to Ruger Vaqueros complete with his own front sight and a custom base pin. All in all, it makes for a very slick sixgun.

In those pre-plastic card days, teenagers could not only buy handguns, they could get the store to carry the bill. So much for today's easy accessibility "problem." The Colt was history, but the Ruger was the future, so I went with the Blackhawk. I still have it and it has been a 6 1/2-inch sixgun as original, a 4 3/4-inch easy-packin' pistol, and now wears a 7 1/2-inch barrel. It is one of those "not for sale" sixguns," but oh, how I wish I had purchased that Colt. It was a prime example of the custom sixgunsmiths' art. My Blackhawk is now worth about $500, and I don't even want to think about the current value of that Colt.

A custom sixgun in 1957 may have seemed unattainable for me, but today I am blessed with custom Colts, Smiths, Rugers and several other makes breathed upon by the top names in the business. It is my good privilege to know the top single-action sixgunsmiths and pistolsmiths today. Men that simply are the best that ever were at their craft, who have worked on my guns, who have built custom guns for my personal use, and who provided me with prized possessions as well as everyday working sixguns. Most assuredly, they are all not found in these pages, space constraints being what they are, and the reader is advised that more custom handguns will be found in my two previous books, *Big Bore Sixguns* and *Action Shooting Cowboy Style*.

Custom sixgunsmiths

Alpha Precision: Elmer Keith would have loved the work of many of today's top sixgunsmiths, including, and especially, Jim Stroh of Alpha Precision. Stroh, named in the past as "Pistolsmith of the Year" by The American Pistolsmiths Guild, understands sixguns, especially single-action sixguns, as few pistolsmiths do. Seventy years ago Keith chose the strongest single-action available at the time, the Colt Single Action Army. Today, Jim Stroh does his work with the workhorse Rugers, the Vaquero, the Blackhawk, and the Bisley. Often when not starting with the Bisley, Stroh adapts the Bisley grip frame to his big-bore sixguns as it is the best for handling heavy loads in Ruger sixguns. It has been my good pleasure to test several of Stroh's best sixguns, as well as have him build one for me personally.

Stroh is recognized as a master working in metal who can fit factory cylinders to tighter specifications or provide totally custom cylinders in either five or six-shot versions in .44 Magnum and .45 Colt and five shots in .475 and .500 Linebaugh. Ruger factory cylinders, unlike the First and Second Generation Colt Single Actions, have never utilized a base pin bushing. Stroh uses a press fit base pin bushing that is cut absolutely square at both ends to eliminate premature cylinder end play. To also combat end play and provide a very tight cylinder with virtually no side-to-side movement of the cylinder, Stroh fits an oversize locking bolt that completely fills in the locking slot in the frame and the slots in the cylinder itself. In addition, Stroh adds a locking block in the interior of the frame to support the cylinder locking bolt.

One of the problems inherent with single actions and heavy loads is the inertia factor that comes into play with ejector rod housings. When the sixgun is fired, the recoil tends to separate the barrel from the ejector rod housing. It is a rare single-action sixgunner who has not lost an ejector rod housing at some time. Stroh combats this by installing two heat-treated dowel pins in the underside of the ejector rod housing and into the barrel. This is an extremely strong solution to a common problem. I would be very surprised if anyone ever loses an ejector rod housing from a Stroh sixgun.

Stroh performs one operation on New Model Rugers that will endear him to the hearts of traditional sixgunners everywhere. He incorporates a Colt-style half-cock notch while maintaining the transfer bar safety. One of the chief complaints about New Model Rugers is the fact that the cylinder chamber does not line up naturally with the opening in the loading gate. If one waits to hear the click, it is too late. The cylinder has already advanced too far. Stroh, through careful fitting and timing, eliminates this problem. At the click, the cylinder chamber is lined up to perfection in the loading gate area.

This is as good as it gets. This five-shot .45 Custom Ruger by Jim Stroh features Bisley Model grip frame hammer and trigger, Stroh front sight with interchangeable sight blades, total tuning and tightening of the action, satin blue finish, and a Colt-style trigger. Ivory micarta grips are by Charles Able.

Stroh also features full free cylinder rotation in both directions. That is, with the loading gate open, the cylinder can be freely rotated either clockwise or counter clockwise. This is extremely helpful when loading and especially if a bullet should jump the crimp, protrude from the end of the cylinder and hit the back of the barrel, preventing forward rotation. This has happened to me several times over the past four decades and I always had to figure out a way to push the bullet back into the case. With Stroh's special feature you simply open the loading gate, rotate the cylinder backwards, and remove the round with the ejector rod.

Stroh cylinders are line bored, meaning each chamber is cut with the cylinder locked in place in the frame, thus assuring nearly perfect alignment. This is a slow and expensive proposition that is also used on Freedom Arms revolvers. Blued steel custom five-shot cylinders are made from aircraft certified 4140 and cut to a diameter of 1.780 inches, and specially heat treated before they are chambered and machined. For stainless-steel cylinders, Stroh uses 13-8 aircraft grade PH stainless steel. This is tougher than 17-4PH and both are stronger than 4140.

What does a Ruger Vaquero need to make it even more usable? Adjustable sights. Stroh has come up with a slick conversion for an adjustable-sighted Vaquero by using the Smith and Wesson rear sight. This sight arrangement is much more compact than the standard Ruger Blackhawk sight and allows the maintenance of the eye-pleasing rounded top strap. Because the new-style Smith and Wesson rear sight with its rounded edge at the front does not reach the total length of the top strap, Stroh welds up and re-shapes the top strap to remove the hog wallow cut out rear sight that is standard on Colt Single Actions and Ruger Vaqueros. With Stroh's touch, the S&W rear sight looks as if it was custom made for the Vaquero. His six-shot .44

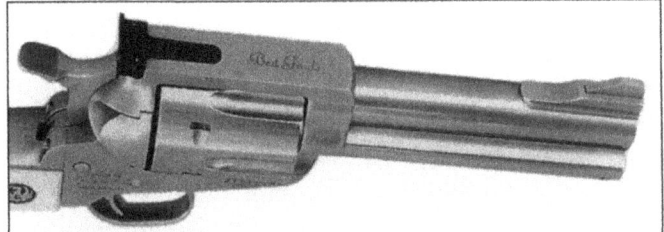

Top view of one of Jim Stroh's "Best Grade" Ruger Models shows the Flat-Top profile, reshaped hammer, Stroh front sight, and Bowen rear sight.

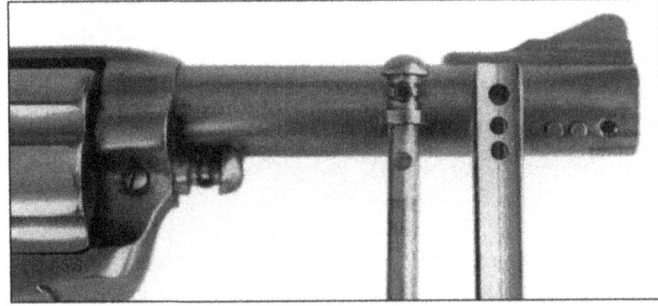

Ejector rods from Jim Stroh do not come off! Shown is his double-dowel system as well as a shortened base pin for use on less-than-standard-length barrels.

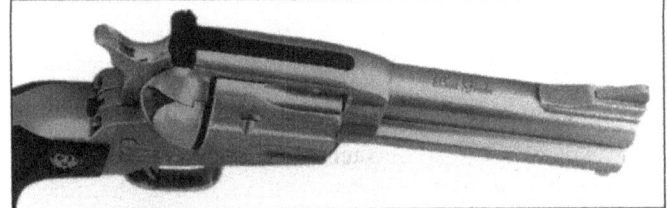

The installation of a Smith & Wesson rear sight on a Vaquero by Jim Stroh includes welding and reshaping the top of the frame in front of the rear sight, as well as the addition of a Stroh front sight.

Magnum comes very close to filling what has been my life-long quest for the "perfect packin' pistol." With my favorite packin' pistol loads for the .44 Magnum of 10 grains of Unique under a 260- or 295-grain Keith style hard cast bullet, the Stroh .44 Vaquero in my hands does 1,135 fps and 1,130 fps, respectively, with groups of 1 1/2 and 1 3/8 inches.

My personal Stroh sixgun is a .45 Colt built by Alpha Precision. Every sixgunner should have at least one great sixgun and this is one of my all-time greats with every feature I could think of that Stroh offers to make it nearly perfect. All of the above features are found on this sixgun, including blued front sight blades of the flat post persuasion. Somewhat different than the normal Stroh finish is the requested satin blue finish for use in heavy-duty hunting situations. The addition of ivory micarta grips, fitted and scrimshawed by Charles Able, makes it a sixgun anyone can be proud to pack.

With its smooth 2 1/2-pound trigger pull, this gun will shoot! Bullets in the 300-grain weight range at 1,100 to 1,150 fps make nice little tight groups of around 1 inch at 25 yards. The recoil factor has a lot to do with this as once the muzzle velocities with heavy bullets are moved above 1,200 fps my groups start to open up. NEI's 310- and 325-grain Keith bullets and RCBS's #45-300 SWC all will stay in the magical 1-inch grouping with 21.2 grains of H110 for 1,120 to 1,170 fps. An old load that is still a good one is Lyman's #457191 300-grain .45-70 bullet sized to .452 inch and loaded over 18.5 grains of #2400. The first of the heavyweight loadings for the .45 Colt, it does 1,170 fps and shoots 1-inch groups with this sixgun. Keith had his Last Word sixgun and Jim Stroh his Alpha (First) Precision. Stroh could easily advertise his work as the Alpha and Omega, the beginning and ending of sixgun perfection.

Bob Baer: Nearly 15 years ago I did an article for *American Handgunner* about the L'il Rugers of Andy Horvath, and a .44 Special in particular. When this article appeared I received a great letter from John Wootters, who has long been one of my favorite writers. John was a close friend of Skeeter Skelton. I quote from the letter: "Your recent piece about the little Rugers inspired me to tell you a tale. The so-called little Ruger and .44 Special was the favorite type of sporting pistol and cartridge of my late buddy, Skeeter Skelton, who spent much of his terminal illness in a hospital here in Houston. Together, with another friend and single-action expert, Bob Baer, we passed a lot of time plotting the creation of just such a pistol, of which he'd done several, only to sell or trade them all away. We even acquired the Three-Screw, .357 Mag Blackhawk for raw material. Sadly, Skeeter had to fold his hand before the last raise, and the project never went further, until recently. Then the gun was rechambered and re-

This custom .44 Special Ruger by Bob Baer not only looks and feels good, it also shoots exceptionally well.

barreled (4 5/8 inches from a slow-twist proven-accurate .44 Douglas premium blank) by Houston pistolsmith Earl Long. Bill Grover (Texas Longhorn Arms) then took over. He re-cut the forcing cone to suit himself, put a Colt-style crown on the muzzle, and installed one of the front sights he makes for his "Grover's Improved No. 5" Keith gun. He also re-bushed the cylinder and adjusted the cylinder gap to less than .002 inch (which makes it the tightest Ruger, even customized, I've ever seen!), and then hand fitted one of his No. 5 base pins. Finally, he broke the leading edge of the cylinder all around to make it easy on holsters.

"Bob Baer took over from there. He installed a bolt block and hand-tuned the action... and he is as good at that as any living man. He also performed his trigger magic, producing an absolutely exquisite 2-pound let-off. Then he flat-filed the frame, removing all markings, and rounded the square corners of the top strap, sort of ala Colt SAA. Many years ago Skeeter and I shared a hunting trip in northern British Columbia, during which we jointly discovered the skeleton of a mature stone ram, probably killed in an avalanche. I've been saving the horn material for the "right gun" for 15 years. This is the right gun. Baer fitted and shaped the grips to my order,

The author and gunsmith Bob Baer admire the .44 Special "Skeeter Gun" at a Shootists Holiday gathering in Colorado.

leaving the aluminum XR3-RED grip frame bright-polished — which was the way Skeeter liked them. That sheep horn is spectacular, a beautiful, creamy, smoky gray with subtle striping. Bob says it's harder than ivory!

"Now the gun went back to Grover for marking and polishing. The only markings are ".44 SPECIAL" on top of the barrel, "T.L.A. INC. RICHMOND TEXAS" in two lines on the top strap, a tiny, stylized longhorn steer head on the right side of the frame (Grover's logo), and the serial number, "S.S. 1" (for Skeeter Skelton), on the underside of the frame. Finally, Grover's man, Lee, did an inspired job of polishing and blueing. The little .44 is a sweetheart, quiet and pleasant to shoot, accurate (naturally, in that chambering), light as a feather, and pretty as a yellow cactus blossom. It leaps to hand of its own will, and seeks a target with the eagerness of a pointer pup. I will cherish it 'til the day I die, and may even have it buried with me.

"I think you'd like what I've come to call 'Skeeter's gun,' in every way. I know Skeeter would have loved it... it's his kind of sixgun...and mine. It's also a sort of tribute to an old and dear friend. He comes to mind every time I buckle in on, which is daily when I'm at my ranch down on the border. He'd have liked this memorial better than any other kind, I expect. Baer told Sally and young Bart about it, and they agree; they're touched. Having been struck by the similarity of our tastes as manifested in your article, and assuming that you are also acquainted, at least, with Skeeter, I thought you might like to hear about S.S. 1"

S.S. 1 is one of most spectacular custom Rugers in existence and this letter inspired six more S.S. Rugers by Bill Grover for Baer, Terry Murbach, Bart Skelton, Jim Wilson, myself, and Grover himself. There will be no more. When Skeeter wrote about his first .44 Special conversion back in the 1970s, I also had a 4 5/8-inch Ruger .44 made up. After my S.S. sixgun, Grover also made me a 7 1/2-inch .44 Special Ruger, and Hamilton Bowen has built three 4 5/8-inch and one 7 1/2-inch .44 Special Ruger for my use. Since receiving that letter I have also shot sixguns and lever guns with Bob Baer many times, discovering in the process that Baer performs exceptional magic on Marlin lever guns

It started in life as a 6 1/2-inch Ruger Old Model Blackhawk .357 Magnum. Bob Baer transformed it into a 3 1/4-inch, nickel-plated, lightweight .44 Special.

and Old Model Rugers. We had often talked about his building a special Ruger for me, but somehow never quite got around to it. Until now.

I recently found an Old Model .357 Ruger Blackhawk and sent it off to Bob Baer with instructions to simply build me a special gun, his choice of style and caliber. I've seen and handled many of Baer's creations from short barrels to long barrels, from round butts to lanyard rings, from .22s to .357s to .44s, with all kinds of artistic touches abounding. I did not know what to expect, but I knew I would not be disappointed.

Baer's conversion is a .44 Special with the front and rear edge of the grip frame tapered to make it more comfortable. Tedd Adamovich of BluMagnum made the fancy walnut grip blanks, which Baer then expertly fitted to the bright polished grip frame. The ejector rod housing is also polished bright, while the rest of this Special sixgun is finished in a very hard nickel plating. Keith DeHart expertly rechambered the cylinder and furnished the 3 1/4-inch barrel. The total package is a very easy-to-pack 30 ounces.

Some other special touches include a shortened base pin head, a thinned ejector rod head with a recess in the bottom of the ejector housing so the housing does not have to be removed to remove the base pin. The hammer spur has been slightly lowered, broadened, and checkered. The top strap has been tapered on both sides as mentioned by Wootters on the Skeeter gun. The front edges of the cylinder have been chamfered, and a very slight offset has been placed at the back edge of each chamber so that one may remove fired cartridges with a thumbnail if so desired. Of course, the entire action has been smoothed.

Special markings on this .44 Special include my initials, "JAT," on the front of the frame, and in front of the trigger guard on the bottom of the frame, we find "RGB," "01 SS SPL." One of the most amazing things is the marking on the bottom of the butt. Bob Baer decided to make a Texas-style brand for me and place it on the butt. What he did not realize is that he duplicated the marking that I have been using on any artwork I have done since my grade school days. In addition, he also crafted an easy-to-carry holster and also marked it with my "brand' and his logo. All together, it certainly is a Special sign for a Special sixgun from a Special sixgunsmith.

Bozeman Trail Arms: Tom Sargis is a one-man shop specializing in making single-action sixguns sing a fine tune. He also is a grip maker who understands how single-action grips are supposed to feel and function. When I found a used Third Generation Colt Single Action Army .44 Special x 7 1/2 inches with one major problem — the front sight had been filed down and was now placing my 250-grain .44 Special bullets about 6 inches high at 25 yards — off it went to Sargis to build up the front sight blade. That seemed like too little work to have done when paying the extortion fees now required by UPS for shipping handguns, so we added an action job and one-piece walnut stocks. To complete the project, Kelye Schlepp of Belt Mountain Enterprises sent over one of his new #5 base pins with the Elmer Keith-designed head.

There is something almost sensuous about cocking the hammer on a properly tuned Colt Single Action Army. The action is smooth, the cylinder locks up tightly with very little play, the trigger pull is light and crisp, the re-cut forcing cone aids accuracy, and the one-piece walnut stocks and #5 Belt Mountain cylinder base pin complete a sixgun package that is near perfect. So good in fact, that a Second Generation Colt New

Two .44 Specials by Tom Sargis. The 7 1/2-inch Colt Single Action has been totally tuned and stocked with one-piece walnut, while the bottom gun, a 5 1/2-inch New Frontier, has been fitted with an oversize bolt resulting in a great reduction in the cylinder side play.

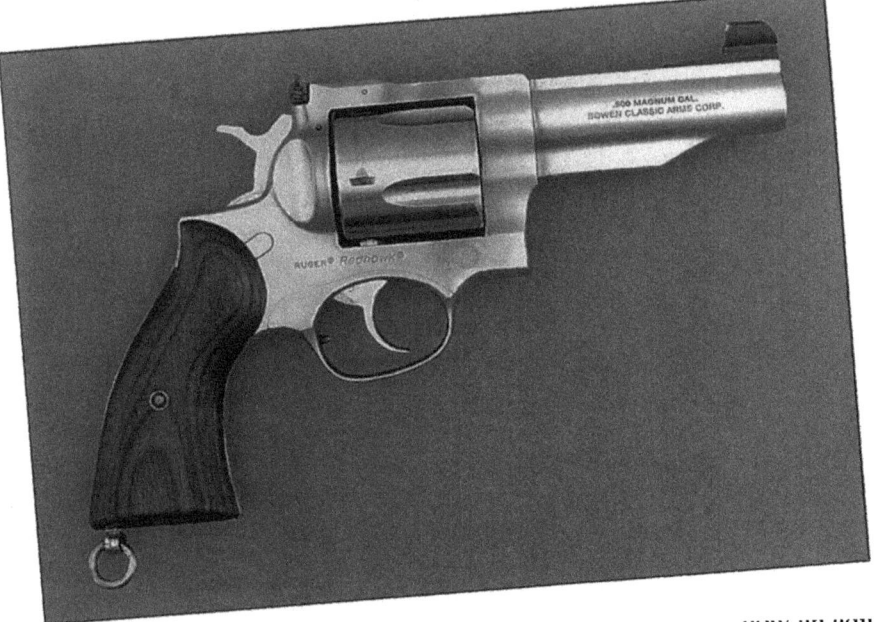

The infamous Ashley Emerson Ruger! This is a Hamilton Bowen-built, 4-inch, five-shot .500 Linebaugh on a Ruger Redhawk. Ashley is one of the few men that can handle it well.

Frontier .45 x 4 3/4-inch barrel and a 5 1/2-inch .357 Magnum New Frontier went off to Sargis to make it into one of my favorite sixgun types — a big-bore packin' pistol. Sargis once again tuned the action, set the trigger pull at 3 1/2 pounds, installed the new barrel, re-cut the forcing cone, and rechambered the original .357 cylinder to .45 Colt. Another #5 base pin from Belt Mountain also completed this project.

This sixgun also shoots like a dream. Every good stool has three legs, so Sargis was once again called upon to complete my single-action search for perfection. Anyone that has had much experience with Third Generation Colt Single Actions and New Frontiers knows that the quality of these beautiful sixguns can be found to be anywhere from absolutely excellent to very second rate. My Third Generation 5 1/2-inch .44 Special fell somewhere in the middle of the two extremes. It shot well enough, but the action was rough and the cylinder was quite loose. Actually, it is surprising that it shot so well. Off it went to Sargis with instructions to tune it, smooth it, and above, all take as much play as possible out of the cylinder. The result is probably one of the finest Colt New Frontiers in existence! Tom fitted an oversize bolt that removes all perceptible play both side to side and fore and aft in the .44 cylinder. Sargis knows single actions!

Bowen Classic Arms: If it is possible to do it to or with a revolver, Hamilton Bowen can accomplish it. I first met Bowen at a Shootists Holiday nearly 20 years ago and he has worked his artistic talent on many sixguns for me over the past two decades. I earlier mentioned that he had converted four Ruger Old Model .357 Blackhawks to .44 Special, and sweet-shooting sixguns they are. Add to this a completely refinished 7 1/2-inch Colt Bisley .44, a Colt Single Action Army that is now an adjustable-sighted 8 1/2-inch .32-20, another Colt Single Action converted to a 5 1/2-inch .41 Special with non-fluted cylinder, and a 586 Smith & Wesson, also now a .41 Special.

The .41 Special is a mild wildcat made by simply cutting back .41 Magnum brass to .44 Special length. The original Ruger Blackhawk, the .357 Magnum Flat-Top, is the perfect candidate for conversion to .41 Special. A call to Hamilton Bowen revealed that he indeed had a pre-warning .41 Magnum barrel on hand so all we needed for a project sixgun was a .357 Flat-Top. Off went the sixgun to Bowen for the conversion after it had been fitted with fancy English walnut stocks by BluMagnum. In addition to converting the .357 to .41 Special, Bowen fitted it with a post-style front sight, the frame and hammer were beautifully case colored, the balance of the gun was deeply blued, and the alloy grip frame was also finished in a deep blue/black. I had not seen the custom grips as they had been sent directly to Bowen by Tedd Adamovich of BluMagnum. He had warned me that they were, in his words, "stunning." He did not exaggerate! The combination of fancy walnut stocks, bluing, and case colored finish not only makes this one of the most beautiful cus-

It appears to be a Colt Flat-Top Target from the 1890s. It is in fact a Colt New Frontier that has been expertly converted to a .32-20 Flat-Top style by Hamilton Bowen.

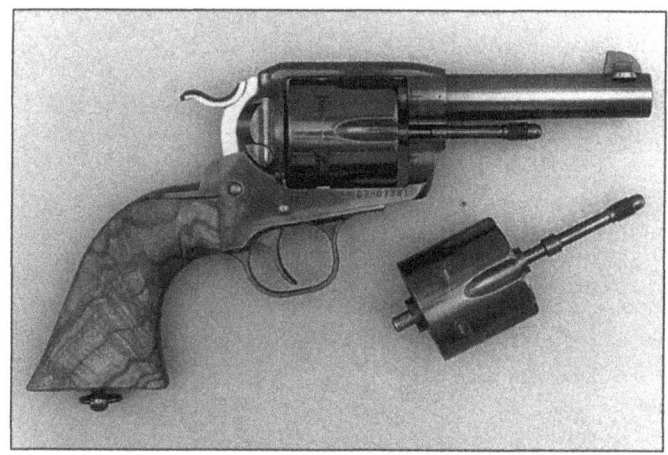 

This unique New Model Ruger by Hamilton Bowen has a Bisley Model hammer, dovetail front sight, and removable cylinders as built by Sedgely on Colt Single Actions in the 1920s.

A lightweight Colt Single Action .45 by Hamilton Bowen, complete with engraving, Bisley hammer, dovetail front sight, and 4-inch barrel. A beautiful and practical sixgun.

tom Rugers in existence, but also a prime candidate for the title of perfect packin' pistol.

Some of the other excellent custom sixguns offered by Hamilton Bowen include a replica of Elmer Keith's #5SA; a Ruger Redhawk in .454 fitted with an L-frame style barrel complete with recoil reducing porting; .32-20 and .41 Special conversions and the Old Model Ruger's; Ashley Emerson's 4-inch five-shot .500 Linebaugh on the Ruger Redhawk; a Vaquero with a Sedgely style removable cylinder; a Ruger Redhawk made to resemble the 1917 Smith & Wesson; and lightweight versions of the Redhawk or Vaquero in chamberings such as the .50 Action Express.

Bowen's rendition of Elmer Keith's famous #5SAA is, as the original, one of the most beautiful sixguns in existence. Bowen not only offers the #5 fully engraved and stocked with ivory as Keith's sixgun was, but also as a workin' sixgun, blued with walnut stocks. Bowen is the complete sixgunsmith in that he can build the most modern of sixguns and also has a very strong traditional side, which is revealed in such projects as the Keith #5 and 1917 Redhawk, as well as Colt New Frontiers turned into Colt Flat-Top Targets

They once were standard Ruger Vaqueros, one a 7 1/2-inch .45 and the other a 5 1/2-inch .44-40. David Clements used QPR grip frames to turn them into 3 7/8-inch Sheriff's Models.

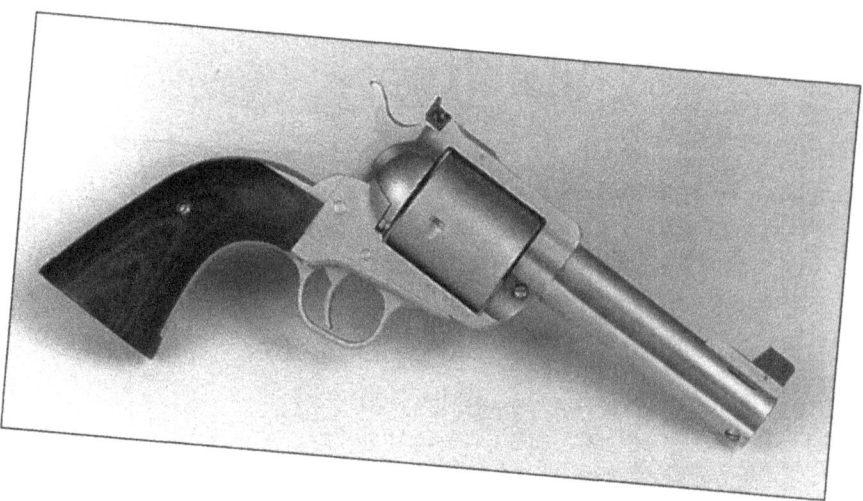

This fully custom five-shot New Model Ruger .45 by David Clements features a Bowen rear sight, blade front sight, and extended stocks.

from the 1890s. Such a sixgun chambered in .32-20 will stir the soul of any true sixgunner. The .32-20 is such a grand little cartridge and Bowen is one of the sixgunsmiths that truly appreciates it. In addition to building target style .32-20s on both Colt New Frontiers and Ruger Colt Model Blackhawks, Bowen also salutes the .32-20 by starting with an Old Model Blackhawk and turning it into a Colt-style sixgun by removing the adjustable rear sight and welding and shaping the top strap to the traditional style. If it is a project worth doing sixgun style, Bowen Classic Arms can do it.

Clements Custom Guns: David Clements has been a custom gunsmith for 10 years and is that rare commodity, a 'smith that can, and will, do sixguns, semi-autos, and all types of rifles as well. Clements recently sent along two of his sixgun packages, both custom Ruger .45s built on the Ruger New Model Blackhawk, built for two different purposes yet both are easy to pack and fit my definition of what a packin' pistol should be. The Ermine is a lightweight, 34-ounce, .45 Colt that will not be noticed when it is carried day in and day out in a holster, be it on a cartridge belt or pants belt. Clements starts with a Ruger Stainless Blackhawk in .357, .44 Magnum, or .45 Colt to build as he says "A short, light-carry gun for outdoorsman." Starting with the basic Blackhawk, Clements installs a 4-inch match grade barrel, weight-saving aluminum alloy grip frame, and ejector rod housing. The action is tuned and smoothed, all end shake is removed, the lock-up is tightened to remove side-to-side play in the cylinder, the chambers are polished, and the throats of the cylinder chambers are properly sized.

Clements also fits a shortened base pin with a flat head to allow the ejector rod to travel as far as possible to eject empties. The cylinder is given the free spinning treatment, which allows it to be rotated in either direction. This allows it to be rotated backwards in case a bullet jumps the crimp, extends from the front of the cylinder, and locks up the gun. With this modification one simply has to spin the cylinder backwards and remove the round. Very handy.

A larger and heavier .45 from Clements Custom Guns is the TAYRA offered in .45 Colt or .44 Magnum. Again, Clements starts with a stainless-steel Blackhawk, but maintains the factory stainless-steel grip frame and ejector housing as the goal is not to reduce weight but build a gun that will hold up to constant use of heavy loads. The weight in .45 Colt with a 5 1/2-inch match grade bull barrel is 46 ounces. It is, of course, much more pleasant to shoot with heavy loads than the little Ermine.

I would not recommend any gunsmith that I would not also trust to work on my own guns and David Clements has worked on several of my big-bore sixguns. When Qualite Pistol and Revolver supplied me with two of its round-butt grip frames for the New Model Ruger, I found it was no great chore to attach them to two Ruger Vaqueros. A brass version was bolted to a Ruger Vaquero 5 1/2-inch .44-40, while the stainless-steel frame version went on to a 7 1/2-inch .45 Vaquero. Now it was time for Clements to do his work. The QPR grip frames are provided slightly oversize to be perfectly fitted to each Ruger main frame, and 5 1/2- and 7 1/2-inch barrels do not mate up aesthetically or practically well with round butts, at least not for me.

Both blued sixguns went off to Clements with instructions to cut the barrels to minimum length and still maintain use of the ejector rods and housings. Clements settled on 3 7/8 inches for the barrel lengths by also altering the head of the base pin as on the Ermine to allow the ejector rod to do its work of shucking fired brass. Two steel ejector rods with crescent heads and two steel ejector housings, also all from Qualite, were sent to Clements and these were also cut to fit the 3 7/8-inch barrels.

After cutting both barrels Clements fitted each sixgun with a new front sight that was high enough that I could file them in to fit my loads, hold, and eyes. Both the Vaqueros, one in .45 Colt and the other in .44-40, had chambers that were much too tight for the best accuracy with cast bullets and the factory barrels, so Clements opened the .45 chamber mouths to .453 inch and the .44-40 to .429 inch. These two sixguns are very easy to pack, will handle heavy loads easily and also

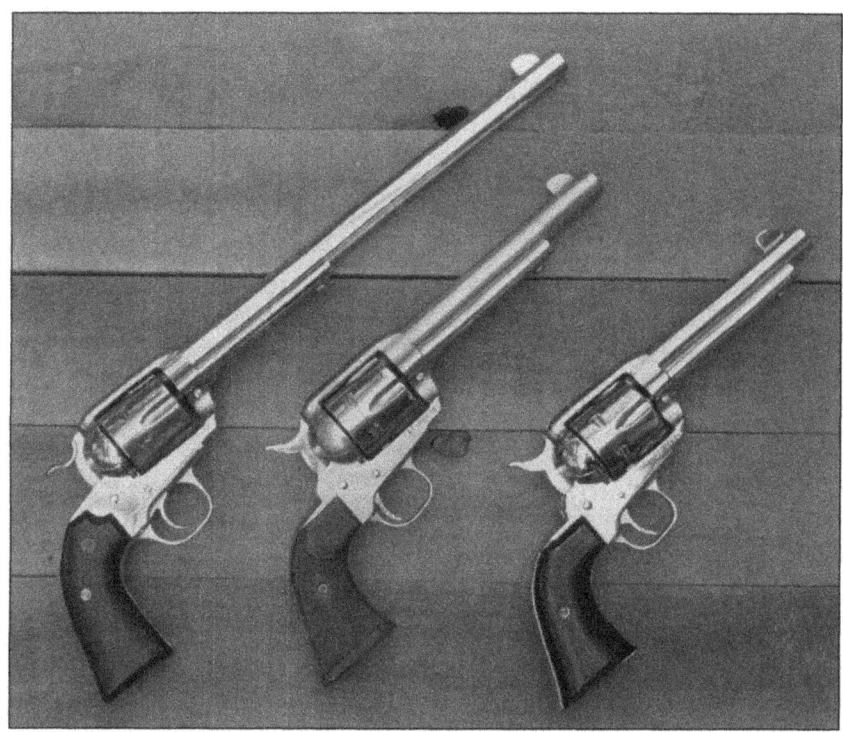

Larry Crow likes the .38-40. These custom .38-40 Vaqueros, a 5 1/2- and 6 1/2-inch, and a 10-inch Bisley Model, are expertly tuned and shoot with the best of them.

make such loads exhibit much less felt recoil because of their QPR round-butted grip frames.

Two other sixguns were sent off to Clements simply to be made easier to use and/or carry. A .44 Special Colt New Frontier was cut from a barrel length of 7 1/2-inch to an easier-to-pack 5 1/2 inches and the factory front sight re-mounted, while a 5 1/2-inch .44 Magnum Super Blackhawk was fitted with a Bisley grip frame, hammer and trigger to make it much more controllable for me with heavy loads. Workmanship by Clements on both of these special .44s was superb.

Clements lists a large number of custom touches for Rugers, Colts, and Smith & Wessons. The latter can be converted from .357 to .44 Special or .45 Colt, and .41s to .45 Colt is also a popular conversion. Custom barreled and cylindered Ruger Blackhawks can be had in .44 Special, .44-40, .38-40, 10mm, .41 Magnum, .45 Colt, .44 Magnum, and .45 Auto Rim, while five-shooters in .45 Colt, .454, .475, .500, and .50AE are offered to tackle the really big stuff. Ruger Redhawks can also be turned into five-shot .45s and .500s. One of the best ideas to come along in many a year is Clements' offering a Elmer Keith style and sized #5 grip frame on New Model Rugers.

Competitive Edge: Larry Crow of Competitive Edge is a cowboy action shooter as well as a custom sixgunsmith who is particularly fond of the .38-40 cartridge. So much so, in fact, that he uses a pair of stainless-steel Vaqueros converted to .38-40 when he shoots cowboy-style. Larry sent three of his custom stainless-steel .38-40 Vaqueros along for testing, one of his 6 1/2-inch competition guns, as well as a 5 1/2-inch and 10-inch "Buntline" Bisley Vaquero. They have all proven to be excellent examples of the gunmakers' art. So much so, that I sent him an Old Model Three-Screw .357 Magnum Ruger Blackhawk to be custom built to my specifications.

The New Model Rugers are larger then I deem necessary for normal use with a .38-40 cartridge. The Vaqueros that Crows uses for his .38-40s are built on Ruger's .44 Magnum frame while the Old Model Blackhawk .357 is the same size as the Colt Single Action Army. This size is much more to my liking for the old .38 Winchester Centerfire.

This .38-40 Ruger will be a one of a kind. A Power Custom Colt-style steel grip frame with custom stocks is being fitted; the match grade barrel will be 7 1/2 inches with a post front sight matched up with one of Bowen's rear sights. The action will be totally tuned and smoothed. Finally, the finish will be by Doug Turnbull with a case hardened frame and hammer, and the balance of the gun deeply blued. This is one of those I-can-hardly-wait type of projects.

Cosby Custom Gunsmithing: Cosby's platform for customized single actions is the Ruger Blackhawk, Vaquero, or Single-Six. He especially prefers the opposite ends of the spectrum, that is, the big-bore .45s and the diminutive .32s. He is also an artist in metal, shortening barrels, remounting front sights, re-shaping top straps, and especially cutting and welding grip frames. There are several sixgunsmiths that "round-butt" the Ruger grip frame by simply working with the metal that exists by filing, grinding, and polishing it to minimum size. Cosby goes further. He cuts and welds the grip frame, be it steel or aluminum, and really round-butts it to absolute minimum size. The result is a grip frame that is very easy to conceal and also handles felt recoil extremely well. Those who have never shot a big-bore sixgun with a rounded butt will be very surprised at how well the recoil is tamed. I prefer the term "Storekeeper" for all of these ejectorless single-action sixguns, and "Sheriff's Model" for those short-barreled sixguns that still have an ejector rod housing.

The first Cosby Custom Cowboy sixgun tested was a true Storekeeper's Model with a 3-inch barrel. Starting with a stainless-steel Vaquero in .45 Colt, Cosby removed the ejector rod housing and also modified the frame to remove the receptacle for the ejector rod, shortened the barrel to 3 inches, re-installed the front sight, and radically round-butted the grip frame by cutting and welding, grinding and polishing. The result is one of the easiest-handling single-action .45 Colts ever, for quick work from the leather or waistband for defensive purposes.

When I first started shooting sixguns, both Second Generation Colt Single Actions and the then new Ruger Blackhawks were available. The Colts were "perfect" in balance and pointability, but with relatively fragile lockwork, while Bill Ruger's revolvers were virtually indestructible. Even at my then young age I could see combining the two sixguns together would really be "perfection." Ruger eventually arrived at the same conclusion, but it was in the 1990s and not the 1950s, and the result was the Vaquero built on the New Model frame and action. The Vaquero has been tremendously successful and is probably the most popular sixgun found in cowboy action shooting circles.

It is possible to come much closer to perfection in building a Colt-styled Ruger, but it takes the skill of a custom sixgunsmith and a different starting platform. Beginning with a .45 Colt Three-Screw Blackhawk, Cosby removes the adjustable rear sight and ramp front sight. The top of the frame is then welded up and reshaped to provide the hog wallow-type rear sight found on a Colt Single Action Army, while the new front sight is also a Colt-style blade.

All the Old Model and Flat-Top Three Screw Rugers were equipped with aluminum alloy grip frames, so this oversight is handled by using a steel grip frame from an Old Army. Cosby sent me a matched pair of sixguns so converted to examine. Both of them were fitted with staghorn grips, beautifully engraved by well-known engraver Michael Dubber. Dubber executes scrolls on cylinder, barrel, and frame along with the proper embellishments on the ejector rod housing, butt, backstrap and even the sides of the front sight; and then the entire package is nickel plated.

For anyone who would like to make a good gun better, Brian Cosby can certainly carry out your wishes. Cosby specializes in Rugers, but his shop is a full-service operation doing repair and custom work on all handguns, rifles, and shotguns. His restored Winchesters and Colts look as good or better than when they first left the factory. When he sent a pair of 4 3/4-inch Colt Single Actions and a Model '92 Winchester, all in .32-20 and all completely restored, refinished in blue and case colors, and barrels re-lined, I found the trip to UPS to send them back extremely painful.

D&L Custom: Dave Lauck has long been known for his tactical weapons, both semi-autos and rifles, but he does much more. So when I had the chance to have two pair of my sixguns worked over by D&L and also

Two junkers rescued from the bone pile and totally restored by Brian Cosby. These two First Generation Colt Single Actions have had the barrels re-lined, actions rebuilt, and then were refinished to match the finish they wore when they originally left the Colt factory.

testdrive another pair from his shop, I jumped at the chance. Several years ago I decided to start watching for nickel-plated Smith & Wesson sixguns that I could pick up at a good price. My first acquisition was a Model 29 4-inch .44 Magnum about eight years ago. I have been watching for a mate for it ever since. My goal was to come up with a pair of double-action sixguns for fast speed shooting from the hip and also using the method of point shooting advocated by the late Rex Applegate. When I found another nickel-plated 4-inch .44 Magnum, it was time to start putting my speed shooting pair together. I had a pair of stag stocks for an N-frame in my parts box and found another pair at a local shop that was going out of business. Both were exceptionally thick and useless for my hands so I turned to my friend Tony Kojis, who thinned them and smoothed them and took all the rough spots out.

It was about this time that D&L entered the picture. I shared with Dave Lauck that I did not like the wide target hammers and triggers found on these sixguns. I wanted both the hammer made smaller and the trigger smoothed and reduced in size and shape. Lauck trimmed the width of the triggers, rounded them off so there were no sharp edges, and removed all the serrations to give me a smooth platform for my trigger finger. It is much easier to shoot double-action with a smooth trigger that allows the finger to slide slightly over the face of the trigger as it is being pulled. He also reshaped the hammer to more closely resemble the hammer found on a Colt Python. They are slightly smaller so the hammers do not hit the back of the hand in double action firing while still giving plenty of area for the thumb should I desire to cock the .44 and shoot deliberately. Hammers and triggers were finished in a mirror hard chrome to match the finish of the rest of the sixguns. Elmer Keith was exceptionally fond of the short-barreled S&W .44 Magnums both for defensive use and for easy packin.' Every time I shoot my pair I will think of him.

Having two stainless-steel Vaqueros on hand, one in .45 Colt and the other in .44-40, both of which needed just a touch to make them personally mine and also easier to shoot and pack, they were first equipped with stag grips from Ajax and then sent off to D&L to be slightly modified. I had Lauck cut the barrels so they were even with the ejector rod housings, remount the front sights, and round the butts ever so slightly. I did not want what is normally thought of as round-butted single actions, but rather just have the sharp corners cut away from the front and back of the grip frame proper.

The simple tasks performed on these Vaqueros improved them tremendously for my use, and I no longer get bit by the sharp edges of the grip frame. Lauck replaced the front sights with ones tall enough for me to file in to hit precisely to my point of aim with my chosen load. These Vaqueros make excellent packin' pistols for woods wandering, mountain rambling, desert exploring, hiking trips, or even to carry as a defensive sixgun.

For my perusal, Lauck also sent along a pair of 1991A1s. These 1991A1s were totally custom built. The finish is matte hard chrome, sights are adjustable MMC Combat Night Sights. Behind the front sight are cocking serrations on each side of the slide to aid in feeding that first round from the magazine to the chamber if the 1991 is carried with an empty chamber and the slide forward. On each .45 is a match aluminum trigger, a high-sweep beavertail safety, and the newest

To make these Smith & Wesson .44 Magnums easier to handle, Dave Lauck slimmed and smoothed the triggers, reshaped the hammers to match those found on a Colt Python, and then hard chromed them all to match the nickel plating found on the rest of the sixguns.

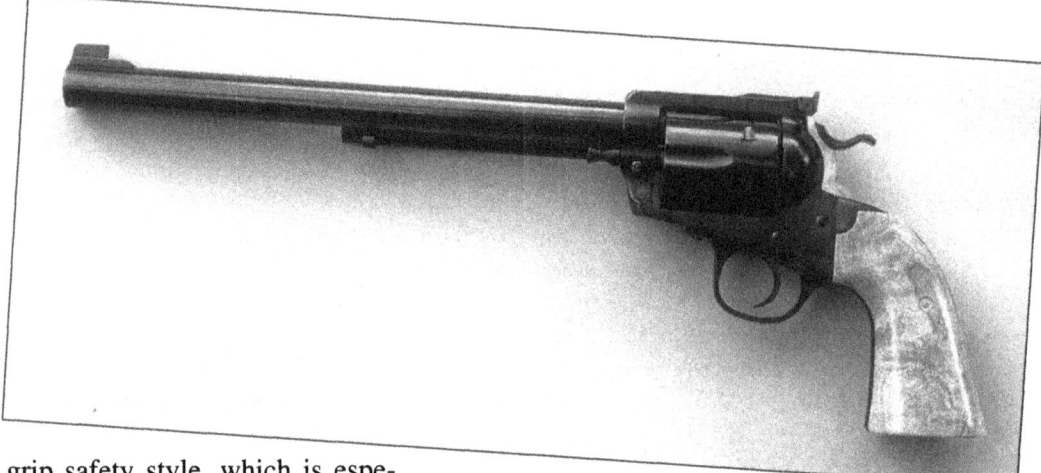

Ben Forkin converted this .357 Maximum Ruger to .445 Super-Mag with Bisley Model grip frame, hammer, and trigger, post front sight, Bowen rear sight, and Belt Mountain #5 base pin. Burl mesquite stocks are by Scott Kolar.

grip safety style, which is especially shaped to aid those whose hand does not automatically depress the grip safety as the 1991 or any 1911 is gripped naturally. The thumb safety has been extended for ease of operation and a thumb guard added along the slide to keep those that use a grip with high riding thumb from getting nailed by the moving slide. Each slide, of course, has been tightened to the frame, a tungsten guide rod installed along with a Bar-Sto barrel, match barrel bushing, target crown on each muzzle, and recoil springs replaced.

At the grip frame, in addition to the new grip safety, we find both front and back of the frame have been stippled to give a secure gripping surface. The mainspring housing is now steel, a Heinie magazine well has been added for quick replacement of new magazines, which are now Wilson-Rogers stainless-steel match magazines, and the grips are now of checkered exotic wood. Finally, to finish off the package, we find a slotted hammer, and an ejection port that has been opened and flared to prevent any empty brass from hanging up as it is ejected. Both Custom 1991A1s were test fired on combat silhouette targets with 185-, 200-, and 230-grain .45 ACP loads. Both guns functioned flawlessly and hit to point of aim. The combination of stippling on the front and back strap and the checkered grips was all much appreciated for rapid fire use. I could carry either or both of these D&L .45s and feel confident in them and my ability to use them.

Ben Forkin: I had been sitting in a deer stand on the Penn Baggett Ranch outside of Ozona Texas for three days with no luck as far as a nice whitetail buck was concerned. I had a turkey, and a javelina, but as yet had not seen that right buck. After spending the morning on stand, Penn picked me up for a late breakfast and a little down time before going back out in the afternoon. Since this was the last day, and I did not want to trust my sixguns to the airlines, I had planned to ship them home by overnight UPS. This, of course, meant I was without a sixgun for the final afternoon into evening hunt. This would be no problem as Penn is a fellow sixgunner and allowed me to use one of his custom sixguns. It turned out to be a double blessing.

The afternoon turned out to be very quiet with nothing moving. The plan was for me to be picked up at 6 p.m. I looked at my watch in the fast-approaching darkness and saw that it was 5:55 p.m. and I started to get ready to go. I looked up and there he was, a beautiful whitetail buck! Lord, please don't let Penn show up early! I waited as the deer moved closer, slowly extended my arms, placed the front sight on the buck's shoulder, and squeezed the trigger. At the shot, the buck dropped in his tracks and Baggett was close enough to hear the shot.

The sixgun I was using was a custom .445 Super-Mag on a Ruger .357 Maximum using Baggett's handloads with the 265-grain Hornady Flat-Point. I had to have a sixgun like this, so I began the search for a reasonably priced Ruger .357 Maximum and a gunsmith who would perform the work. Both turned out to be

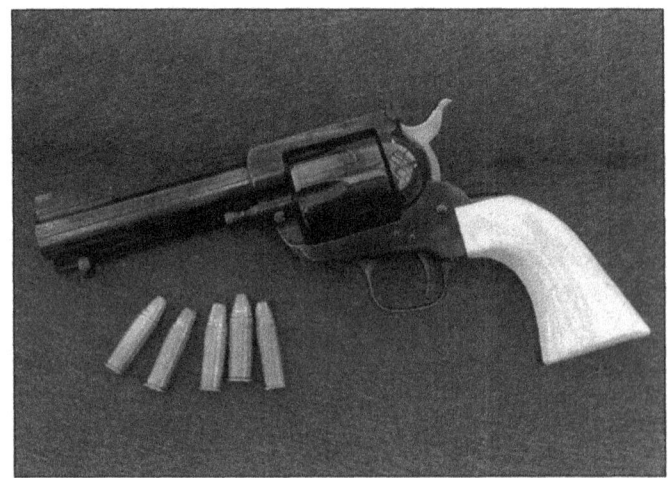

As a tribute to Skeeter Skelton, Bill Grover built this .44 Special on a Flat-Top Ruger. It is serial #SS4 of seven special sixguns. One-piece ivory stocks are by Tedd Adamovich.

When Bill Grover was the master gunmaker at Texas Longhorn Arms, he often provided extra cylinders. This West Texas Flat-Top Target handles .44 Magnum, .44 Special, and .44-40.

exceptionally easy. I found a Ruger quickly and sent the Maximum off to Ben Forkin.

Forkin is a Montana sixgunsmith who learned much of his trade working with Hamilton Bowen, which is certainly a high recommendation. I had been acquainted with Ben's work through Bowen, knew Ben personally and had shot with him and also experienced his .475 and .500 Linebaugh conversions on the Ruger Redhawk. For the custom Maximum, Forkin rechambered the cylinder to .445 and fitted a 101/2-inch heavyweight barrel with the requested Patridge front sight. The touch of two other custom 'smiths is seen on this sixgun also, as it wears a Bowen rear sight and a Belt Mountain #5 base pin. The original Ruger Super Blackhawk grip frame, hammer, and trigger were removed and replaced with Ruger Bisley counterparts, which for me handle recoil much better. Forkin marked the left side of the barrel with "FORKIN ARMS," the right side of the frame now says ".445 SUPER MAG CAL." and the entire sixgun was finished in a dark blue. This the first sixgun made for me by Forkin Arms, but hopefully not the last. As a final touch it now wears custom stocks of beautiful burl mesquite crafted by Scott Kolar of SK Custom Grips. I'm looking forward to the spending of more time in my special stand on the Baggett Ranch with my very own custom .445 SuperMag.

Bill Grover: It was in the mid-1980s at a gathering of the Shootists that I first met Bill Grover. I was struck by the fact that he talked in loving terms of what he called "ma pistols." Actually I "knew" Grover before this meeting from an old article from *Guns Magazine* about a young shooting wizard, one Thell Reed, and the gunsmith that built his Colt Single Actions. That gunsmith was none other than Bill Grover. Since that first meeting, I have shot with, hunted with and, above all, appreciated the guns of Bill Grover.

In 1981 Grover founded Texas Longhorn Arms. Grover, like this dedicated sixgunner, always felt like he was dealing with hallowed ground when it came to Elmer Keith. He could think of no finer tribute to this man than to reproduce the No. 5 S.A. Keith improved the Colt Single Action in 1929; Bill Grover set about to improve the No. 5. And improve it he did! Grover called his company the "Home of the Right-Handed Single Action." When you hold a Texas Longhorn

This beautiful little sixgun, built by Andy Horvath, is a 4-inch .44 Special on an Old Model Ruger .357 platform. Engraving and ivory stocks by BluMagnum, holster by Thad Rybka.

Four of Andy Horvath's L'il Guns. These are great trail guns. They all feature shortened barrels and ejector rod housings and slightly rounded grip frames. Bisley Models are in .32 Magnum and .22 LR, and are matched up with the same calibers in Single-Six Models. They are also great guns for young kids.

Arms sixgun in your right hand your thumb naturally reaches down and flips open the loading gate, which is now on the left side of the Grover gun. For a right-hander, a Texas Longhorn Arms sixgun never leaves the shooting hand whether shooting, loading, or unloading.

I personally own and regularly shoot a pair of Grover's Improved Number Fives in .44 Magnum and .45 Colt. They are among my most prized possessions. The first time I fired Grover's Improved Number Five in .44 Magnum I was totally impressed. Those first five shots got my attention real fast. That first Improved Number Five was on its way to be engraved in the same pattern as found on Keith's .44 Special. However, I was allowed to shoot it first. Five rounds of 250-grain hard cast Keith bullets, naturally, over 20.0 grains of #2400, a load in the 1,200-1,300 fps category, dropped into less than 1 inch at 25 yards. It just doesn't get much better than that! As a hunting sixgun, Grover's Improved Number Five leaves little to be desired and packs perfectly. Elmer Keith would certainly approve.

Bill Grover was the founder, inventor, and master gunmaker for Texas Longhorn Arms from 1981 to 1998. In addition to the magnificent Improved Number Five, Grover also produced several other big-bore sixguns: the South Texas Army, a much-improved version of the traditional Colt Single Action (mine is a 4 3/4-inch .44 Special); the West Texas Flat-top Target, a superb target, hunting, or long-range shooting sixgun; and the Texas Border Special, a round-butted, easy-packin' single action — sixgun that one would not be afraid to bet one's life on. Bill also produced a very limited number of stainless-steel sixguns with folding leaf rear sights. These sixgun masterpieces are known as Grover's Express Model.

The Flat-Top Target built for me by Bill Grover is certainly one of the most special single actions in existence. The grip frame is longer than a traditional single action, more along the lines of the 1860 Army, making it very comfortable to shoot. Plus, this .44 Magnum now has been fitted with three extra cylinders by Bill Grover: .44 Special, .44 Russian, and .44-40. Now that new .44 Colt brass is available someday we'll add a fifth cylinder in this chambering. It's a truly one-of-a-kind single action.

Mention was made earlier of Grover's part in building the Skeeter Gun and subsequent series of SS1 to

SS7. Grover had been instrumental, along with Bob Baer, in building the Skeeter Gun as they call it, the .44 Special sixgun that Skeeter Skelton had commissioned. Its serial number is SS1. Also related earlier John Wootters now has this sixgun. I now have SS4. The second Skeeter Gun, SS2 in the series, is now in Bart Skelton's hands, Bob Baer has SS3, Bill Grover has SS5, friend and fellow writer Terry Murbach has SS6, and Sheriff Jim Wilson, also a good friend and fellow writer, has the last gun, SS7. The Shootists held a special seven-gun salute and memorial service to Skeeter in 1992 and there will be no more .44 Specials built in this series.

Although all seven of us have SS sixguns, they are all quite different and reveal the individual tastes of the owners. My particular SS4 started life as a .357 Magnum Ruger Flat-Top Blackhawk from the 1950s. Grover and I put our heads together on this one so a double influence can be seen. The cylinder has been rechamberd to .44 Special tightly to allow the use of .429-inch diameter bullets, but kept to minimum dimensions for long case life. Barrel/cylinder gap was set at .0025 inches. A Colt backstrap and trigger guard and a Colt ejector rod along with a Bullseye headed ejector rod were fitted. With the installation of the Colt backstrap and trigger guard, it was necessary to machine a special hanger to accept the Ruger mainspring and strut and Grover also replaced the trigger return spring with a new coil spring. By installing a Colt grip frame, we not only went from aluminum to steel, we also now could install one-piece stocks. Tedd Adamovich made the one-piece ivories that will make your mouth water.

For sighting equipment, Grover installed a Number Five front sight, bold, flat, and black, and a Number Five base pin with a large, easy-to-grasp head was also installed. The front of the cylinder was beveled as on the old Colt Single Action Armies and the gun was engraved to read "SKEETER SKELTON .44 SPECIAL" on the left side of the barrel and "TEXAS LONGHORN ARMS INC, RICHMOND TEXAS" on the top of the topstrap. The serial number is marked "S.S.4" in the same three places as the original Colts: the front bottom of the backstrap, in the front of the trigger guard and on the frame in front of the trigger guard screw.

Grover is justly proud of his work and thinks this is one of the finest sixguns in existence. I again wholeheartedly agree. I expect to enjoy it the rest of my life and then pass it on to one of my grandsons.

Andy Horvath: One of my great joys as a gun writer is to introduce relatively unknown craftsmen to the shooting public. Such was the case of Andy Horvath when, almost 20 years ago, I discovered his little ad in a Handgun Hunters International copy of the club newspaper, *The Sixgunner*. At the time Horvath caught my eye he was specializing in .44 Special conversions. We made contact and he sent a Ruger Old Model .357 Magnum that had been converted to .44 Special and a Model 1892 Winchester that he had rescued from the bone pile and also turned into a .44 Special for my examination and test-firing.

I was impressed enough with his work that I sent off a Ruger Old Model .357 Blackhawk with the request to make it into a .44 Special that was just a little different. The barrel, along with the ejector rod and ejector housing, was to be shortened to 4 inches, and the grips and grip frame round-butted. That was in 1985. I was so pleased with it that I took it to the first Shootists Holi-

All four of these "Little Guns" started as full-sized single actions. They are (from top left): a 3 1/4-inch Old Model Ruger .44 Special by Bob Baer; a 3-inch Bisley Model Cimarron .44-40 by Milt Morrison; a 3 1/2-inch Old Model .45, also by Morrison; and a 4-inch .44 Special Old Model Ruger by Andy Horvath.

day in 1986 and it was certainly well received among the knowledgeable sixgunners in attendance. In fact, one very well-known gunsmith at the time looked at it, worked the action several times, turned it over in his hands repeatedly, and then looked up and said, "I have to get better." I felt that was very high praise for the work of Andy Horvath.

The word spread and other sixgunners opted for the same type of sixgun from Horvath in other chamberings such as .45 Colt and .41 Magnum. The .44 Special, along with several of these other "L'il Guns" built by Horvath, were featured in the September/October 1990 issue of *American Handgunner* and the fire was lit around the country and even in Hollywood. Either Don Johnson or Mickey Rourke, or both, saw the article and wanted my little .44 Special for a movie they were doing. There was no way I was about to turn my gun loose, but I did suggest that Horvath be contacted and as a result he not only built guns for the movie, he also made personal guns for both Johnson and Rourke. Horvath has been busy ever since!

A few years later I had Horvath build me two more truly little L'il Guns. This time we started with a Ruger .22 Bisley Model and a .32 Magnum Single-Six. The same basic work that had been performed on the .44 Special transformed these two small frame Rugers into family heirlooms. In addition to the regular work, I had Andy swap grip frames so I wound up with a custom .22 Single-Six and a Bisley Model .32. Both of these guns were written up in *American Handgunner* in the September/October 1995 issue. Andy may be best known for his L'il Rugers, but he is a complete gunsmith and can do wonders with sixguns, including transforming double-action revolvers into Fitz Specials. If you do not know who Fitz was or what a Fitz Special is, your sixgun knowledge needs to be upgraded by reading about J. Henry Fitzgerald, who was "Mr. Colt" in the 1930s. Since those first three little guns were built for me, my family has expanded, so I recently contacted Andy with the idea of building a trio of trail guns designed for easy packin' in desert, foothills, woods, or mountains. I especially wanted sixguns that will eventually belong to my three grandsons, John Christopher, Jason Michael, and Brian John. Three Single-Six Rugers were sent off to Horvath at his Diagonal Road Gunshop to have him perform his L'il Gun magic and to provide three great understudies for my big-bore sixguns and also fun sixguns for the grandkids to shoot and dream of owning someday.

We started with a Ruger New Model .22 Single-Six stainless-steel with a 6 1/2-inch barrel. Andy cut the barrel to 4 inches, reduced the length of the ejector tube and ejector rod and a new base pin was fitted with a larger, but shorter head that is knurled for easy removal. The liability warning was removed from the left side of the barrel, the stainless-steel grip frame was rounded at the back of the butt, and the sharp edge removed from the toe of the butt. An extra-nice touch was the checkering of the front of the ejector rod head. Factory ejector rod heads are very small, often allowing the finger to slip off while removing spent shells. The checkering prevents that.

The second sixgun, a Ruger New Model .22 Single-Six Bisley Model, blued, 6 1/2-inch barrel, received all of the same operations. However, the altering of the grip frame and polishing of the warning label from the left side of the barrel necessitated re-bluing, so the entire little .22 Bisley was refinished in a high polish bright blue. A Ruger New Model Single-Six .32 H&R Magnum, blued, 6 1/2-inch barrel, completed the trio. This sixgun was found used in a gunshop this past year and at an incredibly low price for a high-demand Single-Six. These little .32s are extremely hard to find. As this gun started as a blued model, Horvath also applied one of his beautiful blue finishes after removing the barrel warning. The grip frame, since it is an aluminum alloy as on all the standard Single-Six models, was polished bright, which looks very attractive when mated with the high-polish bright blue. Another nice touch from Horvath was the inclusion of an extra taller front sight just in case the adjustable rear sight did not have sufficient adjustments to compensate for the different bullet

Even before Freedom Arms was chambering the .475 Linebaugh, Jack Huntington was converting .454s to .475, such as this 4 3/4-inch version complete with muzzle break.

Larry Kelly of M-N-P knows hunting handguns well. His Stalkers are built on stainless-steel Ruger or Smith & Wesson .44 Magnums and feature tuned actions, 8 3/8-inch barrels, and scopes on SSK T'SOB mounts.

weights. All of the front sights for these little guns are held on with a screw, so they are easily changed.

Horvath's work is totally top drawer and he not only makes great "L'il Trail Guns," I am convinced he can do just about anything and do it right. I recommend him highly and without reservation

Jack Huntington: Jack Huntington has been quietly building .475 and .500 Linebaugh chambered sixguns for about 10 years now, sixguns with a different twist. Before Freedom Arms chambered the .475 in their Model 83, Huntington offered his .475 conversions. Starting with a Freedom Arms .454, Huntington added a custom barrel and rechambered the cylinder to come up with a .475 Linebaugh.

At first glance, Huntington's .475 looks like a standard Freedom Arms sixgun except for the addition of a muzzle brake. Said brake is mounted on a 4 5/8-inch barrel while the front sight extends the full 4 3/4-inch length of the original barrel and thus fits over the back of the brake. For added control, the brake contains eight rows of ports running lengthwise with the barrel and consisting of alternating rows of four and five holes. It definitely helps tame the felt recoil of the .475 Linebaugh. It does not put the recoil in the pleasant range by any means, but it does help. Everything else is pretty much stock Freedom Arms, including the rear sight assembly and the front sight with its interchangeable blade feature.

Huntington also builds custom .500 Linebaugh five-shooters on Ruger platforms with an oversize non-fluted cylinder that completely fills the cylinder frame window, Bisley grip frame and trigger, and deep-blue finish. Either of these two sixguns with the attending loads will certainly handle anything that walks. Up close against critters that can bite back, they would give the user confidence that he could keep himself out of serious trouble. With the lighter loads, deer, black bear, feral hogs, and the like could easily be handled with authority and a lot less recoil.

Starting with a Super Blackhawk, Huntington also builds a utility single action. The barrel is rebored, a custom five-shot free-wheeling cylinder in .50 AE is fitted, and the entire gun is given a Metalife hard chrome finish. The grips are wooden finger groove from Hogue's. A red insert is placed in the factory front sight, the action is smoothed and tightened, and the trigger pull is set at 3 pounds, and one is into a truly big-bore for the least possible expense. Speer's 325-grain jacketed hollowpoints clock out at 1,355 fps from the 7 1/2-inch barrel of the custom Super Blackhawk.

Huntington also offers complete action work on Ruger, Colt, and replica single actions such as: re-cutting of sear surfaces, speeding up cylinder/hand timing, installing internal over travel stops, full polishing of all mating surfaces, lightening spring tension, setting trigger pulls at 3 pounds, tightening of the cylinder, resetting of barrel/cylinder gap, re-cutting of the barrel throat and forcing cone area. All of Huntington's custom big bores show excellent workmanship and performed flawlessly. It would seem another custom sixgunsmith has been found that can supply the needs of those that want a quality big-bore sixgun.

Mag-Na-Port: Larry Kelly began experimenting with his own personal sixguns and the porting process in 1961, about the same time that he formed a partnership known as Apollo EDM with two friends. His personal sixgun, a Ruger Flat-Top .44 Magnum, was Mag-Na-Ported and a business was about to begin.

The idea of porting a sixgun to reduce muzzle flip was not new. The problem was how to do it without leaving burrs around the slot inside the barrel. Kelly's process made the cuts cleanly without any rough spots or burrs. A patent was approved for Mag-Na-Porting in 1972, and that same year Mag-Na-Porting was featured in an article entitled "Less Kick From Magnum Maulers" and on the cover of *Guns & Ammo*. Mag-Na-Port was off and running. In 1974, gun writer Bob Milek, featured Mag-Na-Port's porting system and gunsmithing as he related the total rebuilding of his favorite Model 27 .357 Magnum in *Handloader* magazine. J.D. Jones was also an early supporter, featuring an article on a custom-built .41 Magnum Ruger Blackhawk in *GunSport*.

I sent off two .44 Magnums to Kelly years ago to have the trapezoidal slots cut in the barrel to aid in reducing recoil and muzzle flip. Kelly called and made a few suggestions. The result was two favorite packin' pistols that have now served for more than two decades. The first .44, a Smith & Wesson 4-inch Model 29, was Mag-Na-Ported, round-butted (before everyone else discovered round butting!), the action was tuned, the trigger rounded and smoothed, a C-More front sight installed, and the entire gun was finished in Metalife SS, a stainless-steel-like finish. The second sixgun, a 7 1/2-inch Ruger Super Blackhawk Old Model, was cut to 4 3/4 inches and set up as the Model 29. I have since replaced the grip frame on the Ruger with a stainless-steel grip frame from Ruger's Old Army along with Eagle's UltraIvory grips. The Smith & Wesson wears custom rosewood stocks by my good friend, the late Deacon Deason of BearHug grips. Both of these sixguns are easy to pack, quick into action, and a pleasure to shoot. They have accompanied me on many a hunting trip and outdoor excursion.

Since those two guns were worked on, I have had the good privilege to meet Larry Kelly, visit in his home, travel through the Mag-Na-Port facility, and see the Handgun Hunter's Hall of Fame and Museum. Kelly is one of my favorite people. He is not only a top handgun hunter and businessman, he is just plain good folks.

Once Mag-Na-Port was established and on its way, Kelly began offering Limited Editions aimed mainly at the Handgun Hunter. The success of Mag-Na-Port has given Kelly the time and money necessary to allow him to hunt all over the world. Kelly probably has more firsthand experience with the hunting of really big game with a handgun than any other individual in history. He has taken all of the African "big five" with a handgun. I doubt very much that he will ever be equaled. Along the way Kelly has come up with some definite ideas on what makes a superior handgun hunting sixgun and these are all offered to hunters through Mag-Na-Port.

The Stalker series was conceived by Larry as the perfect revolver for serious handgun hunting, with the first Stalker, a Ruger Super Blackhawk .44 Magnum, being used by Kelly all over the globe to take many big-game trophies. The Stalker is described by Kelly as "a very special gun offered to meet the requirements of the hunting fraternity — the dedicated handgun hunt-

Mag-Na-Port's finest, a 5 1/2-inch Predator featuring velvet hone finish, decorative bands on the cylinder, totally tuned action, C-More front sight, and trapezoidal porting.

Milt Morrison of QPR starts with a standard Old Model Blackhawk .45 Colt and turns it into a 3 1/2-inch Sheriff's Model with a QPR round-butted grip frame, case colored mainframe, and the balance of the gun finished in QPR's Black Diamond blue.

ers. The Stalker was developed to meet the requirements of these men and women. It's a gun designed by hunters, for hunters. The Stalker is the result of many years hunting experience by the people here. We are proud of the gun, and sincerely convinced it is everything a serious hunter requires, whatever the game."

The Stalker conversion is available on big-bore sixguns, all in stainless steel, such as the Ruger Super Blackhawk and Super Redhawk, the Smith & Wesson Model 629, and the .454 Casull from Freedom Arms. All Stalker conversions have a number of things in common: an 8 3/8-inch barrel, an inverted muzzle crown to protect the muzzle, Mag-Na-Porting, Velvet Hone finish, polished hammer and trigger, a superb action job, Pachmayr grips, SSK scope mount base (except the Super Redhawk which comes factory equipped with scope rings), 2X Leupold scope, swivels and studs, and a carrying sling. Every hunter and outdoorsman I know has to have a packin' pistol. A short-barreled, powerful, easy-to-carry big-bore sixgun. Mag-Na-Port's answer to this need is the Predator. The Predator starts out as a stainless Super Blackhawk. The barrel is cut to 4 5/8 inches and given Mag-Na-Porting and the inverted muzzle crown exactly as found on the Stalker series. The Predator also has the standard Velvet Hone finish, action job, polished hammer, trigger, cylinder pin release, cylinder pin, ejector rod head, and screws. The Predator is not designed as a primary hunting handgun, but a backup, and is fitted with easy-to-see sights consisting of a C-More colored front sight and white outline rear.

At the other end of the handgunning spectrum, Mag-Na-Port also led the way in developing "Mini Magnums" — short-barreled, concealable big-bore sixguns. Mag-Na-Port offered 2 1/2- and 3-inch, round-butted, double-action conversions long before sixgun manufacturers discovered the concept. Model 29 and 629 .44 Magnums and Model 25 .45 Colts from Smith & Wesson were given short barrels, round butts, tuned actions, and the Mag-Na-Port porting process to become big-bore pocket pistols. The latest addition to the Mini Magnum concept is Colt's biggest snake, the Anaconda in .44 Magnum or, .45 Colt.

Two .44s rescued by Milt Morrison of QPR. The New Service .44 Special has been completely rebuilt, while the slick little sixgun on the bottom, complete with QPR's round-butted grip frame and a 3-inch bull barrel, started life as Cimarron Bisley Model. It is now officially known as "Taffin's Toy."

In 1983, Kelly founded the Handgun Hunter's Hall of Fame and Museum. Open to the public, this facility features over 100 specimens, including elephant, Cape buffalo, Alaskan brown bear, lion, and leopard, all taken with a handgun. One year later, Kelly was recognized for his lifetime of dedicated service to handgunning as he was named as the "Outstanding American Handgunner" by the Outstanding American Handgunner Awards Foundation.

Now that Kelly is at least semi-retired, son Ken Kelly has ably taken over the day-to-day task of heading up the business. Ken, starting with Mag-Na-Port at the tender age of 12 in 1973, has literally grown up with the business. By the time the Mark V arrived, the younger Kelly was doing some of the light gunsmithing duties, such as disassembly and sight work. By the age of 16, he was porting the .44 Magnum sixguns. After graduating from high school in 1979, Ken Kelly then attended the Colorado School of Trades, but was mostly trained in gunsmithing by his dad and uncle Jerry, who was a longtime gunsmithing fixture at Magna-Port.

In 1987, Ken took over as president of Mag-Na-Port. He is a hunter in his own right, also taking many species of game both American and African. Most importantly, his father has been able to hunt around the world knowing Ken had everything under control at home. Ken not only inherited the love for good guns and hunting from his dad, he is also good folks and one of my favorite people.

Qualite Pistol & Revolver: Milt Morrison of QPR is a complete pistolsmith. He is former S&W armorer, understands single actions and how they work, provides a Black Diamond blue finish that will make your mouth water, and also can rescue some of the great classic sixguns made before WWII. Everyone who has read any amount of my articles, columns, and books over the years knows of my passion for the .44 Special. With all my Special shooting, the one .44 Special that escaped me was a Colt New Service.

From the late 1890s until 1941 there were more New Service Colts produced than Colt Single Actions from 1873 to 1941 when both models ceased production. Colt Single Actions are easy to find; New Services not so easy. Narrow the search to a .44 Special in either model and it becomes extremely difficult. Only once had I seen a Colt New Service that was marked "RUSSIAN AND S&W SPECIAL 44" on the barrel. I had previously owned a Colt Single Action so marked, but I deemed it so valuable that I swapped it to a collector for all the money in it, plus two shooting Colt Single Actions, a Second Generation .44 Special and a .45 New Frontier. When the second New Service so marked came along I grabbed it, even though it needed a lot of help. The lanyard ring was missing, the action was out of time, the factory grips were gone and replaced by a serviceable but non-excitable pair of Jay Scott imitation rosewood stocks, and someone had fitted the frame with a Smith & Wesson adjustable rear sight while leaving the front sight intact. The result was a sixgun that shot 18 inches high!

The only sixgunsmith I know that is acquainted with the New Service is Milt Morrison. Remember, these sixguns have not been made for 60 years! Mine was shipped off to Milt at Qualite Pistol & Revolver with proper instructions. Morrison would have it for over a year while he tried to find a couple of new parts. Morrison installed a Patridge front sight on a ramp base, tuned the action, reshaped and smoothed the face of the trigger, and re-blued the entire sixgun. This is what one can see and feel. To make everything work, Morrison had to improvise and perform several other operations. And he did this project without benefit of a parts supply for the old Colt.

The ratchet on the back of the cylinder was worn, so Morrison faced it off and set the cylinder back. This required setting the barrel back also and resetting the barrel/cylinder gap. A new gas ring was installed along with a new mainspring. The hand was too short and the bolt needed to be replaced, but neither are available as parts so Morrison stretched and reshaped the hand, repaired and re-cut the cylinder bolt, and also repaired the rebound lever. It took a lot of doing by someone who knew what he is about, but thanks to Qualite Pistol & Revolver I finally have a good-shootin' .44 Special New Service. A replacement lanyard ring was found at Shapels'. I have watched the grip boxes at gun shows looking to come across a pair of stag stocks that would fit a New Service, and I just recently found the pair of stags to complete the project. Another .44 Special has been saved from the bone pile.

This past fall, Milt and his wife, Karen, came over to join my wife and I in a cowboy shoot. In the evening, a few sixguns were pulled out with the idea of coming up with a different kind of custom sixgun. As a result, a Uberti/Cimarron Bisley .44-40 was sent home to Milt's shop to be converted to a 19th-century-style "belly gun," a term used for short-barreled, easy-to-conceal sixguns. I gave Morrison the artistic freedom to do whatever he pleased to come up with the perfect single action for concealment and defensive use, and that is exactly what he accomplished. This little sixgun is so special that Karen has dubbed it "Taffin's Toy."

Morrison removed the ejector rod housing and also removed the ejector mount slot on the right side of the frame, welding and re-contouring the frame in the process. The standard Bisley grip frame was removed and replaced by a brass QPR Bird's Head grip frame adapted to a Colt-style mainframe. At the same time the original Bisley hammer was also changed from its

Beautiful sixguns for a lovely lady. Gary Reeder personalized these New Model .357s for Diamond Dot, while Twyla Taylor scrimshawed the grips.

link system to a roller system to work with the new mainspring. Of course, the entire action was tuned in the process and all cylinder end shake was removed.

The original barrel was discarded and replaced by a 2 1/2-inch-long, .800-inch-diameter barrel. The rear sight notch was changed from its V shape to give a square picture. A new front sight was fitted, and the trigger was contoured to match the inside of the trigger guard. Finally, the mainframe was re-color cased, the rest of the gun was finished in QPR's high luster Black Diamond blue, and an 18K-gold band was inlayed around the cylinder. It is certainly one of the most beautiful and efficient single-action belly guns in existence and one that someone such as Doc Holliday would have appreciated.

Gary Reeder Custom Guns: When my wife decided to get into cowboy shooting, the task fell upon me to outfit her properly. Since she had used a Ruger New Model Super Blackhawk for silhouetting in the early 1980s, I felt it would be easiest to supply her with the type of sixgun she was most familiar with (other than the J-frame she carries daily). We had a stainless-steel New Model .357 Blackhawk on hand, and it was an easy chore to find a mate for it at the local pawn shop. The older New Model was a pre-warning version, however, its mate needed that warning label removed and "DIAMOND DOT" put in its place.

With that primarily in mind, both guns were sent off to Reeder with the instructions to inscribe the barrels, smooth out the actions, and anything else he would do to fancy them up a bit. They came back highly polished, looking much like they were nickel plated; tastefully laser engraved on barrels, cylinders, frames, and grip frames; the grips, which had been scrimshawed with "Diamond Dot" by Twylla Taylor, fitted; the hammers jeweled; and the actions smoothed out. I was highly pleased with these sixguns, but more importantly, so was Diamond Dot. The work by Reeder definitely gave her new pride of ownership and her new sixguns just have to be shown to everyone. She is not the fastest shooter on the line, but she prides herself on not missing many targets. I know I would want her on my side.

Reeder uses five basic platforms to build his guns for handgun hunters, cowboy shooters, and those that want an easy-packin' big bore sixgun that can handle any emergency that may arise in the wild. His guns are built on Thompson/Center single shots (already covered in that chapter), Ruger Redhawks and Super Redhawks, Ruger Blackhawks and Bisleys, Ruger Vaqueros, and the Model 83 from Freedom Arms.

Reeder offers several custom options on the already excellent Freedom Arms sixguns. The "Ultimate Back-Up," mainly in the original .454 Casull chambering, consists of fixed-sighted frame; 3 1/2-inch barrel with ejector rod; Reeder's rendition of the Bird's Head grip, the Gunfighter grip frame; Vapor Hone finish; shooter's choice of animal engraved on the cylinder; and the Ultimate Back-Up logo on the barrel. This little sixgun does right at 1,700 fps with a 265-grain bullet and nearly 1,350 with a 300 grainer. That is a lot of power in a very packable sixgun.

Several Ultimate Models are offered such as the Ultimate .41 chambered in .41 GNR; the Ultimate Fifty, and the Ultimate Long Colt. The latter is chambered in .45 Colt with a custom five-shot cylinder on the .50AE frame. Two models are available, the Hunter Model with soft satin finish and shooter's choice of barrel length;

This Ruger Vaquero Blackhawk .45 has been turned into a lightweight Backpacker by Gary Reeder. With aluminum grip frame and ejector rod housing, and 3-inch barrel, total weight is slightly over 30 ounces.

and the Professional Model with a choice of finishes, Gunfighter grip frame, and adjustable express sights, and an extra cylinder in .454 Casull. Both models feature custom engraving on frame, cylinder, and barrel.

For those that prefer double actions, Reeder starts with a Redhawk to make his Alaskan Survivalist. Offered in either .45 Colt or .44 Magnum, the Survivalist is round butted and fitted with ebony grips; the barrel is cut to 3 inches; action is smoothed; hammer, trigger, and pins are high polished; and the finish is soft satin black or Vapor Hone. Reeder's Long Colt Hunter on the Redhawk is a 5-incher, with soft satin finish, action job, gold dot front sight, V-express rear, jeweled hammer and trigger, and Gunfighter Grip frame with ebony grips. Engraving is offered at no extra charge, including a most attractive version consisting of animal tracks.

Using the super strong Super Redhawk, Reeder comes up with The Master Hunter. Built on a 7 1/2-inch .44 Magnum, The Master Hunter includes a Reeder muzzle brake, smoothed action, Vapor Hone finish, jeweled hammer and trigger, Hogue soft rubber finger groove grips, and express sights as well as the Ruger ring setup for scope mounting. The brake turns full-house .44 Magnums into the feel of .38 Specials in this setup for the serious hunter.

The single-action version of the Redhawk Long Colt Hunter is built on a stainless Blackhawk .45 Colt with 5 1/2- or 7 1/2-inch barrels, gold bead front sights, satin finish, rounded Bisley grip frame with ebony grips, polished pins, and jeweled hammer and trigger. Ruger's Bisley is a very popular hunting handgun and many shooters have been adding the Bisley grip frame, hammer, and trigger to their standard Blackhawks. The Ultimate Bisley from Gary Reeder Custom guns is in .44 Magnum or .45 Colt, fully engraved with a high-polished black Chromex finish with a barrel length choice of 4 1/2, 5 1/2, 6 1/2, or 7 1/2 inches.

Reeder's number one hunting handgun is The African Hunter built on the Bisley or Super Blackhawk. These are serious hunting sixguns chambered in .475 Linebaugh and .500 Linebaugh, The African Hunter is a five-shooter with a 6-inch barrel and Reeder's muzzle brake installed. Finish is all stainless steel on the Super Blackhawk, or black Chromex with stainless cylinder on the Bisley frame. Grip frames are Bisley-style, rounded and fitted with black buffalo horn or laminated grips. Sights are standard Ruger or gold bead front and

Two .357 Rugers personalized and re-blued by Gary Reeder. The Flat-Top features a 10 1/2-inch barrel from a .357 Maximum, while the bottom Bisley has not only been appropriately engraved, but it's also been fitted with an extra cylinder in .356GNR.

express V rear sights, and base pin, trigger and hammer all bright polished.

I've mentioned Diamond Dot's sixguns worked on by Reeder. One of my favorite sixguns is my old stainless-steel 10 1/2-inch Super Blackhawk. It possesses incredible accuracy for an out-of-the-box sixgun, but this is mated with an absolutely awful trigger pull. My RCBS Trigger Scale only goes to 8 pounds and it would not set it off. After all these years I decided to do something about the trigger as well as the warning label on the left side of the barrel. Off it went to Gary Reeder Custom Guns. It came back with the left side of the barrel reading "JOHN TAFFIN THE SHOOTISTS" in script, the action smoothed, the trigger pull set at my request, the hammer and trigger were polished bright along with all the screws and pins, while the entire gun was given the soft satin Vapor Honed finish giving it a somewhat frosty appearance. Beautiful!

Two recent sixguns improved and beautified by Reeder include a Ruger Bisley .357 and a well-worn .357 Flat-Top. The first was sent off to Reeder with a set of genuine stag grips and an extra 9mm cylinder. Gary totally tuned the Bisley, fitted the stags perfectly, slightly rounding the butt in the process, rechambered the extra cylinder to .356GNR, and topped off the whole thing with a deep blue-black finish and gold appointments as well as "JOHN TAFFIN THE SHOOTISTS" inscribed on the left side of the barrel. The Flat-Top was picked up very reasonably as it had a buggered-up front sight in addition to the worn finish. I looked at a 10 1/2-inch heavy barrel from a Ruger .357 Maximum and thought, "Why not?" Gunsmith Mike Rainey, at our local shop Shapels', fitted the Ruger Maximum barrel and ejector rod housing to the Flat-Top and polished the left side of the barrel smooth. It was test-fired with Cast Performance Bullet Co.'s 187-grain, gas-checked, flat-nosed bullets at 1,300 fps and then turned over to Reeder to be refinished. It proudly stands next to the Reeder Bisley.

Dave Sample: Dave Sample knows cowboy action shooters and their single-action sixguns. It is a fact of life that most single actions come through from the factory with rough interiors and heavy trigger pulls. Sample can fix 'em! The action is gone through completely and carefully stoned for smoothness. This takes time and patience as most single-action inner parts are very rough with casting and tool marks still extant. The trigger and hammer give a safe and lasting pull, the springs are reshaped, and the sear and bolt spring, so fragile in Colt Single Actions and even more so in replicas, is replaced by a long-lasting piano wire spring.

Most factory single actions are at least slightly out of time and allow the bolt to drop into place before the hand completes its movement, or on the opposite extreme, not dropping into place until after the hand has been fully extended and requires inertia to complete the task. When parts such as these are out of synch, it really strains the hand and action. Sample adjusts the hand, replacing it if necessary, and adds an over-travel screw to stop the hammer's movement as it engages the full-cock notch. This eliminates the strain on the hand, hammer notch, cylinder ratchet, and cylinder pin.

Sample also performs other custom touches, such as cutting the forcing cone to 11 degrees to help eliminate leading, honing the chambers in the cylinder for smoothness in loading and unloading, and chamfering the edges for easier loading. To prevent the all-too-common breaking of Colt-style hand springs, Sample replaces them with a Ruger-style coil spring. Most replica single actions are authentic down to the "pinched frame" rear sight — a narrow and shallow V notch rear sight that is very hard to see. Sample runs a 3/32 end mill through the V, making it into a much easier to see "U." The back edge of the front sight is then serrated to cut down on offending glare.

Sample can make single actions sing! A matched pair of Cimarron Model Ps in .38-40 with 7 1/2-inch barrels

And now for something completely different! This custom Encore from SSK chambered in the potent .440 Cor-Bon features a barrel shaped like an ancient cannon.

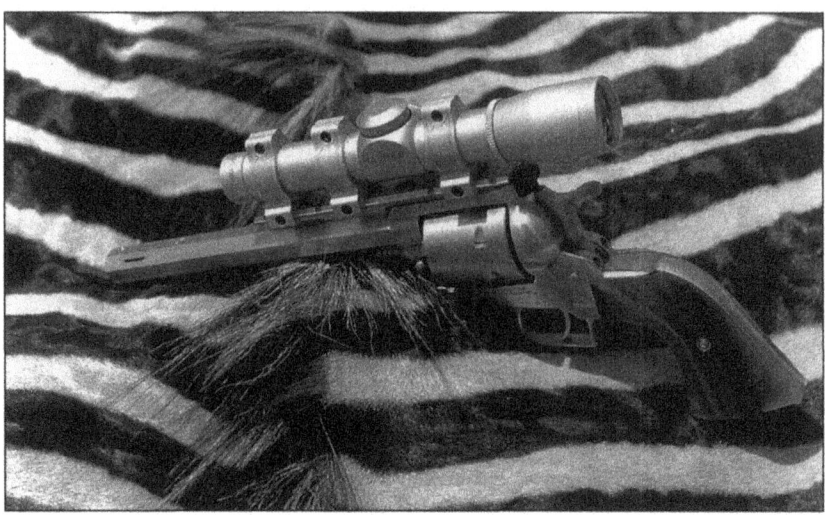

SSK builds custom sixguns as well as single shots. This Ruger Super Blackhawk has an SSK octagon barrel as well as an SSK T'SOB mount.

have now been exquisitely smoothed out. One of the early Lightning .38s had firing pin problems. Sample totally tuned this little sixgun and replaced the firing pin in the process. Result, problems all gone. He took two less-than-perfect replicas of mine, a 4 3/4-inch .44 Special Model P and a 3 1/2-inch New Thunderer .45 and turned them into sweet-singin' sixguns. Both were out of tune, with the .44 Special having a hammer that was suffering from way too much over-travel. On this sixgun Sample installed a hammer stop to prevent the over-travel, which puts a lot of strain on the hand and cylinder ratchet and which will also eventually beat them into submission. Both sixguns are now perfectly tuned examples of what single-action sixguns should be.

SSK Industries: J.D. Jones of SSK is best known for his customizing of single shots that were covered in the previous chapter. However, SSK also performs many custom services on revolvers and semi-automatics. He can turn the little Ruger MK II .22 into a work of art by tuning and either reshaping the barrel exterior or replacing it with a match grade barrel. For the big sixguns from Ruger and Freedom Arms, SSK offers the best muzzle brake, the Arrestor, in existence and also the toughest scope mount available.

The Jones-designed T'SOB scope mount is machined from high tensile strength aluminum and custom fitted for each revolver as a standard-length base or with a full-length barrel rib. Designed to accept Weaver-style scope rings, this mount, which allows the user the choice of two, three, or four rings, is the only mount to seriously consider for the really heavy-kickin' handguns, be they sixguns or single shots. More than one shooter has watched his scope launch into orbit because he used a lesser mount on a hard-kickin' handgun.

SSK specializes in action tuning, setting barrels back, re-cutting forcing cones, re-chambering and rebarreling,

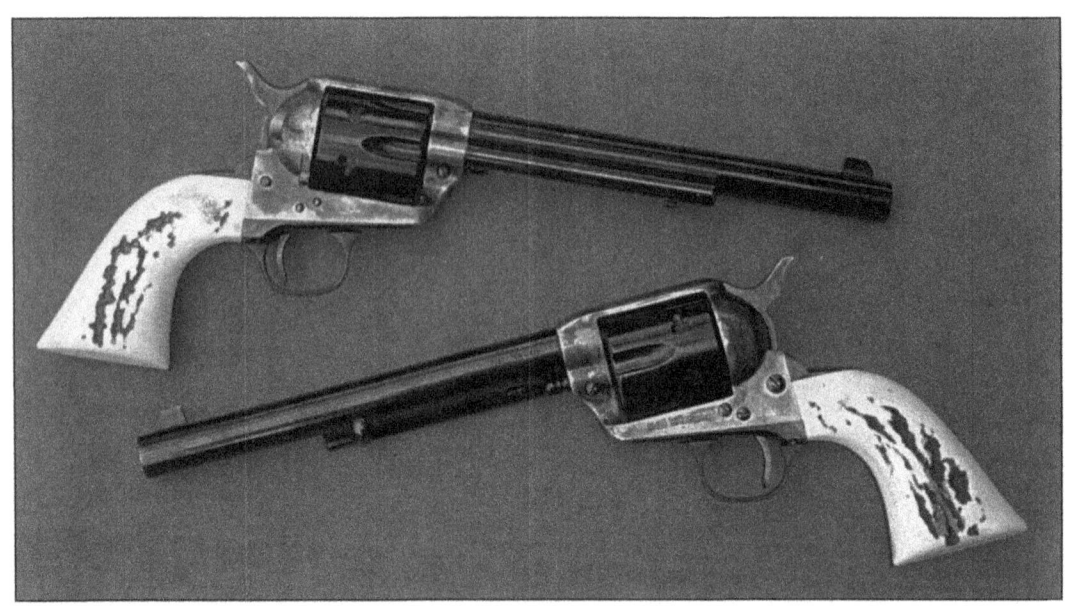

This pair of Cimarron 7 1/2-inch Model P .38-40s has been totally tuned by Dave Sample. Both sixguns will group 1 inch or less from a rest at 25 yards.

This custom Kobra from Ed Brown is appropriately named. Notice the checkering pattern on the slide and front strap. It has custom sights, trigger, hammer, Ed Brown grip safety, bobbed grip frame, totally tuned and tightened. This is a first-class semi-automatic.

specially contoured barrels such as a tapered octagon or diamond shape, re-bluing, custom plating in SSK Chrome, and most assuredly, installing the T'SOB scope mount. A really nice touch offered by SSK is to inscribe custom guns on the barrel in script such as "Custom Made for John Taffin by J.D. Jones." To paraphrase an old advertising slogan, "You're in good hands with SSK" as very few men understand heavy-kickin' handguns like J.D.

Custom pistolsmiths

It would take a book this size and then some to spotlight the work of all the qualified pistolsmiths building custom semi-automatics. For my part, I have chosen to showcase three men I know personally and whose work I am well acquainted with: Ed Brown, Jimmy Clark, and Bill Wilson.

Ed Brown: What do you do when you have a stock .45 Commander that bites you with every shot fired in spite of the Commander hammer that is supposed to eliminate this? I know what I did and that was to send it off to Ed Brown to be fitted with one of his beavertail safeties. Result? Problem disappeared. Ed Brown, like Jimmy Clark, has been one of the recipients of the "Pistolsmith of the Year Award" given by the American Pistolsmith's Guild. Ed Brown Products is a complete shop offering aftermarket parts and accessories for 1911s as well as building some of the best custom 1911s available using Ed Brown barrels, frames, and slides.

The top-of-the-line offering, the Classic Custom, features Ed Brown slide and frame, ambidextrous safety, Memory Groove beavertail grip safety, post front sight mounted in a dovetail, Bo-Mar adjustable rear sight (also dovetailed), two-piece guide rod, Ed Brown Match grade barrel, Commander-style hammer, specially polished slides, all topped off with checkered grips of exotic wood by Hogue. The Class A Limited features a Novak LMC fixed rear sight mounted low into the slide. It is also available in Commander style with Ed Brown's Bobtail grip frame, which is tapered on the back edge for a more compact and easier handling grip.

One of the newest offerings from Ed Brown Products is the Kobra Carry. This compact semi-auto has Novak night sights, Commander-style hammer, Memory Groove beavertail safety, and it has been de-horned, bead blasted, and fitted with the Bobtail grip frame. The Kobra Carry gets its name from the unique Cobra skin "checkering" found on the front and back straps and on the slide above the grips. An excellent choice as a defensive carry sidearm.

Clark Custom Guns: It was my good pleasure to travel to Shreveport, Louisiana, in the fall of 1990 to help honor Jimmy Clark as 1990's Outstanding American Handgunner. While I was there I was invited to spend the weekend with the Clarks, giving me a chance to visit with him and his family, spend some time in the shop, and also visit with Bill Jordan, and Jerry Miculek. I even got to shot Miculek's famous 8 3/8-inch Model 27 that he has used to consistently beat semi-

This Clark Combat Commander .45 Colt features Clark's Pinmaster sights, Accuracy Tuner, trigger job, and tightened slide, all resulting in a .45 ACP that will group with the best of them.

One of the best .45s available is this Wilson Combat Super Grade. Many of the features are on the interior, however, custom sights, trigger, beavertail grip, and ambidextrous safety all testify to a top-notch .45 ACP.

automatic shooters. It did not work quite as fast in my hands as in Jerry's, who has since broken many speed-shooting records using S&W 625s and 627s. Sadly, Jimmy Clark and Bill Jordan are now both gone Home. It was a great pleasure for me to know such fine gentleman and great shooters.

During that visit, I was able to talk with Jimmy as he shared with me that his philosophy in the gun business was to find a need and fill it. When he started there was a dire need for semi-automatics converted to .38 Special from .38 Super. It was 1951 and Clark was broke. He borrowed the money for 20 .38 Supers and ran an ad advertising these guns converted to .38 Special with sleeved chambers, Micro sights and a trigger job for $137.50. A second ad brought in orders for 80 guns and that was the last advertising Clark did until the 1980s, when he began marketing a line of accessories.

Clark is known for numerous developments, such as the Clark .22 Ruger steel trigger. In 1962 Clark made the first long slide that was 1 3/8 inches longer than the standard Government Model. He also started making barrels in the 1960s and one of his innovations was a barrel with an integral feed ramp that supported the case head in the Government Model. Clark's Custom Guns continues to do about 500 centerfire guns per year plus Ruger .22s. The first Pin Gun came from Clark's shop. It was designed for a bowling pin shooter and for maximum loads with minimum recoil. The first Comp Gun consisted of weight only, then ports were added to further reduce recoil.

A few weeks after returning from Louisiana, I received three test guns from Clark's Custom Shop. One of these was a Clark Combat Master made on a Colt Combat Commander. While I found the two Pin Masters sent for testing, one in .45 and the other .38 Super, to be excellent shooting and handling semi-autos, it was the Combat Master that really intrigued me. This is a great-shooting .45 auto and a perfect carry gun cocked-and-locked style.

Clark started with a Colt Combat Commander .45 ACP. Pin Master style sights are fitted as well as the accuracy tuner. The rest of the Colt is pretty much stock on the outside, but of course the slide is tightened and a trigger job is added. The result is a dream packin' pistol in a proven defensive cartridge. This .45 ACP shoots exceptionally well with groups averaging 1 1/2 inches for seven shots at 25 yards in my hands. The barrel is stock Colt, and the accuracy comes from the hand fitting and the accuracy tuner. One of my favorite loads for the .45 is the Bull-X 200-grain semi-wadcutter over 6.0 grains of WW452AA. This load clocks out at 950 fps from the Commander barrel and puts the whole magazine full in 1 1/4 inches. It just doesn't get any better than this!

The Pin Masters had to go back, but you can bet I bought the Clark Combat Commander!

Jimmy is gone but Clark Custom Guns continues headed up by Jim Clark Jr. They still offer many of the innovative semi-autos brought forth by Jim Sr., as well as a complete line of parts. One of its latest creations is the Meltdown. Starting with a 1911, all external surfaces are contoured and blended to remove all sharp edges and angles. This includes the magazine and grips as well. No sharp edges whatsoever. Clark also offers the .460 Rowland Long Slide. This powerhouse pistol has a 6 1/4-inch Match Grade Barrel, 6-inch Caspian slide, Clark Carry Bushing Style Compensator, accuracy and reliability package, choice of iron or scope sights, beavertail grip safety, extended thumb safety, and trigger job with Clark Match hammer and trigger. For those that desire to build their own .460, Clark offers a drop-in kit to be matched up with a quality 1911 frame and slide.

Wilson Combat: I first met Bill Wilson at a Shootists Holiday in the mid-1980s, and I was most impressed with the array of custom semi-autos he brought along. Soon after meeting him, I pulled my poor-shooting .38 Super Colt Commander out of storage and sent it off to him. When it left here it could not be counted on to put a magazine full on a 12-inch target at 25 yards. When it returned, it would keep them all within 2 inches. That certainly made me a believer. In 1988 I was assigned the job of attending The Masters Tournament mainly to cover this prestigious event for both *American Handgunner* and *Guns*. I also went to shoot, and I thought I was ready. I was not. I really went to school, so to speak, by shooting in The Masters, and I learned, boy did I learn! The action event format was entirely new to me as I had never before fired a match with falling targets. I was not ready, but my

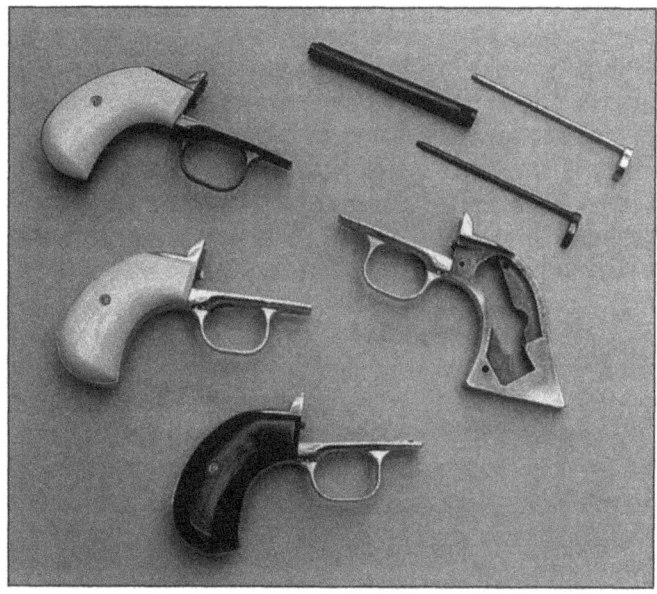

QPR features a full line of Ruger grip frames, both round butt and standard style, in blue steel, stainless steel, or brass, as well as those that fit Old Models and New Models. Steel ejector rod housings and ejector rods with properly sized heads in both blue and stainless are also available.

gun was certainly ready. It was a Wilson Accu-Comp LE in .45 .ACP, a fantastic piece of shooting machinery that would certainly do the job.

Bill Wilson is now fast approaching his Silver Anniversary of providing custom semi automatics. His products are endorsed by such shooters as Clint Smith, headman at Thunder Ranch, Jeff Hoffman of Black Hills Ammunition, Ken Hackathorn, founder of IPSC and IDPA, and well-known competitive shooter Jerry "The Burner" Barnhart. Wilson's catalog features a dozen or so custom .45 semi-automatics, such as the Classic, the Classic Stainless, and the Classic Long Slide. Of this series of semi automatics, slides and frames are mated together in tight tolerances, then fitted with a stainless-steel match grade barrel and hand-fitted bushing. Sights consist of the post front in a dovetail matched up with a Wilson Lo-Mount Adjustable rear sight. Add in checkering on the rear of the slide, ambidextrous safety, ultra-light hammer, high-ride beavertail, patented extractor, extended ejector, throating and polishing of the barrel throat and feed ramp, lowering and flaring of the ejection port, heavy-duty recoil spring on a full-length guide rod, all topped off with Armor-Tuff coating on the slide and hard chrome finish on the frame.

Wilson is heavy into tactical pistols. Two new models offered are the Tactical Carry Pistol and the Close Quarters Battle. Both, of course, are chambered in .45 ACP, with the former, aka the KZ-45, now being

This Ruger .45 Blackhawk has been customized with the addition of Bisley Model grip frame, hammer, and trigger, post front sight, maple grips by Scott Kolar, and a #5 base pin by Belt Mountain.

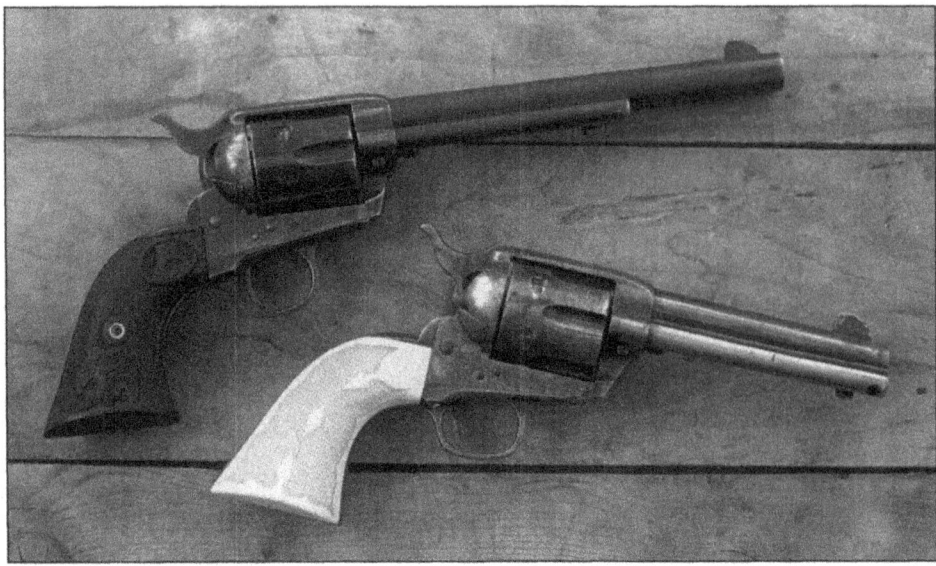

Eddie Janis of Peacemaker Specialists totally rebuilt the 7 1/2-inch Third Generation .44-40, including fitting a new cylinder, while the First Generation 4 3/4-inch .45 received all new interior parts and one-piece ivories.

offered in stainless steel. Wilson Combat is a complete shop for semi-automatics shooters with every possible service and accessory offered in its catalog. Good stuff!

Custom parts

Belt Mountain Enterprises: Early Colt Single Actions had a screw that entered diagonally from the front of the frame and applied pressure against the cylinder base pin. To remove the pin this screw, which held the pin in place, had to be loosened. It was soon replaced with a transversal spring-loaded catch. A screwdriver was no longer needed to remove the pin, but quite often the spring did not provide enough tension and the pin moved forward under recoil. This became more prevalent as single actions were chambered in Magnum cartridges. Belt Mountain addresses this by offering replacement base pins in several types, all of which are .002 inch oversize for a tight fit of cylinder to frame.

Both blued and stainless versions are offered with an Allen screw in the head of the pin that can be tightened against the bottom of the barrel to prevent movement under recoil. The latter comes with a standard-sized head, or a larger, easier-to-remove knurled head. While some pins are too loose, allowing them to escape their spring loaded catch, others are very hard to remove as the head is too small to allow a firm grasp. That is why single actions are often encountered with plier marks on the cylinder pin head. The larger head of the Belt Mountain pin addresses this problem. All styles are available for Colt Single Actions, Ruger Old or New Models, and replicas.

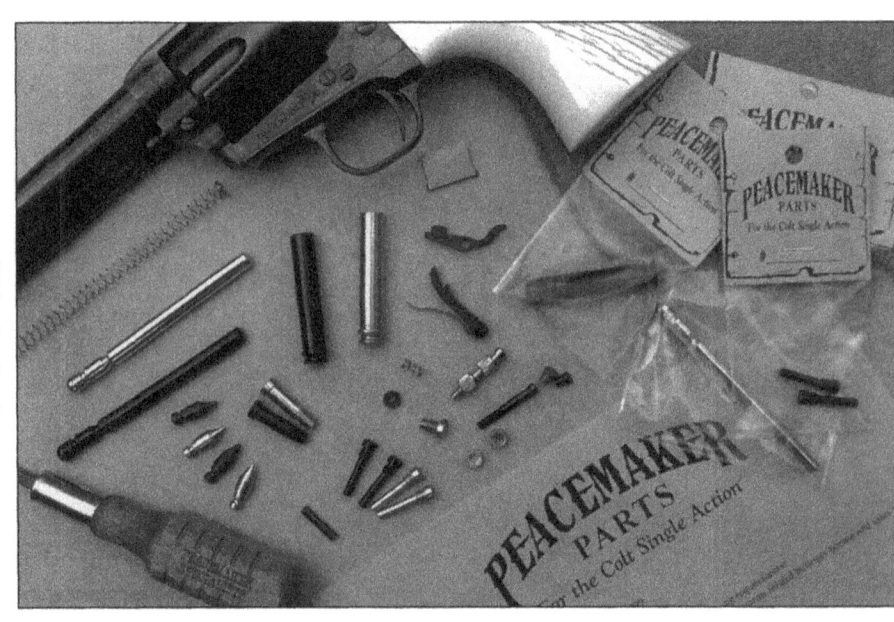

Peacemaker Parts has everything needed to tune or totally rebuild any First, Second, or Third Generation Colt Single Action Army.

Need a barrel for a Colt Single Action? Peacemaker Parts has every length available. This beautiful sixgun was totally rebuilt with Peacemaker Parts by Peacemaker Specialists.

Now Kelye Schlepp has gone even farther at the suggestion of Sgt. Fermin Garza of the Corpus Christi Police Department. Garza suggested that Schlepp offer a base pin that had a head shaped the same as that found on Elmer Keith's old #5SA (as Keith called his favorite .44 Special Colt Single Action). I was able to supply Belt Mountain with pictures and the result is a #5 pin from Belt Mountain. Keith wanted a pin that was both secure and easily removed. To provide the latter, the head of this pin looks as if it is made of several layers of concentric circular discs with the larger discs at both ends coming together with the smallest disc in the middle. Somewhat like two funnels placed end to end. The result is a beautifully shaped pin that not only really dresses up a single action, but is secure and also easy to remove.

Qulite Pistol & Revolver: Ruger's ejector rods little button heads give very little area for the finger to rest upon as empties are shucked and at the end of a long shooting day can result in a sore finger even if no sticky or stuck cases are ever encountered. QPR is now supplying both blued and stainless ejector rods with a crescent-shaped head just like the original Colts from the 1870s. These can be gunsmith installed or done yourself with patience and a small file to be

The specialty of Power Custom is Ruger single actions. The work includes new triggers, Bisley-style hammers, free-spinning pawls, and a replacement grip frame that is identical in size and shape to the Colt Single Action Army.

These two Ruger Blackhawks have been turned into Bisley Models by using Bisley grip frames, hammers, and triggers. They also feature free-spinning pawls from Power Custom and stocks from Lett and Hogue.

sure they fit the ejector rod housing slot correctly. When the original Ruger Single-Six .22 (1953) and .357 Blackhawk (1955) debuted, they carried steel ejector rod housings. Around 1963 these were replaced with aluminum housings that had a dull blue-black finish that wore rapidly. Only recently has Ruger returned to the steel ejector rod housing on their blued Vaquero sixguns. That means there are thousands of aluminum alloy ejector rod housings out there that are simply begging to be replaced by steel.

QPR to the rescue again! Some fitting may be required, again no great chore, and one needs to know if the sixgun has the small 3/16-inch or larger 1/4-inch screw head.

Finally, we come to the pièce de resistance. Again, since 1953, most Rugers have had alloy grip frames. Exceptions have been the Super Blackhawk, very recent Vaqueros, and all stainless-steel guns. QPR offers several ways to remedy this situation. A brass grip frame, which really looks attractive and rich on a

Three from Bill Oglesby for three special purposes: A custom Taurus 431 .44 Special, a Colt Single Action Army .45, and a Ruger Bisley Vaquero .45.

Bill Oglesby's custom-fitted, tuned, and polished .45 Colt Bisley Vaquero with one of his Competition Strut Assembly kits.

blued Ruger sixgun, is available from QPR to fit Blackhawks or Vaqueros, Old or New Models. In addition to standard grip frames, QPR offers its Bird's Head grip frames. These are also offered for the Old or New Model Rugers, and in blued steel, brass, or stainless steel with a choice of micarta grips in white or black. I have made up two "Sheriff's Model" Rugers using these grip frames, one in .45 Colt and the other in .44-40. They make into very easy-handlin' and compact sixguns.

Peacemaker Specialists: I recently came up with a 4 3/4-inch .45 Colt SAA made in 1917. It has an excellent bore and chambers, but several pits and scratches on the surface. The black eagle grips were slightly warped, the cylinder a little loose. This sixgun obviously needed several parts to bring it back to first-class shooting shape. A new bolt and hand were needed for tightening and tuning, the base pin needed to be replaced, as did the base pin latch, and all the exterior screws needed to be replaced just for general appearances. For continued reliability, all springs also had to be replaced.

Many of the First Generation parts are slightly different, especially interior parts. There is a longer bolt and hand and firing pin that is shaped quite differently. Even the old screws were different with domed instead of flat heads. Thanks to Peacemaker Parts we can now acquire newly manufactured parts to fit these old sixguns. Currently, Peacemaker Parts has all the necessary screws, several different styles of base pins, base pin bushings, firing pins, hands, bolts, all springs, and even bolt and trigger screws that are different in length to allow for the tapered frame. In addition to all these newly manufactured parts, both First and Second Generation barrels and cylinders are available for most calibers and models and eventually these may also be offered as newly manufactured parts. It is still economically feasible to pick up an old Colt as I did and use Peacemaker Parts to put it back into excellent shooting shape.

Power Custom: In 1973 Ruger made the first major change in single-action sixgun design since 1836. For nearly 150 years single actions had to be carried with the hammer down on an empty chamber in the case of centerfire models or in a slot provided between chambers in cap-n-ball sixguns. A hammer down on a loaded round or capped cylinder was an accident ready to happen. Ruger changed this by adding a transfer bar safety mechanism, which allowed a single action to be carried fully loaded with the hammer down. The transfer bar makes this possible since it blocks the hammer from contacting the firing pin and allows the contact to occur only when the hammer is cocked, the trigger

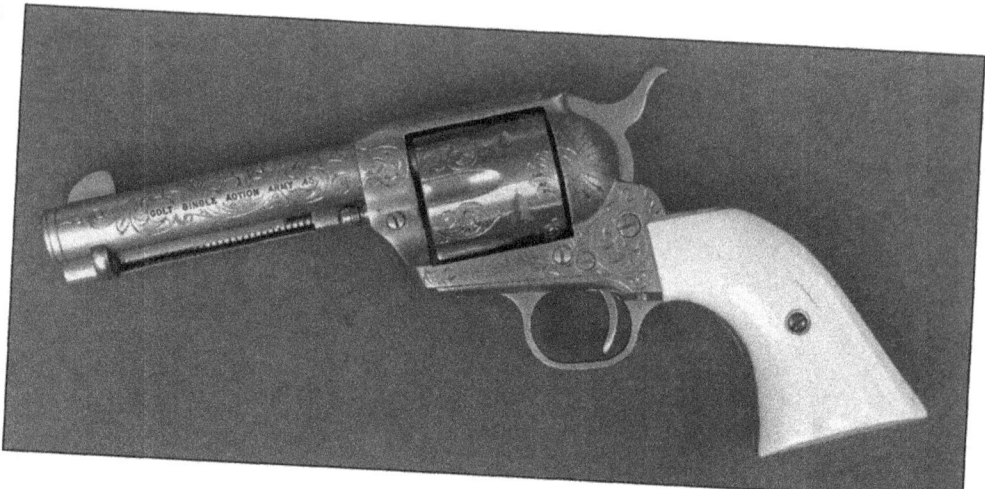

Jim Riggs engraved this Second Generation 4 3/4-inch Colt .45 ... as well as

pulled, and the gun fired.

With the old Colt Single Action and original Ruger Flat-Tops, it was possible to place the hammer on half-cock, rotate the cylinder, listen for the click and know that the chamber was lined up perfectly under the loading gate for either shucking a fired round or reloading a fresh one. With the new Ruger mechanism, when the click is heard it is too late. The cylinder has advanced too far to either remove or replace a round of brass.

Power Custom is offering several custom parts for Ruger Single Actions. The Ruger Single Action Hammer & Trigger Kit is made for all New Model Large and Small Frame Rugers, Blackhawks, Super Blackhawks, and Vaqueros. The kit consists of three parts: a hammer assembly with hammer plunger, plunger spring, and plunger pin; trigger to use with a hammer with a half-cock notch; and the spring kit with three Wolff mainsprings of 17, 18, and 19 pounds to replace the 23-pound factory spring, and both a 30-percent reduced power trigger return spring and a stronger cylinder latch spring.

In addition to this kit, Power also offers a free spinning pawl to replace the hand on Ruger Single Actions. This allows the cylinder to rotate in either direction. If the hammer is left lowered and the gate opened the cylinder will rotate in either direction for loading and unloading. Place the hammer on half-cock and the cylinder rotates only in the traditional direction and also utters an audible click as the chamber lines up with the loading gate opening. Power has also added Bisley hammers and triggers for Single-Sixes and most welcome is a true Colt-style grip frame for both Old and New Model Blackhawks and Vaqueros.

Oglesby & Oglesby: Many single actions, be they domestic or imported replica, come from the factory with a hammer that travels too far to the rear, resulting in undue pressure on the bolt, locking notches, hand, and the cylinder ratchet. On Colt-style sixguns, this problem is often solved by placing an over-travel screw beneath the top of the mainspring. "Badlands" Bill Oglesby has come up with the answer for Rugers. The Competition Strut Assembly kit is the same as that used in Oglesby's custom Rugers and features a built-in stop at the bottom of the strut so the over travel can be corrected. This kit also comes with three different mainsprings: a Competition spring allowing fast cocking and operation; a General Purpose spring, which as its name applies fits most sixgunning chores; and finally, a Hunting spring, for 100 percent reliability in the game fields. Each kit comes with easy-to-follow directions.

Oglesby is a cowboy action shooter, teaches classes in fast

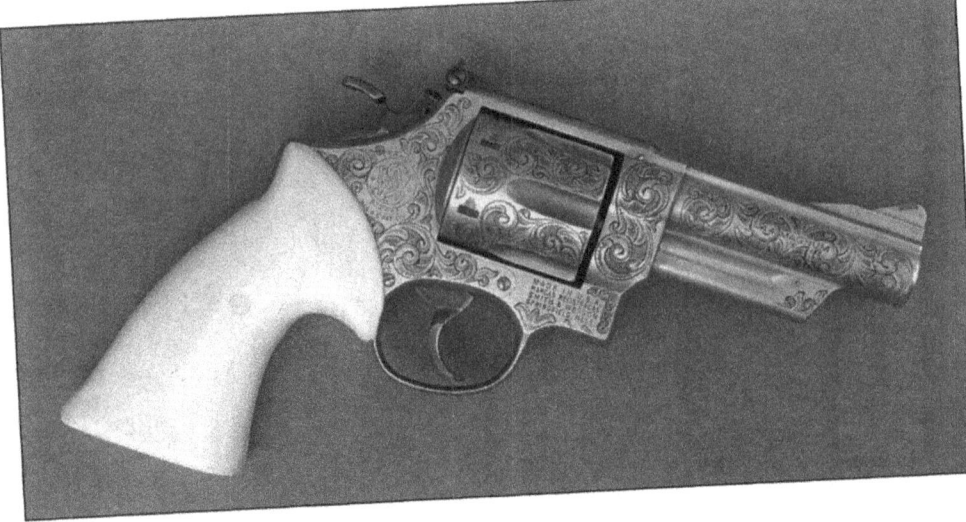

... this Smith & Wesson 4-inch .44 Magnum. Both guns, though beautifully engraved, satin nickeled, and stocked, are shooting guns and will be passed on to grandsons eventually.

One of the few semi-automatics worthy of engraving, this Series '70 Colt has been beautifully executed in scrollwork and then satin nickeled by Ed DeLorge.

shooting, and also provides custom sixgun work. His work on a 4 3/4-inch Colt Single Action .45 delivers a very smooth action, perfectly timed with no over travel on the hammer, and a mainspring that allows for smooth cocking without being so light that ignition suffers. A Ruger single action, this one a stainless-steel .45 Colt Bisley Vaquero, had the same work performed as the Colt Single Action, and if anything it is even smoother despite the fact that it is a Ruger New Model. To give it a distinctive look, all parts are high-polish stainless, except the mainframe and the ejector rod housing, which are a contrasting satin bead-blasted finish.

The factory grips on this Bisley Model have been slightly reshaped to give the gunfighter-style shelf directly beneath the factory emblems, and they have also been beautifully refinished to bring out the character of the factory wood. Finally, the barrel has been re-crowned and the liability warning removed from the left side of the barrel. This turns out to be a very practical do-it-all packin' pistol.

Now comes something completely different. Starting with a Taurus Model 431 five-shot, double-action .44 Special, Oglesby builds an easy-carrying, relatively lightweight sixgun for hiking desert, foothills, woods, or mountains. The exterior finish is now satin stainless, except for a high-polished cylinder and trigger. The hammer has been bobbed, and the trigger smoothed and radiused for quick double-action work. The original front sight has been removed and replaced by a custom rib and an Ashley Outdoors Big Dot Tritium front sight made up with an Express rear sight. Sights are very quick to pick up and especially so in dim light. It is sighted in to hit point of aim with Speer's Gold Dot 200-grain .44 Specials or Winchester's SilverTips of the same weight.

The back of the grip is serrated to help control in double-action work, two detent balls have been placed at the front of the crane to maintain alignment, and all sharp corners have been removed. A very special .44 Special and one that packs very easily in a Bianchi #105 belt slide.

Heritage Handguns: Theodore Roosevelt had one. General George S. Patton had one. Even Pancho Villa had one. All of these men had one thing in common: the sixguns they preferred for fighting were also fancy. With Roosevelt it was a 7 1/2-inch Colt Single Action Army .44-40 with full engraving, nickel plating, and ivory grips with TR carved into them. Carried in an equally fancy carved cross draw holster, the .44-40 was his constant companion on his ranch in the Dakota Badlands in the 1880s.

Young Lt. Patton chose a special sixgun before he joined Black Jack Pershing to pursue Pancho Villa in 1916. That sixgun was a Colt Single Action Army .45 with the "Gunfighter" length 4 3/4-inch barrel also fully engraved and ivory grips with the initials GSP etched into them. This sixgun, carried in a Myres Border Patrol holster, became his authority symbol in World War II. Pancho Villa? What else but a Colt Single Action .45, again with the 4 3/4-inch barrel and full nickel plating with extra-fancy ivory grips that carried a carved steer head with gold horns and ruby eyes.

Texas Rangers routinely carried fancy sixguns and semi-automatics. The early issues of *Guns* magazine often featured articles highlighting such rangers as Clint Peoples and Bob Crowder, both of whom packed a pair of engraved and ivory-stocked 1911 .45s. Ranger Lone Wolf Gonzaullas preferred fancy sidearms as badges of authority. Gonzaullas's engraved and ivory-stocked 1911 .45 also had the trigger guard cut away for speed handlin'. Tom Threepersons, who designed the famous holster that still bears his name, packed a nickel-plated Colt Single Action .45 with pearl grips bearing the Colt factory medallion and a carved steerhead. The stars of the "B" movies of the 1930s and 1940s, such as Tom Mix, Buck Jones, and Tim McCoy, all packed fancy sixguns across the silver screen. Even John Wayne,

A Third Generation 4 3/4-inch Colt Single Action .44-40 that has been turned into a family treasure, thanks to beautiful engraving by Dale Miller.

who also starred in "B" movies at the beginning of his long career, died in his final movie, *The Shootist*, packing a fully engraved .45 Single Action.

Earlier I mentioned passing on a fully engraved Colt Single Action .45 with adjustable sights added for only $150. Now that seems like a pittance and, of course, I wished I had bought it. The Colt was over three weeks' pay in those days, so I passed, much to my eternal regret. Marriage came, then kids, and the decision to go to college. Putting myself through college while raising a family of three kids and a wife who stayed home with them left little money for anything so frivolous as an engraved sixgun.

But time passed ever so quickly. The kids grew and were soon out on their own and I dreamed of that engraved sixgun once again. Finally, my wife said enough is enough, do it and stop talking about it. So, 30 years after the dream started, I contacted Jim Riggs about engraving a sixgun. Now the problem was which sixgun to choose. It did not stay a problem very long as the most natural thing was to do a sixgun that Keith would like — a Smith & Wesson 4-inch .44 Magnum.

My 4-inch Model 29 from the early 1960s was sent off to Riggs and he was given carte blanche to "make me a fancy sixgun." When it came back I could not have been more pleased. Riggs had executed scrollwork on more than 75 percent of the .44 Magnum and then had it satin-nickeled to better show off the engraving. I recommend this subtle finish highly for both protection and good looks.

Engraved sixguns are like potato chips, you can't stop at just one. A second sixgun, this time a Colt Single Action Army, also from the 1960s, was chosen to be sent off to Riggs. I already had a 4 3/4-inch .45 Colt with ivory grips by Charles Able that I had selected years earlier for engraving. This sixgun, as with the Smith & Wesson .44 Magnum, would be a shooter, not a piece to hide away, so I made sure it shot to point of aim with a favorite .45 Colt load. It took a slight bit of filing on the front sight to get the point of impact to point of aim and then the blued Colt with a case hardened frame was also sent south to Boerne Texas to be engraved by Riggs.

On this sixgun Riggs used a style that looks very much like pictures I have seen of sixguns that were engraved in the frontier period. My name is also engraved on the backstrap so this sixgun will, in all probability, eventually go to the oldest grandson who also bears my name. With its satin-nickel finish and ivory stocks the overall effect of this Colt Single Action Army is one that either Buck Jones, Hopalong Cassidy or even Gen. Patton would approve of.

Now enter Ed Delorge. Ed is both a full-blown gunsmith and gun engraver from Louisiana. We first made contact several years ago when I asked him to send some pictures of his work. He went one step further. Not only did I get pictures of several handguns he had engraved, he also sent a picture of himself with his family. A man who is proud of his family immediately gains points with me! The decision was made to send him a Colt MK IV Series '70 .45 ACP to be given the fancy treatment. This is not just an ordinary, run-of-the-mill .45 as it shoots extra ordinarily well. With target loads it will cut a cloverleaf at 25 yards one-handed. I should say it would 30 years ago when my hold was steadier and my eye was keener. I can't do it quite as well anymore, but the .45 still will in the right hands.

Over the years this .45 was fitted with an ambidextrous safety, beavertail grip safety, Colt Commander hammer, and high-visibility fixed sights consisting of a blade notch rear and a post front sight. The beavertail and Commander hammer solved the problem of the fleshy part of my hand getting bit by the standard hammer as the Colt cocked itself upon firing. This was definitely a gun worthy of engraving.

Off this gun went to Delorge, who was also given carte blanche as the expert with only one stipulation. I wanted the finish to be satin nickel to match the Smith .44 and Colt .45 Single Action. The contours of the Government Model are quite different than either the Smith & Wesson or Colt Single Action revolver. Working with flat surfaces for the most part, Delorge executed a smaller scrollwork and leaf pattern than found on the two sixguns. The result is stunning to say the least. The scrolls and leaves are perfectly executed and set off by a very subtle stippled background. Delorge covered the slide, frame, even both sides of the ambidextrous thumb safety, with his pattern. Finish is satin nickel as requested and a pair of milky ivory stocks by Bob Leskovec Grips were added to complete this third special handgun.

Just before beginning my second book, *Action Shooting Cowboy Style*, I was contacted by Milt Morrison of Qualite Pistol & Revolver to tell me that he had found a young man, one Dale Miller, that was doing some fine engraving on firearms. A proper specimen was selected, in this case a nickel-plated, Third Generation 4 3/4-inch .44-40, to send off for engraving. The nickel plating was stripped by Morrison and the sixgun was then sent on to Miller to be engraved. When Miller finished his part of the project, the .44-40 came back to Morrison to be re-nickeled and returned to me. Miller engraved the barrel, cylinder, and frame with tasteful scroll engraving beautifully executed. The back strap has scroll work at the top and bottom with enough room left in the middle to engrave my name should I so choose. The rounded part of the top of the backstrap as well as the recoil shield on both sides of the hammer are all engraved with a pattern that makes it appear as the sun coming up on a beautiful morning. Eddie Janis of Peacemaker Specialists performed one of his Saddle Tramp action jobs, and Milt Morrison of Qualite refinished the sixgun in bright nickel and fitted a pair of Ajax stag stocks to the grip frame. This is a fancy sixgun, but still a workin' sixgun.

In the fall of 2001 a second Colt Single Action, this time a Third Generation 4 3/4-inch .38-40 was sent off to Milt to be disassembled, forwarded to Dale for engraving, and then returned to Milt for refinishing. Milt eventually called to tell me that it was back and his exact words were, "it is beautiful with 75 percent coverage." I had given Dale Miller no instructions, but simply turned him loose. Morrison is now finishing the Colt in his Black Diamond deep blue finish. Miller is another true artist who has given me a sixgun to cherish.

Quite often in my writings I mention purchasing and putting things back for my grandkids as well as guns such as these that will go to them when I am gone. Who knows, they may even get some of them as they come of age and I, hopefully, am still here. There is a reason for my emphasizing passing on part of me to them. My paternal grandfather was killed in Europe while my grandmother was pregnant with my future father. I have nothing that belonged to him. My father was then killed before I was a year old. The only thing I have of his is a broken pocket watch, a belt buckle, and few pictures. I've always felt somewhat disconnected from my family past because of this. My grandkids will never feel the same way.

CHAPTER 13

CUSTOM STOCKS

You have saved your money for several months and finally have enough to purchase the handgun you've been dreaming about. However, if you're a serious shooter, you will soon find that more dollars will need to be spent. In fact, it may be necessary to spend as much for extras, or even more, as you spent on the gun. Three, possibly four, more expenditures are necessary to complete what is basically a good solid handgun.

Which is the most important? The ranking will be different for each one of us. Unless we are going to keep our gun in the original box and only take it to the range to shoot occasionally, we need a holster, a quality holster, to carry our prized possession. This may be anything from a concealment rig, to a shoulder holster for hunting, or even an elaborate western outfit complete with cartridge belt.

Thanks to our liability-driven society, chances are 100 percent, or nearly so, that our new handgun will also need the action smoothed and the trigger brought down from that heavy pull normally found on factory handguns. For some of us, it may also be necessary to change the shape and/or size of the front sight to accommodate our eyes. Finally, we come to what I consider the most important aspect when it comes to actually shooting any handgun, and that is the grips or stocks. I can live with a heavy trigger if the stocks fit my hand.

We would do well to take a lesson from the two greatest handgun writers of all time, Elmer Keith and Skeeter Skelton. If one peruses their articles, Elmer's from the late 1920s through the late 1970s, and Skeeter's, from the late 1950s into the late 1980s, one

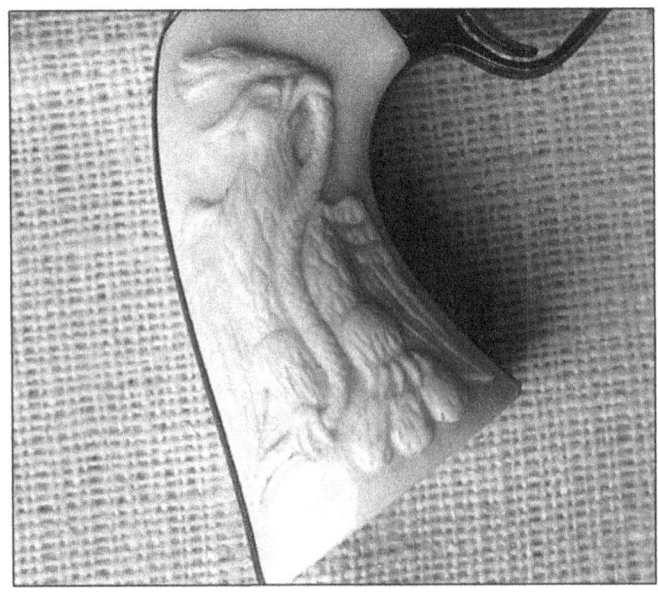

If you been around for awhile you may recognize these custom ivory stocks carved with a Mexican eagle as being on Elmer Keith's #5SAA.

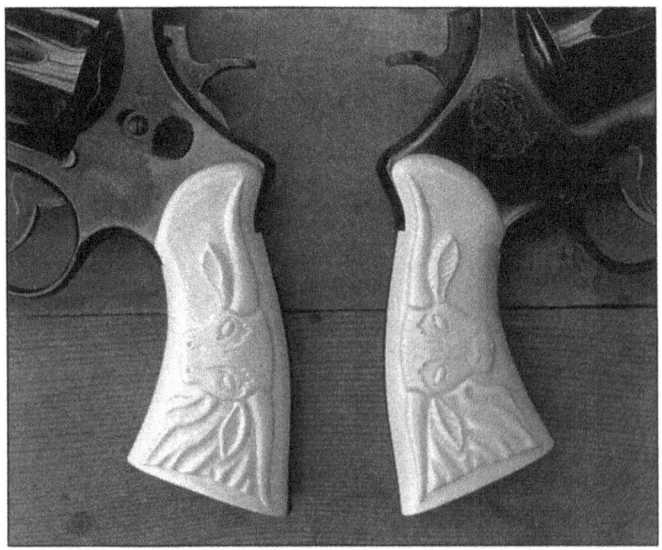

Taffin commissioned Bob Leskovec to carve the ivories on a pair of .44 Specials so that one longhorn skull would be on the left grip panel and the other on the right.

Three of the most desirable grip materials on three generations of Colt Single Actions: First Generation .45, checkered ivory; Second Generation .45, mother of pearl; and Third Generation .44 Special, stag.

finds two common aspects of their writings and handguns. Both men could spiritually pull us into their articles, as no one before or since. And invariably, almost without exception, their personal sixguns always carried custom stocks. In fact, today we can talk of Skeeter Skelton Stocks and Elmer Keith Grips, and most dedicated sixgunners know exactly what we are talking about. Skeeter's grip for the Smith & Wesson double-action sixgun is an improvement on the design by Walter Roper prior to World War II that led to Smith & Wesson's target stocks. Skeeter slimmed them and re-contoured them to make them fit the shooter's hand much better. While they will serve as "target stocks," they are not overly bulky, thus much better suited to everyday use for everything from peace officering to hunting.

Elmer Keith, having small hands, did not like the hand-filling target-type stocks found on most large-framed Smith & Wessons, but rather preferred the Magna-type stocks that were originally found on the .357 Magnum beginning in 1935. Keith called these plainclothes stocks. Unlike Skeeter's preference, there is no filler behind the trigger guard on this style grips and I always wondered how Elmer could shoot the .44 Magnums with his heavy load using these stocks. I found out when I examined his sixguns. His stock material of preference was ivory, for two reasons. The obvious, of course, is the natural beauty of the elephant's tooth, but an even more important aspect is the carving found on his grips. He particularly preferred the longhorn steer head carved on the right side of his grips as that carving perfectly filled in the natural crease in the hand. That is how Elmer could handle the recoil, especially of the 4-inch .44 Special and .44 Magnum sixguns he preferred for concealment use.

Even as I was typing the above paragraph, I had to stop and joyfully opened the door for Fed-Ex as it dropped off a pair of 4-inch .44 Special Smith & Wessons that were coming back from grip maker Bob Leskovec. Since I do not believe in coincidence, this must have been a sixgunning omen of some kind, and surely Elmer is smiling. Leskovec duplicated Elmer's grips for the pair of 4-inch .44 Specials my wife purchased for me for my birthday last year. Since these sixguns are to be worn in tandem in a pair of floral carved El Paso Tom Threepersons holsters, one set of grips is carved on the right side and the other on the left. Bob outdid himself on these beautiful grips and we'll talk more about him shortly in the section on his company, Precision Pro Grips.

Handgun stocks, like sixguns, pickup trucks, dogs, horses, and wives, not necessarily in that order, are highly subjective. Fortunately, we have a large group of grip makers ready to fulfill our needs and wants. Material suitable for grips is also quite varied. We have mentioned ivory as perhaps the finest and also the most expensive material. Ranking right with ivory, as far as quality and expense, are ram's horn, buffalo bone, and with the current ban on exportation, even stag horn. Then comes exotic woods of all kinds, and

These two custom Rugers, a .41 Special and a .45 Colt, deserve very special grips. Fancy-grade walnut by BluMagnum and buffalo bone.

Would you believe that these grips are made of buffalo bone? Unbelievable figure and color.

Single-action or double-action sixgun, or semi-automatic pistol, they all look good with ivory stocks.

These exquisite Tiffany grips by John Adams on a Cimarron 1871-72 Open-Top are reminiscent of the grips Sam Colt supplied on many of his presentation pieces in the 1850s and 1860s.

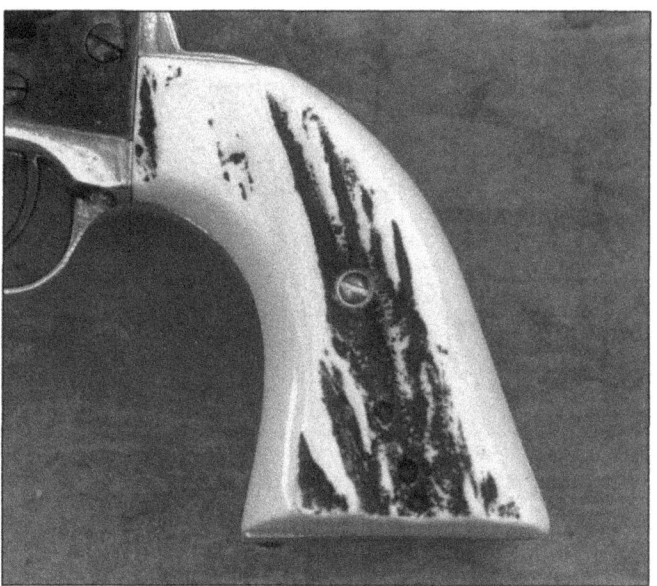

Genuine stag is expensive and very difficult to come by. An easy alternative, especially for cowboy action shooters, are these faux stag by Ajax on a Cimarron .38 Cartridge Conversion.

the synthetics such as micarta, polymers, and even plastic and rubber.

I must admit that, unlike a few years ago, most current handguns are at least equipped with usable stocks. This has happened simply because most makers, especially of double action sixguns, now provide rubber grips on their handguns. The looks of these grips may not excite us, but they usually provide a non-slip gripping surface and also help to tame recoil. Most single-action stocks are also usable with standard loads, but can easily be improved as they are normally too slim at the top and too thick at the bottom. They are also often made of wood that is not even close to awe inspiring. Of all handguns, single-action sixguns especially deserve beautiful stocks. The looks of semi-automatics can also be vastly improved with fancy stocks. Single-shot handguns come ready equipped with decent grips, and for the truly hard kickers rubber stocks are available.

Here we will mostly be looking at some of the newer grips that have become available in the past few years. I also refer the reader to my two previous books, *Big Bore Sixguns* and *Action Shooting Cowboy Style,* for extensive chapters on custom stocks as well.

John Adams: With the abundance of handgun stock makers how does one provide a truly unique grip? Well-known engraver John Adams Sr. fills a niche that as far as I know as not been addressed in well over 100 years. When Sam Colt gave a special presentation sixgun to various dignitaries, he not only had it cased and fully engraved, he also often had it fitted with Tiffany grips. Most of us cannot afford the sixguns these grips were attached to, nor can we afford the grips, but thanks to the tremendous revival of interest in single actions during the last decade of the 20th century, we now not only have virtually every single action from that period of time available once again in replica form, Tiffany Grips are once again available at an affordable price.

I recently sent a replica '72 Open-Top .45 Schofield to Adams for the fitting of a pair of Tiffany-style grips. Working from an original pattern, Adams carves the grips, casts them, plates them, and then fits them to the sixgun. In the process the original backstrap is removed and replaced by the solid Tiffany grip, adding considerable weight to the original sixgun while also providing an extremely solid gripping surface. The total result is a stunningly beautiful sixgun. Of course, one should understand that this style grip is not practical on any heavy-recoiling sixgun.

Ajax Grips: Ajax Custom Grips offers a full line of custom stocks for single actions, double actions, and semi-automatics. Grips are crafted of both natural and synthetic materials, including staghorn stocks from the Indian Sambar Deer. Currently, stag is under an exportation embargo, however, Ajax still has a small amount of stag on hand. To counteract this shortage, Ajax is now offering a polymer grip with a stag pattern somewhat reminiscent of the "stag" stocks found on many Colt Single Actions during the heyday of the "B" western movie as well as on the Great Western sixguns of the 1950s and 1960s. These new stags really help dress up such single

Presentation-grade walnut stocks by BluMagnum grace the grip frame of this custom Ruger single action.

These Skeeter Skelton stocks of exotic wood by BluMagnum are not only beautiful, they also turned this round-butt .45 Colt Mountain Gun into a square butt.

actions as replica cap and ball revolvers and the cartridge conversions. Both my 1861 Navy and 1851 Model Cartridge Conversion now wear Ajax polymer stags.

One of my favorite sixguns is a .44 Special 5 1/2-inch New Frontier totally tuned by Tom Sargis. This single action needed a special pair of grips, which turned out to be genuine stags with a Colt Factory medallion fitted from Ajax. Many of the stag grips I have seen offered have been overly thick and very sharp, so much so that they were painful to use. That is why I started having stag stocks slimmed down and smoothed to a bone appearance. Ajax's stag grips are already of the proper width without the rough surface found on many stag stocks. Their stag stocks for the Colt 1911 are also of a width that does not add to the bulk of the grip frame.

Ajax also offers a line of wood grips for most revolvers and semi-automatics in walnut, cherry wood, and black silverwood. For those that want the best in grip materials, genuine ivory cannot be topped. Ajax is one of the few sources for this rare material. Made of African elephant ivory, these grips must be special ordered and custom fitted to each individual handgun. Ajax is also one of the few suppliers I know of that can fit the original Ruger Blackhawks, the XR-3 grip frames that were standard on the Single-Six and .357 and .44 Magnum Blackhawks from 1953 to 1963.

BluMagnum Grips: Earlier we mentioned the type of stocks preferred by Skeeter Skelton. The number one request I get for grip information concerns these grips that were formerly offered by BearHug Grips. Deacon Deason of BearHug marketed the Skeeter

The late Deacon Deason of BearHug furnished all four of these custom stocks for the four N-frame 8 3/8-inch Smith & Wessons chambered in .357 Magnum, .45 Colt, .44 Magnum, and .41 Magnum.

Skelton Style stocks that were extremely popular with users of Smith & Wesson sixguns both the K-frame, Model 19 size, and the big N-frame .44 Magnum. Roper designed the stocks that were found on Smith & Wesson double actions from before World War II to about the late 1950s. After that they became too blocky and too large for anyone with average-sized hands. Skelton changed the Smith & Wesson/Roper design slightly to conform to his hand and the result is the best grips ever devised for double-action Smith & Wessons.

Deacon Deason went Home in 1994 ending the BearHug line of Skeeter Skelton grips. Tedd Adamovich of BluMagnum was a personal friend of Deacon Deason and learned to make double-action grips from watching Deac. I loaned BluMagnum several pair of Skeeter Skelton stocks made for me personally by Deacon Deason. Adamovich was able to complete the tooling to make the original Skeeter Skelton Style grips as formerly offered exclusively by BearHug, and also to obtain permission from both Jo Deason and Sally Skelton, the two wives of these two sixgunners to call them the Skeeter Skelton Style. They are available in both walnut and fancy woods as finished stocks. Adamovich also offers these as grip blocks completely fitted to the frame but left to be finished at half the normal price. Having several sets of BluMagnum Skeeter Skelton Stocks on both K- and N-frame Smith & Wesson's, I proclaim them to be every bit as good, possibly even better, than the originals.

Buffalo Brothers: When I first started shooting sixguns as a teenager back in the 1950s, the majority of replacement grips being offered were plastic. First we had the imitation stag grips seen so often in "B" westerns. At the time I thought they were terrible and my mind was not changed when they were offered as the standard grip on Great Western sixguns. In those days I discarded them, now I collect them! Times do change.

Then came the Jay Scott lineup of synthetic grips in pearl, ivory, and wood finishes. All of these grips were strictly for looks and offered no improvement over the factory grips. In fact, in many cases they were worse. All that is now changed and some excellent synthetic grips are available.

At the top of the list are the offerings from Buffalo Brothers. These synthetic grips are beautifully molded with many of the old-time carvings found on single actions of the 1870s. The color is also molded in the grip. I first met Buffalo Brothers at the SHOT Show two years ago and was most impressed with the look and feel of their line of grips. A few weeks later at Winter Range I stopped by the Buffalo Brothers tent on Sutler's Row and wound up purchasing a Second Generation Colt Single Action .45 Colt with the coveted 4 3/4-inch barrel and totally tuned by American Frontier Firearms. Since it had to be shipped FFL to FFL, I made arrangements to have Buffalo Brothers first fit it with a pair of one-piece style checkered grips with a Texas Star in the middle. They look like old bone and the color in the butt is particularly striking.

Since that time Buffalo Brothers has greatly expanded its line and has stag, bone, checkered, carved, almost anything anyone could want for a single-action sixgun. I have now fitted stag, bone, and checkered grips to a pair and a spare of Schofields, checkered Fleur-de-lis to a New Thunderer, bone to a Lightning and a Remington 1890, and stag to a Cartridge Conver-

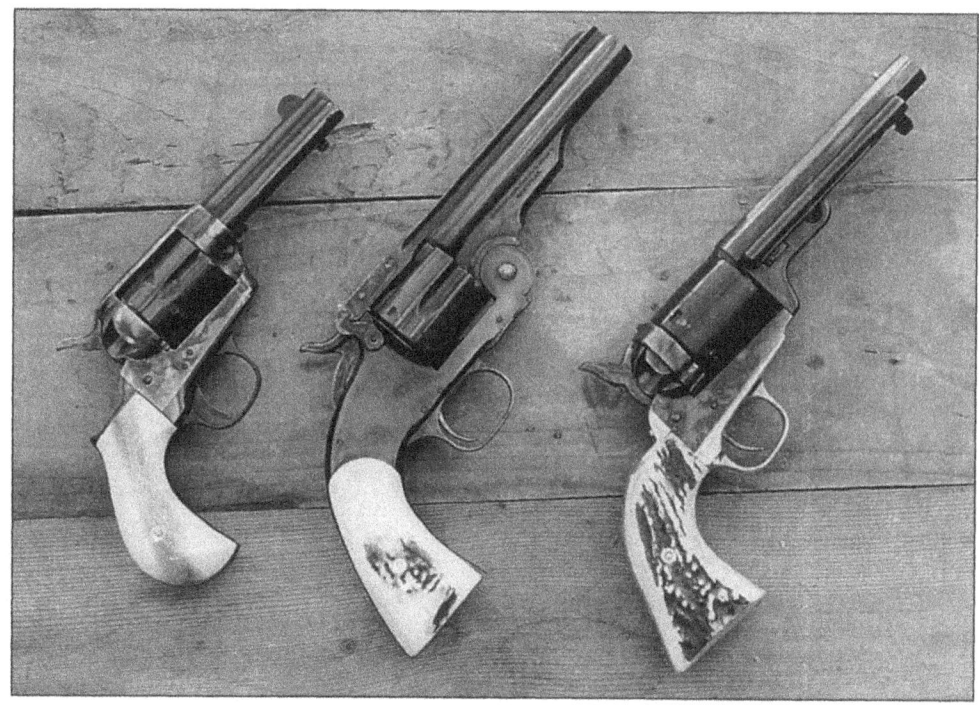

Buffalo Brothers has a full line of grips such as these bone grips on a Cimarron .38 Lightning (left), and stag grips on a Navy Arms Wells Fargo Schofield Model and a Cimarron .38 Cartridge Conversion.

sion. All of these Cowboy Action Shooting replica sixguns are greatly enhanced in appearance by the addition of custom grips from Buffalo Brothers. All grips, whether one- or two-piece style, need to be fitted to each individual sixgun. My gunsmith, Mike Rainey at Shapels', handles this task superbly for me.

Crimson Trace: Remember those first bulky laser sights offered for use on handguns in the last quarter of the last century? Thanks to Crimson Trace, laser sights are now available that are no larger than the handgun grip. In fact, they are contained in the grip itself. Made for most popular semi-automatics and double-action revolvers, the battery-operated laser sight is at the top of the right grip with a switch at the front of the grip that is activated when one takes the normal shooting grip. A second switch at the bottom of the grip allows the battery to be switched off when the handgun is neither in use nor expected to be used immediately. Batteries last about four months when left on constantly.

Crimson Trace Lasergrips are very easy to sight in using a tiny Allen wrench to adjust windage and elevation through two very tiny holes at the top of the grip. Once it is sighted in, simply grasp the handgun in the normal shooting position, which automatically shines a red dot on the target. The dot marks the spot where the bullet will go. These grips have both a serious and a fun application. On a serious side, they are extremely valuable as a defensive proposition, especially at night when sights may be very difficult to see. For my use, they are installed on two sixguns, a Taurus Titanium .38 that normally rides in a jacket pocket, and a Smith & Wesson 4-inch .44 Magnum which is likely to be found next to my bed at night. The latter is also an enjoyable sixgun for point shooting practice, especially when loaded with .44 Specials.

Eagle Grips: To fill in the void caused by the shortage of ivory, and to also supply a grip at a much lower cost than the real thing, Eagle developed a new synthetic that is the closest to the genuine article I have ever seen. Most imitation ivory has a flat plastic look. Not so with Eagle's UltraIvory. Not only do they not look cheap, they also have a wavy, milky pattern throughout similar to real ivory. This milky pattern really shows up in strong sunlight. These grips are offered in three single-action versions: plain smooth, carved, and checkered.

I have had UltraIvory fitted to several single-action sixguns. First, a Second Generation 7 1/2-inch Colt SAA .44 Special that I had totally rebuilt from a .38 Special by Eddie Janis at Peacemaker Specialists; then a custom Ruger .44 Magnum with a 4 5/8-inch barrel and standard grip frame built by Mag-Na-Port on a Three-Screw Super Blackhawk with a stainless-steel looking finish and utilizing a grip frame from the Ruger

The Crimson Trace laser sight on this 5-inch Smith & Wesson 629 makes it very easy to shoot a tight group without using the factory sights.

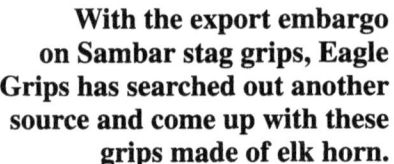

With the export embargo on Sambar stag grips, Eagle Grips has searched out another source and come up with these grips made of elk horn.

The "Coke bottle" grips found on S&W revolvers in the 1950s have now been duplicated by Eagle Grips with its Heritage Grips of rosewood.

Almost as good as a time machine is the use of these two Smith & Wessons, a Schofield Model and a Model #3 Russian with Eagle's UltraIvory stocks and 1870s style Cheyenne Cartridge Boxes.

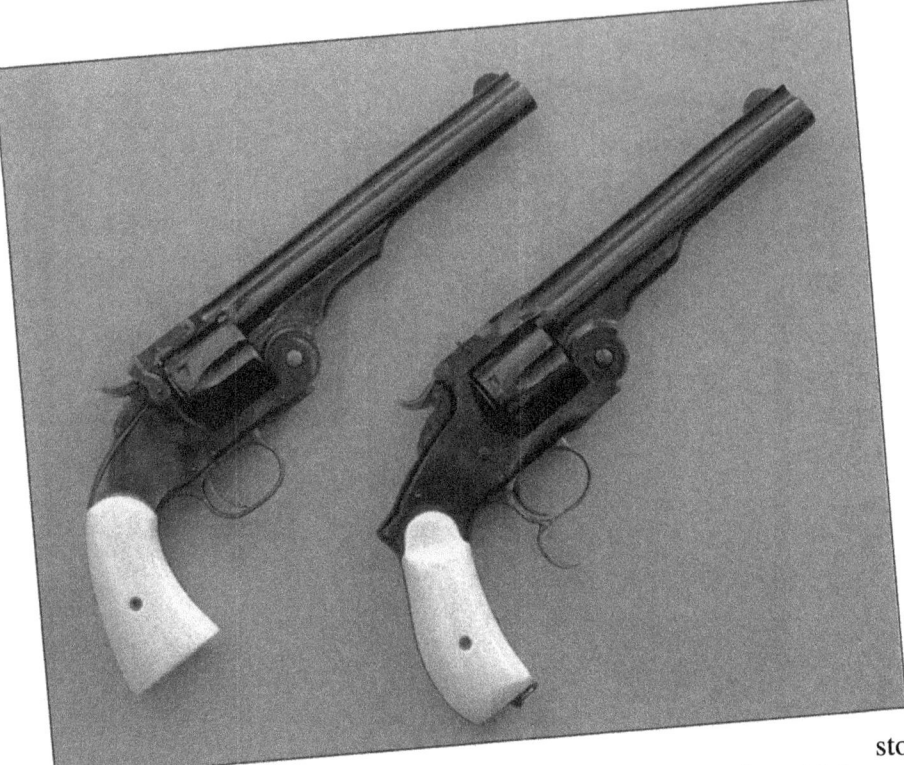

In the 1870s, Smith & Wesson single actions were often fitted with ivory grips. Both of these sixguns, a Smith & Wesson Model 2000 .45 Schofield and a Navy Arms Model #3 Russian, have been fitted with UltraIvory grips by Eagle.

Old Army grip; and a 4 3/4-inch Colt SAA .38-40 now wears a pair of UltraIvories with a carved steer head on the right panel.

Sixgunners have been blessed with an abundance of replica single-action sixguns, however, most literally cry out to announce: "I am a replica." An easy way to correct this situation is to have these sixguns fitted with custom stocks. UltraIvories really dress up the Colt Black Powder series of cap and ball revolvers, the Colt Cartridge Conversions as offered by Cimarron, and even the Smith & Wesson single-action replicas, such as the Schofield from Smith & Wesson and the Navy Arms Model 3 Russian.

With the shortage of real stag horn, several companies have been looking for viable alternatives. Eagle's answer has been elk horn. I picked up two pair of elk antler grips from Raj Singh of Eagle at the last Tin Star Range Wars and have now had them expertly fitted to Vaqureo grip frames and polished by Tony Kojis. They look exceptionally good on the blued Vaqueros and the polishing brings out a lot of color not present in the stag horn grips from the antlers of the Sambar stag. It's an excellent alternative for those that prefer genuine stag rather than a polymer or plastic imitation.

This past week I really took the plunge and had Tony Kojis fit a pair of Eagle's genuine mother of pearl grips to a Colt Single Action. Pearl is very hard to work, but Kojis knows what it is all about and did a superb job making them one-piece style. Finally, we have a return to the past with Eagle's Rosewood "Coke Bottle" stocks for Smith N- and K-frames. These are virtual duplicates of the Goncala Alves stocks found on the Smith & Wesson .44 Magnum and .357 Combat Magnum in the 1950s. They have been sorely missed.

Roy Fishpaw: Anyone who has any interest in grips probably knows and recognizes Roy Fishpaw of Custom Gun Grips as the absolute master in the realm of custom crafting sixgun and semi-automatic stocks. When it comes to making gun grips, Fishpaw understands everything: fit, finish, shape, size, and material.

Fishpaw crafts beautiful grips from some of the most mouthwatering walnut in existence. His grips for Smith and Wesson's big N-frames are masterpieces. Not only is he able to finish the grips to perfection, he can also add nice touches, such as sterling silver inlays. Roy recently completed a pair of walnut grips for one of my .44 Smiths and fitted a silver inlay on one side with my initials engraved, and carried out this theme with a similar

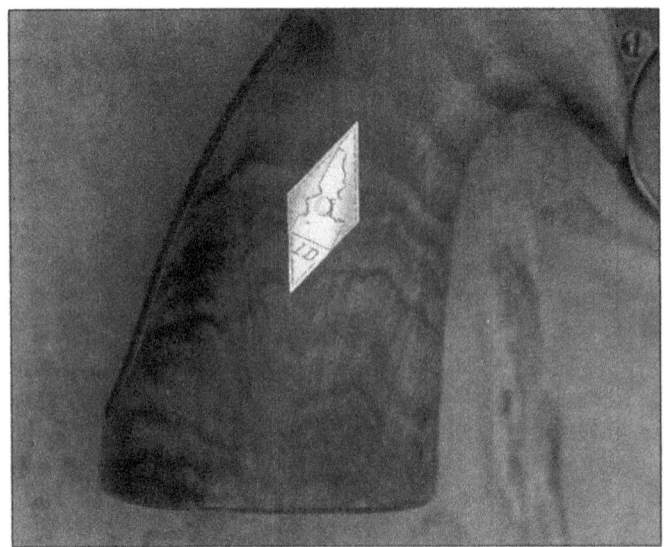

It just doesn't get any better than this! Presentation-grade walnut stocks with silver medallion inlaid by Roy Fishpaw.

Roy Fishpaw went to one of the most exotic materials available, Dall sheep horn, to stock this Texas Longhorn Arms Improved Number Five.

inlay on the other side featuring the outline of the state of Idaho. Beautiful!

New to Roy's lineup of exotic woods is a mysterious specimen known as Snakewood. Just as its name implies, Snakewood has a grain pattern that makes it look like the skin from a snake. Snakewood comes from the area around Surinam, and although the trees grow to a diameter of several feet, only the center, or heartwood, is usable. Trees also grow in inaccessible areas and must be carried out of the jungle by human labor. The basic color is a deep brown interspersed with a snakelike patterning that is black. It is also a very hard and heavy wood, even more so than Lignum Vitae, or Ironwood.

Two of the most exotic materials for custom grips are ivory and ram's horn. One of the finest single-action sixguns in existence is the Texas Longhorn Arms Improved Number Five, which is Bill Grover's salute to Elmer Keith and his original #5SA. Such a sixgun deserves great grips and the solution was Dall Sheep horn from Roy Fishpaw. It looks somewhat like ivory with a straw-like grain pattern, with one grip panel carrying beautiful red streaks. It is a fitting pair of stocks for a great pistol that brings back memories of a grand sixgunner. As this is written, an 1873-1973 7 1/2-inch Colt Peacemaker Centennial .45 Colt has been sent to Fishpaw for re-stocking. This magnificent Single Action Army, one of the best offered by Colt in that particular run of sixguns, came with U.S. Cavalry-style stocks that are way too wide for my hands. Roy will do it right.

Gripmaker: Friend Larry Little purchased the Gripmaker business out of Texas, moved it to Missouri, and greatly expanded the offerings in the process. All of these grips are of ivory urethane and Little says they will age just like original ivory. Gripmaker's grips, which must be hand fitted by the purchaser, are offered for almost every single-action sixgun imaginable, from the 1848 and 1849 Pocket Colts, through the 1851, 1860, and 1861 Colt cap-n-balls, the Colt Single Action Army and Bisley, all both real and replica. The imports, Remington cap-n-ball and 1875 Single

Two classic Smith & Wessons sixguns — a Model 29 .44 Magnum and a Model 27 .357 Magnum — stocked in the classic style by Roy Fishpaw.

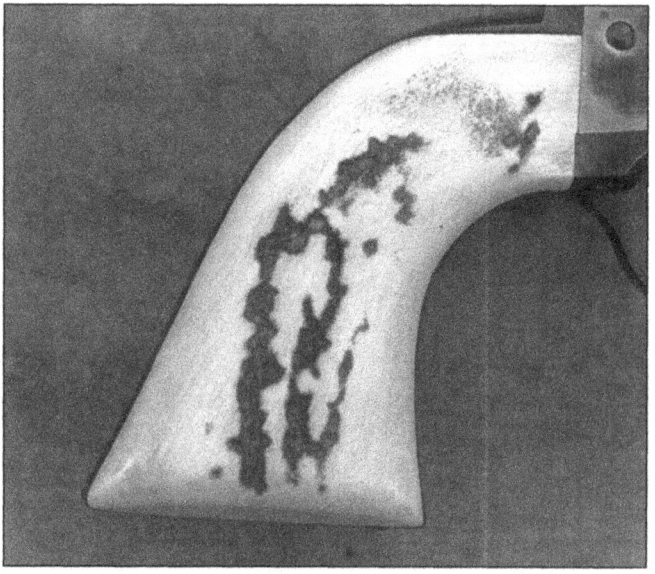

Another good workable solution for the lack of genuine stag horn is replica stag by Gripmaker.

This pair of 7 1/2-inch Cimarron Model P .38-40s have been completely tuned by Dave Sample and stocked with Gripmaker's faux stags by Tony Kojis.

Action, the New Thunderer and Lightning, the S&W Schofield and Model #3, and all of the Ruger Single Actions are also provided for.

In addition to plain "ivory" and a stag-like finish, Gripmaker offers about two dozen carved grips, most of which are replicated from old-time designs such as the Hickok Eagle, the Mexican Eagle, the Texas Star, and the Liberty Head. Of course, all carvings are not available for all grip shapes. I recently ordered up some grip blanks to fit both 1851 Navy and 1860 Army Colt replicas used for cowboy action shooting. Gripmaker provided examples of both plain and carved designs, including the Hickok Eagle and the Texas Star.

In the process we learned something about the grip frames offered on the various 1860 replicas. I could not fit all the Army grip frames with the grips he provided, so when we met at the Shootists Holiday, I took along several grip frames. We found there are several grip frame shapes being offered of varying lengths and widths. When ordering for a particular cap and ball sixgun, provide Gripmaker with the manufacturer's name. A tracing of the grip frame would also be quite helpful.

I was able to fit Gripmaker's grips to a pair of 1860 Armies with a few hours work and the use of a Moto-Tool. Panels were first fitted fairly closely to the frames and then epoxied together to make a one-piece grip. For this operation the frame was heavily coated with Vaseline to prevent the panels from being glued to the grip frame. Using the spacer provided by Gripmaker, the panels and the spacer were both given a light coating of glue, then placed on the sixguns. The

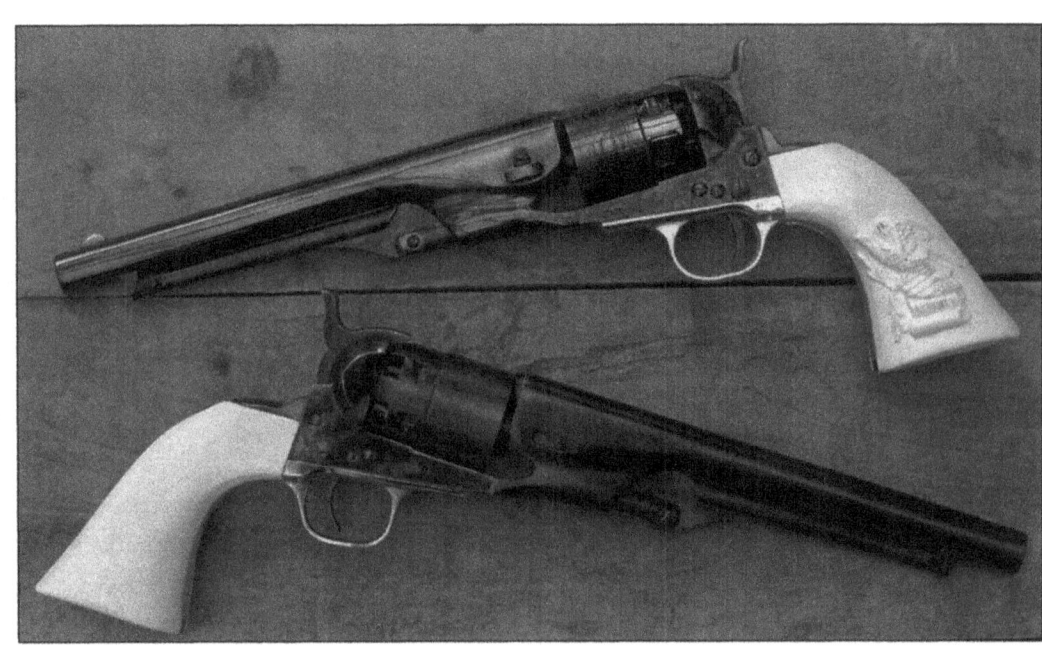

Gripmaker can dress up any single action with smooth or carved ivory-style grip panels. They are supplied slightly oversize for custom fitting.

Herrett's Stocks has been producing grips for two generations. These are checkered and smooth Detective Stocks on round-butted S&W N-frames.

rubber was banded in place, then left to dry overnight. The next day they were ready for final fitting. Carefully. Little's imitation stags have been fitted to a pair of 7 1/2-inch Cimarron .38-40 Model Ps by Tony Kojis, and both sixguns have been expertly tuned by Dave Sample. Replica sixguns simply don't get much better than this!

Herrett's Stocks: Rod Herrett continues to produce excellent stocks of walnut in many exotic woods for most double-action sixguns and semi-automatics. The first pair of custom grips I ever bought were Herrett's Trooper stocks for a Smith & Wesson N-frame more than 40 years ago. They still give excellent service. In addition to the Trooper for Smith & Wessons, Herrett's also offers the Detective for concealment use on both J- and K-frame Smiths. I have found this style to also work well on round-butted N-frames. Many of the currently produced 1911s are equipped with Herrett's grip panels of exotic woods, and those that I have that were not originally fitted with Herrett's grips certainly wear them now.

Rod Herrett is also offering smooth wooden stocks of walnut or several exotic woods for the Dan Wesson large-frame sixguns. They will fit either current production or early .44 Magnum, .41 Magnum, .45 Colt, or any of the SuperMag frames. Wesson sixguns do not have a grip frame and normally take a one-piece grip hollowed out for the grip frame stud to accept. Herrett's stocks are

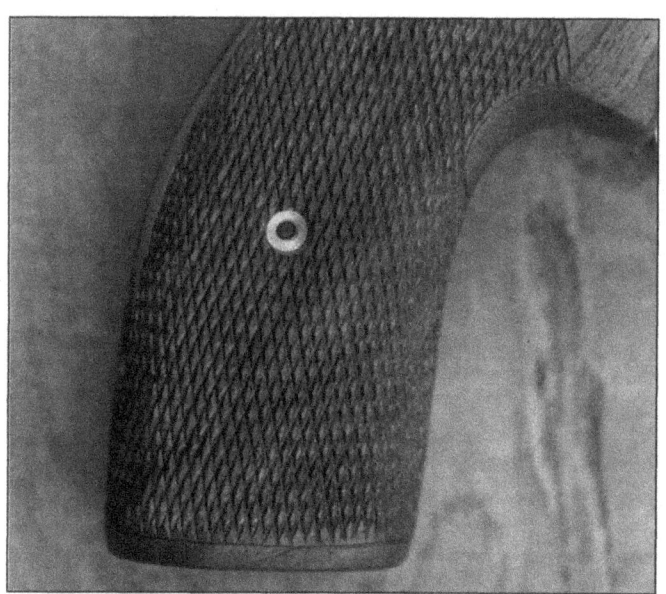

A close-up of the Herrett's Detective Stocks on an S&W N-frame reveals their compactness.

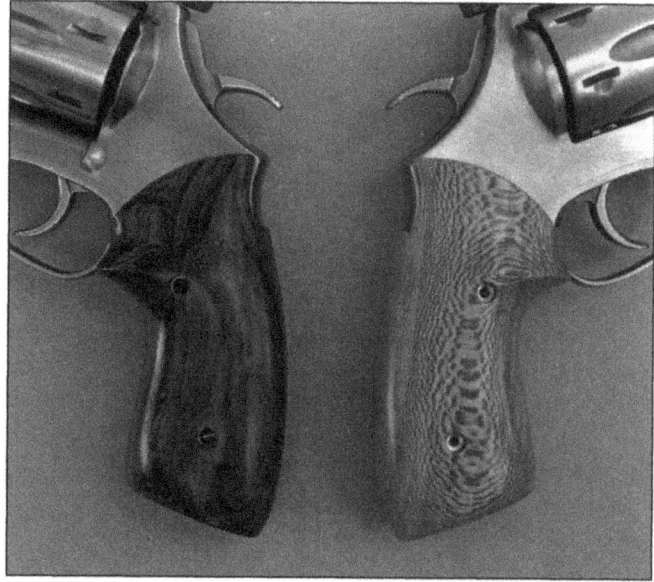

Herrett's Trooper stocks of exotic woods not only add a fancy touch to Dan Wesson sixguns, they are also highly functional.

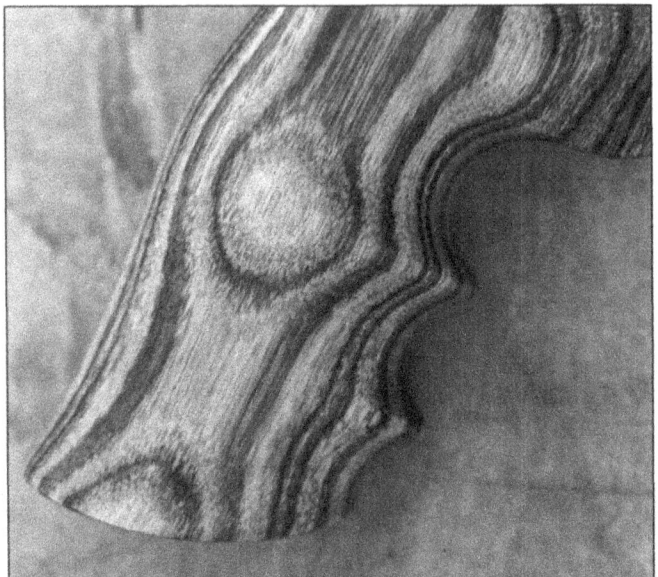

Hogue's finger grooved stocks help to offset the muzzle heavy feel of the current crop of heavy underlugged-barreled sixguns.

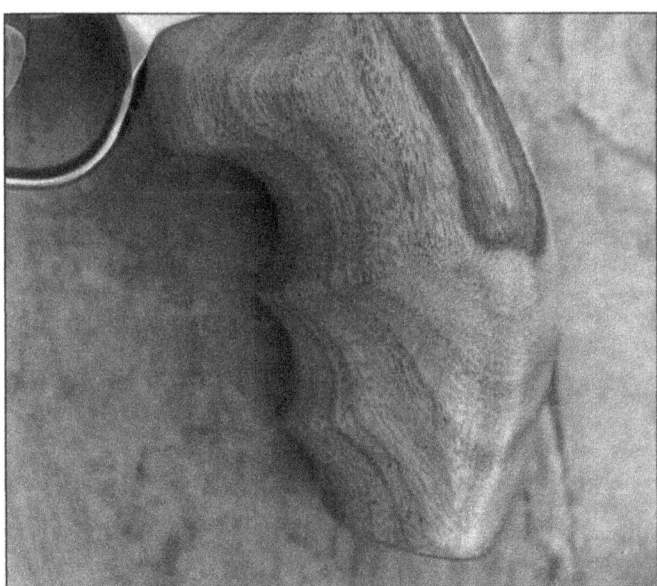

Finger grooved stocks can also be compact such as these Hogue's on a round-butted Smith & Wesson.

two-piece, ingeniously designed and held on securely with two screws. They install easily and if they don't line up the interior nut is backwards. Flip it and try again.

These are high-quality custom stocks offered in several woods. Presentation maple really looks good on a stainless Wesson, and such stocks are even more comfortable than the original stocks found on older Dan Wessons. They are loosely based on the Bill Jordan-style stocks, but the use of a stud instead of a grip frame allows them to fit the hands of us ordinary mortals who do not have Jordan's huge hands.

Hogue Grips: Guy Hogue originally started the business that bears his name to supply police and defensive-style grips for double-action revolvers. They have continually expanded their offering of grips to include all types of handguns. Grips with and without finger grooves are offered in both rubber and exotic woods. Many of the factory grips found on currently produced double-action sixguns are from Hogue. They are much more usable than the wooden stocks found on the guns in the 1980s in 1990s. While I am not normally a fan of finger grooves grips, I do find that Hogue's finger groove grips of exotic woods not only look great, they help control some of the heavyweight, hard-kickin', double-action sixguns available today. They are especially appreciated when

Dustin Linebaugh expertly fitted these Cimarron Cartridge Conversions, an 1860 .44 Colt and an 1851 .38 Long Colt with stocks of ivory micarta.

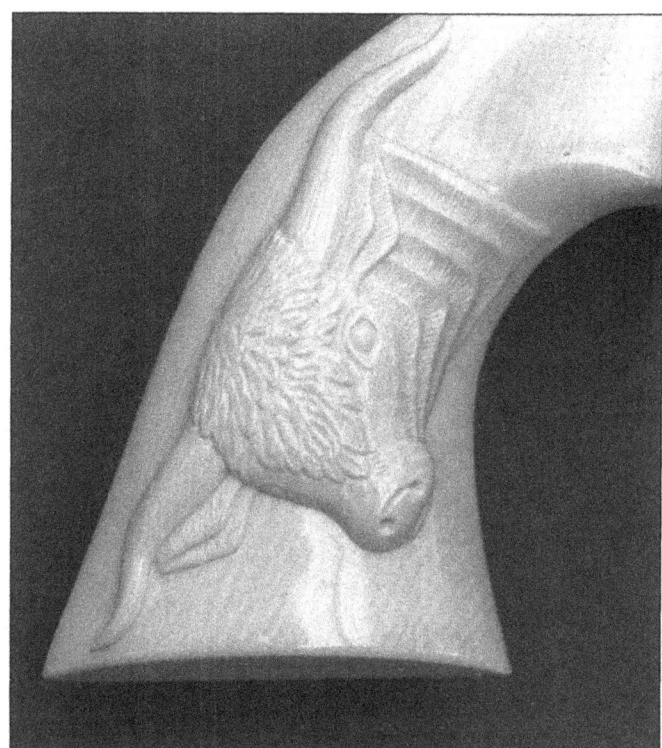

Carved steer head carried out in ivory on an engraved .45 Colt Single Action Army by Paul Persinger.

shooting those sixguns with long, 8-inch or more, heavy underlugged barrels. The newest addition to the double-action line of Hogue grips is the Bantam, a pebble-grained rubber grip of minimum size with finger grooves for S&W J-, K- and L- frame round butts. These are standard equipment on S&W's Scandium .357 Magnum J-frame. I don't think this little sixgun could be controlled without them.

In the past few years Hogue's has branched out, offering sixgun grips for both Colt and Ruger single actions. These grips are offered in exotic woods as well as both black and ivory micarta, and now in a cherry wood color. The line has now been expanded even further with grips in many materials available for the Ruger Bisley. A stainless-steel Blackhawk .45 to Bisley now wears Hogue's of black micarta. All of the Bisley grips I have encountered from Hogue's are well finished and fit extremely well for off-the-shelf grips.

Dustin Linebaugh: Dustin is the son of John Linebaugh of Linebaugh Custom Sixguns, so he has literally grown up around sixguns and sixgunners. The first time I met him he was all of about 6 years old and handling a Smith & Wesson .22 Kit Gun like an adult. He has worked on guns with his dad as well as furnishing the custom stocks for the five-shot .45s, .475s, and 500s from Linebaugh's shop.

As a grip maker, the younger Linebaugh demands the same close tolerances in ivory micarta and fancy woods his dad demands in metal. Linebaugh prefers to polish his custom grips to the grip frame and then refinish the frame after he has a perfect mating of metal and grip material. I recently had Dustin custom craft ivory micarta grips for a pair of Cimarron Colt Cartridge Conversions and found his work to be superb. The ivory micartas really move them up several notches on the sixgun ladder.

Micarta is a very tough material, so these are also an excellent choice to fit to a hard-workin', hard-kickin' sixgun such as a Linebaugh conversion to .475 or .500 on a Ruger, or a Freedom Arms big bore. Dustin can fit either the Bisley grip frame or the Freedom Arms grip frame to perfection.

Paul Persinger: The Colt Single Action Army is one of the few factory sixguns that comes with stocks that fit my hand. The only reason to replace them is to come up with a more exotic material than black rubber eagle grips or the extremely plain Jane stocks found on Third Generation Colts. Once I had that first pair of floral carved El Paso Saddlery holsters, the factory grips on my 7 1/2-inch Colts looked oh so plain. Something drastic had to be done.

The grip frames were pulled off and sent to Paul Persinger with instructions to provide one-piece ivory stocks with one set carved on the right panel and the other on the left. Persinger is another artist of tremendous talent in several mediums. His drawings are unbelievable. He can duplicate any of the carved ivory stocks that were offered by Colt on its cap and ball presentation pieces, and any of several well-known carvings found on Single Action Armies. Or, he can work from a picture or sketch.

Earlier I mentioned the Elmer Keith Grips for double-action revolvers. Keith also did the same thing with

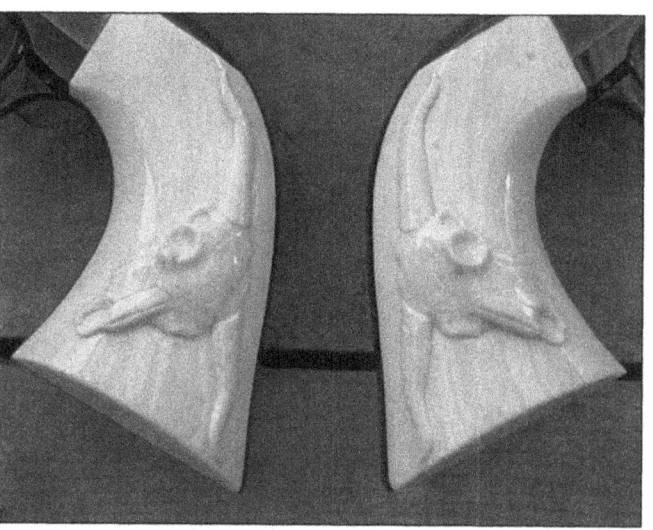

A matched pair of 7 1/2-inch Colt .45s deserve the best, and the best is carved ivory by Paul Persinger.

Bob Leskovec of Precision Pro duplicated these Elmer Keith stocks of carved ivory for a pair of S&W 4-inch .44 Specials.

his single-action sixguns. For these two 7 1/2-inch Colts, I went with the carved longhorn steer skulls as they not only look good, they also naturally fill in the crease in the shooting hand, making it much easier to control the recoiling sixgun. Persinger outdid himself with these stocks. The carving is carried out to perfection and, most importantly, the raw material he started with is of extremely high quality with lots of "marbled milk" showing. Tony Kojis, who fits grips for me often, looked at Persinger's work, studied it, removed the backstrap to look closer, and said, "This guy is the best I have ever seen!" A great tribute to Persinger from a fellow grip maker. Persinger also works with exotic woods and ram's horn. While Roy Fishpaw uses Dall sheep horn, Paul goes with bighorn sheep, resulting in the same straw-like translucent color but with black streaks. A true Western artist.

Precision Pro Grips: Bob Leskovec of Precision Pro Grips works with several media, including exotic woods, silver inlays, ivory, and acrylics, with both of the latter offered in carved motifs. My first stocks from Leskovec were Elmer Keith-style carved in ivory acrylic for an S&W Elmer Keith Commemorative 4-inch .44 Magnum and a 7 1/2-inch New Frontier .45 Colt. Then came a pair of ivory grip panels for an Ed DeLorge engraved 1911. There is ivory, and there is ivory, and the best grip makers look for ivory that is creamy or with a lot of grain showing or both. Leskovec shops carefully for his ivory.

At the beginning of this chapter, I mentioned the pair of 4-inch .44 Specials that have been expertly stocked by Precision Pro Grips. They are exquisite examples of the gripmakers art, and although I have said repeatedly that certain guns are really dressed up

Original stocks from one of Roy Rogers' movie sixguns? No, these grips are the Roy Rogers style by Precision Pro.

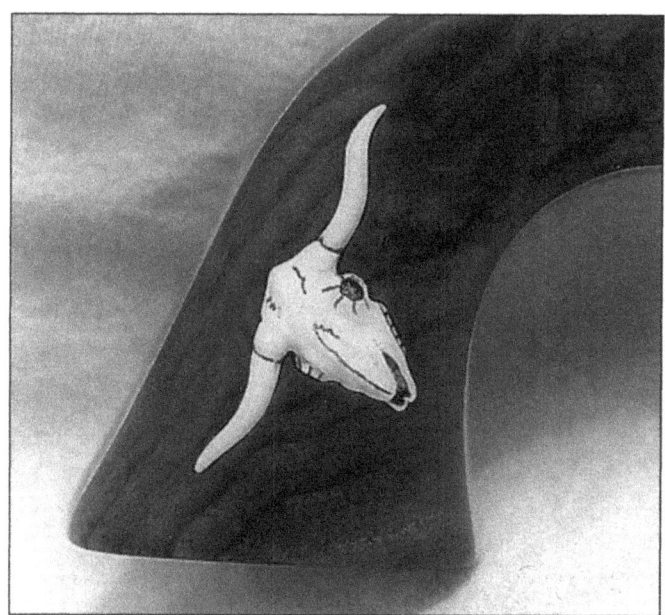

Bob Leskovec of Precision Pro fashioned these stocks of fancy walnut and then inlaid a steer horn carved of ivory.

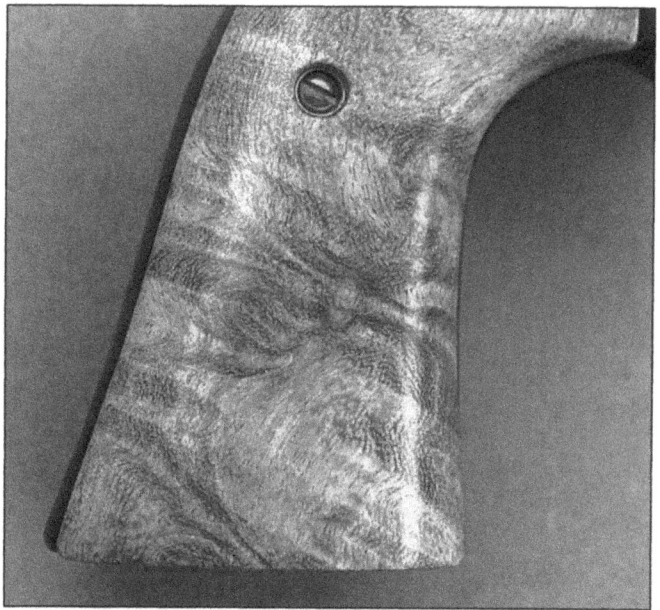

These Bisley Model grips of Burl mesquite have been expertly fitted to the grip. Frame by Scott Kolar of SK Custom Grips.

by certain grips, I must again say that this pair of .44 Special sixguns are now really special. However, I am afraid that I may have to finish this project by having both guns fully engraved. Such great grips deserve engraved sixguns.

We have mentioned several gripmakers' solutions to the difficulty in obtaining genuine stag horn for grips. Bob Leskovec takes a different path with stag, and not necessarily because of the shortage, but rather as a salute to the heroes of the "B" western. Roy Rogers packed sixguns with plastic stag grips in his many movies. Precision Pro Grips offers sixgunners a replica of the Roy Rogers grip expertly carved in acrylic panels. They look better than the originals, are certainly built more solidly, and will not crack or warp like the original plastic stags.

SK Custom Grips: We have mentioned some of the unique services offered by several grip makers and we can add Scott Kolar of SK Custom Grips to the top of the Unique List. I first "met" Kolar over the Net when he posted on my Web site that he would offer to refinish any Ruger stocks with a 2-for-1 offer. For anyone that would send in two pair, he would refinish one pair and keep the other pair as payment. I took him up on this offer, sending him four pair of Bisley and two pair of Vaquero stocks. The three pair that were returned were beautifully finished — so much so that, except for the factory medallions, one would doubt that they were original grips.

I have mentioned my dissatisfaction with the grips found on replica single actions. They fit extremely well, they feel good; however, the finish leaves me cold. Grips were pulled from Patersons, Walkers, Dragoons, 1851s, 1860s, and both Remington and Colt Single Action replicas. Some were refinished in walnut, others with an ebony color. The change in the personality of the sixgun

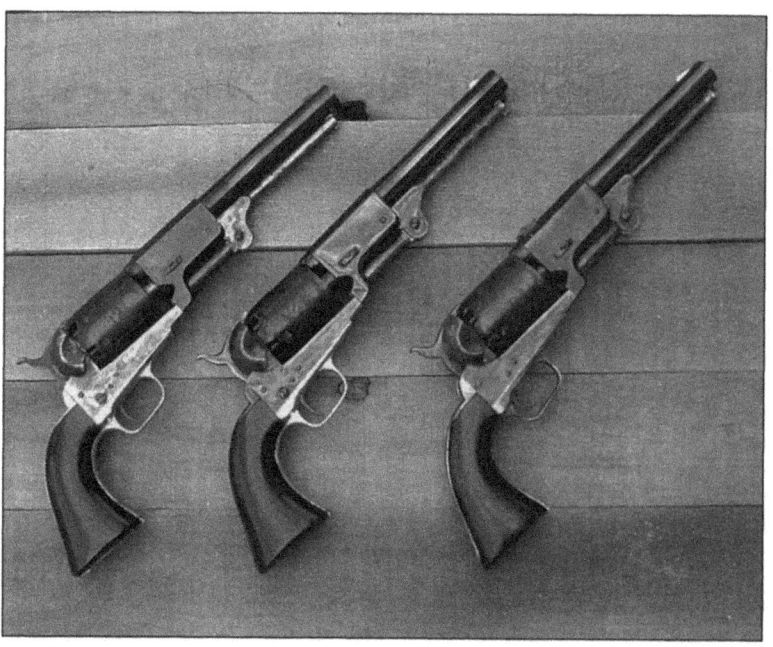

The stocks found on replica percussion revolvers, such as this pair and a spare of .44 Dragoons, deserve a better finish than the factory provides. Scott Kolar refinished all three of these in ebony. Great improvement.

Burl maple grips by Scott Kolar provide the finishing touch to a stainless-steel .45 Colt Ruger Blackhawk that has been fitted with Bisley Model grip frame, hammer, and trigger, as well as a #5 base pin from Belt Mountain.

was dramatic. Scott even managed to find some decent wood under some of the cherry-colored Italian stain.

SK Custom Grips also offers custom-made grips in some of the most beautiful wood available, such as flame-grained maple and burl mesquite. The color and figure in the latter definitely falls into the category of having to be seen to be believed.

TK Custom Grips: TK is Tony Kojis, who I have often mentioned as he is one who fits many of the custom grip panels, or old stags, I find to some of my sixguns. I quite often search out old grip panels at gun shows and they rarely fit the sixgun I want them on. A trip to TK takes care of that. He is also a fine gripmaker in his own right. For me, he has done stag, ivory and pearl. The first pair of grips he ever did for me were one-piece Pau Ferro on a 4 3/4-inch Colt Single Action. That was in 1970 and those one-piece grips, which are actually two pieces with a spacer in between, have never come apart. I can't say that about all other one-piece grips over the years.

Kojis has a method for attaching the panels to the spacer, which I of course cannot reveal, other than to say it works, is very durable, and is extremely strong and secure. He also came up with a pair of wraparound grips made of maple for the original Charter Arms Bulldog .44 Special and built them in such a way that they could be as small as possible and not crack under the stress of recoil. An added bonus with grips by TK is the fact that Tony is also an excellent single-action sixgunsmith and has often been able to bring sixguns to near perfection while stocking them.

There are three possible reasons, four if we include expense, why a shooter may not opt for custom grips. Although highly unlikely, said shooter may be one of those very rare individuals whose hand actually fits the generic grips offered by the factory. The possibility of this happening is about the same as winning the lottery. Secondly, the casual shooter may simply not care if the grips fit his hand or if the sixgun is given a little extra personality and customized according to his personal taste. Finally, one simply may not know what is available. Hopefully, we have at least addressed this final category.

Two by Tony. Tony Kojis crafted these staghorn grips on a 4 3/4-inch Colt New Frontier and one-piece stocks of Pau Ferro on a 4 3/4-inch .44 Special Colt Single Action. The latter grips have been in service for more than 30 years and have never loosened.

CHAPTER 14

EL PASO SADDLERY

"Out in the West Texas town of El Paso, I fell in love with a Mexican girl. Nighttime would find me in Rosie's Cantina, music would play and Felina would whirl." Who can forget those lyrics from Marty Robbins? Both Felina and Rosie's Cantina would lead to our hero's downfall as we soon hear as he mournfully relates his demise. "Down went his hand for the gun that he wore." The young cowboy survives the gunfight and runs but love brings him back to El Paso. As he returns he finds, "Off to my left there were five mounted cowboys; off to my left rode a dozen or more." The end was inevitable and the young cowboy dies in El Paso with one last kiss from Felina. The song may have been fiction, but it is very easy to conceive of this very event taking place in the history-rich town of El Paso, Texas.

It is not hard to imagine that both this young cowboy and the Arizona ranger with "The Big Iron On His Hip" (Robbins's other big hit) both procured their fast sixgun leather from El Paso Saddlery. The firm owned and operated now by Bobby McNellis is celebrating its 113th year of supplying quality leather to sixgunners, saddlemen, cowboys, hunters, outdoorsman, peace officers, and anyone who carries a sixgun or semi-automatic.

Rich history runs throughout the past of El Paso Saddlery with a cast of characters from its many years in business. Texas Ranger John Hughes, lawman Tom

The Tom Threepersons #1920 holster has been made by literally every manufacturer, however, none can surpass the beautiful rigs offered by El Paso, such as this fully carved outfit for the Smith & Wesson .357 Combat Magnum.

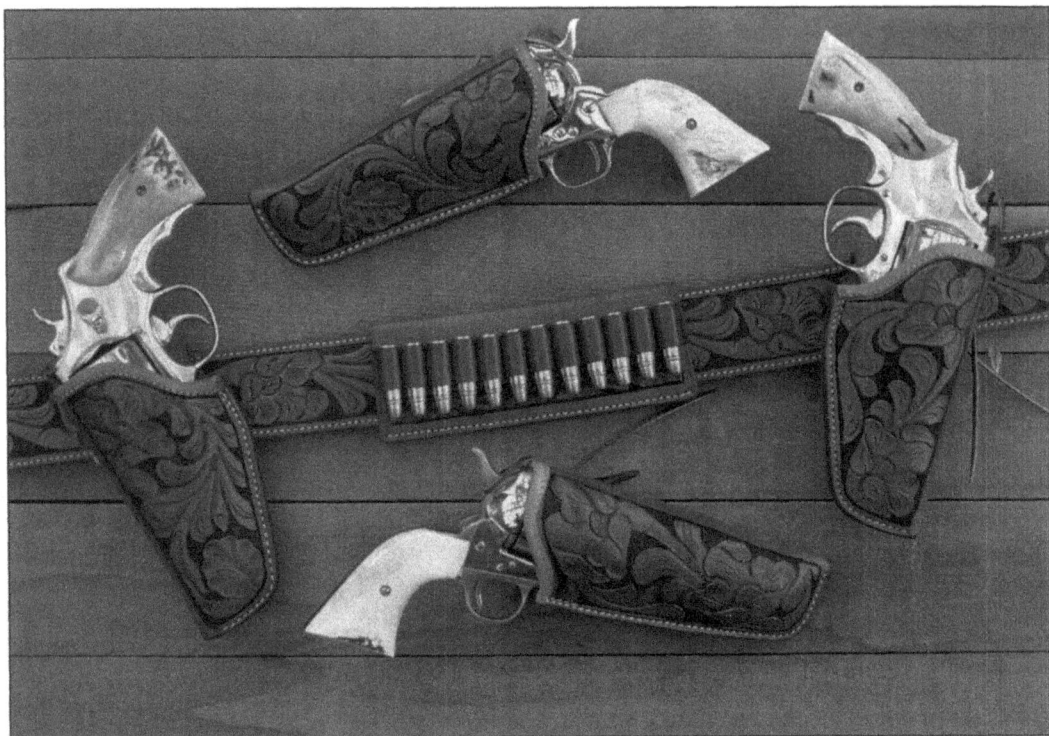

For packin' a pair of sixguns, be they Smith & Wesson 4-inch .44 Magnums or 4 3/4-inch Colt Single Action Army .45's, El Paso's #1920 performs the function perfectly and beautifully when fully carved.

Threepersons, outlaws John Wesley Hardin and Black Jack Ketchum, peace officer Pat Garrett, Doc Holliday, Gen. George Patton, Col. Charlie Askins, and Ed McGivern, fastest man who ever lived with a double-action sixgun until Jerry Miculek; they're just a few famous names connected with El Paso Saddlery. From the make-believe world of Hollywood, we can add in John Wayne, James Arness, Clint Eastwood, and Richard Boone. The easily recognizable rigs they wore to entertain us are also all now offered by El Paso Saddlery.

Bobby McNellis of El Paso Saddlery relates the following about El Paso: "In 1889 El Paso, Texas, was the most notorious town in the West. Gunfighters, gamblers, and outlaws alike found this border town an ideal haven. Its wide-open atmosphere gave rise to such popular pastimes as gambling and prostitution. Saloons lined the streets offering faro, poker, roulette, and craps. On Utah Street, only a few blocks from the original El Paso Saddlery shop at 400 El Paso Street, prostitutes could be found plying their trade around the clock. Only a block north, Dallas Stoudenmire, famed El Paso city marshal, shot three men in as many seconds. Another block farther is the spot where John Wesley Hardin was killed in 1895, and only steps away was the infamous Gem Saloon. It is here, according to legend, that Wyatt Earp witnessed the gunning down of two men in half an hour, then hastily left town abandoning his intention of applying for the city marshal's job.

In those early days the Saddlery's customers ranged from professional gunmen who needed sturdy holsters to house the tools of their trade, to cowboys seeking rugged

Western art at its best. El Paso's #1920 fully carved with a dyed background and custom made to fit a 4 3/4-inch Colt Single Action Army. Tom Threepersons's design wastes absolutely no leather.

When Southwestern pistoleros Tom Threepersons and Lee Trimble put their heads together, they came up with two great holster designs, the #1920 (top) and the #1930 Austin.

saddles for their ponies, to average citizens requiring nothing more than quality belts and leather goods. Among those customers numbered such men as John Wesley Hardin, John Selman, John Milton, Captain John R. Hughes of the Texas Rangers, Bat Masterson, Killing Jim Miller, George Scarborough, and Pat Garrett."

We can trace the roots of El Paso Saddlery back even farther than 1889 as it was in that year that the Andrews and Hill Leather Company became El Paso Saddlery. By 1889 much of the West had been tamed, but not the Southwest. The Mexican border from Texas through New Mexico and into Arizona would remain more than a little wild well into the 20th century and, in fact, is still so in many places today. The phrase "a man to ride the river with" comes from the harshness of the area and having a compagnero, preferably an accomplished pistolero, that could be counted on to be just as tough as the country and its conditions.

El Paso was large enough for two leather shops, El Paso Saddlery and S.D. Myres. Eight years after El Paso Saddlery formed, S. D. "Tio Sam" Myers opened his leather shop in Sweetwater, Texas. That was 1897. The companies would operate separately until the 1920s, when El Paso became part of S.D. Myers after the latter had moved from Sweetwater to El Paso.

In the 1970s, S.D. Myers was sold and moved its operation to Oklahoma. At the same time, Bobby McNellis purchased the El Paso segment of the company and kept it in El Paso, making it the oldest continuously operating company in the city. McNellis modernized the company by adding the latest designs in sixgun leather to go with the western and military holsters being produced by El Paso Saddlery. A comparison of the current El Paso Saddlery catalog with an old S.D. Myers catalog also reveals that McNellis did more than simply purchase El Paso Saddlery. He also obtained the holster patterns of S.D. Myers, which disappeared shortly after the move out of Texas. Sixgunners can now not only find the excellent designs of both companies under the El Paso Saddlery banner, a comparison of the current product with the older versions will reveal that today's leather is not only of better quality, it is also better crafted.

Every bit as practical and beautiful as the #1920 Tom Threepersons is the #1930 Austin, here shown with a 4 3/4-inch .45 Colt Single Action Army from the same time frame as Threepersons and Trimble.

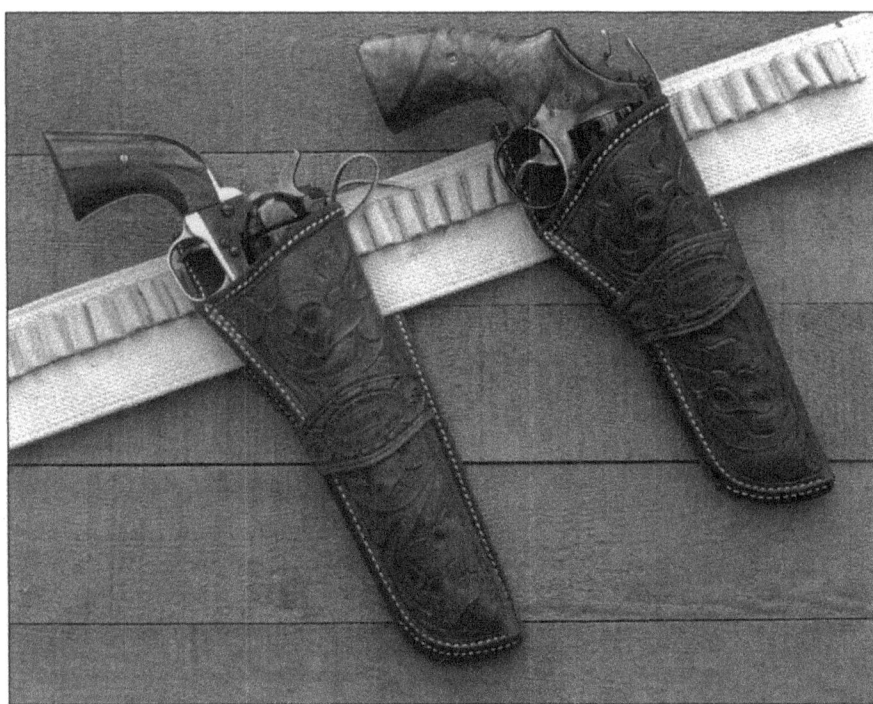

Both the #1920 and the #1930 were made to slant backwards for speed when drawing. The author finds the #1930 more practical for field use when made to hang straight. Sixguns are a 7 1/2-inch Ruger and a 6 1/2-inch Smith & Wesson, both chambered in .44 Magnum.

In 1916, a second lieutenant ordered what would become one of the most recognized sixguns in history. Three decades later he would be one of the most famous leaders of World War II. Who has not seen photos of the colorful General George S. Patton wearing his fully engraved, ivory-stocked, 4 3/4-inch Colt Single Action Army .45 Colt? That sixgun became the symbol of his leadership and every soldier could tell by the ivory gripped pistol that Patton was out front. Patton purchased his beautifully ornate .45 Colt from the Shelton Payne Arms Co. of El Paso. The silver-plated sixgun, serial number 332088, was shipped on March 5, 1916. Four days later Mexican Revolutionaries crossed the border at Columbus, New Mexico. Patton had his sixgun when he joined the punitive expedition under Black Jack Pershing.

Photos exist of Patton wearing his Peacemaker in Mexico, but it is difficult to ascertain what type of holster he is wearing. Not so during his World War II service as a great leader of men and tank commander extraordinaire. In 1935, Patton ordered a second sixgun while stationed in Hawaii. This sixgun, an ivory-stocked, blued 3 1/2-inch Smith & Wesson .357 Magnum, was to supplement his Peacemaker .45.

Sometime in the late 1930s, Patton entered the S.D. Myers shop in El Paso to order leather for his soon-to-be-famous sixguns. For each sixgun he ordered two holsters, one left and one right hand for the Colt and also for the Smith & Wesson so he could wear either sixgun on either side. The outlines of the two sixguns are quite different and the holsters were formed to each individual sixgun size, so it was not a matter of one size fits all. We know from the memory of a worker in the shop at the time that two of each were ordered. Photos that survive also showing him wearing the guns on both sides. Today one set is in the military museum in Fort Knox while the other remains with the family.

The holsters were purchased in plain brown finish with a matching military style belt about 2 inches in width. In addition to the holsters and belt, Patton also ordered a 12-loop cartridge slide for .45 Colt cartridges, and a handcuff case that was used to carry a compass. The holsters were patented by Myers in 1938 and the Border Patrol Model holster was standard equipment for most peace officers until well into the last half of the 20th century.

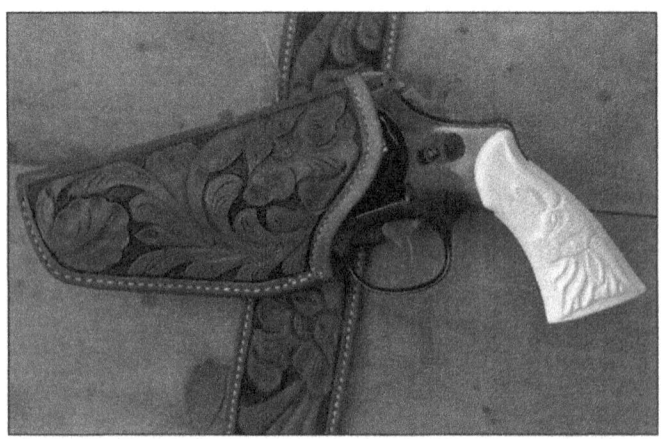

A triple salute to Elmer Keith. A holster he would prefer: El Paso's floral-carved #1920 carrying a 4-inch Smith & Wesson .44 Special with carved ivory grips Keith-style by Bob Leskovec.

The #5 Patton holster, along with the military style belt, still exists in the catalog of El Paso Saddlery. It is available as the original in plain finish, or can be ordered basket stamped or floral carved. The shank of this historically important leather is metal lined so it can be bent to conform to the hip contour. It has a safety strap that can be fastened out of the way around the body of the holster, and also has a sewn-in muzzle plug to prevent dirt and debris from entering the holster from the bottom. Available with a smooth lining to protect the single or double action sixgun, as well as the semi-autos for which it is made, the Patton holster gives me a special feeling of connecting with history any time I buckle it on and strap in an engraved and ivory-stocked Colt Single Action .45.

Several years before Patton entered the El Paso leather shop, another famous sixgunner brought his design for a radical new holster to El Paso and Tio Sam Myers. We back up again to 1916 and the raids across the border by revolutionaries. This time it was at Glenn Springs, Texas, and Lee Trimble was a ranger at the time. Because of the lawlessness around the border country, another sixgunner came from Canada, where he had been in the Northwest Mounted Police, and hooked up with Trimble. The second pistolero was Tom Threepersons.

These two famous lawmen, as many of us do today, sat around discussing sixguns and leather one evening. At the time, peace officering had been changing rapidly, with officers changing four-legged critters to four wheels. Wide belts with two rows of cartridge loops and Mexican or Cheyenne style holsters worked well on horseback, but not when seated in an automobile. Threepersons and Trimble were about to change this.

They both decided less was better and came up with almost identical designs. Threepersons took his design to S.D. Myers in 1920, while Trimble went to Austin and stopped in the shop of W.R. Brill. In all probability, each only expected to see one holster made to fit their individual needs. For both it was essential that as little leather as possible be used to carry out their ideas. Lightweight and quick access to the sixgun were of paramount importance.

Up to this time, sixgun leather was built for maximum protection with most of the gun covered by leather. Trimble and Threepersons cut away all excess leather and raised the holster high on the belt. The hammer and trigger guard are completely exposed with only the cylinder and barrel being encased in leather. The front of the trigger guard rides on a thick welt sewn in between the layers of leather along the back edge of the holster body.

To eliminate any movement of holster on the belt, the belt loop in Threepersons's design is simply folded over and stitched to the back of the holster, making it very tight. The sixgun is formed to the leather so it rides tight, but a smooth, quick draw is not impeded. To also aid in the draw, the holster was slanted with the muzzle to the rear. This has since become known as the FBI slant. One thing was added to Trimble's holster, either by himself or Brill, and that was the addition of very trim back flap. Instead of a sewn belt loop, the

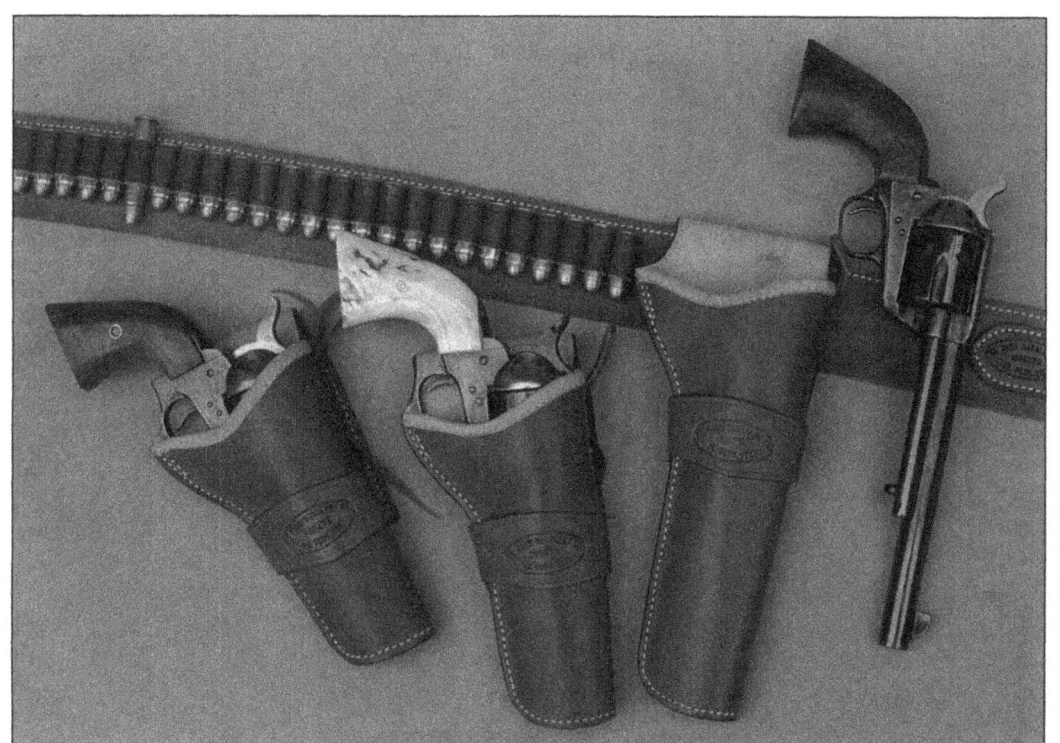

El Paso's Duke is the company's rendition of the holster rig carried by John Wayne for several decades. Shown with Great Western and Colt Single Actions with 4 3/4-, 5 1/2-, and 7 1/2-inch barrels, they make practical field rigs.

Brill/Trimble design used a loop around the holster that fastened to the back flap at a position that was made to conform tightly to whatever belt size was being used. Both designs work fine on a cartridge belt while the Threepersons design works better than the Trimble design when worn on a pants belt.

Both designs, the 1920 Threepersons, and the 1930 Austin, are still found in the El Paso Saddlery catalog. They are, at least to my way of thinking, the two best holster designs ever to come from the mind of man. For decades the Threepersons was worn by thousands of peace officers, especially when the sixgun needed to be concealed. It was the favorite holster of the FBI. It has been copied by every leather manufacturer since the 1920s and was modified slightly by Elmer Keith to become the #120 from the old George Lawrence Co.

The Threepersons is probably even more practical as an outdoorsman's leather than as a peace officer's holster. Light in weight, rides high and secure and, combined with a cartridge belt, makes a great rig for the handgun hunter as it packs a big sixgun as well as one can be carried. No one makes the Threepersons better than El Paso Saddlery. This most famous of all holsters is available for sixguns or semi-automatics in plain, basket, or floral design, with a safety strap or hammer thong, and in the regular muzzle to the rear slant or made to hang straight. For hunters who carry a long-barreled sixgun especially, whether on horseback or in and out of a vehicle, the Threepersons can be ordered in a crossdraw mode. It is the best way short of a shoulder holster to pack an 8 3/8-inch Smith & Wesson. To protect the sixgun's finish, all versions are furnished lined only.

The 1930 Austin also comes lined only in plain, border-stamped, basket-stamped, or floral-carved designs. For use on a cartridge belt I actually like this design even better than the 1920 Threepersons. It has a "Texas Ranger" look and with the back flap simply seems to ride better for me on a wide belt. Either design is a sixgun carrying masterpiece.

Whatever the design, all El Paso Saddlery holsters are crafted the same way. First, the basic holster is cut out of the best leather available and all edges are beveled and hand burnished. If lining is being used it is then sewn in and in many models, such as the Threepersons and Duke, rolled over the edges and sewn so it cannot separate from the main body of the holster. The holster is then sewn or laced together, formed to the exact model of sixgun it will carry, then oiled or dyed. Most models are offered in russet brown or black. No vat dipping at El Paso. All carving and stamping is done the old-fashioned way, by hand. El Paso stamping and floral carving is the finest available anywhere, with most holsters and belts available in any one of seven versions: plain, border stamped, basket stamped, floral,

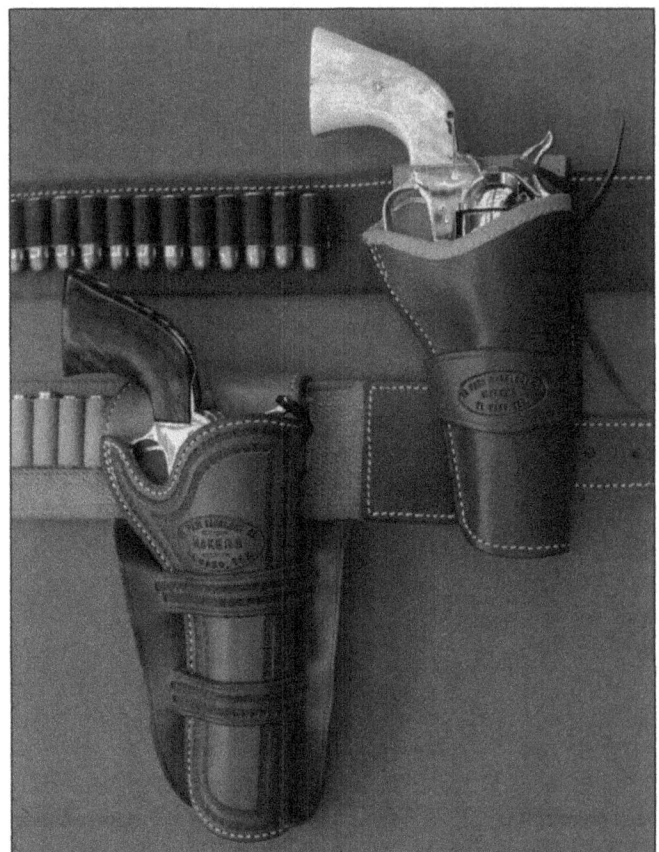

El Paso's Duke (top) compared to the #1880. The former allows quicker access to hammer and grip frame.

plus swirl and fishscale stamping patterns, and the rugged-looking rough-out in which the leather is reversed so the smooth side is inside.

I doubt that that many sixgunners have heard of the name of Adan Saez. But many have seen his work as he is a true artist working in leather. Saez is the number one leather carver at El Paso Saddlery, and in fact, until very recently, has been its only leather carver. He has now been joined by a young man named Manny Aguirre. Aguirre started as an apprentice and is now a fully fledged carver of beautiful Western art in leather.

The past three S.A.S.S. (Single Action Shooting Society) regional cowboy shoots I have attended have all found me searching out the El Paso Saddlery tent on sutler's row. Each of those trips have found me coming away with both a right-hand and left-hand fully floral carved set of holsters for Colt Single Actions. First came a pair of 1897 Sweetwaters for 7 1/2-inch Colts; then two 4 3/4-inch versions of the Cheyenne holster as made by F.A. Meanea in the 1880s; and finally I just returned from Range War at Tin Star Ranch where I found a matched pair of 1930 Austin's in extra fancy floral carving. I was also pleased to know that these were the first items in my collection of working West-

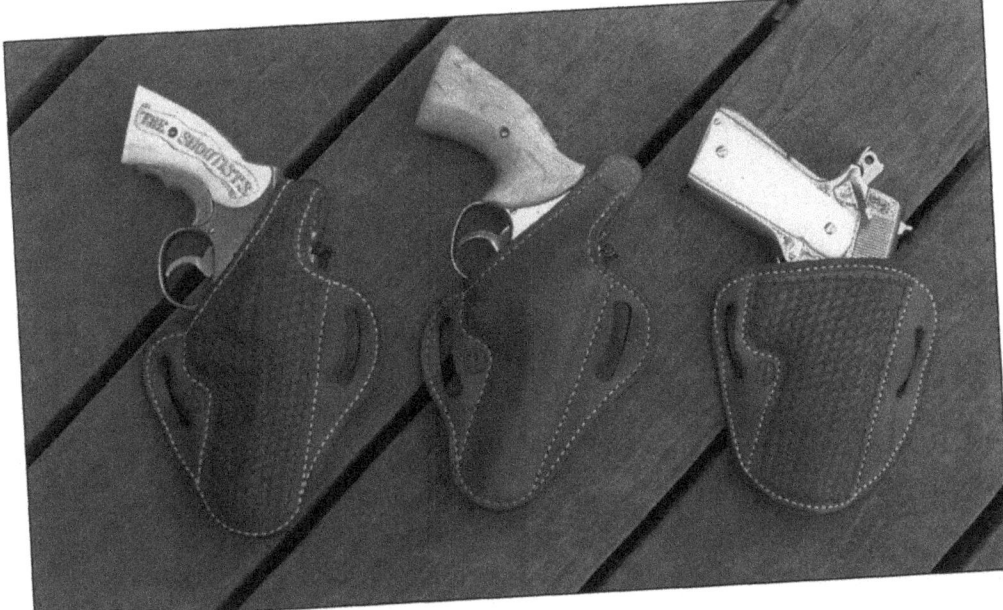

Whether used with a double-action sixgun, such as the 4-inch S&W .44 Special or Magnum, or a semi-automatic Colt Commander, El Paso's #77 Tortilla carries high, tight to the body, and secure.

ern art created by Manny Aquirre. Whether it's standard or floral carving, floral carving with a dyed background, or extra fancy floral carving, and whether the work is done by the old master or the new kid on the block, El Paso Saddlery can provide shooters with all manner of leather representing true works of Western art that are offered at highly affordable prices. In the space allotted we cannot cover every rig offered by El Paso but we can cover some of the most popular, and especially those with which I am most familiar.

Rigs with a Western flair

This is probably the most popular category of El Paso Saddlery leather. At the top of this class we have the aforementioned #1920 Threepersons and #1930 Austin. Also very popular and very practical is the #44 Duke. This holster and belt combination is patterned after the holster created by Ed Bohlin and worn by John Wayne from the *Tall in the Saddle* in 1944 through his last picture, *The Shootist*, in the 1976. The El Paso rendition has a rough-out belt with full cartridge loops, while the holster, fully lined with a minimum back flap, hangs straight. It is a heavy-duty rig for single- and double-action sixguns.

When I first started shooting in the 1950s, another young sixgunner was making his mark in Hollywood with the Hollywood Fast Draw holster. Arvo Ojala not only provided a low-hanging buscadero rig with a metal lined holster to allow a Colt Single Action Army to be cocked in the holster for an extremely fast draw, he was also teaching the stars how to handle a sixgun. Ojala was the man who stepped out on the dusty streets of Dodge City every Saturday night to face Marshal Matt Dillon in the early days of *Gunsmoke*. Ojala made

El Paso's #88 Street Combat works as well with single-action sixguns as it does with double-action revolvers or semi-automatics. They are shown with the #77 for comparison.

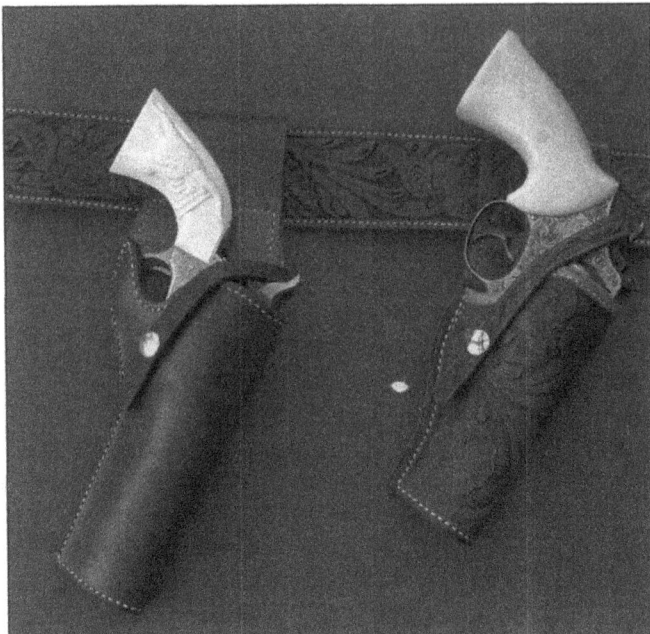

In 1935 soon to be General George Patton ordered the #5 Border Patrol holster that carried his Colt Single Action Army all through World War II. It evolved into the modern version of the Border Patrol rig, shown with a Smith & Wesson, that would become the standard peace officer's holster in the middle of the 20th century.

Dillon's rig as well as the unique rig worn by Paladin in *Have Gun, Will Travel*, one-half hour earlier. El Paso Saddlery has been commissioned by Ojala to continue to produce both the original Model #1 as worn by James Arness and Richard Boone's Paladin rig.

Everyday packin' iron rigs

A majority of states now have concealed weapons license laws that allow concealed carry once the applicant passes an FBI background check. This has made concealment rigs in high demand. In addition to the #1920, El Paso offers two thoroughly modern rigs with the #77 Tortilla, a pancake-style holster with a thumb-break release, and the #88 Street Combat. Both rigs ride high on the belt and out of the way. Lining is standard on both. The #88 does not have a retaining strap, but rather holds the sixgun or semi-auto by tension that is maintained by metal in the muzzle end of the holster. Simply remove the gun and squeeze the holster together to increase the retention security. Both are good rigs for wearing under a jacket or suit coat.

The U.S. Army influence

The #1911 Patton is the #1940 standard World War II G.I. holster with a swivel fitted, while the #1942 is a shoulder rig of the type worn by tank crews in Patton's Army. Going back to World War I we find the #1917, a half-flap holster for Colt and Smith & Wesson sixguns. As we keep going back for flap styles, we find the full-flap Civil War and Frontier #1860 for sixguns, and the #1880 Cavalry holster with a half flap and designed to ride crossdraw style on a military belt.

Rigs from the 19th century

El Paso Saddlery has a big advantage over the other firms that offer traditional leather. The others have had to research, but El Paso has the original patterns going back to the 1880s. Chronologically, we find the #1849, that rides high and conforms to the slim outlines of cap and ball sixguns; the #1870 Slim Jim, a most practical rig for carrying a single action and the rig that ushered in the era of the gunfighter; the #1880, a Mexican loop holster with two loops around the body of the holster; and the #1890, with one loop that is riveted to the back flap. The #1880-S and #1890-S are the two latter rigs with more leather cut away from the trigger guard and hammer. This style was worn by Texas Ranger Capt. John R. Hughes. The 1897 Sweetwater, named after the town and year in which S.D. Myers started his leather-making firm, consists of a low-riding Mexican-style holster with a T-shaped loop that goes around the main part of holster body and also around the bottom of the holster. It's a very practical way to carry a long-barreled single-action sixgun.

One of the most comfortable ways to carry a 7 1/2-inch single action is the Wes Hardin, which is a crossdraw Slim Jim style with three rows of two cartridges each on the body of the holster. The Cheyenne, a fully lined straight-drop holster matched up with a 3-inch lined cartridge belt, is reminiscent of the rig worn by

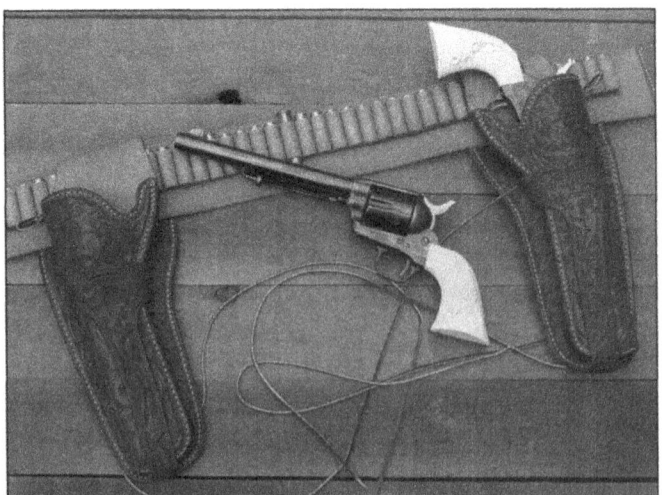

A pair of El Paso's #1897 Sweetwaters carry Taffin's 7 1/2-inch Colt Single Action Army .45s with ivory stocks by Paul Persinger. When worn all day, the web belt proves to be more comfortable than leather.

Truly authentic old West leather carrying a pair of 4 3/4-inch Colt Single Action Army .45s, El Paso's floral-carved Cheyennes.

Theodore Roosevelt in the 1880s, while the Doc Holliday shoulder rig was inspired by Val Kilmer's excellent portrayal of the dentist turned gunslinger.

Want to carry your Hog-Leg shoulder style but remain traditional? El Paso offers three choices, the Tombstone Speed Rig, a skeleton holster with a back flap, small toe to accept the end of the barrel, and a leather lined spring clip around the cylinder; the #1879 Texas, a straight-hanging-under-the-arm pouch holster; and the #1895 Hardin, patterned after the rig worn by the infamous gunfighter, complete with cartridge loops sewn on the shoulder strap.

El Paso offers a full line of belts to carry its leather. The #1 Money Belt is made by folding over a wide piece of leather and then sewing it on one side and the two ends leaving an opening for inserting coins. The #2 Texan is offered lined or of heavyweight single thickness complete with full cartridge loops, and there are several extra-wide belts for carrying rifle cartridges, "modern" bottle-necked bolt gun cartridges or the Frontier straight-sided Sharps cases, or a combination of rifle and sixgun cartridges. A most comfortable option from El Paso is a cartridge belt of the web or canvas style as worn by the military in the 1880s. These conform to the body and are probably the most comfortable ever devised.

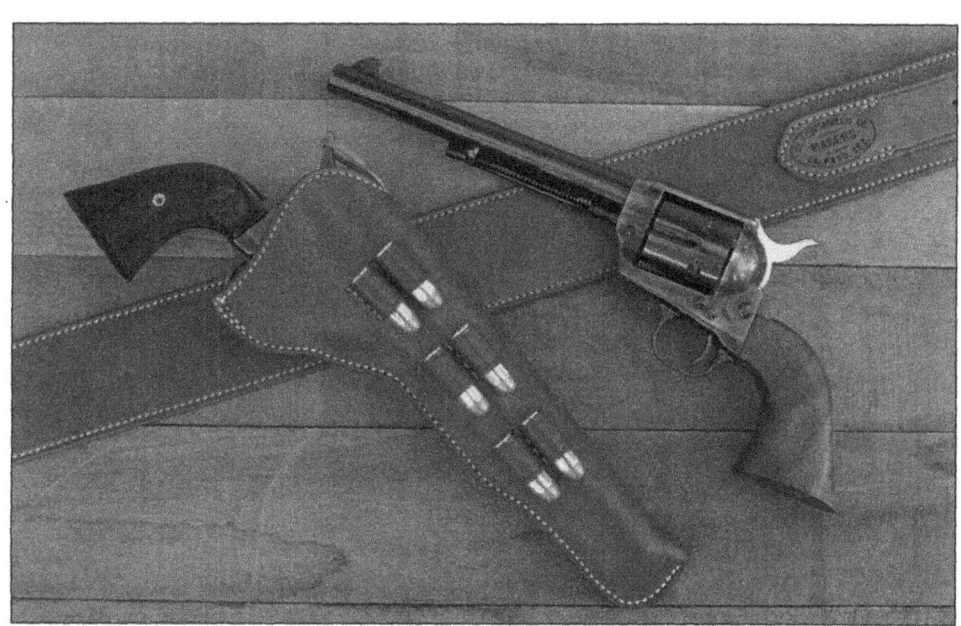

This Slim Jim-style holster with six cartridge loops is the 1895 Hardin and is named after the notorious gunfighter, John Wesley Hardin.

CHAPTER 15

HANDGUN RIGS

Cheap is definitely too expensive when it comes to buying tires, brakes, parachutes, firearms, and holsters. An expensive firearm deserves the best care, and that care will be delivered by a well-designed holster made of the best available materials and crafted by experts who understand what a holster should do and what it must not do. A properly treated firearm will last a lifetime and then some.

The same is true of holsters. Holsters are highly subjective items, perhaps even more so than sixguns and semi-automatics. When it was time for me to choose my first holster, it was relatively simple. The three big manufacturers were George Lawrence, S.D. Myres, and H.H. Heiser with all representing the best quality it was possible to obtain. However, my local dealer only handled George Lawrence. Today's shooters have a much more difficult time. All three of the 1950s major purveyors of leather are gone, but there are dozens of excellent leather craftsman out there with everything from one–man shops, to mom-and-pop operations, to large companies.

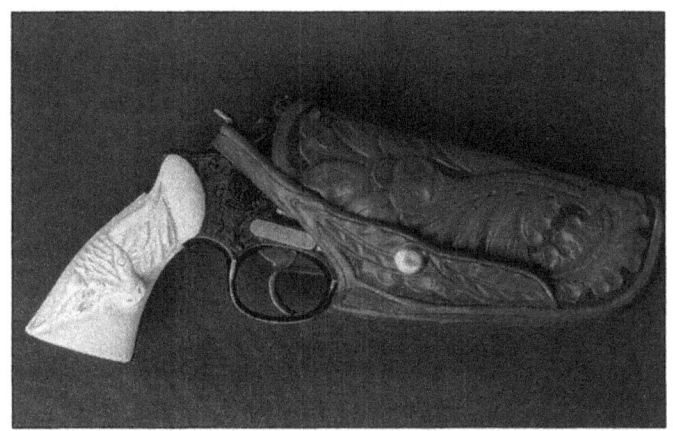

When Elmer Keith went fancy he used this fully carved holster with his fully engraved 4-inch Smith & Wesson .44 Magnum, with carved steer head ivories.

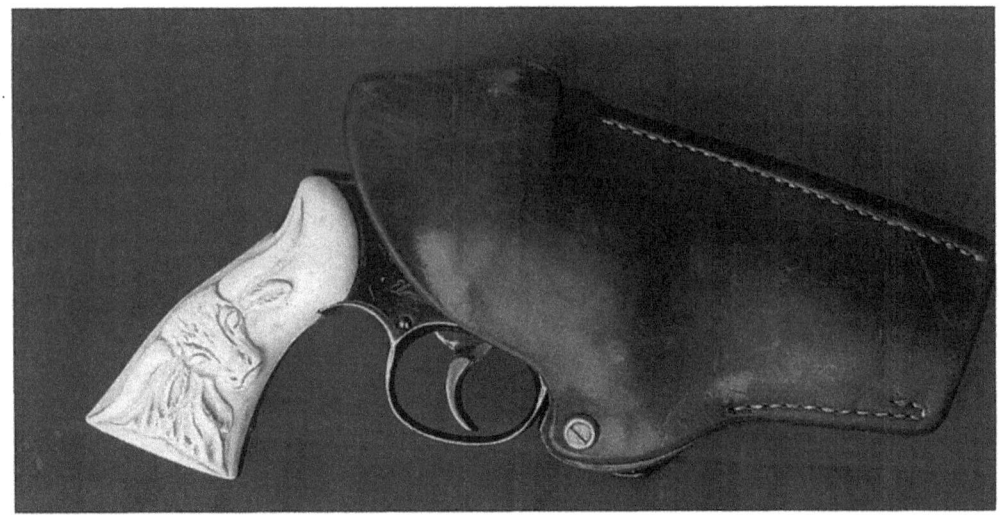

Elmer Keith's everyday packin' rig was this custom holster with a screw for adjusting tension and covered hammer to protect the jacket lining. The sixgun shown is Keith's standard blue 4-inch .44 Magnum with carved ivory grips.

Two practical rigs for packin' .45 semi-automatics concealed: Bianchi's Askins Avenger, with Kimber CDP; and Derry Gallagher's Jeffe carrying a Kimber Compact.

What follows herein is not meant to be an exhaustive treatise of all the great leather available. (I again recommend my first two books: *Big Bore Sixguns* and *Action Shooting Cowboy Style* for more information on leather other than that covered here.) Instead, we will look at some of the leather that I have used successfully for concealed carry, hunting, hiking, backpacking, camping, or just plain old-fashioned woods bumming, which can take place not only in the woods, but sagebrush deserts, rolling foothills, lofty mountains and in the pines. Different situations and handguns will require different holsters but the need always remains the same. The holster must provide comfort, security and, most of the time, easy accessibility. Comfort will depend largely upon each individual, and our choice will also depend upon how we are moving about, be it on foot, by horseback, or in a vehicle.

Any successful holster must retain the handgun by either having a safety strap, thong, or a very tight fit. The best retaining device, or at least the most convenient, is what is known as a safety strap. It consists of sturdy piece of leather that goes over the hammer and then fastens to the front of the holster with a dot snap. It is easily unfastened and can be folded behind the belt when its use is not necessary. I also like the hammer thong, especially for single-action sixguns. However, it can be hard to release in cold weather with equally cold fingers. It is the most unobtrusive of the over-the-hammer style and does not detract from the artistic beauty of the holster itself.

Not using the safety strap can be disastrous to a hunting trip. When in Africa I shot a warthog early on and placed my scoped Freedom Arms in its shoulder holster, leaving it unsnapped. When I bent over to look for the bullet that had exited the warthog and plowed into the mud, my sixgun slipped out of its holster and the scope hit the only large rock around. Fortunately I had backups.

Bianchi: Named after the old pistolero Col. Charles Askins, the Askins Avenger was originally designed for carrying that most serious of all defensive sidearms, the 1911 Government Model .45. Askins knew hand-

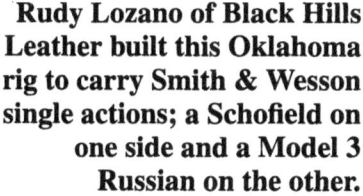

Rudy Lozano of Black Hills Leather built this Oklahoma rig to carry Smith & Wesson single actions; a Schofield on one side and a Model 3 Russian on the other.

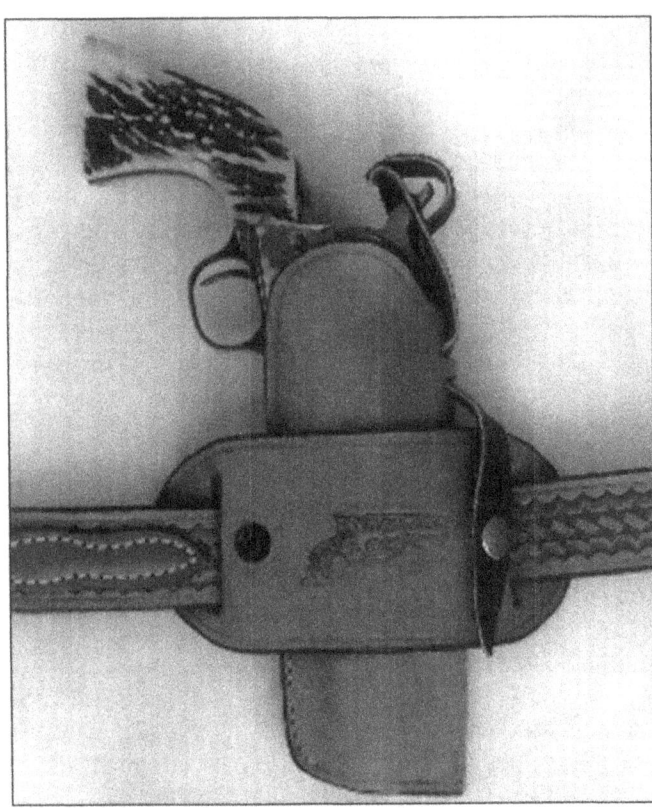

Originally offered as the Texas Hi-Rider by Texas Longhorn Arms, this most practical holster is now offered by Ted Blocker.

guns and carried one in serious situations most of his life. He literally did it all in his lifetime and survived several wars and numerous gunfights along the Mexican Border. He knew what worked. He should have died in a gunfight. Instead he spent several years, as did Elmer Keith, lying in bed as the victim of a stroke.

The Askins Avenger has several features that make it special. First, there is a molded-in sight channel. I like an easy-to-see flat black post front sight on many of my big-bore guns. However, this often presents a problem in a conventional holster. With the Bianchi Sight Channel the front sight does not dig into the leather, thus there is no "fuzz" attached to the front sight when the pistol is drawn. With its slot on the back edge of the holster and a sewed-in tunnel on the back of the holster proper, the Avenger rides close to the body. The top edge of the holster is leather, reinforced to keep it open and to allow easy re-holstering. Finally, a leather security strap is attached to the back of the holster with a dot snap and a slot that goes over the pistol's hammer. This is easily removable if not desired. The Avenger is a favored rig for semi-autos.

Black Hills Leather: This outfit is probably best known for its western gear, but Black Hills Leather also provides excellent concealed-carry leather. A prime example is the BH49 slide for the 1911. This is a two-slot design, fully lined, and hand molded to the exact gun it is to carry. Rudy Lozano of Black Hills also wisely finishes this rig without resorting to oils so there are no stains that will appear on clothing with its use. It's a good rig for minimum bulk with a 1911 or any other semi-auto carry.

Bart Ballew of Circle Bar T provided this unique set, with carving by Marty Overstreet for Cactus Tubbs.

When Navy Arms introduced the S&W New Model .44 Russian, and at about the same time, Smith & Wesson came forth with the .45 Schofield Model 2000, I contacted Lozano and we agreed that the Oklahoma Rig in black leather would be a proper sheath for this pair of single action Smiths. Rudy turned out a most beautiful outfit with a fully lined cartridge belt and twin holsters both made to hang straight. The holsters are of the Mexican style with two loops around the holster body, they have a full back flap, and are also fully lined. Both holsters and the cartridge belt are finished with a double border stamp, and then dyed black. The Navy Arms New Model Russian fitted with Eagle's UltraIvory grips rides in the right-handed holster while the similarly gripped Smith & Wesson Model 2000 Schofield nestles in the left-hand holster. A rig and two sixguns that any shooter can take great pride in.

Ted Blocker: In the 1980s, Bill Grover of Texas Longhorn Arms not only came up with a great sixgun with the Improved Number Five, he also supplied great leather to carry it, the Texas High-Ride holster. Unfortunately, TLA's doors are closed and if you can find one of its sixguns or High-Rider rigs you have virtually struck gold. The sixguns may be gone, but Ted Blocker is offering the Texas High-Ride.

Consisting of a belt slide with two loops and separate holster body that is accepted by the belt slide, the Texas High-Ride is convenient, secure, and rides high and comfortable. If it is necessary to do so, the holster body can be removed from the belt slide by unsnapping the loop along the front edge of the holster while leaving the slide on the belt. The holster can be worn butt to front or back on either side with the same rig, which works for concealment, hunting, or general field use.

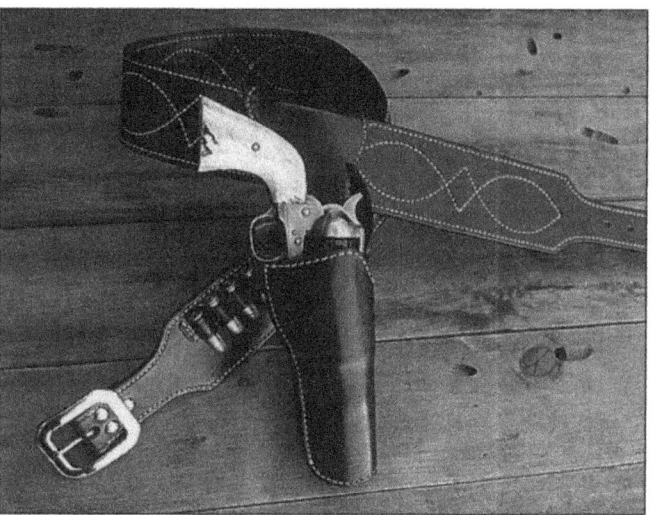

Andy Anderson was a pioneer leather worker in the 1950s and 1960s and one can see his rig often on the hips of such stars such as James "The Virginian" Drury, Steve McQueen, and Clint Eastwood. This Andy Anderson rig was faithfully duplicated by Walt Ostin.

Circle Bar T Leatherworks: Bart Ballew operates Circle Bar T Leatherworks and he and his carver, Marty Overstreet, produce some of the finest cowboy leather that has ever been seen be it in the dusty streets of Laredo or at any cowboy action shooting match. This past month, my friend Butch Glenn, aka Cactus Tubbs, who is also a deputy sheriff, called to tell me about the new double rig he had just received from Ballew. Cactus says of Bart's work: "My wife, Dakota Star, used a very unique word to describe the color and finish by saying the rig looked so "healthy." Well, initially I thought that was a word I wouldn't have used. But the more I think about it, the more it just seems to describe it perfectly. The second thing that was immediately noticeable was the absolutely outstanding quality of leather. You can rest assured I have seen truckloads of other rigs over my years as an outdoor enthusiast, western action shooter, and lawman, and this is as fine a grade of leather as I ever seen. Not a single weak spot, blemish, unwanted bend line, premature cracking, or thin area. I have literally examined this rig with a magnifying glass and I can honestly say the leather is a perfect as nature can produce. Bart takes his sweet time personally hand picking leather at the tannery for his customized rigs.... The holsters are free-hand cut out of 9 to 10-ounce top-quality vegetable tanned leather and lined with senior calfskin. The belt is constructed of the same materials. The holsters are totally hand-stitched, the 40 shell loops are each individually hand-stitched. Of course, high-grade premium leather is only one ingredient in a custom rig. Premium leather requires a true craftsman to turn it into

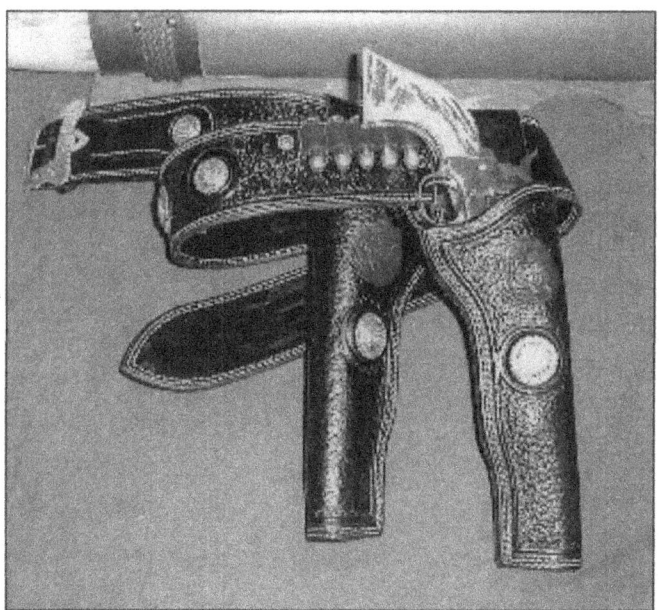

This rig by Circle Bar T is reminiscent of the double rig worn by Gary Cooper as Wild Bill Hickock in *The Plainsman*.

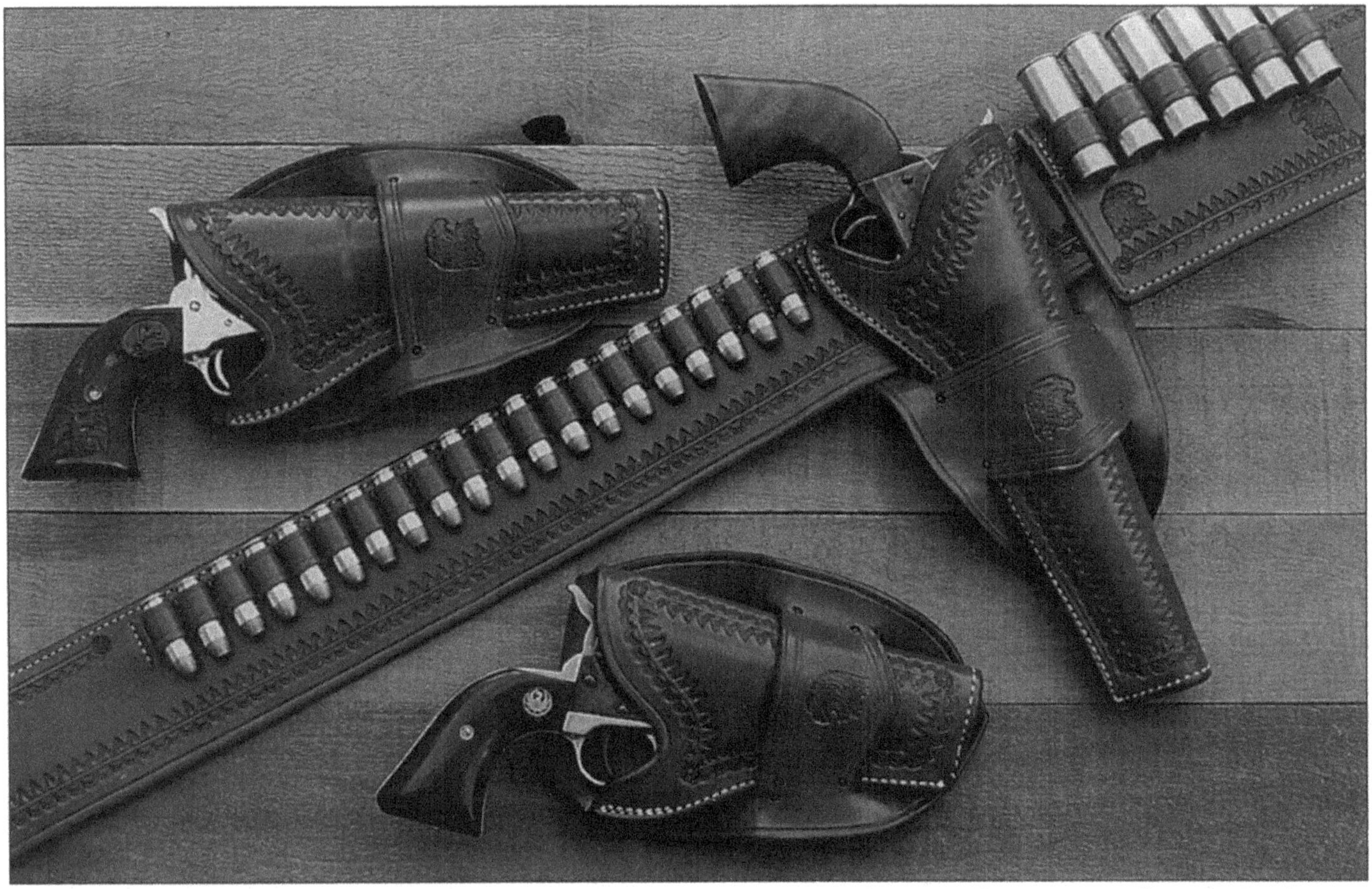

All three of these holsters were built by G. William Davis for gunsmith Dave Sample, aka Captain Eagle. Note the Eagle head on each piece.

the product you want. Bart's quality work shows in such important areas as stitching, borderline placement, stamping, and in the actual floral carving."

I will say that everything he says is right on the money, as I have thoroughly examined this double Mexican loop rig also. It is perfection carried out in leather and I knew it would be for Bart made a rig for me when I was working on my book *Action Shooting Cowboy Style*. I have just returned from Winter Range where it just so happens that Bart was displaying a rig reminiscent of the double butt to the front leather worn by Gary Cooper as Wild Bill Hickock in *The Plainsmen*. It was constructed of pebble-grained black leather. I could not resist so I ordered a rig just like it with Slim Jim holsters with an added loop so they hang lower and straight. These will be made to carry a pair of Cimarron .44 Colt Cartridge Conversions and will be built so they can be worn butt to the front or to the rear. I have no doubt that both work and quality of leather will be as good as it gets.

G. WM. Davis: I recently sent a Cimarron .38 Lightning to gunsmith Dave Sample for one of his excellent tuneups. Dave contacted G. Wm. Davis who then sent me a miniature rendition of the Mexican loop

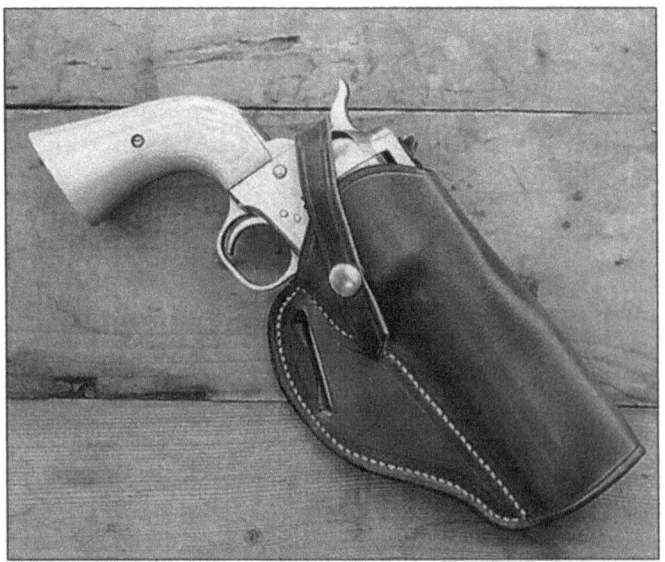

The author considers the Freedom Arms shoulder holster the most practical for carrying a scoped Freedom Arms Model 83. However, for packin' a 4 3/4-inch Model 83, the Freedom Arms Crossdraw is much more practical.

holster to fit on the pants belt and carry the little Cimarron .38 Lightning. As an extra added bonus, I found this same holster works quite well with my custom L'il Ruger Single-Sixes from Andy Horvath. These little sixguns have 4-inch barrels and rounded butts and fit perfectly in the Davis leather. In the past I have highlighted Davis's Rooster Rig as one of my favorites for carrying a Colt Single Action. It still is.

Freedom Arms: Three of my favorite hunting handguns are all scoped 7 1/2-inch Freedom Arms Model 83s in .357 Magnum, .44 Magnum, and .454 Casull. Which caliber I choose depends on what I'm after. In either case I grab the shoulder holster that Freedom Arms offers for its scoped revolvers. Perhaps it is not correct to call this a shoulder holster as a really rides across the front of the body. Whether walking, standing, sitting, or riding this holster works! I wear it so my pants belt enters the loop on the back of the holster taking much of the weight off the shoulder straps. This works out very comfortably.

In addition to the shoulder holster, Freedom Arms now has a new line of belt holsters for all their single actions. Mine is a crossdraw for the 4 3/4-inch Model 83. This high-quality rig, as one would expect from Freedom Arms, is made of minimum bulk yet protects the sixgun well and also has a safety strap for security while hunting in rough terrain. The strap can be easily folded out of the way when not in use. The belt loop is designed to ride high and tight to the body by incorporating one loop as part of the back edge of the holster

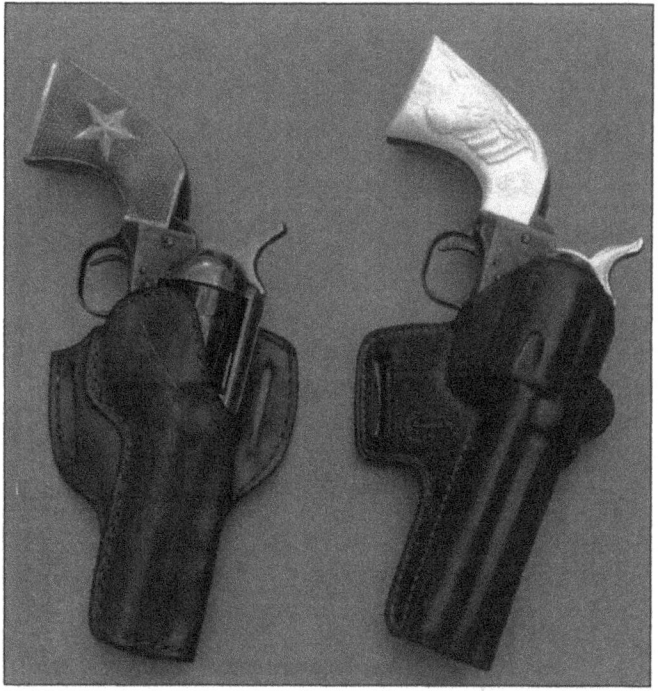

Two solutions to the same problem of carrying a Colt Single Action concealed: the PS6SA by Bob Mernickle, and the Jeffe by Derry Gallagher. They both work. Stocks are by Buffalo Brothers and Eagle Grips.

Derry Gallagher is a genius working in horsehide. Examples of his concealed leather carry 2 1/2-inch Smith & Wesson .357 Magnums with stocks by Eagle and Herrett's.

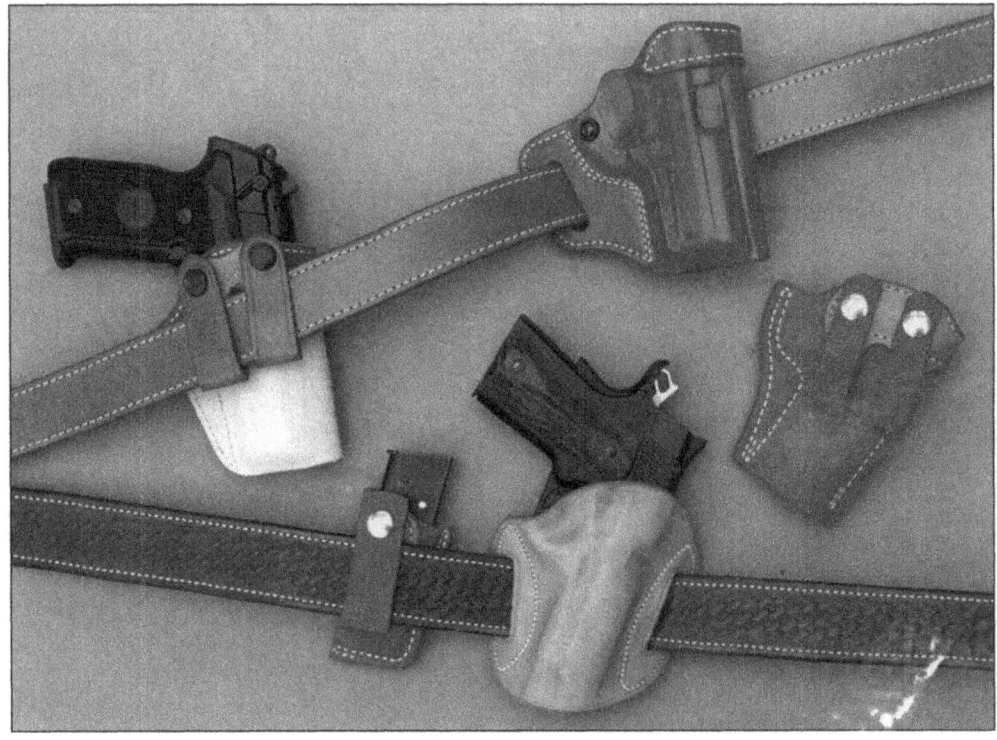

Gould & Goodrich offers a full line of high-quality belt holsters and inside the pants rigs for semi-autos such as the Beretta Cougar and Kimber Compact .45s.

itself. The other provides extra strength and stability as it is made from a piece of leather that nearly transverses the entire back of the holster. It's a very good hunting rig.

Derry Gallagher: Texan Derry Gallagher is now turning out some really fine concealment rigs for both sixguns and semi-automatics, and in talking with others with similar rigs from Gallagher I find agreement that they are top quality all around. Gallagher constructs all of his holsters from horsehide, not the typical cowhide. This makes them not only lighter weight, but tougher also. Each holster is hand finished and boned, again by hand to the exact sixgun or semi-auto it will carry. No generic one-size-fits several-sixguns here! Each holster is dyed, unless it is to be left in a natural color, and then again hand rubbed and waxed. The wax minimizes any transfer of dye to the clothing. I have been wearing, and rotating, three Gallagher rigs for the

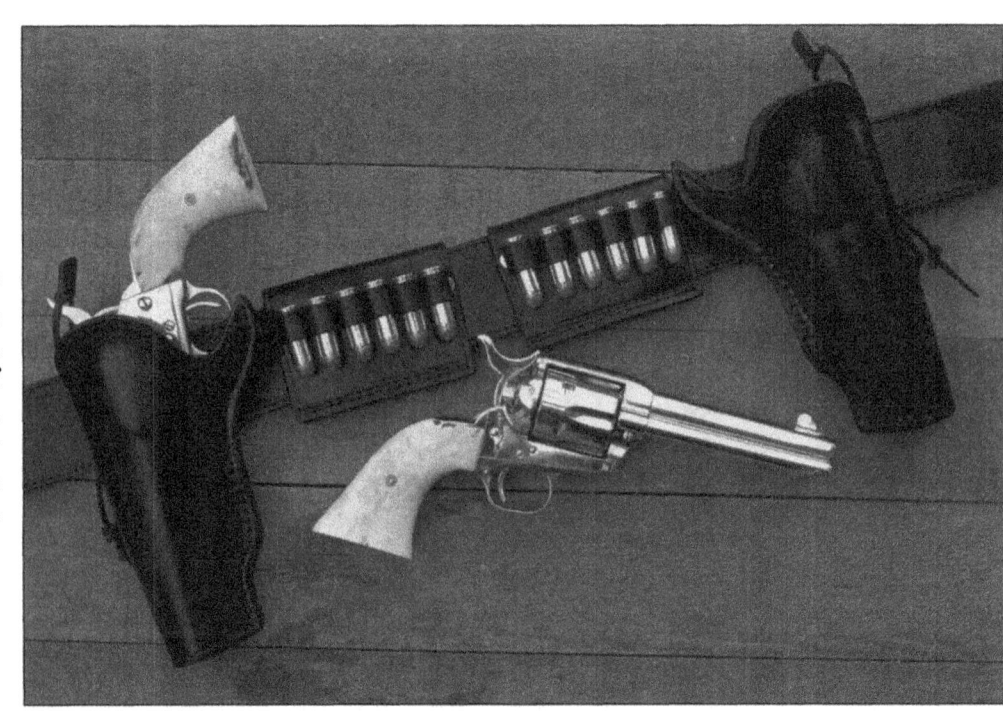

Kirkpatrick Leather's double Prospector rig, custom-built for the author, carries a pair of nickel-plated, stag-gripped Colt Single Action Army .45s for cowboy action shooting or general field use.

past several months. The Smith & Wesson Model 19 .357 Magnum, the original Combat Magnum, has been a favorite of mine, and after trading into a nickel-plated Model 19 and a stainless-steel Model 66, both with 2 1/2-inch barrels, and both too large to be classed as pocket pistols, I had the need for a high-quality concealment rig to pack these original .357 belly guns.

The answer is Gallagher's Jeffe rig. Gallagher calls this a belt slot/tunnel design, which allows the holster to fit not so quite so close to the body as a two-slot holster, thus allowing a faster draw. This rig is made both with and without a covered trigger guard and I have been using both quite satisfactorily. For a Kimber Compact .45 ACP, Gallagher's answer has been the Jeffecito, with a covered trigger guard and a high riding, forward slant position of the little .45. This is good leather. A fourth rig from Derry Gallagher is his answer for the need for good leather for concealed carry of a single action that rides high with an FBI slant and carries a 4 3/4-inch Colt Single Action. Gallagher also offers belts and magazine pouches as well as holsters.

Gould & Goodrich: After 50 years, Smith & Wesson has introduced companion Chief's Specials to its original J-frame, five-shot, .38 Special Chiefs from 1950. The new Chiefs' Specials are all semi-autos in 9mm, .40 S&W, and .45 ACP. The latter, the CS45, which in all likelihood will be the most chosen of the new Chiefs, rides in Gould & Goodrich's #801 Yaqui Slide. This simple design features a holster that is about as compact as leather can be with a belt slot, and a folded-over strip of leather to hold the barrel and trigger guard of the CS45. Two adjustable tension screws are provided at the trigger guard and a loop cut out of the back of the holster allows for perfect placement over a pants belt loop for added security. It is easy to conceal a sixgun or semi-automatic in cold weather, but it becomes much more of a logistics problem as the weather warms up. The tendency is to go to smaller and smaller weapons as less clothing is worn. A travel vest or a mesh vest has become a dead giveaway for concealed carry anymore, but a western-style vest such as those worn by many of the cowboy shooters is not. The combination of the CS45 and the Gould & Goodrich version of the Yaqui Slide can easily be concealed under a vest as the barrel on the CS45 protrudes less than 1 inch below the belt line. To supplement the Yaqui Slide, G&G also offers an excellent inside-the-pants holster with nothing to protrude below the belt on the outside.

Kirkpatrick Leather: Cimarron Firearms has often led the way with replica sixguns and the Colt Cartridge Conversions are no exception. Pickin' leather for carrying these early cartridge-firing sixguns from the 1870s was very easy. A few years ago I had Kirkpatrick Leather build me a double Prospector Rig for a pair of 1860 Armies. These are fully lined, Slim Jim-style holsters that hang straight on the belt, making it easy to wear them butts to the front or to the rear. The matching belt is also lined, with everything basket stamped and a light tan color. Even though they are made for the 1860 Armies, the square and open bottoms also leave enough room for the ejector housings of either the Richards or Richards-Mason Conversions.

Excellent leather, in fact so much so that I have since added a similar double rig, black floral carved, for a pair of 7 1/2-inch stainless-steel Ruger Vaqueros, and I just took possession of a third set of plain black Kirkpatrick Prospectors to carry two 4 3/4-inch Colt Single Actions. I use these with cartridge slides rather than bullet loops on the belt as it makes them so

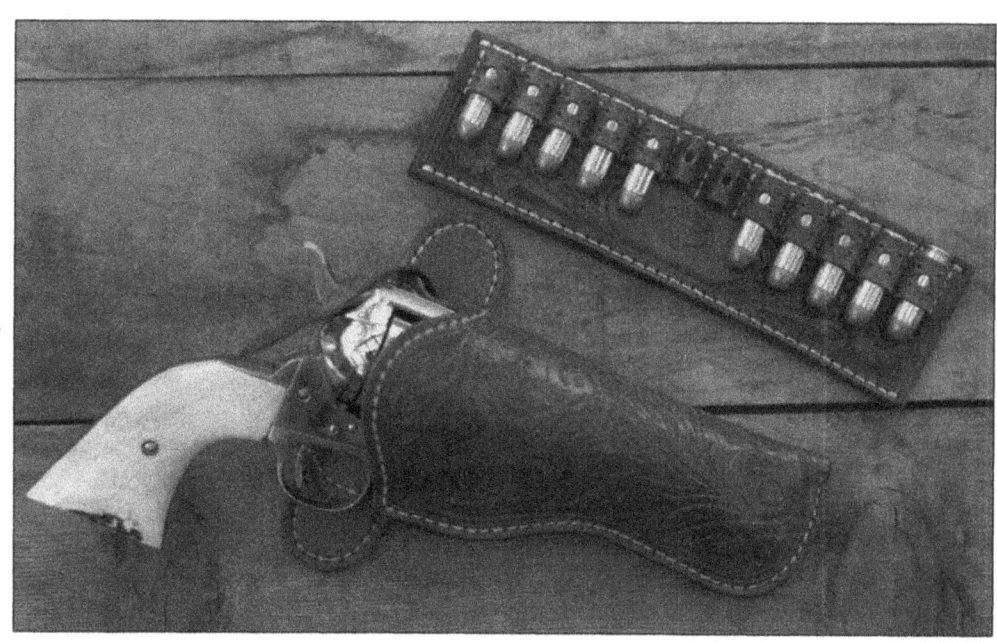

This Legends in Leather concealment rig is based on an old-time design and is named the Billy Old after one of the survivors of Adobe Walls. The 12-loop cartridge slide is carefully designed to conform to the curve of the body.

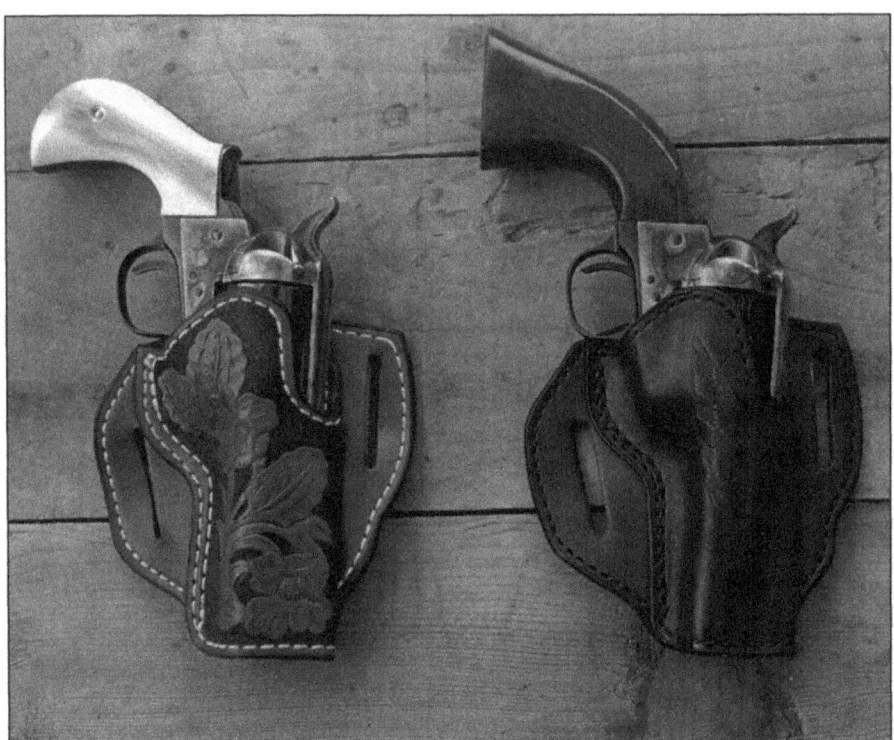

Bob Mernickle's PS6SA, which is especially designed for concealment use, is shown in both fully carved and plain versions with Cimarron sixguns.

much more versatile. If I don't want to carry a lot of cartridges I do not have a lot of empty loops. I can go with no cartridges, or six, or 12, as I prefer. This also allows The Prospector to double as a field rig when wearing one sixgun.

Legends in Leather: Jim Lockwood of Legends in Leather is a master leather craftsman specializing in reproducing exact duplicates of the rigs worn by "B" western movie heroes, big-budget western stars, and the familiar leather seen in TV westerns of the 1950s and 1960s. Even when it comes to carrying concealed, or open for that matter, since Lockwood lives in an open-carry state, he stays with the traditional and recently made up a concealment rig for me to pack a 4 3/4-inch Colt Single Action Army. The concealment holster made by Lockwood is fully lined and floral carved with a neutral cant. It uses a minimum of leather like the TomThreepersons, but rides slightly lower and also features a low cutout in the front of the holster below the hammer for an easier draw and also easy re-holstering with one hand. Rather than being sewn to the holster, the belt loop is secured by two Chicago screws, and this loop also has two stabilizing ears that ride behind the pants belt. An over-the-hammer safety strap is also featured.

To match up with the holster, Lockwood provides a cartridge slide that is also floral carved and holds 12 rounds. Normally such a slide would be too stiff to ride comfortably on a pants belt, however Lockwood cuts a large slot in the back of the slide so it easily contours to the body and also allows the positioning of the pants belt loop in the middle of the slide. A nice added touch features the "see through" holes in the cartridge loops that are reminiscent of the rigs worn by stars in the 1930s. Lockwood has named this rig the Billy Old after a famous Arizona ranger from the early 1900s. Good rig.

Bob Mernickle: Bob Mernickle is a talented Canadian who does it all: authentic western, cowboy action rigs, Hollywood western, fast draw, field holsters, shoulder holsters. With his PS (Personal Series), he also has some of the best in concealment leather, including two holsters suitable for concealed carry of single actions. My Colt SAA 4 3/4-inch rides in his inside-the-pants holster, which is also the model used for packin' a 4-inch Smith & Wesson .44, or his latest high-ridin' rig, PS6SA, with fully exposed hammer, trigger guard, and butt, that is also cut low in the front for easy access.

The PS6DA is made for all frame sizes of double-action sixguns to accommodate barrel lengths up to 6-inches. I have been using one of his new PS6DA models with a 3-inch J-frame Smith &Wesson. It rides high, comfortable, and secure with no need for a safety strap. Mernickle's PS rigs are available in several configurations for most single actions, double actions, and semi-automatics. If your need for concealment leans more to shoulder holsters, Mernickle can furnish a proper rig for just about any single or double action sixgun or semi-automatic.

Walt Ostin/Custom Gun Leather: Ostin, from British Columbia, like many of the rest of us grew up on a diet of "B" westerns, and would often saddle his horse and ride into town on Saturday afternoons to see the latest exploits of favorite movie heroes. After pursuing several careers throughout his lifetime, Ostin found his real niche when he purchased a leather shop in the 1980s and began offering custom leather.

For those of us who prefer the 19th-century styles, Custom Gun Leather provides a skeleton pattern spring clip shoulder holster, and the California Pattern or Slim Jim including a lower-riding, straight-drop version known as the Gunfighter Slim Jim. The most popular holster of the period was the Cheyenne-style or the Mexican Loop style of holster. Those offered by Ostin include his rendition of the Cheyenne, the Russell, the Montanan, the Kansas, the Utah, the Colorado, and the Texas. To all of these holster styles from Custom Leather we can add lever gun and shotgun scabbards, including those that carry two long guns at one time, shotgun and bat wing chaps, saddle bags, shotgun slides, spur straps, wrist cuffs, and bandoliers. Belts include both 3- and 4-inch money belts, canvas prairie belts, and sixgun cartridge belts with everything produced by Custom Gun Leather being of the highest quality.

For a then-new 5 1/2-inch Colt SAA .44 Special, I chose Ostin's Colorado. Of the Cheyenne pattern, this single-weight holster and belt are finished with a stamping design that Walt came up with and resembles basket weave but it is not. It looks more like connected oval spots. The belt and holster are both stamped with this unique design and then border stamped, and the holster is finished off with two small conchos at the back edge of the holster loops. This rig, as the sixgun it now carries, is one of the most attractive I have ever encountered. It is also extremely practical leather for cowboy shooting, woods bumming, hunting, or any activity requiring a sixgun.

One of Ostin's heroes as a kid, as it was for many of the rest of us, was the Lone Ranger as played by Clayton Moore both on TV and in the movies. Ostin has carefully re-created the last rig worn by Moore in his movies and appearances. This black floral carved rig features holsters of the Mexican loop style, but the part of the holster designed to house the bottom of the trigger guard has been sewn to the holster itself so the complete trigger guard

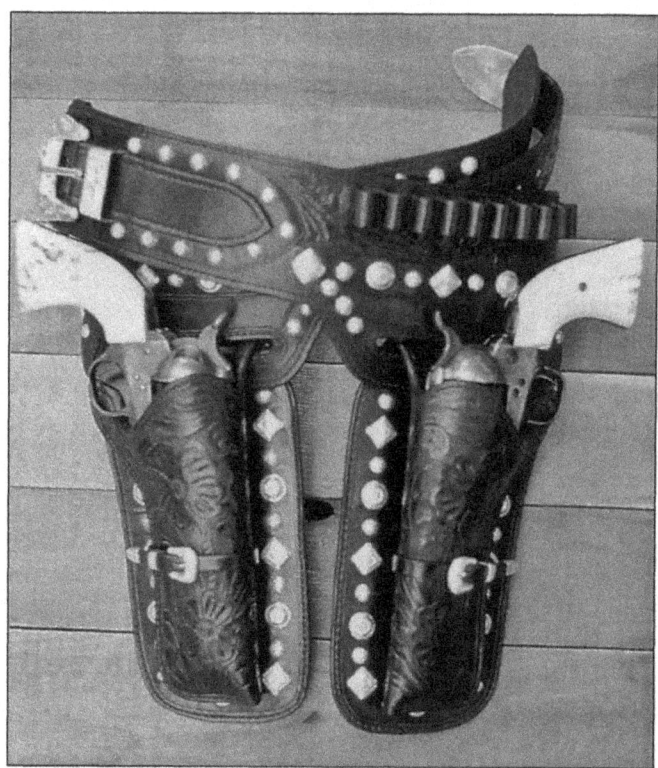

For anyone over 40 this rig from Walt Ostin should be a reminder of the days of "From out of the past comes the thundering hoof beats of the great horse, Silver..." It's a beautiful rendition of a Lone Ranger rig.

The author relaxes in his trophy room while packing a .45 Colt in Bob Mernickle's PS6SA holster.

Walt Ostin studied films and movies to come up with this expertly crafted tribute to the "King of the Cowboys," Roy Rogers.

rides outside the holster for a faster western movie draw. It is a beautiful outfit commemorating a bygone era.

Just about the same time I got really serious about single-action sixguns, a young fellow in Hollywood was not only instructing the stars how to look like they knew what they were doing when drawing and shooting a Colt Single Action, he also began manufacturing his new holster. Arvo Ojala added a metal lining to the holster body, which allowed a single action to be cocked in the holster, and a metal stiffener in the drop loop so the holster would always stay in place as a draw was made. One of the men that worked for Arvo was Andy Anderson, who came up with a different idea and struck out on its own with his Gunfighter Holsters. Anderson made two changes: the holster was taken out of the drop loop and fitted over the belt and riding higher; and instead of the holster hanging straight it was now radically angled barrel forward.

Anderson's rig became very popular with fast-draw artists as well as such stars as Chuck Connors, Clint Eastwood, Steve McQueen, and "The Virginian," James Drury. Now that Andy Anderson has gone Home, Walt Ostin makes a faithful reproduction of the Andy Anderson Gunfighter Rig. I ordered an Arvo Ojala rig in the late 1950s, which I still have. However, I made a mistake and neglected to followup with an Andy Anderson outfit. That has now been corrected, and Ostin has crafted a black Andy Anderson rig for me to fit a 7 1/2-inch Colt. Anderson would approve of Walt Ostin's work.

Von Ringler: Von Ringler is another craftsman that I first met at an early gathering of The Shootists. His offering of Tom Threepersons's design is The Linebaugh to carry the big custom sixguns of John

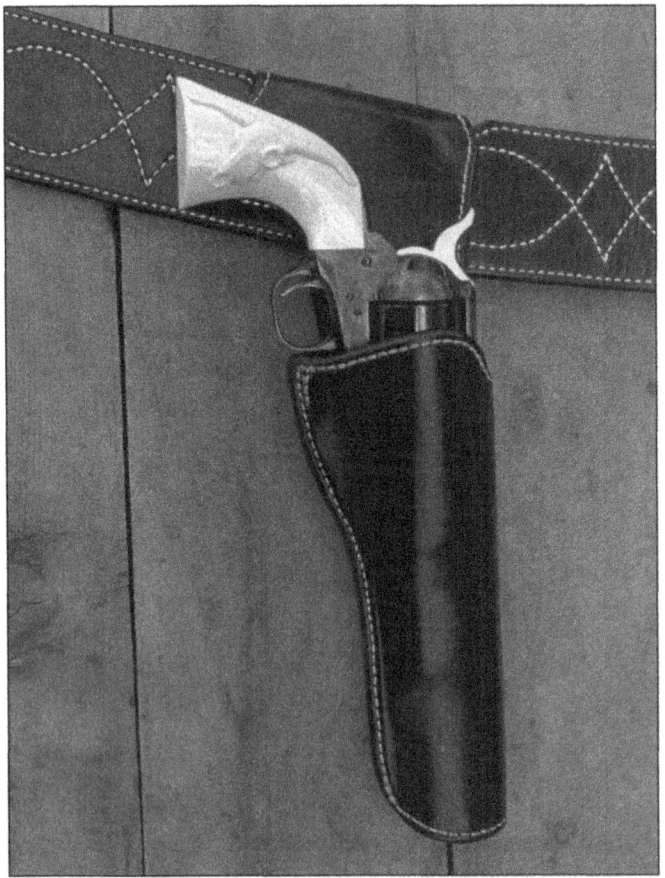

The author liked the idea of an Andy Anderson rig so well that he had Walt Ostin custom craft this rig for a 7 1/2-inch (Anderson's favorite length) Colt Single Action. Carved ivories are by Paul Persinger.

Von Ringler specializes in holsters, such as The Linebaugh, designed to carry the big-bore sixguns pioneered by John Linebaugh.

Linebaugh, and others such as those offered by Freedom Arms. This is a very sturdy holster, lined, with a safety strap. The main seam, unlike the Threepersons design, features a curve as it travels downward from the trigger guard to the end of the mainframe and then into the barrel profile. Ringler also offers an excellent Pancake design for the big single-action and double-action sixguns, as well as trim cartridge slides. All these from Ringler are designed with the handgun hunter in mind.

Ringler Custom Leather also offers a most ingenious design that is not a strong side holster, nor a crossdraw holster, not even a shoulder holster, but actually all three. Known as the Wyoming Combination, this rig consists of a fully adjustable lightweight belt and a holster pouch. The belt has enough adjustment to allow it to be worn as a waist belt or a shoulder strap. One can tighten up the belt and wear it around the waist or lengthen it and wear the rig over the shoulder. I have found it most handy for carrying a 5 1/2-inch Super Blackhawk with a second one that carries the extremely hard to holster Super 14 Thompson/Center Contender.

San Pedro Saddlery: Big Ed Douglas of San Pedro Saddlery offers traditionally crafted Mexican loop holsters that hold single action sixguns tightly without the use of a safety strap or hammer thong. Not only is this design still usable as a field holster, there are still a

Named after William Holden's character in *The Wild Bunch*, this Pike Rig by San Pedro Saddlery is an excellent traditional holster for use with a 1911 such as the Springfield Armory TRP shown here.

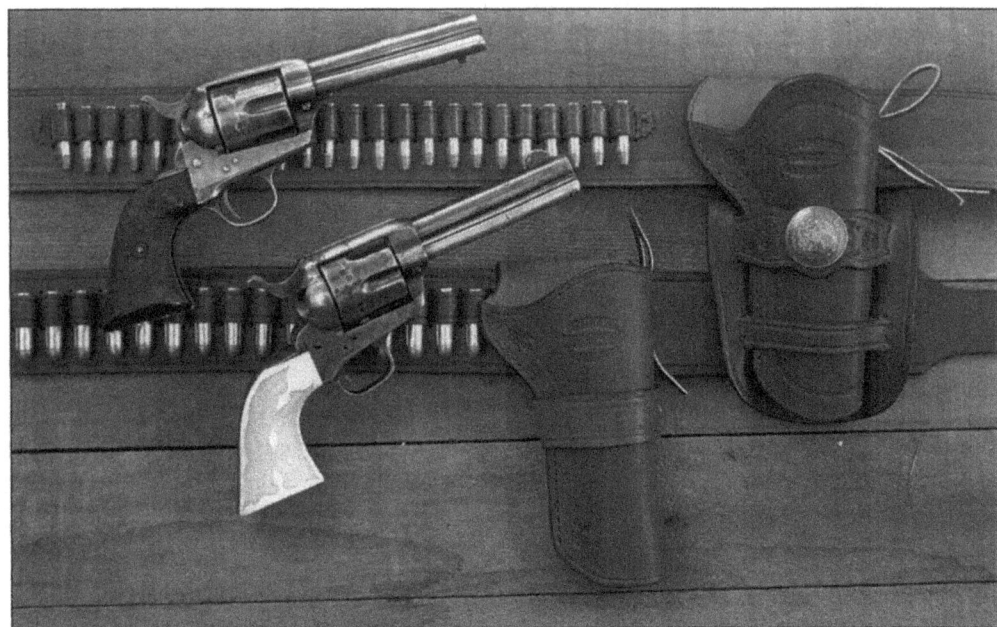

Traditional holsters by San Pedro Saddlery carry First Generation 4 3/4-inch Colt Single Actions, a .32-20 circa 1904, and a .45 Colt circa 1917.

whole lot of sixgunners who prefer to do it the old way. The 1911 .45 was designed to provide the same power as the military black-powder load in .45 Colt Single Action Army in a modern semi-automatic, and as such was the only sidearm that many Texas Rangers deemed good enough to replace the Colt Single Action Army. This theme was carried out in the movie *The Wild Bunch* as Pike Bishop packed and used both a Single Action Army and the 1911. Today I carry Springfield Armory Mil-Specs in a Pike Rig from San Pedro Saddlery. This is a superb rig consisting of a tapered belt, holster, and double-cartridge case all of oiled single-weight leather, except for the Mexican loop style holster which is lined with pigskin. Belt, holster, and cartridge case are all border stamped, while the belt is furnished with a brass gunfighter-style buckle.

Recently I was most fortunate to come into a set of Peacemaker Centennial sixguns made in 1973 to commemorate the 100th anniversary of the Colt Single Action Army. This magnificent set consists a 7 1/2-inch .45 Cavalry Model blued, case hardened, with one-piece walnut stocks, while the other sixgun, also 7 1/2 inches in barrel length, is a nickel-plated .44-40 Frontier Six-Shooter. These came to me just shortly after Big Ed of San Pedro sent a Cavalry Model flap holster and belt, and also a Slim Jim holster for a 7 1/2-inch Colt. Cer-

Great old sixguns deserve traditional leather. A 7 1/2-inch Colt .44-40 Frontier Six-Shooter, circa 1879, and a U.S.-marked 7 1/2-inch .45, circa 1881, with Slim Jim Crossdraw and Cavalry outfit by San Pedro Saddlery.

Rusty Sherrick crafted this high-riding concealment rig of horsehide for a 3 1/2-inch .45 New Thunderer.

tainly looks like a sixgunnin' omen to me! As with all leather from San Pedro Saddlery, both workmanship and material are excellent.

C. Rusty Sherrick: Rusty Sherrick works in horsehide and exotic leather and has come up with a high-riding concealment rig for a 3 1/2-inch New Thunderer in .45 Colt. Being of horsehide it maintains its shape without being bulky and also holds the gun without the need for a safety strap. The holster is boned to the contours of the single action and is basically a belt slide with a holster body incorporated. It rides high and tight and is easily concealed.

Sherrick makes holsters for about any handgun and specializes in easy-to-pack hunting rigs, defensive rigs, and cowboy holsters. The Super Redhawk is a large sixgun weighing nearly 4 pounds with a very long barrel, which would seem to be much too large and heavy to pack comfortably in any hip holster, at least until Rusty entered the picture. For the Ruger Super Redhawk, Sherrick crafted a very lightweight crossdraw holster of horsehide with a half flap covered with sharkskin. It's a most attractive rig that rides high and comfortable on the waist belt on the off-side. Sherrick now calls this Big John's Half Flap Crossdraw.

Milt Sparks: Many of the designs that came forth from peace officers designed for their use or others primarily for carrying concealed also turn out to be excellent field holsters. Both applications require comfort and security for wearing all day long and then some. Special Agent Hank Sloan of the FBI, with some input from Elmer Keith, designed the #200AW for Milt Sparks. This is basically a Tom Threepersons holster with two changes: the leather comes up to cover the hammer to prevent excess wearing of coat linings and the safety strap has been replaced by a tension screw. Turns out to be an excellent field holster.

Sparks literally wrote the book on quality concealment leather and the Sparks catalog is filled with concealment leather designs and the #200AW is one of the best. This rig features ideas from several prominent sixgunners. It has the FBI slant that was probably first advocated by Tom Threepersons in his excellent rig. It was Sloan who added the tension screw at the holster welt to provide adjustable security, and Elmer Keith suggested the leather be extended to cover the hammer to prevent the wearing of the jacket lining.

Add in a covered trigger guard, a high-riding belt slot, and a choice of finishes and lined or unlined, and we once again have an excellent holster for carrying a large sixgun under a jacket. The #200AW is made for both single-action and double-action sixguns and is used personally with a 4 3/4-inch Colt Single Action Army, and two Smith & Wessons, the 4-inch .357 Combat Magnum and the 4-inch N-frame.

Even a sixgun as large as Ruger's 9 1/2-inch Super Redhawk carries easily in this Big John Half Flap Crossdraw by Rusty Sherrick.

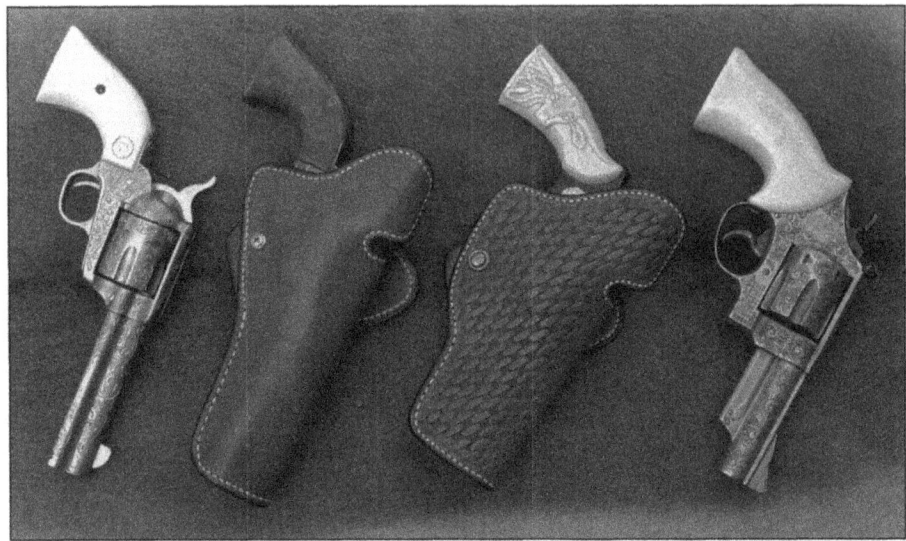

Originally designed as a concealment rig by Hank Sloan and Elmer Keith, this #200AW by Milt Sparks also makes a very practical field rig for both single and double-action sixguns. Engraved sixguns are by Jim Riggs.

Another great rig from Sparks is the Summer Special. This inside-the-pants holster is extremely versatile and can be made for either single-action or double-action sixguns or semi-autos, and anything from the smallest up to the largest for practical defensive carry. The holster itself is made rough-out, so the smooth leather rides against the gun and the rough part of the leather against the clothing helps to keep it in place. Add in a metal stiffener in the top band of the holster to keep it open when the gun is drawn, and one or two snap-off belt loops, depending upon the size and weight of the gun to be carried, and we have a true classic concealment holster from a highly respected company. As with the Askins Avenger, the Summer Special also provides for sharp sights on large semi-autos by using a sewn-in sight rail. Good leather.

Thompson Gun Leather: Forrest Thompson learned leather working from his dad and has now been crafting leather rigs for two decades. He works with heavyweight leather unlined and formed to the gun all with a very traditional look. His Slim Jim style, made for a 7 1/2-inch Colt Single Action, rides high in a cross draw position with an abbreviated flap over the hammer. Instead of a snap, the flap tucks into a loop on the holster body. Neat old-time design.

Thompson's full-flap holster for a 4 3/4-inch Colt rides high on the strong side, has a full border stamping on body and flap, and is also finished in a deep brown color. A different piece from Thompson for the 4 3/4-inch Single Action does double duty as a belt holster or a rig that can be looped over a saddle horn. Five "D" rings on the back of the holster allow the carrier to adjust the angle for carrying on the saddle or the strap can be removed and the pants belt threaded between two loops sewn on the back. There is enough adjustment in the carrying strap that it could also simply be looped over one's shoulder. A most unusual and well-thought-out rig.

A properly cared for firearm will last a lifetime and then some. The same is true of holsters. My Ruger Flat-Top Blackhawk .44 Magnum was purchased new in 1957 and at the same time I also ordered what was the best leather available at the time and a rig recommended by Elmer Keith — a George Lawrence #120 Keith holster and matching belt with 12 cartridge loops for it. The Ruger's 6 1/2-inch barrel was soon cut to 4 3/4 inches and the #120 Keith was also altered accordingly. The Ruger currently wears another barrel, a 7 1/2-inch tube, so the #120 now carries Colt New Frontiers and various short-barreled Ruger Blackhawks, but it is still in excellent shape, albeit with several scratches that show it has been used a lot. It will outlast me. Somehow, over the past four decades, the belt shrunk up to be too small to wear. Had I chosen to save a few bucks in 1957, the holster would have fallen apart years ago. One of my grandsons will inherit this one and I have no doubt that some day he will be able to pass it on to his grandson.

Forrest Thompson designed this unique half-flap holster to carry a Colt Single Action Army.

CHAPTER 16

HUNTING WITH HANDGUNS

As Don Edwards sings, I truly "thank the Lord I wasn't born no later than I was." I turned 13 in 1952 and the 1950s certainly were a near-perfect era to be a teenager. Families were solid, as were family values. Life was relatively simple. It was the age of the custom cars, chopped, channeled, bubble skirted, with flaming paint jobs. Movies were not only not rated, they had easily identifiable good guys and bad guys. TV was in its infancy, had not even arrived in many parts of the country. Ike was in the White House. Elvis, Pat, Perry, and Tennessee Ernie all sang music we could understand and identify with. Instant communication meant talking to your neighbor. And many kids grew up learning about firearms.

By 1955 I knew that sixguns would be a very important part of my life. My very wise old-maid school-

J.D. Jones has been promoting handgun hunting for several decades and was one of the first to take a Cape Buffalo with a Contender, in this case chambered for the .375JDJ, a truly all-around big-game cartridge.

teachers allowed me to read and write about guns, hunting, and the outdoors in nearly every assignment. However, handgun hunting on a large scale had not yet arrived, and the only Magnum sixgun available was a .357 Magnum. That was about to change. For 30 years a cowpoke out here in Idaho had been proclaiming that not only was a sixgun capable of taking big game cleanly, he accomplished it with his custom .44 Special sixgun loads.

For three decades Elmer Keith loaded 250-grain hard cast bullets and #2400 powder and achieved 1,100-1,200 fps from a long-barreled sixgun. I have duplicated his old loads using the balloon head brass, 18.5-grain #2400 that he had prior to 1950 with his hard cast .44 Special "Keith" bullets using modern primers. That load clocks out at more than 1,200 fps from a 7 1/2-inch single-action sixgun. When solid head brass arrived in the 1950s, he dropped his charge of #2,400 to 17.0-17.5 grains.

All Keith wanted was to see his .44 Special offered as a factory load in a new sixgun. It happened at Christmas time in 1955, and was even more than he had wanted. Smith & Wesson teamed up with Remington and the result was the Smith & Wesson .44 Magnum and Remington's first .44 Magnum loading. Keith had asked for a 250-grain bullet at 1,200 fps; he received a 240-grain bullet traveling at well over 1,400 fps and he was ecstatic. Those first 6 1/2-inch bright-blued S&W .44 Magnums that began to arrive at gun shops in 1956 were magnificent, however, the ammunition left a lot to be desired. The bullet was much too soft for the velocity achieved. Keith went to work using his 250-grain hard cast bullet and his favorite #2400 powder and the result was what has come to be known to shooters and reloaders as the Keith load: Lyman's original #429421 Keith bullet over 22.0 grains of #2400 for a full 1,400 fps and, as Keith said, less pressure, no barrel leading, and greater accuracy. It has always been a great handgun hunting load.

The .44 Magnum has been "king of the sixgun cartridges" for nearly half a century. It is not as easy to control as its predecessor, the .357 Magnum, nor even its offspring, the .41 Magnum, and it has been overshadowed in power by several new cartridges: the .454 Casull, the .480 Ruger, and the Linebaughs (both .475 and .500), even the heavy-loaded .45 Colt. However, it still remains the first choice of most handgun hunters and is undisputedly the hunting handgun and hunting cartridge by which all others are judged.

A decade after the .44 Magnum arrived, a small company in New Hampshire began producing a single-shot handgun first chambered in .22 and .38 Special. It wasn't long before the folks at Thompson/Center discovered that they had an action capable of handling any of the lever gun or Magnum sixgun cartridges then in

Another pioneer handgun hunter is Mag-Na-Port's Larry Kelly, here shown with a beautiful Alaskan Dall ram taken with the Contender.

existence. The Contender was soon chambered in such excellent hunting cartridges as .44 Magnum, .30-30, and .35 Remington. When J.D. Jones founded SSK Industries in the 1970s he opened large new doors for the Contender, offering it chambered in .45-70 and then a full lineup a JDJ wildcat cartridges.

The day is long past when handgun hunting was regarded as a stunt and probably every game animal that walks has been cleanly taken with both sixguns and single shots many times over. This includes brown bear, grizzly bear, polar bear, moose, and elk in this country, as well as the African big five. A few years ago, a hunter in Africa found he had a client that wanted to take a Cape buffalo with a sixgun. The hunter, being ignorant of the ways of sixguns, called several of his friends and inquired if they were interested in seeing "a crazy American killed." The crazy American survived; the buffalo died with one shot.

Any accurate handgun with good sights in virtually any chambering from .22 Long Rifle up is suitable for hunting. It is simply a matter of matching the gun and load to the game being pursued. Every hunter must realize that the ammunition being used must, that is, M-U-S-T, be capable of taking game cleanly and

Zebras are surprisingly hard to put down. This stallion went 200 yards before collapsing from one shot out of the author's 6.5 JDJ Contender.

quickly. And along with this, any handgun hunter that cannot realistically judge how far he can shoot accurately should not be in the field. It is one thing to lie on one's back Creedmore style and consistently punch the shoulder area of a steel silhouette ram at 200 meters with an open-sighted sixgun. But when pursuing live game it is quite another matter. Factor in excitement, being out of breath, not having a steady rest, and a live animal, and for most of us, 200 meters quickly shrinks to a maximum of 50 yards. Add a good rest and a scope and we come closer 100 yards. Change the handgun to a super accurate Contender, properly chambered, and 200 yards is not out of the question. The longest shot I have ever made has been 250 yards on a blackbuck antelope using a Contender chambered in 6.5 JDJ. I had a solid rest and I knew what the gun was capable of doing, and the result was an instantaneous one-shot kill. I have also taken African gemsbok with that same

A favorite hunting area is the YO Ranch in Texas; a favorite quarry, a Texas whitetail; and a favorite combination — the Freedom Arms .44 Magnum with 2X Leupold scope and Black Hills 240 gr. JHP load.

The author with friend and guide Frank Pulkrabek with South African impala taken with the 6.5 JDJ. The following spring Frank was killed by a drunk driver as he was taking hunters back to the San Antonio airport.

He is so ugly, he is beautiful, the warthog, that is. One shot from the Freedom Arms .454 dropped him where he stood.

Three of the best powders for assembling heavy-bullet sixgun loads are Hodgdon's H110 and Lil' Gun, and Winchester's 296.

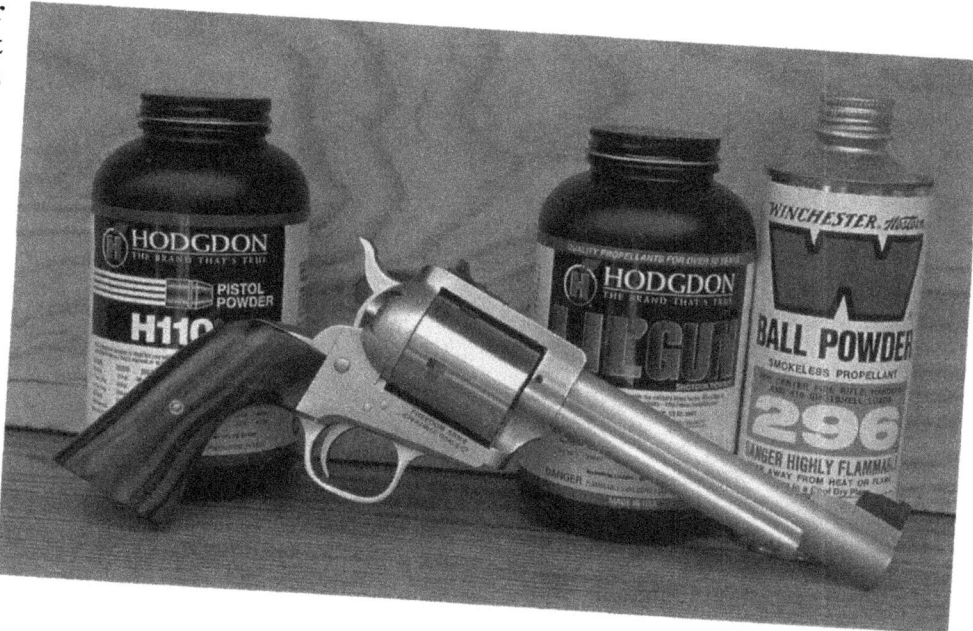

gun and load at 180 yards and zebra with the .375 JDJ at 200 yards. In every case I had a solid rest and a standing, broadside shot.

For any cartridge to be effective, whether it is fired from a sixgun or rifle, the four "P's" must all be in place: placement, power, performance, and penetration. We define these terms as follows:

Placement: where the bullet strikes the intended target
Power: the muzzle energy and/or TKO value
Performance: whether the bullet expands, holds together, or comes apart
Penetration: how deeply the bullet will travel, especially in a large animal

Certainly a solid bullet, whether hard cast or jacketed, can be expected to penetrate much deeper than a jacketed hollowpoint or soft nose. That is a given. The wise hunter decides according to his intended quarry whether he needs ultimate expansion, deepest possible penetration, or a combination of both.

At a recent Linebaugh Sixgun Seminar we ran tests on the penetration of big-bore sixguns and rifles. The results were quite surprising. Using wet newsprint as our test target, Randy Garrett's .45-70 Hammerhead 530-grain hard cast in a lever gun at 1,550 fps went 55 inches; a 495-grain hard cast .500 Linebaugh fired from a 5 1/2-inch sixgun with a muzzle velocity of 1,270 fps was right behind it at 52 inches; the .500 Nitro Express with a full metal jacket and weighing 570 grains came in third at 48 inches, followed by the .458 Winchester with a 500-grain solid traveling at a muzzle velocity of 2260 fps and 47 inches of penetration, and the lowly .45 Colt with a 350-grain hard cast bullet at 1,400 fps with 43 inches of penetration, or only 5 inches less than the .500 Nitro and 4 inches less than the .458! Of course, the .45 Colt load tested is only for use in the Freedom Arms .454 or custom five-shot .45 Colt revolvers. The .44 Magnum, with a 250-grain Keith bullet at 1,200 fps, went 27 inches into the wet newsprint. We also had only one load for the new .480 Ruger, that being Hornady's original factory offering of a 325-grain XTP-JHP at 1,350 fps. This round is not designed for deepest penetration, but did expand well and traveled 17 inches into the newsprint.

How did the truly big bore sixguns, that is, .45 Colt, .454 Casull, and the .475 and .500 Linebaugh's, com-

Single-shot handguns become viable for hunting with dozens of wildcat and factory chamberings. These are some of the best for sixguns (from left): .44 Special Keith Load, .44 Magnum, .45 Colt, .454 Casull, .475 and .500 Lineaugh.

The author gave up on shotguns for turkeys and instead turned to the Freedom Arms .357 Magnum, taking this tom on the Penn Baggett Ranch near Ozona, Texas.

larger than Texas whitetails, I prefer a hard cast bulleted load such as the serious hunting loads offered by Buffalo Bore, Cor-Bon, or Garrett, or similar handloads using hard cast bullets such as those offered by BRP or Cast Performance Bullet Co. If the range or expected shot is anticipated to be 100 yards or longer, my choice becomes a scoped single-shot Contender with the vast majority of my hunting, depending upon the size and toughness of the critter being pursued, being with the .257 JDJ, 6.5 JDJ, or .375 JDJ. When I hunted Africa I took the latter two T/Cs as well as a Freedom Arms .454.

I am often asked what the best handgun and/or load is for hunting a particular animal. The question is usually impossible to answer as there rarely is a best, however, there are certainly better and definitely those that are preferred. In 1935, the best sixgun available was Smith & Wesson's .357 Magnum. In the mid-1950s, the best had become the .44 Magnum either from Ruger or Smith & Wesson. Now we find ourselves in the first decade of the 21st century and our choices are almost endless when it comes to handguns and cartridges. Let's take a look at some of the best available in chronological order.

pare? For the .45 Colt, in addition to the already mentioned load, a 310 Keith at 1,250 fps (one of my favorite loads and safe for use in Ruger's Blackhawk or Bisley) penetrated 36 inches, while the 300 LBT traveling at 1,180 fps penetrated 2 inches deeper. Using Cor-Bon's 360 Bonded Core at 1,500 fps in the .454 yielded 45 inches of penetration. Moving up to the .475 Linebaugh, a 420 LBT at 1,335 fps did 47 inches, while the same bullet at an easy-shooting 1,050 fps still penetrated to 40 inches. When I shot a 1,200-pound American bison with this load I experienced complete side-to-side penetration. In one side, out the other. It is obvious from these tests the .44 Magnum with a 250-grain bullet at 1,200 fps, or a 300-grain .45 Colt at 1,250 fps, will certainly handle any deer that walks.

I have personally hunted extensively with sixguns and single shots over the past two decades. For smaller big game, such as Texas whitetails and javelinas, I prefer a jacketed hollow point with my load of choice being Black Hills 240 JHP. For Texas turkeys, I go with the same company's 125 JHP in the .357 Magnum. For game

Less than five minutes of shooting light were available when the author connected on this Texas whitetail on the Baggett Ranch using Penn Baggett's custom .445 Ruger.

A most unusual trophy from Mark Hampton's Show Me Safari Ranch in Missouri. A yak taken by Mike Figueroa with a custom five-shot .45 Bisley Model.

.45 Colt: I would not want to count all the game taken with the original black-powder load of a 255-grain conical bullet at around 900 fps. For nearly a century this was the standard loading level for the .45 Colt mainly due to the fact that the original sixgun, the Colt Single Action Army, has paper-thin cylinder walls when chambered in the big .45. With the advent of the large-framed Ruger Blackhawk in the 1970s, we had a factory-chambered .45 Colt that could handle heavier loads, such as 250-grain bullets at 1,300 fps and 300-grain bullets at a full 1,200 fps.

Ruger still offers the Blackhawk in .45 Colt with either a 7 1/2-inch or easier-packing 4 5/8-inch barrel, and with either the original blued finish or weather-beating stainless steel. In any caliber for a packin' sixgun I prefer the shorter barrels, but where hunting is the main activity I feel much better with a 7 1/2-inch sixgun simply because for me it is so much easier to shoot accurately. My favorite of the Ruger line when it comes to the .45 Colt, in fact in any hunting handgun chambering, is the Bisley Model. Offered only in blue and with a 7 1/2-inch barrel, the Bisley Model combines the best features of the original Colt Bisley Single Action, Freedom Arms, and Ruger Super Blackhawk grip frames. For those that prefer double-action sixguns, Ruger offers the .45 Colt in its bull-strong Redhawk. Offered in stainless steel only with a choice of 5 1/2- and 7 1/2-inch standard models, or a 7 1/2-inch scope-ready model complete with Ruger scope rings, the Redhawk will handle heavy factory .45 Colt loads with ease.

The Mouflon is regarded by many as the world's most beautiful sheep. Mike Figueroa scored on this trophy with a five-shot .45 Colt Bisley Model.

Ruger's Bisley Model .45 Colt is an excellent choice for handgun hunting when properly loaded.

From Freedom Arms comes the easy-packing Mid-framed Model 97 in .45 Colt in barrel lengths of 4 1/4, 5 1/2 and 7 1/2 inches, all with adjustable sights and scope ready (by removing the rear sight).

Two companies, Buffalo Bore and Cor-Bon, offer .45 Colt loads suitable for hunting big game where deep penetration is required. All of Buffalo Bore's .45 Colt loads are advertised as "Heavy .45 Colt" and are for use only in modern heavy-duty .45 Colt sixguns. There are three standard offerings: for maximum penetration, a hard cast 325-grain LBT-LFN at 1,325 fps; penetration combined with expansion, a 300-grain Speer PSP (Plated Soft Point) at 1,300 fps; and for smaller critters where expansion is more important than deep penetration, Buffalo Bore offers a 260-grain jacketed hollow point at 1,450 fps. The fourth offering from Buffalo Bore was designed with the mid-framed Freedom Arms Model 97 .45 Colt in mind and is a 300-grain Speer PSP at 1200 fps. This is also a good choice for those that hunt deer-sized critters with Ruger's

Buffalo Bore offers heavy-duty handgun hunting ammunition in .44 Magnum, .45 Colt, .480 Ruger, .475 and .500 Linebaugh.

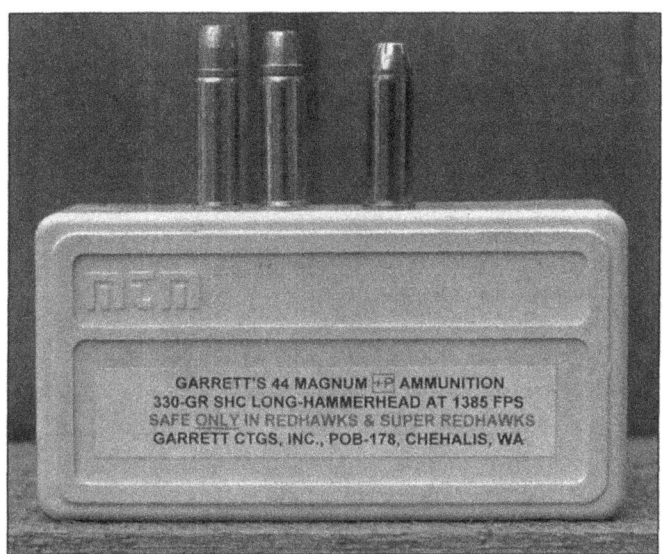

Garrett's caters to the handgun hunter who prefers to use the .44 Magnum with two loads, a 330-grain hard cast for Redhawks and Super Redhawks, and a 310-grain hard cast for heavy-duty .44 Magnums with shorter cylinders.

Blackhawk because, although it is a potent loading, it is fairly mild, relatively speaking, in recoil. Currently, Cor-Bon offers three .45 Colt Magnum +P loadings for handgun hunters. Notice both Buffalo Bore and Cor-Bon distinguish their serious .45 Colt hunting loads from the normal .45 Colt factory loads by using the terms "Heavy .45 Colt" and ".45 Colt Magnum +P" and I cannot emphasize enough that these loads are for currently manufactured large-framed .45 Colt sixguns. Cor-Bon's .45 Colt hunting loads include a 265-grain Bonded Core HP at 1,350 fps, a 300-grain Bonded Core jacketed soft point at 1,300 fps, and a 335-grain Hard Cast rated at 1,050 fps. Cor-Bon's Bonded Core process fuses the interior lead core to the outside jacket to keep both together for maximum penetration combined with expansion. Its Hard Cast and Penetrators are designed to perform as solids, giving the most possible penetration on large and/or dangerous game.

.357 Magnum: I do not normally recommend using the .357 Magnum for big-game hunting. Although I have taken deer-sized animals with it, it was up close and with hard cast bullets designed for maximum penetration. I do use the .357 Magnum a lot for hunting, but it is for turkeys, where legal, and my choice is Black Hills 125-grain jacketed hollow points, a scoped sixgun, and the placing of the shots where the head meets the body.

Smith & Wesson offers the .357 Magnum in the L-frame Model 686, a stainless-steel, heavy underlug-barreled sixgun offered to hunters with either a 6- or an 8 3/8-inch barrel length. It has a well-deserved reputation for both durability and accuracy, and is also scope ready when the rear sight assembly is removed. For those that prefer single-action sixguns, Ruger offers the extremely strong Bisley Model with a 7 1/2-inch barrel, as well as the standard 6 1/2-inch Blackhawk in either blue or stainless. Freedom Arms has two frame sizes in .357 Magnum: the large-framed Model 83 with a five-shot cylinder, and the mid-framed Model 97 with a six-shot cylinder.

Virtually every ammunition manufacturer offers .357 Magnum loads. For hunting with the .357 Magnum I only know of three loads that are offered for deep penetration. Those loads are: Cor-Bon's 180-grain Bonded Core at 1,265 fps and 200-grain Hard Cast at 1200 fps, and Federal's 180-grain hard cast known as a Cast Core rated at 1,250 fps.

.44 Magnum: Smith & Wesson offers the .44 Magnum in the stainless-steel 629 in both 6- and 8 3/8-inch versions, as well as two heavy underlug-barreled 629s, the 6 1/2-inch PowerPort with factory-ported barrel and an excellent black post front sight, and a just-announced HiViz fiber optic front sight; and the Classic DX sans porting, but offered in either a 6 1/2- or 8 3/8-inch version. The latter is one of the most accurate .44 Magnums it has been my pleasure to shoot.

For Ruger single-action style we have the legendary Super Blackhawk, which since 1959 in its 7 1/2-inch blued version has been, and remains, probably the greatest bargain offered to handgun hunters. Shooters now have a choice of blue or stainless-steel versions and barrel lengths of 4 5/8, 5 1/2, 7 1/2, and 10 1/2 inches. I have found the latter to be especially accurate and easy shooting. However, when it comes to Ruger single

BRP's 290-grain Keith-style GC is a superb performer in Ruger's Bisley Model when combined with Hodgdon's Lil' Gun for around 1,335 fps.

actions in .44 Magnum, I much prefer the Bisley Model, although it is only offered in a 7 1/2-inch blued version. Ruger recently reintroduced its Super Blackhawk Hunter Model, one of the best .44 Magnum hunting sixguns available. All it needs to be near perfect is the addition of a Bisley grip frame, hammer, and trigger.

While Smith & Wesson used an existing frame, the .44 Hand Ejector, as the platform for the .44 Magnum in 1955, Ruger was able to build a larger, stronger sixgun, the Redhawk, around the cartridge in 1979. The Redhawk was joined by the Super Redhawk in 1987. Redhawk fanciers have a choice of blue or stainless-steel versions in 5 1/2- and 7 1/2-inch barrel lengths with the latter also being offered scope ready with integral scallops on the barrel rib to accept Ruger rings. Those that prefer the larger Super Redhawk have only two choices, a 7 1/2- or 9 1/2-inch scope ready, stainless-steel, massive brute of a sixgun. Excellent double-action .44 Magnums are also available from Taurus with its Raging Bull. Wesson Firearms offers its New Generation Large Frame .44. Even Colt has recently reintroduced the .44 Anaconda.

Freedom Arms also offers its Model 83 in .44 Magnum only in stainless steel and in all four standard barrel lengths. My most-used hunting handgun for whitetail deer is a scoped Freedom Arms 7 1/2-inch .44 Magnum combined with above mentioned Black Hills Ammunition's .44 Magnum offering consisting of a 240-grain jacketed XTP bullet from Hornady loaded to 1,350 fps.

Virtually every ammunition manufacturer offers quality .44 Magnum ammunition loaded with 240-grain jacketed hollow points that are certainly adequate for the hunting of small deer. I have already cited my choice of Black Hills Ammunition's .44 Magnum 240-grain JHP for this duty. For heavy-duty use, both Speer and Winchester take the standard .44 Magnum loading up a step with the former's 270-grain Gold Dot Hollow Point at 1,250 fps and the latter's 250-grain Partition Gold at 1350 from the same Ruger .44 Magnum. Both Black Hills and Federal contribute to 44 Magnum hunting loads with a 320-gain Hard Cast and a 300-grain Cast Core, respectively, both at 1,250 fps, and Hornady joins the heavy bullet brigade in .44 Magnum with its 300-grain XTP-MAG at 1,150 fps.

Buffalo Bore's offerings in .44 Magnum consist of three heavy .44 Magnum loadings. First there is the above mentioned 270-grain Speer Gold Dot loaded to 1,450 fps. Then a 300-grain Speer PSP (Plated Soft Point) at 1,300 fps. Finally, for maximum penetration, a 305-grain hard cast LBT-LFN (Long Flat Nose) rated at 1,325 fps.

Cor-Bon has six .44 Magnum loads for specific purposes. The 240-grain jacketed hollowpoint has a full 1,500 fps velocity for small deer. The tougher 260-grain Bonded-Core hollowpoint (1,450 fps) will work for most hunting situations. The 280-grain Bonded-Core soft point (1,400 fps) works for larger deer, including elk and moose. The heavyweight heavy-duty loads from Cor-Bon for the .44 Magnum include a 300-grain jacketed soft point at 1,300 fps that is designed for expansion on soft-skinned game; the 305-grain Flat-Point Penetrator (1,300 fps), a copper-jacketed solid for maximum penetration; and the 320 grain Hard-Cast Flat Point (1,270) that combines a wide frontal surface for maximum shocking power combined with deep penetration.

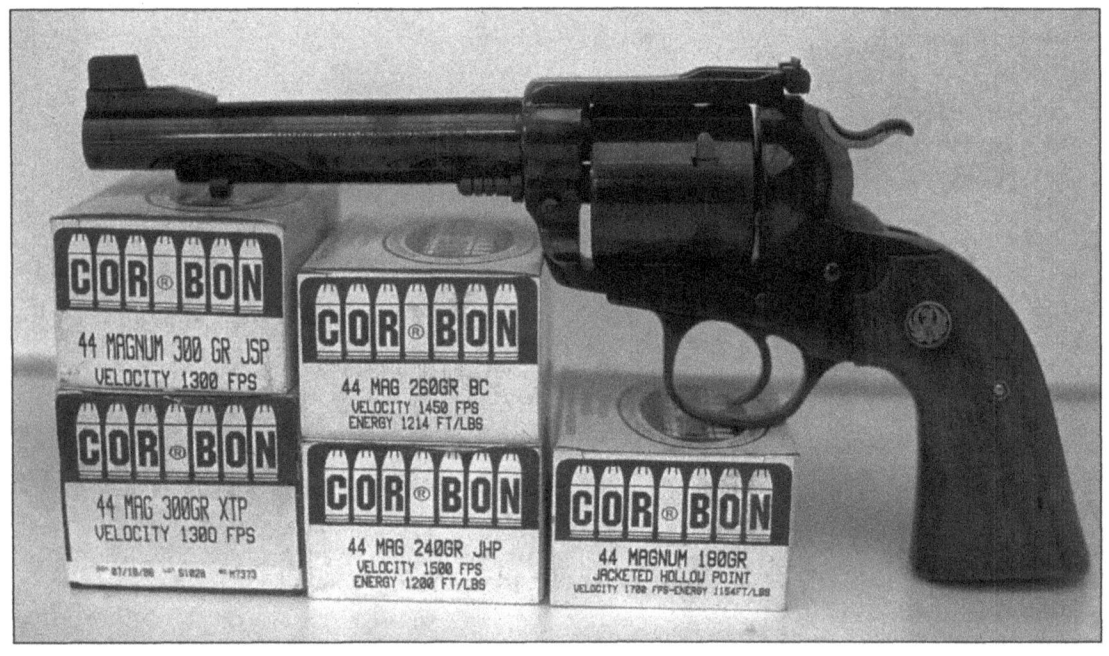

Cor-Bon specializes in both defensive and hunting ammunition with a wide range of hunting loads for single shots as well as sixguns from .357 Magnum through .454 Casull.

Bill Buckman hunts almost exclusively with the 7 1/2-inch Freedom Arms .454. This New Mexico bull elk was taken with his handload of a 260-grain Freedom Arms JFP at 1,800-plus fps.

Randy Garrett was one of the first to offer sixgunners heavy-duty .44 Magnum ammunition for use on large and/or dangerous critters. Currently, Garrett Cartridges offers two Super Hard Cast Hammerhead loadings: a 310-grain bullet at 1,325 fps for use in all currently manufactured .44 Magnums, and 330-grain +P Long Hammerhead at 1,385 fps for use in Ruger's long-cylindered Redhawk and Super Redhawk. These loads are too long to fit in the cylinders of other .44 Magnum sixguns. Both loads are designed for maximum penetration and will shoot through most animals broadside and penetrate deeply into the vitals from a frontal shot. Garrett's .44 Magnum bullets are of the LBT style rather than the Keith style and are cast from specially designed molds that give a meplat or frontal surface of .320 inch in diameter for maximum shocking power.

.41 Magnum: The .41 Magnum survives today in Smith & Wesson's Model 657, Ruger's Blackhawk, the Dan Wesson, as well as both Freedom Arms models. In the future, it will also be produced in both the Taurus Raging Bull and the Colt Anaconda in .41 Magnum Both of the sixguns offered by Freedom Arms are five shooters with the large-framed Model 83 capable of handling much heavier loads than any manufacturer is offering. The standard 210-grain jacketed hollow point .41 Magnum load offered by several manufacturers is certainly capable of handling small deer. However, Federal is the only company that now offers a .41 Magnum loading with a heavyweight hard cast bullet. Its load features a 250-grain bullet at 1,250 fps and compared to the standard 210-grain jacketed hollow point is certainly a better choice for hunting with the .41 Magnum when penetration is desired.

.454 Casull: Available in standard barrel lengths of 4 3/4, 6, 7 1/2, and 10 inches, the .454 from Freedom Arms has become the truly serious hunter's hunting sixgun. For 15 years, except for a few sixguns from U.S. Sporting Arms, the Freedom Arms was the only game in town when it came to the .454 Casull chambering. Now, within the past few years both Taurus and Ruger have introduced double-action revolvers chambered for the 454.

Buffalo Bore offers two hard cast and one jacketed bullet load for the .454 Casull. The jacketed version consists of Freedom Arms' 300-grain jacketed flat nose at 1,625 fps; while the two hard cast bullet loads are a 325 grain LBT-LFN at 1,525 fps and a 360-grain LBT-WFN at 1,425 fps. These loads will handle anything that walks!

They said it couldn't be done, however Bill Buckman is a dedicated handgun hunter and took this trophy pronghorn on the Whittington Center in Raton with a Freedom Arms .454.

Lynn Thompson of Colt Steel has hunted Africa extensively with an iron-sighted 7 1/2-inch .454. This rhino is an exceptional and rare trophy.

The ultimate handgun hunting trophy! Lynn Thompson took this bull elephant with a .454 from Freedom Arms.

Cor-Bon offers six loads for the .454, three that are designed for expansion plus penetration and three for the ultimate in penetration. Cor-Bon says of its first two Bonded Core designs, the 265-grain BC Hollow Point at 1,800 fps, and 285-grain BC Soft Point at 1,700 fps: "Upon impact they will expand, creating a devastating mushroom — plowing through tough hide and bone." These two are followed by a 300-grain jacketed soft point at 1,650 fps. For deepest penetration with the .454, Cor-Bon's 320-grain Flat–Point Penetrator, 335 Hard Cast Flat Point, and 360 grain Flat Point Penetrator are rated at 1,600 fps, 1,600 fps, and 1,500 fps, respectively.

.500 Linebaugh: This biggest of the big and John Linebaugh's first wildcat is still not offered as a factory-chambered revolver, but is well represented by custom five-shot revolvers from John Linebaugh himself as well as sixgunsmiths such as Hamilton Bowen, David Clements, Ben Forkin, Jack Huntington, Gary Reeder, and Jim Stroh. Factory loads are available from Buffalo Bore. Three hard cast LBT designs, a 435-grain LFN at an easy-shootin' 950 fps, the same bullet at a full-bore 1,300 fps, and a 440-grain WFN for maximum shocking power combined with penetration at 1,250 fps, are joined by a 400-grain jacketed hollowpoint at 1,400 fps.

Ashley Emerson, originator of the ghost ring rifle sight that bears his name, is also a dedicated handgun hunter, taking this wild boar with his Bowen-built, five-shot, 4-inch Redhawk chambered in .500 Linebaugh.

.475 Linebaugh: When Buffalo Bore decided to offer the .475 Linebaugh ammunition as a factory chambering it trimmed the rim diameters to fit in the Freedom Arms-sized cylinders. So we now have the excellent Model 83 offered in .475 Linebaugh in all standard barrel lengths, as well as six versions of .475 ammunition from Buffalo Bore.

As with the .500 Linebaugh, Buffalo Bore starts with an easy-shootin' loading of a 420-grain LBT-LFN at 950 fps. Next comes the two heavy-duty cast bullet loads, both at 1,350 fps, and both weighing in at 420 grains, one an LBT-LFN for maximum penetration and the other an LBT-WFN (Wide Flat Nose) for maximum shocking power. For those that prefer jacketed bullets there is a 400-grain jacketed softpoint at 1,400 fps and finally two "custom" loadings of a 350-grain JHP at 1,500 fps and a 440 LBT-WFN at 1,325 fps.

The .480 Ruger: Finally we have the newest big-bore sixgun cartridge, the .480 Ruger. It's the first cartridge to bear the "Ruger" name. Chambered in the .454-styled Super Redhawk, the .480 is the .475 cut back to 1.275 inches and loaded by Hornady with a 325-grain XTP-MAG hollowpoint bullet to 1,350 fps. We used this load on wild hogs in Texas ranging in weight from 125 to 190 pounds. Penetration was complete with a broadside shot on the 125-pound boar, but not on the 170- or 190-pound specimens. From this small sampling I would classify this most interesting cartridge in its original factory loading as a deer-sized cartridge with the same capabilities as a .44 Magnum

Ashley Emerson's .500 Redhawk scored again, this time on a New Mexico mountain lion.

Bob Baker, president of Freedom Arms, took this magnificent bull bison in early testing of the .475 Linebaugh.

loaded with a 300-grain JHP. Hornady now has a load with a jacketed flatpoint and Buffalo Bore's hard cast offerings include a 370 at both 1,000 and 1,300 fps, and a 410 at 1,200 fps.

With single-shot handguns such as M.O.A.'s Maximum, RPM's XL, or Thompson/Center's Contender or Encore, there is virtually no limit to the choices — everything from .22 Long Rifle up to .45-70. When chambered in such cartridges as the 7-08 or .308, they will often shoot more accurately than similarly chambered bolt-action rifles. A hunter using a scope-sighted, single-shot handgun with a solid rest will not give up anything to a rifle shooter.

For those that may prefer semi-automatics for hunting the standard 1911, either .45 ACP or .38 Super will suffice, IF AND ONLY IF, both handgun and load are very carefully tailored to the game. They are not recommended for anything above the size of very small whitetails. Better choices are a custom 1911 in .460 Rowland, which is in the .44 Magnum class, or the Magnum Research Desert Eagle chambered in .41 or .44 Magnum, or .50 Action Express. The newest semi-auto suitable for hunting is the Casull 3800. This long-slide 1911 uses a 125-grain JHP or 147 grain JHP at 1,600-1,800 fps. It shoots very flat and should do the job on varmints, coyotes, and small deer.

My first handgun hunting adventures began in the 1960s using the 6 1/2-inch Smith & Wesson .44 Magnum and Ruger 7 1/2-inch Super Blackhawk. When I finished graduate school in 1971, my reward was a Ruger Flat-Top Blackhawk in the very rare 10-inch version. It was carried for many Idaho seasons and miles in a Goerg shoulder holster. All three of these have now

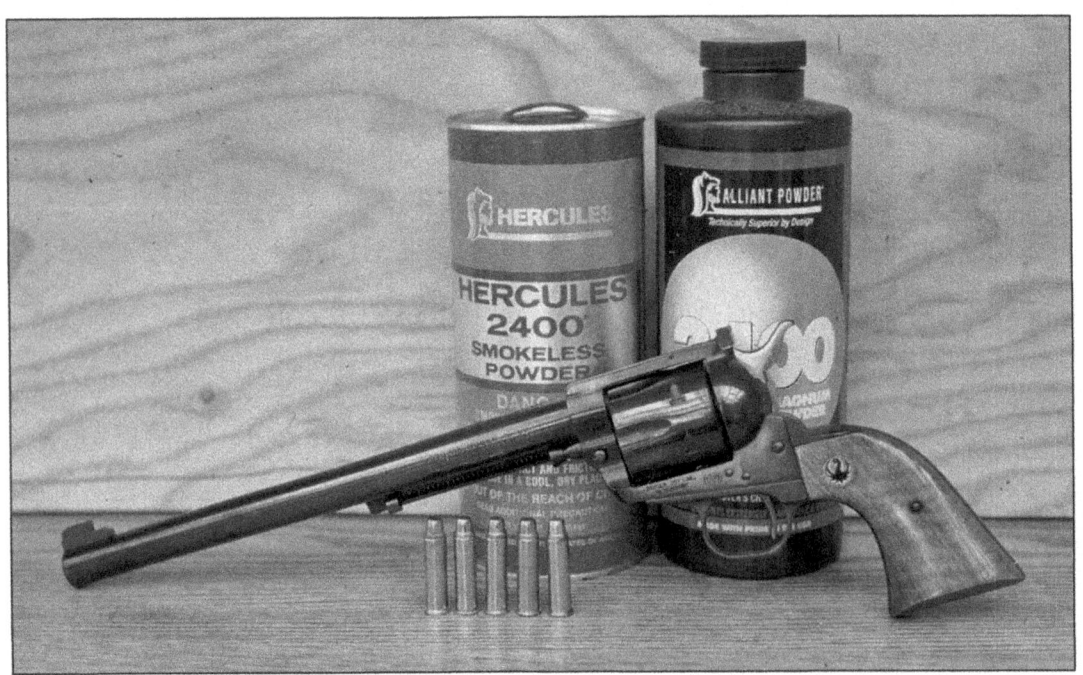

One of the author's early hunting handguns was this original 10-inch Ruger Flat-Top .44 Magnum. In those days it was mostly used with the Keith .44 Magnum load using #2400. Now it gets more relaxed treatment with a 250 Keith or 290 BRP over 10.0 grains of Unique for around 1,150 fps.

Two shots, two trophies. These two ibexes fell to the author's .375 JDJ Contender in less than 30 seconds.

been at least semi-retired. Most of my handgun hunting sixgun-style is now accomplished with 7 1/2-inch scope-sighted Freedom Arms revolvers chambered in .357 Magnum, .44 Magnum, 454 Casull, or .475 Linebaugh. My favorite single-shots include the Contender in the above mentioned JDJ wildcat chamberings, .257JDJ, 6.5 JDJ, and .375 JDJ as well as the Encore in 7-08, .308, and the 6.5 JDJ Mini-Dreadnaught.

For most of us handgun hunters, the vast majority of our handgun hunting consists of deer and/or wild hogs. For these any properly loaded sixgun from .41 Magnum up, or any single-shot handgun with performance equal to or greater than a .30-30, will suffice. A thorough understanding of what both shooter and handgun are capable of will do much to ensure handgun hunting success.

CHAPTER 17

SIXGUN/LEVER GUN COMBINATIONS

Since the great rise in handgun hunting and also the golden days of long-range silhouetting, both of which began in the late 1970s/early 1980s, it has been commonplace to see handguns chambered in rifle cartridges. While it is true that many of today's handguns can handle the most powerful of rifle cartridges, chambering rifle cartridges in handguns goes way back to the 1860s, even further back to 1852 if we consider the ill-fated Volcanic lever-action pistols and revolvers that used bullets with the powder in the base. They were anemic to be sure, and they failed, but they were a start and served to help launch two giants, Winchester and Smith & Wesson.

The first truly successful repeating rifle using fixed ammunition was the 1860 Henry chambered in .44 Rimfire. When Smith and Wesson introduced its first single-action big bore sixgun in 1869, it was chambered in .44 Rimfire; and when Colt submitted its first single-action to the Army tests of 1872, it was also chambered in .44 Rimfire. Both the S&W Model 3 and the Colt Single Action Army of 1873 were soon chambered in centerfire cartridges. The 1860 evolved into the 1866, still firing

Sixguns, lever guns, boys, and dogs go together. Grandsons John Christopher Taffin and Jason Michael Seals, along with Red, relax after the morning's shooting.

It is never too young to start them in the shooting sports. Grandson Brian John Panzella is already an accomplished pistolero with a Ruger .22 Single-Six, and is learning with a companion lever gun, a Marlin 39 Mountie.

the .44 Rimfire, however, by the time it became the Winchester 1873, the lever gun cartridge would be the .44 Winchester Centerfire, or .44 WCF, or as it is most commonly known today, the .44-40.

By 1878, Colt had also chambered its Single Action Army in .44-40 and it would not be too long before shooters could have sixgun/lever gun combinations with a Winchester 1873, and then a Model 1892 chambered in .44-40, .38-40, or .32-20 and a matching Colt or Smith & Wesson sixgun. It is true that many pistoleros stayed with a .45 Colt sixgun and a .44-40 lever gun, but it is equally true that many opted for the convenience of the same chambering in both firearms.

From the 1870s up to the advent of World War I, sixgun/lever gun combinations were commonplace, but many rural peace officers had swapped their .44-40 lever guns for the new Winchester 1894 .30-30 or 1895 .30-40 Krag. As rifle cartridges became more powerful, the idea of a sixgun and lever gun chambered in the same cartridge pretty much disappeared. By the time World War II arrived, the Winchester Centerfires, .32-20, .38-40, and .44-40, were all pretty much dead cartridges for either the short gun or the long gun.

In the 1950s, it was nearly impossible to come up with a sixgun/lever gun combination, especially when the most popular sixgun cartridges by then were the .357 Magnum and the .44 Magnum. I well remember an article in one of the early issues of *Guns* by one of my favorite writers, Kent Bellah. The article was entitled "The Two-Gun Man Comes Back," and Texan Bellah, who dearly loved the Smith & Wesson .357 Magnum, wrote of gunsmith Ward Koozer and his converting of the Model 1892 Winchester to .357 Magnum. By the time the .44 Magnum really got going in the late 1950s, the same type conversions were being performed on both Winchester '92s and South American El Tigre lever guns that had originally been .44-40s.

We take so much for granted today as it is possible to find lever guns in a matching chamberings for nearly every sixgun cartridge. This has only been true on a large scale since the last quarter of the 20th century. In the late 1960s I can well remember the excitement shared by sixgunners with the news from both Marlin and Winchester that they were chambering their respective lever guns for the .44 Magnum. For my part,

A original .38-40 sixgun/lever gun combination from the turn of the 20th century: Winchester's Model 92 and the Colt Bisley Model.

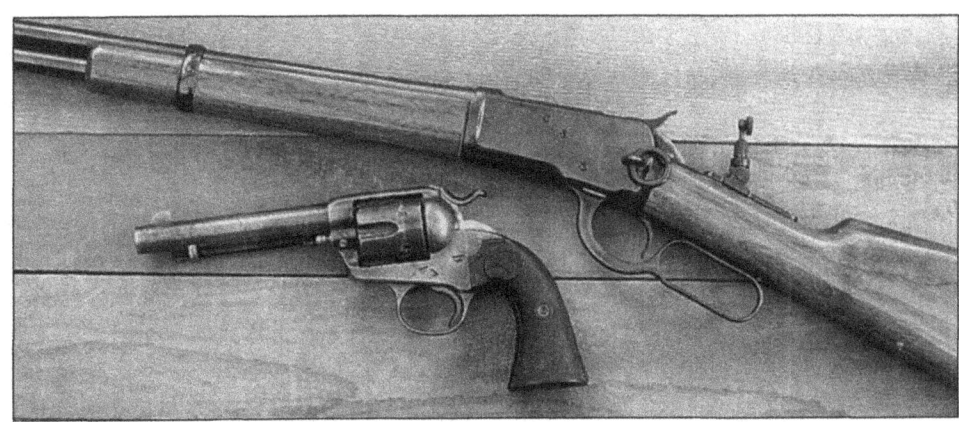

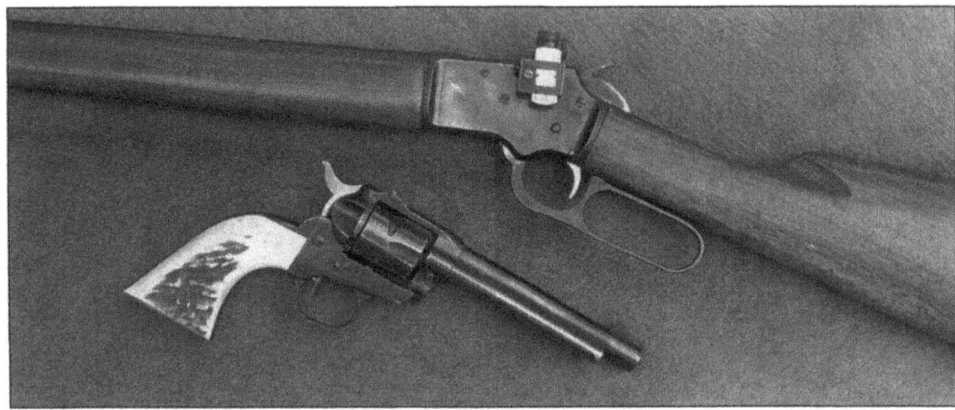

An excellent starting sixgun/lever gun combination for kids is the Ruger Single-Six and the Marlin 39 Mountie. This pair dates back to 1956 and shows no signs of wearing out.

I purchased the first Marlin 336 .44 Magnum in my area and it is still in the family.

Actually, my beginning with sixgun/lever gun combinations goes back about 10 years before the advent of the Marlin .44 Magnum. My first personally purchased firearm was the Marlin Model 39 Mountie, one of the slickest .22s ever produced, lever gun or otherwise, and it was soon joined by a companion Ruger .22 Single-Six. If I could somehow capture the great joy experienced in those days just shooting these great little .22s, and bottle it, I could cure all of the world's ills. The .22 combination was soon joined big-bore style by two .38-40s from the 1890s, a 4 3/4-inch Colt Single Action Army and a Marlin Model 1893. I wasn't smart enough at the time to realize what a great combination this was and they went the way of all foolish gun trades.

If Kent Bellah were alive today and writing, his article would be entitled, "The Two Gun Man IS Back!" I could not stop in at my local gun shop and choose a sixgun/lever gun combination in the late 1950s/early 1960s, however, today the choices are virtually endless. Consider this, Navy Arms alone offers Winchester replicas on all the patterns for 1860, 1866, 1873, and 1892, and when we look at all possible configurations as to barrel length and type, round or octagon; style, rifle, short rifle, sporting rifle, carbine; finish, brass, iron blue, case colored, stainless-steel; and calibers, we have 49 choices!

Taking three importers, Navy Arms, Cimarron (1860, 1866, 1873), and EMF (1892), we can choose from the fol-

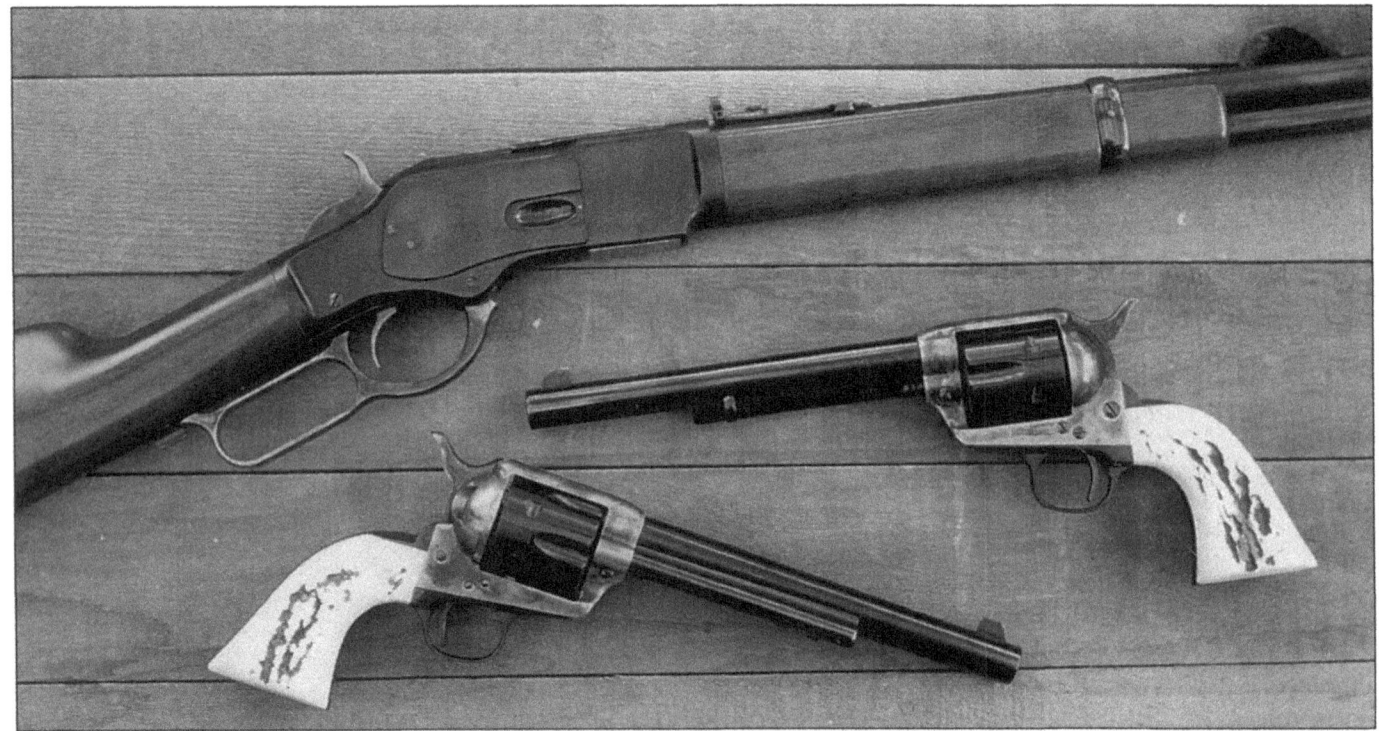

Thanks to modern replicas, cowboy action shooters can have a combination from the 1880s, such as this Cimarron 1873 and a pair of 7 1/2-inch Model Ps, all chambered in .38-40.

In original form all of these would be too valuable to shoot. However, it is now possible to have a .45 S&W sixgun/lever gun combination thanks to Taylor's & Co.'s Spencer Carbine, Smith & Wesson's Model 2000, and Cimarron's 1871-72 Open-Top. All are chambered in .45 Schofield.

lowing: 1860 (.44-40, .45 Colt), 1866 (.32-20, .38 Special, .38-40, .44-40, .44 Special, .45 Colt), 1873 (same as 1866 plus .357 Magnum), and 1892 (.357 Magnum, .44 Magnum, .44-40, and .45 Colt). From Winchester we have the Model 1894 in three barrel lengths in each of .357 Magnum, .44 Magnum, and .45 Colt chamberings, with the same calibers offered in Marlin's 1894 Cowboy as well as its new .38 Special Cowboy Competition. The Marlin has also been recently chambered in .44-40 and from time to time the .41 Magnum surfaces. In addition to all these, it is relatively easy to still find replica Model 1892s bearing the Winchester or Browning label in .357 Magnum, .44 Magnum, .44-40, and .45 Colt; and with a little diligent searching, locate good, solid-shootin' specimens of the original 1892 in .32-20, .38-40, and .44-40. I have found the first two, still searching for the latter. Factor in all the replica sixguns, plus the modern offerings from Colt, Freedom Arms, Smith & Wesson, Ruger, Taurus, Wesson Firearms, and the number of possible combinations become astronomical. Sometimes, progress is really on our side.

Just recently, the Spencer Carbine has become available in .44 Russian and .45 Schofield; Winchester has considered offering the Model 94 in .480 Ruger; and one importer is at least advertising the Model 1892 Rossi

Not only would an original 1860 Henry be cost prohibitive to shoot, it is also nearly impossible to find original .44 Rimfire ammunition. This Navy Arms Henry is chambered in .44-40 and matches up well with an "antiqued" Third Generation Colt .44-40 and an original Colt Frontier Six-shooter.

Shooters can once again enjoy shooting a .44 Colt using a pair of Cimarron Cartridge Conversions with a Cimarron 1866 chambered in .44 Special.

Puma in .454. Whether we will actually see the latter remains to be seen. I would expect that they will have to go back to the drawing board on this one and add some steel plus a few other modifications to make it work, if it ever does. I do know that the .454 is way too much cartridge to work without stretching things in either the Marlin 336 for the Winchester 1894. What we really need is a beefed-up Model 1892 designed around the cartridge.

Of course, we cannot cover all possible combinations, but we can take a brief look at some of my favorites separated into two categories: the old traditional lever guns, Spencer Carbine, 1860 Henry, 1866 Winchester Yellow Boy, and 1873 Winchester, all basically designed for Cowboy Action Shooting, reenactments, and just plain fun; and the modern lever guns: the 1892s, and the current Marlin and Winchester offerings which not only work in the above situations but also serve well in the hunting field.

Replicas of Traditional 19th Century Lever Guns

Spencer Carbine: The original Spencer was a seven-shot rimfire lever action carbine with a tubular magazine in the butt stock. When one pushes down and forward on the lever, which surrounds the trigger, the fired case is ejected and a new round is fed from the butt stock tube straight into the chamber, however, the hammer must then be cocked before the Spencer is ready to fire. President Abraham Lincoln fired an early Spencer and was duly impressed, with the result being that the United States Government ordered 10,000 Spencers with the first guns delivered in December 1862.

The original Spencers were loaded one cartridge at a time in the butt stock. Blakeslee's Patented Cartridge Box speeded the process up by providing 10 ready loaded tubes of seven rounds each to allow for faster reloading. Although Spencers would remain in use long after the Civil War, the Spencer company itself disappeared in 1869. Rimfire ammunition for Spencer lever guns was still being made after World War I.

Spencers are of course antiques today, ammunition is nearly impossible to find and most of us have very little chance of ever shooting an original Spencer. However, thanks to Taylor's & Co., new Spencers, as well as Blakeslee's Cartridge Box, are available for re-enactors, cowboy action shooters, and anyone else who simply wants to connect with the 19th century. Taylor's & Co.'s Spencer Repeating Carbine is manufactured by Armi Sport of the renowned gun making area of Brescia Italy. Current models are available in either .44 Russian or .45 Schofield with a third chambering of a "modernized" .56/50 Spencer being promised.

For those who choose the Spencer chambered in .44 Russian, Navy Arms gives us a grand sixgun companion, the Smith & Wesson Model 3 Russian cham-

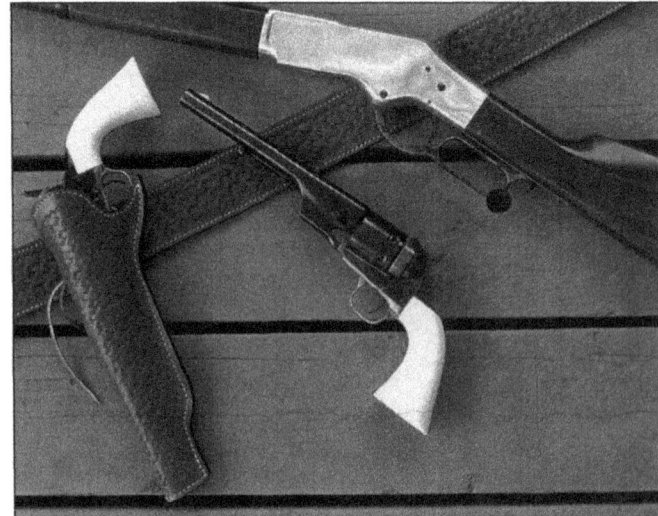

Cowboy action shooters can experience real old-time sixgun/lever gun fun using black powder .44 Colt's in an 1866 Yellow Boy and a pair of Colt Cartridge Conversions.

bered in the original .44 Russian. For those who choose the .45 Schofield, Smith & Wesson's Schofield Model is available only in .45 S&W, or as it is more commonly known, .45 Schofield. Both are excellent representations of the original single action Smith & Wessons from the 1870s. It is also possible to match the Spencer .45 Schofield with an 1871-72 Open-Top in the same chambering.

Model 1860 Henry: B. Tyler Henry received a patent in October of 1860 covering both a new lever-operated rifle as well as a rimfire self-contained cartridge to replace the ill-fated Volcanic with its bullet containing powder and primer in the base. Henry was the shop foreman for Oliver Winchester, who purchased the Volcanic from two young fellows by the names of Horace Smith And Daniel Wesson in 1855. Two years later Smith & Wesson would begin with their first handgun and Oliver Winchester would use the 1860 Henry as the basis for a long line of Winchester lever guns.

The Henry rifle did not have a long history. It was in production only from 1860 to 1866 with somewhere around 13,000 having been produced. The replica 1860 Henry, be it from Navy Arms or Cimarron, is a very true to the original replica. It is offered in three versions, all with 24-inch barrels and holding 13 rounds. The original held 16 rounds. And as with the Spencer Carbine, the ammunition has been "modernized" and the brass-framed Military Henry Rifle is available in both .44-40 and .45 Colt. One also has the option of a case-colored receiver version, while a blued receiver is available only in .44-40. Sights, also as on the Spencer, consist of blade front matched up with a long-range, flip-up, ladder-style rear sight. With the rear sight down in its normal position, the

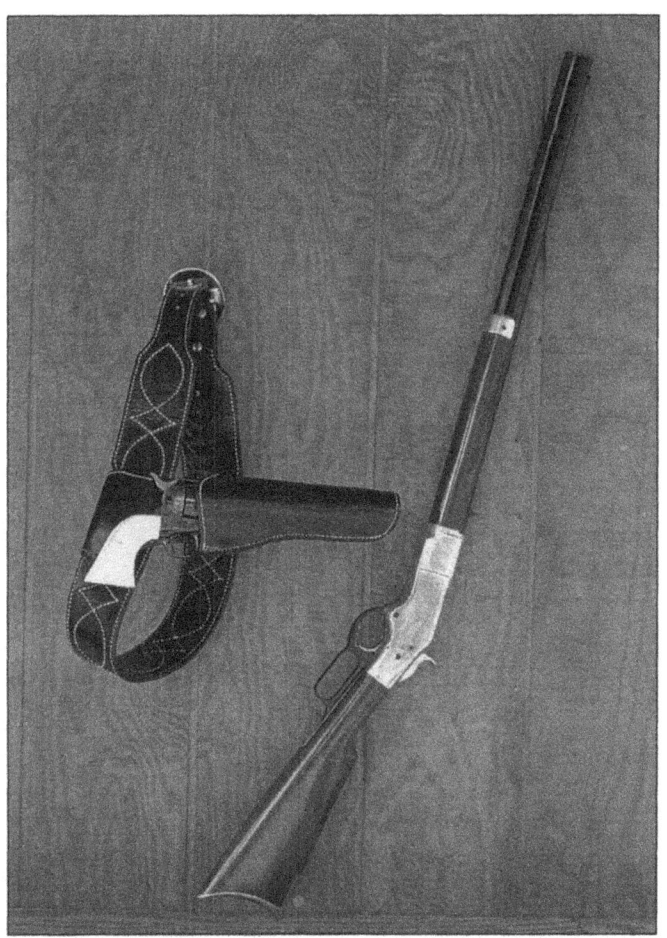

If you choose to go with a .44 Special in Cimarron's 1866, an excellent sixgun choice is a 7 1/2-inch Second Generation Colt in an Andy Anderson rig by Walt Ostin.

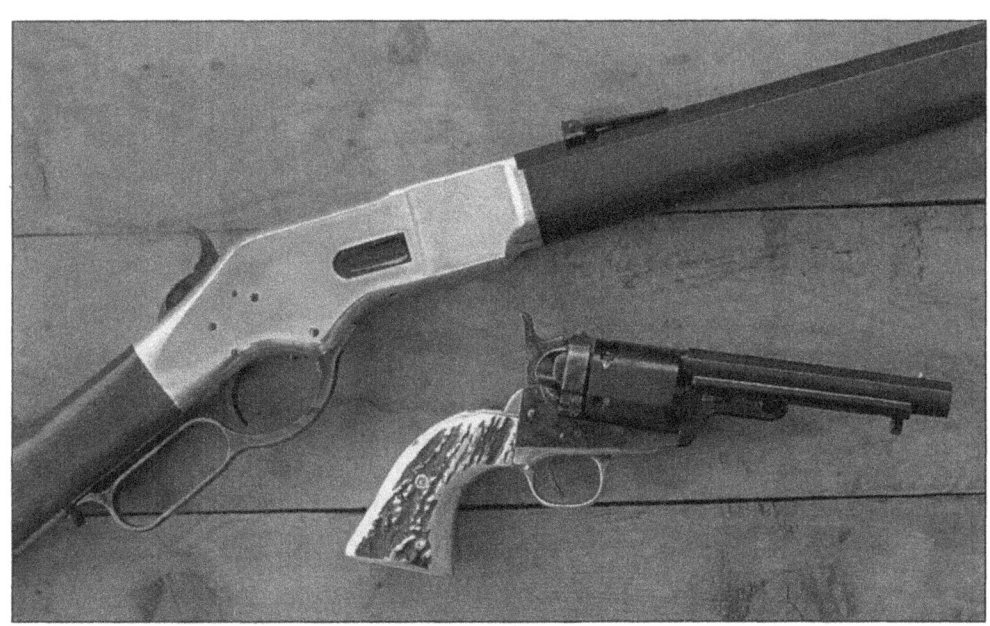

For those that prefer the gentleness of a .38 Long Colt, there is Cimarron's 1866 Yellow Boy and the 1851 Navy Cartridge Conversion, both chambered in .38 Special. Grips are by Buffalo Brothers.

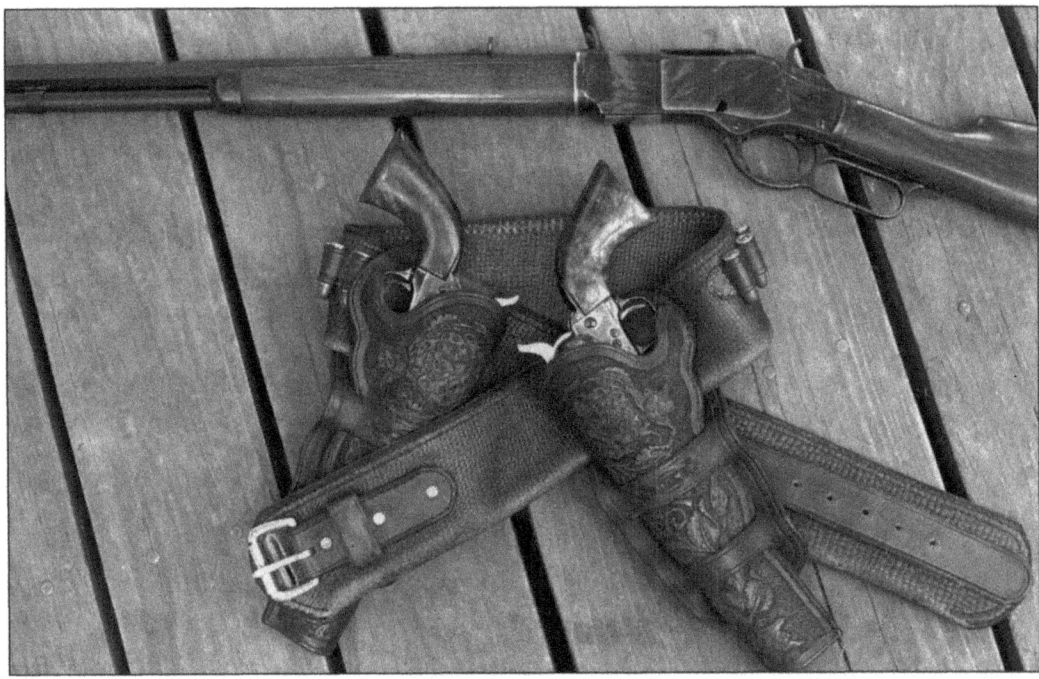

A pair of 7 1/2-inch .44-40's in a double carved rig from Chaparral along with an 1873 Winchester can do wonders for the spirit and the soul.

Navy Arms 1860 Henry is right on the money at 50 yards. All three versions weigh right at 9 pounds.

Although not truly authentic to the 1860, the .44-40 is closer than the .45 Colt so it is my number one choice. For black-powder use, to match the 1860 Henry, I chose an original 1879 Colt Frontier Six Shooter 7 1/2-inch .44-40. For smokeless or black powder, I use a Second Generation 1873-1973 Peacemaker Centennial Edition in the same configuration.

Model 1866 Yellow Boy: In 1866, the Henry was improved with King's Patent, named for Nelson King, who followed B. Tyler Henry as Oliver Winchester's shop foreman. This first Winchester, the 1866 Yellow Boy, used the same .44 Rimfire ammunition, but it was loaded through what has now become the traditional loading gate on the right side of the receiver. Since the follower no longer had to travel the length of the magazine tube, the 1866 was also fitted with a wooden forearm.

I really mess with tradition with this one and select .44 Special for the 1866. Not because I want to use heavy loads, which would be dangerous in this lever gun, but rather .44 Colt, the same chambering found in the Richards, and Richards-Mason Cartridge Conversions, which matches up great with the 1866. The 1866 feeds and shoots the shorter .44 Colt just fine if 230-grain bullets are utilized.

Model 1873 Winchester: The 1873 Winchester rifle itself had an iron and then steel frame rather than the brass frames of the 1860 Henry and 1866 Yellow Boy lever guns, plus the new cartridge was a centerfire. All of the early Winchesters, the 1860 Henry, the 1866 Yellow Boy, and the 1873 Winchester, have buttery-smooth actions. The cartridge is lifted straight up and then into

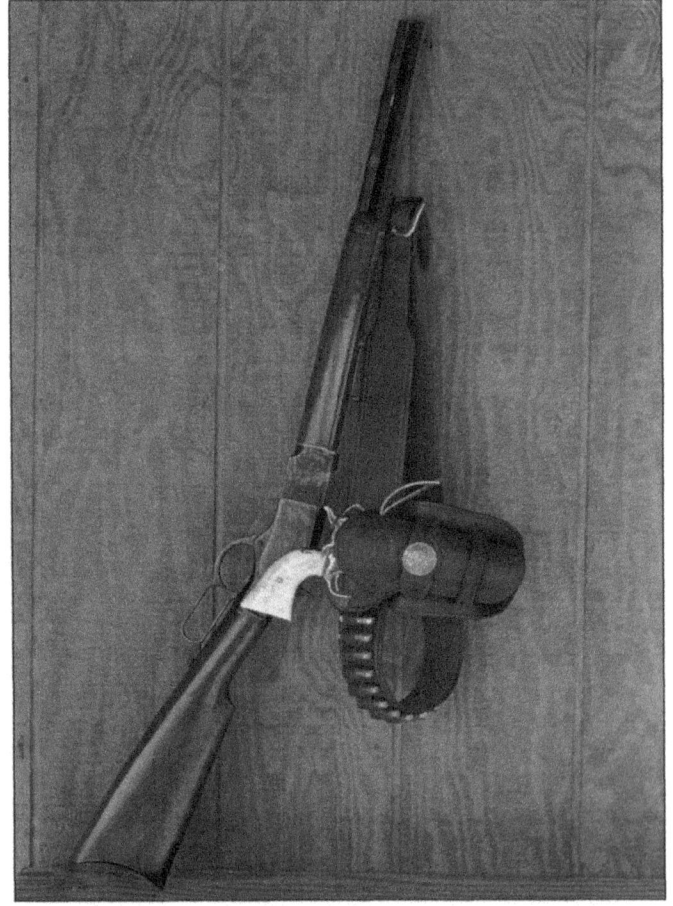

Everyone doesn't opt for the same chambering in sixgun and lever gun. Many in the last quarter of the 19th century stayed with a Winchester Model 1873 and .44-40, while the sixgun that was belted on stayed a .45 Colt. Leather is by San Pedro Saddlery.

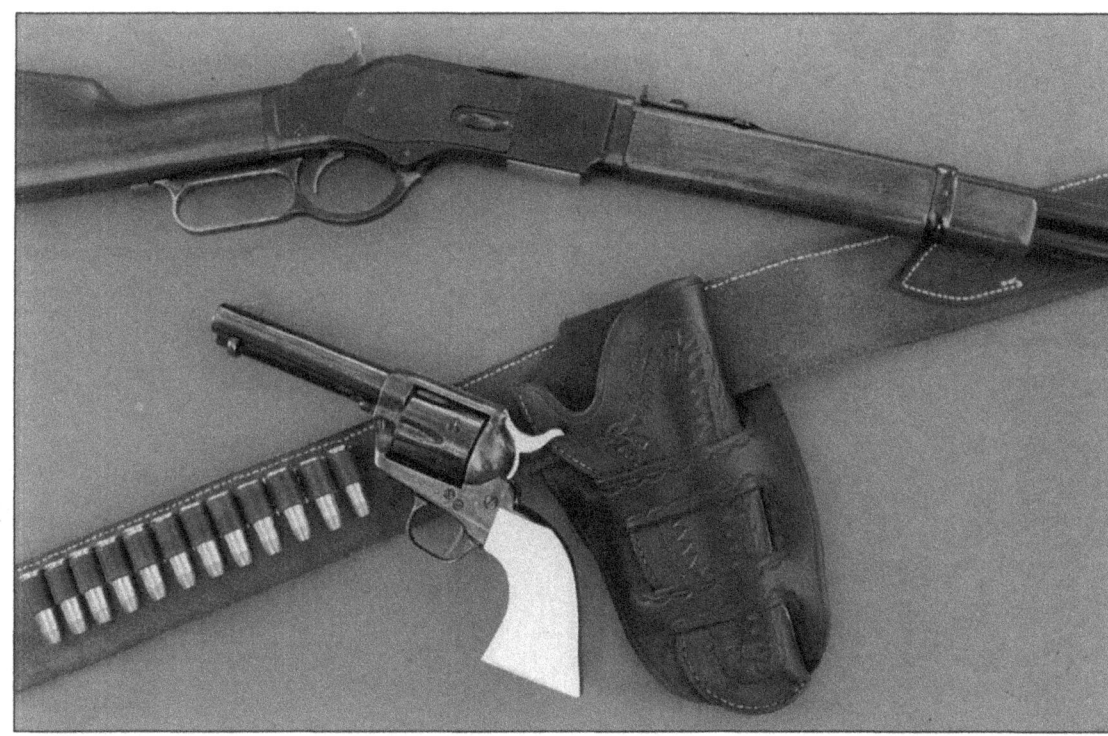

Guaranteed to take you 125 years into the past: A Winchester lever gun, a Colt Single Action, and a Mexican double loop.

the chamber rather than coming in at an angle. Working the lever on a '73 and chambering a .44-40 round is pure joy. The original chambering was joined by the .38-40 in 1879, and this was followed by the .32-20 in 1882. When Colt added these three cartridges to the Colt Single Action Army, it became possible for a shooter of that age to have a sixgun and saddle gun that chambered the same cartridge and at three different power levels. Such a combination was useful then, and even today, with most saddle horses replaced by pickups and 4x4s, the combination idea is still desirable. It definitely is for cowboy action shooting participants.

Replica Model '73 Winchesters, made by Uberti of Italy, are offered by both Cimarron and Navy Arms. My 1873 lever guns of choice are a .44-40 Border Model from Navy Arms with a brilliantly case-colored receiver mated up with red-colored wood for the forearm and butt stock, and a blued barrel and crescent-shaped butt plate. With its short, heavy, octagon barrel, the 1873 balances very well and comes right up on target. It's hard to stop with just one 1873, so my second '73 is a round–barreled Short Rifle from Cimarron chambered in .38-40. Unlike the Navy Arms 1873, this version has a plain blue receiver and, like the Navy Arms .44-40, it also shoots superbly.

My combinations of choice with these two '73s are acquired by matching them with a Third Generation Colt Single Action Army 7 1/2-inch .44-40, totally rebuilt and antiqued by Peacemaker Specialists, and for the .38-40 '73, a matched pair of 7 1/2-inch Cimarron Model Ps in .38-40.

FAVORED LOADS FOR THE REPLICAS 1860, 1866, AND 1873

.44-.40 (.44 WINCHESTER CENTERFIRE):

BULLET	LOAD	MV/7 1/2"	MV/24"
Oregon Trail 200 RNFP	8.0 gr. Unique	915	1,226
Oregon Trail 200 RNFP	35.0 gr. Pyrodex P	909	1,450

.38-40 (.38 WINCHESTER CENTERFIRE):

BULLET	LOAD	MV/7 1/2"	MV/24"
Oregon Trail 180 RNFP	8.0 gr. Unique	993	1,278
Oregon Trail 180 RNFP	35.0 gr. Pyrodex P	1,118	1,252

.45 COLT:

BULLET	LOAD	MV/7 1/2"	MV/24"
Oregon Trail 250 RNFP	8.0 gr. Unique	945	1,062
Oregon Trail 250 RNFP	35.0 gr. Pyrodex P	987	1,045

A salute to Kent Bellah — Browning's B92 and the 3 1/2-inch Smith & Wesson, both chambered in .357 Magnum.

In the late 1950s and early 1960s, Winchester 1892s were often converted to .44 Magnum. Browning made this unnecessary with the introduction of the B92 in .44 Magnum, shown with a companion Ruger Flat-Top .44.

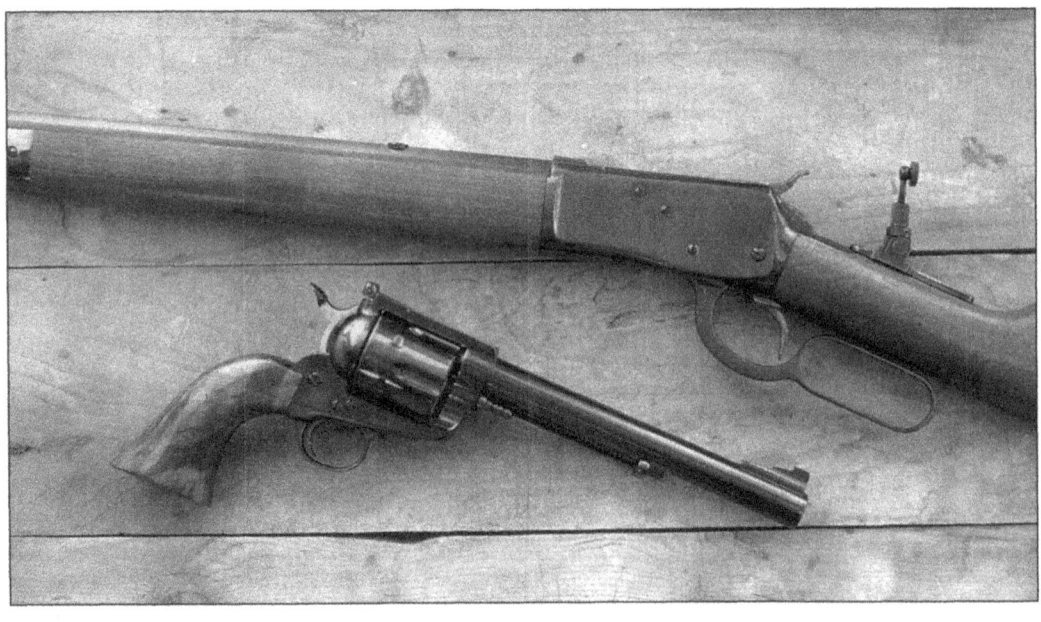

An excellent combination for hunting that will safely get everything possible out of the old .44 Winchester Centerfire, Navy Arms octagon-barreled 1892 and a Texas Longhorn Arms West Texas Flat-Top Target, both chambered in .44-40.

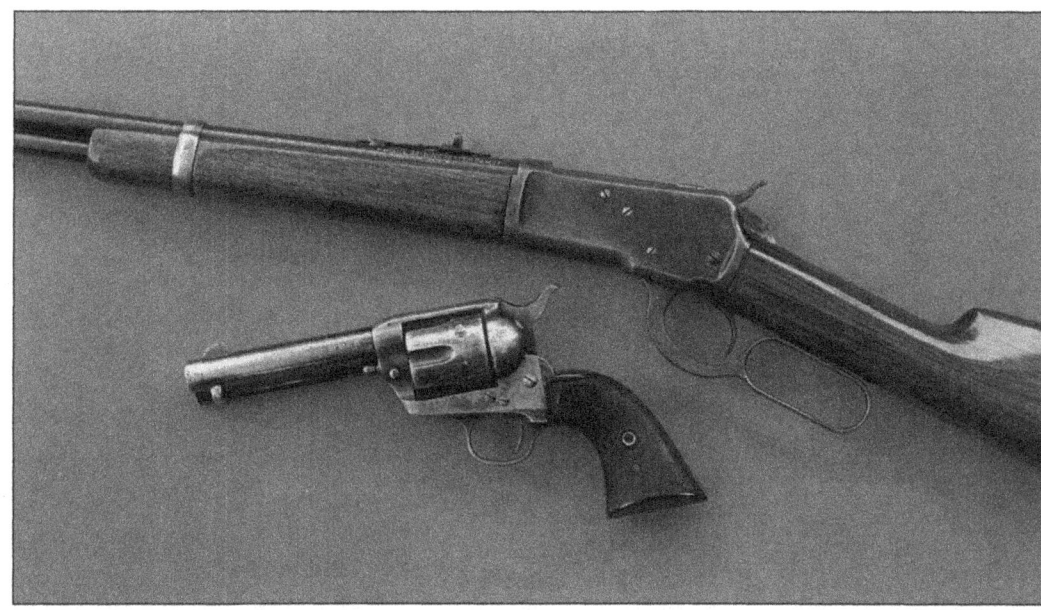

By the late 1890s a popular combination became the Winchester 1892 and the Colt Single Action Army, both in the easy-handling .32-20.

Modern lever guns and replicas

Model 1892 Winchester: The slickest Winchester ever, the Model 1892 is well represented in replica form having been imported from Italy, Brazil, and Japan at various times over the past three decades by Browning, Cimarron, EMF, Interarms, and Navy Arms. The 20-inch round-barreled carbine is the most popular of all as it is the same configuration as the original Model 1892 seen by millions of us in four decades of John Wayne movies. Name the caliber and it is probably available in a Model 1892. Originals can be found in .32-20, .38-40, and .44-40; Browning B92's in .357 Magnum and .44 Magnum; late-manufactured Japanese replicas through Winchester in .357 Magnum, .44 Magnum, .45 Colt, and .44-40; Inter-Arms Rossi's in the same four offerings as Winchester; and currently through Navy Arms or EMF, also in the same four chamberings.

It just seems natural to me that the first choice for caliber and configuration in a Model 1892 should be a .44-40 with a 20-inch full octagon barrel. The Navy Arms version has a blued barrel, receiver, lever, fore end cap, and crescent-shaped butt plate all set off well by the good quality American Walnut used for stocking this new-old model. Both the dovetail mounted front sight and the walnut used in the stocks are upgrades by Navy Arms from the previous models offered by Interarms. The operation of the action is also much smoother than Rossis I have worked with in the past.

The Model 1892 is a much stronger action than the 1860, 1866, and 1873 being, in fact, a miniature 1886. In my old Lyman Cast Bullet Manual there are loads for the .44-40 in the Winchester '92 consisting of a

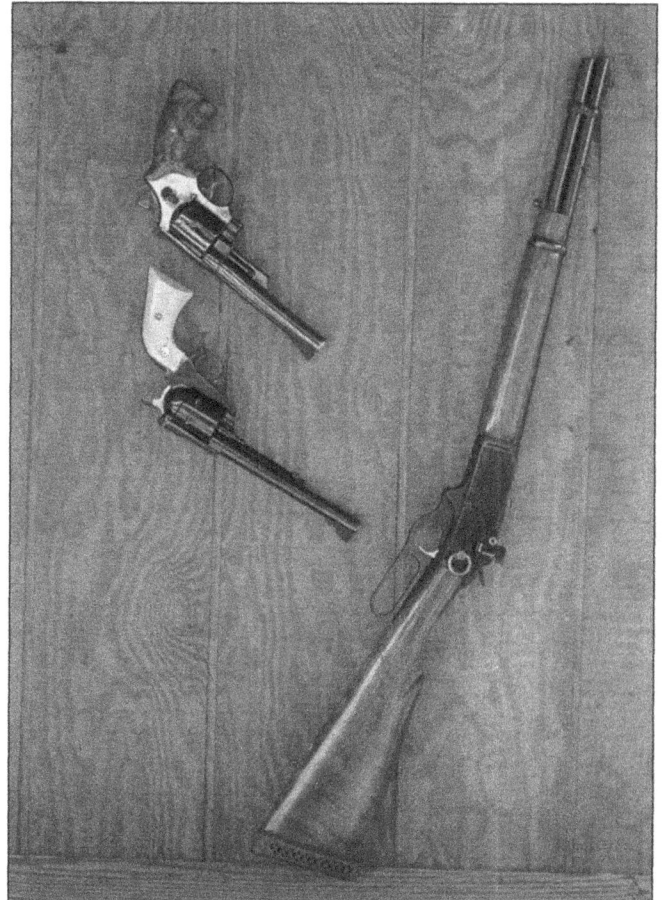

Three great .44 Magnums from the middle of the 20th century: the Ruger Super Blackhawk, the Smith & Wesson Model 29, and the Marlin 336.

One of the handiest lever guns in existence is Marlin's .357 Magnum Model 1894C, shown here with two excellent companions, a Smith & Wesson Combat Magnum and a Ruger Flat-Top Blackhawk.

205-rain cast bullet at 1,900 fps, a 215-grain gas check at 1,850 fps, and a 200-grain jacketed bullet at 2,100 fps! All loads were assembled with #2400.

With the 1892, one has a lever action that can be seriously considered for hunting. With the mild loads that are required for use of the 1860, 1866, and 1873 Winchesters and the Spencer, it is no great chore to come up with a load that is suitable for use in both sixgun and lever gun. However, by the time we get to the Model 1892, with an action that will handle Magnum-level loads, excellent shooting loads to use in tandem are not so easily arrived at. Most sixguns will shoot most loads very well. However, lever guns can be picky. You can save a lot of time and energy if a load is settled upon for use in the lever gun, first and then checked to see how it performs in the companion sixgun, rather than vice versa.

When choosing a sixgun to go with the modern lever-action rifles, my first choice is always a sixgun with adjustable sights. For the 357 Model 1892, I bow to Kent Bellah's choice and go with a 3 1/2-inch Smith & Wesson .357 Magnum Model 27. Moving up to the big bores, in .44 Magnum, a Ruger Flat-Top cut to 4 3/4 inches; for a '92 .45 Colt, Colt's New Frontier 4 3/4 inches; and finally for the .44-40, a Texas Longhorn Arms 7 1/2-inch West Texas Target.

I earlier mentioned how fortunate I have been to come up with original 1892s in both .32-20 and .38-40 chamberings. That good fortune also extends to their mates, from the first decade of the 20th century, a 4 3/4-inch Colt SAA .32-20, and a 5 1/2-inch Colt Bisley Model .38-40. It just doesn't get much better than this, at least until I find that just-right original Model 1892 with the barrel marked ".44 WCF."

Marlin 1894 Cowboys: I've been a fan of Marlin lever guns for nearly five decades, ever since I bought a pair of Marlin shooters, original Model 1894s chambered in .38-40 and .25-20. In my foolish life as a teenager I let both guns slip through my hands. I would love to have them back now! In the 1960s, Marlin's 336, a long-time deer hunter's favorite offered in .30-30 and .35 Remington, was introduced as a sixgunner's companion in .44 Magnum. As mentioned, I purchased the first one to hit town and it has now served me well for more than 35 years. With its 20-inch barrel, full magazine tube, and straight-gripped stock it is the near-perfect woods carbine. However, a real joy found in firearms is taking "near-perfect" sixguns or lever guns and making them even more perfect. To accomplish this with the Marlin 336 .44 Magnum, it was sent off to gunsmith Keith DeHart to have the barrel cut to 18 1/2 inches and the overly abundant forearm and butt stock, both made of too much quality walnut, slimmed down. The result is an even easier and faster-handling big-bore carbine.

In 1969, the Marlin 1894 was resurrected and offered in .44 Magnum, and then in subsequent years, .357 Magnum (a truly great lever gun), .45 Colt, .41 Magnum, .25-20, and .32-20. The last four chamberings are gone in the standard 1894, with the .41 and .45 commanding premium prices at gun shows. They have been replaced with the 1894 Cowboy, a 24-inch octagon-barreled lever gun designed primarily for cowboy action shooters with the added benefit of being an excellent hunting lever gun. It is available in .45 Colt, .44 Magnum, .357 Magnum, and .44-40. To make them handier in the field, I have had both a .44-40 and a .45 Colt Cowboy cut back to an easier-handling 19 1/2-inches.

Several years ago Marlin offered two special runs of 16 1/2-inch Trapper-style carbines in .45 Colt and .44 Magnum with a total of 2,600 being manufactured. The .44 Magnum version is back with a ported barrel and is an excellent shooter and easy on the shoulder. All Marlin lever guns are drilled and tapped for scope mounts, and also drilled and tapped to accept Williams or Lyman receiver or peep sights. They also work well with tang sights.

I do not normally like to participate in the "what if you could have only one gun" scenario, but if I were forced to choose two rifles, one a .22 Rimfire, and the other a Centerfire, those two choices would be a Marlin 39 Mountie and Marlin 1894C .357 Magnum. There simply is not much I need to do with a rifle that I could not accomplish with either one of these little lever guns. In fact, I like my originals so well that I have found duplicates of both and put them away for the grandkids. Companion guns are also easy to pick for these lever-gun classics. From pure nostalgia and for old-time's sake, an original Flat-Gate .22 Single-Six goes with the Mountie, while the 1894C's partner is either a 4 5/8-inch Ruger Flat-Top Black Hawk or a Smith & Wesson Combat Magnum, the 4-inch Model 19.

The original 336 .44 Magnum lever gun just goes very naturally with Ruger's 7 1/2-inch Super Blackhawk, while for the 1894 .45 Colt it would be hard not to pick the Freedom Arms Model 97. Switching to the Trapper Model Marlins, I select double-action with two 4-inch Smiths, a Model 29 .44, and a Model 625 .45 Colt Mountain Gun, all designed for easy packin'. Finally, with the two 1894 Cowboys cut to 19 1/2 inches, the .45 Colt rides with a Texas Longhorn Arms Improved Number Five, and the .44-40 partners up with a 7 1/2-inch New Frontier .44 Special fitted with a .44-40 cylinder.

Winchester 1894: The 1894 Winchester is to long gunners what the Colt Single Action is to sixgunners. Its looks, feel, and performance stir the heart, mind, and soul as no other rifle. Even though it was not yet in existence at the time period depicted by most Hollywood tales, it is still the rifle must of us saw in countless western movies as we grew up. The Colt Single Action and the Winchester rifle were synonymous with the "B" movies of the 1930s and '40s, and the TV Westerns of the 1950s. Perhaps that is why both are still so popular today. The most popular version of the Model 1894 is the "standard" carbine, or the 20-inch barrel, full magazine tube, straight-gripped stock version. The perfect saddle gun. Early versions are marked .30 W.C.F. for Winchester Center Fire, instead of the .30-30 marking found on all current Model 1894s so chambered.

With the advent of the .44 Magnum sixguns from Smith & Wesson and Ruger in the 1950s, the demand soon rose for a companion lever gun. As we have mentioned, gunsmiths made a comfortable living converting Model 1892 Winchester .44-40s to .44 Magnum. Then in the 1960s, both Winchester and Marlin introduced lever guns in .44 Magnum, with Winchester's being on the tried-and-true Model 1894. Since that time, the Winchester '94 has been offered in a commemorative version in .44-40, as well as current sixgun cartridge chamberings of .357 Magnum, .44 Magnum, and .45 Colt.

The Trapper versions of the Model 1894 with 16 1/2-inch barrels, full magazine tubes, and chambered in .30-30, .357 Magnum, .44 Magnum, and .45 Colt have been very popular as woods guns that pack very easily and also go well with pickup trucks and jeeps. Their short barrels and compact size make them imminently more practical than a long-barreled bolt action, especially for the 4x4-riding farmer and rancher.

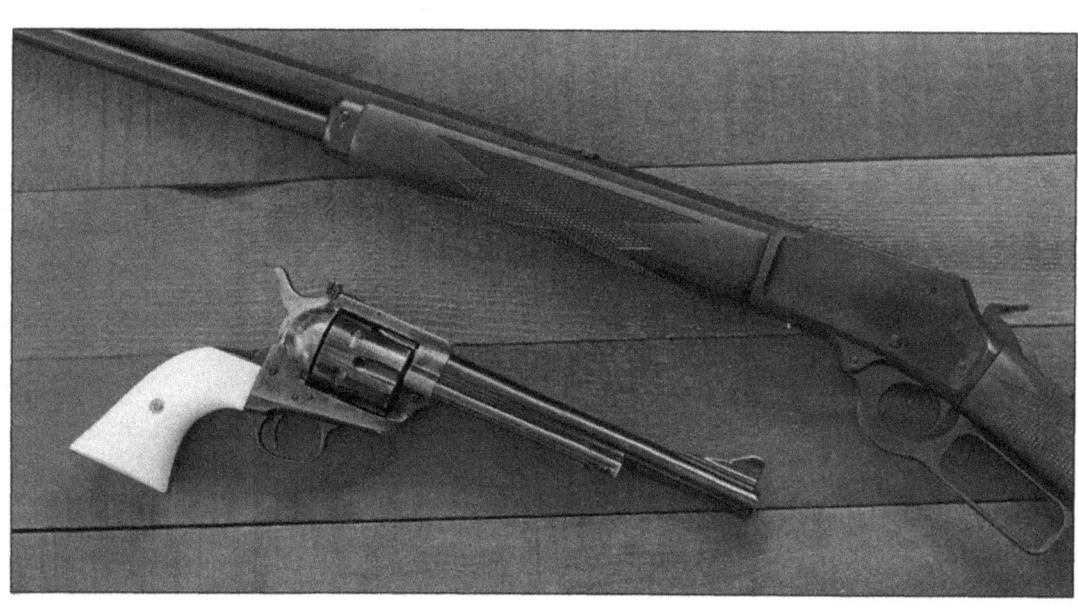

The .44-40 has been given new life in several lever guns, not the least of which is the Marlin 1894, which is paired up with a 7 1/2-inch Colt New Frontier.

A Ruger Bisley Model and a Winchester 94, both chambered in .44 Magnum, will handle most serious hunting chores.

With the great popularity of cowboy action shooting, Winchester introduced the 20-inch Trails End version capable of carrying 11 rounds, available in .357 Magnum, .44 Magnum, and .45 Colt. Many local cowboy shooters pick their lever gun with an eye on also using it for close-range hunting as we have general seasons on mule deer and elk as well as a spring and fall season for black bear. Both the .44 Magnum and the .45 Colt Trails End or Trapper versions fit in quite well here. For hunting loads in the .44 Magnum, Garrett's 310-grain semi-wadcutter Keith bulleted factory load clocks out at 1,520 fps and Winchester's Partition Gold 250 at 1,700 fps, and two reloads, a 250-grain gas check Keith and 300-grain flat point both over 10.0 grains of Unique for 1,400 and 1,300 fps muzzle velocity, respectively.

Switching to the .45 Colt, my favorite hunting load for use in heavy-framed sixguns such as the Ruger Blackhawk has long been a 300-grain bullet over 21.5 grains of either H110 or WW296 for 1,200 fps. Using RCBS's excellent Keith-style gas checked 300-grain bullet #45-300SWC-GC over 21.5 grains of H110 yields a muzzle velocity of 1,400 fps from the Trails End .45 Colt, and shoots remarkably well with groups at 1 inch. This is just the ticket for close-range work on deer, black bear, and even elk.

Companion sixguns for the Winchesters? In .45 Colt or .44 Magnum it is Ruger's New Model Blackhawks, both of which have been "Bisley-ized" with Ruger Bisley Model grip frames, hammer, and triggers being installed. With the Trapper .357, Smith's 5-inch Model 27 or 8-shot 627 gets the nod.

Although not a lever gun, a very interesting and useful .44 Magnum has recently arrived. Three years before the advent of the 10/22, Bill Ruger brought out

An early Winchester 1894 Trapper in .45 Colt with a case colored receiver goes well with a pair of Colt Single Action .45s with leather by El Paso Saddlery.

FAVORED LOADS FOR SIXGUN/LEVER GUN COMBINATIONS
(FOR USE IN STRONG MODERN SIXGUNS AND LEVER GUNS ON THE 1892 AND 1894 PATTERNS ONLY!)

.357 MAGNUM:

BULLET	LOAD	MV/14 5/8"	MV/18"
Hornady 140 XTP	17.5 gr. #2400	1,478	2,008
Hornady 140 XTP	19.5 gr. WW296	1,423	1,962
Speer 158 JFP	15.5 gr. #2400	1,305	1,742
Speer 158 JFP	17.5 gr. WW296	1,344	1,748
Lyman #358156GC	15.0 gr. #2400	1,425	1,880

.44 MAGNUM:

BULLET	LOAD	MV/5 1/2"	MV/20"
Speer 240 JSP	22.0 gr. #2400	1,362	1,672
Speer 240 JSP	24.5 gr. WW296	1,342	1,681
Hornady 265 JFP	23.5 gr. WW296	1,317	1,621
Lyman #431244GC	20.0 gr. #2400	1,228	1,624
NEI 310KT	21.5 gr. WW296	1,304	1,547

.45 COLT:

BULLET	LOAD	MV/5 1/2"	MV/16"
Hornady 250 XTP	25.0 gr. H110	1,148	1,741
Lyman #454424	18.0 gr. #2400	1,151	1,489
NEI 310KT	21.0 gr. WW296	1,147	1,446

his first rifle, the .44 Magnum Deerstalker. The Deerstalker held four .44 Magnum rounds in its tubular magazine and was very popular, especially for the hunting of deer and black bear in heavy cover at close range. When the Deerstalker was issued the list price was $108, complete with the genuine walnut stock. Elmer Keith reported in 1961 that Bill Ruger used the Deerstalker successfully in Africa, taking a leopard at 100 yards as well as wart hog, topi, hyena, bushbuck, kob, and waterbuck. Keith also reported a few months later on his use of the new .44 Magnum carbine. "… I cannot readily think of a handier and more deadly little gun for all timber and reasonable range shooting of animals that are wanted for the table. It would also make a most excellent fighting weapon in close combat for any peace officer or for the military."

Alas, the Deerstalker was dropped from production in 1985, only to arrive in 1999 as the Deerfield. Catalogued as the Model 99/44, this new gas-operated .44 Magnum has an 18 1/2-inch barrel with a 1 in 20 twist, instead of the slower 1:38 too often found on .44 Magnum carbines, and the rear sight is now a folding aperture. Instead of a tubular magazine, the new Deerfield operates from a four-round rotary magazine. Due to its gas operation and well-designed stock, it is one of the most enjoyable .44 Magnum rifles I have ever shot and it has no trouble whatsoever fitting right in with my lever guns. Ruger's Mini 14-style semi-auto .44 Magnum is a great brush rifle for close-range shooting, and by "brush rifle" we mean a rifle that is easy to carry in woods or heavy brush, not one that can shoot through the latter. Elmer Keith liked the original Ruger .44 semi-auto, so this carbine deserves a very special sixgun as its companion, that being a 4-inch Elmer Keith Commemorative Model 29 .44 Magnum.

As we said at the beginning, there are literally endless combinations and choices when it comes to selecting a sixgun/lever gun combination. These are not necessarily the best, they are simply those that I enjoy tremendously.

EPILOGUE

With this we have come to the end of another book on big-bore handguns and related items that help us enjoy them even more. I would again recommend my first two books, *Big Bore Sixguns* and *Action Shooting Cowboy Style*, for more of the same type information and especially for other examples of custom sixguns, custom stocks, custom leather, and custom 'smiths.

It has been more than 45 years since a young kid purchased his first .22 lever gun and matching .22 sixgun and began the journey down a great path. I have been truly blessed all along the way. Yes, I have accumulated many guns as I moved along, and I have also done a lot of shooting and hunting, but more importantly I have met so many great people and gained so many true friends among those who enjoy shooting and hunting. I doubt that one could ever find a greater bunch of people anywhere. May your journey even exceed mine.

Good shootin' and God bless,
John Taffin,
Boise Idaho

HANDGUNNER DIRECTORY

Six-guns-U.S. manufactured, and replicas

Cimarron Arms, P.O. Box 906, Fredericksburg, TX 78624

Colt's Mfg., P.O. Box 1868, Hartford, CT 06144

EMF, 1900 E. Warner, Suite 1-D, Santa Ana, CA 92705

Freedom Arms, P.O. Box 150, Freedom, WY 83120

Marlin Firearms, P.O. Box 248, North Haven, CT 06473

M.O.A., 2451 Old Camden Pike, Eaton, OH 45320

Navy Arms, 689 Bergen Blvd., Ridgefield, NJ 07657

Sturm, Ruger & Co., Lacey Place, Southport, CT 06490

Smith & Wesson, 2100 Roosevelt Ave., Springfield, MA 01102

Taurus International, 16175 NW 49th Ave., Miami, FL 33014

Taylor's & Co., 304 Lenoir Dr., Winchester, VA 22603

Thompson/Center, P.O. Box 5002, Rochester, NH 03866

USFA Co., P.O. Box 1901, Hartford, CT 06106

Winchester, 275 Winchester Ave., Morgan, UT 84050

Custom six-gunsmiths, parts, and engraving

Actions By T, 16315 Redwood Forest Ct., Sugar Land, TX 77478

Adams & Son Engravers, 87 Acorn St., Dennis, MA 02638

Alpha Precision, 3238 Della Slaton Road, Comer, GA 30629

Belt Mtn. Enterprises, P.O. Box 3202, Bozeman, MT 59772

Bowen Classic Arms, P.O. Box 67, Louisville, TN 37777

Bozeman Trail Arms, 28 Lake Dr., Livingston, MT 59047

Ed Brown, 43825 Muldrow Tr., Perry, MO 63462

Brownell's, 200 S. Front St., Montezuma, IA 50171

Clements Custom Guns, 2766 Mt. Zion Road, Woodlawn, VA 24381

Clark Custom Guns, 336 Shootout Lane, Princeton, LA 71067

Competitive Edge, Rt. 1 Box 140, Bogard, MO 64622

Cosby Custom Gunsmithing, 111 W. Lincoln, Chandler, IN 47610

D&L Custom, P.O.Box 651, Gillette, WY 82717

Ed DeLorge, 6734 W. Main St., Houma, LA 70360

Ben Forkin, P.O. Box 444, White Sulphur Springs, MT 59645

Bill Grover, P.O. Box 703, Richmond, TX 77469

Andy Horvath, 14131 Diagonal Road, LaGrange, OH 44050

Jack Huntington, 44633 Sierra Hwy, Lancaster, CA 93534

Linebaugh Custom Sixguns, Rt 2, Box 100, Maryville, MO 64468

Mag-Na-Port, 41302 Executive Dr., Harrison TWP, MI 48045

Dale Miller Enterprises, Box 73, Hawk Springs, WT 82217

Munden Enterprises, 1621 Samson St., Butte, MT 59701

Oglesby & Oglesby, 744 W. Andrew, Springfield, IL 62707

Peacemaker Specialists, P.O. Box 157, Whitmore, CA 96096

Power Custom, RR2 Box 756AB, Gravois Mills, MO 65037

Qualite Pistol & Revolver, 15461 E. Batavia Dr. Suite B, Aurora, CO 80011

Gary Reeder Custom Guns, 2601 E. 7th Ave., Flagstaff, AZ 86004

Jim Riggs Engraving, 206 Azalea, Boerne, TX 78006

RPM, 15481 N. Twin Lakes Dr., Tucson. AZ 85739

Dave Sample, 804 Oak Terrace Dr., Prescott, AZ 86301

Shapel's Gun Shop, 1708 N. Liberty, Boise, ID 83704

SSK Industries, 721 Woodvue Lane, Wintersville, OH 43952

Wilson Combat, 2234 CR 719, Berryville, AR 72616

Six-gun stocks

Ajax Custom Grips, 9130 Viscount Row, Dallas, TX 75247

BluMagnum, 5825 Hemingway, Colorado Springs, CO 80930

Buffalo Brothers, 8315 E. Quill St., Mesa, AZ 85207

Crimson Trace, 8089 SW Cirrus Dr., Beaverton, OR 97008

Eagle Grips, 460 Randy Road, Carol Stream, IL 60188

Roy Fishpaw, 793 Mt. Olivet Church Road, Lynchburg, VA 24504

Gripmaker, P. O. Box 511, Mt. Vernon, MO 65712

Herrett's Stocks, P.O. Box 741, Twin Falls, ID 83303

Hogue Grips, P.O. Box 1138, Paso Robles, CA 93447

Dustin Linebaugh, P.O. Box 2735, Dept. G, Cody, WY 82414.

Paul Persinger, 10441 Mackinaw, El Paso, TX 79924

Precision Pro Grips, 5142 Hardt Road, Gibsonia, PA 15044

SK Custom Grips, 160 Richmore Dr., Verona, PA 15147

TK Custom Grips, 6210 Edgewater, Boise, ID 83709

Six-gun leather

John Bianchi, P.O. Box 2038, Rancho Mirage, CA 92270

Black Hills Leather, 410 W. Aurora, Laredo, TX 78041

Ted Blocker, 14787 S.E. 82nd Dr., Clackamas, OR 97015

Circle Bar T Leatherworks, 2213 State Rt. W., Fayette, MO 65248

G. Wm. Davis, 1120-D S. Hwy 89, Chino Valley, AZ 86323

El Paso Saddlery, P.O. Box 27194, El Paso, TX 79926

Freedom Arms, P.O. Box 150, Freedom, WY 83120

Derry Gallagher, P.O.Box 720536, McAllen, TX 78504

Gould & Goodrich, P.O. Box 1479, Lillington, NC 27546

Kirkpatrick Leather, P.O. Box 3150, Laredo, TX 78044

Legends in Leather, 1353 Coyote Road, Prescott, AZ 86303

Bob Mernickle, 32552 Bobcat Dr., Mission, BC, Canada V2V5L1

Walt Ostin/Custom Gunleather, 1260 Fisher Road, RR#2, Cobble Hill, BC, Canada, V0R1L0

Von Ringler, 31 Shining Mtn., Powell, WY 82435

San Pedro Saddlery, 506 E. Fremont, Tombstone, AZ 85638

C. Rusty Sherrick, 507 Mark Dr., Elizabethtown, PA 17022

Milt Sparks, 605 E. 44th St., Boise, ID 83714

Thompson Gunleather, 11078 W. Jewell Ave. B-4, Lakewood, CO 80232

Ammunition, bullets, molds, reloading, etc.

Black Hills Ammunition, P.O. Box 3090, Rapid City, SD 57709

Buffalo Bore, P.O. Box 78, Carmen, ID 83462

BRP Bullets, P.O. Box 9220, Tulsa, OK 74157

Cast Performance Bullet Co., P.O. Box 153, Riverton, WY 82501

CCI/Speer P.O. Box 856, Lewiston, ID 83501

Cor-Bon, 1311 Industry Road, Sturgis, SD 57785

Dillon Precision, 8009 E. Dillon Way, Scottsdale, AZ 85260

Federal Cartridge, 900 Ehlen Dr., Anoka, MN 55303

Garrett Cartridges, P.O. Box 178, Chehalis, WA 98532

Hornady, P.O. Box 1848, Grand Island, NE 68802

Lee Precision, 4275 Hwy U, Hartford, WI 53027

Lyman, 475 Smith St., Middleton, CT 06457

NEI, 51583 Columbia River Hwy., Scappoose, OR 97056

Oregon Trail, P.O. Box 529, Baker City, OR 97814

RCBS, 605 Oro Dam Blvd., Oroville, CA 95965

Redding, 1089 Starr Road, Cortland, NY 13045

Remington, P.O. Box 700, Madison, NC 27025

Sierra Bullets, 1400 W. Henry St., Sedalia, MO 65301

Starline, 1300 W. Henry St., Sedalia, MO 65301

Winchester Div., Olin Corp., 427 N. Shamrock, E. Alton, IL 62024

INDEX

Symbols

#1860 for sixguns, 298
#1870 Slim Jim, 298
#1879 Texas, 299
#1880 Cavalry, 298
#1880-S, 298
#1890-S, 298
#1895 Hardin, 299
#1911 Patton, 298
#1940 Standard World War II G.I., 298
#1942, 298
#200AW, 313
#2400, 75, 121
#358156, 100
#358156GC, 109
#358627, 103
#401043, 105
#40188, 105
#429215, 100
#429244, 100
#431244, 77
#452490, 100
#5 Patton holster, 295
#5SA, 102
#77 Tortilla, 298
#88 Street Combat, 298

Calibers

.22 Rimfire, 13, 23, 31, 50, 60, 92, 209, 341
.221 Fireball, 231
.22-250, 229, 231, 234
.223, 229, 234
.225 Winchester, 230, 235, 237
.256 Winchester, 55, 231
.270, 231, 235
.30 Carbine, 98, 104
.30 Herrett, 226
.30/06 JDJ, 235, 237
.30-06, 137, 201, 229, 231, 237
.30-30, 137, 193, 225-227, 230, 231, 237, 316, 329, 331, 340, 341
.30-40 Krag, 83, 331
.308, 229-231, 234, 328, 329
.309 JDJ, 227, 235, 237
.32 Long Colt, 48
.32 Magnum, 104, 105, 129, 172, 186, 199, 252, 254
.32-20, 28, 30, 38, 50, 51, 105, 129, 171, 172, 186, 199, 244-246, 248, 312, 331, 333, 337, 339, 340
.338 JDJ #2, 235, 237
.35 Remington, 193, 224, 226, 230, 231, 316, 340
.356 Winchester, 226, 233, 234
.357 Herrett, 226
.357 Magnum, 11, 30-32, 34, 39-41, 46, 47, 51, 53-56, 59, 67-75, 77-87, 93, 94, 96-98, 100, 101, 103, 104, 106-109, 111, 112, 115, 116, 119, 122, 123, 133, 136, 141-144, 162, 167-172, 183-186, 190, 192-200, 202, 204, 207, 218, 221, 222, 225, 242, 244, 247, 253, 256, 275, 283, 287, 294, 305, 307, 316, 320, 323, 324, 329, 331, 333, 338-343
.357 Maximum, 115, 140, 142, 143, 192, 193, 250, 261
.357 SuperMag, 142, 184, 190, 192, 193, 194, 195, 196, 197, 199, 232
.358 Winchester, 234
.360 DW, 198, 199
.375 H&H, 234, 235
.375 JDJ, 227, 235-237, 319, 320, 329
.375 SuperMag, 190, 193-195, 199
.375 Winchester, 193, 194, 225-227, 230, 231
.375/06 JDJ, 235, 237
.38 Casull, 203, 204
.38 Long Colt, 47, 48, 50, 51, 82, 286, 335
.38 Special, 30, 31, 34, 38, 39, 47, 51, 53-55, 67-72, 77, 79, 82, 98, 100, 108, 109, 111, 116, 142, 167, 172, 186, 217, 218, 224, 235, 260, 264, 280, 307, 316, 333
.38 Super, 29, 31, 68, 201-203, 206, 211, 212, 226, 264, 265, 328
.38 Super Police, 68
.38/44, 68, 69, 82
.38/44 Heavy Duty, 68
.38/44 Outdoorsman, 69
.38-40, 18, 28, 30, 31, 38, 41, 42, 44, 50, 51, 53, 62, 63, 83, 105-107, 111, 205-208, 247, 261, 262, 273, 282, 284, 285, 331-333, 337, 339, 340
.40 G&A, 205, 206
.40 S&W, 84, 87, 208, 218, 220, 222, 307
.400 Cor-Bon, 205
.401 PowerMag, 83
.401 Winchester, 83
.41 GNR, 259
.41 Long Colt, 30, 48, 49, 50, 51, 83, 111
.41 Magnum, 55, 82-86, 88, 89, 91, 98, 103, 104, 106, 107, 109, 119, 144-146, 169, 170, 172, 180-184, 187-190, 193, 196, 197, 205, 207, 221, 224, 226, 237, 244, 247, 254, 256, 278, 285, 316, 325, 329, 333, 340
.41 Special, 83, 244, 245
.414 SuperMag, 190, 192, 196, 197, 199
.416 Taylor, 235
.416/348 JDJ, 235
.416 GNR, 237
.44 Colt, 20, 252, 286, 304, 334, 336
.44 Double Action First Model, 62
.44 Douglas, 241
.44 Magnum, 15, 45, 55, 56, 58, 59, 73, 77-86, 89-91, 93-109, 111-116, 118-130, 133-137, 140-142, 144, 162, 164, 165, 169, 173, 174, 176, 177-181, 183-188, 190, 193-197, 199, 200, 203-205, 221, 222, 224-228, 238-241, 246, 247, 249, 251, 252, 255-258, 260, 270, 272, 275, 278-280, 282, 283, 285, 288, 292, 294, 300, 305, 314, 316, 317, 319, 320, 322, 323, 324, 325, 327-329, 331-333, 338-343
.44 Rimfire, 24, 26, 61, 330, 331, 333, 336
.44 Russian, 14-16, 18, 26, 50, 60-63, 74, 82, 252, 303, 333-335
.44 S&W, 24, 26, 61, 88
.44 S&W American, 14
.44 Schafer UltraMag, 194
.44 Special, 15, 29, 30, 33-35, 38-44, 51, 53, 54, 61-70, 74-79, 82, 84, 86, 89, 91, 94, 96, 98, 99, 104, 108, 120, 130, 133, 134, 166, 171-173, 180, 186, 200, 203, 225, 238, 241-244, 247, 250-254, 257, 258, 262, 267, 271, 274, 275, 278, 280, 288-290, 294, 297, 309, 316, 319, 333-336, 341
.44 Special Triple-Lock, 29
.444 Marlin, 194, 227, 230, 235, 237
.444 Schafer Magnum, 194
.44-40, 14, 18, 20, 21, 25-27, 30, 37, 38, 40, 41, 44, 50, 51, 53, 62, 63, 96, 105, 107, 111, 245-247, 249, 251-253, 258, 266, 269, 271-273, 312, 331, 333, 335-341

.445 SuperMag, 190-192, 194, 250, 251
.45 Auto Rim, 53, 89, 90, 100, 197, 198, 247
.45 Colt, 14, 17, 18, 20, 21, 26, 27, 29-31, 33-35, 38-41, 43, 44, 49-51, 53, 54, 56-59, 61-63, 83, 86, 88-92, 94, 96, 98, 100-113, 116, 120-123, 127, 128, 130, 133-137, 139, 143, 165, 167, 169, 171, 172, 177, 180, 182-184, 186-188, 190, 194, 212, 224, 225, 239, 241, 244, 246-249, 252, 254, 257, 259, 260, 263, 269, 271, 272, 276, 278, 279, 283, 285, 287, 288, 290, 293, 294, 309, 312, 313, 316, 319-323, 331, 333, 335-337, 339-343
.45 Government Model, 29, 90
.45 Magnum, 121, 133, 134
.45 S&W, 18, 333, 335
.45 Schofield, 16, 18, 88, 277, 283, 303, 333-335
.450 Boxer, 27
.450 Eley, 27
.450 GNR, 237
.454 Casull, 82, 120, 124, 126, 127, 129-131, 134-137, 140, 144, 164, 169, 173, 174, 176, 177, 180, 221, 222, 234, 237, 257, 259, 260, 305, 316, 319, 324, 325
.454 Casull Raging Bull, 174
.455 Eley, 27, 53
.45-70, 129, 162, 164, 166, 225, 227, 230, 231, 237, 241, 316, 319, 328
.458 WinMag, 236
.460 Rowland, 197-199, 204, 205, 328
.460 Rowland Long Slide, 265
.475, 82, 103, 127, 129, 130, 162-166, 172, 180, 197, 221, 222, 237, 239, 247, 251, 254, 255, 260, 287, 316, 319, 320, 322, 327-329
.475 GNR, 237
.475 Linebaugh, 129, 130, 162, 164, 166, 172, 254, 255, 260, 320, 327, 329
.476 Eley, 27
.480 Ruger, 124, 128-132, 162, 163, 165, 166, 177, 179, 180, 182, 316, 319, 322, 327, 333
.50 Action Express, 141, 144, 169, 219-222, 237, 245, 328
.500 Alaskan, 235
.500 Linebaugh Longs, 127, 165
.500 Linebaughs, 82, 149, 222

Numerics

1836 Paterson, 9
1847 Walker Colt, 10
1851 Navy, 11, 12, 24, 26, 60, 284, 335
1860, 11-13, 23-26, 47, 60, 61, 82, 91, 330, 332, 333, 335-337, 339, 340
1860 Henry, 24, 60, 61, 330, 332, 334-336
1863 Model, 18
1866, 332
1866 Winchester Yellow Boy, 334
1871-72 Open Tops, 20
1873, 332
1873 Winchester, 27, 334, 336, 340
1875 Remington, 20
1878 Model, 50
1889 Navy Model, 50
1903-A3 Springfields, 200
1911 Government Model .45 ACP, 201
1917 Model, 53, 54, 63, 92
1920 Threepersons, 296, 297
1930 Austin, 293, 296, 297
1950 Target Models, 64, 78
209X50 Magnum, 228
360Sc Chief's Special, 86
396Ti, 86
4506, 207
4516, 218
45-250FN, 156
586, 85
6.5 JDJ, 235
625-2, 90
625-5, 90
686, 85
7-08, 229
7BR, 229

A

Able, Charles, 39, 240, 241, 272
Accurate Arms, 162, 194
Accurate Arms #9, 125
Adamovich, Tedd, 243, 244, 250, 253, 279
Adams, John Sr., 277
African Hunter, 260
Aguirre, Manny, 296
AimPoint, 130
Ajax Custom Grips, 277
Alaskan, 50, 137, 165, 191, 235, 237, 258, 316
Alaskan Survivalist, 260
Alliant, 122
Alpha Precision, 239, 241
American Handgunner, 241, 254, 258, 263, 265
American Pistolsmith's Guild, 263
American Rifleman, 77, 238
AMT's Javelina Hunting Model Long-Slide, 206
Anaconda, 56-59, 158, 257, 324, 325
Anderson, Andy, 303, 310, 335
Andrews and Hill Leather Company, 293
Applegate, Col. Rex, 70, 249
Arness, James, 29
Arrestor, 231, 262
Artillery Model, 26
Askins Avenger, 210, 301, 302, 314
Askins, Col. Charles, 30, 70, 71, 211, 216, 301
Autry, Gene, 29

B

Baby Dragoon, 11
Baer, Bob, 241-243, 253
Baggett, Penn, 172, 250, 320
Baker, Bob, 137, 142, 144, 165, 167, 328
Baker, Wayne, 135
Ballew, Bart, 302, 303
Balloon Head, 76
Balloon-Type, 134
Bangor Punta, 80, 184
Barrel/cylinder Gaps, 103, 138
Bar-Sto, 204, 250
Baughman, 72
Baughman front ramp, 90
Bausch and Lomb, 126
Beals, Fordyce, 18
BearHug, 54, 58, 69, 74, 81, 84, 86, 88, 90, 116, 121, 256, 278, 279
Bearhug, 55, 56, 59
Beavertail, 263
Beery, Wallace, 54
Bellah, Kent, 331, 332, 340
Belt Mountain, 114, 243, 244, 250, 251, 265-267, 290
Beretta, 216, 219, 306
Bianchi Sight Channel, 302
Bill, Buffalo, 15, 50, 61
Billy Old, 307, 308
Birdshead, 48
Bishop, Pike, 212, 312
Bisley Model, 28, 30, 45, 48, 100-104, 106, 109, 111, 113-115, 127, 129, 132, 140, 240, 245, 247, 250, 252-254, 257, 265, 268, 271, 289, 290, 321-324, 331, 340, 342
Black Chromex, 260
Black Diamond, 257-259, 273
Black Hills, 109, 140
Black Hills Leather, 301, 302
Black Jack Pershing, 294
Blocker, Ted, 302, 303
BluMagnum, 40, 74, 104, 243, 244, 251, 276, 278, 279
Bohlin, Ed, 101, 297
Bo-Mar Silhouette, 138, 139
Bonded Core, 122, 128, 166, 178, 320, 323, 326
Bonney, William, 49
Bonnie and Clyde, 28
Boone, Richard, 292, 298
Border Patrol, 70
Boser, 105
Boser, Gordon, 83, 93
Bowen Classic Arms, 244, 246
Bowen, Hamilton, 103, 141, 242, 244, 245-247, 250, 251, 326
Bozeman Trail Arms, 243
Bren Ten, 206
Brill, W.R., 295, 296
Brown, Ed, 204, 263
Browning, 201, 203, 205, 206, 220, 222, 333, 338, 339
BRP, 59, 83, 106, 108, 113, 115, 123, 125, 126, 128, 132, 141, 143-162, 166, 176, 178, 187, 188, 190, 194, 320, 323, 328
Buffalo Bore, 121, 122, 128-131, 136, 164-166, 178, 182, 320, 322-328
Buffalo Brothers, 25, 279, 280, 305, 335

Buntline Specials, 27, 41
Burris, 121, 127, 166, 158, 187

C

Cassidy, Hopalong, 29, 272
Cast Performance Bullet Company, 122, 189, 197, 199
Casull Arms Model CA3800, 204
Casull, Dick, 120, 133-136, 158, 204
Cavalry Model, 26, 27, 312
CCI Blazer, 92, 210, 212, 213, 215, 219
CDP (Custom Defense Pistol), 208-210, 301
Chester, 29
Cheyenne, 296
Chicago Chopper, 68
Chief's Special, 79, 86, 217-219, 307
Chrome-Moly, 116
Cimarron, 17, 113, 131, 253, 257, 258, 261, 262, 277, 279, 282, 284-287, 304, 305, 307, 308, 332-335, 337, 339
Circle Bar T Leatherworks, 303
Civil War, 24
Civilian Model, 27, 37, 51, 111
Clark Combat Commander, 263, 265
Clark Custom Guns, 197, 204, 263, 265
Clark Drop-in Kit, 205
Clark, Jimmy, 201, 263, 264
Classic, 81
Classic DX, 81, 323
Clements, David, 103, 245, 246, 326
CNC, 74, 85, 196
Cody, William F. "Buffalo Bill", 15
Coke Bottle, 282
Colt, 299
Colt .357 Magnum, 45, 55
Colt .38 Super, 29
Colt and Smith & Wesson 1917 revolvers, 200
Colt Cartridge Conversions, 20, 282, 287, 304, 307, 334
Colt Frontier Sixshooter, 27, 40
Colt Government Model, 43
Colt Lightning, 43, 48
Colt, Samuel, 9, 12, 13
Combat Magnum, 46, 71-74, 81, 85, 90, 200, 282, 291, 307, 313, 340, 341
Commander .45 ACP, 201, 264
Compact, 90, 132, 138, 171, 173, 200, 208, 210-213, 217-219, 240, 263, 269, 285, 286, 301, 306, 307, 341
Competition Strut Assembly kit, 269, 270
Competitive Edge, 247
Connors, Chuck, 310
Contender G2, 231
Contender Super, 225
Contender Super, 14 225
Cooper, Gary, 303, 304
Cooper, Jeff, 203, 206, 211
Cor-Bon, 121, 122, 128, 130, 136, 142, 161, 176, 177, 178, 186, 205, 206, 208-210, 212, 213, 216, 218, 219, 231, 261, 320, 322-324, 326

Cosby Custom Gunsmithing, 247
Cosby, Brian, 248
Cougar, 216, 219, 306
Crane, 116
Creedmore, 225, 317
Crimson Trace, 280
Croft, Harold, 101, 238
Crow, Larry, 247
Crowder, Bob, 271
CS40, 219
CS45, 219
CS9, 219
Custer, George Armstrong, 15
Custom Gun Grips, 282
Custom Gun Leather, 308

D

D&L Custom, 248
Dall Sheep Horn, 283, 288
Davis, G. Wm., 304
Deane and Adams, 47
Deason, Deacon, 55, 90, 121, 256, 278, 279
Deerfield, 343
Deerstalker, 343
DeHart, Keith, 243, 340
Delta Elite, 206
Derry Gallagher, 73
Desert Eagle, 141, 219-222, 328
Detective, 285
Diagonal Road Gunshop, 254
Dillinger, John, 66
Dillon, Matt, 29, 31, 297
Doc, 29
Dominator, 232, 233
Dornaus & Dixon, 206
Dot Snap, 301, 302
Dougan, John, 96
Douglas, Ed, 311
Dragoons, 10, 11, 24, 26, 60, 289
Drury, James, 310
Dubber, Michael, 248
Duplex, 134

E

Eagle Grips, 11, 41, 269, 280, 281, 287, 305
Earp, Wyatt, 28, 29, 292
Eastwood, Clint, 56, 80, 292, 303, 310
Edwards, Don, 315
Eimer, Pop, 83
El Paso Saddlery, 39, 208, 210, 287, 291-298, 342
Eliphalet Remington, 18
Elliott, W. H., 18
Elliott, Wild Bill, 29
Elmer Keith Grips, 275
Emerson, Ashley, 244, 245, 327
EMF, 10, 21, 113, 332, 339
Encore, 223, 229, 231, 235, 261, 328, 329
Endurance Package, 81
Equalizer, 27

F

Fast Draw, 155
FBI, 307
FBI Slant, 295, 307, 313
Federals, 90, 109, 210, 218, 323
Festus, 29
Field Grade, 138-140, 162, 165
First Model Hand Ejector, 62, 63, 68
Fishpaw, Roy, 67, 69, 78, 86, 104, 282, 283, 288
Fitz Special, 254
Fitzgerald, J. Henry, 254
Fitzgerald, J.H., 49
Flat-Point Penetrator, 324
Folded Head, 76, 134
Ford, Glenn, 29
Forkin, Ben, 250, 251, 326
Fourth Model Hand Ejector, 66, 75, 89
Freedom Arms Collectors Association, 160
Frontier Six-Shooter, 14, 25-27, 312
Full-Moon Clips, 90, 91, 197, 206

G

Gallagher, Derry, 73, 211, 301, 305-307
Garrett, 108, 109, 119, 130, 178, 186, 196, 320, 323, 325, 342
Garrett, Pat, 292, 293
Garrett, Randy, 319, 325
Garza, Sgt. Fermin, 267
Gaston Glock, 213
Gates, Elgin, 190, 193, 194
George Lawrence #120 Keith holster, 314
George Lawrence Co., 296
Glenn, Butch, 303
Glock, 206, 213, 214, 215
Goerg, Al, 223
Gold Dot, 92, 141, 178, 199, 210, 260, 271, 324
Gould & Goodrich, 219, 306, 307
Gould, Chester, 55
Government Model .45s, 200
GP-100, 117, 118, 122, 123, 126, 132
Grand Duke Alexis, 15, 61
Gripmaker, 283
Grover, Bill, 241, 242, 250-253, 283, 303
Grover's Express Model, 252
Grover's Improved No. 5, 241
Gun Digest, 203
Gun Re-Blu Company, 78
Gunfighter-Style, 271
Guns & Ammo, 83, 256
Guns Magazine, 93, 100, 251, 271
Gunsmoke, 29, 297
Gunther, Al, 55

H

H.H. Harris, 80
H110, 121
H4227, 193
Hackathorn, Ken, 265
Half-Moon Clips, 53, 87

Hamer Jr., Frank, 29
Hamer, Frank, 28, 29
Handgun Hunter's Hall of Fame and Museum, 256, 258
Hardin, John Wesley, 28, 292, 293, 299
Hatcher, Major, 79
Hawkeye, 231
Hays, John Coffee, 8, 9, 60
Heard, Charles McDonald, 29
Heavy .45 Colt, 82, 148, 155, 322
Heiser, H.H., 300
Hellstrom, Carl, 184
Hellstrom, Doug, 84
Henry Model 1860, 24
Henry, B. Tyler, 335, 336
Heritage Models, 91
Herrett, Rod, 285
Herrett, Steve, 223, 226, 227
Herrett's Trooper, 285
Herter, 83
Hickok Eagle, 284
Hickok, Wild Bill, 12
Highway Patrolman, 66, 85, 111
Hi-Viz, 86
Hoenig, George, 232
Hoffman, Jeff, 214, 265
Hogleg, 27
Hogue, 81
Hogue grips, 71, 73, 286, 287
Hogue, Guy, 286
Hogue, Pat, 158
Holliday, Doc, 12, 28, 48, 49, 259, 292, 299
Hoover, J. Edgar, 70
Hopkins & Allen, 22
Horn, Tom, 50
Hornady, 59, 72, 83, 85, 88, 103, 106, 108, 113, 122, 123, 128, 130-132, 141-143, 162, 163, 165, 167, 180, 182, 187, 193, 194, 196, 198, 199, 205-207, 210, 212, 213, 215, 216, 218, 227, 230, 231, 234, 250, 319, 324, 327, 328, 343
Horvath, Andy, 241, 251-255, 305
Houchins, 238
Hoxie, Jack, 54
Hughes, John R., 291, 293, 298
Hunter Model, 113-115, 231, 259, 324
Hunter Packs, 197
Huntington, Jack, 254, 255, 326

I

IHMSA, 82
Improved Number Fives, 252
Interarms, 339
Iron Sight Gun Works, 142
ivory, 80, 287

J

Jacobsen, Teddy, 57, 58, 89
James, Jesse, 28
Janis, Eddie, 38, 266, 273, 280
Jeffe rig, 307
Jeffecito, 307
J-frame 340Sc Centennial, 86
Jones, Buck, 271, 272
Jones, J.D., 125, 225, 235, 236, 256, 262, 263, 315, 316
Jordan, Bill, 29, 72, 73, 83, 84, 263, 264, 286
Jungkind, Reeves, 55

K

Keith Bullet, 76, 98, 109, 126, 193, 196, 241, 252, 316, 319, 342
Keith, Elmer, 29, 49, 64, 69, 75, 83, 93, 101, 102, 120, 133, 203, 223, 238, 239, 243, 245, 247, 249, 251, 252, 267, 274, 275, 283, 287, 288, 294, 296, 300, 302, 313, 314, 316, 343
Kelly, Ken, 258
Kelly, Larry, 106, 255, 256, 258, 316
Ketchum, Black Jack, 292
Keys, General Bill, 59
K-frame, 71, 84, 85, 173, 279, 282, 285
Kimber and Springfield Armory, 203
King Cobra, 55, 56
King Custom SAA, 76
Kirkpatrick Leather, 306, 307
Kobra Carry, 263
Kojis, Tony, 33, 39, 249, 282, 284, 285, 288, 290
Kolar, Scott, 11, 250, 251, 265, 289, 290
Koozer, Ward, 331

L

L'il Guns, 254
Lachuk, John, 77, 93
LAR's Grizzly, 206, 220, 221
Lauck, Dave, 248, 249
LBT, 59, 108, 115, 122, 123, 128, 130, 141, 161, 162, 166, 178, 182, 187, 188, 190, 197, 320, 325, 326
Legends in Leather, 307, 308
Leskovec, Bob, 33, 75, 101, 201, 202, 273-275, 288, 289, 294
Leupold, 129, 140, 143, 257, 317
L-frame, 85, 86, 245, 323
Liberty Head, 284
Linebaugh 82, 103, 104, 127, 129, 130, 141, 162, 164-166, 172, 221, 222, 239, 244, 245, 251, 254, 255, 260, 287, 310, 311, 316, 319, 320, 322, 326-329
Linebaugh Custom Sixguns, 287
Linebaugh Sixgun, 319
Linebaugh, Dustin, 286, 287
Linebaugh, John, 103, 162, 166, 287, 311, 326
Linebaugh, The, 310
Line-Boring, 140
Little, Larry, 283
Lockwood, Jim, 308
Loc-Tite, 135
Lone Ranger, 309
Lone Wolf Gonzaullas, 64, 271
Lozano, Rudy, 301-303
Lyman, 42, 44, 59, 72, 74, 76, 77, 83, 85, 98-100, 103, 105, 106, 108, 109, 113, 123, 126, 139, 141, 143, 161, 164, 188, 193, 216, 241, 316, 341, 343
Lyman's #429421, 109
Lyman Cast Bullet Manual, 339
Lyman's, #429421, 75
Lyman's #358429, 69
Lyman's #358477, 69
Lyman's #410459, 103

M

M.O.A., 234, 328
Madsen, Chris, 28
MagnaClassic, 82
Mag-Na-Port, 104, 255-258, 280, 316
Mag-na-Port, 106, 258
Magnum Research, 220, 328
Marlin 1894, 340, 341
Marlin 336, 226, 332, 334, 339, 340
Marlin Model 39 Mountie, 332
Mason, William, 26, 47-50, 203
Masters Tournament, The, 265
Masterson, Bat, 27, 293
Maximums, 127, 165, 197
McCoy, Tim, 271
McGivern, Ed, 30, 292
McNellis, Bobby, 291-293
McQueen, Steve, 310
Meanea, F.A., 296
Meprolight Tritium, 209
Mernickle, Bob, 305, 308
Merrill, 232
Merwin and Hulbert, 22
Metalife SS, 256
Mexican Eagle, 274, 284
Miculek, Jerry, 263, 292
Mid-Frame Model, 97 167, 169
Milek, Bob, 226, 256
Military & Police Model, 62, 71
Miller, Dale, 40, 272, 273
Miller, Killing Jim, 293
Mil-Specs, 210, 211, 212, 312
MIM, 74, 81, 85
Mix, Tom 271
MMC Combat Night Sights, 249
Model 12, 184, 186
Model 15, 186
Model 1860 Army, 12
Model 1877, 48, 49, 83
Model 1890, 17, 20
Model 1892, 253, 331
Model 19, 73, 74, 85, 279, 307, 341
Model 1926, 64, 68
Model 1950 Target, 75-77, 89
Model 1955, 89, 90
Model 24, 64, 66, 75, 89
Model 25-2, 88, 89, 91, 92, 206
Model 25-5, 88-92
Model 26, 89
Model 27, 70-72, 80, 85, 186, 256, 263, 283, 340, 342
Model 28, 85

Model 3, 14-16, 18, 26, 282, 301, 330, 334
Model 386Sc, Mountain Lite 86
Model 41, 187
Model 44, 56, 173, 174, 187
Model 57, 84, 85, 88
Model 610, 87, 88, 206
Model 629, 85, 205, 257
Model 65, 73
Model 657, 85, 325
Model 66, 74, 85, 307
Model 696, 86
Model 715, 186
Model 741, 187
Model 83, 104, 129, 133, 135-163, 165-167, 168, 171, 172, 182, 195, 255, 259, 304, 305, 323-325, 327
Model 97, 104, 135, 142, 151-156, 322, 323, 341
Model HEG, (Hand Ejector Gold) 91
Model Number 1, 13
Model Number 1 1/2, 13
Model Number 2, 13
Model of 1878, 49, 50
Model P 23, 26-28, 30, 31, 39, 40, 43, 44, 49, 50, 262, 284
Moore, Clayton, 309
Moran, Jerry, 55
Morrison, Milt, 53, 96, 258, 273
Moto-Tool, 284
Munden, Bob, 29, 34, 36, 39, 40
Murbach, Terry, 120, 242, 253
MV, 343
Myers, S.D., "Tio Sam" 293-295, 298
Myres, S.D., 28, 70, 293, 300

N

Nahas, Richard, 92
Navy, 11, 12, 17, 18, 20, 21, 24, 26, 50, 51, 60, 224, 278, 279, 282, 284, 303, 332-339
NEI, 59, 99, 103, 123, 187, 188, 241, 343
NEI #451.310, 109
NEI 429.260KT, 109
New Century, 62, 74, 75, 87, 128
New Frontier Single Action Army, 39
New Haven Arms Company, 13
New Model, 16, 61, 62, 75, 94, 98, 100, 104-109, 114, 115, 239, 245-248, 254, 259, 265, 266, 269-271, 303, 342
New Model .44, 18
New Model Army .44, 20
New Model Number 3, 18
New Service, 45, 46, 51-56, 58, 59, 69, 89, 106, 187, 257, 258
New Service Target Revolver, 54
Newly, 29
N-frame, 45, 53, 55, 68, 69, 71, 72, 84-87, 186, 249, 278, 279, 282, 285, 313
Niles, M.A., 83
Novak Low Mount, 213
Novak, Wayne, 207
NRA, 70, 79, 118

O

O'Connor, Jack, 238
Oehler Model 35P, 122, 127, 128, 143, 218
Officer's Model Match, 55
Oglesby & Oglesby, 270
Ojala, Arvo, 297, 298, 310
Old Lucky, 28
Old Model, 98, 99, 104, 106, 107, 109, 115, 135, 242-248, 251, 253, 256, 257, 265, 339
Oliver Winchester, 13, 335, 336
Omega Star, 219
Ostin, Walt, 303, 308-310, 335
Outers Pistol Perch, 158
Overstreet, 302
Overstreet, Marty, 303

P

P.O. Ackley, 134
P-90, 215, 216
Pachmayr, 138, 229, 232, 233, 257
packin' pistol, 89, 97, 102-104, 107, 109, 111, 134, 139, 162, 239, 241, 244-246, 257, 264, 271
Paladin, 31, 298
Parkerized, 212
Partition Gold, 108, 109, 128, 176, 178, 324, 342
Paterson Model, 9
Patridge, 54, 71, 138, 142, 251, 258
Patridge sight, 90
Patriot, 223, 228
Patton, General George S., 28, 68, 70, 71, 271, 272, 292, 294, 295, 298
Peacemaker, 13, 23, 27, 38, 71, 91, 266, 267, 273, 280, 283, 294, 336, 337
Peacemaker Centennial, 312
Peacemaker Parts, 269
Peacemaker Specialists, 269
Pearce, Brian, 130, 131
Pender, Jack, 55
Penn Baggett Ranch, 250
Peoples, Clint, 271
Performance Center, 71, 91, 92
Persinger, Paul, 36, 39, 40, 287, 288, 298, 310
Philippine, 50
Pi, Peter of Cor-Bon, 205
Pin Master, 264
Pistol Packs, 197
Power Custom, 247, 267-270
Precision Pro Grips, 288
Predator, 104
Premier Grade, 136
Pretty Boy Floyd, 66
Prospector Rig, 307
PS6DA, 308
Python, 45

Q

QPR, 246, 258
Qualite Pistol & Revolver, 258

R

Rainey, Mike, 261
Raj Singh, 282
Ranger Lone Wolf Gonzaullas, 271
RCBS, 141
RCBS #45-201, 218
RCBS's #38-150KT, 69
RCMP, 54
Redhawk, 118
Redhawk Long Colt Hunter, 260
Reed, Thell, 251
Reeder, Gary, 106, 109, 236, 237, 259-261, 326
Reloader, 7 226
Remington, 17-23, 26, 77, 99, 136, 143, 178, 193, 201, 210, 212, 219, 223, 224, 226, 230-232, 234, 279, 283, 289, 316, 340
Richards Conversion, 23, 25
Riggs, Jim, 270, 272, 314
Ringler Custom Leather, 311
Ringler, Von, 310, 311
Robbins, Marty, 291
Rock, Jim, 232, 233
Rogers, Roy, 29
Rogers, Walter, 93, 97, 98, 100
Roosevelt, Theodore 28, 50, 271, 299
Rossi Puma, 333
Rowland, Johnny, 197
Royal Blue, 47, 107
RPM XL, 232, 234
Ruger Blackhawk, 44, 94, 104, 105, 121, 169, 182, 192, 197, 238, 240, 243, 244, 247, 256, 321, 342
Ruger Flat-Top, 96, 99, 100, 253, 256, 314, 328, 338, 340, 341
Ruger Single-Six .22, 31
Ruger Super Blackhawk, 11, 99, 114, 135, 173, 185, 251, 256, 257, 321, 339
Ruger, Bill, 93, 248, 342, 343
Ruger, Tom, 120
Russell, Sam, 49, 83
Russian Model, 15, 16, 61

S

S&W bright blue, 78
S.A.S.S. (Springfield Armory Single Shot), 230, 232
Sadowski, Fred, 55
Saez, Adam, 296
Safe Action trigger, 214
Sample, Dave, 261, 285
San Pedro Saddlery, 212, 311
Sargis, Tom, 243
Scandium, 86
Scarborough, George, 293
Schafer, Lew, 194
Schlepp, Kelye, 243, 267
Schofield Model, 15, 16, 18, 279, 281, 303, 335
Schofield, Col. George, 15
Scott, Jay, 258, 279

Scout, 223, 228
Second Generation 1873-1973 Peacemaker Centennial Edition, 336
Second Model Hand Ejector, 63, 64
Second Models, 63
Security-Six, 116, 117, 118, 123, 132
Sedgely, 238, 245
Selman, John, 293
Serva, Bob, 196, 197
Seville, 193
Shapel, 209
Sharpe, Phil, 69
Shelton Payne Arms Co., 294
Sheriff's Models, 27, 245
Sherrick, Rusty, 131, 132, 313
Sierra, 59, 85, 88, 103, 123, 126, 141, 143, 187, 194, 196, 197-199, 206, 207, 218
Silver Tip, 91
Single Action Army (Colt), 14, 17, 18, 20, 23, 26-31, 36, 39, 41-44, 48-51, 56, 61, 71, 76, 79, 88, 94, 97, 101, 102, 106, 107, 109-113, 120, 121, 135, 168, 169, 171, 200, 203, 212, 215, 222, 238, 239, 243, 244, 247, 248, 267, 271, 272, 283, 287, 292-294, 297-299, 306, 308, 312-314, 321, 330, 332, 337, 339
Single Action Army Flat-Top Target, 30
SK Custom Grips, 251, 289, 290
Skeeter Gun, 253
Skelton, Bart, 242, 253
Skelton, Skeeter, 29, 55-58, 68, 70, 77, 82, 84, 86, 241, 242, 250, 253, 274, 275, 278, 279
Slim Jim, 12
Sloan, Hank, 313, 314
Smith, Clint, 265
Smith, Horace, 13, 335
Snakewood, 283
South Texas Army, 252
Spanish American War, 26, 50
Sparks, Milt, 220, 313, 314
Speer, 59, 72, 74, 83, 85, 88, 91, 92, 103, 108, 121, 123, 126, 128, 132, 141, 143, 165, 171, 178, 182, 187, 193, 194, 198, 199, 206, 207, 210, 212, 213, 215, 216, 220, 222, 227, 228, 231, 234, 235, 255, 271, 322, 324, 343
Spencer Carbine, 333-335
Springfield Armory, 90, 91, 197, 203, 205, 209-213, 230, 232, 311, 312
Springfield Armory's Omega, 206
SS1, 253
SS2, 253
SS3, 253
SS4, 253
SS5, 253
SS6, 253
SS7, 253
SSK, 103, 106, 108, 109, 123, 125, 126, 128, 139, 141, 144-162, 166, 171, 187, 188, 194, 205, 225, 227, 229, 231, 233-236, 255, 257, 261-263, 316
Stalker Conversions, 106, 257

Star Valley, 135, 142, 162
Starline, 145, 164, 166, 194, 198, 199, 205
Storekeeper's Models, 27, 41
Stoudenmire, Dallas, 292
Stroh, Jim, 55, 103, 104, 109, 239, 240, 241, 326
Sturm, 120, 128, 200
Summer Special, 314
Super Hard Cast Hammerhead, 325
Super Ram Silhouette, 196
Super Redhawk, 56, 82, 120, 122-132, 180, 182, 257, 259, 260, 313, 323-325, 327
SuperMags, 190, 191, 193, 197
Supica, Jim, 92

T

Target Grey, 127, 128
Target Model of 1950, 66, 75
Taylor Knockout Formula, 222
Taylor, John "Pondoro", 222
Taylor, Twyla, 109, 259
Taylor's & Co., 333, 334
Texas Border Special, 252
Texas High-Ride, 303
Texas Longhorn Arms, 106, 241, 251-253, 283, 302, 303, 338, 340, 341
Texas Rangers, 9, 271
Texas Star, 284
Third Model, 60, 64, 66, 68, 75, 89
Thomas, Heck, 28
Thompson, Forrest, 314
Thompson, Ray, 77, 100, 103
Thompson/Center, 194, 206, 223, 225, 226, 228, 231, 232, 235, 236, 259, 311, 316, 328
Thompson/Center Contenders, 193
Threepersons, Tom, 58, 109, 210, 271, 275, 291-293, 295, 310, 313
Thuer Conversion, 25
Thunderer, 48, 49, 131, 262, 279, 284, 313
Tiffany-style, 277
Tigre, El, 331
Tilghman, Bill, 28, 63
Tombstone Speed Rig, 299
Top-Break, 14, 24, 60
Tracy, Dick, 55
Trails End, 342
Transfer Bar Safety, 98, 100, 106, 107, 239, 269
Trapper-style, 341
Trimble, Lee, 293, 295
Triple-Lock, 29, 43, 61-64, 67, 69, 75-78, 89, 91, 180, 215
Triplex, 134
Trooper, 47, 55, 285
Trooper Mark III, 55
Trooper Mark V, 55
TRP, 211-213, 311
Tyler T-grip, 68

U

Uberti, 258, 337

Uncle Mike, 121, 131
United States Border Patrol, 54
Unlimited Silhouette, 225

V

V-10 Ultra Compact, 213
Vaquero, 101, 109-113, 115, 239-241, 245-249, 259, 260, 268-271, 282, 289, 307
Villa, Pancho, 28, 271
Volcanic Repeating Arms Company, 13

W

Walker, Samuel, 9
Walters, Ray, 128
Warren Center, 224
Wayne, John, 29, 271
Weaver, 158, 231, 262
Wells Fargo Model, 12
Wesson, Dan, 13, 56, 81, 82, 103, 142, 182-199, 285, 286, 325
Wesson, Doug, 70
Wesson, Seth and Carol, 195
WFN, 128
White, Rollin, 13, 14, 23, 24
Whitney, Eli, 10
Wiegand, 174
Wild Bill Hickock, 304
Wild Bunch, 212
Williamson, Lt., 83
Wilson, Bill, 211, 263, 265
Wilson, Jim, 29, 131, 242, 253
Wilson, R.L., 126
Wilson-Rogers, 250
Winchester Model 1866, 24
Winchester's, 90, 109
Winter Range, 279
Wolf and Klar, 63, 66
Wood, Leonard, 50
Wootters, John, 241, 243, 253
WW296, 59, 83, 103, 104, 106, 108, 113, 115, 121, 123, 125, 126, 128, 136, 141, 143, 176, 178, 186-188, 193, 199, 222, 342, 343
Wyoming Combination, 311

X

XP-100, 230-232
XR-3, 107, 278
XR3-RED, 107, 109, 242

Y

Yaqui Slide, 219, 307
YO Ranch, 142, 204
Younger, Cole, 28

About the author . . .

John Taffin has been handgun writer for the past 50+ years as and a staff writer for the *American Handgunner* and *Guns* for the past 36+ years assigned to do feature articles as well as regular columns, "Taffin Tests", "The Sixgunner", "Handloading", and "Campfire Tales". He has also contributed regular columns and features to *Shoot! Magazine, The Freedom Arms Collectors Journal,* and *Handgun Hunters International* as well as the *Digest Annuals* from Krause Publications. His main interests are big bore sixguns, lever action rifles, and single-shot rifles and pistols, and he has hunted extensively with handguns in America and Africa.

Taffin is also the founder, 1986, and first chairman of The Shootists and past chairman of the Outstanding American Handgunner Awards Foundation. He has also served on the board of the Handgun Hunters Chapter of SCI, and is a NRA Life Member. He considers only five things in this life to be important, namely, Faith, Family, Friends, Firearms, and most assuredly Freedom.

Author of eight books and more than 2,000 articles, Taffin and his wife Dot have three children and 14 grandchildren and reside in Idaho. The kids are all grown-up and on their own, however, Taffin's constant companions during his writing chores are Chloe, a Pomeranian, and Molly, a Shih Tzu, who also serve as doorbells and watchdogs. He still misses his two Malamutes, Red and Wolf.

Other John Taffin Titles from
Echo Point Books
You May Enjoy

Single Action Sixguns
No firearm is more easily recognizable than the 1873 Colt Single Action Army Revolver, but the famed weapon is just one of hundreds of models of single actions revolvers that have been used in battles across the continent. Packed with photos and facts about revolvers from 1850 to today, this guide is a must-have for every gun enthusiast.

HARDCOVER ISBN 978-1-63561-691-0

Big Bore Sixguns
In this comprehensive guide, firearms expert John Taffin follows the development of big bores from 1870 to today. His fascinating model to model review includes more than 300 photos and fine details about the pioneering sixguns, as well as the influence those guns have had on each other and the field of competitive shooting.

HARDCOVER ISBN 978-1-63561-690-3